Study Commentary on Ezekiel

A Study Commentary on Ezekiel

Peter Naylor

EP Books

EP Books
Faverdale North, Darlington, DL3 0PH, England
e-mail: sales@epbooks.org
web: www.epbooks.org

EP Books USA
P. O. Box 614, Carlisle, PA 17013, USA
e-mail: usasales@epbooks.org
web: www.epbooks.us

First published 2011

British Library Cataloguing in Publication Data available

ISBN-13 978 0 85234 726 3 ISBN 0 85234 726 X

Unless otherwise indicated, Scripture quotations are the author's own translation.

Printed and bound by the MPG Books Group

Contents

Part 2

Part 3

Illustrations

Foreword

A tribute to Peter Naylor

Dr Peter Naylor was one whom I counted as a good friend and a respected Christian brother. When I had a question on the hermeneutic of a passage of the Scripture text he readily shared his expertise with me; there were also occasions when he honoured me by discussing some problem that he was grappling with. He taught both Greek and Hebrew. I was present in one of his Greek lessons when he read from his Greek Testament in the manner that he thought it would have been read originally, bearing in mind the breathing and accents as indicated in the text. It sounded like pleasant music! He was awarded a doctorate in London in 2001.

I recall one Sunday when I had preached at Wellingborough Tabernacle, where he was pastor, that after lunch he suggested a walk in the town. As we walked he began asking me questions concerning my view of the relationship between the Old Testament law and the law of Christ from the New Testament. As the questions proceeded it slowly dawned on me that the challenges he was posing were from a different Peter than the one I had come to know. Perhaps my expression indicated that I was puzzled for, with a disarming smile, he said, 'It's all right; I'm acting as a devil's advocate.' That was Peter — constantly probing and testing in order to find God's truth.

When I was responsible for the Grace Baptist Mission literature work, Peter helped us with certain projects, notably preparing a workbook briefly tracing the history of God's people through the Old Testament and New Testament years, and with the book published by Grace Publications entitled *Picking up a pin for the Lord*. It was in those years that we were able to work with him on a simple English commentary on Ezekiel's prophecy, in language that was easier to understand, for translation into a Third-World language. At least from the year 2000, if not before, Ezekiel's prophecy was engaging his mind. Now, at last, as the final result of years of study, writing and rewriting, the work sees the light of day in the Evangelical Press series of Study Commentaries. It is the cream of Peter's academic ability, joined with the savour of his Christian experience.

Over the years Peter visited the Philippines, South Africa and, on the trail of William Carey, Serampur, near Calcutta in North India. He was also a loyal member of the council of the Strict Baptist Historical Society for some years. His unexpected death in August 2007 meant that, sadly, he never saw the publication of his commentary. But I am sure that whoever reads *Ezekiel* now will find that, as the prophet often said, quoting the prophetic words of his God, 'they will know that I am the LORD'. *That was always Peter's desire for people too.*

John Appleby
formerly a joint managing editor for
Grace Publications Trust

Author's preface

This commentary seeks to give a verse-by-verse exposition of the prophecy of Ezekiel. In the suggested translation of the Hebrew text, 'Yahweh' transliterates the Hebrew term behind 'LORD', as normally found in the versions, because it is the name by which God made himself known to Israel.[1] References to the book of Ezekiel usually give chapter and verse numbers only.

The principal thesis of these pages is that the prophecy falls into three main sections. The first, chapters 1 – 33, concerns Israel before and during Ezekiel's time. About this there can be no dispute. But interpretations of the suggested second and third divisions, chapters 34 – 39 and chapters 40 – 48, are not so easy. I would make two propositions: firstly, that chapters 34 – 39 refer to the spiritual renewal of Israel, Abraham's natural children, at some time prior to the Second Coming of Christ; secondly, that chapters 40 – 48 have to do with the heavenly scene, after the Advent of the Lord and when sin and conflict are no more.

I am grateful to Evangelical Press for encouraging me to undertake this study, to those who have offered important comment and to Chris Duncan, my son-in-law, for his invaluable help with the graphics.

Peter Naylor
Wellingborough,
Northamptonshire

Introductory matters

There are two preliminary matters (at least) that might be mentioned: the nature of the Hebrew text of Ezekiel and the oft-discussed question of editorial redaction.

The Hebrew text of the prophecy is not always easy reading.[1] Nevertheless, the English translation offered in this book is almost always based on the vocalized Hebrew script as it stands, and problems concerning the text are only mentioned where they seem necessary for purposes of exposition.

Many textual scholars have considered that the book of Ezekiel is the fruit of various editorial redactors living at the time of, or shortly after, Ezekiel and that it may not emanate directly from the prophet's pen.[2] Typically, L. C. Allen has noted that it 'is the book, of course, that has canonical authority', and that it 'shows evidence of much editorial activity, undertaken by Ezekiel and his successors'.[3]

The present commentary does not subscribe to the theory of later redaction. We are concerned with what we believe to be the word of the Lord as delivered to and relayed by his servant Ezekiel, and we shall proceed on this basis.

Interpretations of chapters 40 – 48

1. A practical renewal programme for national reorganization

According to some scholars, chapters 40 – 48 attained their final form through the labours of disciples of Ezekiel who, like their mentor, anticipated the return of the Jews to their homeland, as related in Ezra and Nehemiah.[4] R. E. Clements observes that these chapters constitute 'an immediate and well-directed summons to build a temple in Jerusalem on the site where the ruins of the old building lay, torn down and burnt by Babylonian enemies'.[5]

But could this have been so?[6] To quote J. B. Taylor:

> If this were an architect's specification we should have expected much more detail about materials to be used, and even though many measurements are given, the ground plan leaves dozens of details to the imagination of any prospective builder, as those who have tried to reconstruct Ezekiel's temple have found to their cost. Moreover, this whole vision (40 – 48) must be taken as a unity and there are elements which are so impracticable that a completely literal interpretation of the vision must be ruled out.[7]

What he means is that no one who intends to build a house can go ahead without an exact three-dimensional plan and precise material specifications. Ezekiel's outline contains neither.

Further, as L. E. Cooper remarks, '... if this [theory] is true, then his [Ezekiel's] hope was never realized. Nothing that took place after the return from Babylon matched the details of these predictions.' And, 'There has been no literal fulfilment down to the present that compares to what Ezekiel saw.'[8]

It is also inconceivable that, upon this theory, in Haggai and Zechariah and in the historical books of Ezra and Nehemiah there should be no reference to Ezekiel or any suggestion that the returning exiles attempted to conform to his directives.

In that Ezekiel beheld the temple 'in the visions of God' (40:2), words that the prophet always applies to symbolic representations rather than to realities, it may be concluded that these chapters are prophetic, looking to an ideal fulfilment at some time in the future. But this begs two questions: what fulfilment, and at what time?

2. The 'church age'

Over the years not a few commentators have considered that chapters 40 – 48 point to the age in which we find ourselves now, the era of the non-ethnic churches.[9] P. Fairbairn observes that from 'the Fathers downwards this has been the prevailing view in the Christian Church'.[10] William Greenhill, an English Congregational minister who died in 1671, discounted the view that Ezekiel's temple was meant to be constructed in Jerusalem by Zerubbabel and his fellow-Jews after the Babylonian captivity. He concluded that 'This vision, therefore, points out the introduction of a better hope, viz. the church of Christ under the gospel.'[11]

Against this, the references that Greenhill employs to make his point are largely from Revelation 20 – 22, chapters that in the main do *not* relate to the progress of the churches during the present age.

J. B. Taylor, describing this type of interpretation as '*symbolic Christian*', comments that

> ... it is overstating the case to refer Ezekiel's vision directly to a Christian 'fulfilment', without seeing that it has a real context for the readers of his own day, and this original context must be the prime concern of the Old Testament exegete.[12]

Fairbairn is also critical, claiming that writers such as Greenhill have 'failed in a correct appreciation of the nature of the vision' and have introduced 'much of an arbitrary and fanciful kind ... into the explanations they gave of particular parts'. Nevertheless, he concludes that these chapters 'present a grand outline of the good in store for God's Church and people', yet without telling what the good will be or when it will occur.[13]

A further argument against the 'church-age' theory is that it is not easy to discern within the New Testament any employment of chapters 40 – 48 bearing upon the life and beliefs of the emergent churches. This point will be developed in the body of the present commentary.

3. The 'prophetic-apocalyptic' view

L. E. Cooper may be quoted because he presents a third approach succinctly:

> The prophetic-apocalyptic view of the passage regards the chapters as an essentially literal description of a real future kingdom. This restored

kingdom is not the church but Israel. While describing literal features of a restored kingdom, Ezekiel also conveys spiritual truth. The very objects he describes, such as a literal temple, priesthood, and sacrifices also function as symbols of the character of the kingdom and its King. For example, the eight steps that lead to the inner court of the sanctuary (40:31,34,37) will be eight literal steps, but they are also a symbol of the Messiah, who is 'the way' of access to fellowship with God (John 14:6).

Again he writes:

> Chapters 40 – 48 present details of the millennial temple, priesthood, sacrifices, and tribal divisions to be set up on earth during the millennium as forerunners of the eternal state.[14]

The same author tells us that:

> Since the church will be taken out of the world, or raptured, prior to the tribulation (Rev. 4:1), the tribulation will be the era of conversion for Israel (Rev. 7:1ff.), and the millennium will afford them the opportunity to reinstate their covenant to celebrate and commemorate the redemptive work of Jesus the Messiah.[15]

Yet the following points should be noted:

I. Concerning the 'millennium'

If, with the present author, one does not accept the view of Cooper and others that there is a fundamental distinction between the Gentile churches and an eventually regenerate Israel, and if one does not believe that there is to be a millennial period during which the visible Lord will reign *on earth*, any approach of this type must be seriously weakened.

II. The old and new covenants

The relationship between the old and the new covenants, as set forth by the New Testament, makes it difficult to believe that there will ever be a reversion to 'the weak and beggarly elements' of Jewish ritual.[16]

Were it to be so, the central thesis of the letter to the Hebrews would be mistaken.[17]

III. The restored temple and Jerusalem

In both the Old and the New Testaments there is an intimate connection between Jerusalem and the temple within it. How is it, then, that in chapters 40 – 48 the temple is situated a considerable distance to the north of the city?'[18] (This criticism only applies if, as accepted by the present commentary, the principal measurement of the central oblation is the reed and not the cubit.)[19]

With its precincts, the area covered by Ezekiel's temple is much larger than that of Solomon's temple, or even that of Herod, within ancient Jerusalem. Neither is it possible that the ground plan of such a temple could embrace the hills and valleys of the land, nor could a temple in any other location than Mount Moriah be that of Jewish expectations.[20]

IV. The central oblation

As the diagrams that appear towards the end of the commentary may show, the description of the central oblation is also physically impossible.

Although Ezekiel's city is nowhere said to be Jerusalem, and is not placed geographically where the terrestrial Jerusalem now is, it is nevertheless the heart of the renewed theocracy. It must, therefore, be an ideal representation. On the other hand, if it is to be understood literally, so must many other prophecies, including some in Ezekiel that tell of the future of Zion and Jerusalem. This being so, figurative interpretations seem much more realistic.[21]

V. The division of the land

The division of the land among the twelve tribes, the allocation of extensive territories to the priests and the Levites, plus the vast size both of the temple and of the city, with an allotment of land for the latter's support, have no historical precedent.

This being so, there would have to be clear evidence within the prophecy to show that a literal fulfilment is intended. Such evidence is lacking. Further, the geographical order of the tribes bears only a passing relation to the settlement outlined in Joshua. In that there are no cities of refuge,[22] there is a fundamental alteration to Moses' legislation concerning manslaughter and murder.

VI. Sacrifices and feasts

Concerning Ezekiel's variations in the temple offerings and, on numerous occasions, in the number of the sacrificial animals, it would be hard to provide an explanation if he meant these to be taken literally. After the restoration there was no attempt to modify Moses' legislation, although it could have been done without much difficulty. Further, why is there no mention of the high priest or of the Day of Atonement?

VII. Waters flowing from the temple

The flow of water from under the eastern threshold of the temple (47:1-12) towards the Dead Sea would be physically impossible in that the watershed of the hilly country is to the east of Ezekiel's temple. Moreover, however great the input of fresh water, the salt in that sea could never be eliminated unless there was an outlet, a notion excluded by 47:11. The complete description must be ideal.

For each and all of these reasons, this book does not accept that Ezekiel predicts the establishment of a literal temple in the land of Israel.[23]

4. That Ezekiel anticipates the church triumphant

The interpretation of chapters 40 – 48 adopted here is that Ezekiel anticipates and expounds the blessedness of Israel in eternity, when this world will be past and gone, and does so in terms of an idealized theocracy.

Do we not have here an anticipation of the many mansions, or apartments, to which Jesus entered when he ascended in order to prepare a place for us?[24] Is this not an Old Testament picture of the heavenly kingdom that is opened to all true saints?[25] Surely, we have here an Old Testament presentation of the New Testament's 'New Jerusalem'.[26] 'And its brilliant glory,' questions C. F. Keil, 'is it not a picture of the unspeakable glory of ... eternal life?'[27]

If so, the prophecy of Ezekiel divides into three elements that concern themselves respectively with, firstly, Israel apostate and exiled; secondly, Israel restored, renewed, persecuted and ultimately vindicated; and, thirdly, Israel glorified and exultant. In hindsight, we are now able to say that ultimate glorification and triumph will occur only when the Messiah shall be revealed to overthrow darkness and to lead his people into a realm in which sin and death are no more.

One would agree with Block when he observes that 'although Ezekiel's restoration oracles predict literal events, not all his descriptions portray the events literally'.[28] The reality appears to be that because the prophet knew that Israel was uniquely the covenant nation of Yahweh, that Canaan had been granted to Israel as a perpetual homeland, that Yahweh would dwell among them for ever and that Yahweh's commitment to David, his servant and their king, would endure,[29] Ezekiel concerns himself with the destiny of a people who would outlast time itself.

This approach to the prophecy will be detailed as the exposition proceeds.

'I am'

Throughout the prophecy of Ezekiel there is a magnificent statement that occurs again and again: 'I am Yahweh.' The assertion that 'then you will know that I am Yahweh' is thematic and tells out the plan of the God of Israel behind the events of time and history.[30]

1. Exodus

About four centuries after Jacob and his children had travelled to Egypt, the pharaoh of the time persecuted that family. This had already been revealed in principle to Abraham.[31] When these predictions were being fulfilled, such affliction could not have been a total surprise to the Hebrews.

The people cried out to God because of their slavery, and their prayer was heard: God remembered his covenant with Abraham, Isaac and Jacob; he saw their family; he knew.[32] Yahweh responded to their plight by introducing Moses, who delivered to the elders of Israel the revelation he had received from God. With their backing, Moses then confronted the pharaoh and demanded that Israel be allowed to depart to the wilderness to serve God.

Pharaoh was truculent: 'Who is Yahweh that I should listen to his voice to send Israel away?' This was followed with an arrogant assertion: 'I do not know Yahweh and I shall not send Israel away.' In the event, Pharaoh made Israel toil even harder. Their predicament seemed insoluble and led the people to turn against Moses and Aaron.[33]

Moses was in an impossible situation. Now spurned by his own nation, he also found himself at odds with Pharaoh. Sensibly, he told Yahweh everything, and the Lord responded.

Firstly, Yahweh promised that because of the 'mighty hand' of God Pharaoh would send the children of Israel away from Egypt.

Secondly, the Lord explained what he had previously revealed to Moses at the burning bush. Although he had appeared to Abraham, Isaac and Jacob centuries before as 'God Almighty', he had not revealed himself by the name 'Yahweh'. 'Yahweh' is probably a variant of a Hebrew verb which may be translated as 'he is', implying the continuous existence, or eternal being, of Israel's God above and beyond time. He was no local, land-tied cultural deity like the fictional gods of Egypt, Canaan and elsewhere. In his plight, Moses was reminded that it was the true God who had established his covenant with the fathers and who had bound himself to grant the tenure of Canaan to their posterity.

Thirdly, for his comfort Moses was told that the Lord had heard and that he would respond to the groaning of the children of Israel.[34]

Moses was instructed to return to the elders and to inform them that Yahweh would bring them out of Egypt and that they would know by experience that he was their God. But although obedient Moses reported this to Israel, they refused to hear him.[35]

For the moment, the children of Israel were uncertain about Moses' assertion concerning a fresh self-revelation of 'Yahweh' in the Sinai desert. What appeared obvious to them in their distress was that this 'Yahweh' had not redeemed Israel; his promises seemed to have collapsed.

But Yahweh insisted that appearances had not told the whole story: soon, both Pharaoh and Israel would 'know' that Yahweh existed and that he was truly the God of Israel. This comes to expression in Exodus 6:7.

In context, Yahweh is described explicitly as the one who had established a covenant with the fathers of Israel and with their family in perpetuity, and who now proposed to honour that covenant by saving the nation and developing his relationship with them.

Moses was intended to infer from this statement that, one way or another, Egypt and all the nations must be brought to know that Yahweh — 'he is' — was uniquely the God of Israel. On the one hand, this acknowledgement would be wrung from the hearts of unrepentant men when enduring the judgements of Yahweh; on the other, it would become a glad confession upon the lips of the redeemed Israelites when constituted formally as God's own special people.

In sum, the deliverance of the family of Abraham from Egypt was brought about by the divine requirement for all men to know that Yahweh is: it was the purpose of God that all must admit that he had committed himself to a binding and lasting relationship with Israel.

And so it came to pass. Because of the judgements of God upon them, eventually the pharaoh and Egypt knew that 'Yahweh is'.[36]

Israel, too, became aware of this truth. In the wilderness and when the people were insubordinate, Moses and Aaron, and then Yahweh himself, predicted that in time 'you will know that it was Yahweh who brought you out of Egypt' and that 'you will know that I am Yahweh your God'. Further, the presence of Yahweh in the tabernacle was designed specifically to ensure that the congregation would 'know that I am Yahweh their God, who brought them out of Egypt so that I might dwell among them'. The Sabbath was planned as a sign 'between me and you for the generations to come so that you may know that I am Yahweh who sanctifies you'. Prior to his death forty years later, Moses recalled that God had supplied every need so that travelling Israel 'might know that I am Yahweh your God'.[37]

2. Time moved on

Centuries passed by. The prayer and the promise that men might know that Yahweh 'is', whether through salvation or in judgement, occur from time to time throughout the Old Testament. Hezekiah's petition, when his people were suffering the Assyrian incursion, is a case in point.[38] The king prays that Yahweh might show himself the God of the covenant both by saving his people and by overthrowing their enemies, the deliverance of the former presupposing the ruin of the latter.

3. Ezekiel: a shift in emphasis

Within the prophecy of Ezekiel we discern a subtle but most important change in emphasis. The principle that Yahweh upholds his own and brings down his and their opponents appears uniformly as a prediction rather than as a prayerful hope: Ezekiel does not desire that this might happen — he anticipates that vindication will occur because it must.

4. A remarkable statistic

Moreover, this truth is presented more than seventy times in chapters 1 – 39, although *never* in chapters 40 – 48. This is quite extraordinary and calls for an explanation. We might even suspect that it could provide us with a key to the interpretation of the complete prophecy.

5. Ezekiel and Exodus

It appears that Ezekiel develops the confrontation situation outlined in Exodus, and does so in two ways. Firstly, he considers the immediate and tragic situation faced by Jerusalem in his day; secondly, he looks down the centuries to distant times.

According to Ezekiel, apostate Israel must come to know that 'Yahweh is' and to understand that the Lord honours his covenant. Tragically, a majority within Israel had never loved their God. Therefore, the sanctions held out by Moses' law would at long last be applied. Ezekiel served due notice to the exiles in Babylon and those then remaining within Jerusalem about what would soon happen: the city must fall. Then they would be convinced that 'Yahweh is'.[39] According to 2:5, when Jerusalem is seized by the enemy, the Jews will realize that Ezekiel had been a true prophet among them.

Ezekiel 20:12,20 tell that the Sabbath had been granted to Israel so that they might know that 'Yahweh is'.[40] Tragically, this sign had been desecrated over the years. Hence, according to 20:38, those who go into exile but who do not repent will never be allowed to return to the land of their fathers to appreciate the seventh-day rest. In this negative fashion they will come to know that 'Yahweh is'.

6. Other enemies

In Moses' time, the lawgiver's predictions were given rapid fulfilment: Egypt soon came to know that Yahweh is the true and only God. Then, after they had left the land of the Nile, Israel attracted other enemies, some apparently more implacable than Egypt. What of them? Are they to escape divine judgement? Ezekiel indicates that they also must come to know that 'Yahweh is'. Exactly like Egypt in Moses' time, they are to be judged by the Lord.

It is true that the motivation for universal hostility to Israel varied. There was ancestral hatred, as in the case of Edom; and there was commercial rivalry, as with Tyre. Egypt, as ever, desired to patronize. Ezekiel points to the distant future when a coalition of the nations, epitomized by Gog and Magog, will be consumed by an evil and irrational desire to annihilate Israel. Whoever they may be, all concerned must be brought to know that 'Yahweh is', and this by his activity against them on behalf of his covenant people. This is spelled out in chapters 25 – 39.

Furthermore, Israel, when renewed spiritually, resettled in the promised land and protected by Yahweh against the hostility of the world powers, comes to know that Yahweh 'is'. To their delight, they are to be assured that the God who entered into covenant with their fathers very many centuries before is still the God who honours that original commitment; Yahweh remains in truth ever the same.[41]

During the earlier part of Ezekiel's ministry, when the destruction of Jerusalem was imminent, he declared that throughout the passage of time the nations would come to know that Yahweh brings down the tall tree and raises up that which is low (17:24). They must realize that Israel's God is in control of all events: not only does he establish the nations, he can destroy them at his will.

In sum, Ezekiel looks both to the immediate future and also far, far ahead. Israel's realization concerning the being of Yahweh occurs not only in 586 BC, when Nebuchadnezzar's hordes destroy Jerusalem, but also — and especially — at the end-time. Then, the nations of the world also accept that Yahweh is God when he honours himself by vindicating Israel (36:23,36; 37:28; 39:23).

7. Moses' ideal becomes Ezekiel's anticipation

Surely this unique clustering of predictions that men everywhere must come to know that 'Yahweh is' has to be thematic. Ezekiel lived at a time when the crumbling earthly kingdom of God — the theocracy of Israel — was on the point of disintegration. This was because of judgement by Yahweh, a judgement predicted by Moses as inevitable because of the anticipated apostasy of that people.

But Moses saw further than judgement, expecting the emergence in time of a God-fearing Israel resettled in the land of promise. Yahweh did not call a nation into being only to cast it off because of a long-standing yet temporary recalcitrance: by grace, there would be a national regeneration.

For Ezekiel it was true that the soul that sins shall die (18:4; 33:1-20). But he also tells that the evil ways of many in Israel cannot permanently frustrate the gracious purpose of God for his people.[42] Ezekiel anticipated that in time Yahweh would ensure that an obedient people would worship and serve him within their own land, a land that would be a blessing to them rather than a curse. Then, all men, both saints and sinners, would know that 'Yahweh is'.

This is the message of a prophecy with a scope that is as long-range as it is narrow. Unlike others of his fellow-prophets, Ezekiel was concerned with one matter only: the ultimate realization of the ideal of a regenerate people subject to Yahweh and living within the decreed bounds of their land. By this means the world, too, must come to acknowledge that 'Yahweh is'.

8. Chapters 40 – 48

Strikingly, in chapters 40 – 48 Ezekiel does not refer overtly to this fulfilment. Rather, he outlines the dimensions and rituals of an ideal temple situated within the land of Israel. As noted above, following the overthrow of Gog and Magog (chapters 38 – 39), no situation arises in which God acts so that men might know that 'Yahweh is'. We perceive an eloquent silence that cries for attention.

9. Beyond the horizon

To anticipate, I suggest that chapters 40 – 48 cannot be concerned with a residence in the land of Israel as we now know it and prior to the end of the world. As this commentary seeks to demonstrate, the justification for this view is that the descriptions of temple, land and settlement given in these chapters simply do not fit such a background. Nor do I accept that these chapters allow themselves to be spiritualized as somehow descriptive of the New Testament churches.

What, then, is the culmination of Ezekiel's message? I believe that the burden of the closing part of the prophecy relates to another age, an age that even for us has not yet appeared. Picking up the observation of Hebrews 11:10, I suppose that Ezekiel, like Abraham, looked forward to 'a city which has foundations, whose builder and maker is God', a city, therefore, that stands on the other side of the horizon separating time and eternity.

The validity of this approach would appear to be borne out by the book of Revelation, as may be seen if we draw a parallel between 47:12 and Revelation 22:1-2. Clearly, John's vision is a development of that seen by Ezekiel. In this glorious situation-to-be there are no tensions; all is at peace and Eden is restored.

Nor, in Ezekiel, is the security of Israel a temporary phase in expectation of a final onslaught by the powers of evil, following which Yahweh destroys his enemies by the breath of his mouth.[43] No more does Yahweh need to declare himself both to a sinful world by judgement and to his own struggling people by their vindication that 'he is'. This he has done once and for all. Gog and Magog were the final enemies, and they have been swept away.

Symbolism

But perhaps there is a problem for us who live in times other than, and far later than, those of Ezekiel. If the prophet glimpsed the eternal blessedness of the Israel of God, why does he describe what he saw in terms of what is for Christians the redundant symbolism of the tabernacle and temple? The question may be critical.

This commentary suggests that Ezekiel's prediction concerning a new city, a new temple and a secure family, all within the land of promise, was the only means by which he could have expounded ultimate heavenly realities.

Look at it like this: Ezekiel was not the apostle John detained on the island of Patmos, a man who had stood near the cross of Calvary, who had seen the risen Christ and who had rejoiced in the earliest triumphs of the gospel.[44] The sixth-century BC exile in Babylon was a prophet of Israel agonizing over the destruction of his city and the temple. Then and there God disclosed to him the eternal future of Israel in terms of the Mosaic dispensation, and in a manner that Ezekiel must have well understood and appreciated. I hope to develop this point.

The failed kingdom of Judah, misled by the usually degenerate family of David, collapsed in 586 BC. Ezekiel knew that in time this nominal theocracy would be replaced by a regenerate nation to be led and shepherded by the Messiah. It was revealed to him that Israel, when truly the people of God, would be established in their land prior to the events of the end-time. Further, Ezekiel reveals that this terrestrial glory will not exhaust the original promises to the patriarchs: there must be an eternal dimension.

In other words, Ezekiel lived in an end-time, although not *the* end-time. Aware that the sanctions of Moses' law were coming to fruition, he anticipated the realization of the ideal held out by this same law, the fulfilment of a long-term promise concerning both an obedient people settled in Canaan, and its continuation — the eternal habitat of the Israel of God in a world other than this.

I recapitulate in order to clarify the present interpretation.

The prophet Ezekiel survived the trauma of a collapsed kingdom. But not abandoning the prospect of the established kingdom of God, his prophecy holds forth the assurance of a new, regenerate Israel governed by Yahweh through the shepherd-prince-king emanating from the family of Jesse.

This expectation works out in two distinct and successive stages. Firstly, Israel is to be resettled in the promised land prior to the end of the world. Secondly, Ezekiel beheld a scene different from anything that could be realized in this world: the kingdom of Israel would be established in perpetual glory following the overthrow of every enemy. Then, Israel worships in the eternal state where nothing disturbs communion between Yahweh and his own.

The three principal divisions of the prophecy

As has already been mentioned, the prophecy might be said to fall into three principal divisions, each marked explicitly by a reference to the captivity of the Jews.

In detail, Ezekiel dates his revelations from the time when he was taken as a prisoner from Jerusalem to Babylon in company with Jehoiachin, then king of Judah. This would have been in 597 BC. Significantly, throughout the body of the prophecy there are only three occasions when the prophet dates his visions with explicit reference to the exile of Judah. These are 1:1-2; 33:21 and 40:1. We shall proceed on the basis that these references are deliberate.

1. The Jewish captivity and Ezekiel's visions

The first part of the prophecy is a ministry of condemnation: degenerate Israel is to be evicted from the land of promise. In 1:1-2 Ezekiel begins to pour forth judgements upon a faithless nation. The date is unambiguous: 'the fifth of the month in the fifth year of King Jehoiachin's exile', the fifth year being 597 BC. Chapters 1 – 33 tell of the explosion of divine wrath upon the apostate kingdom of Judah.

Secondly, 33:21 marks a new phase of ministry for the prophet. This was 'in the twelfth year of our exile', 585 BC. Chapters 34 – 39 unfold the establishment and vindication of Israel, regenerate and now resident in the promised land.

Finally, 40:1 commences a series of fresh visions. These expound the splendour of a city-temple in a setting that patently cannot belong to this world. The date for the opening of this new range of predictions is the 'twenty-fifth year of our exile', which appears to have been 572 BC.

In short, the prophet Ezekiel, who lived to see the warnings of Moses' law come to realization, was convinced that the original covenant between God and Abraham, Isaac and Jacob would ultimately be fulfilled. He believed that the conditional blessings promised by Leviticus 26:1-13 and Deuteronomy 30:1-10, and the final vindication of Israel anticipated by Deuteronomy 32:36-43, would become realities — realities conceived in eternity past, cradled in history and extending into a future eternity. To repeat, the prophecy is concerned with the condemnation, restitution and, finally, the glorification of the twelve tribes of Israel.

Block notes that:

> Israelite confidence in Yahweh was founded on an official orthodoxy, resting on four immutable propositions, four pillars of divine promise: the irrevocability of Yahweh's covenant with Israel (Sinai), Yahweh's ownership of the land of Canaan, Yahweh's eternal covenant with David, and Yahweh's residence in Jerusalem, the place he chose for his name to dwell.[45]

I would identify with this, except that, as I see it, the first of the 'four pillars of divine promise' was not the irrevocability of the Sinai arrangement, but that of the unilateral covenant between Yahweh and Abraham.[46] It was upon this that the Jews who remained in Judah after the destruction of Jerusalem relied, albeit having entertained a serious misapprehension of the matter, believing falsely that the city could never fall (see 33:24). Ezekiel was concerned with the destruction of these pillars during his lifetime and their ultimate and permanent re-erection at a future period.

2. The Old Testament and the New Testament

We know more about the matter than Ezekiel did when he was here. For us, the ancient mystery that the kingdom of heaven would in due time embrace Gentiles as well as Jews is no longer a secret, according to, for example, Ephesians 3:4-6. But although he was not completely unaware of it (see 47:22-23), Ezekiel was not primarily concerned with this truth.

Whereas John on Patmos wrote that 'the leaves of the tree were for the healing *of the nations*',[47] it was Ezekiel's mission to warn and then, following the holocaust of 586 BC, to comfort the family of Abraham. This is why he states that the leaves are for the healing of (presumably) the twelve tribes (47:12), declining to tell out that the blessing would embrace the world.

The godly Jew may rejoice in this grand picture of heaven — and the converted Gentile may lift up his head: he will not be shut out. In the words of our Lord, he may hope to feast with Abraham, Isaac and Jacob in the kingdom of heaven.[48]

3. The usual approach

Commentators often divide the book into three divisions: chapters 1 – 24, issued before the fall of Jerusalem; chapters 25 – 32, containing oracles delivered to foreign nations; and chapters 33 – 48, issued after the fall of Jerusalem.[49] One problem with this is that such a scheme fails to distinguish between the scene of chapters 34 – 39 (Israel resettled, attacked and vindicated) and that of chapters 40 – 48 (Israel glorified).

Nevertheless, the division is not entirely inaccurate. This is because at the end of chapter 24 Ezekiel is told that, even as his wife has died, so the exiles in Babylon will lose the delight of their eyes, the temple in Jerusalem. From chapter 25 the prophet is concerned with matters other than the condemnation of his own people and the predicted fall of Jerusalem. Immediate tragedy is past; reconciliation and light approach. Then follows an anticipation of glory.

Even so, it might be better to consider the complete book as focusing upon Israel both before and after the fall of Jerusalem *at the time* when news of that disaster was broken to Ezekiel (33:21). At this point the tenor of the remaining oracles alters dramatically. Now that the divine wrath has been poured out, the prophet devotes himself to promises and consolation. This fits precisely with the suggestion that the book falls into three distinct sections (1:1 – 33:20; 33:21 – 39:29; and 40:1 – 48:35), each being dated explicitly from 597 BC, when Ezekiel was taken into exile.

4. Solomon in all his glory

Approximately one thousand years before the birth of Jesus, Israel had arrived at a pinnacle of glory. Solomon was king in Jerusalem, the people knew peace, and their God had provided the opportunity for the monarch to erect the temple of Yahweh in the city of Yahweh's choice. The building, of course, was not meant to be desecrated by idolatry. Neither in the temple's holiest place nor in its precincts, any more than in Jerusalem or in any part of the land, was God to be represented by painting or sculpture.[50] Were Israel to be obedient, the situation of the people would be blessed.

Sadly, there was a considerable problem. At least since the departure of the twelve tribes from Egypt, the overwhelming majority of Israelites had been addicted to idolatry. 'How often they rebelled against him in the wilderness, and grieved him in the desert! And they turned and tempted God, and provoked the Holy One of Israel,' laments Psalm 78:40-41. Because idolatry was certain to repel the mercies of God, future blessings depended upon whether or not Israel would be obedient to the law.

5. A broken covenant

Tragically, and as we now know, it never worked out like this. Even before Jacob's family had gone down to Egypt, they inclined to false worship. Both in Egypt and after the meeting between Yahweh and Israel at Sinai, when they were constituted as the covenant people of God, they had persisted in their evil ways.[51] Provoked by his numerous foreign wives, even Solomon fell prey to this sin.[52]

The inevitable consequence was that Yahweh recruited the world to bring disaster upon Israel. After the time when the tribes had split into two parts,[53] the ten in the north ('Israel') were governed by rebel kings, while Judah, together with diminutive Benjamin, was ruled from Jerusalem by the dynasty founded by David.

Later, the northern tribes were overrun by the Assyrians. This was about 722 BC. Over a hundred years later, the empire of Babylon, Assyria's successor as the dominant world power, began to make inroads upon Judah. In 586 BC Jerusalem was devastated by Nebuchadnezzar's armies, the temple was destroyed and the throne of David cast into temporary oblivion.

6. The fellowship of the prophets

During those fateful years God did not leave his unhappy people without help, but raised up prophets to teach and guide them.

One such prophet was Jeremiah, like Ezekiel a priest.[54] His ministry had commenced about 627 BC, almost half a century before the reduction of the theocracy of Israel. Within Jerusalem and when Nebuchadnezzar's hordes had broken through the walls, he was finally abducted to Egypt, where presumably he died.

Although Ezekiel and Jeremiah never mention each other by name, it is probable that the former, then a youthful priest far away by the Chebar canal, knew of, or perhaps had been in personal contact with, the older man in Jerusalem. It is likely that Ezekiel had been there in 622 BC, when a copy of the 'book of the law' was discovered and when the temple was being repaired.[55] And he must have been sadly aware that Josiah's attempted reformation had proved fruitless.

Then there was Daniel. As a young man he had been deported to Babylon in the wake of Nebuchadnezzar's first descent upon Judah. This was in 606 BC. Ezekiel, of course, was also taken into exile, in about 597 BC, the eighth year of the reign of Nebuchadnezzar. In all, some ten thousand Jews were then led away from Jerusalem. This date is important because, as we have observed, it provides a mark from which Ezekiel dates many of his prophecies. By this time Daniel may have attained relatively high office in the Babylonian administration.[56]

Daniel lived until at least 539 BC, when a Persian emperor's decree for the Jews to go back to their shattered land and city was put into action.[57] Like Daniel, Ezekiel never made the homeward journey. Unlike Daniel, it appears that he died before his people's return to Jerusalem, having spent his last thirty years in Babylonia (29:17). It is remarkable that at a time when Israel was passing through unprecedented distress, God should have given such an unusual fulness of prophetic revelation to Jeremiah, Ezekiel and Daniel. A comparable situation might have been the joint labours of Isaiah, Micah, Hosea and Amos more than a century earlier. Neither Jeremiah nor Daniel nor Ezekiel, all removed from Jerusalem by force, found their last resting place there.

Although he never mentions Ezekiel, it is likely that Daniel would have been aware of the fortunes of the incoming waves of exiles from Judah and of the ministry of his fellow-prophet. Indeed, Ezekiel refers to Daniel three times, remarking upon the latter's holiness and wisdom (14:14,20; 28:3).

7. Ezekiel serves the God of strength

Ezekiel's name is significant, meaning 'God strengthens'. In order to serve Yahweh in the situation in which he found himself, the prophet needed and received strength greater than his own. Because he was only a man, the strong hand of Yahweh came upon the prophet when he commenced his difficult ministry of condemnation among truculent exiles in Babylon (3:14).

He was granted an astonishing series of visions — visions that were the fruit neither of a vivid imagination nor of clairvoyant powers (as some have alleged). Ezekiel was no heathen like Balaam, who employed divination to tell the future;[58] nor was he like Nebuchadnezzar, who cast lots with arrows, examined animal entrails and consulted his idols in order to ascertain his military operations (cf. 21:21).

Like other prophets, Ezekiel was borne along, so to speak, by the Holy Spirit.[59] Therefore he speaks to us directly for and from God. As we travel through the forty-eight chapters of his prophecy, we discover that his enduring ministry is one both of warning and of promise. His book addresses the sins and problems of the people of God in his time, but looks forward to and beyond our time and, as this commentary would see it, to the end of time and then into eternity. This is why the man and his message are so important.

8. Ezekiel and the apostle John

Years after Ezekiel's day, Jerusalem and its rebuilt temple were again destroyed and the Jews scattered. Another Jew, John, an apostle of Jesus, was held prisoner on the island of Patmos in the Aegean Sea. He had done no wrong and was there solely because of his Christian activities.[60] He has been mentioned already. Like Ezekiel six hundred years earlier, John was given to see the future sufferings and the eventual triumphs of the church of God in this world, and something of the glory of eternity.

What is important for us is that much of Ezekiel's ministry is embraced by John in his prophetic book. The prisoner in Babylon foretold strange, wonderful, sometimes sad and often glad, but always true things — things that were revealed more clearly to, and outlined in greater detail by, the Christian apostle.

This means that if we want to understand the book of Revelation and see how it is that God will maintain his people until Christ comes again in glory, we must give careful attention to the prophet Ezekiel. John knew this well. But it also works the other way around. As we noted earlier, if we want to understand Ezekiel, and particularly chapters 40 – 48, we have to take into account John's great book.[61]

9. Ezekiel's prophecy: long in vision; restricted in scope

Other prophets in Israel were concerned with the inauguration of the new covenant (e.g., Jeremiah) and with the admission of the nations to the people of God (e.g., Jonah, Micah, Isaiah, Hosea and Amos). Ezekiel's vision, although taking us beyond the end of the world, is more focused. At a time when the kingdom of God upon earth was apparently vanishing, albeit temporarily, Ezekiel looked ahead to the residence of a regenerate, holy Israel settled in the land of promise.

This is why (to repeat) the present commentary suggests that chapters 40 – 48 are not to be spiritualized as somehow descriptive of the Gentile church within this gospel dispensation. Nor should they be taken to refer somehow to an alleged post-advent millennial kingdom centred at Jerusalem. Having introduced the point already, I shall seek to show that they predict the bringing together of the family of Abraham towards the end of this age, then the emergence and downfall of the one whom we often term the 'antichrist', and finally the advent of Christ and the inauguration of the eternal state.

The historical background

Ezekiel lived in a time of sweeping political changes during which the map of the territories surrounding Israel was being redrawn. The Assyrian Empire had long since been the major force in world events and had even extended itself westwards as far as Egypt. But contemporarily with the wane of the Assyrian power, a new empire was emerging on the world stage: Babylon. Nabopolassar (625–605 BC) defeated the Assyrians at the gates of Babylon in 626 BC and ten years later advanced up the Euphrates. This alarmed the Egyptians, who joined forces with Assyria in order to repel the new enemy. They were signally unsuccessful, and in 612 BC Babylon, aided by the Medes, overran Nineveh. In the year 605 BC a decisive battle was fought at Carchemish, where Egypt was repulsed by the armies of Babylon under the leadership of Nebuchadnezzar II, Nabopolassar's successor (605–562 BC).

Jeremiah makes special mention of this conflict in addressing the defeated foe: 'Against Egypt, concerning the army of Pharaoh Necho, king of Egypt, which was by the Euphrates River at Carchemish, which Nebuchadnezzar, king of Babylon, defeated in the fourth year of Jehoiakim the son of Josiah, king of Judah.'[62] Babylon was now dominant in the affairs of the Near East, and would remain so until eclipsed by Persia some seventy years later.

Manasseh, king in Jerusalem for fifty-five years until 642 BC, had shown himself to be the most perverse of all the descendants of King David, notwithstanding his late conversion.[63] His grandson Josiah (640–609 BC), who ascended the throne at the age of eight, strove to set matters right by cleansing the nation of cult objects, abolishing divination, restoring Jerusalem as the focal point of worship and reintroducing the Passover.[64] Tragically, his efforts seem to have achieved no more than a superficial reform, and Jeremiah's reluctance to comment positively speaks volumes: the prophet knew that godliness is never the child of legislation, however right and good the latter may be.

Josiah was slain in battle when endeavouring to repulse Pharaoh Necho, who was leading his armies north and east to aid the Assyrians against the ascendant Babylonians.[65] Jehoahaz, a foolish youth, succeeded him. He reigned for no more than three months before being deposed, when he was carried away to Egypt by Necho. The pharaoh replaced him with a brother, Eliakim, whom he renamed Jehoiakim in order to assert Egyptian dominance over the Jewish monarchy.[66] An irresponsible individual who attracted the contempt of Jeremiah,[67] Jehoiakim lasted as king from 609 until 597 BC, during which period he submitted for a time to Nebuchadnezzar of Babylon, who had advanced westwards against Egypt.

The yoke of servitude irked, and when Jehoiakim rebelled against Babylon Nebuchadnezzar took decisive action. Initially, he sent small contingents, supported by Syrian, Ammonite and Moabite vassals, to harry Judah, and then followed up with a direct assault on Jerusalem. After a three-month siege the city was overpowered. Jehoiakim was apprehended and taken to Babylon, whence he appears to have returned to Judah at a later date.[68] The influence of Egypt had now waned to vanishing point and Judah became a vassal of Babylon. Nebuchadnezzar installed a son of Jehoiakim, the eighteen-year-old Jehoiachin, also called Coniah or Jeconiah,[69] as a puppet ruler in

Jerusalem, but he endured for no more than a brief three months. Apparently he looked to Egypt for military aid,[70] but this ploy failed. Nebuchadnezzar sent his armies back to Jerusalem and deported Jehoiachin, the queen mother, numerous dignitaries and about ten thousand others to Babylon.[71] This was in 598/597 BC. Among these was the youthful Ezekiel, who found himself resettled in a Jewish enclave near Nippur not far from the Chebar canal (1:1-3). Jehoiachin ended his days peacefully in Babylon, where thirty-seven years later (*c.* 560 BC) he was eventually freed from prison to be made a life pensioner at the royal table.[72]

Meanwhile, Judah had continued as a client state of Babylon, and Zedekiah, a brother of Jehoiakim and son of Josiah, was Nebuchadnezzar's nominee for the throne. An indecisive man, he would not accept, contrary to the counsel given to him by the prophet Jeremiah,[73] that Jerusalem would fall to the might of Babylon. His folly was bolstered by the fact that the Egyptians still entertained aspirations for military conquest in Palestine.[74] A strong pro-war party in Jerusalem encouraged Zedekiah to rebel.

Nebuchadnezzar lost patience and in the ninth year of Zedekiah's reign he attacked. The siege lasted for about two years, culminating in 586 BC with the destruction of Jerusalem and its temple. Zedekiah the insurgent was punished by being compelled to witness the execution of his sons prior to having his eyes gouged out. He was then deported to Babylon, where he eventually died.[75] What remained of Judah became a Babylonian province. The nation of Israel and the Davidic monarchy were no more.[76]

Ezekiel's chronology

Unlike any other Old Testament prophet, Ezekiel provides a sequence of dates for his oracles. In terms of our own chronology, they would appear to be as follows:[77]

1:1-2	Ezekiel's call	31 July 593
8:1	Vision of idolatry in Jerusalem	17 Sept. 592
20:1	Deputation of elders	9 Aug. 591
24:1	The siege commences	15 Jan. 588
26:1	Prophecy against Tyre	12 Feb. 586
29:1	Prophecy against Egypt	7 Jan. 587
29:17	Nebuchadnezzar, Tyre and Egypt	26 April 571
30:20	Pharaoh's arm	29 April 587
31:1	Prophecy against Pharaoh	21 June 587
32:1	A lament for Pharaoh	3 March 585
32:17	Pharaoh in Sheol	17 March 585
33:21	The fall of Jerusalem	8 Jan. 585
40:1	The new Jerusalem	28 April 573

With the exception of the oracles against the nations (chapters 25 – 32), the dates occur in an exact chronological order. Ezekiel's ministry lasted, therefore, for slightly more than twenty years.

This commentary divides into three main sections, chapters 1:1 – 33:20; 33:21 – 39:29 and 40:1 – 48:35, all of which subdivide into the thirteen parts indicated by these dates.

Part 1:
From 'the fifth of the month (it was the fifth year of the exile of King Jehoiachin)'

1. The first series of prophecies

(Ezekiel 1:1 – 7:27)

This series of prophecies dates from about 593 BC, the fifth year of King Jehoiachin's exile, and commences with chapters 1 – 3 telling of the vision of God revealed to Ezekiel and of his commission as a prophet to Israel.

Ezekiel introduces himself (Ezekiel 1:1–3)

The opening three chapters of the prophecy serve two functions. Firstly, they tell of the circumstances of Ezekiel's call to the prophetic ministry; secondly, they serve as a necessary introduction to the whole book. The total prophecy is so remarkable and far-reaching that without chapters 1 – 3 it would be defective. The opening chapter of the prophecy of Jeremiah serves as a parallel: such was the character of his ministry that it was essential for him to be confirmed in his call. Now, to Ezekiel will be granted revelations concerning the departure of God from Israel and the Lord's eventual return to be with them in an eternal Jerusalem. It is for this reason that the vision of Yahweh seated upon the throne-chariot is so appropriate: the Lord will never surrender his crown rights.[1]

1:1-3. And it was in the thirtieth year, in the fourth, on the fifth day of the month, and I was among the exiles by the Chebar canal. The heavens were opened and I saw visions of God. On the fifth of the month (it was the fifth year of the exile of King Jehoiachin), the word of Yahweh came immediately to Ezekiel, the son of Buzi, the priest, in the land of the Chaldeans by the Chebar canal, and the hand of Yahweh was upon him there.

Within verses 1-3 the first verse is couched in the first person singular (**'I'**) and the last in the third person (**'him'**). There is a reason for this: not only does

Ezekiel stamp his prophecy as in some sense autobiographical, he becomes a personification of his message, as, for example, in his bereavement (24:15-27). This, too, is why he provides a precise historical backdrop for his initial call. The dates are all significant.

'In the thirtieth year' probably refers to Ezekiel's age.[2] Nearly a thousand years earlier Moses had to number and enlist all the male Levites between thirty and fifty years old for the transport of the tabernacle furniture in the wilderness. Standing service at the tabernacle could begin at the age of twenty-five, but in later years was reduced to twenty. Ezekiel may hint that his position was analogous to that of a Levite commencing his labours during the forty-year wilderness journey.[3]

This notice of date would indicate that Ezekiel regarded his call as occurring at a crucial point in his life. Denied his priestly vocation in Jerusalem, he was commissioned as a prophet.[4] In W. Eichrodt's words:

> At the age at which he would under other circumstances have entered priestly office, Ezekiel was transplanted into unclean heathen soil, experiencing the first major disappointment of his life. The judgement which threatened his people first struck him, thus beginning at the house of God.[5]

By introducing himself in these terms, Ezekiel implies that the family of Aaron, whose representative he had become, would recommence its ministry within a new tabernacle complex, but a tabernacle situated no longer in Judah. The point is that the collapse of David's royal house and the extinction of temple worship in Jerusalem were not seen as a finish: the worship and service of the God of Israel would continue. The tabernacle had been transferred, as it were, to another site, even as it had been relocated again and again during the wilderness journeys. In other words, the tragedy then occurring in Judah is seen as a beginning rather than a dismal end, the inauguration of a new epoch in the history of Israel.

Ezekiel, deported from Jerusalem and the temple where Yahweh's presence had once been manifest, was in a land where Yahweh had not been known to reveal himself. Yet the God of Israel *was* there: **'the heavens were opened'** because he remained the God of heaven, unable to be confined to a geographical locale.[6]

But Ezekiel did not see directly: he beheld **'visions of God'**. This means that he gazed upon a resemblance of heavenly reality rather than upon the reality itself. As Numbers 12:6-8 makes plain, the prophets without exception saw indirectly, by means of visions and dreams, because no man is able to see the fulness of God directly and live.[7]

The **'Chebar canal'** was probably part of a complex irrigation system conducting water from the rivers Tigris and Euphrates to the city of Nippur.[8] Whether Ezekiel was by the canal when he received his vision or found himself where other Jews were settled is unclear (1:1).

The prophet's thirtieth year coincided with **'the fifth year of the exile of King Jehoiachin'**, about 593 BC. As has been noted earlier, Jehoiachin, grandson of King Josiah, after holding the throne for only three months and ten days, had been taken to Babylon from Jerusalem in 597 BC.[9] 'Jeconiah' means 'Yahweh will establish', but the Lord chose not to establish him, in that, young as he was, he 'did evil in the sight of Yahweh'.[10] Even youngsters need to repent and believe — but he did not. Yet in the event Jeremiah, as well as Jehoiachin's Babylonian captors, preferred to regard him rather than Zedekiah as the legitimate king.[11] Although Jehoiachin was followed by Zedekiah, who reigned for eleven years, the latter was not his son.[12] In effect, with the deposition of Jehoiachin the Davidic line of succession ceased, the deportation marking a crisis in Israel's history. As Jeremiah 22:28-30 had predicted, it was an end (many would have thought, *the* end). Yahweh, having shown that he was determined to close down the kingdom of Judah, would in time open up a new epoch for his people.

According to Jeremiah 51:59, Zedekiah went to Babylon in the fourth year of his reign (i.e. in 593 BC), which may have given the exiles some reason to hope that they would soon return to Judah.[13] But it was not to be, Ezekiel being raised up to show that the immediate future for Israel was centred upon Babylon rather than upon the homeland.

The opening of Ezekiel's prophecy dates, then, to this year, 593 BC, Ezekiel introducing himself as a priest — that is, of the family of Aaron from the tribe of Levi — filling out the reference in 1:1 to 'the thirtieth year'. Throughout his book Ezekiel displays an intense interest in all matters relating to the priesthood, Yahweh having selected the right man to deliver his word at this critical point in the destiny of Israel (1:2).

'The hand of Yahweh' is an anthropomorphism, Ezekiel acknowledging that from the commencement of his ministry his God was in control, even in **'the land of the Chaldeans'**, by which is meant the Babylonian Empire (1:3).[14] A literal hand descending from the heavens did not alight upon Ezekiel's shoulder.

Application

If Ezekiel received his call to the prophetic ministry when Zedekiah went to Babylon,[15] it is probable that at that point the hopes of the exiles were raised high concerning an early return to Judah. It was part — but only a part — of Ezekiel's ministry to disenchant them: for the time being, the temple, the Davidic monarchy, Israel's retention of the promised land and, indeed, the very presence of God in Jerusalem would be no more.

The Lord casts down before he raises up. His ways are surprising in the extreme,[16] yet he never allows apostasy to triumph among his people. Had Ezekiel's contemporaries known it, Leviticus 26:21-39 was about to find a fulfilment in Babylonia. (Do read this chapter from Leviticus. It will feature again and again in Ezekiel's prophecy.)

As noted, in his earlier years Ezekiel would probably have heard Jeremiah's preaching in Jerusalem and must have mulled over Josiah's unsuccessful reformation.[17] All the while he anticipated that he would be a serving priest within the temple. In the event, his hopes were dashed. By the time of his thirtieth birthday he had been in remote exile for five years with little or no prospect of returning to Jerusalem. It was then that the Lord bestowed upon him a ministry far, far more important than that of officiating at the temple altar. Sometimes the Lord takes away so that he might give. For Christians, disappointment often precedes the dawn. When we are weak, then we are strong.[18]

'There' (i.e. the land of heathen Babylon) in 1:3 is eloquent. There is no situation to which the hand of the Lord cannot reach, even when the prosperity of the churches is scarcely visible.

The living creatures (Ezekiel 1:4–14)

The God of Israel appeared to Ezekiel, and the revelation is expounded in 1:4-28. The prophet beheld four living creatures which formed a hollow square and which were accompanied by moving wheels. When the creatures' wings were raised, they touched, but did not support, a platform, or 'firmament' (cf. 1:9,23,25), upon which was situated the throne of Yahweh.

We shall consider the complete vision in three sections: first, the living creatures (1:4-14); secondly, the wheels (1:15-21); and, thirdly, the throne (1:22-28).

1:4-14. And I saw, and, look, a stormy wind came from the north — a great cloud, and fire taking hold of itself and radiance surrounding it. And from its centre there was as the gleam of glowing metal — from the centre of the fire. And from its centre, the likeness of four living creatures, and this was their form: they had the likeness of a man. But there were four faces to each one, and four wings to each one of them. And their feet — a straight foot; and the soles of their feet like the sole of the hoof of a calf, and as the gleam of burnished bronze. And the hands of a man under their wings on their four sides. And their faces and their wings, for the four of them: their wings were joined one to another. They did not turn when they moved; each was going straight ahead.

And the likeness of their faces: a man's face, and a lion's face to the right for the four of them, and an ox's face on the left for the four of them, and an eagle's face for the four of them. And their faces — and their wings were spread out upwards: for each two wings joining each, and two covering their bodies. And each went straight ahead: where the spirit would go, they went. They did not turn when they went. And the likeness of the living creatures: their appearance was like burning coals of fire, as the appearance of torches. It was moving among the living creatures. The fire was brilliant, and from the fire lightning came out. And the living creatures ran forward and back — as the appearance of sparks.

The prophet beheld a stormy cloud, dark and threatening, moving **'from the north'**. This was almost certainly because, like Jeremiah, Ezekiel knew that divine judgement upon Judah was emanating from that direction, and with special reference to Jerusalem.[19] The reader is reminded of the awesomeness of the Sinai revelation: the God of Israel is righteous in his dealings with the unrepentant.[20] From the heart of the cloud appeared the **'gleam'**, or possibly 'appearance', of **'glowing metal'** (*hashmal*, 1:4):[21] the vision was brilliant yet foreboding and mysterious. Lightning flashed across the sky.

'Fire taking hold of itself and radiance surrounding it' (1:4) possibly tells, in Gardiner's words, of flames 'succeeding one another so rapidly that each seemed to lay hold on the one that had gone before'.[22] The same expression occurs in Exodus 9:24: 'there was hail, and fire mingled with the hail', the reader being invited to imagine a powerful thunderstorm seen at a distance, the immense, towering black cloud being lit up from within by continuous lightning flashes.

'And from its centre, the likeness of four living creatures' indicates that Ezekiel saw an indirect vision. The principal characteristic of the creatures was that they were alive (1:13,14,15,19,21, etc.). Each possessed a human form, which suggests that they stood upright. Yet each had four faces, looking in different directions, and four wings, unlike the six wings of the seraphim in Isaiah 6:2 and Revelation 4:8. **'Four'** probably corresponds to the number of the creatures and is suggestive of universality, life and reverence: **'and their wings were spread out upwards: for each two wings joining each, and two covering their bodies'**. John Calvin wrote that:

> As for the number of cherubim, I have no doubt that God wanted to teach that his power is diffused through all regions of the world. We know that the world is divided into four parts [north, south, east and west], and therefore in order for the people to know that God's providence rules everywhere in the world, four cherubim are presented.[23]

Their legs, which sparkled like polished brass or bronze, stood upright, and the soles of their feet were each like the **'sole of the hoof of a calf'**, a figure which may symbolize nimbleness. The prophet does not tell us at this point what these creatures were, but in 10:15,20 he recognizes them as cherubim, supernatural beings never far from God.[24] Yahweh will suffer none to violate his holiness (1:5-7).

Beneath the four wings and on the four sides of each of the cherubim were **'hands'**. The upper right wing of each creature contacted the raised left wing of the being immediately to its right, recalling the touching of the outstretched wings in the temple of Solomon.[25] Moving in harmony, the four creatures never swerved, proceeding directly to where they were intended to go. Ezekiel noticed that the four **'faces'** of each of them were respectively that of a **'man'**, with that of a **'lion'** to its right and that of an **'ox'** to its left. That of an **'eagle'** pointed away from the prophet. The two wings of each creature not in contact with the wings of the two adjacent beings covered its body (1:8-11).

Although they moved together, the creatures were not autonomous, travelling wherever **'the spirit'**, or wind, led them. They were servants of God and moved at his bidding (1:12). Moreover, they appeared to be incandescent, Ezekiel introducing two similes to stress the brightness of the vision: **'And the likeness of the living creatures: their appearance was like burning coals of fire, as the appearance of torches.'** Fire and lightning surged among them (1:13-14). It seems that, because archaeology has not discovered any analogues to Ezekiel's creatures, the symmetry displayed in the vision anticipates that of the architecture of the ideal temple (see chapters 41 – 44). The God of Israel is the God of order and precision.

So far, the vision has exhibited the essential holiness of the God of Israel, his inexhaustible power and the harmony of his purposes. In that the fiery cloud came from the north, Yahweh was revealing himself as the God of judgement. Supporting his throne, it may be that the cherubic beings reminded Ezekiel that Yahweh was as strong as the lion, as swift as the eagle, as energetic as the bull, and that he was personal, exercising a rationality reflected (dimly) by the mankind that he had created.

Application

The prophecy of Ezekiel is essentially theocentric. That is, it commences with a vision of the God of Israel, even as it closes by stating that Yahweh is with his people in the heavenly city (48:35). As the prophecy opens, its reader is directed to consider the attributes of the God who will cast down ere he raises up. 'Look,' said Simeon to the mother of our Lord, 'this child is destined for the fall and rising of many in Israel.'[26]

Ezekiel lived at a time when, as ever, armies were on the move and some leaders were planning to redraw the map of the world in their favour. But the prophet saw that the politics and militarism of his day were no more than tools in the hand of the Lord. Potentates might fulminate against Israel, but God was above them and, indeed, was using them for his own blessed purposes. It was so, too, when Augustus decreed that all the world should be taxed, and when Pilate surrendered Jesus to the wrath of the Jews.[27] Our God reigns, and Christ is Lord over all in the interests of the churches of his grace.[28]

The wheels (Ezekiel 1:15-21)

Prior to the 1700s, since time immemorial man-made vehicles had of necessity to be pushed, pulled or carried, whether by man, beast or sail. Human ingenuity had been unable to contrive a power-source that could be installed within, say, a wagon, chariot or ship. Even in relatively modern times, Leonardo da Vinci (1452–1519) could only sketch plans for a *man-powered* military fighting vehicle or aircraft.

Remarkably, Ezekiel beheld a four-wheeled vehicle that was self-propelled, its power-source being within it. Moreover, it contained its own guidance system and was able to move freely on the surface of the earth and also to fly. What he saw was in effect a composite development of the theophany of Exodus 19:9-16, of the vision recorded in Exodus 24:10 and of that recorded by Isaiah 6:1-6.

The passage may also recall 2 Samuel 22:9-13:

> Smoke went up from his nostrils,
> And devouring fire from his mouth;
> Coals were kindled by it.
> He bowed the heavens also, and came down
> With darkness under his feet.
> He rode upon a cherub, and flew;
> And he was seen upon the wings of the wind.
> He made darkness canopies around him,
> Dark waters and thick clouds of the skies.

From the brightness before him
Coals of fire were kindled.[29]

Furthermore, Yahweh's presence was witnessed far beyond the limits of the promised land.

Ezekiel must have been astonished by what he saw, and his hearers by what they heard from him.

1:15-21. And I saw the living creatures, and, look, one wheel upon the ground next to the living creatures for its four faces. The appearance of the wheels and their workmanship were as the gleam of chrysolite, and there was a single likeness for the four of them. Their appearance and their workmanship were as a wheel within a wheel. They went in their four directions when they moved; they did not turn as they went. And their rims! They were both majestic and fearful, and their rims were full of eyes round about for all four of them. And when the living creatures moved, the wheels next to them moved; and when the living creatures ascended from the earth, the wheels ascended. Wherever the spirit would move, they went there — the spirit would go! — and the wheels ascended alongside them because the spirit of life was in the wheels. When they moved, they too went; and when they stood still, they too stood; and when they ascended from off the earth, the wheels ascended alongside them, for the spirit of life was in the wheels.

As he gazed at the creatures, Ezekiel saw a **'wheel'**, **'one'** (collective) wheel in the sense that the living creatures were one, yet four wheels in that the living creatures were actually four.[30] Placed on the ground, each wheel was adjacent to the human face of one of the four beings (1:15). The wheels resembled a precious stone, *tarshish*, **'chrysolite'**, or perhaps another mineral also having the lustre of gold. It seems that each wheel was double, maybe like a wheel inserted **'within'** another wheel with (presumably) their two axles at right angles to each other. They were in effect castors that could swivel in any direction. Like the creatures, the wheels moved straight forward, by which is meant that they could be guided without any deflection from the path marked out for them (1:16-17). When the creatures were raised up from the earth, the wheels were lifted up because the **'spirit'** of **'life'**, that of the creatures, was in them to grant life. The prophet tells that the outer circles of these wheels, when elevated, were fearful in their splendour. Moreover, their **'rims'** were **'full of eyes'** (1:18-21).

The wheels served the living creatures, and, as 1:22-28 will reveal, the living creatures were beneath, and therefore subservient to, the God of Israel upon his throne.

In sum, the wheels were visionary and symbolic (see **'appearance ... as'**, 1:16) and were reflections of the magnificence of golden **'chrysolite'** (1:16). They enabled the chariot to move in any direction, indicating that God in heaven is active in this world. Thus, **'one wheel** [was] **upon the ground next to the living creatures'**. Further, **'when the living creatures ascended from the earth, the wheels ascended'** (1:15,19,21), demonstrating decisiveness, a unity of purpose in all God's actions. In that they had **'eyes'** in their outer rims, they manifested intelligence and omniscience, and were the location of the **'spirit of life'**. Unlike, say, the gods of Babylon, such as Bel and Nebo,[31] the God of Israel was neither confined to any particular territory nor was borne by man or beast. The wheeled means of transport beheld by Ezekiel was an autonomous vehicle upon which was to be seen the God of Israel.

The throne (Ezekiel 1:22-28)

In addition, Ezekiel saw something like a firmament, an expanse, above the living creatures. And above the appearance of the firmament there was the resemblance of a throne upon which was seated the semblance of a human form. It was radiant, as is white-hot metal. Surrounding the enthroned human appearance was that of a rainbow. The prophet, beholding the manifestation of the glory of Yahweh, heard God speaking and fell upon his face.

It is important to observe the frequency with which terms such as **'likeness'** (*d'mut*), **'appearance'** (*mar'eh*) and **'as'** (*k*) occur in 1:1-28, and particularly in verses 22-28. Ezekiel is determined to show that what he witnessed was visionary, a symbolic representation of divine reality. In no way does the vision trespass upon the demands of the Second Commandment.[32]

1:22-28. And a likeness was over the heads of the living creature: a firmament as the gleam of awesome crystal, stretched out over their heads, on top. And underneath the firmament their wings extended straight out, each one to its companion. To each were two wings covering them, and to each were two wings covering them, even their bodies. And I heard the sound of their wings, like the sound of many waters, like the sound of the Almighty, when they went; the sound of a tumult, as the sound of a camp. When they stood they let their wings sink down. And there was a sound from above the firmament that was over their heads. When they stood they let their wings sink down.

And from above the firmament that was over their heads there was as the appearance of a stone of sapphire, the likeness of a throne, and above the likeness of the throne a likeness as the appearance of a man above it, on top of it. And I saw as the gleam of amber, as the appearance of fire within and around, from the appearance of his loins and upwards. And from the appearance of his loins and downwards I saw as the appearance of fire, and brilliance surrounded him, as the appearance of the bow which would be in a cloud on a rainy day — thus the appearance of the surrounding brilliance. It was the appearance of the likeness of the glory of Yahweh. And I saw and fell upon my face and heard a voice speaking.

The **'likeness'** of an expanse resembling crystal rested over the heads of the creatures: **'a firmament as the gleam of awesome crystal, stretched out over their heads, on top'**. **'Firmament**' derives from *raqia*, meaning something that is stamped or beaten out.[33] In this case, the expanse was immense in its extent. *Qerah*, the Hebrew word behind **'crystal'**, normally denotes ice or frost,[34] the meaning here being that the platform, sparkling and glistening, was fearful in aspect. Beneath the firmament the creatures' wings were extended, though not necessarily to support it, the reason probably being that (of course) Yahweh did not need support. Further, the wings of these flying creatures were not designed for bearing loads. Some were in free motion, others covering the cherubim's bodies (1:23 repeating 1:11 for emphasis).

Clearly, Ezekiel's vision was a development of that granted to the prophet Isaiah about 150 years earlier.[35] Both men served the one, unchanging God. As we shall see, both visions were based on the gold-covered ark situated within the holiest place of the tabernacle (1:22-23).[36]

When the creatures were in motion their wings conveyed the impression of extraordinary yet controlled power. The throb of their reverberations was simultaneously like that of the **'sound'**, or torrent, of **'many waters'** (imagine Niagara), **'like'** the voice, or **'sound'**, of **'the Almighty'** (*shaddai*; cf. 10:5) and the clamour of an army camp. That their movement sounded like God speaking signifies that they were the attendants of Yahweh. Occasionally the creatures remained still, possibly because the God before whom they hid themselves restrained their exuberance. Then their wings sank down (1:24-25).

Above the heads of the creatures and above the expanse Ezekiel could see the appearance of an enormous gem, or semi-precious stone, shaped like a **'throne'**. It might have been lapis lazuli, bright blue in hue, although **'sapphire'** corresponds to the background Hebrew *sappir*.

Then, **'above the likeness of the throne a likeness as the appearance of a man above it, on top of it'**. Not beholding an actual human form, Ezekiel saw a vision of God, above whom there is no other.

From the **'loins'** upward the appearance of the human form was like incandescent metal, possibly brass or bronze (cf. 1:4). Ezekiel beheld radiant fire surrounding the appearance, a radiance that, perhaps strangely, was like a **'bow'**, or rainbow, **'in a cloud on a rainy day'**. The complete vision was nothing other than a manifestation of the glory of Yahweh. Ezekiel tells us that he collapsed. Then, prostrate, he heard a voice (1:26-28).

The prophet was granted this vision on other occasions during his ministry (3:23; 8:1-4; 10:1-22; 43:1-3). Chapter 10 declares that the four living creatures beneath the sapphire firmament were 'cherubim'. Just like the wheels, they were filled with eyes (10:12,15,20).

1. The significance of the vision of the throne

This vision was, of course, given to the prophet for a purpose, telling that Yahweh was glorious and powerful. Thus, the Hebrew term *kabôd* (1:28) signifies the weight of the divine majesty: in a pagan land, Ezekiel had seen the overpowering glory of the Lord.[37] Further, as noted, Ezekiel beheld a development not only of the vision of Isaiah 6:1-7, but also a variant of Exodus 24:10 and Exodus 25:10-22. Yahweh, who had committed himself to Israel at the time of the Exodus, was revealing himself as the same God in far-away Babylon nearly nine hundred years later.

In that the chariot of fire approached from the north, Jeremiah 1:13-16 comes to mind. There, 'north' represents Babylon, appointed as the weapon of God's judgement upon apostate Israel. So it does here.

The living beings and the wheels were replete with eyes, signifying that the chariot was self-directing, marking out its own path. The God of Israel revealed himself as omniscient and free to move at will.

Furthermore, the vision proclaimed that the relationship between the Lord and his people was *not* at an end, notwithstanding the impending destruction of Jerusalem and of its temple.

In previous times, the ark of the covenant symbolized, yet never assured, the presence of Yahweh with Israel.[38] In the arrangement seen by Ezekiel, God was present in person, the reality minus the material shell.[39]

Because the wheeled and winged throne of God was seen in Babylonia rather than in Judah, the vision announced that the land of Israel was not to be regarded by Ezekiel as the unique and necessary focus for the worship of God. And, if the throne of Yahweh spoke of his power and authority over all men, Ezekiel learned that, although Israelite exiles were defeated, disabled, disgraced and distant from home,[40] not only was the Lord with them *in* Babylon, but mighty Babylon was no more than a temporary instrument of the Lord, Yahweh showing himself to be free from all earthly limitations. The figure four, probably standing (as noted) for universality, seems to expound this truth. Ezekiel's four creatures, each with four faces and four wings, looked everywhere. The four wheels were able to move the chariot effortlessly in any direction.[41] In this fashion the revelation sets the scene for the drama to be unfolded in the first twenty-four chapters of the prophecy.

Furthermore, Ezekiel saw God in human form upon his throne, a figure said specifically to be like that of a man. If, as was the case, Adam was made in the image and likeness of God,[42] here there was a role-reversal. **'And above the *likeness* of the throne a *likeness as* the *appearance* of a man above it, on top of it'** is specific. Since this was a theophany, no representation of Yahweh other than that of the human form could have been possible.[43]

By means of the sign of the rainbow, the Lord showed himself faithful to his Genesis 9 covenant.[44] In a time of widespread war, when men were intent on damaging the environment, Ezekiel was reminded that the promise to Noah still held good: God would not forget his word and his world. Ecology mattered to him — and still matters.

It needs to be remembered, too, that this vision was seen by Ezekiel on four occasions during his lengthy ministry: firstly, when he was called to the prophetic ministry (1:4-28); secondly, when he was called upon to predict the destruction of Jerusalem and the temple (3:23); thirdly, a year and a half later, when he beheld the evils perpetrated in the temple and the departure of the glory of Yahweh from Jerusalem (8:4; 10:15-22); and, finally, when he witnessed the presence of Yahweh returning to his house, never to depart (43:1-4).

This being so, the vision relates to the whole prophecy of Ezekiel, telling that the God of Israel decrees and controls the destinies of nations, that he is alike the God of judgement and of salvation, and that he is to be, and will be, worshipped, feared and adored.

2. A theophany or Christophany?

In that Ezekiel was given to see the appearance of a man seated on the throne, did he behold the pre-incarnate Christ, as did, for example, Gideon and then Samson's parents?[45] Some of the older commentators are adamant.[46] More modern writers tend not to make the identification. Nor, with a slight hesitation, would this book.

Firstly, Isaiah 6:1, which is a precedent, is anthropomorphic: 'I saw Yahweh sitting on a throne, high and lifted up, and the train of his robe filled the temple.' Ezekiel's vision recapitulates and develops that of Isaiah. Daniel 7:9,13 also employ an anthropomorphism, telling that 'the Ancient of Days', who was other than the 'Son of Man' — the latter being the pre-incarnate Messiah — was robed and that on his head was white hair. Was it so in Ezekiel's vision too?

Secondly, within the New Testament the book of Revelation distinguishes between the enthroned God and the Lord Jesus Christ (which is not to say that Christ is not God).[47] In that John, prisoner on Patmos, recalls Ezekiel, likewise a captive, it would be hard to interpret the latter's vision as that of Christ.

Why, then, the anthropomorphism? May it not be that, even as Adam was created in the image and likeness of God, God may be measured by his own image in that Yahweh possesses all the attributes of personality? Ezekiel learned that the God of Israel was no impersonal, irrational force. And yet, may it not also be that Ezekiel's vision anticipated an incarnation?

'Emmanuel' would come to his earthly people because Christ is in the Father, and the Father in him.[48] John 12:41, with its recall of Isaiah 6:1-7, would seem to bear this out.

Application

The vision of God vouchsafed to Ezekiel is without parallel in the Old Testament. Nevertheless, it was inferior to the revelation granted to us in the person of our Lord Jesus Christ.[49] To the prophets — Ezekiel not excluded — 'it was revealed that, not to themselves, but to us they were ministering the things which now have been reported to you through those who have preached the gospel to you by the Holy Spirit sent from heaven.'[50] Whereas, for example, Ezekiel predicted the coming of the Good Shepherd (chapter 34), we know far more about him. Indeed, he is our incarnate Lord and Saviour.

Although Christian ministers are not prophets, they will never serve effectively unless, like Ezekiel, they begin their life's work with a true knowledge of him who sits upon the throne, who gives strength, who will judge every man according to his works, and who delights in mercy. Ezekiel commences his book by recounting his inaugural vision of God and ends by telling that Yahweh will ever be with his people (48:35). In the intervening chapters his concern is to expound the mind of the Lord. The pulpit should be dedicated to the proclamation of the one who is grace and truth.[51]

Forewarned is forearmed
(Ezekiel 2:1-10)

Chapters 2 and 3 tell of the call of Ezekiel to the prophetic ministry. When we arrive at 2:1, Ezekiel is still by the Chebar canal (see 1:1). There, in a visionary state, he is lifted up to behold for a second time the throne of Yahweh (3:12). After this he travels elsewhere to remain with some fellow-exiles for seven days (3:14-15). Then he receives fresh instructions concerning his responsibilities as a watchman (3:16-21) and is directed to go to the plain (3:22). There he again beholds the enthroned Yahweh. He prostrates himself, but is made to stand up (3:23-24). Further instructions are given (3:24-27).

The commissioning process may have taken eight days, if we draw a comparison with the period of consecration of Aaron and his sons.[52] And those days were eventful: apart from Moses, no other prophet was ever granted such a vision of the divine glory.[53]

It may be unfortunate that the content of 2:1 – 3:27 falls rather artificially into two chapters, in that both tell of Ezekiel's commissioning as a prophet. They should, therefore, be read together.

2:1-10. And he said to me, 'Son of man, stand upon your feet and I shall speak with you.' And the Spirit entered me as he spoke to me and stood me on my feet. Then I heard him who was speaking to me.

And he said to me, 'Son of man, I am sending you to the sons of Israel, to rebellious nations, who have rebelled against me. They and their fathers have transgressed against me to this very day. And the sons are hard of face and strong in heart. I am sending you to them, and you will say to them, "Thus says the Lord Yahweh." And they, whether they will hear or refrain (for they are a house of rebellion), will know that a prophet had been among them. And you, son of man, do not be afraid of them, nor be afraid of their words, because briars and thorns are with you, and you sit with scorpions. Do not be afraid of their words and do not be shattered on account of their faces, because they are a disobedient house. And you will declare my words to them, whether they listen or whether they refrain — for they are disobedient.

'And you, son of man, hear what I am telling you. Do not be rebellious like the house of rebellion. Open your mouth and eat whatever I give to you.' And I saw, and, look, a hand stretched out to me, and, look, in it was a scroll of a book. And he spread it out before me, and it was written, front and back, and written on it were lamentations, moaning and wailing.

Ezekiel the priest had collapsed when he saw the vision of Yahweh (1:28). Now he is told to stand up. Declining to address someone flat on the ground, the Lord would communicate with a servant in a posture appropriate for receiving a commission to speak for his God to the sons of Israel. But, although commanded to arise to hear God's word, in the presence of holiness Ezekiel could not summon the strength. Therefore **'the Spirit'** enabled him to obey (2:1-2). When overcome by the glory of their revelations, the prophets were invariably sustained by the Lord.[54]

Ezekiel was addressed as **'son of man'**, literally 'a son of Adam', one who partakes of the nature of the first man.[55] This ascription, which occurs sparingly in the Old Testament, is found over ninety times in Ezekiel. The expression may be a prophylactic, warning Ezekiel against the snares attendant upon inherent human frailty. As noted by R. W. Klein, who employs 'mortal' as a rendering for the Hebrew *ben Adam*, 'son of man':

> Ezekiel was profoundly influenced by the presence (or absence) of God and by the presence (or absence) of God's glory. In comparison with the glorious deity, the prophet himself is a mere mortal, a lowly, virtually anonymous channel through whom the word of Yahweh came... The name Yahweh, rather than the name or personality of Ezekiel, gives authority to the prophet's message.[56]

Because Ezekiel was a prophet-priest he must have been vulnerable to the sin of spiritual pride. Therefore he needed to appreciate more keenly the gulf between his weakness and the glory of God. It was Yahweh, rather than his own not inconsiderable abilities, who would enable him to serve as a prophet. The principle extended, too, to the experience of our Lord. In the Gospels, Jesus repeatedly describes himself as 'the Son of Man' in order to emphasize his true humanity, yet a perfect humanity overshadowed by the Spirit of God. He learned to be obedient.[57]

Yahweh informed Ezekiel that he was being sent to **'the sons of Israel'**, said to be **'rebellious nations'** (2:3, plural; not 'nation', as in some English versions). The meaning is that because the forefathers of Ezekiel's generation had alienated themselves from their God, their posterity possessed a dignity and stature no higher than that of idolatrous Gentiles. Following the captivity of the ten northern tribes, the two remaining tribes of Judah and Benjamin had been considered as representative of all Israel,[58] and it is so here.

In particular, these descendants are said to be **'a house of rebellion'**, rather than, say, 'the house of

Israel' — 'Israel' meaning something like 'a prince with God'.[59] This they were definitely not. They are said to be **'hard of face'** as well **'strong in heart'**, flatly refusing to lower their eyes in shame before Yahweh.[60] To such people Ezekiel must go. Whether they hear him or not (and they will not because they are rebellious), in time they shall acknowledge through the fulfilment of his words that **'a prophet'** had **'been among them'** (2:4-5). In previous years Isaiah had also been called to be faithful in the face of his countrymen's opposition.[61] Deuteronomy 18:22 stated that the predictions of a true prophet would always be honoured, and now the Lord informs Ezekiel that the false prophets who were presenting themselves to the people will never be vindicated (see 12:21 – 13:23). The time must come when Israel will be compelled to accept that Yahweh had sent Ezekiel.

Unlike Moses and Jeremiah, Ezekiel is not allowed an opportunity to excuse himself from his ministry. Nor, unlike Jonah, does he seek to evade his call.[62] Although the exiles are like **'briars'**, **'thorns'** and **'scorpions'**, Ezekiel is to fear neither them nor their words, nor their undisguised hostility. Their refusal to hear him is no more than an act of rebellion on their part, rather than an honest response to any supposed inadequacy in Ezekiel. So, because God has sent him, he is to be faithful to his commission.

'Shattered on account of their faces' (2:6) suggests profound disappointment, and even nervous shock, occasioned by addressing fellow-exiles who would display their contempt for the prophet's words. In later centuries, Paul and his gospel were a fragrance to some people, yet to others they were a stench. But he never deviated.[63]

The prophet was informed that he must not turn against Yahweh, as would **'the house of rebellion'**: the exiles simply did not represent the 'house of Israel'. It is tempting to suspect that an embittered

Ezekiel was on the point of opposing his call to the prophetic ministry. Yet he had to devour **'whatever'** would be given to him, this command probably being a test of his obedience; at that moment he could not have known what he would be required to consume and might have objected to eating anything unclean (2:7-8).[64]

Of course, there was no literal eating. The meaning is that the prophet had to absorb the declared word of God, making it a part of his whole being.[65] A **'hand'** holding a **'scroll'**, the latter either of papyrus or skin,[66] was stretched out in his direction (2:9).

Yahweh **'spread ... out'** the roll so that Ezekiel could see all of it before examining it in detail. He perceived that **'lamentations, moaning and wailing'** were written on both sides, possibly indicating that there was so much for the prophet to declare, or that there was no space for him to add any words of his own. But what was written on the scroll? One not unreasonable suggestion has been that the scroll might have symbolized Leviticus 26 and Deuteronomy 28, which project covenant curses against Israel in the event of the people being unfaithful.[67] It certainly signified that, until the destruction of Jerusalem and its temple, his ministry would be nothing other than condemnation, there being nothing else for him to declare. Yet, after the unthinkable had happened, his utterances would be none other than consolation (2:10; cf. 33:33 onwards).

Application

For some ten years, from 597 BC until 586 BC, Ezekiel was to announce to the exiles the impending desolation of the kingdom of Judah. Therefore, they were to prepare to mourn, weep and wail.

Such a ministry must have been an immeasurable burden for a weak, fallible 'son of man'. To be faithful, he would need help. The next chapter tells us that he received it. The Lord never allows faithful servants to fend for themselves.

The Christian pastor should spend much time with his God in prayer and strive to set his mind on 'things above'.[68] If he does not live, as it were, in the context of eternity, he will fail to warn the unrepentant of their immense peril and to remind the saints of their certain hope.

Over the years, the writer of this commentary, when in pastoral harness, spent far too much time in what he now considers to have been diversions. Beware of too many committees, of too much attendance at conferences and of too many administrative duties. When Paul counselled Timothy to give himself to reading,[69] was he not advocating a regime of intense ministerial study?

Ezekiel's responsibility (Ezekiel 3:1-27)

This chapter reveals Ezekiel as a man who the Lord knew would not back away from what would be, certainly in its initial stages, an entirely negative ministry. Although the word of Yahweh was sweetness to the prophet (3:3), upon reflection he was embittered in his heart and spirit (3:14). He must have asked himself whether he really wanted to be a mouthpiece for the God of Israel. In the event, yet again he saw the throne-chariot of Yahweh (3:23) and accepted that in the years ahead he must tell out only what Yahweh would reveal, and only when Yahweh would speak with him (3:24-27). When we arrive at the end of this third chapter we behold a prophet now prepared for a lifetime of service.

1. Courage (3:1-11)

3:1-11. And he said to me, 'Son of man, eat whatever you find; eat this roll, and go, speak to the house of Israel.' So I opened my mouth and he fed me this scroll. And he said to me, 'Son of man, feed your stomach and fill your bowels with this scroll that I am giving you.' And I ate, and in my mouth it became like honey for sweetness. And he said to me, 'Son of man, go. Come to the house of Israel, and you will speak to them with my words. For you are not being sent to a people of unintelligible speech and with a dull language, but to the house of Israel. Nor to many peoples with unintelligible speech and dull language, whose words you do not hear. Surely, if I had sent you to them they would hear you. But the house of Israel is not willing to listen to you because they are not willing to listen to me, because all the house of Israel are of a strong forehead and they are hard in heart. Look, I have given your face to be strong alongside their faces, and your forehead to be strong alongside their forehead. I have made your forehead like emery, harder than flint. You will not fear them and you will not be shattered in their presence, because they are a disobedient house.'

And he said to me, 'Son of man, all the words that I shall speak to you, take into your heart and hear with your ears. And go, come to the exiles, to the sons of your people, and you will speak to them and you will say to them, "Thus says the Lord Yahweh" — whether they hear or whether they refrain.'

When Paul travelled to Antioch in Pisidia on his first missionary journey, he was invited to preach in the local synagogue on the Sabbath day. He informed his Jewish hearers that Jesus Christ was the one of whom their Scriptures spoke. Seven days later, Paul returned — by invitation — to repeat what he had said. Sadly, because the Jews displayed their usual antagonism the apostle informed them that henceforth he would turn to the Gentiles. Those non-Jews who were present and who heard his words rejoiced.[70]

Ezekiel, of course, never lived to see this day, and was informed by the Lord that he would end his life among fellow-exiles who would not receive his ministry. Had he been sent to foreigners, they would have given him their serious attention (3:6; cf. 33:31-32) — but the time had not yet arrived.

So the prophet **'ate'** the scroll. In doing this, he absorbed the word of God into his innermost being. Because it was the word of God it **'became like honey for sweetness'**; the man rejoiced to be chosen as a mouthpiece for Yahweh (3:1-3). As noted by J. L.

Berquist, 'The scroll with bitter words tastes sweet to this prophet... He dedicates his life to announcing God's presence, which gives meaning and purpose to Ezekiel's life.' This was also the experience of Ezekiel's contemporary Jeremiah and, centuries later, of the apostle John.[71] Although Ezekiel does not actually say that the sweetness turned to bitterness, this may be inferred from 3:14, in that he 'went, bitter in my spirit's wrath'. Nevertheless, not disobedient, he stands alongside Jeremiah and John, among others.[72]

The **'son of man'** was instructed to **'come to the house of Israel, and you will speak to them with my words'**, in the knowledge that they would be able to appreciate the thrust of his message. Whatever other difficulties he might experience, there would be no communication problem. Nor was the prophet allowed to add to or subtract from what Yahweh instructed him to relay to the people.

To highlight the inevitable collision between prophet and hearers, the Lord reminded Ezekiel of the obvious: that he would not be approaching non-Jews, **'people of unintelligible speech and with a dull language ... whose words you do not hear'**. **'Unintelligible speech'** occurs in Isaiah 33:19, referring to barbarous nations whose speech was incomprehensible, and **'dull language'** in Exodus 4:10, where Moses professes to lack necessary eloquence. The burden of the charge is that Ezekiel's fellow-Jews would be obliged to respond to what they could understand perfectly well (3:4-6).

Yet, sadly, **'the house of Israel is not willing to listen to you because they are not willing to listen to me, because all the house of Israel are of a strong forehead, and they are hard in heart'**. Ezekiel was informed that they would resist him, not because of any inadequacy in his person or ministry, but because they were biased against the word of God.[73] Not only were they hard in their hearts, their perverse obstinacy would manifest itself even in the way they stared at Ezekiel (3:7). Whereas the forehead was the location where a minuscule section of the law of the Lord should have been tied as a symbol of obedience,[74] it would now manifest perversity. It had been like this for Isaiah, and Jesus would be faced with similar opposition.[75]

Yet Ezekiel will be granted strength to prevail: his **'face'** and **'forehead'**, too, will be **'strong'**. When they butt against him, he will push them back. He will be like **'emery, harder than flint'** (**'emery'** = *samīr*, perhaps 'diamond'; cf. Jer. 17:1): as diamond can cut into glass and as a flint knife is extremely sharp,[76] so the prophet will fearlessly cut away their resistance. Furthermore, he **'will not be shattered in their presence'**. Ezekiel will never suffer nervous collapse because he will always bear in mind that they are **'are a disobedient house'** (3:8-9).

Confronted with the prospect of such hostility, Ezekiel is promised God-given courage and firmness: whereas they harden themselves against God, Yahweh will strengthen, or harden, him, which may be why his name was 'Ezekiel', meaning (as has been noted) 'God strengthens'. Other prophets found themselves in a similar case.[77]

The son of man was told to **'take'** into his **'heart'** **'all the words that I shall speak to you'** and to **'hear'** them; seemingly, there would be future revelations (3:10). Then he must approach the communities of exiled Jews. Significantly, Yahweh informs him that they are the children of **'*your* people'**, meaning that, as God had in principle repudiated them because of their apostasy, they did not belong to him! Compare this with what the Lord said to Moses after Aaron had fabricated a golden calf: '... *your* people, whom *you* brought up from the land of Egypt, have corrupted themselves.'[78]

In spite of this, Ezekiel is required to speak, whether or not his hearers will attend: rejection by Ezekiel's generation and their rejection by Yahweh do not imply the Lord's permanent rejection of Israel (3:11).

2. Caught up in the Spirit (3:12-15)

3:12-15. And a wind raised me up, and I heard behind me the sound of a great earthquake — 'Blessed be the glory of Yahweh from his place' — and the sound of the wings of the living creatures touching one another, and the sound of the wheels alongside them — the sound of a great earthquake. And the wind raised me up and took me, and I went, bitter in my spirit's wrath, and the hand of Yahweh was strong upon me. I came to the exiles at Tel Abib, who were dwelling by the Chebar canal where they were living, and for seven days I sat there devastated among them.

After receiving this disturbing commission, Ezekiel was lifted up by the **'wind'** — that is, by the Spirit of God — presumably in vision.[79] He heard **'behind'** him a voice reverberating like the rumbling of a severe earthquake, saying, **'Blessed be the glory of Yahweh from his place'** (3:12). Although some commentators suggest that these words should not be retained in the background Hebrew text, in that they do not constitute a formal doxology,[80] such radical surgery does not seem necessary. The provenance of the voice would be the surround to the throne of Yahweh,[81] as might be suggested by 3:13: **'I heard ... the sound of the wings of the living creatures ... and the sound of the wheels alongside them — the sound of a great earthquake.'**

In this vision Yahweh discloses himself from the place where he is, from above the chariot of fire and glorified by all who find themselves in his holy presence. By this token the prophet is made to realize that he must publish the word and the attributes of the God of Israel, however depressed the spirituality of the people. He is reminded forcibly that truth must not be trimmed to satisfy the whims of men who have never given serious attention to the voice of Yahweh. The Lord remains the same in his glory even though the world and also Israel are in hopeless confusion.

Such encouragement was needful because Ezekiel proceeded **'bitter in my spirit's wrath'**. Sweet though the word of God might have been to him, he was aware that the call of God would involve much personal sorrow, and this knowledge overwhelmed him. What he could or, as he may have seen it, should, have been — a serving priest in Jerusalem — would never be. Or it may be that Ezekiel began to comprehend the righteous anger of the Lord towards an apostate people, and could see nothing in the foreseeable future other than 'lamentations, moaning and wailing' (cf. 2:10).

The first approach seems preferable. The shock of exile, an unprecedented vision of God, the awareness that he would minister among an insensitive people, and that he would always be a man standing alone, drained him. Yet although there was anger and resentment, he recounts that **'the hand of Yahweh was strong upon me'**. Divine power overcame Ezekiel's reluctance and he had no alternative but to obey (3:14). In the words of Amos:

A lion has roared!
Who will not fear?
The Lord GOD has spoken!
Who can but prophesy?[82]

In his vision, the son of man discovered himself in the company of some fellow-exiles at **'Tel Abib'** (meaning 'mound of spring produce' or, better, 'mound of the flood debris')[83] by the **'Chebar canal'**. Possibly they were living in light huts that they had built for themselves upon the elevation. He **'sat there devastated among them'**. The apparent clash between 1:1 and 3:15 may be resolved if the former points to the general area where the exiles were settled, and the latter to their specific location.

It might be that sitting was a conventional posture in times of grief and that a period of **'seven days'** was usual for displaying sorrow.[84] Further, this week of quiet meditation among those to whom he had been commissioned to speak would have corresponded to the consecration of priests to their office.[85] If so, the prophet identified with men who were on the point of losing just about everything they had. But there was more to it than sympathy and consolation: Ezekiel knew that before he could be a source of comfort to his fellow-Jews, he must be a messenger of sorrow. For this task, thoughtful preparation of mind and heart was essential. Understandably, he was distraught (3:15).

3. Ezekiel, a watchman (3:16-21)

3:16-21. And at the end of the seven days the word of Yahweh came to me, saying, 'Son of man, I have appointed you a watchman for the house of Israel. When you hear a word from my mouth you will warn them from me. When I say to the wicked person, "You will certainly die," and you do not warn him and you do not speak to warn the wicked person away from his wicked path in order to live, he, the wicked person, will die in his iniquity — but I shall seek his blood from your hand.

'And as for you, when you warn a wicked person and he does not turn from his wickedness and from his wicked path, he will die in his iniquity — but you will have delivered your soul. And when a righteous person turns from his righteousness and practises evil, and I set a stumbling block in front of him, he will die. Because you did not warn him he will die for his sin, and his righteous acts that he did will not be remembered — but I shall seek his blood from your hand.

'And as for you, when you warn him — the righteous man — that the righteous should not sin, and he does not sin, he will surely live because he was warned, and you will have delivered your soul.'

After the seven-day silence, Ezekiel, now recovering from the shock of the initial revelation, received the final part of his commission: he would be a **'watchman'** (3:16-17).[86] The same charge, albeit amplified, is repeated in 33:1-16. He can be contrasted with the prophet Habakkuk, called to be a watchman in the sense that he was to expect a word from Yahweh.[87] Ezekiel was a watchman in that, like Jeremiah, he had to guard his people by warning them of impending danger.[88]

Ezekiel was solemnly informed that, should he fail to warn the inveterate sinner who lacked respect for the covenant between God and Israel,[89] that person must die in recompense for his iniquity. Yet in that situation Ezekiel would be considered as a murderer, having shed the man's blood, albeit indirectly.[90] Conceivably, had the foolish man been told about his danger he might have been reclaimed. Therefore the prophet must discharge his personal responsibility and deliver his own **'soul'** by telling out the truth of God (3:18-19). 'Soul' does not stand for man's undying spirit but his complete self, his whole being.

Similarly, if a **'righteous person'** lapses into sin and if Ezekiel fails to rebuke him, the former must die, his righteous conduct not being taken into consideration by God: accrued guilt will have to be paid for. But, again, Ezekiel's silence will be tantamount to homicide in that he could have spoken but had failed to do so. Therefore the prophet must preserve his hands from the blood of the degenerate sinner by giving him timely warning. If he does so and if the offender repents, Ezekiel will deliver himself from danger. Equally, Ezekiel was instructed to warn the relatively 'righteous man' who had not as yet deviated from his path — but who might. No eventuality could be overlooked.

The act of turning from righteousness is associated with a God-given obstacle, or **'stumbling block'**. The meaning could be that Yahweh permits those who are called by his name to be tempted by evil even though he never directly invites men to do wrong. But if they wish to sin, they are given opportunity to do so and must reap the just consequences.[91] Or, a stumbling block might have been a blessing from God that renders a sinner complacent or even hostile. Perhaps this is what is meant when we read in Isaiah that Christ would become a stumbling block to both the houses of Israel.[92]

It is to be noted that Ezekiel's commission to address those who had abandoned, or would abandon, righteousness had nothing to do with any speculation about whether or not godly people can fall finally from grace. Ezekiel's reader must be careful not to attribute to him the rounded New Testament doctrine of justification by faith. Deuteronomy 24:13, in commenting on the treatment of a debtor by his creditor, states that mercy shown to the destitute 'shall be righteousness to you before Yahweh your God'.

That is to say, Old Testament practical righteousness meant fidelity to the demands of the Ten Commandments, the heart of the Sinai covenant, and all their numerous applications. Thus Zachariah and Elizabeth 'were both righteous before God, walking blameless in all the commandments and ordinances of the Lord'.[93] All that is taught here, in chapter 3, is that there are inseparable bonds between repentance and life and between deliberate sin and death. If men persist in evil, they die — even if they are ostensibly members of the covenant community. If they turn from sin, they live (3:20-21).

Ezekiel's commission gives much emphasis to the principle that every Israelite to whom he would communicate the word of God was individually responsible to Yahweh. The covenant relationship between Israel and God retreats, and the priest/prophet becomes virtually a pastor of souls.[94]

In sum, the emphasis of this passage is upon Ezekiel's responsibility, whether or not his hearers respond positively to his warnings being almost a secondary issue.

4. Movement (3:22-24)

3:22-24. And the hand of Yahweh came upon me there, and he said to me, 'Rise, go out to the plain and there I shall speak with you.' So I rose up and went out to the plain, and, look, the glory of Yahweh was standing there, like the glory that I saw by the Chebar canal, and I fell on my face. And the Spirit entered me and made me to stand on my feet, and he spoke with me and said to me, 'Come, shut yourself up inside your house.'

Here we are told about a further extended silence enforced upon Ezekiel, and are introduced to four prophecies which he was instructed to enact rather than utter.

Again **'the hand of Yahweh came upon'** Ezekiel. Firstly, the prophet was commanded to depart from the exiles in Tel Abib, where they and he were (cf. 3:15). Accordingly, he left them in order to proceed to **'the plain'**, perhaps an alluvial river plain, a wasteland, where he saw again the vision given to him by the Chebar canal (1:4-28). Overawed (**'and, look,'**), yet again the prophet fell prostrate to the ground (3:22-23).

And yet again (cf. 2:2) **'the Spirit'** raised him upon his feet in order to receive a further revelation.

The Lord instructed his servant: **'Come, shut yourself up inside your house.'** Did Yahweh intend that Ezekiel should be given space for further contemplation prior to entering upon an exceptionally difficult ministry? Almost certainly not. Rather, the prophet will sally forth to meet his fellow-exiles only if and when he has a word from the Lord to share with them, as suggested by 3:25-27. So, if he has nothing to say he must remain quietly in his residence (3:24).

5. A future ministry (3:25-27)

3:25-27. 'And you, son of man, look — they have placed cords on you and have tied you up with them, and you will not go out among them. But I shall make your tongue stick to the roof of your mouth. So you will be dumb and will not be a prosecutor for them because they are a rebellious house. But when I speak with you I shall open your mouth, and you will say to them, "Thus says the Lord Yahweh." He who hears, let him hear; and he who refrains, let him refrain — for they are a rebellious house.'

The ensuing revelation divides into three sections, each commencing with the address **'and you, son of man'** (3:25; 4:1; 5:1). Ezekiel was commanded to act out symbolically the siege of Jerusalem, and in chapter 5 to assume the collective role of the inhabitants following the reduction of the city.

Although Jeremiah, a contemporary of Ezekiel, was actually thrown into prison,[95] there is no evidence that Ezekiel received similar treatment. It follows that the binding of the prophet with **'cords'** in his own house might be best understood as a non-physical, figurative restraint placed upon him by spiritual powers commissioned by Yahweh (**'they'**; cf. the check mentioned by 4:8). Accepting the discipline, his lips are constrained. Apparently, it is Yahweh who will **'make** [his] **tongue stick to the roof of** [his] **mouth'**, rendering him **'dumb'**, so that Ezekiel will not be **'a prosecutor for them'** — the reason being that the exiles **'are a rebellious house'**. The verdict had already been passed, and there was no more time for rebuke with a view to national restoration. The silence was intended to persist until Ezekiel received tragic news about the destruction of Jerusalem six or seven years later, in 586 BC. This non-literal interpretation is supported by 24:27 and 33:22.[96] Then, his mouth will be open, even though not all will take him seriously (3:25-27).

'He who hears, let him hear; and he who refrains, let him refrain,' anticipates our Lord's words in Matthew 13:9 following the parable of the sower: 'He who has ears to hear, let him hear.' As Taylor observes, Ezekiel's message will 'confirm men in their attitude to the God who inspired it: they will either hear it and obey; or ignore it and be condemned'.[97] Henceforth, Ezekiel will be the mouthpiece of the Lord, speaking in public only when God has something for him to say (3:27).

Application

Ezekiel's ministry was exercised at a time when most Israelites refused to believe that Jerusalem could, would, or should be destroyed. Moreover, within the New Testament there appear to be only two verses — 2 Corinthians 6:16-17 — which give direct quotations from the prophecy (20:34,41; 37:27), although the vision of the chariot-throne finds plentiful allusion in the book of Revelation. It might, therefore, be somewhat difficult to deduce specific lessons from the experiences of the pastor-prophet at this point in his ministry to apply to contemporary ministers of the gospel.

Nevertheless, certain principles stand out.

Firstly, when he was inducted to the office of prophet, Ezekiel beheld the glory of the Lord no less than three times (1:4-28; 3:12-13,23). Imbued with a sense of the transcendent majesty of the God of Israel who would not be confined to the land of Canaan, the prophet would persevere in his ministry as the years rolled by. The minister of the gospel who lacks an appreciation of the greatness, holiness and righteousness of his God may find it hard to give his heart to his work. Those who, like Ezekiel, fall before their God rather than into sin will find that he grants strength to overcome.

Ezekiel had to be warned against personal rebellion, chapters 2 – 3 reminding an apparently reluctant 'son of man' (3:14) that he was only a man and had no option but that of obedience. Although we all sin, sin is, nevertheless, unthinkable because it offends God. Yet we can (and often do!) go to 1 John 1:9.

In later years the apostle Paul almost certainly alluded to Ezekiel's commission when he addressed the Ephesian elders, testifying that he was 'innocent of the blood of all men',[98] believing that he had been faithful to his call. It follows that the charge given to Ezekiel relates to all who handle the word of God. Ministers who do not preach the truth have a problem for which, in time, they will have to give their answer. Woe to us if we do not proclaim the counsel of God![99]

Like Ezekiel, the minister of the gospel is called to be faithful to the Bible rather than to be obviously successful (although numbers are never unimportant). Whether or not others heed, he has to remain a watchman. But truth must always be communicated in love, and sometimes this can be difficult. Moreover, we should always ask what more there is that we might do to spread the word. Ezekiel himself was never short of ways and means to communicate, as we shall see from 4:1 onwards.

A minister must be careful to be neither more nor less than a servant of the word: Ezekiel was commissioned to speak for the Lord and was denied any opportunity to communicate with his fellow-exiles about other matters. There are far too many ministers who employ their pulpits to speak about anything and everything apart from the gospel of the grace of God.

Judgement upon Israel
(Ezekiel 4:1 – 7:27)

Ezekiel's ministry now commences with a series of seemingly bizarre acted signs. Firstly, there is his symbolic siege of a clay brick or tablet and the placing of a barrier between the brick and himself (4:1-3).[100] Then the prophet is instructed to lie on his left and right sides respectively for specified periods (4:4-6), this to be followed by the baring of his arm (4:7) supplemented by a species of divine restraint (4:8). Following this, Ezekiel is required to consume minimal quantities of ritually unclean food and water (4:9-15) and then to shave and dispose of his hair (5:1-4). Judgement over Jerusalem is announced (5:7-10), and there is a second pronouncement to the same effect (5:11-17). Yahweh then proclaims his judgement upon the mountains of Jerusalem (6:1-14), issuing an alarm that takes the form of a song of lamentation (7:1-27).

In sum, these four chapters proclaim the impending doom of two bastions of Jewish hope: the city of Jerusalem with its temple, and the land of Israel.

1. The first symbolic act: the clay brick (4:1-3)

4:1-3. 'And you, son of man, you will take for yourself a brick and place it before you. You will engrave a city upon it — Jerusalem. And you will lay a siege against it and will build a siege wall against it. You will pile up a siege mound against it, place camps against it and set battering rams against it all around. And you will take for yourself an iron plate and place it as an iron wall between you and the city, and you will set your face towards it so that it is under siege. You will besiege it. It is a sign for the house of Israel.'

The first action involved Ezekiel's employment of readily obtainable materials from everyday life. He was to inscribe upon a **'brick'** of clay a simple line drawing of the contours of the city of **'Jerusalem'**. (By analogy, imagine an outline logo of London, perhaps depicting the Tower of London, Tower Bridge, Big Ben and St Paul's Cathedral.) Perhaps Ezekiel was to perform this act in an open space in front of his house, where a large crowd would have quickly assembled. His sketch would undoubtedly have featured an outline of Solomon's Temple, still standing at that time (4:1).

Then he would **'lay a siege against it'**, an action which may have involved small models, in that he had to **'build a siege wall** [representations of siege towers or of an encircling wall] **against it'** and **'pile up a siege mound** [a small ramp of earth] **against it, place camps** [standing for military divisions] **against it and set battering rams** [named from the butting tendency of that animal] **against it all around'**. Presumably reclining on the ground (cf. 4:4-6), Ezekiel was to demonstrate in a most vivid fashion that Jerusalem would remain under siege with no possible relief forthcoming (4:2).

Then he had to place an **'iron plate'**, by which is meant a kitchen pan or griddle, between himself and the brick. This would represent an impregnable wall of partition between, on the one hand, the besieging Babylonians and the God who had sent them and, on the other, the blockaded city.

The charge given to Ezekiel, which text and context assume he obeyed, was so unusual that his disquieted fellow-exiles must have gaped at him in astonishment.

Perhaps the clay of the brick and the iron of the griddle represented, respectively, the weakness of Jerusalem and the strength of the besiegers. Yet, in that it was Ezekiel, as the prophet of Yahweh, who was told to **'set your face towards it'** — that is, against the brick — the Lord was showing in a most graphic manner at the outset of his servant's lengthy ministry that it was he, the God of Israel, who was the omnipotent adversary of the wicked city and all its evil.

If those who beheld Ezekiel accepted that he was a genuine prophet (and there is no reason to doubt this), they would have been profoundly shocked by what they saw and the inference they derived from it. Could Yahweh ever turn against the site of David's throne and against his temple? But Ezekiel indicates that it would be so: his actions were **'a sign for the house of Israel'** — for all the covenant people, whether within the land of promise or elsewhere (4:3).

Even so, perhaps the majority of Ezekiel's spectators, and those who were told about his weird action, still believed that the Lord would soon terminate the siege of Jerusalem.[101] If so, Ezekiel's next action must have relieved them of the delusion.

2. The second symbolic act: lying down on each side (4:4-8)

4:4-8. 'But you, lie down upon your left side, and you will lay the iniquity of the house of Israel upon it. For the number of the days that you will lie upon it, you shall bear their iniquity. And I myself have designated the years of their iniquity as the number of days for you: 390 days, and you will bear the iniquity of the house of Israel. And you will complete these and lie down a second time, upon your right side, and shall bear the iniquity of the house of Judah for forty days: a day for a year, a day for a year I have assigned to you. And you shall set your face towards the siege of Jerusalem and with your arm bared you will prophesy against her. Look, I have placed cords upon you, and you will not turn yourself from side to side until you have completed the days of your siege.'

Symbolically enacting the siege of Jerusalem, Ezekiel personified the immediate future of its populace by being made to **'bear'** their sins, though not as a sacrificing priest. That the two actions, siege and sin-bearing, were synchronous is borne out by verse 7.

Ezekiel was commanded to **'lie down'** on his **'left side'** for 390 days without turning over, and on his **'right side'** for forty days. If these periods were consecutive, totalling 430 days, they seem to clash with 8:1, which records that Ezekiel's next vision began fourteen lunar months — 413 days — after this (cf. 1:2).[102] It is possible, then, that the two were concurrent, or that the vision recorded in 8:1 onwards overlapped. It is impossible to be dogmatic about this.

Apparently, the prophet was to stretch out with his head pointing towards the west and his feet to the east. This strange posture was deliberate, although humiliating in the extreme: Ezekiel was required to communicate a vital lesson to his fellow-Jews because they needed to humble themselves. He could not have reclined during the whole twenty-four hours of each day for more than a year because such an exercise would have been physically impossible and because, as shown by 4:9-17, he had, among other matters, to prepare his own food.

The 390 days would represent **'the years of their iniquity'** — that is, **'of the house of Israel'** — while the forty days are said to represent **'the iniquity of the house of Judah ... a day for a year'**.

To understand the significance of the 390 and forty-day periods, let's note what seems to be reasonably clear and then to try to look at the matter through the eyes of Ezekiel:[103]

1. The period between the building of the temple in, say, 966 BC until its destruction in 586 BC was very nearly 390 years.

2. The stated number of day-years stands for periods during which the prophet would **'bear the iniquity of the house of Israel'** and **'the iniquity of the house of Judah'**. According to Leviticus 16:21-22, on the Day of Atonement the high priest was to acknowledge the 'iniquities', the 'transgressions' and the 'sins' of Israel, and would lay them symbolically upon the head of the scapegoat, which would 'bear' 'all their iniquities' away. It seems that Ezekiel was to inform apostate Israel by act and by deed that they would be inflicted for their sins inasmuch as there was no scapegoat.

3. There appears to be a deliberate recall of Numbers 14:34: 'According to the number of the days in which you spied out the land, forty days, for each day you shall bear your iniquity one year, forty years, and you shall know my rejection.' In a reversal of the procedure of Numbers 14:34, one day now represents one year.

4. Even as the forty-year period predicted by Numbers 14:34 was intended to remove a sinful generation in order to prepare for the second-generation conquest of Canaan, so the destruction of the apostate theocracy appears as a prelude to a new beginning (so chapter 34 onwards). If so, Ezekiel was to declare that both punishment and preparation were on the horizon.[104]

5. It follows that the period of 390 + 40 day-years is related to the siege of Jerusalem and the collapse of the Israelite theocracy. Acting in place of Yahweh, who was attacking the city (4:3), Ezekiel also represented Jerusalem as it suffered beneath the Babylonian scourge.

6. The period totalling 430 days seems to end at 586 BC, when Jerusalem was destroyed.

7. According to Exodus 12:40-41, Israel spent 430 years in Egypt prior to the Exodus.

8. Although Ezekiel's action was not expiatory, since no Old Testament prophet or priest was ever required to be an actual sin-bearer, in that he would bear the iniquity of Israel and Judah he was performing a legitimate priestly function. This, when explained, would have been understandable to his spectators.[105]

Taking all this into account, it may be that Ezekiel knew that, according to Scripture, were Israel to invalidate the Sinai covenant (in spirit, if not formally), banishment to a foreign land would be their lot, such an exile being modelled by the 430-year servitude of Jacob and his family in Egypt.[106] He would also have been aware that the sum of 390 and 40 is 430.[107]

And he must have known that the period from the inauguration of the temple until its destruction was almost 390 years, and that during those years the northern tribes and also Judah were advancing to a state of virtual apostasy.[108] Finally, Ezekiel knew that whereas Israel went into exile in 722 BC,[109] Judah, the sole remnant of David's united kingdom, had endured until at least 592 BC, up to the occasion of his first sign-act.

For the prophet, all this must have crystallized into a dramatic association of ideas. Ezekiel's actions informed all who had ears and eyes that there would be another sojourn in an unclean land (prefigured by the residence of Israel, then a slave nation, in Egypt); that (like the wilderness journey) the anticipated exile would be punitive — the Lord's response to the degeneracy of the twelve tribes following the time of David; and that Judah might expect a restoration to the land of promise. However, the duration of the exile is not specified. Ezekiel's lesson was that past iniquities must lead to a penal eviction, there being no immediate hope for the people, for the Davidic monarchy, for Jerusalem, or for its temple.

Significantly, he would announce that the judgement must be suffered by Judah,[110] upon the assumption that 'Israel' and 'Judah', although formally distinct, were not to be considered separately. Prior to and following 4:4-6, the term **'house of Israel'** refers consistently to the twelve tribes, with little or no reference to the division of the kingdom. For example, 17:2 assumes typically that Judah-in-exile represents 'the house of Israel'.[111]

In sum, what Ezekiel offered his people were emotive numbers: 390, 40 and 430 individually and in concert recalling past miseries and predicting more to come, but also anticipating a restoration (4:4-6).

When lying upon his right side, Ezekiel must **'set** [his] **face towards the siege of Jerusalem'** and, with his **'arm bared'**, he would **'prophesy against her'**. 'To set one's face' is a common Old Testament expression for steadfastness of purpose, even hostility,[112] and with his arm bared he would exhibit the resolution of a warrior prepared for battle.[113]

Thus his eyes were to remain fixed upon the sketch of Jerusalem inscribed on the clay brick, his undeviating gaze portraying the unrelenting character of the promised judgement. Moreover, it seems that the prophet had to allow himself to be trussed with **'cords'** so that the allotted time span for the symbolic siege could not be reduced: attackers and defenders had all been set in place by Yahweh. By comparison with 3:25, it may be that these cords were metaphorical, the prophet being bound (so to speak) to say nothing to his hearers other than the declared word of the Lord.

It is probable that Ezekiel would have spent only a part of each day lying on his right and then left side.

Otherwise, as noted, he could not have carried out the instructions of 4:9 – 5:4. Yet the self-restraints placed upon both tongue and body must have intimated to all and sundry that he would not deviate from his mute but powerful warning **'until you have completed the days of your siege'**. By **'your'** (singular), Yahweh insists that Ezekiel will identify with the divine purpose (4:7-8).

3. The third symbolic act: survival rations (4:9-17)

4:9-17. 'But take for yourself wheat, barley, beans, lentils, millet and emmer, and you will put them into a single vessel and shall make them into bread for yourself. You will eat it the number of days that you lie on your side — for 390 days. And your food that you will eat will be by weight: twenty shekels a day. From time to time you will eat it. And you will drink water by measure: one-sixth of a hin. From time to time you will drink. And you will eat it as a barley cake and it will be cooked in their sight with lumps of human excrement.'

And Yahweh said to me, 'Thus shall the sons of Israel eat their bread, defiled, among the nations where I shall expel them.'

And I said, 'Ah, Lord Yahweh. Look, my soul has never been defiled; and since I was a youth until now I have never eaten what died of itself or was torn, and impure meat has never entered my mouth.'

Then he said to me, 'See, I have given to you the dung-pats of an ox instead of the lumps of a human, and you will make your bread over them.'

And he said to me, 'Son of man, look, I am breaking the staff of bread in Jerusalem, and they will eat bread by weight and with anxiety, and will drink water by measure and in desolation — so that bread and water may fail, and a man and his brother be desolated and be consumed by their iniquity.'

The prophet was instructed to enact a third sign, in which he would portray not only the sufferings of the city of Jerusalem under prolonged siege by consuming drastically reduced quantities of food and drink, but also the afflictions of deportees carried off into exile by eating food prepared in a manner abhorrent to Jews (or, indeed, to anyone). The cooking of food with sun-dried excrement for fuel would be an analogue to the horror of surviving on an alien diet in an idolatrous land (4:9). Daniel and his three friends were confronted with that problem and, in later centuries, Christians at Corinth were faced with the same issue.[114]

During the 390 + 40 days (although only 390 days are mentioned here), **'from time to time'**, possibly once or twice a day, the prophet-priest would eat different kinds of grain and vegetables which, in their scarcity, had to be baked into cakes over a fire fuelled by **'lumps of human excrement'**. This means that, lacking utensils, Ezekiel would bake the dough by laying it directly upon the glowing ashes of burnt faeces, the resultant lump of bread bearing the marks of the ashes. One can well appreciate Ezekiel's repugnance. **'Emmer'** was a kind of wheat with bearded ears, now grown mainly for fodder and cereals.

Moreover, this food would be cooked **'in their sight'** — that is, publicly. We are nauseated when we try to imagine the details of preparation. Ezekiel's drink was to be water only. The stated quantities are meagre in the extreme: of food, **'twenty shekels a day'**, perhaps about 230 grams, and of water, **'by measure: one-sixth of a hin'**, about half a litre.[115] When observed outside (or within?) his house and lying on his side, Ezekiel had to be seen to chew and sip starvation rations. In that it would have been impossible for a man to survive on such a meagre diet for much more than a year, it may be that Ezekiel was allowed these quantities for public consumption only, in that his actions were no more than a parable. In any event, his cumulative suffering must have been intense (4:10-12).

This diet, although not necessarily unhygienic, was ritually unclean as well as (to say the least) obnoxious. Such a diet constituted **'defiled'** food because lands beyond Israel were reckoned to be besmirched and because human excrement, upon which his food had to be cooked, would normally have been given careful disposal.[116] It is no surprise, then, that an Israelite priest who loved Yahweh and his law protested, much like Simon Peter at a later time.[117] But whereas Peter was informed that the Old Testament dietary regulations had been cancelled, for Ezekiel they remained in force.

Therefore Ezekiel declared that he had never eaten flesh from animals that had died naturally, from animals that had been killed by beasts of prey and from which the blood would not have been drained,[118] or from that which was **'impure'** (*piggûl*), probably meaning sacrificed flesh left over to the third day and beginning to putrefy,[119] such meat being as anathema as the flesh of the pig.[120] For this reason, permission was given to him to use dried cow-dung as fuel instead of human waste. None the less, the regime was loathsome (4:13-15).

The term **'staff of bread'** is enigmatic, unless it is a deliberate allusion to the covenant curse of Leviticus 26:26: 'When I break your *staff of bread*, ten women will bake your bread in one oven, and they will bring back your bread by weight, and you will eat and not be satisfied.' The ancient warning must be fulfilled in that the people of Jerusalem will eat their bread **'by weight'** — that is, in carefully measured amounts — so scarce will it be. Far from Yahweh having broken his agreement with Israel, he will be faithful to what he had declared at Sinai. Possibly, Leviticus 26:39 is recalled in 4:17: 'And those among you who are left will be *consumed* in their iniquities in the lands of their enemies; and also in the iniquities of their fathers, which are with them, they will be *consumed*' (4:16-17).

4. The fourth symbolic act: Ezekiel's hair (5:1-4)

5:1-4. 'But you, son of man, take for yourself a sharp sword: as a barber's razor you will take it for yourself, and you will pass it over your head and your beard. And you will take for yourself a weighing scale and divide them up. A third you will consume with fire in the centre of the city, when the days of the siege are fulfilled. Then you will take a third: you will strike with the sword all around it. And a third you will scatter to the wind, and I shall draw out a sword after them. From there you will then take a few in number and bind them in your gown. And you will take from them again and shall throw them into the centre of the fire, and you will burn them with fire. Fire will go out from it to all the house of Israel.'

The final symbolic action involved the cutting of Ezekiel's hair. The **'son of man'** would take a **'sharp sword'** and, apparently, whet it until it had the edge of a razor. Then, he would shave off his hair and his beard or, perhaps, seek the services of a barber (5:1).

One can imagine the astonishment of those who beheld Ezekiel performing this strange action. Although in Old Testament times cutting the hair was both a mark of mourning and a part of the Nazirite vow,[121] shaving as a ritual act of worship was strictly forbidden.[122] On one occasion it became a mark of dishonour and ridicule, when David's envoys had part of their beards removed by Ammonites.[123]

So what would Ezekiel's spectators have made of it? Perhaps they recalled Isaiah 7:20, in which judgements upon Israel are described as a shaving of the head and facial and bodily hair with a mercenary razor. In context, Isaiah predicted that Yahweh would conscript the Assyrians into his service to chastise the ten tribes. In Ezekiel's situation, because priests were forbidden to shave either the head or the beard,[124] his shaving must have symbolized desolation and judgement from Yahweh.

When cut off, Ezekiel's hair had to be divided into three equal parts. One third was to be burnt, possibly on top of the clay sketch of Jerusalem. Another third was to be chopped up into little pieces and placed around the sketch. Nearly all of the remaining third was to be scattered to the winds. **'And I shall draw out a sword after them'** (5:2) derives from the warning of Leviticus 26:33: 'I shall scatter you among the nations and draw out a sword after you.'

Ezekiel was to retrieve a small quantity of the hair lying around the clay tile and tuck it in his robes (5:3).[125] From this remnant a minute quantity would be committed to a fire ignited near the brick representing Jerusalem.

The burden of Ezekiel's action was that what he did with his hair God would do to Jerusalem. Firstly, the Babylonian aggressor was destined to put the city to the torch. Many would perish within the gates, others dying by the sword beyond the walls. Those who remained were to be scattered in exile where, far from home, they would not find relief, war pursuing them wherever they tried to settle. Surprisingly, among the few survivors there must be a further refinement, this time by fire: a flame would spread **'to all the house of Israel'** (5:4).[126] In fulfilment of Leviticus 26:36-39, the long arm of divine justice would stretch beyond the borders of Israel.[127]

5. The signs explained (5:5-17)

5:5-17. 'Thus the Lord Yahweh has said: "This is Jerusalem: I have set her in the centre of the nations, and around her are lands. But she rebelled against my judgements more wickedly than the nations, and against my statutes more than the lands around her; for they rejected my judgements, and as for my statutes, they did not walk in them."

'Therefore, thus says the Lord Yahweh: "Because you are more tumultuous than the nations that are around you — you have not walked in my statutes and you have not performed my judgements, nor have acted according to the judgements of the nations that are around you" — therefore, thus says the Lord Yahweh: "Look, I, even I, am against you, and I shall perform judgements in your midst in the eyes of the nations. And I shall do in you what I have not done, and the like of which I shall not do again, because of all your abominations. Therefore, fathers will eat sons in your midst, and sons will eat their fathers, and I shall perform judgements among you and shall scatter all your remnant to every wind."

'"Therefore, as I live," says the Lord Yahweh, "Surely, because you have defiled my sanctuary with all your pollutions and with all your abominations, I also will withdraw. Neither will my eye be piteous, nor will I spare. A third of you will die by the plague and will fail by famine in your midst; and a third will fall by the sword around you; and I shall scatter a third to every wind, and I shall draw out a sword after them.

'"Then, when my anger is spent and I rest my fury among them, I shall be comforted, and they will know that I, Yahweh, have spoken in my jealousy when I have discharged my fury among them. And I shall make you a desolation and a reproach among the nations that are around you, in the eyes of everyone who passes by. So it will be reproach and derision, discipline and horror for the nations around you when I execute judgements among you with anger and with fury, and with raging rebukes. I, Yahweh, have spoken.

When I dispatch the evil arrows of famine against them, which will be for destruction — which I shall dispatch to destroy you, I shall intensify famine upon you and I shall break your staff of bread. And I shall send famine on you, and the wild beast, and they will make you childless; plague and blood shall pass among you, and I shall bring the sword upon you. I, Yahweh, have spoken."'

Through his servant, Yahweh now explains the signs. Symbolism ceases. For the first time in his ministry the prophet is to speak in plain terms, doing so until he records another vision, given to him one year later (see 8:1). Ezekiel's exposition involves parallelism, a distinctive feature of Hebrew literature.

The prophet declares that Yahweh had **'set her** [Jerusalem] **in the centre of the nations, and around her are lands'** (5:5). That is, Israel was situated strategically at a mid-point between Africa, Europe and Asia, and was able to communicate by sea or by land north, south, east and west (cf. 38:12). Further, there was a degree of geographical isolation affording protection: desert to the east and south, sea to the west and mountainous northern borders. The twelve tribes were granted ample opportunity to settle, to thrive, and to be a light to the nations. Yet the geographical situation of Jerusalem was a secondary matter, in that God had chosen this city as his habitation and the seat of the throne of David. In the words of Psalm 132:13-14, 'For Yahweh has chosen Zion; he has desired it for his habitation: this is my resting place for ever; here I shall dwell, for I have desired it.'

The election of Israel explains the following indictment: sadly, Israel had **'rebelled against my judgements more wickedly than the nations, and against my statutes more than the lands around her'** (5:6). In an absolute sense this could not have been the case because the surrounding nations were not in receipt of Moses' written law and hence could not formally rebel against it. And evidence does not prove that the twelve tribes were more debased than, say, Egypt or Assyria. The meaning is that Israel had sinned against the greater light, that of special revelation.[128]

This condemnation is now given expansion: the surrounding nations were not without some understanding of right and wrong and, to a point, observed the light of conscience.[129] A comparison may be made with 11:12: 'And you will know that I am Yahweh; for you have not walked in my statutes, and my judgements you have not executed, but have done according to the judgements of the nations which are around you.' Likewise 16:47: 'But you have not walked in their ways [those of the nations] or have done according to their abominations. In such a short time you have caused ruin in all your ways more than they.'

What was worse, states Yahweh, had Israel never received Moses' law, this insensitive people would have proved themselves more depraved than their neighbours: **'you have not ... acted according to the judgements of the nations which are around you'** (5:7).

But how could this be? To quote Gardiner:

> The various religions of the heathen were alike in imposing little check on the passions and selfishness and self-will of man; in fact, they often not only encouraged but deified the worst traits of human nature. The law of God, on the contrary, set before men as the object of their worship a Being of absolute purity and holiness, and made the devotion to Him of heart and soul and strength its first and most absolute command.[130]

So Jeremiah 2:11:

> Has a nation changed its gods,
> Which are not gods?

But my people have changed their Glory
For what does not profit.[131]

The sins of Jerusalem were aggravated because God had placed this people in the centre of the nations that were around her. Light should have proceeded from Jerusalem to give revelation to the world. Canaan had been selected as a strategic home for the family of Abraham for this very purpose, and it was to Israel alone that God had revealed himself.[132] It should have been the wisdom of this redeemed people, in the presence of nations immersed in depravity, to honour the written law of God. But it did not happen. Instead of emitting light, Israel had absorbed darkness.

Habitual apostasy meant that Israel had become unfit for her high calling. Therefore, since Jerusalem was more evil than less privileged peoples, God would judge her **'in the eyes of the nations'**. Exodus 12:12 and Numbers 33:4, which refer to the judgements of Yahweh upon Egypt, are recalled.[133] In heart and spirit Jerusalem had made herself like the land of the pharaohs, and must suffer accordingly. Even as Yahweh had formerly acted for Israel, now **'I, even I, am against you.'** The Lord emphasizes that he has become the implacable enemy of his own people (5:8).

There is more. Because of its awfulness, the destruction of Jerusalem will be unrepeatable: **'And I shall do in you what I have not done, and the like of which I shall not do again, because of all your abominations'** (5:9). This predicts the collapse of the city as a gathered community. The nature of these **'abominations'** will be made clear by chapter 8, although in Deuteronomy all idolatry is reckoned as an abomination,[134] and it was the manifest idolatry of Jerusalem that had provoked Yahweh.

Thus the shearing and division of Ezekiel's hair becomes a vivid and realistic token of what the city is about to suffer: one third of the population will starve;

one third will die by the sword; and the rest will be scattered. No fraction can survive. The prophet even predicts cannibalism: men who once worshipped Yahweh in the temple erected by Solomon will soon butcher their children to obtain meat, an abomination that had been anticipated by Moses (5:10).[135]

The unrepeatable nature of the imminent destruction of Jerusalem by the Babylonians needs our further consideration. When Jerusalem and the temple were destroyed in the Jewish-Roman war of AD 66–70, the Christian churches were in the main not affected. This was because they were situated for the most part in other lands. Simply expressed, at the turn of the ages apostate Israel was considered by the New Testament as not even being representative of the people of God in name. Paul observes that because the young churches in Judea were suffering from the hands of unbelieving Jews, judgement would be poured out upon the latter.[136]

In Ezekiel's day, Jacob's family included the true Israel, and this because the grace of God operated almost solely among Abraham's natural children, a circle within a circle.

It follows that Ezekiel's predicted collapse of Israel, then the sole manifestation of the church of God, pointed to a unique event. Such a tragedy had never happened before and it would never occur again in the same way. **'Neither will my eye be piteous, nor will I spare'** (5:11) refers to the charge not to be lenient in the execution of a punishment.[137] Compassion will not temper divine justice.

The 'fire' of 5:2 is explained not as the burning of the city, but as **'plague ... famine ... sword'**. And it would happen (5:12).[138]

5:13-17 reflect in plain language the symbolism of 5:1-4. Because the besetting sin of Jerusalem was gross idolatry, Yahweh proposes to exchange kindness for wrath, in consequence of which God will be

'comforted', meaning that he consoles himself through exacting a just vengeance.[139] Dishonoured publicly by his chosen people in the land and city of his choice, the Lord will see to it that he is vindicated publicly in the same land and city: his **'fury'** will, at last, be **'discharged'**. The God who exercises **'jealousy'** is passionately concerned about the misdeeds of his covenant people (5:13).

Although by means of Abraham's family all the nations of the earth were to be blessed,[140] now Israel becomes **'a desolation and a reproach'** among the surrounding nations. They will regard this people as a **'reproach and derision, discipline and horror'**, recognizing the Babylonian scourge as an instrument in the hand of Israel's God.

Ezekiel's choice of words is as powerful as it could be. Instead of Israel's being exalted among the nations,[141] the world will ridicule the erstwhile people of Yahweh (5:14-15). Lamentations 2:15-16 tells that it came to pass.

Some are to die within the city by plague and famine; others must perish by the sword and by wild animals in the environs of the city; and those who survive are to be pursued everywhere, again by the sword. Now a wilderness of devastation, Jerusalem becomes a mockery to all the nations — in fulfilment of Moses' warnings (5:16-17).[142]

It seems probable that Deuteronomy 32:23-25 is given a deliberate recall, in that these sombre verses mention arrows, famine, plague, ferocious beasts and the sword as instruments of divine retribution in the event of Israel's denying the covenant. That which Moses anticipated, Ezekiel could see as being fulfilled; it was the word of Yahweh (5:16-17).

6. A prophecy against the mountains of Israel (6:1-14)

The shearing of Ezekiel's hair is now explained in more detail. This chapter, which is a distinct oracle in itself, ought to be read in conjunction with Leviticus 26, and particularly Leviticus 26:27-33.[143] Leviticus 26, which anticipates the settlement of Canaan by the twelve tribes following the departure from Egypt, may be conveniently subdivided:

Lev. 26:1-13. Yahweh issues prohibitions against idolatry and promises of blessing in the event of obedience.

Lev. 26:14-20. Warnings are given of judgements within the land of Canaan in the event of Israel's rejection of the covenant.

Lev. 26:21-26. In the event of further hostility to Yahweh, notwithstanding the inflictions mentioned in verses 14-20, more severe judgements are promised, again within the borders of Canaan.

Lev. 26:27-34. Should there be ongoing recalcitrance, Israel, still settled within the land, will suffer military conquest, the destruction of all idolatrous sites and finally exile 'among the nations' (26:33).

Lev. 26:34-39. In the event of complete apostasy, the desolated land 'will enjoy its sabbaths' (v. 34), by which is meant relief from the depredations of unfaithful Israel. But any who may remain will be unable to resist their enemies, and the exiles will suffer further afflictions.

Lev. 26:40-45. If (or, better, when) the exiles repent, Yahweh will remember his covenant with Abraham, Isaac and Jacob. He will never surrender the land or the people of Israel permanently. This most important point is elaborated in the comments and endnotes covering Ezekiel 33:10-16, and particularly 33:12.

The considerable disproportion between the relatively few verses that promise blessing in the case of covenant obedience (Lev. 26:1-13) and those that threaten judgement in the event of disobedience (Lev. 26:14-45) indicates that Moses anticipated Israel's apostasy, exile and ultimate spiritual renewal.[144] Deuteronomy 32:1-43 virtually expects that in the shorter term the people will repudiate their covenant responsibilities because they were 'a perverse and crooked generation'.[145] But compare Deuteronomy 32:43 and Romans 15:10. Light will follow darkness.

Thus Ezekiel's ministry was established on the terms of the covenant inaugurated by Yahweh at Sinai, which covenant the people said they would accept gladly, but which they soon broke.[146]

As for the prophet, during a lifetime of ministry he would show that the God who had become the opponent of Jerusalem and of Israel was acting in strict accordance with the warnings issued at Sinai, warnings that must have been well understood by the twelve tribes. Hence, in Ezekiel's day the remnant had only themselves to blame for their misfortunes.

The two prophecies of chapters 6 and 7 develop the dramatic symbolism of chapter 5. During the fourteen months between 1:2 and 8:1 their contents may have been uttered at intervals, thunderclaps designed to shock the people into repentance.

I. The mountains (6:1-7)

6:1-7. And the word of Yahweh came to me, saying, 'Son of man, set your face towards the mountains of Israel and prophesy against them. And you will say, "Mountains of Israel, hear the word of the Lord Yahweh. Thus says Yahweh to the mountains and to the hills, to the ravines and to the valleys: 'Look, I, even I, am, bringing a sword upon you and I shall destroy your high places. Your altars will be desolated and your sun-pillars will be broken, and I shall cause your slain to fall before your idols. And I shall lay the corpses of the sons of Israel before their idols and shall scatter your bones around your altars. In all your dwelling places the cities will be devastated and the high places will be desolated — in order that your altars may be devastated and desolated, your idols be broken and made to cease, your sun-pillars be cut down and your works be wiped out. And the slain person will fall in your midst, and you will know that I am Yahweh.'"'

The prophet was required to address the **'mountains of Israel'**, contaminated in that they had become sites for sanctuaries that defiled the land.[147] In a sense, the mountains were guilty because of the people beneath whose sin they lay.

During the period before Solomon's temple, high places were innocuous (for example, Samuel at Ramah and Solomon at Gibeon[148]) and were excused because there was as yet no temple. Then, after the consecration of the temple, the high places were outlawed. Sadly, although Hezekiah and Josiah attempted to remove them,[149] their reforms were negated by Manasseh.[150]

'Set your face' is an expression that can be used with respect to direction or purpose,[151] or to manifest opposition, as here.[152] And, if some exiles were turning their faces towards Jerusalem for prayer,[153] the prophet's condemnation would have been ironic (6:1-2): the turning of *his* face indicated that Yahweh was antagonistic to the land of the fathers.

Ezekiel, a herald, was instructed to declare, **'Mountains of Israel, hear the word of the Lord Yahweh.'** Occurring first in Joshua 3:9, the formula 'hear the word' introduces an official pronunciation, and at this point may reflect the conflict over authority between Ezekiel and other local (false) prophets.[154]

'I, even I' stresses that these judgements were from Yahweh, the prime mover: **'a sword'**, that of Babylon, will be employed by Israel's God to eliminate **'your high places'** once and for all. No longer will hilly Israel (as viewed from the perspective of flat, alluvial Mesopotamia) bear the shame placed upon it by the twelve tribes (6:3).

The verbs **'desolated'** and **'broken'** (6:4) tell that Yahweh was inexorably opposed to the **'altars'**, **'sun-pillars'** and **'idols'** that his apostate people had employed in their worship. It has been suggested that the Hebrew behind **'sun-pillars'** means a chapel or shrine of some sort.[155] If so, here is more irony: Israelite worship was repugnant to Israel's God.

That **'your slain'** are to **'fall before ...** [their] **idols'** would be an act of justice, dead men collapsing before lifeless deities and compounding the latter's desecration.[156] The Hebrew *gillûlim* behind **'idols'** is possibly a word containing the vowels of the Hebrew *shiqqûtz*, 'disgusting thing', and the consonants of a noun meaning faeces (cf. 4:12,15): Yahweh was revolted by Israelite idols, which he considered as virtual lumps of excrement.[157] As with the deity opposed by Gideon,[158] because they were false they would be unable to defend themselves.

Leviticus 26:30 is given recall: 'I will destroy your high places, cut down your incense altars and cast your carcasses on the lifeless forms of your idols; and my soul will abhor you.' The reader is also reminded of Josiah's action in incinerating human bones upon the altars of high places in order to defile them, the scattering of bones being a punitive sacrilege.[159] Yahweh proposes to exact just retribution (6:5).

That **'your works'** are to **'be wiped out'** recalls what Israel should have done to the nations within Canaan at the time of Joshua's conquest, but did not;[160] so her deeds, performed in imitation, must be obliterated. Jerusalem will be wiped clean, as a dirty plate would be, and left to dry (6:6).[161]

The final verse is terse: when the cultic sites have been destroyed by the Babylonians, then **'you will know that I am Yahweh'**. If there is a change of pronoun, as is frequent in Ezekiel, the people rather than the mountains are being addressed. Deuteronomy 28:26 may have been in Ezekiel's mind: 'Your carcasses shall be food for all the birds of the air and the beasts of the earth, and no one shall frighten them away.'[162] Yahweh desires that his apostate people be compelled by force of arms to acknowledge that he is the only God whom they should have worshipped in the manner that he required (6:7).

II. Yahweh's broken heart (6:8-10)

6:8-10. '"'Yet I shall leave a remnant in that there will be some of you among the nations who escape the sword — when you are scattered in the lands. Then those of you who escape will remember me there, among the nations where they are captive, in that I was broken by their adulterous heart which turned from me, and with their eyes which played the harlot after their idols; and they will loathe themselves in their own sight for the evils that they have done — that is, for all their abominations. And they will know that I am Yahweh: I did not say in vain that I would execute this evil upon them.'"'

Through Ezekiel's lips Yahweh repeats his prediction that some of the people are to be scattered, yet stressing that from them he will leave a **'remnant'** (6:8): the Lord is in control of every individual, whether for life or for death.

When exiled among unclean nations, they will **'remember'** Yahweh — that is, will convert — in that they give serious attention to him. For the first time in his prophecy Ezekiel likens Israelite apostasy to sexual infidelity: **'I** [Yahweh] **was broken by their adulterous heart which turned from me, and with their eyes which played the harlot after their idols,'** a metaphor to be developed in chapters 16 and 23. In that Israel's sin was a species of adultery, Yahweh is passionately resentful, not because the people transgressed impersonal law, but because they abandoned him and were guilty of lese-majesty, hostility to their rightful Lord. In earlier years, Hosea 1 – 3 had likened the ten northern tribes to a married woman who abandoned her husband in favour of numerous lovers. Ezekiel does not innovate.

When in exile, some survivors **'will loathe themselves in their own sight'**, experiencing revulsion because of **'the evils that they have done — that is, for all their abominations'**. Job declared that 'my soul loathes my life' — but not because of any known sin. The case of Israel in exile will be different. In 20:43 and 36:31 the people are said to be nauseated because they remember their ways; here, they are disgusted with themselves because they remember Yahweh, who had been **'broken by their adulterous heart'**. Although some commentators suggest that **'broken'** (*nishbarti*) takes a middle and transitive sense, 'Because I have broken their whorish heart', the suggested translation may be valid: Yahweh's heart had been broken by Israel's infidelity, and here he pours out his feelings. Now they are aware of what they had done (6:9). In company with the hills, witnesses of their misdeeds, they realize that **'I am Yahweh'**, who did not **'say'**, or speak, **'in vain'** the warnings of Leviticus 26 (6:10).

III. Stamping and clapping — but not in joy (6:11-14)

6:11-14. 'Thus says the Lord Yahweh, "Strike with your fist and beat with your foot, and say, 'Ah,' for all the evil abominations of the house of Israel who will fall by the sword, by famine and by the plague. He who is far away will die by the plague, and he who is near will fall by the sword, and he who remains and is guarded will die by famine, and I shall discharge my fury among them.

'And you will know that I am Yahweh when their slain are amid their idols around their altars — on every high hill, on the tops of the mountains, beneath every green tree and underneath every thick oak, the place where there they gave a pleasing aroma to all their idols.' And I shall stretch out my hand upon them and shall render the land more devastated and ravaged than the wilderness of Diblah — in all their dwelling places. And they will know that I am Yahweh."'

Before Ezekiel announces the word of Yahweh, he is bidden to **'strike with your fist and beat with your foot'**. Clapping the hands and beating with the feet obviously display strong emotion.[163] Considering himself to have been wronged, the Lord has an unchangeable purpose. But he does not gloat, unlike the Ammonites who had also clapped and stamped (see 25:6). Those who saw and heard Ezekiel would have been dumbfounded, not for the first time, at the weird actions of one who deemed himself to be a mouthpiece of Yahweh.

We have to imagine three concentric circles with Jerusalem as their common midpoint: the exiles in Babylonia (**'he who is far away'**), those beyond the walls of Jerusalem (**'he who is near'**) and those trapped in that city (**'and he who remains and is guarded'**). All will be the objects of a **'fury'** that Yahweh will **'discharge'**, or bring to completion, **'among them'**. They drop dead because of **'sword'**, **'famine'** and **'plague'** (6:11-12).

The fact that the burial of the dead will occur beneath oak trees suggests the existence of shrines for ancestor-worship at such sites.[164] Now various localities are selected to give vividness to the eventual judgement: **'on every high hill, on the tops of the mountains, beneath every green tree and underneath every thick oak'**. Ezekiel might be alluding to Deuteronomy 12:2 and Hosea 4:13, suggesting that since the time of Moses it was accepted that apostate Israel would select pleasant places in which to indulge themselves. If so, such locations will be given macabre employment. **'Pleasing aroma'** — fumes arising from idolatrous sacrifice — is ironic in that the expression often refers to the sacrifices that Yahweh *had* commanded;[165] the sin of Israel has been great.

'The wilderness of Diblah' would have abutted the north-east border of Israel. 'Diblah' might be mentioned in Numbers 33:46-47 and in Jeremiah 48:22. 2 Kings 23:33, yielding Riblah in the Hebrew text, becomes Diblah in the Septuagint, and was situated in the far north, 'in the land of Hamath'. Apparently, it was a city on the eastern border of Moab, beyond which lay the great desert stretching towards the Euphrates. It was usual to call any wilderness by the name of the nearest town.[166]

All will be devastated, no part of the land escaping the sword of Yahweh. The sense of absolute desolation will be worse than that of being lost in a wilderness. Yet, notwithstanding the carnage, a few remain alive. In concert with the hills and the penitent exiles, the survivors finally assent to the truth that **'I am Yahweh'**.

Considered as a married woman, Israel had been consistently unfaithful to her God. Worse, adultery had always occurred within the land of promise, the abode that Yahweh had granted her and in which he had been pleased to dwell with her. Therefore the marital home will be broken up and the erring wife be cast out to survive as best she may in lands and cultures to which she had never belonged. For his part, Yahweh, the God of the broken heart, insists that the small print of the covenant stipulations, as in

Leviticus 26, must be satisfied. Ejected from Canaan, the wife will remember her aggrieved husband, and in time will repent (6:13-14).

7. Israel is to be overthrown (7:1-27)

This new collection of pronouncements opens with the same formula that began chapter 6: **'And the word of Yahweh came to me, saying'**. The revelation divides into two main parts, 7:1-4 and 7:5-27. Both commence with the assertion, **'Thus says the Lord Yahweh'**.

The prophecy focuses upon the nearness and the completeness of the predicted judgement. It is to some extent a song of lamentation, more poetic in its structure than anything that has gone before.

That there is so much reiteration (see 7:2-4,5-9) suggests that most of the exiles, together with those who remained behind in Jerusalem, believed that their city would never fall to the Chaldeans. They reckoned that the land, the monarchy, the city and the temple must, and therefore would, remain inviolate. In his day Isaiah had proclaimed that the Assyrians would never enter Jerusalem,[167] and he spoke the truth. But Ezekiel's people were living in the past, whereas God was judging the present. Times and attitudes had changed.[168]

Two centuries earlier the prophet Amos had denounced Israel's longing for 'the day of Yahweh'.[169] Whatever the nature of popular expectations, Amos stated that it would 'be darkness, and not light'. Ezekiel follows in the footsteps of this prophet, as also in those of Isaiah and Zephaniah, who both refer to 'the day of Yahweh' as a time of judgement for an apostate people.[170] In particular, Ezekiel reflects Zephaniah, who around 630 BC prophesied concerning the destruction of Judah. The 'son of man' now tells that 'the day of Yahweh' is imminent and irreversible. Thus, verses 2-13 contain three short oracles, linked together by somewhat similar expressions: **'the end has come'** (7:2-4), **'an evil ... has come'** (7:5-9) and **'the day has arrived'** (7:10-12).

I. The end (7:1-4)

7:1-4. And the word of Yahweh came to me, saying, 'And you, son of man, thus says the Lord Yahweh to the earth of Israel: "An end! The end has come upon the four corners of the land. Now the end is upon you, and I shall send my anger against you, and I shall judge you according to your ways and I shall set all your abominations against you. My eye will not have pity on you and I shall not be compassionate, for I shall set your ways against you and your abominations will be in your midst, and you will know that I am Yahweh."'

Ezekiel had been informed in chapter 3 that he would be a watchman to his people. Now, it is as if he blows the trumpet in alarm — short, staccato sentences characterizing verses 1-9. In that Yahweh addresses **'the earth of Israel'** rather than, say, 'the people of Israel', Ezekiel warns his constituency that, whereas some had already been driven from the land of promise, the deportation was far from complete: the people of Israel must be deprived of that territory where over the centuries they had lived and by which they had been supported.

The expression 'earth of Israel' — **'earth'** translating *adamah* (rather than *eretz*, or 'land') — is unique to Ezekiel.[171] Recognizing an intimate link between the chosen people and the chosen land, he knew that if the Jews repudiated the covenant, the 'earth' would, in a sense, acknowledge their shame and must disclaim them. Thus, **'the four corners of the land'**,[172] meaning every part, is almost an eschatological term.

Accordingly, in the later part of the prophecy Ezekiel declares that when (not if) Israel repents and honours Yahweh, the people must be restored to their 'earth': true Israel will never lack her own territory. **'End ... end'** is repeated to give a sombre emphasis. Whereas Amos had also declared that 'the end has come',[173] he was addressing the apostate northern tribes; now, Yahweh reckons Judah to be in a similar case (7:1-2; cf. 7:6).

In that Judah had programmatically violated the terms of the Mosaic covenant, time had finally run out. As heaven saw the tragedy, there was no point in further delay: Judah, were she to remain *in situ*, would never come to her senses. There had to be an end to it all. **'I shall send my anger'** is vivid: divine wrath will be shot forth as a missile or dispatched as a messenger.[174] **'I shall set ...'** (or, 'I shall give ...') in verses 3 and 4 carries the sense of just retribution: the sad fate in store for the people of Judah will be no more than a compensation for their evil deeds. There will be neither pity nor compassion.

In the parable of the prodigal son the young man 'came to himself' before he 'came to his father'.[175] That is, his repentance was triggered by affliction when in a far country. Although the analogy between his situation and that of the Jews in Ezekiel's day is not exact (he wanted to leave his home; they did not), there is a parallel. The Lord knew that Israel would only face reality when they were deprived of all those benefits that they took for granted and which they regarded as inalienable. Only thus would they **'know that I am Yahweh'** (7:3-4).

The second main section, 7:5-27, divides into four parts that anticipate the gruesome and shocking details of an imminent judgement (7:5-9,10-13,14-22, 23-27).

II. Evil will come upon evil (7:5-9)

7:5-9. 'Thus says the Lord Yahweh: "An evil, a unique evil — look, it has come. An end has come; the end has come. It has wakened upon you; look, it has come. The leash has come to you, inhabitant of the land. The time has come; the day is near — tumult and not joy on the mountains. Now, soon, I shall pour my fury upon you and expend my anger in you, and I shall judge you according to your ways, and shall set all your abominations upon you. And my eye will not spare and I shall not be compassionate: I shall requite you according to your ways, and your abominations will be in your midst, and you will know that I Yahweh am smiting."'

It is impossible to reflect in English the staccato style of the Hebrew of 7:5-9. **'Thus says the Lord Yahweh'** opens the second call to the exiles. **'An evil, a unique evil'** — an evil so all-embracing that it is complete in itself and needs no repetition — **'has come.'**[176] Disaster after disaster is on the way (7:5). This is amplified in the next verse, in which the Hebrew words translated as 'end' and 'awaken' or 'rouse' are similar. Ezekiel gives a play upon both: **'An end** [*qétz*] **has come; the end** [*qétz*] **has come. It has wakened** [*héqitz*] **upon you.'** Judgement has stirred from slumber and will bring Judah to its end (7:6).[177]

'The leash' [*tz^{e}phira*] occurs elsewhere only in 7:10 and in Isaiah 28:5, which tells that 'In that day Yahweh of hosts will be for a *crown* [*tz^{e}phira*] of glory and a diadem of beauty to the remnant of his people.' The probable root meaning is something like 'circuit': 'The *circuit* has come to you, inhabitant of the land.' Matters have come full circle, Isaiah's circlet of 'glory' becoming Ezekiel's cord of slavery that will lead the people away into exile.

This verse should be compared with Zephaniah 1:14-16 and Isaiah 22:1-5. About fifty years earlier, the former prophet predicted the advent of 'the great day of Yahweh', 'a day of wrath'; the latter, over a century before Ezekiel, anticipated 'a day of trouble' bursting forth against the 'Valley of Vision'. Ezekiel knew that he was pronouncing the imminent end of the old order. There would be **'tumult and not joy on the mountains'**. **'Joy'** (*hêd*; the only occurrence of this word in the Old Testament),[178] will be displaced by confusion upon those mountains that had endured idolatrous worship (7:7).

Expanding 7:3-4, the next two verses promise that the eyes of Yahweh will gaze pitilessly upon the sufferings of an apostate people; he will spare them nothing. Although Nebuchadnezzar is assumed to be the human instrument, he is no more than that — an instrument. It is Yahweh who will smite in an act of judgement. Ezekiel regards the Babylonian descent upon Judah as more than a military incursion.

The imagery of judgement is vivid: Yahweh is **'soon'** — that is, in the near future — to **'pour'** out his **'fury'** upon the land, a land to be brought to account for its evil ways. The metaphor is repeated in Jeremiah 1:13-15; 6:11, concerning fluid from a boiling cauldron being poured upon unfortunate victims. There will be no compassion, Yahweh in person afflicting Jerusalem. In consequence, **'you will know that I Yahweh am smiting'** (*makkeh*). Taylor notes that:

> ... to hearers and readers who were used to names of God like 'Jehovah-jireh' ['Yahweh will provide'] and 'Jehovah-nissi' ['Yahweh is my banner'][179] it must have come home with tremendous force to have Him described as 'Jehovah-makkeh'. The Lord who had provided and protected would strike.[180]

Ezekiel seeks to shock his hearers into contrition (7:8-9).

III. The day has nearly arrived (7:10-13)

7:10-13. '"Look, the day! Look, it has come! The leash has gone out; the rod has blossomed; insolence has bloomed. Violence has risen up for a staff of wickedness: none of them and none from their multitude, and none from their tumult — and no eminence among them. The time has come; the day has arrived: let not he who acquires rejoice, and let not the seller mourn: because wrath is upon all her multitude. For the seller will not return to what was sold, even though both live among the living, for a vision is for all her multitude: it shall not turn back, and the man whose life is in iniquity will not strengthen himself."'

'The end' (7:6) is now termed **'the day'**: **'Look, the day! Look, it has come!'** The focus narrows and in a near repeat of 7:7 Ezekiel declares that **'the leash has gone out'**, the 'leash' (*tz^{e}phira*) probably being a chain of captivity. Now matters are on the move and there is no more time.

Further, **'the rod has blossomed'** (7:10). Although this might refer to the Babylonian conqueror, it is more likely a play on words, an allusion to the rods of the tribes mentioned by Numbers 17:8-10. In Ezekiel's situation the rod representing the tribe in Jerusalem has budded and blossomed in its pride, eventuating in self-destruction. Even as Aaron's blossoming rod was 'to be kept as a sign against the rebels', the imminent day is proclaimed as a portent.

'Violence has risen up for a staff of wickedness' (7:11). Here, the **'staff'** is not a rod for punishment but a wicked people who may be either the Chaldeans or, better, Israel.[181] There is **'no eminence** [*nôah*] **among them'**. *Nôah* (not Noah, the patriarch) occurs only here,[182] probably meaning that which is glorious or beautiful: Israel has run its circle; prosperity has led to pride, and pride to wickedness. The tumult or multitude will vanish: **'none of them and none from**

their multitude, and none from their tumult' will remain. The prophets of Israel were realists who understood the horrors of war, and here Ezekiel predicts that nothing of overweening Israel shall be left. The disjointed language in what is a difficult verse is alliterative and deeply emotive, the Hebrew conveying the sense of 'nothing ... nothing ... nothing ... nothing'.

The oracle continues as a deliberate hotchpotch of irony and wordplay.[183] In a land at war, the peacetime operation of the law of the jubilee is inoperative.[184] Therefore, neither should the buyer rejoice at his temporary acquisition, returnable at the time of jubilee, nor should the seller contemplate regaining his loss. It is all out of the question: **'wrath is upon all her multitude'** (7:12) and **'a vision is for all her multitude'** (7:13). Here, Ezekiel reports his anticipation of Israel's impending destruction. The seller will not go back to his land because the prophetic vision of judgement cannot be reversed. In that the year of jubilee will be no more, the people cannot revert to their old ways. Nor can any man preserve his life by his iniquity because Yahweh is beyond bribery (7:12-13).

IV. Destruction (7:14-22)

7:14-22. '"They have sounded with the horn and have prepared everything, but nobody goes to the battle because my wrath is against all her multitude. The sword outside and plague and famine within. He who is in the field will die by the sword, and he who is in the city — famine and plague will devour him. And their escapees will escape and be on the mountains as doves of the valleys, all of them cooing, each man with his iniquity. All hands will hang limp and all knees will flow with water, and they will don sackcloth and shuddering will cover them; on every face there will be shame, and on all their heads, baldness.

'"They will cast away their silver in the streets and their gold will be as filth; their gold and their silver will be unable to deliver them in the day of the rage of Yahweh; they will not satisfy their souls and will not fill their bellies because their iniquity has become a stumbling block. And they set the beauty of his ornament into pride, and with it they made the images of their abominations and their detestable things. Because of this I shall bestow it upon them as filth. And I shall give it for plunder into the hand of strangers, and to the wicked of the earth for plunder, and they will profane it. And I shall turn my face away from them and they will profane my hidden place, and vandals will come there and profane it."'

Ezekiel's words are dramatic in the extreme. Because the destruction about to fall upon Jerusalem will be total, none can escape: **'but nobody goes to the battle'**. The people are so emotionally weak that they cannot fight. Picking up 7:12-13, it is declared that **'my wrath is against all her multitude'** (7:14). So the inflictions of Leviticus 26, **'sword'**, **'plague'** and **'famine'**, will take their toll on an enfeebled people. None shall escape (7:15).

'As doves of the valleys', like tame birds flying to avoid the hawk or the fowler, frightened men and women who escape the catastrophe take to the mountains.[185] There, they sigh for want of rest, and this because of their **'iniquity'** (7:16). Such is the sense of extreme weakness that **'all hands will hang limp'** and **'all knees will flow with water'** (7:17), possibly meaning that the fugitives urinate involuntarily because of fear (so the Septuagint). Grief encapsulating them, they don **'sackcloth'** and — again involuntarily — remain **'shuddering'**, exuding **'shame'**. They will tear their hair, rendering themselves 'bald' (7:18).[186]

'Their gold and their silver will be unable to deliver them.' Because there will be no food to buy, the wealthy must starve along with the poor. Every man cloaks himself with misery, knowing now that precious metals and valuable ornaments, from which he fabricated his objects of worship, are unable to feed or save. There is a direct parallel between this verse and Zephaniah 1:18: 'Neither their silver nor their gold shall be able to deliver them in the day of the wrath of Yahweh.' Ezekiel sees prophecy being fulfilled.

Escapees are ashamed and fling away their valuables **'as filth'**, the Hebrew behind 'filth' representing female impurity (*niddah*). Language could not be more violent, the material wealth that precipitated their downfall and which became a **'stumbling block'** now being an object of extreme revulsion (7:19).

Not only will they abhor their materialism, but Yahweh himself will ensure that because they had employed the sacred materials of worship for their crude idolatry (as stated in 16:17), or, possibly, had erected pagan images within the temple precincts,[187] he will cause them to consider their **'abominations'** and **'detestable things'** as **'filth'** (again, *niddah*), although how this will come about is not stated (7:20). Genesis 31:33-35 speaks of Rachel sitting upon Laban's household gods during her menstrual cycle, and Ezekiel may allude to this.

In consequence, Yahweh delivers the temple, or precious materials — those employed either in the construction of the temple or in the fabrication of idols within the temple — to **'the hand of strangers'** (cf. 28:7; 31:12), who are **'the wicked of the earth'**, meaning the most wicked.[188] It is delivered to them by Yahweh **'for plunder'**, and they will **'profane it'** (7:21). The reference is to Nebuchadnezzar's hordes and their anticipated misdeeds.

Because Yahweh turns his **'face'** from Judah, the Chaldeans **'profane my hidden place'**, the Holy of Holies, the heart of the worship and of the national life of Israel. In that an apostate church profaned it, an invader shall in turn despoil it (7:22).

V. Chains (7:23-27)

7:23-27. '"Make a chain, for the land is full of the judgement of blood and the city is full of violence. And I shall bring the evil of the nations and they will possess their houses, and I shall cause the pride of their strength to cease, and their holy places will be profaned. Destruction has come and they will seek peace — but there is none. Disaster will come upon disaster and rumour will be upon rumour, and they will seek a vision from the prophet. But law will perish from the priest and counsel from the elders. The king will mourn, the prince will don devastation and the hands of the people of the land will be agitated. I shall deal with them on account of their way, and with their judgements I shall judge them, and they will know that I am Yahweh."'

Because those who escape death on the streets must go into exile, their captors are bidden by Yahweh's messenger **'to make a chain'** to link captives together in a column as they are marched away.[189] In addition to multiple idolatries, the leaders of Judah have been guilty of **'the judgement of blood'**, by which would be meant the unjust employment of the death sentence, and of **'violence'**, as shown by 19:3,6; 22:6,27 (7:23).

'The evil of the nations' refers to the power and ruthlessness of the enemy.[190] Pitiless and bloodthirsty aliens will put an abrupt end to the objects of the people's confidence, **'their holy places'**. The Masoretic vocalization of the Hebrew behind **'holy places'** (*m'qadshéhem*) is unusual and may indicate that, as the rabbis interpreted the matter, the Lord reckoned that the temple had become an assemblage of pagan shrines belonging to the people but not acknowledged by Yahweh. These profane places will themselves be **'profaned'** (7:24).

At the same time as ruin is being inflicted stroke by stroke, bad news accumulates: **'destruction'** (*q'phadah*, related to the Hebrew word for hedgehog, an animal that can injure the skin) arrives. Hearts will be punctured with fear, and the wretched community lies helpless.[191] There is neither prophetic vision nor any word from Moses' law to encourage them; nor have the elders any counsel to give. All feel themselves abandoned because, in truth, they are abandoned.[192] Although they may **'seek peace'**, it is too late (7:25).

The awfulness of the matter is exacerbated by the collapse of the conventional means of divine guidance. Prophetic **'vision'** will be denied the people,[193] and the **'prophet'**, **'priest'** and **'elders'** will be unable to proffer counsel and comfort. Micah 3:5-7, issued a century and a half before Ezekiel, had much the same message for the ten northern tribes when they were about to be taken into exile. Is Ezekiel refuting the pretensions of those in Judah who opposed Jeremiah, his contemporary, and who asserted that 'the law shall not perish from the priest, nor counsel from the wise, nor the word from the prophet'?[194] They believed that the priests were even yet reliable exponents of Mosaic law and that the elders were fitted to advise the king in matters of state. Not so, believed Jeremiah, and Ezekiel stands with him (7:26).

'The king' of Judah, Zedekiah, goes into mourning. Further, **'the prince'**, the singular possibly representing the totality of the Jerusalem nobility, is clothed in desolation, and the hands of common folk, **'the people of the land'**, twitch in terror. Justice demands that what they have done be done to them. So, when every earthly prop has collapsed, they will accept that Yahweh is the true God who had brought all this to pass (7:27).

The initial series of Ezekiel's prophecies, extending from the beginning of the fourth to the end of the seventh chapter, closes. Uttered within the period of a year and two months, like the next series (chapters 8 – 19), they began with a remarkable series of symbolic acts and continued with plain declarations. Ezekiel's fellow-exiles had now been in captivity for five to six years, and many still looked to Jerusalem, the Davidic monarchy and the temple as their united source of strength. Many probably hoped and trusted that they would soon be sent home and that the war would be over.

Ezekiel has shown that such was the perversity of his apostate nation-church that there would be no true reformation among the people, whether at home or in exile, unless and until their earthly hopes were dashed and they had been utterly humiliated.

Application

With regard to 4:1-3, Ezekiel's opening act signalled to those who had eyes to see and ears to hear that at that time Yahweh was implacably antagonistic to Jerusalem, the city which, centuries before, he had chosen as the site for the temple.[195] But, it may be asked, does the Bible ever portray God as the opponent of men?

The reply is 'yes': Romans 5:10 tells that 'when we [that is, Christian believers] were enemies we were reconciled to God through the death of his Son, much more, having been reconciled, we shall be saved by his life'.[196] Reconciliation involves the settlement of a quarrel, and reconciliation between God and sinners means that the quarrel commenced by men against God is at an end: no longer is he angry. The offending party (the believer) has sought peace with God through Jesus Christ and has found it.[197]

But let it be said that divine antagonism is always holy and just. Mysteriously, it can coexist with love. Romans 5:8 shows that the God who loves his people demonstrated that love for them when he was their adversary!

The lesson of Ezekiel 4:1-3 (and, of course, of the whole of Scripture) is that if men will abandon the one true God they need not be surprised if, eventually, they experience his anger and hostility.

Concerning 4:4-8, Ezekiel had no good news to convey to the exiles prior to the fall of Jerusalem, people whose false hopes had to be dashed before they would be prepared to hear good news. Today's minister of the gospel must (graciously) inform the unconverted that unless they repent they not only have nothing that can last, but will lose all that they do have.

Furthermore, the pastor should be no impersonal relay for what he knows to be the truth. Ezekiel's strange actions were '*his*' siege of Jerusalem, and his was a costly discipline, lying on his side and consuming repulsive food every day for more than a year of his life. At Thessalonica it was said of Paul and his colleagues that it was *they* who had 'turned the world upside down'.[198] By his demeanour the true preacher of the gospel will be, to an extent, the message as well as the messenger. Communication is all his business.

In 4:9-17, Ezekiel's cry of protest concerning his diet was not unheard. The Lord never lays on us more than we are able to bear,[199] and we are permitted to tell him all our sorrows and needs. Correction — we *must* tell him all our needs;[200] it is sin not to do so.

The employment of a set of balances by Ezekiel (5:1-4) stresses that God's judgement upon Israel would be exact. Similarly, at the end of this age the unrepentant will be recompensed 'according to their deeds'.[201]

Regarding 5:13-17, Moses was informed by Yahweh that were Israel to honour the stipulations of the covenant into which they were being brought by God, they would 'be a special treasure to me above all people; for all the earth is mine. And you shall be to me a kingdom of priests and a holy nation.'[202]

Tragically, Israel was faithless to her God from at least the inception of the covenant at Sinai. Godly men and women, such as Deborah and David, Joshua and Jeremiah, and Hannah and Haggai, were no more than exceptions to the rule. Therefore God rejected his nominal people by expelling them from the land of promise. Although Moses' administration would remain in force for another half-millennium after Ezekiel's time, it was in effect a dead letter, awaiting a better covenant.[203] Hebrews 10:28-29 informs us that 'Anyone who has rejected Moses' law dies without mercy on the testimony of two or three witnesses. Of how much worse punishment, do you suppose, will he be thought worthy who has trampled the Son of God underfoot, counted the blood of the covenant by which he was sanctified a common thing, and insulted the Spirit of grace?'[204] These verses allude to apostasy by those who have professed the faith.

If we believe that we are in Christ and Christ in us, our duty to honour our relationship with the Lord is of paramount importance, even if — as has happened so often to so many, and will happen again — our lives are placed in prejudice. Ponder Luke 12:48.

Concerning 6:1-14, the fact that some would survive the holocaust and come to their senses tells of the grace of God. Notwithstanding the judgement that culminated in 586 BC with the destruction of the Jerusalem temple, there would be a remnant. Grace would reign. In today's world, the churches are shot through with error, ignorance and superficiality. But there must always be a remnant. Let us rejoice that Christ will continue to build his church upon the firm foundation of gospel truth.[205]

7:1-27 is sombre because war is truly dreadful. Sadly, throughout human history there have been, and always will be, men and nations who, like the ultimate Antichrist, 'honour a god of fortresses'.[206] Ezekiel lived through the agony of seeing his beloved land and church ravaged by barbarians, and, had he not known the Lord, he might have been in despair. But he did know the Lord, and he knew too that the appalling catastrophe was taking place so that the people might in time come to know their God. Behind Nebuchadnezzar was the God of Israel.

Affliction, whether it be macro-, even on the international scale, or micro-, smiting just one individual, should drive us to hide under the shadow of the divine wings.[207] Where else is there to go? And those sovereign wings afford much shade.

2. The second series of prophecies

(Ezekiel 8:1 – 19:14)

The first series of visions, together with their explanatory messages, dated from the fifth day of the fourth month of the fifth year of the exile of King Jehoiachin (1:1-2). A further series of revelations is now given to Ezekiel one year and two months later (8:1), and will open up during a period of eleven months and five days (see 20:1). It commences with visions (chapters 8 – 11) and is followed by messages that interpret and apply them (chapters 12 – 19).

The first series of prophecies was directed to the exiles and to those who had been left in Jerusalem. Now, so that the exiles might understand why a final catastrophe is so certain, they have to be told about the extreme sinfulness of Jerusalem. The whole section is concerned mainly with those who were resident in the city and who had been sucked into a vortex of astonishing wickedness.

Ezekiel is taken to the temple (Ezekiel 8:1-18)

Some months earlier the prophet was instructed to go to his home and remain there. He was told that his tongue would be bound (3:24,26). Now his house becomes the scene where he receives another vision. Some elders of the people visit him, presumably to learn what Yahweh had shown him, or perhaps to consult him about what was happening in Jerusalem (8:1; cf. 11:25). Fourteen months after the first vision, Ezekiel was transported in vision, rather than physically, to the temple in Jerusalem (8:1-4), where he witnessed various forms of idolatry (8:5-18).

Did Ezekiel actually see with his own eyes what was happening in Jerusalem? And, even at this late date, was it possible that the temple authorities would have condoned the practices described here? In both cases, possibly so, but it may be better to interpret Ezekiel's vision as symbolic of the utter degradation and disintegration of the nation, extending from the king of the day and the people to the elders, the women and, worst of all, to the priesthood.

1. The unholy temple (8:1-4)

8:1-4. And in the sixth year, in the sixth, on the fifth of the month, I was sitting in my house and the elders of Judah were sitting in front of me. And the hand of the Lord Yahweh fell upon me there. I observed, and, look, a likeness as the appearance of fire — from the appearance of his loins and downwards, fire. And from his loins and upwards as the appearance of brightness, like the gleam of glowing metal. And he sent out the form of a hand and grasped me by a lock of my head, and the Spirit lifted me up between earth and heaven and brought me to Jerusalem in the visions of God to the entrance of the inner gate facing north, where there was the seat of the image of jealousy that arouses jealousy. And, look, the glory of the God of Israel was there, as the appearance that I had seen in the plain.

Remarkably, Ezekiel became the spectator of gross idolatry within the temple of Yahweh in distant Jerusalem. **'The sixth year ... the sixth ... the fifth of the month'** would translate to 17 September 592 BC, fourteen months, or 420 days (14 x 30) after the first vision. The record of the date is important because, as noted by Wright, 'the final destruction of Jerusalem would confirm the validity of his claim to have truly spoken from Yahweh'.[1]

This date appears to conflict with the 390 + 40 days, totalling 430 days, for the symbolic act mentioned in 4:4-6. However, as noted earlier, if Ezekiel did not lie on his left side and then on his right side consecutively, he might have received this new vision at some point during the forty-day period.

It would appear that Ezekiel the priest had now been accepted as a prophet and that he was residing in his own house. Thus, **'the elders of Judah'** were seated before him to hear what he might have to say, perhaps concerning the predictions of Hananiah in Jerusalem and others to the effect that the exile would soon end.[2] **'Judah'** is specified because, although the elders represented Israel, they would probably have stemmed from Judah, the only surviving tribe. Although Jehoiachin was by that time in Babylon, he appears to have lacked any influence over the exiles.[3] It was then that **'the hand of the Lord Yahweh'** fell upon the prophet, Ezekiel being overcome by the presence of God (8:1).

Yet again he saw the Lord, apparently in human form upon his throne (note **'likeness'**, **'as'** and **'appearance'**). The vision is assumed to be similar to that recorded in 1:4-28 (cf. 3:23). The manner of expression is deliberate because Ezekiel wanted the reader to know that he was not hallucinating: what he beheld was from Yahweh, although he did not literally view Yahweh face to face.[4] The vision occurred while the elders were sitting before the prophet. Although they saw nothing they must have witnessed his ecstasy and would have been eager that he should disclose what he had seen (cf. 11:25). **'The gleam of glowing metal'** (8:2) repeats from 1:4.

'The form of a hand' extended from the throne and, in vision, grasped Ezekiel by the hair. The prophet did not actually leave Chaldea, as indicated by 11:24. Borne **'between earth and heaven'**, in spirit the prophet was transported by the **'Spirit'** of God to Jerusalem **'to the entrance of the inner gate facing north'**. This was the gate leading from the court of the people to the court of the priests on a higher level. The accounts of the temple building in Kings and Chronicles do not mention gates leading from one to the other, but they must have been there.

Ezekiel witnessed **'the seat of the image** [*semel*] **of jealousy that arouses jealousy'**. This is a descriptive name for an image which provoked Yahweh's jealousy. There is an allusion to Exodus 20:5: 'For I, Yahweh your God, am a jealous God.' *Semel* occurs in Deuteronomy 4:16, which suggests that Ezekiel was being referred to a fundamental condition of the now shattered covenant. The image was probably that of an alien god, something like Manasseh's icon of Asherah, or Astarte, in Canaanite religion the consort of El, the highest god in the pantheon,[5] rather than a perverted representation of Yahweh. Although such a gross sin is not attributed to Zedekiah, it is possible that he made use of the temple for idolatrous worship, and if so this is what Ezekiel saw. That the image was seated at the entrance to the heart of the temple was a direct affront to the God whose residence it was meant to be (8:3).

The prophet also observed that **'the glory of the God of Israel was there, as the appearance that I had seen in the plain'**. Because God and the gods were irreconcilable, a violent conflict was imminent (8:4). Now Ezekiel will be shown a number of idolatrous performances within the temple, the display possibly coming ever nearer to the Holy of Holies, and thereby highlighting the offensiveness of the various activities.[6]

2. Four abominations (8:5-18)

8:5-18. Then he said to me, 'Son of man, raise now your eyes towards the north.' And I raised my eyes towards the north. Then, look, from the north of the gate of the altar was this image of jealousy in the entry. And he said to me, 'Son of man, do you see what they are doing, the great abominations which the house of Israel does here, to be far from my sanctuary? But turn again: you will see greater abominations.'

So he brought me to the entrance of the court, and I observed and, look, a hole in the wall. And he said to me, 'Son of man, dig now through the wall.' Then I dug through the wall, and, look, a single entrance. And he said to me, 'Come and see the evil abominations which they are committing here.' And I came and saw, and, look, every form of creeping thing and detestable beasts, and all the idols of the house of Israel, engraved upon the wall all around. And seventy men from the elders of Israel were standing before them, and Jaazaniah the son of Shaphan stood in their midst. A censer was in the hand of each man and the scent of the cloud of incense went up. Then he said to me, 'Have you seen, son of man, what the elders of the house of Israel are doing in the darkness, each man in his statue's apartments? For they are saying, "Yahweh does not see us; Yahweh has deserted the land."' And he said to me, 'You will turn again. You will see greater abominations than those they are doing.'

So he brought me to the entrance of the gate of the house of Yahweh that was towards the north, and, look, there the women were seated, weeping for Tammuz. Then he said to me, 'Have you seen, son of man? You will turn again — you will see greater abominations than these.'

And he brought me to the inner court of the house of Yahweh, and, look, the entrance of the temple of Yahweh. Between the porch and between the altar were the like of twenty-five men with their backs to the temple of Yahweh and their faces to the east, and they were prostrating themselves eastward to the sun. And he said to me, 'Have you seen, son of man? Is it too light a thing for the house of Judah to commit the abominations that they have committed here? For they have filled the land with violence and have returned to provoke me. And, look, they are putting the branch up their nose. And I also will act in fury: my eye will not spare and I shall not be compassionate. Then they will cry in my ears with a loud voice, and I shall not hear them.'

Yahweh instructed the **'son of man'** to raise his eyes and look. Could he not see an abomination placed between where he was and the altar? Could he not see what the house of Israel was doing? Yes, he could. The prophet must have concluded that this extraordinary misconduct in the temple would lead to God removing himself far from his people in anger and disgust. As 11:23 shows, it eventually happened.

Sadly, this idolatry was only the initial evidence of the apostasy of Judah. It might be that **'from the north of the gate of the altar'** recalled an action of Ahaz a century earlier,[7] when he relocated Solomon's altar to the north of the alien construction that he had imported. Further, although the image of Asherah placed by Manasseh in the temple was removed by Josiah,[8] it might have been brought back after Josiah's death. But whatever Ezekiel saw, it is described as the **'image of jealousy'**, that which had provoked the Lord to anger (8:5). Perhaps it was the 'queen of heaven' mentioned by Jeremiah.[9] Traditionally, the north gate had been honoured because the royal palace was on the north side of the temple and monarchs would have passed through it when entering to worship, and also because sacrificial victims were killed on the north side of the altar.[10] The aggravation was intense.

The **'son of man'** was asked if he had taken into account **'what they are doing ... to be far from my sanctuary'** (8:6). Because **'to be far'** is, in Hebrew, an infinitive without an expressed subject, it could mean the removal of the people far from the temple, or Yahweh's abandonment of the sanctuary. The latter gives the better sense: it was generally felt that Jerusalem could not fall because God would never abandon the city. But, if it was the Lord who is said to be distancing himself from Jerusalem because of its **'abominations'** (cf. 8:9,13,15,17), all hope was lost.

Ezekiel was then conducted to **'the entrance of the court'** (8:7), a place other than that where he found himself in the initial stage of the vision. Perhaps the location was somewhere in the open space beyond the north gate of the inner court, yet within the boundary marked by the north gate of the outer enclosure (cf. 8:14).

Observing a hole in the wall too small for entrance, the prophet was instructed to enlarge it so that he could crawl through, possibly into a storage room.[11] This he did. He beheld **'a single entrance'** which, again, he was told to enter. The detail emphasizes the furtiveness, and even the extreme secrecy, of the sinful actions that the prophet was about to witness. Yahweh summoned Ezekiel to **'come and see the evil abominations which they are committing here'** (8:7-9).

He gazed upon a wall covered with graffiti, crude representations of every form of reptile and ritually unclean animal plus various idols venerated by the people (8:10). The description points to the influence of foreign cults, particularly those of Egyptian origin, upon worship in Jerusalem, an interpretation supported by the political orientation of the time.

'Seventy men' from the **'elders'** — the latter representing the leaders of the house of Israel in the years following the deportation of Jehoiachin[12] — were present, among them **'Jaazaniah the son of Shaphan'**. This Jaazaniah — the name meaning 'Yahweh listens' — is not necessarily to be identified with the Jaazaniah mentioned in 11:1. But Shaphan might have been the Shaphan who was active in the reformation instituted by Josiah.[13] Another of his sons was Ahikam, a supporter of Jeremiah.[14] If so, this Jaazaniah would have been regarded by Ezekiel both as an apostate and as the black sheep of a worthy family.[15]

Given these family connections, the identification would give dreadful emphasis to the shamelessness of the leaders as they burned **'incense'**, an activity reserved for the priesthood.[16] The number seventy is evocative, raising the suspicion that all those of influence in Israel were, without exception, apostate,[17] in contrast to the priests who had been chosen to draw near to Yahweh. In this instance they may have been burning incense in order to ward off evil, perhaps on the precedent set by Numbers 16:46-48. Even so, they could not avert divine wrath.

Yahweh informed Ezekiel how these evil men justified their rampant idolatry: they made out that the God of Israel had quit the land and therefore was unable to observe them, a charge repeated in 9:9.[18]

This being so, why should the elders of Israel afford Yahweh, the absentee deity, their worship? But, as Ezekiel must have realized, they had wilfully denied two of the eternal attributes of God — that he is everywhere and that he knows everything.

We must imagine the large room in which the seventy elders assembled as being divided into seventy carrels, as in a study library. In each there was an elder who burned incense to his own particular object of worship. Such would have been carved on the four walls (cf. 8:10). The language recalls Leviticus 26:1,[19] which prohibits such activities. Perhaps these leaders, protesting that **'Yahweh does not see us; Yahweh has deserted the land,'** made their claim privately, **'in the darkness'**, because most of the people seem to have held that their city would never fall and would have resented such activity (8:12).[20] Perhaps, too, they concluded that they would have to seek help elsewhere. Of course, they were in profound error. Yet Ezekiel would see **'greater abominations'** than these (8:13).

Nor was he disappointed. Taken to the entrance of the north gate of the outer enclosure, his astonished gaze focused upon **'women'** who were **'weeping for Tammuz'** (8:14). 'Tammuz', a deity not mentioned elsewhere in the Bible, was almost certainly the Sumerian god of vegetation and the divinity known by the Greeks as 'Adonis', the mythological lover of the equally mythological Venus.[21]

Ezekiel adds this detail without giving any explanation of who Tammuz may have been, assuming that his readers would understand. In effect, Yahweh, as Lord of field and forest, was being informed in *his* temple that he had been displaced in favour of an eastern fertility god.

Assuming a similarity between the rites associated with Tammuz and Adonis, it might appear that Tammuz-worship involved mourning for his death followed by jubilation for his alleged return to life. All this must have been bound up with sordid nature and fertility rites, the tenor of which can be inferred. That women were at that time involved in idolatrous worship is indicated by 2 Kings 23:7 and Jeremiah 7:18. Perhaps the women seen by Ezekiel honoured Tammuz instead of Yahweh in that they felt that the Lord was as good as dead — seemingly, he had abandoned his people to the Chaldeans. But Tammuz, they held, was alive — or would be.

Thus far Ezekiel had beheld the idolatry of the people, the creature-worship of the elders and now the follies of the women. But he would **'turn again'** and **'see greater abominations than these'** (8:15).

He was conducted back to the court of the priests, between the entrance to the Holy Place and the altar. In this area, which the priests alone were allowed to tread, **'the like of twenty-five men'** ('the like of' from the Hebrew particle *kaph,* meaning 'like' or 'as') were seen **'prostrating themselves eastward to the sun'**, displaying their rear parts rather than their faces to the holiest place and its God. Their posture was obscene. Even as the whole nation seems to be represented in Ezekiel's vision by the seventy elders, here the twenty-five probably symbolize the body of the Aaronic priesthood: twenty-four standing for the various classes of priests, with the high priest at their head making up the sum.[22]

In that they turned their backs upon Yahweh to worship a created star, they displayed an apostasy of a degree without parallel elsewhere in the Bible. Moses' prohibition counted for nothing.[23]

Two hundred years earlier, Joel had declared that the priests ought to weep between the temple porch and the altar and pray that Yahweh might spare his people.[24] Now Ezekiel has seen an opposite state of affairs (8:16); the sin of the priests was absolute.

Yet there was worse. In addition to flagrant idolatry, the whole land is said to have been **'filled ... with violence'**, the inhabitants returning again and again to provoke their God. Perhaps there is a deliberate recall here of Genesis 6:13, which records that God stated that 'The end of all flesh has come before me, for the earth is filled with violence through them; and, look, I shall destroy them with the earth.' And he did.

'Putting the branch up their nose' during worship is an obscure expression, possibly referring to a custom well understood at the time (8:17). Most commentators suggest that **'their'** should be replaced with 'my',[25] in which case the men concerned were deliberately insulting Yahweh with what might have been another obscene gesture: pointing a stick at his face. What seems certain is that someone was being hurt, whether Yahweh or Israel, or both.

For his part, Yahweh will refuse to spare them: when they eventually cry to him in their misery he will not **'hear them'**. If it is possible to sin beyond the reach of grace,[26] prayer would be futile. In 5:11 Yahweh had declared that he would not tolerate idolatry; in this situation, idol-worship must lead to God abandoning temple, city and land. There is deliberate irony because, as noted, 'Jaazaniah' means 'Yahweh hears': now the Lord remains deaf to all pleas (8:18).

Application

During the forty days when Moses was initially in the presence of God upon Sinai, the children of Israel manufactured a golden calf as a surrogate for Yahweh, and worshipped it.[27] For his part, the Lord informed Moses that the twelve tribes would be destroyed and that he, Moses, would head up a reconstituted Israel. Moses interceded and was heard.[28] Later, Moses petitioned Yahweh to show him his glory, in reply to which God made all his 'goodness' pass before Moses and proclaimed his name to his servant, stating that he would be gracious to whom he would be gracious. This meant that although he, the Lord, would preserve Israel, he was under no necessity to do so.[29]

An analogous situation occurred six centuries later when the prophet Elijah was confronted by the gross idolatry of the ten northern tribes.[30] Following the denouement at Carmel, he fled in fear for his life and was directed by Yahweh to journey to Horeb, where God passed before him. After the wind, the earthquake and the fire, there was 'a still small voice', bespeaking compassion.[31] The time had not yet arrived for the theocracy of degenerate Israel to vanish.

However, matters would run their course. In Ezekiel's day, the overwhelming majority of the sons of Israel had shown again and again that they had no intention of honouring the terms of the Sinai covenant and that there was no hope that they would repent. Therefore, unlike his statement in Exodus 33 and his action and words in 1 Kings 19, Yahweh announced that the period of grace would soon end, that Israel must be banished from the land promised originally to Abraham[32] and that the Davidic monarchy and the temple must be consigned, albeit temporarily, to oblivion. It is to this historical process of establishment and then judgement that the first chapter of the Gospel of Matthew refers.[33]

Implicit in Ezekiel 8 is the expectation that the Lord would honour the original covenant with Abraham — but not by delivering the throne of David back to Jehoiachin or to his immediate descendants; the fulfilment would have to await another age. This also is anticipated by Matthew 1:17: 'So all the generations from Abraham to David are fourteen generations, from David until the captivity in Babylon are fourteen generations, and from the captivity in Babylon until the Christ are fourteen generations.'[34]

Ezekiel 8, a mournful chapter, assumes that God will always claim some for his own.[35] Yet divine sovereignty never cancels human responsibility, in that if men will persist in repudiating the good news of Jesus Christ, the time must come when God will repudiate them.[36] We bow before the one eternal God in awe and humility.

D. Thomas notes cogently that whereas 'Darwinian evolution is worshipped as the explanation for all reality', 'it is in essence a worship of nature's powers, differing little from what the women bewailed beside the north gate of the temple'.[37] Our generation is no less idolatrous than that of the Jewish deportees (8:14).

The slaughtering angels (Ezekiel 9:1-11)

This chapter is a continuation of chapter 8, as indicated by the Hebrew '*vav*-consecutive' sequence (= **'then'** followed by **'he cried'**) connecting 8:18 and 9:1: 'They will cry ... then he cried.' The judgement announced in 8:18 is now executed in visionary form. The ascension of **'the glory of the God of Israel'** (9:3) anticipates the departure of Yahweh from the temple and from Jerusalem, as recorded in chapter 10, and, following chapter 10, the destruction of Jerusalem itself.

1. The men with clubs and the scribe clothed in linen (9:1-6)

9:1-6. Then he cried in my ears with a loud voice, saying, 'Draw near, they who have charge of the city, each with a weapon of destruction in his hand.' And, look, six men were coming from the way of the upper gate facing the north, each with his bludgeoning weapon in his hand. One man was in their midst, clothed in linen and at his loins a scribe's case. So they came and stood beside the bronze altar. And the glory of the God of Israel ascended from above the cherub, on which it had been, to the threshold of the house. Then he called to the man, he who was clothed in linen with a scribe's case at his loins. And Yahweh said to him, 'Pass through the middle of the city, amid Jerusalem, and stamp a mark on the foreheads of all who are sighing and groaning for all the abominations that are being committed in her midst.' And to these he said in my hearing, 'Pass through the city behind him, and strike. Let not your eyes pity and let them not be compassionate. Old man, young man and maiden and child and women you will slay utterly, but do not come upon any man who has the mark on him — and commence from my sanctuary.' Then they began with the older men who were in front of the house.

Yahweh turned from speaking directly to Ezekiel. In the prophet's hearing he summoned those angelic beings who had **'charge of the city'** to **'draw near'**.[38] Each was to grasp a **'weapon of destruction'**, their station presumably being on the walls. The **'loud voice'** mirrored Yahweh's indignation: they would approach the heart of the temple (9:1).

Ezekiel invites his readers to **'look'**: **'six men'** were seen to penetrate the inner court from the direction of the **'north'** gate separating the outer and inner courts, each grasping **'his bludgeoning weapon'**, some sort of mace or club with which to smash the heads of his victims. That the angels are described as human is not unusual,[39] and here they are represented as the executioners of divine vengeance. **'Facing the north'** is significant because this was the direction from which Ezekiel had been shown the idolatrous practices within the temple and from which the Babylonian armies were even then approaching Jerusalem.[40]

Among these supernatural beings was a seventh, an individual clothed in linen, a material representing purity,[41] carrying a **'scribe's case'**,[42] possibly a container replete with pen, inkhorn and parchment. All seven came near and stood by the bronze altar of burnt offering placed by Solomon at the heart of the temple complex but which, as noted, had been relocated by Ahaz to the north of the court to make room for his own importation (9:2).[43] The north side of the inner court would have evoked painful memories.

'The glory of the God of Israel' ascended from **'above the cherub'** — **'cherub'** probably being a collective term for the four living creatures beneath the firmament (cf. 10:2,4) — to transfer to **'the threshold'** of the temple. From this it becomes apparent that the vision seen by Ezekiel when he was called to the prophetic ministry (1:5; cf. 3:13) was a development of the cover of the ark within the Holy of Holies.[44] The God of the covenant, unsettled because of the apostasy of Jerusalem, was preparing to leave the city to its own devices.

Yahweh then summoned the man clothed in linen as the superintendent of the destroying angels (9:3). Significantly, the call emanated from the temple itself, from which God was beginning to depart. As noted by Taylor,[45] there is some uncertainty about the movement of the divine glory, the glory apparently representing the one who was Ezekiel's guide and also the one seated on the throne. Yet because we have here a record of a visionary experience precise detail is not to be expected.

Yahweh gave instructions to the scribe. Proceeding throughout Jerusalem, he would place **'a mark'**, a *tau*, upon the foreheads of all who were **'sighing and groaning'** in sorrow because of the abominations performed in the city and because of the disaster that would surely come.[46] Shaped like a small cross, *tau* was the final letter of the primitive Hebrew alphabet. Disassociation would be the sole qualification for deliverance, birth and social status being irrelevant.

The forehead was chosen because it is the most obvious part of the body,[47] such people being recognized easily by the executioners (9:4).[48] It is also possible that the mark would have served as a sign of ownership.[49] As at the time of the Passover, Yahweh had claimed his own before smiting Egypt.[50]

The six were commanded to follow the recording scribe throughout the doomed city. Without pity, they had to club to death all men and women, all the old and the young, both married and single, who had not been marked on their foreheads. Seemingly, Yahweh specified those who would take refuge within the city walls, able-bodied males presumably having fallen in battle. The gruesome task would begin at Yahweh's **'sanctuary'**, where the appalling evils of the people had reached their peak (8:5-18).[51] The procedure was the same as at the destruction of Sodom and Gomorrah, when Lot had to depart before judgement could proceed.[52] As ever, Yahweh cared for his own.

The obedient executioners commenced by killing **'the older men'**, perhaps the seventy elders (cf. 8:11) or the twenty-five sun-worshippers of 8:16 (9:5-6).

2. The formal deconsecration of the temple (9:7-8)

9:7-8. So he said to them, 'Defile the house and fill the courts with the slain. Go out!' Then they went out and smote within the city. And it came about that as they were smiting I was left by myself. I fell upon my face and cried and said, 'Ah, Lord Yahweh, are you destroying the whole remnant of Israel by pouring out your fury on Jerusalem?'

The angelic instruments of wrath were then commanded to **'defile the house'**, the temple. No longer is it said to be 'my sanctuary' (cf. 9:6). Because it had been desecrated by the residents of the city and their idolatries, it had to be formally deconsecrated by Yahweh and decommissioned as his residence. The obvious method to achieve this was by piling the temple courts high with bloodstained corpses, thus rendering those courts unfit for any holy purpose. According to Moses, contact with human remains led to ritual uncleanness and exclusion from the worshipping community. Accordingly, Yahweh desecrates the temple permanently.[53] As with the execution of Joab,[54] justice had to override all other considerations.

Perhaps the angels were reluctant to undertake this horrific task, which might explain the abrupt instruction to **'go out'**. But go out they did, killing their victims everywhere in the city (9:7).

As they did so, Ezekiel remained by himself in the presence of Yahweh. Prostrating himself, he enquired if, in **'pouring out** [his] **fury'** upon Jerusalem, now a virtual necropolis, the Lord intended to make an end of **'the whole remnant of Israel'**. Like Abraham on behalf of Sodom, and Amos on behalf of the ten northern tribes, Ezekiel interceded for his people.[55] He had no pleasure in the death of the wicked any more than did Yahweh (cf. 18:23). **'Remnant'** must signify the theocracy of Israel as it existed in its diminished state following the numerous judgements of God in previous years. In the time of Solomon it had been truly great, but with the loss of Galilee and Gilead and the end of the northern kingdom, and then the conquest of Judah by the Chaldeans,[56] Israel had been reduced almost to nothing. Now it would vanish completely (9:8).

3. No mercy (9:9-11)

9:9-11. Then he said to me, 'The iniquity of the house of Israel and Judah is exceedingly great; the land is filled with blood and the city is full of exploitation — for they have said, "Yahweh has abandoned the land and Yahweh does not see." But as for me, my eye will not spare and I shall not be compassionate: I shall bring their ways down upon their heads.' And, look, the man clothed in linen with an inkhorn at his loins reported back, saying, 'I have done just as you commanded me.'

An immediate answer was given by Yahweh to the prophet, reminding him of the colossal proportions of **'the iniquity'** of **'Israel'** and **'Judah'**, Judah now representing the complete nation. In addition to the gross idolatries perpetrated by all strata of society, the land had been **'filled with blood'** — the imagery is grim in the extreme — and Jerusalem had become **'full'** of perverted justice; there was no space left for virtue (9:9). No mention is made of the innocent, the impression being that they were remarkably few, if any, although 9:11 implies that there may have been some, in that the man in linen had obeyed his instruction.

The popular excuse given in 8:12, that Yahweh had abandoned the land and did not care what the people did, or what became of them, is reiterated for emphasis. But this was misplaced logic: ironically, Yahweh *did* have an eye and *had* taken notice. Therefore, his **'eye'** would **'not spare'** when it beheld the executioners slaying all and sundry, irrespective of age and gender. There would be no call to hold back, unlike the restraint placed upon the destroying angel in the time of David.[57] Now, the Lord will show no compassion (9:10).

As soon as Ezekiel received this stern reply the angel clothed in linen reported back to Yahweh, having fulfilled his grim task (9:11). We are left to imagine the city reeking with blood and the temple piled high with mangled bodies. How could Yahweh continue his residence in this terrestrial hell? He could not, and he would not.

Application

The ways of God are always right. In his day, Noah 'found grace in the eyes of Yahweh' and 'was a just man, perfect in his generations', who 'walked with God'. Astonishingly, he seems to have been unique in this respect. In consequence, the rest of mankind perished because 'all flesh had corrupted their way on the earth'.[58] Men, women, children and infants suffered. But this was not genocide. If it were, we would find the motivation for the Flood revolting if we did not to bring to mind the principle of solidarity. There is such a thing as corporate guilt, the penalty of which all share unless they disassociate.[59] In Ezekiel's Jerusalem the Lord was keen to seek out and spare those who would not identify with the prevalent apostasy, though we are not told how many there were.

Chapter 9's analysis of the sinfulness of Jerusalem makes it evident that spiritual declension was the parent of moral breakdown. It is so in all societies. Where the true God is wilfully ignored, sin will escalate. And the God who is thought to be unreal sees all and will eventually judge. This means that we must save ourselves from an increasingly evil society.[60]

The glory of Yahweh departs (Ezekiel 10:1-22)

The six executioners vanish from the scene, their departure being followed by a further description of the chariot-throne of Yahweh, adding to that presented by 1:4-28. The man clothed in linen reappears, his role now being that of an agent of destruction rather than of preservation (10:2).

The main feature of the second description of the throne of Yahweh is that the living beings of 1:15 are identified as **'cherubim'** (cf. 9:3), their commission being to escort the God of Israel as he leaves his now profaned temple. Before delving into the chapter, we retrace the path taken by the glory of Yahweh up to the point of the final departure.

We learn from 8:4 that Ezekiel beheld the divine glory 'there', probably at the entrance of the gate leading from the court of the people towards the court of the priests on a higher level on the northern side of the temple complex (cf. 8:3). Or 8:4 might suggest that the divine glory had settled above the Holy of Holies, where the Lord normally took his station.

According to 9:3, the divine glory had ascended from the throne above the cherubim and come to stand over the threshold. This might suggest that the throne seen by Ezekiel in 10:1 was still vacant, Yahweh remaining at the threshold. If so, the first part of 10:4 is parenthetical, 'And the glory of Yahweh *had* risen up from the cherub,' taking us back to the events of 9:3.[61] This would fit with 10:18: **'And the glory of**

Yahweh went away from the threshold of the house and stood over the cherubim.' The apparently complicated sequence of events indicates that the departure of Yahweh from the city was even then in motion. The translation offered here may clarify matters.

1. Fire from the throne (10:1-8)

10:1-8. Then I observed, and, look, with the firmament that was over the head of the cherubim was something like a sapphire stone — as the appearance of the likeness of a throne. It was seen above them. And he spoke to the man clothed in linen, and said, 'Come among the wheels, beneath the cherub, and fill your hands with coals of fire from among the cherubim and scatter them over the city.' So he entered in my sight. And the cherubim were standing on the right side of the house when the man entered, and the cloud filled the inner court.

(And the glory of Yahweh had risen up from the cherub to be over the threshold of the house, and the house was filled with the cloud and the court was full of the brightness of the glory of Yahweh. And the sound of the wings of the cherubim was heard as far as the outer court, as the voice of the Almighty when he speaks.) And it came about that when he commanded the man robed in linen, saying, 'Take fire from between the wheels, from between the cherubim,' that he entered and stood beside the wheels. Then the cherub stretched out his hand from among the cherubim to the fire that was among the cherubim. Picking it up, he placed it in the palms of him who was clothed in linen. He took it and went out. And the cherubim appeared to have the form of a man's hand beneath their wings.

Again, Ezekiel saw a resemblance of the sapphire **'throne'** above the crystal **'firmament'** over the heads of the creatures. Described here as **'cherubim'**, they were none other than the living beings previously seen by the prophet at the Chebar canal (10:1; cf. 9:3; 10:15,22). It would appear that the throne was awaiting the occasion when Yahweh would reoccupy it (see 10:18). Following the first appearance of the throne-chariot, Ezekiel had fallen upon his face (1:28); now, somewhat more calm, he describes in a selective fashion what he saw, giving additions to the initial record and omitting what was not essential to his narrative.

The son of a priestly family, Ezekiel must have been aware of the cherubim situated within the innermost sanctuary of Solomon's temple, and that there were carvings of cherubim within the Holy Place.[62] He would also have known that, in the language of 2 Samuel 22:11 and Psalms 18:10 and 104:3, the God of Israel was enthroned above flying cherubim.[63] Now, in distant Babylonia, he realized that what he saw in vision was the heavenly antitype to the temple representations: the living creatures *were* cherubim (cf. 10:20). Although Ezekiel is not specific, it would appear that the chariot-throne remained vacated in that the glory of the Lord had moved temporarily to the heart of the temple (10:1).

Yahweh, now at the threshold of the temple (cf. 9:3), gave the man robed in linen a new instruction: he was to **'come among the wheels'**, take glowing coals from **'among the cherubim'** beneath the throne **'and scatter them over the city'**. **'Wheels'** translates *galgal* (singular rather than plural), meaning 'round' (cf. 'Golgotha') and possibly a collective noun and a near-synonym for *ôpannim* in 10:10 and elsewhere. The meaning may be something like 'castors'. If so, Ezekiel became aware that the wheels were able to transport the chariot in any direction: Yahweh would not be confined to Jerusalem.[64]

According to Isaiah 6:6-7, a burning coal was employed to purge the prophet's sin; here, coals become a symbol of impending judgement, a conflagration not unlike that of Sodom and Gomorrah.[65] Ezekiel was being informed that the inferno about to burst upon Jerusalem was from God, notwithstanding the Babylonian armies that would amass themselves around the walls for a final onslaught. And, as 2 Kings 25:9 and 2 Chronicles 36:19 relate, it eventually happened: the God of Israel would show himself to be a consuming fire.[66] In accordance with his order, the man went among the wheels to receive the deadly conflagration (10:2).

At the time **'the cherubim were standing on the right side of the house'**, the south flank of the temple as one looks eastward, the **'cloud'** of the divine glory having already moved to **'the inner court'** (again, see 9:3). Apparently by way of explanation, **'the glory of Yahweh'** is said to have ascended already to hover over the threshold of the temple filled with cloud, the court being full of **'the brightness of the glory of Yahweh'** (10:3-4).[67]

'The wings of the cherubim' moved so rapidly that their sound, like the **'voice of the Almighty'** (literally, *El Shaddai*), was audible in the outer court (10:5). Apparently, the creatures were preparing for the return of the divine glory to its normal abode prior to its, and their, final departure from the temple.

As suggested, verses 3-5 seem to be a flashback to 9:3. Now the narrative picks up from 10:2: **'the man robed in linen'** found himself among the whirling **'wheels'** or castors (again, *galgal*) and **'the cherubim'**. One of these creatures transferred glowing coals to his hand, whereupon he departed. It is to be assumed that the angelic scribe did scatter the fire over Jerusalem, although the action is not mentioned.

The coals received from a **'cherub'** had been extracted by the latter from among the four living creatures, of which he was one. In this fashion Ezekiel was made even more aware that the doom descending upon Jerusalem came from God, irrespective of the human agency of destruction, in this case Nebuchadnezzar: the hands of the cherubim were manipulating the hand of Babylon. In that the cherubim were guardians of the divine presence,[68] they were seen by Ezekiel to fulfil their office (10:6-8).

2. The cherubim and the wheels (10:9-17)

10:9-17. When I saw, look, there were four wheels by the cherubim, one wheel by one cherub, and one wheel by one cherub, and the appearance of the wheels was as the gleam of a chrysolite stone. And as for their appearances, there was one likeness for the four of them — as it were, a wheel within a wheel. When they moved, they moved along their four sides; they did not swerve when they moved, moving after the direction to which the head faced. They did not swerve when they moved. And all their flesh and their backs and their hands and their wings, and the wheels, were full of eyes all around — for the four wheels.

As for the wheels, in my hearing they were named 'the wheel'. And there were four faces for each one: the face of the one was the face of the cherub; the second face, the face of a man; and the third, the face of a lion; and the fourth, the face of an eagle. Then the cherubim raised themselves up. This was the living creature that I had seen by the Chebar canal. And when the cherubim went, the wheels went beside them; and when the cherubim were lifting their wings to rise up above the earth, the wheels did not swerve from beside them. When they stood, the others stood, and when they rose, the others rose with them. For the spirit of the living creature was in them.

Verses 9-12 almost parallel 1:15-18. Ezekiel's renewed sight of Yahweh on the sapphire throne was a repetition of the vision that he had seen at the Chebar canal fourteen months earlier (see 10:15,20). Recording what he saw because the chariot-throne would accompany Yahweh's departure from the temple, he adds several additional details.

Firstly, **'cherubim'** replaces 'living creatures'.

Secondly, 10:12 states that **'all their flesh and their backs** [*gabbéhem*] **and their hands and their wings, and the wheels, were full of eyes all around — for the four wheels'**. In that 1:18 states that the 'rims' (*gabbéhen*) of the wheels 'were full of eyes round about', does the present verse single out the living beings or the wheels? If the former, their **'backs'** were filled with eyes, which seems — to say the least — bizarre. But, as Block notes, this surrealistic feature occurs in a visionary experience, Ezekiel pointing out that the chariot was propelled by an all-seeing intelligence (10:9-12).[69]

Thirdly, in 10:13 two different Hebrew words for 'wheel' are used, one of which stresses whirling or rotary motion: **'As for the wheels** [*ôphanim*], **in my hearing they were named "the wheel"** [*haggalgal*].**'** This tells out the infinite energy of the chariot of fire.

Fourthly, the faces of each of the cherubim were those of a cherub (apparently, not that of an ox; cf. 1:10), of a man, of a lion and of an eagle. Perhaps a solution to the apparent discrepancy between cherub and ox lies in the fact that **'cherub'** is preceded, unusually, by the Hebrew definite article, giving, literally, 'the face of *the* cherub' (10:14). This cherub could have been the being mentioned in 10:7 who handed fire to the man clothed in linen. If so, the ox-like face is not specified because Ezekiel knew that its identity could be inferred from the earlier vision.

The movements of these beings are detailed in order to emphasize their submission to the will of God. Indeed, they had no independent existence, in that their spirits resided in the wheels. When the cherubim were still, the wheels did not move; when the cherubim spread their wings and ascended, the wheels revolved beside them (10:15-17).

3. Yahweh abandons the temple (10:18-22)

10:18-22. And the glory of Yahweh went away from the threshold of the house and stood over the cherubim. The cherubim raised their wings and rose up from the earth before my eyes. When they went away, the wheels were by them, and it stood at the entrance of the east gate of the house of Yahweh, with the glory of the God of Israel over them. This was the living creature that I saw beneath the God of Israel by the Chebar canal, and I knew that they were cherubim. For each there were four faces and four wings, and the likeness of the hands of a man underneath their wings. And as for the likeness of their faces, they were the faces whose appearance I had seen upon the Chebar canal. Each moved straight ahead.

Finally, **'the glory of Yahweh'** moved away from the temple threshold and came to rest **'over the cherubim'** who were ready for departure (10:18). In response, these creatures elevated their wings in flight and the chariot-throne was seen by Ezekiel to rise up and then alight **'at the entrance of the east gate of the house of Yahweh'** — that is, at the main entrance of the eastern outermost court. Yahweh was now ready to transfer to the mountain east of Jerusalem (see 11:23). Yet before this happened Ezekiel would witness more of the evils of Jerusalem.

The title **'God of Israel'**, rather than 'Yahweh', is employed in 10:20. Although Yahweh remained the God of Jacob, in Ezekiel's day the Lord regarded himself as no longer the covenant God of apostate Jerusalem. In principle, the unholy city had been abandoned to destruction. This explains why 10:20-22 repeats 10:15 in telling that Ezekiel **'knew'** that what he beheld was what he had seen in his inaugural vision: **'they were the faces whose appearance I had seen upon the Chebar canal'**, notwithstanding the problems about the substitution of 'cherub' for 'ox' in 10:14. God was transferring himself to the exiles in Babylonia. Here, in the seat of majestic heathendom and at the heart of a worldwide tyranny, Ezekiel would observe the throne, itself the antitype to the ark of the covenant (10:19-22).

Application

Previously, the man clothed in linen had been employed in a work of mercy and preservation (9:4), but in chapter 10 he is seen as an agent of judgement. The principle extends to our New Testament age: although the gospel and its messengers are to some the fragrance of life, to others they are the reek of death.[70] Neutrality in the things of God is impossible.

In a sense, Ezekiel may well have been encouraged by the vision of chapter 10: he learned that, although for the foreseeable future the God of Israel had terminated his relationship with Jerusalem and the land of promise, Yahweh had not abandoned his people for ever. The chariot-throne would travel east to dwell with the exiles in a strange land. In later years, our Lord informed the chief priests and elders in Jerusalem that 'the kingdom of God will be taken from you and given to a nation bearing the fruits of it'.[71] That is, the apostate ethnic church would fade away in favour of a non-racial, and therefore omni-racial, church. In the sixth century BC Ezekiel was helping to lay its foundation. We should thank the Lord that the kingdom of heaven is open to all who desire to come and that those who repent and believe are welcome.

Judgement descends upon the leaders of Israel (Ezekiel 11:1-25)

This chapter concludes the series of visions commencing at 8:1. Chapter 8 records that Ezekiel was shown numerous abominations in Jerusalem, and in chapter 9 he tells that all who were not marked for deliverance were to be slain by the destroying angels. Then chapter 10 announced that Jerusalem must be put to the torch. Now, almost by way of recapitulation, the wicked leaders of that city are seen as the objects of condemnation. Although some commentators conclude, as Wevers claims, that 'this section is secondary to the original narrative' because there is a 'total lack of connection with the context', and is 'a separate ecstatic experience',[72] it does integrate nicely with chapters 8 – 10,[73] which suggests that Ezekiel's predictions in this chapter are to be taken as part of the complete temple vision.

There would seem to be three main divisions to the chapter: firstly, the destruction of the evil rulers (11:1-13); secondly, a promise concerning a new Israel (11:14-21); thirdly, the withdrawal of the presence of Yahweh from Jerusalem and Ezekiel's return (in spirit) to the exiles in the land of Babylon (11:22-25).

1. The destruction of the evil rulers (11:1-13)

11:1-13. Then the Spirit lifted me up and brought me to the eastern gate of the house of Yahweh, facing eastward; and, look, in the entrance of the gate were twenty-five men; and I saw among them Jaazaniah the son of Azzur and Pelatiah the son of Benaiah, princes of the people. And he said to me, 'Son of man, these men are devising iniquity and counsel evil advice in this city, who say, "The time is not near to build houses: it is the pot and we are the flesh." Therefore, prophesy against them. Prophesy, son of man.' Then the Spirit of Yahweh fell upon me, and he said to me, 'Say, "Thus says Yahweh: 'Thus you say, house of Israel, and I know the thoughts that arise in your spirit. You have multiplied your slain in this city, and you have filled its streets with the slain.'"

'"Therefore, thus says the Lord Yahweh: 'Your slain whom you have set within it, they are the flesh and it the pot, but he will bring you out from its midst. You have feared a sword, and a sword I shall bring upon you,' says the Lord Yahweh, 'and I shall bring you out of its midst and will deliver you into the hands of strangers and will execute judgements against you. You will fall by the sword. I shall judge you at the border of Israel and you will know that I am Yahweh. This will not be to you for a pot, nor shall you be for flesh in its midst: I shall judge you at the border of Israel. And you will know that I am Yahweh, for you have not walked in my statutes, and my judgements you have not executed, but have done according to the judgements of the nations which are around you.'"'

Then it was that as I was prophesying, Pelatiah the son of Benaiah died. And I fell upon my face and cried out with a loud voice and said, 'Ah, Lord Yahweh! Will you make a complete end of the remnant of Israel?'

Ezekiel was conducted from the inner court, where he had been stationed, to the outer entrance of the **'eastern gate'** of the temple, where the people could gather.[74] The glory of Yahweh had already transferred to this position (see 10:19). The prophet tells us that he saw **'twenty-five men'**, possibly secular leaders rather than the twenty-five priests mentioned in 8:16. This second group of twenty-five might have been the twelve princes of the tribes of Israel, together with twelve royal officers,[75] all accompanying the king himself. In that most of the leading citizens of Jerusalem had been deported along with Ezekiel in 597 BC, these twenty-five might not have been, as Taylor remarks, 'of high quality'.[76]

'Jaazaniah the son of Azzur' and **'Pelatiah the son of Benaiah'** are named, possibly because Jaazaniah means 'Yahweh hears'; Pelatiah 'Yahweh rescues', or 'Yahweh causes to escape'; and Benaiah 'Yahweh builds' (11:1). Jaazaniah would not have been the Jaazaniah mentioned in 8:11, nor the son of Jeremiah the Rechabite,[77] nor the son of the Maacathite.[78] The names might indicate the misplaced hope in Yahweh entertained by complacent leaders in Jerusalem. If so, Ezekiel was being informed that God would not help these iniquitous men.

But what was their sin? Yahweh specifies: they had been guilty of **'devising iniquity'** and had counselled **'evil advice'**, saying that **'The time is not near to build houses.'** Idolatry is seen to have gone hand in hand with immorality.

The reference to **'the pot'** may best be interpreted by comparison with Jeremiah 29:5. Jeremiah, writing from Jerusalem, was calling upon the deportees in Babylonia to build houses, knowing that there could be no early return to the land of Israel and that the exiles had to prepare themselves for a long wait.

For his part, Ezekiel was aware that the leaders in Jerusalem chose to believe that their city would survive the heat of conflict with Babylon, calculating that, just as a pot protects its perishable contents from external harm, so Jerusalem would insulate its inhabitants. Their claim would have been that, although 'the time' was 'not near to build houses' with the enemy battering at the gates, when the war was over they could engage in lucrative redevelopment. But they were wrong, as indicated by the employment of the similar figure in 11:7 and 24:3,6. In short, the people, self-confident in proportion to their ignorance, had rejected the warning of Jeremiah that resistance to Babylon would be disastrous,[79] preferring to trust in the long history and strong walls of their city.

Martin Luther, the Reformer (1483–1546) put it like this:

> ... the law or the Old Testament containeth only conditional promises; for it hath always such conditions as these are, joined to it: If ye hearken to my voice, if ye keep my statutes, if ye walk in my ways, ye shall be my people, etc. The Jews, not considering this, laid hold of those conditional promises as if they had been absolute and without all conditions: which they supposed God could never revoke, but must needs keep them.[80]

So it was that those who remained in Jerusalem believed that they would enjoy tenure, the exiles having been removed from the land and therefore from the blessing of God. To rectify this erroneous perception, Ezekiel was commanded to respond, the imperative verb **'prophesy'** being repeated because the situation was urgent: Yahweh had been provoked and it was time to repent (11:2-4). In 7:2,3,12 and 12:23, Ezekiel warns of the early overthrow of the city.

'The Spirit of Yahweh fell' upon Ezekiel, meaning that he became the actual mouthpiece of Yahweh. He was commanded to inform the **'house of Israel'**, as represented by 'the elders of Judah' who were sitting before him (8:1), that God knew **'the thoughts that**

arise in your spirit' (11:5).[81] The omniscient Yahweh was aware that the policy of resistance advocated in Jerusalem was futile, particularly because homicide had been common in the city. Such atrocities might have been the result of political purges (cf. 19:3,6; 22:27), in that **'slain'** (*chalal*) usually signifies someone killed violently. Thus it had been *within* the walls of Jerusalem (11:6).

Yahweh hurls the Jerusalemites' metaphor back at them, though with an ominous new sense: Jerusalem is, indeed, a container, but not an earthenware pot able to preserve its contents. Rather, it becomes a cauldron piled high with the flesh of the victims of their leaders' cruelty: **'Your slain ... are the flesh, and it** [Jerusalem] **the pot.'**

The meaning is that because the surviving leaders within Jerusalem had murdered not a few of the inhabitants, the city could offer no security to them. The metaphor was not new in that, in the eighth century BC, the prophet Micah had employed it with reference to Samaria.[82] Yahweh will overturn and empty the cauldron, causing those whose hands were stained with blood to tumble **'out from its midst'**, away from Jerusalem (11:7). **'"You have feared a sword, and a sword I shall bring upon you," says the Lord Yahweh'** (11:8).

And away from Jerusalem they will be met by **'a sword'** wielded judicially by agents of Yahweh, specified as **'strangers'** (cf. 7:21; 28:10; 30:12). Even as they had oppressed their fellow-Jews within the city, hostile aliens will afflict them elsewhere (11:9), the site of execution being specified as **'the border of Israel'**. In the event, the place was Riblah, about sixty miles north of Damascus. The 'border' is mentioned possibly because it would be realized that Yahweh's power extended throughout a land that remained his freehold possession and that he was perfectly able to get rid of those whom he considered to be unsuitable tenants.

Then those who survive **'will know that I am Yahweh'**. All this actually occurred, and 2 Kings 25:18-21 tells the story.[83] Jerusalem, therefore, will not be a **'pot'** or container preserving its occupants — **'flesh'** — from disaster. Repeating himself, Yahweh declares that **'I shall judge you at the border of Israel'** (11:10-11).

Years earlier, the elders of the people had approached the prophet Samuel and virtually demanded that he provide a king for Israel.[84] In so doing, they were effectively repudiating the covenant bond between Yahweh and Israel.[85] In the Jerusalem of Ezekiel's day the leaders were guilty of the same sin: ignoring Moses, they had **'done according to the judgements of the nations which are around you'**. Very well! Yahweh declares that if they want to be like the surrounding nations, to the surrounding nations they shall go (11:12).

While Ezekiel **'was prophesying'**, one of the Jerusalem leaders, **'Pelatiah the son of Benaiah'**, died. This may mean that Ezekiel, about 1,000 kilometres from the city, was informed immediately about the death of this man, who was probably an important personage not unknown to Ezekiel and those with him. Vision and reality merge.

As has already been observed, Pelatiah means 'Yahweh rescues', and Benaiah 'Yahweh builds'. The moment of death was timed to show the prophet that what had been declared would certainly occur: Yahweh would *not* rescue and would *not* build Jerusalem.[86] Ezekiel was terrified, much as in 9:8, and asked Yahweh if he purposed to destroy the whole nation. It is likely that the prophet communicated Pelatiah's decease to the elders so that later, when what he said was confirmed by news from Jerusalem (cf. 33:21-22),[87] his predictions in 11:1-12 would have been accepted as authentic (11:13).

2. A new Israel (11:14-21)

11:14-21. Then the word of Yahweh came to me, saying, 'Son of man, your brothers, your brothers your kinsmen, and all the house of Israel, all of them, are they to whom the inhabitants of Jerusalem have said, "Get far away from Yahweh. The land has been given to us for a possession."

'Therefore say, "Thus says the Lord Yahweh: 'Though I have removed them far away among the nations and though I have scattered them in the lands, yet in small measure I shall be for a sanctuary to them in the lands to which they have come.'" Therefore say, "Thus says the Lord Yahweh: 'I shall gather you from the peoples and shall assemble you from the lands in which you were dispersed; and I shall give to them the earth of Israel. Then they will go there and will remove from it all its detestable things and all its abominations. And I shall give them one heart and shall put a new spirit within them, and I shall remove the heart of stone from their flesh and give them a heart of flesh, so that they will walk in my statutes and observe my judgements and do them, and they will be to me for a people and I shall be to them for a God. But as for those whose heart walks after the heart of their detestable things and their abominations, I shall bring their way upon their heads,' says the Lord Yahweh."'

Ezekiel's plaintive intercession elicited an immediate statement from Yahweh concerning the long-term future of the descendants of the exiles *within* the land of promise.

Yahweh spoke in order to reassure the despondent prophet, informing him that his true **'brothers'** were **'all the house of Israel'**, in effect his companions in exile rather than the (temporary) survivors in Jerusalem. For the former there would be consolation rather than condemnation. Ezekiel was reminded that he was responsible for them in that they were his **'kinsmen'**, literally 'the men of your redemption' (from *gôel*).

During the Old Testament period, a *gôel* had numerous responsibilities: he was obliged to purchase his kinsman's liberty if the latter were enslaved to a foreigner, to reclaim family property that had passed beyond family ownership, to marry a relative's widow in order to preserve his line, and to avenge the death of a near relative by seeking the blood of the murderer.[88] By means of this striking metaphor Ezekiel was being told that his ministry would uphold Israel, as represented by the deportees in Babylon.

Sadly, those who reckoned that they were fortunate to be in Jerusalem looked askance at the exiles, believing that in a far country the latter were separated from Yahweh and from the land that remained to those who were there. Therefore they hurled abuse at the exiles: **'Get far away from Yahweh. The land has been given to us** [by Yahweh] **for a possession.'**[89]

In short, these Jews believed that their apparent retention of the land was an integral part of Yahweh's covenant with Israel and that he was defending them.[90] In Babylon, the situation of the deportees was humiliating because they were aware that their fellow-countrymen were scoffing at them (11:14-15). But the ensuing verses show Yahweh's reaction.

The Lord confounds the Jerusalem leaders. It was true that he had **'removed them** [the deportees] **far away among the nations'** and had **'scattered them in the lands'**, but it was not the case that their removal meant that he had alienated himself from them in favour of those who were left behind in Jerusalem.

In fact, he would be **'in small measure ... a sanctuary** [*miqdash*] **to them** [that is, to the deportees] **in the lands to which they have come'**. This statement is unparalleled in the Old Testament,[91] and the closest analogues are in the New Testament.[92]

In Ezekiel's day, Yahweh was promising the exiles that what the Jerusalem temple, Yahweh's *miqdash* (8:6; 9:6), had once been for the twelve tribes, so he would be for them in distant Babylon, an inherently unclean land (cf. 4:13).

'In small measure' is probably adverbial: Yahweh will be the exiles' **'sanctuary'** for a limited period only, implying the dawn of a new and better era (11:16). And it is to this that the following verses point. Then, at an unspecified time, the twelve tribes will be re-united: **'I shall gather you from the peoples and shall assemble you from the lands in which you were dispersed.'** They will be granted again **'the earth of Israel'**.

There is to be, in fact, a new exodus and a new settlement, a promise to be repeated several times later in Ezekiel's prophecy (20:34,41; 34:13; 36:24; 39:27). Eventually, the covenant with Abraham will find a permanent fulfilment.[93] Apparently, unlike the initial refusal of the children of Israel to take possession of the promised land,[94] the settlers will be unhesitant (11:17).

In time to come, regathered Israelites will distance themselves from the misdeeds of their remote forefathers (11:18),[95] doing so because they now possess **'one heart'**, meaning that they entertain a single purpose,[96] and a **'new spirit'**, a determination to honour Yahweh. This 'heart' is said to be of living **'flesh'** rather than of hard, inert **'stone'** (cf. 2:4; 3:7): they will respond positively to everything that God requires from them.

Like his near-contemporary Jeremiah,[97] Ezekiel was given to understand that the prediction of Deuteronomy 30:6 would come to an ultimate fulfilment. With regard to a repentant Diaspora, 'Yahweh your God will circumcise your heart and the heart of your seed, to love Yahweh your God with all your heart and with all your soul, that you may live.'

Although it is not said in as many words, the desired object of the exercise is the renewal of the covenant relationship between God and his people, as indicated by **'so that'** at the commencement of verse 20. The reader is taken back to Genesis 17:7-8, where Yahweh promises Abraham that he will be 'God to you and to your seed after you', and to Exodus 6:7, 'I shall take you as my people, and shall be God to you.'[98]

If this promise is considered in the light of Jeremiah 31:31-34[99] as pertaining to the 'new covenant',[100] it must be borne in mind that this covenant will be new in both of two senses: firstly, that the *whole* people will be renewed, rather than a relatively small remnant (as had been the case, say, in Elijah's day);[101] and, secondly, it will be new in that the Sinai arrangement proffered demand and promise but never provided therapy, neither forensically nor with regard to spiritual regeneration. We see here the glimmering promise of a church in which no individual would *not* know the Lord (11:19-20).

The threat of 9:10, 'I shall bring their conduct upon their heads,' is repeated by 11:21 for those whose hearts lingered after the old abominations. The exiles may not expect that Yahweh's smile will rest upon them just because they are far distant from sinful Jerusalem; they, too, must repent (11:21).

3. Yahweh and Ezekiel leave Jerusalem (11:22-25)

11:22-25. Then the cherubim raised their wings, with the wheels beside them and the glory of the God of Israel over them, above. And the glory of Yahweh ascended from over the centre of the city and stood above the mountain that is to the east of the city. Then the Spirit lifted me up and brought me in a vision by the Spirit of God to Chaldea, to the exiles, and the vision that I had seen went up from me. And I spoke to the exiles all the words of Yahweh that he had shown me.

The first vision, relating to abominations within Jerusalem and commencing at 8:1, now concludes. Departing from the east gate, to which the chariot had previously removed (10:19), **'the glory of the God of Israel'** abandoned the entire city. Bearing its divine rider, the fiery throne alighted on what we know as the Mount of Olives to oversee the downfall of Jerusalem. For someone standing on the temple site in Jerusalem and looking eastwards, Olivet would represent the far horizon, and it must have signified to Ezekiel that God had repudiated the bond between him and the city (11:22-23).[102]

Finally, the son of man was transported in his spirit back to Chaldea. During the whole event he had remained *physically* with the elders of **'the exiles'** who, according to 8:1, had come to listen to him. The **'vision ... went up'** from him to the God who gave it, and Ezekiel disclosed to his hearers **'all the words of Yahweh'** that he had been **'shown'**, his message being that the deportees should place their trust in the word of God rather than yearn to go back to the doomed city (11:24-25).

Application

1. Redefining God

The elders of Jerusalem who survived the first Chaldean onslaught in 597 BC chose to believe that they were secure within the walls of Jerusalem. In effect, they put their trust in the fortifications of their city rather than in the God of that city. But there was a problem: time and again, their predecessors and they had shattered the covenant stipulations that bound Yahweh to his people.[103]

Security cannot be found in prosperity and property, but only in God.[104] Those who redefine God redefine their morality (or, better, generate their own brands of amorality). According to 11:7,12, within Jerusalem spiritual apostasy had manifested itself in gross evil and social injustice. So it must always be, in that societies which refuse to give attention to the Word of God will inevitably succumb to sin. Since the end of the Second World War (at least), within the UK there has been a serious declension in the popular acceptance of evangelical truth. Alongside this, commonly received moral standards have been ignored, often with catastrophic results.

2. The fulfilment of 11:16-18

Chapters 8 – 11 show that the Lord planned to restore a faithful people to the land of Israel.[105] But what of the historical fulfilment? Has it occurred already, or will it happen at some future time?

Although some Jews returned from the Babylonian exile under Zerubbabel,[106] and although after their exile they abandoned formal idolatry, few showed the grace of repentance. Ezra testifies that many Jerusalemites married foreign wives, and Nehemiah was vociferous in his condemnation of this and other evils.[107] It seems difficult, then, to relate the fulfilment of Ezekiel's prediction to the end of the seventy-year captivity.[108]

Nor can this prophecy find its realization in the genesis of the New Testament churches. With the possible exception of 2 Corinthians 3:3 (which may, however, allude to Jeremiah 31:33), not only does the New Testament not apply Ezekiel 11 to the new-covenant status of the churches, it never cites from this chapter.

There remains, then, the possibility that Ezekiel 11 points to the heavenly scene (as does Ezekiel 40 – 48, according to the interpretation offered by the present commentary). Yet this approach may also be discarded, in that 11:17-20 seems to posit a new exodus from captivity to the land of promise at some future time, a conclusion strengthened by 20:33-38.

Nevertheless, whatever view we may prefer, an answer to the question appears to be pressing in that commentators seldom address the matter;[109] consensus fails because there is little debate. May it not be, then, that Ezekiel 11 predicts a return of the Jews as the constituent members of a spiritually and socially united Israel to the land promised to Abraham and his posterity? That is to say, the chapter offers a very long-term prediction concerning what we now know to be events occurring towards the end of the Messianic era.

In New Testament times Paul testified that within Israel there was a remnant that had been chosen graciously by God, and also that most Jews were rejecting the truth of the gospel.[110] But he also indicates that the day will come. Romans 11:25 is explicit, and Appendix ‘C’ considers the matter.

Following the establishment of the throne of David one millennium before Christ, Jewish confidence in Yahweh rested on belief in the permanence of his covenant with Abraham, on Yahweh’s bestowal of the land of Canaan to his chosen people, on his covenant with David and on his choice of Jerusalem. In chapter 11, Ezekiel is concerned with the early destruction of these pillars *and* with their ultimate re-erection in this world. A regenerate, united people will require and will be granted their own habitat.

From this it follows that Ezekiel 11, although primarily addressed to the situation of Jerusalem and of the deportees in the early sixth century BC, beckons to the future.

Signs of the impending catastrophe (Ezekiel 12:1-28)

Linked to the premonitions of judgement in chapters 8 – 11, chapters 12 – 19 portray the worthlessness of the confidence in the security of Jerusalem and its temple that gripped those in the city and the exiles so far away. Ezekiel announces that Babylon must prevail because Yahweh intends to judge sinful Israel. The sequence of vision followed by interpretation in chapters 8 – 19 is not unlike that of the visions of chapters 4 – 5 and the prophecies that follow them in chapters 6 – 7.

In chapter 12 Ezekiel tells how he was required to act out a remarkable drama (12:1-7) and how he had to explain its meaning to his hearers (12:8-16), then how he was to offer to his compatriots another action which would symbolize the distress of the people of Jerusalem (12:17-20) and, finally, his response to the objections that divine judgement would never happen, or that it would be delayed for a virtually indefinite period (12:21-28).

By this time, Ezekiel's actions (see chapters 4 – 5) may have become the subject of ribald comment and ridicule among his fellow-exiles. When in chapter 12 he assumes the mantle of the Jerusalemites, and even of the king, Zedekiah, entering into captivity, many would have been eager to gaze at another bizarre performance.

1. Ezekiel packs his bags (12:1-7)

12:1-7. Now the word of Yahweh came to me, saying, 'Son of man, you dwell in the midst of a rebellious house, who have eyes to see but do not see, who have ears to hear but do not hear, for they are a rebellious house.

'And you, son of man, prepare for yourself baggage for exile and go into exile by day in their sight, and in their sight go into exile from your place to another; perhaps they will see, even though they are a rebellious house. You will bring out your baggage as the baggage of exile by day in their sight. Then you will go out in the evening in their sight, like they who are going out into exile. In their sight dig for yourself a hole in the wall and go out by it. In their sight you will carry it by shoulder and will go out by dusk. You will cover your face and you will not see the land, for I have appointed you for a sign to the house of Israel.'

Then I did this, as I had been commanded. I brought out my baggage by day as the baggage of exile, and in the evening I dug through the wall with my hand. I brought out the baggage by darkness and carried it in their sight.

Although this prophecy is undated, it must have originated prior to the seventh year of Ezekiel's captivity — that is, before 590 BC (see 20:1) and therefore prior to the fall of Jerusalem. In the light of Deuteronomy 18:21-22 it was important for Ezekiel to utter a prediction which, through its fulfilment, would confirm his status and give him credibility for further prophetic ministry (cf. 33:21-22).

Yahweh reminded the **'son of man'** that he lived **'in the midst of a rebellious house'**, a people who had **'eyes to see'** and **'ears to hear'**, but who remained oblivious to the word of the Lord (12:1-2; cf. 2:3-7). The point of 12:2 is that the exiles were no better than those who remained in Jerusalem, even though the former were (presumably) not outwardly idolatrous: they could have perceived the truth had they desired. There is here a recall of Deuteronomy 29:4,[111] and the Lord adds by way of emphasis that they were **'a rebellious house'**. Ezekiel does not expound further, but perhaps they refused to accept that the captivity would last for a full seventy years and, deceived by their local prophets, they believed that there would be an early return to Jerusalem.[112] Here there is a nice balance between divine sovereignty and human responsibility: God blinded them, and they desired to be blind. And perhaps they had already in principle rejected Ezekiel's ministry, as suggested by 33:30-32.

The Lord instructed Ezekiel to gather up his belongings by daylight in the same way that a captive might hastily put into a bag whatever he could seize before his exodus.[113]

Then the prophet was required to carry his bag out of his house, although it is not said what he had to do with it. Presumably, he set the container down outside his door, or by someone else's house, in full view of the spectators who would have gathered to see what was happening, as indicated by the words, **'by day in their sight'** (12:3-4). Yahweh's exclamation that **'perhaps they will see'** suggests that there might be some who would comprehend the significance of Ezekiel's activity and who would repent. But, as Taylor comments, 'even though the result may still be negative, the obligation to speak [in Ezekiel's case, to act] is still there, if only to justify the hearer's condemnation'.[114]

The instruction continued: in the evening of the same day the prophet would tunnel through the sun-dried mud or brick wall of his house, digging from the outside (**'go out in the evening'**). This constituted a change in roles:[115] by packing his bag and leaving by day he represented Jews in Jerusalem going into exile, and then by digging through the wall of his house from the exterior he may have represented the attacking Babylonians.[116] In chapters 4 – 5, too, he symbolized both the aggressors (the sign-act of the inscribed brick surrounded by models of a besieging army) and the besieged (his starvation diet and the shaving of his hair).

Then, presumably having returned to his own house with his travel-bag, he would leave through the hole, this being his second exit. His curious fellow-exiles would still be watching intently (12:4-5).

The second departure mentioned by 12:5 is given further reference, but with more detail. Ezekiel must leave his house **'by dusk'** as if departing in secret,[117] covering **'his face'** so that he could not see the ground clearly. And all this because Yahweh had appointed Ezekiel as **'a sign** [*môphét* = 'omen'] **to the house of Israel'**, representing both the Judge — Yahweh — and the judged — the people of Jerusalem (12:6).

Ezekiel records that he obeyed (cf. 24:18; 37:7), adding that he **'dug through the wall'**, **'in the evening ... with my hand'**, and that when he removed his bag from the house **'by darkness'**, or 'at dusk', he did so **'in their sight'** — that is, he was seen by his fellow-exiles (12:7).

2. The explanation (12:8-16)

12:8-16. Then, in the morning the word of Yahweh came to me, saying, 'Son of man, have not the house of Israel, the rebellious house, said to you, "What are you doing?" Say to them, "Thus says the Lord Yahweh: 'This burden is the prince in Jerusalem, and all the house of Israel who are in their midst.'" Say, "I am your sign: even as I have done, so it will be done to them. They will go into exile and captivity. And the prince who is in their midst will carry his baggage in the darkness and go out. They will dig through to carry him out through it. He will cover his face because he himself cannot see the land. I shall also spread my net upon him and he will be caught in my snare. Then I shall bring him to Babylon, the land of the Chaldeans. But he will not see it, and there he will die. And I shall scatter all who are around him, his helpers, and all his armies to every wind, and I shall draw out a sword after them. Then they will know that I am Yahweh when I disperse them among the nations and scatter them among the lands. But I shall spare a few of them from the sword, from famine and from the plague so that they might declare all their abominations among the nations where they have gone, and may know that I am Yahweh."'

Apparently, both Ezekiel and his spectators returned to their homes and pondered overnight what the prophet had been doing during the previous day. Perhaps he knew what his actions meant; perhaps not. Either way, the next morning Yahweh revealed to Ezekiel exactly what to say to startled fellow-Jews who observed him going out through the wall of his house with a few meagre possessions (12:8).

He would let it be known that his strange deed was an acted parable, addressed to **'all the house of Israel'**, foreshadowing imminent events in Jerusalem. **'Israel'** stands for the existing nation, although at that time composed mainly of the tribe of Judah.

There is a verbal assonance between **'prince'** (*nasi*) and **'burden'** (*massa*), reading somewhat literally, 'the prince — the burden'. The tone is vivid, the individual concerned being Zedekiah, the then incumbent of the throne of David. However, he is not termed 'king' because Ezekiel did not consider him to be anything more than a king in name only (cf. 19:1; 21:25), which is why he dates his oracles by the captivity of 'King Jehoiachin' (see 1:2). But the prophet also addresses the complete nation, in that both Zedekiah and all who remained in Jerusalem and Judah would carry their baggage into exile.

Nor was this prophecy in vain. Zedekiah attempted to escape from Jerusalem but was captured. Later, when he had been compelled to witness the execution of his children, he was blinded. Taken to Babylon, he died in captivity.[118] In effect, Ezekiel's role changed yet again, from representing the besieged and then the besiegers to speaking for Yahweh, the Judge (12:9-10).

Just like those who remained behind in Jerusalem, their notional secure 'pot' (see 11:3), many exiles believed that their captivity would soon be terminated and that they would return to the land of Israel. Therefore, Ezekiel had to inform them that he was **'your sign'** to convince the exiles that the deportation in 597 BC was only the first: **'as I** [Yahweh] **have done, so it will be done to them'** — that is, to the survivors in Jerusalem. Even as Ezekiel had carried his knapsack away from his house, so the inhabitants of Jerusalem would be compelled to evacuate their city (12:11), the following verses telling that Yahweh, rather than the Chaldeans, would make it happen.

Yahweh further instructed Ezekiel to inform his compatriots that **'the prince** [Zedekiah] **who is in their midst** [that is, in Jerusalem] **will carry his baggage'** and will leave the city **'in the darkness'**, meaning that he will attempt to escape under cover of night. Further, **'they'**, the Chaldeans, will penetrate the city walls in order to seize Zedekiah, and the latter will **'cover his face because he himself cannot see the land'** (12:12). This might mean that the king would disguise himself so as not to be seen and that, having fled from Jerusalem, he would never return.[119] Or the meaning might be that, when captured, he would be blinded, never again to see Jerusalem (cf. 12:13). Or both meanings might be intended.

The Lord informed Ezekiel that he must relay to his hearers the grim truth that he, Yahweh, rather than Babylon, was the ultimate opponent of Zedekiah and of Jerusalem: **'I shall also spread my net upon him** [again, Zedekiah] **... I shall bring him to Babylon.'** This is the first time in the book that Babylon is mentioned explicitly, highlighting the fact that the human agents who had deported Ezekiel and others in 597 BC had not finished with the city. Yahweh will resemble a hunter, and Zedekiah, along with his people, a hunted animal (cf. 19:8; 32:3).[120]

Nevertheless, Zedekiah will never **'see'** Babylon, although he will **'die'** there (12:13). Having escaped from Jerusalem as a fugitive with his head covered (see 12:12), he will be deprived of eyesight — as indeed happened. When the exiles learned of the tragedy, their confidence in Ezekiel as a genuine prophet of Yahweh could only have been enhanced.[121]

By Zedekiah's **'helpers'** may be meant his own armed forces plus foreign allies, if any.[122] With his **'armies'** scattered, he will be helpless. But Ezekiel predicts that Babylon is not to be the only place to which the fleeing Jews must be led; they will be scattered **'to every wind'** and will suffer the **'sword'** in lands where they thought that at last they would find refuge. Egypt would be one such place.[123] In consequence, when God has scattered them **'among the nations'** and **'among the lands'**, they appreciate what they had never understood or wished to understand — that **'I am Yahweh'** (12:14-15).

Yet, emerging from **'the sword, from famine and from the plague'** (cf. 5:12; 7:15) will be some who are permitted by Yahweh to escape. It is stressed that, not delivered because of their own righteousness, they acknowledge that God had brought about the collapse of Jerusalem, the temple and the monarchy, and that he was righteous in so doing. In fact, they will **'declare all their abominations among the nations where they have gone'**. If this were not the case, receptor nations, such as Babylon, would have claimed that Yahweh, bowed down by inherent weakness, had been unable to protect his own.

The situation will be a polar opposite to Moses' intercession following the debacle of the golden calf.[124]

Following the ratification of the Sinai covenant, Yahweh declined to wipe out the people, thus defending himself against anticipated criticism by the Egyptians.

Now, in that the covenant relationship had been shattered irretrievably by all Israel, Yahweh, known to be the God who had raised up Israel in the first place, will permit a **'few'** survivors to justify him by acknowledging their own and their nation's apostasy. Then both the escapees and the peoples who receive them will **'know that I am Yahweh'** (12:16).[125]

3. Siege rations (12:17-20)

12:17-20. And the word of Yahweh came to me, saying, 'Son of man, you will eat your bread with quaking and you will drink your water in trembling and anxiety. And you will say to the people of the land, "Thus says the Lord Yahweh to the inhabitants of Jerusalem upon the earth of Israel, 'They will eat their bread with anxiety and shall drink their water in desolation, because its land will be made desolate from its fulness on account of the violence of all who dwell in it. And the inhabited cities shall be laid waste and the land be desolate. And you will know that I am Yahweh.'"'

Ezekiel was instructed to undertake yet another curious action, this time to assume an air of terror when eating and drinking, as if frantically snatching a bite to eat amid the rigours of a siege.

This sign-act would have brought to his hearers' minds the bizarre consumption of starvation rations outlined in 4:9-17, although the two actions must have been distinct. Now, apparently within his own house, Ezekiel will **'eat** [his] **bread with quaking'** and **'drink** [his] **water in trembling and anxiety'** (12:17-18). The point to be made was that for one's hands and body to quake when eating and drinking would lead to a failure to insert food into the mouth and to a spilling of fluid onto one's face and clothing, thus indicating extreme emotional disturbance. We are to imagine the consternation of those who gazed at Ezekiel. Perhaps they thought that he was crazy.

But he was not. Remarkably, Yahweh instructed the prophet to address **'the people of the land'**. Although this expression normally refers to owners of property or to the common people in Israel,[126] here it points to the exiles, those who had been taken from their homeland. Irony is present: residents in the homeland would be denied the land, and those who were distant would not thereby be refused the presence of the Lord.

Concerning **'the inhabitants of Jerusalem'**, Ezekiel must inform his hearers that the situation of those who were still in Judah would deteriorate. Just as he had been allocated miserable rations, they would eat and drink in similar fashion.

And Ezekiel must reiterate the truth that because of their **'violence'** (cf. 7:23; 9:9) those at home were bringing destruction upon themselves in what would soon be a **'desolate'** land. Leviticus 26:43 is probably being recalled: 'The land also shall be left empty by them, and will enjoy its Sabbaths while it lies desolate without them.'[127] Violent men — the Chaldeans — will ravage the land (12:19). Then, when the **'cities'** of Judah have succumbed, **'you** [exiles still dubious that God would allow the unthinkable] **will know that I am Yahweh'** (12:20).

It is no wonder that Ezekiel would be likened to a public entertainer (see 33:30-33). Yet he was only a medium of communication, undoubtedly praying that his hearers might comprehend his message.

4. The vision fulfilled (12:21-28)

12:21-28. Then the word of Yahweh came to me, saying, 'Son of man, what is this proverb that you have concerning the earth of Israel, saying, "The days are prolonged and every vision has perished"? Therefore, say to them, "Thus says the Lord Yahweh: 'I shall make this proverb cease and they will no longer use it as a proverb in Israel.'" But tell them, "The days are near, and the word of every vision! For there shall not again be any false vision or flattering divination in the midst of the house of Israel. Because I, Yahweh, shall speak, and the word that I shall speak will be performed; it will no longer be drawn out because in your days, rebellious house, I shall speak a word and shall perform it," declares the Lord Yahweh.'

And the word of Yahweh came to me, saying, 'Son of man, look, the house of Israel is saying, "The vision that he envisions is for many days, and he prophesies for far-off times." Therefore, say to them, "Thus says the Lord Yahweh: 'None of my words will be drawn out any longer. The word that I speak, it shall be done,' declares the Lord Yahweh."'

Ezekiel was given a fresh word that divides into two sections, each responding to a popular criticism of his message. Like others before and after him, he was discovering that his words seemed incredible to his hearers.[128] In his case, until it was known that Jerusalem had fallen to the Chaldeans, few would take his ministry seriously.

The first complaint, **'The days are prolonged and every vision has perished'**, might have been proverbial. Although prophetic warnings had been circulating for many years, it was being claimed cynically that because there had never been a terminal judgement, what was being prophesied **'concerning the earth of Israel'** would never take place. Bearing in mind the severe statement of 7:2-9 concerning an imminent 'end', and if Ezekiel's words were being relayed to

Jerusalem, it may be that both Ezekiel and Jeremiah had been under attack.[129] If so, it was being put about that **'every vision has perished'**, a 'vision' here signifying a prophet's alleged reception of a word from Yahweh.[130] What Ezekiel, for example, had predicted had apparently fallen to the ground (12:21-22).[131]

Nor were the exiles in Babylon the last to misinterpret God's long-suffering as a lack of concern and an inability to act, as indicated by 2 Peter 3:3-4.[132] When people gaze at the sunshine, as bright in summer as it was last year and no doubt the same as it will be in twelve months' time, they tend to conclude that, although God might conceivably be in heaven, he will not intrude in their world.

'The Lord Yahweh', the covenant God in control of the situation in Jerusalem, responds with a sombre promise in order to uphold the integrity of his appointed servants, and thus his own veracity. The Lord does not assert in a somewhat simplistic fashion that his word will be fulfilled; rather, on the assumption that it will be seen to have been honoured through the downfall of Jerusalem, the impious proverb will fall out of use: **'they will no longer use it as a proverb in Israel'**.

Furthermore, Yahweh, having given attention to the mocking criticisms uttered in Jerusalem against his servants, hurls the cynics' words into their faces: **'But tell them, "The days are near, and the word of every vision!"'** Ezekiel had to inform his people that the fulfilment of his predictions and those of Jeremiah was impending (12:23).

Similarly, the time must arrive when **'there shall not again be any false vision or flattering divination'** within **'the house of Israel'**. Divination (*miqsam*) was a blanket term for techniques intended to discern the will of the gods (cf. 21:22), and Deuteronomy 18:10-14 had strictly forbidden the practice in Israel. So, when the unimaginable has occurred, all concerned will be compelled to accept that, whereas visions and divinations emanating from some so-called prophets had failed so conspicuously, men such as Ezekiel had been fully vindicated (12:24).

That Jerusalem would be swept away was certain because God had spoken and his declared word could not fail.[133] For extreme emphasis, the trilateral Hebrew root *dbr*, meaning 'word' or, in verbal form, 'to speak', now occurs no less than five times: **'"Because I, Yahweh, shall speak** [*a'dabbér*]**, and the word** [*dabar*] **that I shall speak** [*a'dabbér*] **will be performed ... I shall speak a word** [*a'dabbér dabar*] **and shall perform it," declares the Lord Yahweh.'** And, what Yahweh had announced will **'no longer be drawn out'**: the **'rebellious house'** will live to see it happen in their own **'days'** (12:25).

A second disparaging criticism raised against the prophets and, it would appear, particularly against Ezekiel (thus, a derogatory **'he'** twice in verse 27), is that although what he and others were saying might have reflected some semblance of truth, there was no immediate necessity for their hearers to act upon it. All that they had heard would be fulfilled, yet in **'far-off times'**. This is why Yahweh associates the exiles with those in Jerusalem as **'the** [rebellious] **house of Israel'** (12:26-27).

The Lord instructed Ezekiel to repeat, albeit in condensed form, the content of verses 23-25: his word **'shall be done'**, the assertion ending with a repetition of the solemn pronouncement of verse 25: **'... declares the Lord Yahweh'**. What Ezekiel declared was stamped with the imprimatur of Almighty God (12:28).

Application

The influence of a minister of the gospel ought to increase as time goes by. Conceivably, Ezekiel's first sign-acts (chapters 4 – 5) may not have attracted too many spectators. But when we reach 8:1, we find that the elders of the people were sitting under Ezekiel's ministry. They, apparently men of moment in their community, understood that he had something to say that they needed to hear. By the time we come to the sign-acts of chapter 12, the Lord was reminding Ezekiel that the people had lost no time in asking what he was doing (12:8-9) and that he had to give an explanation. Ezekiel, priest and prophet, had become a pastor.

Let not younger ministers be discouraged if not many are immediately converted through their work. If they remain faithful, the gracious Lord will stand by them and the fruit will come.

The present chapter shows that those who inherit a distorted spiritual tradition, like many Jews then in Jerusalem and in exile, may suffer spiritual hardening, which shows that sometimes men have to unlearn untruth before they can appreciate reality. The writer of this commentary has learned to appreciate the importance of teaching children the rudiments of the gospel before they become sceptical, and to some extent hardened, as are so many young people today.

Cynics in Jerusalem and in the exile were claiming that God's word was either untrue and could be discarded, or was so futuristic that it could safely be ignored. They were, of course, wrong. Christians have to live in the light of the promise of the second advent of Christ, even though we do not know the day or the hour.[134] Our lives should be dominated by predictive prophecy. Conversion is just the commencement of our pilgrimage; glory is its conclusion.

False prophets and prophetesses (Ezekiel 13:1-23)

Yahweh has warned Ezekiel about the 'false vision' and 'flattering divination' which were deluding the remnant in Jerusalem, as well as the exiles, into the belief that the city would remain impregnable against siege (12:24). In similar vein, all who were prophesying **'from their hearts'** are now condemned (13:2,17). There were some, both men and women, charlatans, whose declamations roundly contradicted Ezekiel's message.

In Jerusalem, Jeremiah had already uttered a condemnation of false prophets operating there,[135] and had sent a letter to the Jewish elders in Chaldea warning them that they were not to 'let your prophets and your diviners who are in your midst deceive you', nor to 'listen to your dreams which you cause to be dreamed. For they prophesy to you falsely in my name: I have not sent them, says Yahweh.' Two such individuals were a certain Ahab and Zedekiah.[136] Jeremiah continued immediately with the assertion that the exile would continue for a full seventy years.[137]

We find, then, that both in Jerusalem and in Chaldea there were those who insisted vociferously that the Babylonian assault on Jerusalem must terminate, that the war would soon be over and that those who had been deported would return home. Ezekiel was to rebut the heralds of such folly.

1. The false prophets: their misconduct (13:1-7)

13:1-7. And the word of Yahweh came to me, saying, 'Son of man, prophesy against the prophets of Israel who are prophesying, and say to those who prophesy from their hearts, "Hear the word of Yahweh", "Thus says the Lord Yahweh: 'Woe upon the foolish prophets who walk after their own spirit according to what they have not seen. Your prophets are as jackals among the ruins, O Israel. You have not gone up among the breaches, nor did you build a fence for the house of Israel to stand in battle in the day of Yahweh. They envision futility and lying divination, who are saying, "Thus declares Yahweh", and Yahweh has not sent them — yet they expect the confirmation of the word. Have you not envisioned a futile vision and have uttered a lying divination? Yet you are saying, "Thus declares Yahweh," and I have not spoken.'"'

Again, the **'word of Yahweh'** came to Ezekiel, who had no choice (or desire) other than to relay the divine communication to a hostile constituency. He records that what he had to tell was an authentic word from God (13:1).

And, as if to confirm the office of the **'son of man'**, Yahweh reminded him that the **'prophets of Israel'**, a phrase employed only by Ezekiel (cf. 13:16; 38:17), were prophesying from **'their** [own] **hearts'**, bidding men to **'hear the word of Yahweh'**. This is remarkable in that the prophets operating both in Jerusalem and in Babylonia are lumped together as **'foolish'** (13:3).[138]

Worse still, they are said to have been **'prophesying'**, a sarcasm revealing that these misguided folk just could not refrain from opening their mouths in the name of Yahweh, a dangerous procedure in that they were speaking **'from their hearts'**. Although they no doubt chose to assert that they were inspired, their utterances were the product of their own speculation in that their 'hearts' were obviously the seat of their intellectual faculties; manipulating God, they elected to publish their own views about what would happen (13:2).[139] So Yahweh speaks to the **'foolish prophets'**. 'Foolish' translates the background Hebrew *nabal*, a word that, remarks Taylor, 'covers much more than mere stupidity'.[140]

All of which, Ezekiel 13 implies, are accurate descriptions of the false prophets at work both in Jerusalem and in Chaldea. They had not **'seen'** their situation from Yahweh's perspective, in that he never called them and had not communicated with them (13:3). But it was otherwise with Ezekiel, a man who knew the truth of Amos 3:8: 'The Lord GOD has spoken! Who can but prophesy?'[141]

The false prophets known to Ezekiel were far from being sincere yet misguided souls. He likens them to **'jackals'**, or perhaps foxes in the cities that scavenge whatever they can find.[142] As Eichrodt comments, 'A fox makes a comfortable den among fallen ruins, and is in his element there.'[143] Further, rebuking them directly, Yahweh states that **'You have not gone up among the breaches, nor did you build a fence for the house of Israel to stand in battle in the day of Yahweh.'** That is, they had neither attempted to put right what was wrong in Israel, nor — in a change of metaphor from the broken fence, or wall, to that of a city under attack — had they sought to protect their people from the divine marauder. The **'day of Yahweh'**, in this case the sack of Jerusalem in 586 BC, would soon approach, and they had done nothing to reconcile the people to their God and avert disaster (cf. 22:30). Like the hirelings of John 10:12, they cared only for themselves (13:4-5).

Now Ezekiel switches from the second person to the third: **'They envision futility and lying divination,'** the switch being a vivid and not infrequent device in this prophecy. The false prophets' sin was great in that they confirmed their utterances with the divine imprimatur: **'Thus declares Yahweh'**. Although Yahweh had not **'sent them'**, they chose to **'expect the confirmation of the word'**.[144] It was as if they had written what purported to be an official document, doing so in their favour and in that of their friends, and had attached the seal and name of Yahweh to give it binding force. But he refuses to be manipulated, and the day will declare that what they had to say was vain (13:6).

Back, now, to the second person plural. The God of Israel appeals to their consciences with a rhetorical question: **'Have you not envisioned a futile vision and have uttered a lying divination?'** They had, sealing their guilt — and their doom — by forging the divine signature: **'Yet you are saying** [even now, as Ezekiel was issuing the word of Yahweh], **"Thus delares Yahweh."'** But Yahweh remonstrates: he has **'not spoken'** (13:7).

2. The false prophets: their nemesis (13:8-16)

13:8-16. '"Therefore, thus says the Lord Yahweh: 'Because you have spoken futility and have envisioned falsity, therefore, look, I am against you,' says the Lord Yahweh. 'And my hand shall be against the prophets who envision futility and who divine falsity. They will not be in the council of my people, nor be written in the record of the house of Israel, and shall not come to the earth of Israel. Then you will know that I am the Lord Yahweh. Because, indeed, because they have led my people astray, saying, "Peace," and there is no peace, and someone builds a wall and, look, they are plastering it with whitewash, say to those who plaster it with whitewash that it will fall. There shall be overflowing rain, and you, hailstones, will fall; and a tempestuous wind will tear down. And, look, when the wall has fallen, will it not be said to you, "Where is the coating that you applied?"

'"'Therefore,' thus says the Lord Yahweh, 'I shall make a tempestuous wind break out in my fury, and in my anger there shall be overflowing rain, and hailstones in fury for annihilation. Then I shall tear down the wall which you have coated with whitewash and shall bring it to the ground, so that its foundation is laid bare; it shall fall, and you will be annihilated in its midst. Then you will know that I am Yahweh. Thus shall I accomplish my wrath upon the wall and upon those who cover it with whitewash, and I shall say to you, "The wall: it is not!" and they who covered it, "They are not!" — the prophets of Israel who prophesy to Jerusalem and they who envision a vision of peace for her, when there is no peace,' declares the Lord Yahweh."'

The false prophets have been charged and found guilty, the grim verdict of 13:7 being repeated. Now the Judge will declare his sentence. Although the atmosphere is that of a court, the scene is like none that we could imagine in our own society: the King of Israel, Yahweh himself, rather than a delegated servant, pronounces and, as it were, stamps his word with that seal which they had misappropriated: **'"I am against you," says the Lord Yahweh.'**

Neither will their misleading prophecies come to fruition, nor will they prosper; God, against whom they have offended, is against them (13:8).

There is irony in the continuation of Yahweh's pronouncement. In that Ezekiel sometimes refers to the 'hand of Yahweh' initiating true prophecy (1:3; 33:22), now the divine **'hand'**, far from being 'upon' the false prophets, will be **'against'** them.[145]

Firstly, they will no longer form part of the **'council of my people'**. This may mean that the charlatans will never form part of the community of those who belong to the Lord and who perceive his mind.[146]

Secondly, their names will never be entered **'in the record of the house of Israel'**. In that the Hebrew behind 'record' is *k'tôv*, rather than *sépher* — by which latter term is meant 'book' or 'register', possibly that 'of life'[147] — it seems that the false prophets are being informed that their names will not be found in the genealogical lists of the children of Israel. Ezra 2:62 and Nehemiah 7:64 indicate that exclusion was a most severe matter.

Thirdly, they will never **'come to the earth of Israel'**, the territory promised centuries earlier to the fathers: they will end their days in the unclean land to which they had been deported, hopelessness being their only prospect.

And all this will be because when pontificating about the certainty of peace they had deliberately misled their hearers, encouraging them in effect to remain in their sins.[148] Although they will never know Yahweh (in the sense that a Christian believer 'knows the Lord'), they will nevertheless **'know that I am the Lord Yahweh'** (13:9). The prediction is sombre.

A most solemn affirmation opens 13:10, possibly recalling Leviticus 26:43: '... because they rejected my ordinances and their soul abhorred my statutes'. Ezekiel presents an easily understood picture, the people being likened to someone who has built a flimsy **'wall'** (*hayitz*, found only here in the Old Testament, and probably meaning a 'partition' or 'screen').

The false prophets had then smeared **'whitewash'**, a sort of dilute stucco, on it so that the construction appeared attractive and strong. The Hebrew word in 13:10,11 for **'plaster'** is unusual and is similar in form to another word meaning 'silly' or 'absurd' (*taphel*).[149] This is another play on words, in that the encouragement given by these prophets was sheer folly: plastered with error, Israel imagined that all was well, a spurious **'peace'** reigning for a while. In short, these individuals were hypocrites (13:10). Paul may have alluded to this verse when responding to Ananias the high priest.[150]

But whitewash or, as Block puts it, 'hogwash',[151] cannot protect. Ezekiel was commanded to predict that there would be a judgement resembling a violent tempest of **'rain'**, **'wind'** and **'hailstones'** (13:11).[152] The flimsy wall must be hurled to the ground, exposing the inadequate foundations. The meaning is that the cosmetic surgery offered by the false prophets could never cure spiritual and moral decadence.[153]

Ezekiel does not leave his hearers in any doubt: within the doomed city the prophets will perish, recognizing too late that his God was, indeed, Yahweh. Ezekiel makes himself clear: the plastered wall, a symbol of Jerusalem, may look attractive but in its collapse it will, so to speak, bury the prophets of peace. All will ridicule them: **'Where is the coating that you applied?'** (13:12).

The devastation will involve the overthrow of Jerusalem in that **'the wall which you** [the false prophets] **have coated with whitewash'** will be torn down and its foundations exposed.[154] Nebuchadnezzar will raze Jerusalem to the ground and it is to be **'laid bare'**. Again, as in an oft-repeated litany, it is said that **'you** [this time, the false prophets] **will know that I am Yahweh'** (13:13-14).

The denunciation of these impostors reaches its climax. Yahweh will **'accomplish'** — that is, will complete or terminate — his **'wrath'**, in the sense that his anger will be satisfied: **'The wall** [that is, Jerusalem], **"it is not!"'** and **'they who covered it** [that is, the false prophets]**, "They are not!"'**. **'It is not!'** and **'They are not!'** translate a single, expressive Hebrew word meaning 'No!' That it must be so is certified with the divine stamp: **'... declares the Lord Yahweh'** (13:15).

That the Lord targets the false prophets is made clear: **'the prophets of Israel who prophesy to Jerusalem and they who envision a vision of peace for her'**. There had been no peace because the people were not at peace with God, or he with them. Again, the divine confirmation is added: **'... declares the Lord Yahweh'** (13:16).

3. Evil women (13:17-23)

13:17-23. 'And you, son of man, set your face against the daughters of your people who are prophesying out of their hearts, and prophesy against them. And you will say, "Thus says the Lord Yahweh: 'Woe to those who sew covers upon all wrists and who make veils for the heads of every size to hunt down souls! Will you hunt for the souls of my people and preserve your own souls alive? And you have profaned me to my people for handfuls of barley and for fragments of bread to put to death souls who should not die, and to preserve alive souls who should not live, by your lying to my people who listen to lies.'

'"Therefore, thus says the Lord Yahweh: 'Look, I am against your covers with which you hunt souls there to make them fly, and I shall tear them from your arms and shall send away the souls whom you hunt — those souls — to make them fly away. And I shall tear away your veils and deliver my people from your hands, and they will no longer be in your hands for a prey. Then you will know that I am Yahweh. Because you have discouraged the heart of the righteous with deceit — and I did not cause pain — but have strengthened the hands of the wicked so that he should not turn from his evil way to preserve his life, therefore the women will no longer envision futility nor practise divination; for I shall deliver my people from your hands, and you will know that I am Yahweh.'"'

This section may be compared with Isaiah 3:16 – 4:1 and Amos 4:1-3, which criticize affluent women. Yet Ezekiel's castigations, which open with a reflection of 13:2, suggest that he did not have a separate class of female prophets in mind, in that he does not refer to them formally as 'prophetesses'.[155] Nevertheless, he must have known that, unlike genuine prophetesses, these anonymous women were self-appointed. Allowing their fertile imaginations to run riot, they failed to deliver the word of Yahweh.

Even as he wrote he knew that they were busy **'prophesying out of their hearts'**, meaning that they lacked divine inspiration and authority. In referring to them as **'the daughters of *your* people'**, Yahweh disassociates himself from them and from Israel.[156] Firstly, the true character of these foolish females will be exposed; secondly, Yahweh declares that he will overthrow them (13:17).

Yahweh instructed Ezekiel to address **'those who sew covers upon all wrists and who make veils for the heads of every size to hunt down souls!'** Because there are some words in this verse — including those translated as **'covers'** and **'veils'** — which are either unique in the Hebrew Old Testament or are unusual, it may not be possible to be sure about the details. Nevertheless, it seems likely that these women were sewing fabrics with which to cover arms ('covers', *k'satôt*; from *kasah*, 'to cover' or 'conceal') and were devising garments of some sort for people's heads ('veils', from *mispachôt,* 'to join' or 'admit'). They resembled seamstresses making up costumes according to their own picturesque designs. Perhaps they indulged in enchantments, imitating Babylonian magical practice (13:18).[157] If so, this would go some way to explaining the next verse.

Maybe these garments were attached to the **'wrists'** (literally, 'joints of my hands') to create a tactile bond between the women, their spells and their victims.[158] But if 'my hands' is the correct reading, the assertion might be that the prophetesses would (metaphorically) sew coverings together to wrap around the hands of Yahweh so that he, so to speak, could not touch the people directly; they covered up the accusing word of

God, thus concealing the absolute need for repentance. Either way, they sought to **'hunt for the souls of my people'**, preserving their **'own souls alive'**.

Israel, Ezekiel's 'people' according to 13:17, are now claimed by Yahweh as **'my people'**,[159] indicating that he will not finally surrender the covenant nation when it is vulnerable (13:18). Will these women, then, be allowed to live to tell the tale?

If it was the case that these practitioners imitated some (unknown) Babylonian occult practices, they were demeaning Yahweh, the God of Israel, reducing him to the level of a Chaldean deity to be manipulated by spell and incantation. As Block notes, he would have become like the genie in Aladdin's lamp, at the beck and call of his controllers.[160]

Thus, **'you have profaned me to my people'**. And for what? **'For handfuls of barley and for fragments of bread.'** This could mean either that grains of barley and small pieces of bread were instruments of divination ('for', repeated twice, meaning 'by' or 'with', translating the Hebrew *beth*), or that the unfortunate clients (or victims) of these women were required to pay for services rendered.[161] In the latter case, the witches must have enjoyed a meagre livelihood.

That they endeavoured to pressurize Yahweh is suggested by the identification of their motive: **'to put to death souls who should not die'** and **'to preserve alive souls who should not live'**. They affirmed that their deceptive pronouncements to those who would **'listen to lies'** had a binding effect on them — hence the fabric artefacts that symbolized alleged truth. But why should **'my people'** perish through giving court to such falsehood? (13:19).

The Hebrew of 13:20 is difficult although the sense is clear.[162] Yahweh declares his mind, metaphors changing rapidly. If, like bird-catchers, these women strain to trap souls, Yahweh will see that the material bandaging their victims will be ripped off to allow them to fly away. Likewise the veils: the deluded people are not to be denied true prophetic vision. Finally, the women will be compelled to acknowledge that Yahweh is God. Exactly how these unhappy creatures are to be deprived of the tools of their trade is not stated, but it might have been through the Babylonian destruction of Jerusalem — in hindsight their comfortable prophecies would have been seen to be spurious. **'Then'**, the practitioners of magic **'will know that I am Yahweh'** (13:20-21).

The activities of these prophetesses had had a double effect. Firstly, they **'discouraged'** the hearts of **'righteous'** people;[163] secondly, they confirmed the **'wicked'** in their sins instead of urging them to repent and thereby to preserve their lives. Ultimately, when Jerusalem falls these women will see that all their predictions had come to nothing. Consistently with Deuteronomy 18:20-22, Ezekiel warns that the false prophets and their predictions can be expected to fail. Then the parasites will **'know that I am Yahweh'** (13:22-23).

Application

The apostle Peter informs us 'that no prophecy of Scripture is of any private interpretation, for prophecy never came by the will of men, but holy men of God spoke as they were moved by the Holy Spirit'.[164] 'Interpretation' translates the Greek *epilyseôs*, which can mean 'loosing' or 'liberation'. The meaning is that, while genuine prophecy never bypassed the human 'heart', the seat of the emotions and the organ of thought, God-given prophets were led along by the Holy Spirit, although in a fashion that we cannot understand because the gift of prophecy is no longer with the churches. The false prophets addressed by Ezekiel were not inspired, yet chose to adorn their utterances with a 'Thus saith the Lord'. They spoke from their hearts — but not from the heart of God (13:2,17).

As with those prophets, so in later times. Apart from the Bible, which, being true and complete prophecy, is all that we need and all that we have, false prophecy is inherently selfish, emanating from men like those described by Ezekiel as 'jackals' (13:4). Wherever and whenever and however it manifests itself, it is invariably mistaken, usually telling men what they want to hear. In time it must collapse because only the word of the Lord can endure.[165]

Historically, heresies more damaging than persecution by the world have always taken root in the churches. But the Lord knows, 'There must also be factions among you, that those who are approved might be recognized among you.'[166] God gives us enemies to compel us to think and to fight back, which is why Christians have to contend for their faith.[167]

There can be little doubt that the women mentioned by Ezekiel were dabbling in magic (13:18-22). Whereas a degenerate society will always lean towards the occult, the people of God will reject it in favour of the Bible. Luke says concerning the first Ephesian converts, 'Many of those who had practised magic brought their books together and burned them in the sight of all. And they counted up the value of them, and it totalled fifty thousand pieces of silver.'[168]

The condemnation of idol-worshippers (Ezekiel 14:1-23)

Chapter 13 has indicted false prophets. Now Ezekiel turns his attention to their numerous patrons among the deported elders of Israel. Perhaps they resembled those ridiculed by Paul who strained to have 'their ears tickled', scenting novelty and excitement by dabbling in religious controversy.[169]

Ezekiel's condemnation divides into two connected parts. Firstly, 14:1-11 is directed to the elders and their favoured prophets in the exilic communities. Although they seemed to be genuine in that they approached Ezekiel to ascertain the mind of Yahweh on matters relevant to them, they were idolatrous in heart. It followed that the only answer they could receive from the Lord was a declaration of judgement. Secondly, 14:12-23 shows that, even if there were a few righteous men left in Jerusalem, the city would not be spared for their sakes.

These oracles appear to date from the sixth year of Ezekiel's captivity, 891 BC (cf. 8:1).

1. The elders and their favourites (14:1-11)

14:1-11. Then there came to me men from the elders of Israel and sat down before me. And the word of Yahweh came to me, saying, 'Son of man, these men have set up their idols in their hearts and have set the stumbling block of their iniquity before their faces. Should I really be enquired of by them?

'Therefore, speak to them and say to them, "Thus says the Lord Yahweh: 'If any man from the house of Israel sets up his idols in his heart and places the stumbling block of his iniquity before his face and comes to the prophet, I, Yahweh, will be brought to answer him in the matter according to the multitude of his idols, that I may seize all the house of Israel by their heart because they are estranged from me by their idols.'"

'Therefore, say to the house of Israel, "Thus says the Lord Yahweh: 'Turn and return from your idols, and from all your abominations turn your faces. For any man from the house of Israel or of the migrants who stay in Israel and who separates himself from me and sets up his idols in his heart and places the stumbling block of his iniquity before his face, and then comes to the prophet to enquire of me by him — I, Yahweh, shall be brought to answer him by myself. And I shall set my face against that man and shall make him a sign and a proverb, and shall cut him off from the midst of my people. Then you will know that I am Yahweh.

'"'But if the prophet is enticed and speaks a word, it is I, Yahweh, who have enticed that prophet, and I shall stretch out my hand upon him and destroy him from the midst of my people Israel. And they will bear their iniquity: as the iniquity of him who enquires, so will be the iniquity of the prophet, so that the house of Israel will no more stray from me and will no more defile themselves with all their transgressions. Then they will be to me for a people, and I shall be to them as God,' declares the Lord Yahweh."'

Some of the **'elders of Israel'**, senior representatives of the exiled communities rather than a deputation from Jerusalem, came to Ezekiel and sat before him, no distinction being drawn between the tribe of Judah and the rest of Israel (cf. 8:1). Without doubt, the elders in question desired to be given a word from

Yahweh concerning their own future and that of Jerusalem, although this is not made explicit. In view of Ezekiel's ministry among them thus far, it would have been natural for them to seek further counsel from him (14:1).

While in their presence Ezekiel did receive a **'word'** from Yahweh, the Lord not intending to leave his servant without guidance about what to declare to these senior men. The **'son of man'** was informed about the spiritual condition of the elders and was posed a rhetorical question: because they had **'set up their idols in their hearts'** and had **'set the stumbling block of their iniquity before their faces'**, should Yahweh **'really be enquired of them'**? That is, although they had not been guilty of open idolatry, they had alienated themselves from the God of Israel, possibly hankering after pagan modes of worship (cf. the elders in Jerusalem, 8:10-12), and perhaps had envisaged what they might do were they given an opportunity. (The reader is expected by the text to draw his own conclusions.) We could draw a comparison with Lot's wife.[170] This being the case, Ezekiel was not to expect that Yahweh would allow the prophet to be an intermediary between him and them (14:2-3).

Ezekiel had to announce that the Lord would answer the secret idolater in kind. Because Yahweh was not respected, he refused flatly to give straight answers to such folk; if they masked their intentions, so would he. Thus, **'I, Yahweh, will be brought to answer him in the matter according to the multitude of his idols'** (14:4).

The verb **'I ... will be brought to answer'** translates the *Niph'al* form of the Hebrew verb *anah*, 'to answer' or 'respond', meaning that Yahweh would answer to *himself*, being true to his character. A 'characteristic of *Niph'al* is its frequent use to express emotions that react upon the mind'.[171] Compare with 14:7 where, as here, the Lord declares that he will virtually compel himself to be wily towards those of like disposition.

This being so, all concerned must wait and see what the Lord has planned to do, instead of receiving a direct, immediate answer (14:4). The tactic is not dissimilar to that employed against Balaam, a lover of money, who had to wait for a word,[172] and even to the situation in which Micaiah found himself, a (true) prophet who held back before telling out a genuine message that he knew would not be applauded.[173] Likewise, note the statements of 2 Samuel 22:27 and Psalm 18:25-26: 'With the devious you will show yourself shrewd,' where 'shrewd' translates the verb *taphal*, meaning 'to be insipid', or even 'unsavoury', as with 'whitewash', *taphel*, in 13:11. The principle threads through the Old Testament. For example, Isaiah 44:20 castigates the idolater: 'a deceived heart has turned him aside'.

How Yahweh intends to respond to these scheming people is disclosed. He proposes to **'seize all the house of Israel by their heart'**, meaning that, as is a man's heart, so is his outward personality: if there is no inner renewal there must be eradication from society, external reformation being inadequate.[174] By comparison, although Jeremiah never suggested that King Josiah should abort his reforming activity in Judah, evidence fails to suggest that he ever viewed it as likely to be successful. For that prophet, only a renewed heart would suffice.[175]

There might be an allusion in 14:5 to Leviticus 26:41, which predicts that ungodly persons whose hearts have been humbled through suffering will confess their sin.

Ezekiel summoned **'the house of Israel'**, as represented by the Jewish elders seated before him, to avert their **'faces'** from the **'idols'** and **'abominations'** within their hearts, whether they were living in

Jerusalem or in the land of exile (14:6-7). Sadly, a tragic solidarity in unbelief remained firmly in place.

Although the prophet remains adamant that 'an end has come' (see 7:2), in that Jerusalem must fall, he issues a further summons in the name of **'the Lord Yahweh'**. It is emphatic, employing the Hebrew *shûb*, 'to turn', or 'return', three times.[176] **'Turn ... return ... turn your faces'** indicates that the Lord extends a last-minute lifeline to an apostate people: it is never too late to repent (14:6).

Moreover, Yahweh's summons, an echo from Leviticus 17:8,10,13; 20:2; 22:18, is extended to all **'migrants'**, foreigners who happen to identify, perhaps as proselytes, with the exiles from Judah.[177] They are included because they resemble leaven pervading a loaf, their cultural idolatry being imitated by notoriously fickle Jews.

So, whether Israelite or alien by birth, if any man commits idolatry in his heart and then approaches Ezekiel **'to enquire'** of Yahweh, God will **'be brought to answer him by myself'**. This apparently enigmatic affirmation means that the Lord will respond to their request, yet not through a prophetic intermediary. He will act immediately and with decision (cf. the similar construction in 14:4) because he will have no choice other than to commit himself to judging them (14:7).

Firstly, Yahweh will **'set** [his] **face against that man'**, meaning that such an individual will be deprived of the favour of God. In the Old Testament, the expression always occurs with Yahweh as the subject and is often followed by the verb 'to cut off', which action is specified here: the impenitent sinner who takes it upon himself to enquire from Yahweh is to be **'cut ... off'** from the congregation, meaning that somehow he will perish.[178] Further, the Lord will **'make him a sign and a proverb'**, divine judgement marking the individual out as a warning to others.[179] The severity of divine judgement will be, as Deuteronomy 28:37 had predicted, a cause of astonishment to those who witness it. In consequence, all come to realize that **'I am Yahweh'** (14:8).

But what of the false **'prophet'**, a self-appointed individual who had been **'enticed'**, responding positively to men of the limited spiritual calibre of the elders who were presenting themselves before Ezekiel? In that such a person predicted an early cessation of hostilities between Jerusalem and Babylon, he was deluded because Yahweh, no less, had **'enticed that prophet'**. Even so, notwithstanding the sovereign will of God, the man's error remained his alone; he, and no other, had given vent to the delusions of an evil heart. He should not have fantasized about what would, could or ought to be. Yet having allowed himself to fall into the trap, he remains without excuse: Yahweh will **'destroy him'** so that he will no longer be in **'the midst'** of Israel (14:9).[180]

In the situation in which Ezekiel and his hearers found themselves, the challenge of Deuteronomy 13:1-3 was being applied: 'If there arises among you a [false] prophet or a dreamer of dreams ... you shall not listen to the words of that prophet ... for Yahweh your God is testing you to know whether you love Yahweh your God with all your heart and with all your soul.'[181]

Therefore, the false prophets and their hearers alike **'will bear their iniquity'** (14:10), an expression which occurs in the Old Testament to imply judgement by Yahweh. Leviticus 19:8 links the sentence with removal from the congregation.[182]

Yahweh looks to the long term. Although Jerusalem and its temple must soon fall, although the throne of David will crash and although the state of Israel will cease to be, there is hope: imminent judgement will be a precursor to an eventual restoration of the covenant relationship between Yahweh and Israel. Never again will they **'stray from me'** and never again will they

'defile themselves with all their transgressions' (14:11).

Bearing in mind that the present chapter is concerned with what might be termed 'heart idolatry', Yahweh's promise points to spiritual regeneration rather than to mere external reformation. Accordingly, in time **'they will be to me for a people, and I shall be to them as God,'** a declaration sealed by the divine affidavit: **'declares the Lord Yahweh'**. Although when and how this will occur is not stated, groundwork is being laid for the massive declarations of 16:60-63; 17:22-23 and chapters 34, 36 and 37.

2. Jerusalem will not be spared (14:12-23)

14:12-23. Then the word of Yahweh came to me, saying, 'Son of man, if a land sins against me by acting treacherously and I stretch my hand upon it and break the staff of bread, send famine into it and cut off man and beast from it, and these three men were in its midst, Noah, Daniel and Job, they would deliver their souls by their own righteousness,' declares the Lord Yahweh. 'If I were to cause wild beasts to pass through the land and they depopulate it, and it becomes desolate so that no one passes through it because of the beasts, though these three men were in its midst, as I live,' declares the Lord Yahweh, 'they would deliver neither sons nor daughters. They alone would be delivered — and the land would become desolate.

'Or if I were to bring a sword upon that land and I were to say, "A sword shall pass through the land and I shall cut off from it man and animal," and these three men were in its midst, as I live,' declares the Lord Yahweh, 'they would not deliver sons and daughters, but they alone would be delivered. Or if I were to send a plague to that land and I were to pour out my wrath in blood upon it to cut off man and animal from it, and Noah, Daniel and Job were in its midst, as I live,' declares the Lord Yahweh, 'they would deliver neither son nor daughter. They would deliver only themselves by their righteousness.'

'For thus says the Lord Yahweh: "How much more shall it be when I send my four evil judgements — sword, famine, evil beasts and plague — to Jerusalem to cut off man and animal from it! Yet, look, a remnant will be left who shall be brought out — sons and daughters. Look, they will come out to you and you will see their way and their deeds. Then you will be comforted for the evil that I have brought upon Jerusalem, even all that I have brought upon it. Then they will comfort you when you see their way and their deeds. And you will know that I have not done in vain all that I have done in it," declares the Lord Yahweh.'

As noted, these verses tell that if there were only a few righteous men in Jerusalem, even so the city would not be delivered. It may be that Ezekiel was responding to the claims of some that Yahweh had been unjust to expose the city to the armies of Babylon. If so, as Taylor notes, 'This attitude [was] nothing less than using the saints as an insurance policy to cover the sinners.'[183]

Would the exiles not have recalled Abraham when he was promised the salvation of Sodom and Gomorrah on condition that a minimal number of righteous men and women were found there?[184] It is not unlikely, given that Ezekiel's contemporaries were prepared to clutch at any straw, particularly if it took the form of an apparent precedent for their situation.

Yahweh again spoke to Ezekiel, presenting a governing principle (14:12-20) to be applied to Jerusalem (14:21-23). It was as if the prophet needed to be convinced that the city did merit the judgement that, as he had told his fellow-exiles, would soon descend.

'Acting treacherously' (14:13) stems from the Hebrew *ma'al*, which occurs, for example, in Numbers 5:12,27 concerning marital infidelity, and in Joshua 7:1 with respect to Achan's violation of the ban.[185]

Ezekiel will employ the term several times in his prophecy,[186] stressing that Israel had sinned in shattering its institutional covenant with Yahweh. How this had come to pass is expounded in the previous chapters.

So Yahweh will **'stretch** [his] **hand'** against the **'land'** which had been unfaithful — 'land' standing for its treacherous residents (cf. 6:14; 14:9) — and will do so by breaking or shattering **'the staff of bread'**, the supportive food supply, by sending **'famine'**, thereby cutting off **'man and beast'** and so depopulating the land (14:12-13). It seems clear that these words, reflecting as they do Leviticus 26:26 and Deuteronomy 28:38-40 and also Jeremiah 15:2-3, tell that, although it was not Yahweh's fault, the covenant relationship between him and Israel was now at an end.

And, Yahweh **'declares'**, if **'Noah, Daniel and Job'** were found **'in** [the] **midst'** of such a city, although they would **'deliver'** themselves through their righteousness, the city itself would not be spared. There is a sad irony here, in that 'deliver' (from *natzal*) is sometimes associated with the deliverance of Israel from Egypt.[187] Now the Lord's own city cannot deliver itself from Yahweh.

Noah is mentioned in Genesis 5 – 10 and is said by Genesis 6:8-9 to have 'found grace in the eyes of Yahweh', being 'just', 'perfect' (or 'complete') and someone who 'walked with God'. Daniel, an Israelite, a contemporary of Ezekiel and also a deportee from Jerusalem, was deemed righteous by Yahweh and was an eminently wise man.[188] Job, a non-Israelite, is said to have been 'blameless and upright, and one who feared God and shunned evil' and who was an acknowledged servant of God.[189]

Concerning Noah and Job, each man survived disaster because of his righteousness. Furthermore, Noah was the instrument of his family's salvation and Job interceded successfully for his three unwise counsellors.[190] Daniel, who must have been well known to the Jewish exiles, was instrumental in the deliverance of his three godly friends.[191] To speculate a little, perhaps the Jews felt that his influence with Nebuchadnezzar might avert the catastrophe predicted by Jeremiah and Ezekiel.

To repeat, the essential point now being conveyed to Ezekiel is that were these three men resident within such a sinful society, presumably Jerusalem, even so it would not escape judgement (14:14).

Again, should **'the land'** be subjected to wild animals, in pursuance of the warning of Leviticus 26:22, although **'these three men'** would save themselves, not even their sons and daughters would be spared. For Ezekiel, the sombre fact was that Judah was in such a state of spiritual and moral degradation that land and people were beyond the intercession of men of this calibre, were they to be present. The divine imprimatur confirms the matter: **'declares the Lord Yahweh'** (14:15-16).

The litany of doom reverberates. Again in pursuance of Leviticus 26 in general, and 26:25 in particular, should Yahweh cause **'a sword'** to **'pass through the land'**, **'these three men'**, Noah, Daniel and Job, **'alone would be delivered'**. The Lord places himself under oath: **'"as I live," declares the Lord Yahweh'** (14:17-18).

Similarly, as anticipated by Leviticus 26:25, were Yahweh to **'send a plague'** to such a **'land'**, cutting off **'man and animal from it'**, and were **'Noah, Daniel and Job'** to dwell **'in its midst'**, they would save themselves, yet not their families. Although on the surface God speaks hypothetically to Ezekiel (**'or if'**), it is clear that the reference is to Jerusalem and Judah.

Through these predicted four punishments Ezekiel shows that the Israel of the old covenant was in a state of collapse: what Moses expected, Yahweh was bringing to reality nearly a thousand years later (14:19-20).

Thus far, the Lord's word to Ezekiel has been hypothetical, in that reference has been made to a sinful 'land' (14:13-16,17-18,19-20). Now Yahweh is specific: if a righteous person resident in a wicked land ('land' standing for its population; cf. 14:13 etc.) is unable to save his own children, what hope can there be for **'Jerusalem'**: the four disasters, or **'judgements'**,[192] anticipated by Leviticus 26 and enunciated in 14:12-20 will be inescapable (14:21).

At this point Ezekiel might have been taken by surprise, as today's reader may perhaps be, in that, notwithstanding dire predictions concerning the fall of Jerusalem and the impossibility of even a righteous man being able to deliver his children, Yahweh announces that **'look, a remnant will be left who shall be brought out'**, and that these will include **'sons and daughters'**. Words are selected with care: survivors will **'come ... to you** [the exiles] **and you will see their way and their deeds'** (14:22). But it is not said that those who escape will be delivered.

The meaning is that when the new intake of unrepentant deportees joins Ezekiel and the exiles, it will dawn upon the latter that there had been a divine judgement upon Jerusalem and that, from the point of view of their God, it had not been unjust. They will **'see their way and their deeds'**, by which is meant those of the fresh deportees, and conclude that **'I** [Yahweh] **have not done in vain all that I have done in it'** — that is, in Jerusalem. In Ezekiel's prophecy, **'deeds'** stand for unrighteous activity, and, as here, are usually accompanied by 'ways'.[193]

Therefore, the exiles will **'be comforted for the evil that I have brought upon Jerusalem'** because **'they** [again, the new deportees] **will comfort you'**. Any lingering doubts concerning the essential righteousness of the God of Israel will be dispelled.

To read between the lines, it is not unlikely that more discerning souls would have recognized that the covenant warnings of Leviticus 26 and Deuteronomy 28 were finding their fulfilment: far from being perverse, the God of Israel had been true to himself.[194] Yet again, the declaration is sealed with the divine imprimatur: **'declares the Lord Yahweh'** (14:23).

Application

It is striking that the elders who approached Ezekiel were refused a word from God, the reason being that they were known to be idolatrous in their hearts (14:3-7). Although they were formally members of the congregation of Israel, they were not true Israelites.[195] One of the driving principles of evangelical Christianity is that the sinner must approach Christ in true repentance and humble faith before he can be accepted into the church, no man being deemed by others to belong to the church until he can testify by life and lip that Christ has already accepted him.

As in Ezekiel's situation, not all ostensibly monotheistic worship is acceptable to God. For example, should a Christian consume 'halal' meat if he knows that it has been slaughtered according to Muslim law in veneration of Allah? But Allah is not the God of the Bible. One would need to bear in mind Paul's teaching in 1 Corinthians 10:19-20.

Because it is possible that our familiarity with the text of Scripture may sometimes dull our senses, we need to remember that the four plagues given reference in 14:13-21 — famine, man-eating animals, military conflict and plague — were sent by God. In our day, may it not be that such tragedies should be seen as symptoms of an underlying problem, that of sin, and that when men suffer they should seek the true God? Asa, king of Judah, for example, never learnt the lesson.[196]

Together with his near-contemporary Jeremiah, Ezekiel predicted that, for its sins, Judah would fall. Five centuries later, our Lord stated that had wicked Sodom, which flourished about two millennia previous to his day, witnessed his miracles, the people would have repented. And had they repented their community would have remained.[197] That is, Sodom would have survived Egyptian incursions and Assyrian, Babylonian, Persian, Greek and Roman hegemony. A society, be it a village or an empire, which steeps itself in sin cannot last. What, then, of our own nation?

Verses 9 and 10 of the present chapter present a dreadful warning to the minister of religion who bends vital teaching according to the wishes of his hearers. For his part, because Ezekiel was called to be faithful to the Lord when ministering to a faithless society (cf. 3:7-11), he remains a shining example.

Strangely, perhaps, a minister of the gospel might find himself offered deference by unconverted members of his family circle, to whom he may become a sort of religious 'lucky charm'.[198] But 14:14-20 implies that, just like Noah, Daniel and Job, although his faith may be the instrument of his own salvation, it can never suffice for his relatives' deliverance. He must pray for the right occasion to tell them so.

The vine, dangerously unique (Ezekiel 15:1-8)

Chapter 14 has shattered the hopes of those who, even though they were not outward idolaters, did not know the Lord. Theirs was a superficial religion that did not touch the heart. In their complacency they fancied that a few righteous men in Jerusalem could ensure the security of the whole city. The present chapter goes further, extending the denunciation and hurling to the ground the delusion that the nation would never fall.

15:1-8. Then the word of Yahweh came to me, saying, 'Son of man, of all the trees of the wood, what becomes of the wood of the vine — that is, the branch among the trees of the forest? Can wood be taken from it to make a product, or will they take a peg from it to hang on it any vessel? Look, it is given to the fire for fuel; the fire devours the two ends and its middle part is burned. Will it be useful for manufacture? Look, when it was complete it was not made into any workmanship. How much less, when the fire has consumed it and it is burned, will it still be made into a product?

'Therefore, thus says the Lord Yahweh: "Just like the wood of the vine among the trees of the forest which I have given to the fire for fuel, thus I have given the inhabitants of Jerusalem. And I have put my face against them. They will come out from the fire, and the fire will devour them. Then you will know that I am Yahweh when I set my face against them. Thus I shall make the land a devastation, because they have acted treacherously," declares the Lord Yahweh.'

Again **'the word of Yahweh'** came to Ezekiel, posing a question to which the answer must have been obvious: **'... of all the trees of the wood, what becomes of the wood of the vine**[199] **— that is, the branch among the trees of the forest?'** Although the figure of Israel as a vine is not uncommon,[200] the metaphor often expands as a figure for degenerate Israel. Here, the fact that Israel had not produced evidence of repentance is assumed, the comparison being between the ultimate fate of the wood of a useless wild vine and that of other trees in the forest. The expected response from the **'son of man'** is that it must be fit only for burning (15:1-2).

Questions heap up: **'Can wood be taken from it** [a barren vine] **to make a product, or will they take a peg from it to hang on it any vessel?'** Ezekiel is bidden to **'look'**: one glance will be sufficient to confirm that such wood, useless for any domestic purpose, is suitable only **'for fuel'**. Can Ezekiel imagine a peg made of such wood attached to a wall to bear a load? When thrown into the fire, a branch, intrinsically worthless **'for manufacture'**, will burn at each end, the fire advancing to the **'middle part'** and finally reducing the whole to ash (15:3-4).[201]

If when the vine branch was intact it could not serve any purpose, **'how much less'** when it is burned? The tragic metaphor has climaxed (15:5).

Rather like Isaiah 5:1-7, in which the first six verses speak of a fruitless vineyard, verse 7 then giving the interpretation, so 15:1-5 provides the metaphor and 15:6-8 the application. The text of chapter 14 implies that Ezekiel was not instructed to relay the word of the Lord to the elders who had been approaching him (cf. 14:1,6), unless **'you'** (plural) in 15:7 indicates otherwise. Perhaps Yahweh sought to reinforce the prophet's conviction that the centuries-old relationship between Yahweh and Israel-in-Canaan was now at an end.

Accordingly, God had **'given the inhabitants of Jerusalem'** to be **'fuel'** for **'fire'** (15:6). Ezekiel was to envisage the city, its inhabitants, its royal palace and its temple engulfed in flames. To the Lord, they were of the same value as a branch from a fruitless vine when tossed into a fire. It is little wonder that Yahweh took trouble to ensure that his servant would assimilate the reality of the situation before proclaiming it to his fellows.

Exactly like this maverick vine, over the years the people of Israel had demonstrated their unfitness for their unique calling at Sinai when the twelve tribes had assembled as one family under God. Righteousness was meant to be the fruit of this unique vine among the trees of the forest. But it did not happen. In consequence, morally unfruitful Israel, scorched already by means of numerous judgements, has to be consumed. Jerusalem will be devastated.

Soon, therefore, this renegade tree will not be seen in the forest. It is Yahweh, rather than, say, Nebuchadnezzar, who will have **'put'**, or 'set', his **'face against them'**, an assertion repeated for emphasis. Afterwards, when all has become ash, they **'will know that I am Yahweh'**, meaning that the warnings of Leviticus 26 and Deuteronomy 28, integral elements within the covenant arrangement, should not have been spurned (15:7).

The original promises to Abraham always drew a connection between the patriarch's 'seed' and the promised land.[202] Therefore, **'because'** the people of Israel have **'acted treacherously'**, **'the land'** will be made **'a devastation'**, **'declares the Lord Yahweh'** (15:8). Happily, chapter 34 onwards will show that the ideal union between a regenerate people and the land will be brought about. But down to 586 BC all was darkness. Treacherous Israel would have to fall before a new Israel could rise.

Application

Almost certainly alluding to Ezekiel 15, Jesus taught that the branch of the vine that does not bear fruit by abiding in him must be thrown into the fire.[203] In context, the Lord presents himself implicitly as the God of Israel. Do not believe that in the Gospels the Lord Jesus does not proclaim his own deity.

Further, in Romans 2:17-29 the apostle Paul teaches that birth-membership of Israel cannot bring about individual salvation. To find peace with God, the sinful heart, whether Jewish or Gentile, must be changed. And in Romans 11 did the apostle have Ezekiel 14 in mind when he indicates that unbelieving Israelites, not being spared, have been broken off from the vine of the true Israel?[204]

Six hundred years earlier Ezekiel had taught that principle. Whether then, or in Paul's day, or now, those who profess to belong to the Lord have always been required to manifest 'the fruit of the Spirit' rather than 'the deeds of the flesh'.[205]

A dissolute girl and an unfaithful wife (Ezekiel 16:1-63)

Chapter 15 compared Israel to a wild and useless vine, fit only for burning. Even so, because Israel was God's special vine, some might have argued that it could never be rejected permanently. Accordingly, since Yahweh had raised up Israel, the people must remain his own, come what may, even if (as was the case) they were antagonistic to him and to his laws.

This plausible, and probably widespread, fallacy is addressed by the present chapter, which considers the relationship between God and Israel under the figure of what happens when a marriage collapses. It is an allegory, a tale understood by teller and hearers alike to refer to a reality other than the characters and the plot of the story.[206] Although the theme was not new,[207] Ezekiel enlarges it in what is the longest prophetic oracle in the Old Testament. Retrospectively, looking back to the past, and prospectively, sketching the immediate future and then Yahweh's final plan for his people,[208] Ezekiel occasionally employs language which would appear at first sight to be virtually obscene, but does so to bring into relief the awfulness of the manner in which, historically, Israel had abrogated the Sinai covenant with Yahweh.[209]

It was for this reason that the blatant, repetitive adultery of Israel had to be brought to an end by a temporary dissolution of the covenant — temporary, because, true to the terms of that covenant, there would be a future for the marriage. But in the short term it was wrong for Israel to conclude that because Yahweh had committed himself to the family of Jacob, no action could be taken against them. Because Israel, considered as the wife of Yahweh, was thoroughly dissolute, the union would have to be suspended. How could Yahweh tolerate the formality of a marriage in which he had been repeatedly betrayed?

A key word in the chapter is the Hebrew verb *zanah*, 'to commit whoredom', or 'to fornicate', which, with some derivatives, occurs twenty-one times. Shockingly, Israel is likened to a married woman who is a serial nymphomaniac rather than an adulteress.

Although the chapter breaks down into three main sections, Israel's sin (16:3-34), punishment inflicted by Yahweh (16:35-52) and Israel's final restoration (16:53-63), there are further logical subdivisions.

Firstly, the prophet likens this grievously erring family to a baby girl rejected by her Canaanite parents, their origin indicating that they lacked integrity (16:1-5). Secondly, cast onto open ground at birth, she was discovered by Yahweh, who took her home as his adopted child (16:6-7). Then, years later, when the foundling had grown up, he loved her, though not now as a daughter, and made her his wife (16:8-14).

Fourthly, the marriage eventually fell apart because the unfaithful girl habitually favoured the numerous male admirers who came her way. The narration of this disaster occupies most of the chapter (16:15-34).

Fifthly, Yahweh, the aggrieved partner, takes action, his daughter-wife being surrendered by him to public condemnation and execution. This is because Israel's sinfulness had been notorious, far in excess of that of other women, nations that had not been blessed as she had been (16:35-43).

Furthermore, the sinfulness of the faithless wife is highlighted in that in their time Samaria to the north and Sodom to the south had been less evil than Judah (16:44-59).

This leads into the seventh and final section of the chapter, which predicts that Yahweh's covenant with Judah will be revived and — startlingly — that Samaria and Sodom will be co-beneficiaries. Ezekiel looks to the long-term future when Israel, accompanied by formerly repugnant nations, is to be restored to favour. This innovative covenant will involve a transformation of the heart and affections of the restored wife so that she will never again be unfaithful. Israel will love her husband (16:60-63).

1. Israel's lowly origin (16:1-5)

16:1-5. Then the word of Yahweh came to me, saying, 'Son of man, make known to Jerusalem her abominations. And you will say, "Thus says the Lord Yahweh to Jerusalem: 'Your origin and birth are from the land of Canaan; your father was an Amorite and your mother a Hittite. As for your birth, on the day you were born your navel cord was not cut and you were not washed smooth with water; you were not salted with salt nor swathed in cloths. No eye took pity on you to do any one of these things for you, to have compassion on you. But you were cast into the open field, your person loathed on the day you were born.'"'

Ezekiel was instructed to **'make known'** the **'abominations'** (another key word in this chapter) of Jerusalem by means of the figure of an outcast baby girl discovered, adopted and then loved by Yahweh, the Lord charging his people with gross ingratitude and infidelity. Their spiritual parents are said to have been **'an Amorite'** and **'a Hittite'**, mentioned because, as 16:45 implies, these peoples represented all that was worst in the land of Canaan.[210]

Although Jerusalem was originally Jebusite and although David purchased land for sacrifice from a Jebusite,[211] Jerusalem's **'origin'** and **'birth'** are said to have been in **'Canaan'**. This was literally true in that the city's origins predated the emergence of Israel by many centuries.[212] In truth, the Hebrews were of Aramaean descent through the patriarchs.[213] The implication behind these verses is that Jerusalem's residents possessed no innate advantage that could fit them to be the people of God (16:1-3).

Newly-born, the child was denied the love due to her from her parents: neither was the umbilical cord cut and tied, nor was the baby washed **'smooth'**[214] and rubbed with **'salt'** — possibly as a protection from infection[215] — nor wrapped in cloth. Parental neglect amounted to a formal denial of responsibility for the child (16:4).

The infant was **'cast'** by her mother and father into an **'open field'** to die, in that she would succumb to the severities of the weather and to predators. Part of the reason for exposure would have been that she was a girl, deemed to be a useless expense. Stifling any lingering **'pity'**, they refused to **'do any one of these things'** for her, a child **'loathed'** by them at the moment of birth (16:5).

2. The cast-off baby girl (16:6-7)

16:6-7. '"'Then I passed by you and saw you squirming in your blood, and I said to you while you were in your blood, "Live!" Yes, I said to you while you were in your blood, "Live!" I made you great like a plant of the field, and you grew and became great and most beautiful; your breasts were formed, your hair grew — but you were naked and bare.'"'

That Israel survived was due solely to the grace of God. The sight of a cast-off baby girl lying in a field drew his attention. Because the umbilical cord had not been severed, the child was **'squirming'** in her **'blood'**, wallowing in the fluids discharged by her mother at birth. Exposed as she was to the elements, death would have been imminent. So, as if to emphasize the certainty of the matter, Yahweh declared twice, **'Live!'** This may mean, 'In spite of your blood, live,' or, 'Though bleeding to death, you will live.' Although he was under no necessity to retrieve her, when he beheld the baby Yahweh decreed that she should survive, issuing what was in effect a declaration of adoption (16:6). Perhaps this is an allusion to the affliction of Israel in Egypt prior to the Exodus.[216]

Although the Hebrew of 16:7 is difficult, the meaning is clear. As time passed, the healthy child attained puberty, becoming **'great'** and developing **'breasts'** and **'hair'**. She turned into an exceptionally attractive young woman. This vivid metaphor may point to the patriarchal period, or to the enlargement of the nation during the 430 years spent in Egypt prior to the inauguration of the covenant at Sinai.[217] Yet she remained **'naked and bare'**, meaning that Israel had not as yet been granted a formal opportunity to belong to the Lord. As expounded thus far, the metaphor anticipates a double danger — not only might a naked girl become an object of unworthy attention, if she does not accept protection she could be led astray. As the following verses show, this is what happened.

3. Marriage (16:8-14)

16:8-14. '"'Then I passed by you and saw you, and, look, it was your time, a time for love, and I spread my skirts over you and covered your nakedness. I swore to you and entered into a covenant with you', declares the Lord Yahweh, 'and you became mine. Then I bathed you with water, rinsed your blood from off you and covered you with oil. And I clothed you with woven fabric and shod you with leather; I wrapped you in fine linen and covered you in costly material. I adorned you with ornaments and placed bracelets on your hands and a chain on your neck. Also, I put a ring on your nose, earrings on your ears and a crown of splendour on your head. Thus you were adorned with gold and silver, and your raiment was of fine linen, costly material and woven fabric. You ate fine flour, honey and oil. You were exceedingly beautiful and advanced to royalty. Then your name went out among the nations for your beauty — for it was perfect because of my majesty which I bestowed upon you,' declares the Lord Yahweh."'

Yahweh **'passed by'** the girl and realized that because she was no longer a child, the time had come for her to marry. But to whom? To himself! He **'spread'** his garment over her and **'covered'** her **'nakedness'**, betrothing her to him and swearing on his oath to the girl, entering **'into a covenant'** with her.

Nor did she object. She willingly became his, the **'covenant'** probably being the relationship inaugurated at Sinai.[218] Not only is marriage considered as a covenant,[219] spreading a garment signifies betrothal.[220] In 20:5-6 Yahweh declares that in former times he had sworn to bring Israel out of Egypt into the land of promise, and it is to this act of deliverance that the present verse would point. Consequently, the girl-bride **'became'** the Lord's (16:8). The emphasis here is upon the gracious love of God to his people, rather than upon any love that they should have had for him.

Now the language becomes graphic, possibly referring to post-nuptial intimacies, the husband washing away blood that had been shed in consequence of initial intercourse.[221] Bathing and anointing by her divine Husband, rather than her bathing herself,[222] declared his love and esteem for her, the one who was now his queen (16:9).

Yahweh then clothed his bride with the finest of garments, **'woven fabric'**, and footwear of high-quality **'leather'** (*tachash*),[223] possibly from the skin of the dugong, a seal-like animal found in the Red Sea.

She was swathed in **'fine linen'** and **'covered'** in **'costly material'**, although what this latter material (*meshi*) was is unknown. She was dressed in a manner that would befit a queen (16:10).

As was appropriate for the young bride, she was adorned with costly jewellery,[224] the **'ring'** on her **'nose'** probably being clipped to a nostril.[225] The **'crown of splendour'** demonstrated her new-found royalty, and **'adorned with gold and silver'**, robed in **'fine linen, costly material and woven fabric'**, she was provided with cuisine from the palace and **'advanced to royalty'**.[226] Who would have known what she once was, or could have suspected what she would become? (16:11-13).

As Yahweh's consort, her name and fame spread among the other **'nations'**.[227] Her **'beauty ... was perfect'** because of the **'majesty ... bestowed'** upon her. The Lord declares that it was so (16:14).

Some of the intimacies of married life described here show that the covenant bond between Yahweh and Israel was real. Although the Mosaic arrangement anticipated the glory of the Messianic dispensation, yet provided neither justification (there being no effective sacrifice) nor inward sanctification (because the Spirit had not yet been poured out), it was a truly marital relationship between God and the people of Israel: they committed themselves to each other to the exclusion of all others.

4. Gross infidelity (16:15-22)

16:15-34 expounds by means of lurid metaphor Judah's rupture of the marriage bond, and may be subdivided into three parts: 16:15-22; 16:23-29 and 16:30-34.

The first part tells that because the bride had exploited her beauty and the garments, jewellery and food granted to her by Yahweh, they become the means of her disgrace.[228]

16:15-22. '"'But you trusted in your beauty and fornicated because of your name, and you poured out your fornications upon every passer-by: it was for him! And you took some of your clothes and made for yourself gaudy high places and fornicated upon them — things that should not come about nor happen. Then you took your beautiful ornaments — from my gold and from my silver that I had given to you — and made for yourself male images and fornicated with them. You took your clothes of woven fabric and covered them, and presented my oil and my incense before them. And my bread that I had given to you — fine flour and oil and honey with which I fed you — you gave it to them as a pleasing fragrance. And it happened', declares the Lord Yahweh.

'"'Then you took your sons and your daughters whom you had borne to me, and you sacrificed them to them as food. Was it less than your fornications that you slaughtered my sons and gave them up by making them pass through [the fire] for them? And along with all your abominations and fornications, you did not remember the days of your youth when you were naked and bare and were squirming in your blood.'"'

Disaster was waiting just over the horizon. The marriage disintegrated, but not because Yahweh had become weary of the relationship. Rather, the young wife displayed gross infidelity because she had never genuinely loved her benefactor.

Now wanton Israel has placed her joyful confidence in her possessions and in her undeniable capacity to attract men. Deliberately spurning her gracious Husband, she has allowed herself to be seduced repeatedly by the surrounding nations. Natural desire knew no bounds of decency: **'you trusted ... fornicated ... poured out your fornications ... took some of your clothes ... made for yourself gaudy high places ...**

fornicated upon them' — the **'high places'** pointing both to spiritual apostasy (cf. 6:3) and to the conspicuous places where harlots would proffer their services. The **'clothes'** would have bedecked such couches.[229] It was abominable — **'things that should not come about, nor happen'** (16:15-16).

As the Old Testament records, the rot set in during the later years of Solomon. When that monarch took numerous wives he exposed his nation and himself to every variety of idolatry, leading Israel to early division and ultimate ruin.[230]

Historically, it was this perversion of the good things of God that became Israel's characteristic sin. The fabrication of **'male images'** from Yahweh's **'silver'** and **'gold'** is a reference to Canaanite fertility worship, to which the people had become addicted.[231] The metaphor of unnatural sexual activity (**'fornicated with them'**) highlights the perversity inherent in such apostasy (16:17).

The 'male images' mentioned in 16:17 were decked with the queenly garments formerly bestowed upon his bride by Yahweh, and the **'oil'** and **'incense'** that rightfully belonged to him were given to them as food, the oil probably being poured out before a statue and the incense being burned before its face as if the image were alive (16:18). Further, the **'fine flour'**, **'oil'** and **'honey'** which were part of the queen's diet were bestowed by her upon the idols **'as a pleasing fragrance'**, the smoke of sacrifice ascending to their fabricated and insensitive nostrils. It actually **'"happened," declares the Lord Yahweh'**, who gives expression to his shock that such things had ever occurred (16:19).

Even the queen's children whom she bore to Yahweh for his pleasure were killed and offered to the false deities as food. Divine indignation rises to the surface in 16:21: '*my* children'.

It is known that some of the kings of Judah had indulged in human sacrifice.[232] Appalling as this was, for Ezekiel the sheer cruelty of the practice was overshadowed by the ingratitude of the twelve tribes in that they forgot the wretchedness from which they had been rescued.[233] Such apostasy demonstrated that the queen was a Canaanite at heart, choosing not to **'remember'** the time of her **'youth'** when she had been cast out and was in imminent danger of death (16:20-22).

5. Lovers from afar (16:23-29)

Here Yahweh, drawing more deeply upon the metaphor of the wife who became worse than a whore, directs attention to the political alliances formed by Israel and Judah with some of the surrounding nations. The language seems to be semi-pornographic in places, reflecting the emotional trauma and disgust felt by the divine Husband at his wife's nymphomania.

16:23-29. '"'Then it came about after all your evil — Woe, woe to you,' declares the Lord Yahweh, 'that you built a mound for yourself and made for yourself a high place in every avenue. At the top of every road you constructed your high place and made your beauty abominable and spread your feet to all who passed by, and multiplied your fornications. Then you fornicated with the sons of Egypt, your neighbours, great in flesh, and you multiplied your fornications in order to provoke me.

'"'And, look, I have stretched out my hand against you and have withdrawn your prescribed due, and I have delivered you to the appetite of those who hate you, the daughters of the Philistines, who are ashamed of your lewd intention. Then, because you were not satisfied you fornicated with the sons of Assyria. Moreover, fornicating with them you were still not satisfied. And you multiplied your fornication towards the land of merchandise, towards the Chaldeans — and also in this you were not satisfied.'"'

Israel's ingrained spiritual infidelity had derived from the way of life of the previous inhabitants of the land, the Canaanites. Now Ezekiel details other abominations imported eagerly by Israel from more distant nations. Yahweh announces that **'after all** [her] **evil'** there can be nothing but repetitive **'woe'**; although she should have come to her senses, her dissolution knew no bounds (16:23).

In detail, she constructed **'a mound'** for herself, possibly a convex structure, arch-like in appearance, and a **'high place in every avenue'**. The mind boggles, in that the depraved wife fornicated in every available public place (16:24).

There would be an allusion here to Ahaz, who during the sixteen years of his reign constructed 'for himself in every corner of Jerusalem ... in every single city of Judah high places to burn incense to other gods, and provoked to anger Yahweh, the God of his fathers'.[234] **'At the top of every road'**, possibly at the crossroads (cf. 21:19,21), there were built 'high places' to be a focus for yet more immorality. There the woman exposed her private parts (**'spread your feet'**) to any male who happened to be passing. Her **'fornications'** were **'multiplied'** (16:25).

The next few verses point to political and military intrigue with some of the surrounding nations, a practice condemned by the prophets.[235] The Egyptians head the list because Israel seems to have retained an affinity for the land of the Nile, as suggested by the golden-calf incident at Sinai, Jeroboam's golden calves and even by Solomon's marriage to a daughter of a pharaoh.[236]

Further, Egypt had been singled out by this erring woman because it was a nation portrayed as particularly lustful, **'great in flesh'** being a euphemism for the male reproductive organ.[237] Ezekiel mentions this because Egypt had always been a seat of sophisticated idolatry and her gods long the object of divine wrath.[238] Although he reports that Zedekiah sent envoys to Egypt to obtain military help (cf. 17:13-17), the prophet Jeremiah knew that nothing would come of it.[239] Appearances belied reality.

But there was more to Israel's licentiousness than the gratification of her senses. Her waywardness was deliberate, designed to infuriate her God. She became faithless in order **'to provoke me'** (16:26).

'The Philistines' are introduced under the figure of covetous women to whom Israel's licentiousness caused shame. Yahweh had **'delivered'** Israel **'to the appetite of'** these females **'who hate you'**, meaning that, from the period of the judges, the Philistines had been permitted to ravage the south-west corner of Israelite territory.[240] In consequence, Israel's food supply or land, or both, had been diminished: **'I have stretched out my hand against you and have withdrawn your prescribed due'** (16:27).

Furthermore, the Egyptians were not the only men in her life; there were also Assyrians and Babylonians.[241] The Assyrian connection was particularly nauseating. **'Land of merchandise'** renders *eretz c'naan*, which might be translated as 'land of Canaan' in that *c'naan* bears both meanings (17:4).[242] The burden of this verse, then, is that Queen Israel commenced her fornication in geographical Canaan, then extending it to the **'Chaldeans'** at the commercial heart of the world. But even then she was **'not satisfied'** (16:28-29).

6. A harlot who was not a harlot (16:30-34)

16:30-34. '"'How sick is your heart!' declares the Lord Yahweh, 'while you do all these things, the action of a domineering whore. In that you construct your mound at the top of every road and have made your high place in every avenue, and by disdaining money, you have not been like a harlot.

'"'O adulterous wife, who takes strangers instead of her husband! To all the whores they present a gift, but you have presented your gifts to all your lovers and have bribed them to come to you from every direction with your fornications. And in you there has been a perversion with your harlotries more than [such] women in that after you there is no such whoredom. In that you grant hire and hire is not granted to you, you have become a pervert.'"'

None of these men satisfied her because Israel was both saturated with desire and hopelessly arrogant. Although an adulteress may be driven by passion, and a prostitute by financial necessity, Queen Israel had no excuse: **'How sick is your heart!'** Her regal beauty enabled her to attract lovers from far and wide, thus becoming **'a domineering whore'** (16:30). And the next verse shows that she was worse than a whore.

In detail, she degraded herself in that she had become unnaturally different, and in a spectacular manner. This erring wife, driven ever onwards by a combination of malice and lust, hired as many lovers as she could. Offering herself indiscriminately **'at the top of every road'** and **'in every avenue'**, she had disdained **'money'** (*etnan*, elsewhere employed as the payment due to a prostitute for services rendered).[243] Her womanhood was perverted in that she demanded nothing from her men for favours bestowed upon them. Although likened by 16:30 to an imperious whore, now she is said to be *unlike* a professional lady of the streets: concerned for immediate gratification, she had no thought of maintaining herself (16:31).

Thus she had taken **'strangers** [or foreigners — Egyptians, Assyrians, Babylonians] **instead of her**

husband' (Yahweh), which is why she is now addressed as **'O adulterous wife'** (16:32).

Worse, not only had she not demanded money from the foreigners who came to her, she would remunerate them: **'You have presented ... gifts to all your lovers and have bribed them to come to you from every direction.'**

The many good things granted to her by Yahweh, her Husband, were deployed as bribes to attract gigolos and thus to defile her marriage bed (16:33). As mentioned earlier, an instance of this evil must have been the action of King Ahaz, recorded in 2 Kings 16:8-9, who 'took the silver and the gold that was found in the house of Yahweh, and in the treasuries of the king's house, and sent it as a present to the king of Assyria'.

The queen was a **'pervert'** (*hefek*, from *hafak*, 'to turn' or 'overturn'), unlike any conventional harlot or even a non-promiscuous adulteress. And she had isolated herself in that **'after you there is no such whoredom'**, no woman of the street electing to follow her example. She became a unique exponent of extreme female degradation. Thus, **'there has been a perversion with your harlotries'** (16:34).

7. Death by stoning (16:35-43)

These verses are sombre: those whom she seduced and who seduced her will become her executioners.

16:35-43. '"'Therefore, whore, hear the word of Yahweh.' Thus says the Lord Yahweh: 'Because your discharge was poured out and your nakedness was made bare through your fornications with your lovers and upon your abominable idols, and in accordance with the blood of your children which you offered to them, therefore, look, I shall gather all your lovers to whom you were pleasing and all whom you loved along with all whom you hated, and will gather them against you from round about and expose your nakedness to them, and they will behold your nakedness.

'"'Then I shall judge you with the judgements of adulteresses and they who shed blood, and shall appoint to you the blood of wrath and jealousy. I shall also give you into their hands and they will tear down your mounds and devastate your elevations. They will strip your clothes from you and will take your beautiful ornaments and let you lie naked and bare.

'"'Further, they will raise an assembly against you and will kill you by stoning and will cut you in pieces with their swords. They will burn your houses with fire and execute judgements against you in the eyes of many women, and I shall stop you from being a fornicator and you will not offer hire any more. Then I shall rest my fury against you, and my jealousy will turn away from you. I shall be quiet and no longer be angry. Because you have not remembered the days of your youth, but have enraged me with all these things, aha!, I in turn shall bring your way upon your head,' declares the Lord Yahweh, 'and I shall not commit lewdness in addition to all your other abominations.'"'

The faithless, degraded woman had travelled as far as she could down the broad path of sin, with none imitating the enormity of her actions. **'Therefore, whore, hear the word of Yahweh,'** the Lord addressing her in terms of what she had become. The aggrieved Husband takes up the figure of speech of a woman who had become worse than an unfaithful wife (16:35).

Ezekiel describes the queen's sexual passion in erotic terms: she had poured out her **'discharge'** — possibly meaning genital fluid when aroused[244] — had exposed herself to her lovers and her disgusting **'idols'**, and had offered the **'blood'** of her children to these abominations (16:36).

Therefore Yahweh proposes to gather together her paramours, some whom she had enjoyed and some whom she had detested. The language is shockingly graphic. Whereas the infant girl had been naked when discovered by Yahweh and had been naked when she exposed herself to all who wished to gaze, in their presence the wretched woman will now be stripped naked prior to death by stoning, the agents being the armies of Mesopotamia.[245] Her shameful demise will be the antithesis to the divine Husband's covering his bride-to-be with his garment, as in Ruth 3:9 (cf. 16:8), her final exposure being tantamount to Yahweh's repudiation of her. Hosea 2:2-3,10 gives a vivid commentary on the procedure.

Then her erstwhile lovers **'will behold your nakedness'**. The reader is left to imagine the shock and horror felt by the aggrieved royal Husband because of his queen's misdeeds and the shock and horror experienced by Egyptian, Philistine, Assyrian and Chaldean paramours when they gaze at her in her disgrace. Historically, Yahweh's stripping of Israel was the final destruction of the theocracy by the forces of Nebuchadnezzar, Yahweh's unwitting agent (16:37).

It is now made clear that Israel's previous lovers will be the executors of her degradation. In such cases, the traditional method of capital punishment was by stoning, and an apostate city would be put to the sword.[246] Not only will the fallen queen's painful execution lack the swiftness of decapitation, but her shame will be aggravated in that she dies at the hands of her previous lovers rather than by a disinterested public servant: it is *they* who hurl the rocks and crush the life out of her. Having accomplished their task, they hack her disfigured corpse to **'pieces with their swords'** (16:38-40).

Finally, even as the punishment for apostasy and certain forms of immorality was accentuated by incinerating the corpse,[247] Jerusalem, the principal site of indiscriminate adultery, must be burned down, and this in the presence of **'many women'**, by whom are meant other nations. No longer will Jerusalem be immoral; no longer will she pay others to aid her in sin; no longer will Yahweh be jealous. Through Ezekiel's lips the Lord declares that **'I shall rest my fury'** and **'shall be quiet'**, meaning that when the storm of divine wrath is spent, Yahweh will be satisfied with what he did through the agency of Babylon. His holy anger will have been exhausted (16:41-42).

Of course, at the time of the exile Jerusalem could not have forgotten her humble origins. However, she had **'not remembered'**, had not taken to heart, the grace and favour of her God. To illustrate by antithesis, Genesis 8:1 states that 'God remembered Noah', which does not suggest that the Lord had ever forgotten him, but means that he took Noah's righteousness into consideration.

Therefore Yahweh **'declares'** that **'Aha!, I in turn shall bring your way upon your head'. 'Aha!'** is exclamatory: the God of Israel is determined.

In keeping with the Hebrew text, the verb in the second part of 16:43 should probably be in the first person singular, **'I'**, rather than — as yielded by the Septuagint — the second person, 'you': **'and I shall not commit lewdness in addition to all your other abominations'**. By devastating Jerusalem, Yahweh will in no way intensify or compound the wrongs committed by the city. The infliction of the sword of Babylon is to be an act of divine righteousness: were Yahweh *not* to judge the sins of Israel, he personally would be at fault, in effect condoning the error of their ways. As it is, his wrath is a just retribution and an expression of his inherent righteousness. Because God is God he must do it, sin attracting its inevitable price. As R. V. G. Tasker has observed:

> Just as human love is deficient if the element of anger is entirely lacking ... so too anger is an essential element of divine love. God's love is

> inseparably connected with His holiness and His justice. He must therefore manifest anger when confronted with sin and evil.[248]

And, as noted by J. Galambush, '... the use of the marriage metaphor may itself contribute to the reader's perception that Jahweh has been deeply humiliated and consequently must act to avenge his honor.'[249]

8. Bad blood always shows itself (16:44-52)

Instead of condemning Jerusalem for her sins, Yahweh asserts that the errant bride has shown herself to be what she always was because she stemmed from a delinquent, non-Hebrew family. Therefore, nature and nurture would lead to her eventual downfall. Considered as a daughter, she has reflected her Hittite mother's evil character, and considered as a sibling she is worse than her two notoriously degenerate sisters, Samaria and Sodom, both of whom had borne equally decadent daughters. Any pretensions to a security based on descent from Abraham through Isaac and Jacob are now stripped away.

16:44-52. '"'Look, everyone who speaks in proverbs will make a proverb concerning you, saying, "Like mother, like daughter." You are the daughter of your mother who loathed her husband and her children. And you are your sisters' sister — they who loathed their husbands and their children. Your mother was Hittite and your father Amorite. Now, your big sister is Samaria, who lives with her daughters to your left, and your sister who is smaller than you and who lives to your right is Sodom, together with her daughters. But you have not walked in their ways or done according to their abominations; in such a short time you have caused ruin in all your ways more than they.'"'

"'As I live,' declares the Lord Yahweh, 'Sodom your sister, her daughters and she, have not done as your daughters and you have done. Look, this was the iniquity of Sodom your sister: her daughters and she had arrogance, bread to satisfaction and quiet security, and she did not strengthen the hand of the poor and needy. Thus they were haughty and committed abomination before me, and I removed them when I saw it. Nor has Samaria committed half your sins. You have multiplied your abominations more than they and have justified your sisters with all your abominations that you committed. You also, bear your disgrace in that you have arbitrated for your sister with your sins in which you have been more abominable than they. They are more righteous than you. So you, be ashamed and bear your disgrace in that you have justified your sisters.'"'

The outcome of divine chastisement is that all who witness Israel's disgrace will apply to her the **'proverb ... "Like mother, like daughter"'**. That is, others will find cause to say that her innate character, her behaviour — and her downfall — were predictable, given her family background (16:44).

Resuming from 16:3, Yahweh implies that just as Israel's **'mother'**, the immoral **'Hittite'**, despised her husband the **'Amorite'** and also **'her children'**, so Israel has despised her own Husband, Yahweh, and also her offspring. How exactly the Hittites were 'married' to the Amorites (if that is the meaning), and how the former **'loathed'** her husband and her children is not stated, but the assertion is consistent with the contempt shown to infant Israel by her parents, as stated by 16:3-5.

Further, and somewhat surprisingly, Israel is said to have been a **'sisters' sister'** — these women, in sad imitation of their Hittite mother, having **'loathed their husbands and their children'** (16:45). Who these children were will emerge in the next verse.

As one looks towards the east, **'Samaria'** was geographically larger and to the left, or north, of Jerusalem, and **'Sodom'** was geographically smaller and to the right, or south, of the city. Samaria was **'big'** in that the city of that name was the capital of the larger kingdom to the north, and Sodom was **'smaller'** in that it was not the capital of any more extensive kingdom. Clearly, Judah and Samaria were related in that they were divisions of the kingdom of Israel formerly united under Solomon, but it is less easy to see why Sodom is reckoned as Judah's sister. Perhaps, as suggested by the prohibition of Deuteronomy 7:1-5 and the narrative of Judges 2:6-23,[250] there had been intermarriage between some Jews and non-Hebrews in that region following the destruction of Sodom.[251]

If the neglected husband of Samaria and Sodom is taken as Yahweh, whom — it seems to be assumed — even non-Hebrews were expected to serve, there is a disjunction between the present verse and the statement of 16:45 that the Hittites and the Amorites enjoyed some sort of matrimonial relationship (16:46). But, as Taylor notes, 'Perhaps we must not press the details too closely when Ezekiel is saying no more than that there was a family tendency to rejection of the Lord and His standards by virtue of their mixed, Canaanitish ancestry'.[252]

True to ingrained family traits and prior to being swept away in judgement, they had despised their husbands and children. Samaria had been taken into exile one hundred years earlier than Ezekiel's time, and Sodom had been destroyed more than a thousand years before that. Over the years Jerusalem's behaviour had become worse than theirs, having **'caused ruin in all your ways more than they'** and doing it **'in such a short time'** (16:47).

Divine scrutiny now falls upon Sodom. According to Jesus, that city would have survived had its inhabitants been righteous.[253] But it fell because there had never been any show of repentance. According to Ezekiel, the principal fault of Sodom and her daughters (Gomorrah, Admah and Zeboim?) was material selfishness. But, as those to whom Ezekiel was ministering must have concluded, if Sodom had fallen so quickly,[254] could Jerusalem expect deliverance? It may not be without significance that among the sins of Sodom is *not* mentioned the vice to which the city's name has been given, perhaps suggesting that greed, if unchecked, will generate immorality (16:48-49).

Because the principal sin of Samaria, idolatrous image-worship,[255] must have been obvious to Ezekiel and his constituency, it is unmentioned. Nor does the prophet specify the punishment inflicted, namely, the deportation of the ten tribes by the Assyrians.[256] But this would have been at the back of his mind. The dreadful reality to which he points is that Judah's sins had ripened to a degree altogether unknown in the northern kingdom. The suppressed thesis of the present verse is that pride generates all manner of evil, whether idolatry, as in the case of Samaria and Judah, or gross materialism, as in the case of Sodom — or both. Either way, **'I removed them when I saw it'** (16:50).

Can, therefore, Judah survive, bearing in mind that Samaria did not commit **'half your sins'** and that the former had **'multiplied'** her **'abominations more than they'** — that is, more than the combined offences of Samaria and Sodom? **'You have ... justified your sisters'** (16:51), which occurs also in the next verse, is comparative: the total of the sins of Samaria and Sodom had been less than **'half'** those of Judah. Therefore, if their transgressions were not unpunished the fate of Judah is certain.[257]

The intensity of Judah's sins has had the effect of making Samaria and Sodom appear whiter than white, by contrast appearing to be righteous. **'You also, bear your disgrace in that you have arbitrated**

for your sister with your sins' is meant to shock, and Ezekiel's hearers must have been aghast when they heard this. **'Arbitrated'** translates the Hebrew *pillél* which, when followed by the preposition *lamed* — corresponding to the English 'L' — as here, means 'to intercede for', or even 'to come to a decision'.[258] Accordingly, Judah's sins had the effect of averting the divine scrutiny away from Sodom and Samaria in that they were deemed to have been **'more righteous than you'**. Having **'justified'** her **'sisters'** and then having been commanded to **'be ashamed'**, she must (repeat) **'bear'** her **'disgrace'** (16:52).

9. Israel restored (16:53-63)

At this point the thrust of the prophecy alters dramatically. Now there is good news.

Yahweh predicts that he will put an end to the misfortune of Sodom and her daughters, and that of Samaria and her daughters. At the same time, the distress of Judah and of her daughters will terminate. Remarkably, Sodom and Samaria, together with their children, are to be comforted by Judah, and all will be ashamed of their evils (16:53-55). One wonders how the Jews of Ezekiel's time might have reacted to this revelation.

Historically, a literal restoration of Sodom and Samaria has never happened. Sodom vanished, never to be seen again, and the ten tribes of Samaria were never recovered from their Assyrian exile. From this it seems that Ezekiel's predictions stretch towards a time yet to come. But how can this be? One possible answer is that Sodom and Samaria typify a future conversion of the Gentile world, along with the Jews, to the God of Israel. If so, Ezekiel anticipates the universal spread of the good news of Jesus Christ.

During the centuries prior to the destruction of Jerusalem in 586 BC, when Syrians, Philistines and others were pressing hard upon Judah,[259] Jerusalem seemed never to have appreciated that these strokes were from Yahweh. Moreover, the people failed to take to heart the overthrow of Sodom in an earlier age. Ezekiel declares that arrogant and unrepentant Zion will soon fall because it must suffer for its pride and sinfulness. But a once-for-all payment is enough: after the stroke Israel may look ahead to a new dawn. Then the marriage between Yahweh and his people will be renewed, never again to be sundered by her wilfulness and his judgement (16:56-63).

16:53-63. '"'Nevertheless I shall restore their captivity, the captivity of Sodom and her daughters and the captivity of Samaria and her daughters, and I shall restore your captivity in their midst, so that you may bear your disgrace and be ashamed for all that you have done when you console them. And your sisters, Sodom and her daughters and Samaria and her daughters, will return to their former state, and your daughters and you will return to your former state. But was not Sodom your sister a byword in your mouth in the day of your pride, before your evil was exposed? Like that time, you have become the taunt of the daughters of Aram and all who surround her, the daughters of the Philistines, who scorn you. Your wickedness and your abominations — you have borne them,' declares Yahweh.

'"For thus says the Lord Yahweh: 'I have dealt with you even as you dealt, in that you despised the oath, breaking the covenant. Nevertheless, I myself shall remember my covenant with you in the days of your youth and shall establish an everlasting covenant for you. Then you will remember your ways and be humiliated when you receive your sisters — they who are bigger than you with those who are smaller — and I shall grant them to you as daughters, but not from your covenant. Then I myself shall establish my covenant with you and you will know that I am Yahweh, so that you may remember and be ashamed, and that there may never more be an opening of the mouth because of your disgrace when I have atoned for you for all that you have done,' declares the Lord Yahweh."'

The prophet expounds good news: the relationship between Yahweh and his erring bride will not terminate with the overthrow of Jerusalem. Yahweh's original commitment to his pledged word constrains him to restore the union, in fulfilment of Moses' expectation.[260] It is true that because Israel had despised him, Yahweh must deal with her accordingly. But he cannot and does not dismiss her from his heart, the ultimate reality having been foreshadowed by the bond at Sinai.

To **'restore ... captivity'** translates a Hebrew idiom, *shûb shebût,* meaning the re-establishment of former happiness. The sense is brought out by Job 42:10: 'And Yahweh *brought back* Job's losses when he prayed for his friends', Job's 'losses' being what had been taken from him by numerous disasters.[261]Ezekiel employs the expression again in 29:14 concerning Egypt and in 39:25 concerning Jacob. Here there is no suggestion of an early return to the promised land from foreign exile, text and context looking to the long-term future. As shown by 39:25-26, accompanying restoration there will be a removal of the underlying causes of previous misfortune.[262]

The present verse may imply a reunion between the land and its people, in pursuance of the promise to Abraham[263] and as is made explicit in chapters 36 – 39. Eventually, Israel will be aware that Yahweh is the God of covenant mercies when, having scattered the people among the nations, he will reconvene them to settle on their own earth.

It could be that **'Sodom'** is mentioned along with **'Samaria'** because later in the prophecy Ezekiel will predict that the area is to be revived (47:3-12), or possibly because, in the light of Jeremiah 12:14-17, Sodom represents the Canaanites who remained in Israel following Joshua's conquest. Of these, some will turn to Yahweh (16:53).

The sentence commencing at 16:53 flows on. **'Sodom'**, **'Samaria'**, their **'daughters'** and Jerusalem with her **'daughters'** are to be restored — but so that Jerusalem **'may ... be ashamed for all that you have done'**. That is, the greater sin of that city puts the others in the shade: **'you console them'** in that they realize that their shortcomings were relatively light in contrast to those of the city of David. The latter must **'bear'** her **'disgrace'** (16:54).

The promises of 16:53-54 are recapitulated. The dissolute women, along with Jerusalem, the worst of the trio, and their **'daughters'** will **'return to their former state'**, by which is meant their forfeited comfort (16:55).

There was a time when Sodom had been **'a byword'** (*sh'muah*, an object of derision) in the **'mouth'** of Jerusalem in the **'day of'** the latter's **'pride'**, when Jerusalem had been a city wilfully unmindful of eventual judgement (16:56).[264] But this was before her **'evil was exposed'** by the prophets of Yahweh, one of whom was Ezekiel. Since then, and in the context of the progressive reduction of Judah by the armies of Babylon, **'the daughters of Aram'** (Syria)[265] and those of the **'Philistines'** had made Jerusalem their favoured object of ridicule. The tragic fact was that the city of David had been rejected and scorned not only by Yahweh, *but also* by the surrounding world: **'"Your wickedness and your abominations — you have borne" declares Yahweh.'** This being so, the Jews of the exile and those still remaining in Judah may not reckon that because of a supposed moral superiority they will be maintained by their God (16:56-58).

Now comes the concluding section of this very long oracle. Yahweh speaks as if the fall of Jerusalem is a fait accompli: **'I have dealt with you even as you dealt.'** Since Judah has elected to withdraw from the obligations of the exclusive Sinai covenant, so Yahweh feels free to withdraw from the relationship.

In detail, Jerusalem had **'despised the oath'**, meaning that she had voluntarily brought upon herself the curse inherent in withdrawing from a solemn commitment to the Lord. Nehemiah 10:28-29 provides illumination:

> Now the rest of the people ... and all those who had separated themselves from the peoples of the lands to the law of God ... joined with their brethren, their nobles, *and entered into a curse and an oath to walk in God's law*, which was given by Moses the servant of God, and to observe and to do all the commandments of Yahweh our God, and his ordinances and his statutes.

In Nehemiah's day, the people of Jerusalem determined to submit themselves to Moses' law on pain of a divine curse in the event of apostasy. But in the years prior to 586 BC this commitment had been cast aside, the city having despised the oath, thereby **'breaking the covenant'**. Justly, therefore, Yahweh has cursed her, considering himself absolved of any marital obligation (16:59).

Now light shines. Yahweh states that he will **'remember my covenant with you in the days of your youth, and** [will] **establish an everlasting covenant for you'**. This covenant will be resurrected in such a manner that it will never fall into desuetude.

It is true that the blessings of the Sinai covenant were provisional, in that they depended upon the obedience of Israelites who would soon demonstrate their infidelity, as in the golden-calf episode.[266] For this reason, and not through any fault of its own, Moses' covenant became a curse to Israel.[267] Yet the Sinai arrangement was neither the beginning nor the end of the matter. Originating centuries after the foundation covenant that God had established with Abraham,[268] it led in time to the establishment of the Davidic monarchy, all the while anticipating the Messiah.[269] This is why Isaiah speaks about the 'everlasting covenant' with Israel in fulfilment of earlier promises.[270]

When the Sinai covenant was instituted, Yahweh seems to have anticipated that it would be scorned by the twelve tribes of Israel, which is why solemn warnings against apostasy are recorded in chapter 26 of Leviticus, almost at the conclusion of that book. But there is also an expectation that at some future time, in the aftermath of apostasy and inevitable chastisement, there will be Israelite renewal.

Hence, Leviticus 26:42 states that if a scattered and humbled Israel comes to repentance, 'then I [Yahweh] will remember my covenant with Jacob, and my covenant with Isaac and my covenant with Abraham I will remember.' The 'if' in Leviticus 26:40 is virtually a 'when'. Thus, in the present verse it would be the original covenant with Abraham that Yahweh promises to honour, and perhaps with a reflection of Jeremiah 31:31.[271] Jeremiah's 'new covenant' will be 'new' in distinction to Moses' earlier and provisional arrangement, which, with the advent of the Messiah, will pass away.[272] And the new settlement will be no more than the efflorescence of the covenant with Abraham (16:60).

'Then', when the covenant has been renewed, **'you will remember your ways and be humiliated when you receive your sisters.'** When forgiven, Jerusalem will be ashamed of the past. Not only will Yahweh receive the people back, he will bestow upon them a new, holy attitude of heart so that they want to be his. Yet even this is not the whole of the matter: Judah will receive her greater and her smaller sisters (typically, Samaria and Sodom and their daughters) as coequals with her in the one family of God. But although considered as Judah's 'sisters', in a sense they will also be her **'daughters'**.

Originally, the family of Abraham had been the unique recipient of God's covenant promise, the patriarch being given to understand that it would lead to blessing for the whole world. Ezekiel's prediction, then, is that within a non-ethnic church of the future, Israel will retain seniority, rather as an older girl might 'mother' her younger sisters.[273]

And the basis of the triangular relationship between (1) Yahweh, (2) Jerusalem (representing Israel) and (3) Sodom and Samaria will not be **'from your covenant'**. This appears to mean that converted aliens will not accommodate to the Sinai covenant, in that it had been rejected by Israel and in time would be declared redundant by Yahweh (see 16:59). Perhaps this verse shows a glimmer of the 'new covenant' (Jer. 31:31), itself the blossoming of the covenant with Abraham, but with Israel embracing 'sisters', now 'daughters', who were once considered as outcasts. For their part, because they had never had any part in the covenant between God and Israel, they had no claim to participate in the relationship between the Lord and his people. That they do participate is because of divine grace. Eventually, Jerusalem and they will accept that the wall of partition has been broken down (16:61).

These words seem to anticipate Romans 11:32, in which Paul predicts that God '[will have] shut them all [Jews and Gentiles alike] up to disobedience, that he might have mercy on all'.

The oracle climaxes. With the fruition of the **'covenant'** made with Abraham, Jerusalem **'will know that I am Yahweh'**, acknowledging that the God of Israel is the God of grace as well as of judgement (16:62). Through Yahweh's remembrance of his 'covenant' with the patriarchs (16:60), the collective seed of Abraham, now in relationship with the Lord, will

'remember and be ashamed'. No more will Israel 'open' the **'mouth'** to complain that, as the matter had once been perceived, Yahweh was unjust in abandoning Jerusalem to the Babylonian invaders.

The theology of these verses anticipates the New Testament. Although shame is always a condition of forgiveness, the forgiven sinner never ceases to be ashamed of himself: he remembers that it was necessary for Christ to die for him. As years pass and as heaven approaches, remorse and gratitude become more acute, the believer remembering what he was like and intensely aware that he does not deserve the mercy shown to him. Nevertheless, together with all those in 'Israel' embraced by the new covenant, he rejoices that the Lord has **'atoned'** for him.

How Yahweh will atone for his people's offences ('atone', from *kaphar*, 'to cover'; hence, 'to purge') is not specified. But perhaps Ezekiel and his constituency enjoyed access to the prophecy of Isaiah, and specifically to chapter 53. Perhaps, too, they suspected that Yahweh would atone personally for the sins of men by becoming one of them and suffering in their place. It ought not to be forgotten that Ezekiel was a priest as well as a prophet, well comprehending the implications of the tabernacle and temple ritual. To repeat, does not the present verse (16:63) anticipate the New Testament's understanding of Calvary?

Application

Chapter 16's outrageous metaphor of the nymphomaniac was designed to shock Ezekiel's contemporaries into an awareness of the magnitude and intensity of collapsing Israel's sinfulness. Because our own society seems to have forgotten how to blush, we may not expect to be happy nor hope for national security unless there is widespread repentance.

One of the most vivid illustrations of the grace of God in the whole Bible is to be found in 16:6-14. Firstly, the love of God for sinners is undeserved: Christians have done nothing to merit his grace. Secondly, divine mercies deliver and exalt. Thirdly, redemption demands that the redeemed strive to be holy.

Syncretism, the adoption by churches of religious and philosophical practices and beliefs that are alien to the Bible, is always a problem for professing Christians. This is because the Bible is our *sole* authority in all matters of faith and practice rather than our highest authority. We should always listen to others, yet never imitate them unless we judge that what they do and believe is useful and that it measures up to Scripture.

In that nymphomaniac Jerusalem was never content, the fallen city tells out the perennial truth that false religion never satisfies its adherents. Nor can there be any such thing as honest atheism: if men refuse to serve the true God they will serve false gods, and false religion can never generate holiness.

The union between Yahweh and his bride is depicted by 16:8 as a 'covenant'. So are all marriages, which means that they are not to be entered into unadvisedly or too quickly. And matrimony should never be considered as a temporary relationship.

Under the old covenant, not even Israel's status as a nation under God provided personal inner sanctification, the reason being that the Spirit had not yet come. This is why chapter 16 anticipates a new covenant, itself (presumably) the fulfilment of that between God and Abraham. Whereas the 'marriage' between God and Israel fell into abeyance, that between Christ and his bride will never fade.[274] The bride will be eternally exalted (16:63).

We Christians need to remember what we used to be and what we would still be had not the grace of God reached us. Jerusalem's main problem was that she had forgotten (16:43).

The eagles, the vine and the cedar twig (Ezekiel 17:1-24)

Although this chapter is a distinct oracle, it is integral to the series of revelations commencing at chapter 8 and continuing to chapter 19. It is a prediction falling into four parts: firstly, a riddle — that which, lacking an immediate explanation, should excite its hearers to work out its meaning (17:1-10); secondly, the historical interpretation of the riddle (17:11-18); thirdly, the underlying truth that Yahweh, who had been affronted, was precipitating the collapse of Jerusalem (17:19-21) and, finally, a Messianic prophecy (17:22-24).

The Old Testament background to Ezekiel 17 is essential reading.[275] 2 Chronicles 36:13 records that Zedekiah, king of Judah, rebelled against King Nebuchadnezzar, who previously had made him 'swear by God' to maintain his allegiance. But 'he stiffened his neck and hardened his heart against turning to Yahweh, the God of Israel'. That is, Zedekiah's rebellion against Nebuchadnezzar was fuelled by his lack of fear of the God of Israel, whose name he had invoked. It was this problem of attitude which is the key to the interpretation of the present chapter, which should be paralleled with chapter 12 in that both predict the king's demise.

1. A riddle (17:1-10)

In his vision Ezekiel saw two birds. Both were eagles and both were powerful. But one was more powerful than the other.

17:1-10. Now the word of Yahweh came to me, saying, 'Son of man, propound a riddle and make up a parable for the house of Israel. And you will say, "Thus says the Lord Yahweh: 'The great eagle, large in wing, long of pinion, full of multicoloured plumage, came to Lebanon and took away the top of the cedar. He plucked off the topmost of its shoots and brought it to the land of merchandise; he set it in a city of traders. Then he took from the seedlings of the land and placed it in a field of seed — a stalk beside abundant waters; he set it like a willow. And it sprouted and became a spreading vine, low of height turning its branches towards him, and its roots were under it. Thus it became a vine; it yielded shoots and sent forth boughs.

'"'Now there was another great eagle, with great wings and much plumage. And, look, this vine bent its roots towards him and sent its branches to him to water itself from the beds where it was planted. It had been transplanted to a good field, by much water so that it might produce branches and bear fruit, to become a splendid vine.'"

'Say, "Thus says the Lord Yahweh: 'Will it prosper? Will he not tear out its roots and strip off its fruit so that it dries up — so that all its sprouting leaves wither? And neither by a great arm nor by many people is it to be lifted from its roots. And, look, transplanted, will it survive? Will it not be that when the east wind touches it, it will wither completely? On the beds where it flourished it will dry up.'"'

Yahweh declared a new word to the **'son of man'**, who would **'propound a riddle and make up a parable for the house of Israel'**. His hearers were to consider the prophetic word-picture and attempt to work out the meaning (17:1-2). Because it was expected that they would fail to do so, an interpretation is provided. The ploy was not without parallels, as, for instance, the experience of certain Philistines who heard Samson's strange tale about bees, a dead lion and some honey, and who knew that it was in their interest to get to the bottom of the matter.[276] Jesus used parables in profusion,[277] stories designed to captivate the attention of genuine disciples.

The riddle commences. **'The great eagle'**, with large wings and extended talons, **'came to Lebanon and took away the top of the cedar.'** Neither is there an identification of the person or empire represented by the bird (although the definite article, **'the'**, might give a hint), nor a motive given for its action (unless **'took away'** implies an act of rapacity), nor an identification of the **'top of the cedar'** in **'Lebanon'**. The curiosity of Ezekiel's hearers is being stirred (17:3).

'The top of the cedar' is defined as **'the topmost of its shoots'** that was carried off to **'the land of merchandise'** (literally, *eretz c'naan*, 'the land of Canaan'; cf. 16:29),[278] 'Canaan' not being the land settled by Israel under Joshua, but **'a city of traders'**. However, the city is not identified (17:4).

The imagery changes, the 'great eagle' becoming an agriculturalist and the 'top of the cedar' a native seedling **'of the land'**. It is planted in well-irrigated earth, **'a field of seed'**, just as someone might plant a **'willow'** twig (17:5).

In due course, the seedling **'sprouted'** and **'became a spreading vine'**. It took root, **'turning its branches'** towards the planter, alias the great eagle. Established in the earth, **'it yielded shoots and sent forth boughs'**. Having done all that was essential, the planter had every right to expect fruit (17:6).

Ezekiel's hearers must have been wondering what the prophet was saying to them, by now their curiosity being fanned into a flame. Ezekiel continues: there appeared **'another great eagle, with great wings and much plumage'**. **'Look'**, says Yahweh, **'this vine'**, alias the top shoot of the cedar of Lebanon, **'bent its roots towards him and sent its branches to him to water itself'**, and this even when it remained in the **'beds'** where it had been **'planted'** in the land of the first eagle, in the land of the traders (17:7).

The intended implication is that for some reason the vine was perverse. Supplied with both soil and irrigation by the first eagle, it could have had no good reason for seeking nourishment from elsewhere: **'It had been transplanted to a good field ... to become a splendid vine.'** Why, then, the affront to the first eagle-cum-husbandman? (17:8).

The riddle has come to its end, to be followed by rhetorical questions. Yahweh himself wishes to be told whether or not the vine will **'prosper'**. Will not the husbandman, alias the first, greater eagle, uproot it and remove its leaves and fruit so that it **'dries up'**? Assuming a positive answer from his hypothetical hearers, the Lord states that if (or when) it happens, no great effort will be needed to cause it to be **'lifted from its roots'** (17:9). This is a warning, and Ezekiel's hearers, if they had any inkling of the solution to the riddle, may have trembled.

More questions: **'... transplanted, will it survive?'** That is, although the cedar twig-cum-vine had been replanted in the land of the merchants and had been given every attention, **'will it survive'**, in that it has bent its roots towards the second eagle and has extended its branches in its direction? When exposed to the searing heat of an **'east wind'**, must it not wither? Yes, says Yahweh, **'On the beds where it flourished it will dry up'** (17:10).

2. The historical interpretation of the riddle (17:11-18)

Ezekiel was instructed to ask his fellow-exiles if they had understood the significance of the riddle. On the prior assumption that they would return a negative answer, Yahweh provides his own interpretation.

17:11-18. And the word of Yahweh came to me, saying, 'Say now to the rebellious house, "Do you not know what these things are?" Say, "Look, the king of Babylon has come to Jerusalem and has taken its king and its princes and has brought them to himself to Babylon. And he has taken from the royal seed, has cut a covenant with him and has brought him under oath. He also took the mighty of the land — that the kingdom might be low and that he might not lift himself up, so as to observe his covenant, that it might stand. But he rebelled against him in sending his messengers to Egypt to grant him horses and many people. Will he prosper? Will he who does such things escape? Can he break the covenant and escape? 'As I live', declares the Lord Yahweh, 'surely in the place of the king who made him king, who despised his oath and whose covenant with him he broke, in the midst of Babylon he will die. Pharaoh will not act for him in war with a large army and with a great assembly when they cast up siege mounds and construct siege walls in order to cut off many lives. He despised the oath to break the covenant, and, look, he has given his hand and has done all these things. He will not escape.'"'

Conceivably, Ezekiel's hearers might have offered a variety of identifications for the greater and the lesser eagles, and for the cedar twig that became a vine.

Now Yahweh gives definitive clarification. Although the individuals who stand behind the riddle / parable are not named, their identities would have been obvious. The greater eagle represents Nebuchadnezzar of Babylon.[279] Like a bird of prey with outstretched wings and long feathers, this man had, as it were, flown in conquest over many lands. The full, multi-coloured plumage given to the creature stands for the many different races held together by force in the empire of Babylon.

The eagle swooped upon Lebanon and snatched away the top of a particular cedar tree. Lebanon represents Jerusalem, where the royal palace (the cedar tree) had over the years been enriched with Lebanese timber (see 17:1-3), and the twig is Jehoiachin, who after reigning for three months was deported to Babylon along with his family and some of his leading men (17:11-12).[280] Although 2 Kings 24:9 records that Jehoiachin 'did evil in the sight of Yahweh', 17:4-6 suggests that he was well received in Babylon.

At this point it may be helpful to note once again Josiah's immediate descendants. Josiah (639–609 BC) was succeeded by one of his sons, Jehoahaz, who reigned for three months. This was in 609 BC. Then Jehoahaz was followed by his brother, Josiah's son Eliakim. His name was altered to Jehoiakim and he reigned for eleven years (608–598 BC), to be succeeded by his son Jehoiachin, Josiah's grandson. He reigned for three months, in 597 BC.

After Jehoiachin came his uncle Mattaniah.[281] Nebuchadnezzar changed his name to Zedekiah, and he reigned for eleven years before being deported to Babylon in 586 BC.

The eagle, alias Nebuchadnezzar, selecting someone from **'the royal seed'**, **'cut a covenant with him'** and **'brought him under oath'** (17:13). This was done to ensure that Judah would remain as a client kingdom subservient to Babylon. The procedure may have included the drawing up of a solemn treaty between Judah and Babylon ('cutting a covenant') and then an oath of allegiance sworn by Zedekiah personally. To judge by 2 Kings 24:15-16, Jehoiachin's brief tenure of the throne ended when the royal family (**'the**

mighty of the land') and the nobility, together with skilled artisans and craftsmen, were deported — royalty and aristocracy as hostages and the second group probably to boost the receptor economy.

Overall, the deportation was intended by Nebuchadnezzar to reinforce the status of Judah as a vassal kingdom of Babylon, to ensure that Zedekiah, who succeeded Jehoiachin and who remained in Jerusalem, would not **'lift himself up'**,[282] and to make certain that the **'covenant'** between Judah and Chaldea would **'stand'** (17:14).

Furthermore, although a power-hungry despot who appeared to be lord of all, the Babylonian monarch had need of Judah as a puppet state in his intercontinental struggle with Egypt. Fundamentally, this is why he brought Zedekiah under tribute.

Unhappily, Zedekiah **'rebelled against'** Nebuchadnezzar by **'sending his messengers to Egypt to grant him horses and many people'** (17:15). Although the details of this rebellion are unknown, the background seems clear. Zedekiah, a monarch who 'did evil in the sight of Yahweh',[283] travelled 'to Babylon in the fourth year of his [eleven-year] reign', about 592 BC,[284] perhaps to give a suspicious Nebuchadnezzar reassurances about his allegiance. Further, Jeremiah 37:5-8 states that when the Babylonians were investing Jerusalem, an Egyptian army advanced towards the city, causing the Chaldeans to retire. But Pharaoh's forces did not press their attack.

Jeremiah predicted that the Chaldeans would return to Jerusalem and eventually raze the city — which is what happened. Already, the Chaldeans had repulsed the Egyptian armies at Carchemish in 605 BC, which meant that as far as Judah was concerned the latter were useless allies.

It may be assumed that for a number of years Zedekiah intended to renege on his oath of subjection to Babylon, that he had sent emissaries to Egypt to enlist mercenary help and that his treachery had become known to Nebuchadnezzar. The celebrated 'Lachish letters', dating from the time of the Babylonian invasion, may throw some light upon the Egyptian connection. Letter 3, from a slave, Hoshaiah, to a military commander in Lachish, 'my Lord Jaush', states that 'the commander of the army went down ... to come to Egypt', this statement followed by a reference to a letter sent by one Nedebiah, 'the grandson of the king', 'from the prophet [Jeremiah?], saying, "Beware!"'[285] At this eleventh hour was Zedekiah pleading for Egyptian aid when the Chaldeans were so near Jerusalem?

Therefore, **'Will he prosper? Will he who does such things escape? Can he break the covenant and escape?'** (17:15). The only possible answer is that Zedekiah must bring his people and himself to ruin.

Because Zedekiah had broken his oath, Yahweh would place himself under his own oath: **'"As I live,' declares the Lord Yahweh'**, Zedekiah will end up in the **'place'**, or territory, of Nebuchadnezzar, the one who had **'made him king ... and whose covenant ... he broke'**. Therefore, **'in the midst of Babylon he will die'** (17:16). 2 Kings 25:7 narrates that, following his capture, Zedekiah was transported to Babylon, after which no more is heard of him, except here.

The divine oath is expanded. Although having promised much, the Egyptian pharaoh **'will not act for him** [Zedekiah] **in war'**,[286] failing to oppose the Babylonians when the latter invest Jerusalem. According to Jeremiah 44:30, the pharaoh alluded to here was Hophra (589–570 BC), 'pharaoh' meaning 'great house' — that is, the royal palace and the court of Egypt combined — yet applied to the person of the monarch himself. Perhaps these words were uttered by Yahweh at the same time as the prophecy of Jeremiah 37:6-10. If so, both in the homeland and in the land of exile the Lord declared through two eminent servants that Babylon must prevail, would **'cut off many lives'**, and that Zedekiah's pro-Egyptian manoeuvrings must come to nothing (17:17).

Zedekiah's offence is placed under greater magnification. In despising his **'oath'** and breaking his **'covenant'**, to which he had **'given his hand'**, **'he will not escape'** (17:18). He never faced up to the certainty that Nebuchadnezzar, the object of Jewish treachery, would return in wrath.

3. Yahweh, Zedekiah and Nebuchadnezzar (17:19-21)

Yahweh declares that the violation of the oath of fealty sworn by Zedekiah to Nebuchadnezzar was a sin against heaven, for which Zedekiah must be held responsible.

17:19-21. '"'Therefore,' thus says the Lord Yahweh: 'As I live, surely, it is my oath which he despised and my covenant that he broke. I shall bring it upon his head. I shall spread my net upon him, and he will be seized in my snare, and I shall conduct him to Babylon and enter into judgement with him there for the treachery that he has committed against me. And all his fugitives in his armies will fall by the sword and those who remain will be scattered to every wind. Then you will know that I, Yahweh, have spoken.'"'

These verses have to be interpreted in the light of 2 Chronicles 36:13, which has already been quoted: 'And he [Zedekiah] also rebelled against King Nebuchadnezzar, who had made him swear by God; but he stiffened his neck and hardened his heart against turning to Yahweh, the God of Israel.'

Because the Jewish king had called upon his God to judge him in the event of his breaking the terms of the covenant, Yahweh will now call him to account.

The Lord declares that it was **'*my* oath which he despised and *my* covenant that he broke'**.

In Israel, the taking of an oath was always a sacred matter.[287] Zedekiah's broken promise meant that he could not prosper. As a hunted animal he will be tracked down by Yahweh, will be deported to Babylon and there will **'enter into judgement'** with Yahweh, no less (17:19-20). All this, it is assumed, will be undertaken by Yahweh's involuntary agent, Nebuchadnezzar. What the nature of the judgement will be, if other than dying in captivity (cf. 17:16), is not stated.

But prior to this reckoning, the **'fugitives in his armies will fall by the sword'**, Zedekiah presumably learning of the collapse of all resistance to the Chaldeans. **'Then'**, when any survivors have been scattered in all directions, **'you** [the exiles in captivity] **will know that I, Yahweh, have spoken.'** It will be accepted that Yahweh had been the prime mover behind the Chaldean holocaust (17:21).

4. A Messianic prophecy (17:22-24)

In the earlier part of the riddle a twig from a cedar of Lebanon was transported to a land of merchants, where it was planted. Metamorphosed into a vine, it flourished, but treacherously shifted its allegiance, bringing ruin upon itself. Now, Ezekiel's parable reconsiders the selfsame cedar: Yahweh himself, rather than an imperial eagle, will transplant a twig, with astonishing consequences. These three verses are Messianic to the core.

17:22-24. '"Thus says the Lord Yahweh: 'I myself shall take from the top of the lofty cedar and shall establish it. From the topmost of its shoots I shall pluck a tender sprig and I shall transplant it upon a high and lofty mountain. On the high mountain of Israel I shall transplant it that it may bear branches and yield fruit and become a splendid cedar. Then birds of every kind will abide beneath it; in the shadow of its boughs they will dwell. So all the trees of the field will know that I am Yahweh: I make low the tall tree and exalt the low tree; I wither the moist tree and cause the dried-up tree to flourish. I, Yahweh, have spoken, and I shall act.'"'

Yahweh declares that he personally will **'take'** a shoot from **'the top of the lofty cedar'**. In effect, if the God of Israel has brought about the downfall of the house of David (see 17:19-21), it is he who will resurrect the Davidic monarchy. Unlike the greater eagle, alias Nebuchadnezzar, who snatched away Jehoiachin, the topmost twig, from the cedar of Lebanon (17:3-4), Yahweh will not employ violence. It is implied that the whole process will be innocuous — initially, at least, unexposed to the glare of publicity.

And the **'sprig'** from the cedar, **'from the topmost of its shoots'**, will be **'tender'** (17:22). A century earlier Isaiah had employed a similar metaphor,[288] and it was taken up by Jeremiah in Ezekiel's lifetime.[289] It would occur again in Zechariah 3:8; 6:12, following the Babylonian exile. The references in Jeremiah declare, and those in Zechariah imply heavily, that the 'branch' will restore the throne of David.

And Yahweh will plant it upon **'the high mountain of Israel'**. According to 17:6, the earlier transplanted twig — the throne of David when Zedekiah was its incumbent — was intended to become a 'spreading vine, low of height, turning its branches towards' Nebuchadnezzar. But the latter-day tender twig will become a **'splendid cedar'**, subservient to none, so much so that **'birds of every kind will abide beneath it; in the shadow of its boughs they will dwell'**, which is more than would ever be said for Israel in exile.

Through the instrumentality of Babylonian military might, Yahweh was bringing the throne of David and the theocracy of Israel to nothing, was removing the temple from the face of the earth and was withdrawing his presence from a people who had been settled in Canaan for one thousand years. Now Ezekiel predicts that the throne of David will be established again[290] — this to be achieved by Yahweh's direct action. In short, the ancient promises to Abraham will attain an astonishing fulfilment (17:23).

The riddle-cum-parable (see 17:2) reaches its climax. Surprisingly, the **'trees of the field'** do not bow down before this magnificent cedar. Rather, they accept that **'I am Yahweh'**, the God who is capable of bringing down **'the tall tree'** and exalting **'the low tree'**, of withering **'the moist tree'** and revivifying **'the dried-up tree'**.[291] In effect, because this particular tree is somehow different, in that its growth is not the consequence of human enterprise, the trees in the field, alias the kingdoms of this world, acknowledge the glory and power of the Davidic, Messianic kingdom, a kingdom *not* of this world.[292] And in so doing they accept that Yahweh will have been true to earlier promises and that he had never finally surrendered his commitment to the seed of Abraham, to the land of promise and to the throne of David. He had never finally deserted his people.[293]

When Ezekiel issued this parable many Jews in exile, along with those who were holding out in Jerusalem, must have hoped that the throne of David would blossom again in the persons of Zedekiah's immediate family. This chapter shows that, although it could not be, the throne of David would not only survive but would one day be dominant, yet not as an imperialistic, militarist power. **'I, Yahweh, have spoken, and I shall act'** (17:24). In Daniel 4:20-27 Nebuchadnezzar is compared to a gigantic tree which heaven commands to be chopped down. According to

Matthew 13:32, Jesus considered his own empire as a tree with small beginnings but with a splendid destiny. Scripture is internally consistent.

Application

Most of the Jews in Ezekiel's time considered that the Babylonian invasion of their sacred homeland was a disaster of vast proportions for which they might expect the imminent help of Yahweh. But they were wrong. The real problem was that over the centuries Israel had chosen to deride the covenant between God and themselves at Sinai. True to the terms of that covenant, Yahweh was withdrawing his presence and many other blessings from Israel, a people who would be abandoned to the mercies of an alien, cruel empire.

In our world, war and other afflictions are symptomatic of a deep-rooted problem — that of human sin. We often hear about human rights, yet neglect to consider our ultimate human responsibility — the duty of all men everywhere to repent and seek God.[294] Our priorities need to be realigned.

The agreement between Zedekiah and his Babylonian overlord was essentially a commitment by the Jewish king to Yahweh (17:19). When men break their promises to one another, they sin against the God of heaven.

Christ's kingdom cannot fail. Since the time of his death and glorification men everywhere have had good cause to admire the gentle shoot of David's line who, unlike any other empire builder, conquers and cleanses hearts.

The parable of the sour grapes (Ezekiel 18:1-32)

Jerusalem, the city of God, was under attack when this oracle was issued, and it was obvious to the wise, such as Ezekiel and Jeremiah, that woe would be heaped on woe. But why were these miseries the lot of the elect nation?

Thus far in his prophecy Ezekiel has warned that Jerusalem must soon suffer for its sins, yet — to judge by the present chapter — it appears that those in captivity were unready to admit their corporate and personal guilt. Ascribing to their forefathers the sins for which Judah was being punished, they developed a proverb: **'The fathers ate sour grapes, and the children's teeth are blunted?'**

That it was an adage also current in the homeland is indicated by Jeremiah 31:29:

> In those days [that is, in the age of the new covenant] they shall say no more:
>
> 'The fathers have eaten sour grapes,
> And the children's teeth are set on edge.'
>
> But every one shall die for his own iniquity; every man who eats the sour grapes, his teeth shall be set on edge.[295]

Lamentations 5:7 also reflects this popular yet false theodicy: 'Our fathers sinned and are no more, but we bear their iniquities.'[296]

Ezekiel gives Yahweh's response even though his words must have been unpalatable to many. His message is a biting rebuttal of a biased and erroneous interpretation of Israelite suffering.

Notwithstanding Ezekiel's message, on the surface the proverb must have seemed to many to hold some truth. Firstly, Exodus 20:5 states that 'I, Yahweh your God, am a jealous God, visiting the iniquity of the fathers on the children to the third and fourth generation of those who hate me,'[297] apparently telling that parental sin must inevitably have its account paid by the children in later times. As Wright observes, 'One generation's wickedness affects the quality of life for the next.'[298] But why this must be so would have been understood in more than one way.

Secondly, to travel no further than chapter 16, Ezekiel himself had taught that the Chaldean reduction of Israel was due to the latter's persistent infidelity: as far back as the Sinai covenant the twelve tribes had been perverse. It is not hard to see that the proverb must have seemed to some to encapsulate truth, a direct inference being that Yahweh was dealing unfairly with Ezekiel's immediate generation.

1. The proverb (18:1-2)

18:1-2. And the word of Yahweh came to me, saying, 'What is it to you, that you use this proverb against the earth of Israel, saying, "The fathers ate sour grapes, and the children's teeth are blunted?"'

So flagrant was the Jewish misunderstanding of exactly why Jerusalem was suffering that the Lord required Ezekiel to address his fellow-exiles: **'the**

word of Yahweh' came to him. Although it was not disputed by the Jews that the Babylonian incursion was an act of God, what was in dispute was *why* Yahweh had seen fit to grant the infliction, and whose sins in particular were responsible for these disasters. In Judah and among the exiles in Babylon it appears that many refused to accept that they personally were at fault. Rather, they cosseted themselves with the notion that their generation was sustaining a legacy of guilt handed down to them by sinful forefathers: they were being made to writhe because their forebears had been evil. Fallen men always tend to blame others for their own troubles.

In order to cement this convenient fallacy in the popular imagination, a proverb had been devised. It had a ring to it and caught the ear: **'The fathers ate sour grapes, and the children's teeth are blunted?'** The meaning is that the parents had sinned — that is, had unwisely devoured unripe grapes — but that the children's teeth were set on edge because of the acid taste for which they had no responsibility. Was it not so? The proverb seems to have been cast in question form, demanding an affirmative answer. The implication was that the fathers, rather than their innocent offspring, should have tasted the bitterness of their misdeeds, and that there had been something amiss with the divine economy (18:2).

At this point it may be useful to consider the Bible's overall teaching about inherited guilt.

It is true that Moses did teach the visitation of the sins of fathers upon their children: what parents had done, their offspring would also pay for. Indeed, Yahweh predicted this with reference to Israelite adulation of the false gods worshipped by the nations.[299]

Thus it was with the incident of the golden calf, fabricated by Aaron when the people complained that Moses had spent too long on the summit of Mount Sinai.[300] Yahweh informed Moses about what had happened in the camp and was told that the Lord keeps 'mercy for thousands, forgiving iniquity and transgression and sin; by no means clearing the guilty, visiting the iniquity of fathers on the children and on the children's children to the third and the fourth generations'.

Nor was this ever forgotten. At the time of the exile to Babylon, nearly one thousand years later than Moses, it was believed by some that Yahweh was applying the principle. Jeremiah wrote that the God of Israel shows 'loving-kindness for thousands', *yet* repays 'the iniquity of fathers into the bosom of their children after them — the Great, the Mighty God, whose name is Yahweh of hosts'.[301]

This prophet, almost contemporary with Ezekiel, had predicted that Yahweh would make Judah an object of horror among all the kingdoms of the earth because of Manasseh, the son of Hezekiah, for the atrocities he had earlier performed in Jerusalem.[302]

Centuries later, Jesus recognized that the sins of parents can be charged to their children:

> Therefore, indeed, I send you prophets, wise men, and scribes: some of them you will kill and crucify, and some of them you will scourge in your synagogues and persecute from city to city, that on you may come all the righteous blood shed on the earth, from the blood of righteous Abel to the blood of Zechariah, son of Berechiah, whom you murdered between the temple and the altar. Assuredly, I say to you, all these things will come upon this generation.[303]

Yet in Scripture there is another fundamental principle that runs in parallel, and this must not be forgotten. Deuteronomy 24:16 states specifically that 'Fathers shall not be put to death for their children, nor shall the children be put to death for their fathers;

a person shall be put to death for his own sin.' That is, an innocent son must never pay the price for his parent's offences. King Amaziah of Judah executed the men who murdered his father, Joash, but because Moses had forbidden further action he refrained from putting their sons to death.[304]

In reality, neither in the Old nor the New Testament is there a contradiction between what might be termed, on the one hand, collective and, on the other, individual responsibility. The warning that the sins of the fathers must be visited upon their children applies to succeeding generations of evil men who, from father to son and from son to grandson, and so on, habitually refuse to turn to the Lord in shame and repentance.

This is the crux of the issue. Throughout their generations such a family exercises a determined opposition to truth, none desiring to honour the terms of the greatest commandment and all conniving in a persistent and hearty aversion to the one God.[305] The family tree is infected from the deepest root to the topmost branch.

This is why at Pentecost the apostle Peter exhorted his penitent hearers to 'be saved from this perverse generation'.[306] His message was that if they refused to face up to their sins, they must suffer along with habitually impenitent Israel.

Because this was how it stood with Israel in the time of Ezekiel, how would Yahweh respond? Could he do no more than stand to one side and allow a people called by his name to continue in their apostasy?

Clearly, no. There would be a consequence, as dire as it was inevitable and just. Even as the sins of the children of Israel were cumulative, being heaped up generation by generation, so judgement, when it finally materialized, would be a reaction to apostasies both previous and contemporary. When the time came for a reckoning, the wrath of God would be levelled at the most recent exponents of the evils of their ancestors.

The current generation must suffer the displeasure of God both for its own sins and for the sins of those who had gone before, evils with which it had identified.

In Ezekiel's time, the decreed judgement was the destruction of Jerusalem and its temple, together with the overthrow of the throne of David and a mass deportation to Babylon, all betokening the withdrawal of the presence of Yahweh from the elect nation. This was seen to be in harmony with the truth that each man would suffer ('die') for his own sin. The deceased fathers had eaten sour grapes *and* their children had imitated them. Therefore, the teeth of the children would be set on edge for what their parents and they had shared.

This is the truth urged by Ezekiel upon his hearers. He has already stated that were '"these three men ... in its [Jerusalem's] midst, Noah, Daniel and Job, they would deliver their souls by their own righteousness," declares the Lord Yahweh' (see 14:14). An individual's personal faith and righteous conduct will save him — but only him.

One effect of this fallacious proverb and its perverse fatalism must have been a numbing of the consciences of the exiles, as well as of those who remained in Jerusalem. Given that divine judgement for the sins of previous generations was just over the horizon, as inexorable as it was unrelenting, why respond to the ministry of the likes of Jeremiah in Jerusalem and of Ezekiel in Babylonia? In that the God of Israel was a disappointment to them, why should they seek to honour his law as revealed through Moses? Let them eat, drink and be merry — for they were doomed to die.[307]

But Yahweh would have none of this shallow reasoning. As in 12:22, where another spurious maxim is challenged, he faces his antagonists: **'What is it to you, that you use this proverb?'** Ezekiel's hearers are brought back to reality. As indicated by 3:18-21;

9:4-6; 14:3-9; 33:1-20, God will condemn an individual if he remains unrepentant (18:1-2).

2. Individual responsibility (18:3-20)

18:3-20. '"'As I live', declares the Lord Yahweh, 'you will never again employ this proverb in Israel. Look, all souls are mine. As the soul of the father, so the soul of the son: they are mine. The soul who sins, it shall die.

'"'But if a man is righteous and practises judgement and righteousness, does not eat on the mountains and does not raise his eyes to the idols of the house of Israel, does not defile his neighbour's wife and does not approach a woman who menstruates; if a man does not oppress but restores the pledge of someone's debt, does not commit robbery but gives his bread to the hungry and covers the naked with clothing, and does not give money on interest and does not take profit; if he averts his hand from iniquity and executes true justice between man and man; if he walks in my statutes and observes my judgements to act truly — he is righteous. He will surely live,' declares the Lord Yahweh.

'"'Now, should he beget a violent son who sheds blood and who does any of these things (though he himself has not done these things) — that is, he eats upon the mountains and defiles his neighbour's wife, oppresses the poor and needy, commits robbery and does not return a pledge but raises his eyes to idols and commits abomination, gives money with interest and takes money with profit — shall he live? He will not live. He has committed all these abominations; he will surely be put to death. His blood shall be upon him.

'"'And, look, he begets a son who sees all his father's sins that he committed and he observes but does not do likewise. He does not eat on the mountains and he does not raise his eyes to the idols of the house of Israel; he does not defile his neighbour's wife and he does not oppress any man; he does not take a pledge and does not commit robbery; he gives his bread to the hungry and covers the naked with clothing. He keeps his hand from the poor, does not accept interest and profit and executes my judgements and walks in my statutes. He shall not die for his father's iniquity. He will surely live.

'"'As for his father, because he practised extortion, has robbed a brother and has done what is not good among his people — look, he shall die in his iniquity. Yet you are saying, "Why should not the son bear the guilt of his father's iniquity?" But the son has performed judgement and righteousness, has kept all my statutes and does them; he will surely live.

'"'The soul who sins, he shall die. A son will not bear the guilt of his father's sin, and a father will not bear the guilt of the son; the righteousness of the righteous will be upon him, and the wickedness of the wicked will be upon him.'"'

Whereas Jeremiah had anticipated a time when Israel would not want to employ this proverb,[308] Yahweh insists that it must be abandoned forthwith in that imminent events will lay bare its falsity: **'"As I live", declares the Lord Yahweh, "you will never again employ this proverb in Israel"'** (18:3).

The principle underlying divine judgement is presented. Because **'all souls'** belong to Yahweh, he is under no necessity to punish one individual in the place of another for his sins. **'The son'** is not necessarily accountable for his parent. As Wright comments, 'Human beings, far from living in the grip of fatalistic and impersonal laws, actually live in relation to the personal God, Yahweh, to whom all lives belong.'[309]

'Soul' translates the Hebrew *nephesh*, which, as in 13:20 and Genesis 2:7, means the totality of an individual's being. The equivalent New Testament word would be *psyché*, as in Acts 27:37: 'and all of us in the ship were two hundred and seventy-six *psychai* [souls]'. Ezekiel denies the fatalism of his contemporaries: Jews in Jerusalem and in exile are not to blame their misfortunes on their forefathers' sins. To **'die'** would mean, as in Genesis 2:17,[310] separation from God and all his benefits (18:4).

Four cases are now discussed in order to establish the principle: that of a just man who seeks to honour Yahweh (18:5-9); that of his evil son (18:10-13); that of the righteous son of a wicked man (18:14-20); and that of a change of attitude in an individual, whether from evil to righteousness or vice versa (18:21-29).

It has sometimes been suggested that these verses allude to the lives of the kings Hezekiah (who was righteous), Manasseh, his son (who was not), and Josiah, Manasseh's grandson (who, like his great-grandparent, was righteous).[311] Although this cannot be proved, we can imagine Ezekiel's hearers inferring a connection.

Firstly, Ezekiel introduces the case of someone who, in general terms, **'is righteous and practises righteousness and judgement'**, proceeding to clarify the typical lifestyle of such a person, 'righteousness' and 'judgement' typifying Yahweh himself, as every Jewish worshipper would have known (18:5).[312]

Taylor remarks that:

> This is no statement of justification by works; it is saying that a man's life is a matter of his heart. God does not average out a man's life; it is the direction of his commitment that counts. And basic to Ezekiel's analysis of the whole issue is that the Lord has no pleasure in the death of the wicked (18:23,32); He wants him to turn and live.[313]

Because values were blurred within the Israel of Ezekiel's time, the prophet had to restate ancient principles. True justice will spurn all forms of idolatry (**'does not eat on the mountains'**, presumably in honour of false gods; cf. 18:11) and will repudiate adultery and sexual uncleanness.[314] Leviticus 18:24-30 warns that moral abomination must lead to the expulsion of Israel from the land of Canaan, and the present verse (18:6) probably has this in mind.

Righteousness of this calibre is kind to a neighbour, will refuse a poor man's pledge for a loan, declines interest and spurns unlawful possession of another's property. It provides food and clothing for the poor in Israel.[315] Amos 2:6-8 and Malachi 3:5 remind us that orphans, widows and resident aliens were always vulnerable. Lending money at interest to a poor Israelite was evil because the debtor, being unable to repay, would have been forced into slavery. **'True justice between man and man'** is required at all times, the righteous Israelite not abusing the legal process in favour of dishonest personal gain (18:7-8).

So, where these conditions are honoured, there will be life rather than death. The Lawgiver blesses the one who honours his law. Yet again, the divine imprimatur seals the declaration: **'declares the Lord Yahweh'** (18:9). For Ezekiel, as in the Bible generally, morality is the outward expression of true religion: when God is ignored, behaviour degrades. In time, the 'secular' society will implode.

Ezekiel now contemplates a second case, that of the **'violent'** son of a righteous man. The significance of this term is that, whereas the father had done all in his power to uphold the interests of the vulnerable, the son is destructive. He **'sheds blood'** and **'does any of these things'**, by which are meant the offences detailed in 18:5-8. The point is that the integrity of the parent cannot shield the son from judgement, salvation not being communicated by their blood relationship (18:10).[316]

Ezekiel excludes all possible exceptions to the principle. Should an evil son be guilty of the sins mentioned previously, he must perish even though his father had committed none of them (18:11). Because his death is his own fault he can blame no one apart from himself.

Ezekiel understood that Moses' law was a unity. When one part is broken, the offender is accountable for his rejection of the whole.[317] The prophet asserts roundly that the immorality of the hypothetical son is an **'abomination'**, no less evil than the abomination of idolatry referred to in chapter 8 and the spiritual apostasy detailed in chapter 16 (18:12). Nor is this linkage coincidental: when men abandon the true God, they have the potential to sink into all manner of sin.

If, then, the evil son of a righteous father **'has committed all these abominations'**, having placed himself among those for whom God is their enemy, **'he will not live ... he will surely be put to death'**. By comparison with Leviticus 20:9-27, in which being 'put to death' occurs frequently, it appears that Ezekiel's point is that judicial execution may only be inflicted where there is personal guilt, the legal innocence of a parent not being imputed to an evil son.

Therefore, the latter's **'blood shall be upon him'** (18:13). But, since execution was tantamount to summary expulsion from Israel, and hence from the society in which God was pleased to dwell, Ezekiel anticipates the New Testament doctrine of eternal alienation from God and from his heavenly abode.

Ezekiel offers a third hypothetical case. As if to emphasize the inflexibility of the principle of personal accountability, he bids his hearers to **'look'**. Suppose that **'he'**, by which Ezekiel means an evil child of a righteous father, **'begets a son who sees all his father's sins ... but does not do likewise'** (18:14). Because the third-generation offspring ponders his immediate parent's misdeeds and, like the Christian convert of 1 Peter 1:18, disassociates from the evils commended to him by his own family, he will not be charged for his father's sins. Even though the latter must die, **'he'**, the son who is faithful to the terms of the covenant between Yahweh and Israel, **'will surely live'** (18:14-17).

Glancing back to the second case, that of the situation of the second-generation evil son of a righteous parent, Ezekiel anticipates that his hearers will criticize his teaching. Why, they will object, should *his* righteous, third-generation, son not bear some responsibility for the sins of his immediate parent? Why should he not be asked to pay something? After all, close blood relationships cannot be denied, and a family, whether it stands or falls, cannot be divided. If one member is honoured, all benefit. Conversely, if one member disgraces the family name, all should be expected to share the reproach.

As if to demolish the fallacy that guilt is a corporate matter irrespective of the righteous attitude of some, Ezekiel notes that even if the hypothetical second-generation parent had **'practised extortion'**,[318] had **'robbed a brother'** and had **'done what is not good among his people'**,[319] his righteous son who **'has kept all my statutes'**, whose heart is in conformity with the demands of the covenant, will not be held accountable: **'he will surely live'**. There is no such thing as blanket guilt any more than there can be blanket innocence, according to which fallacy the elect status of Israel would cover up the impenitence of many within the nation (18:18-19).

So it is only **'the soul who sins'** who **'shall die'**. The notion that a righteous person must suffer for the sins of someone who is wicked in heart and conduct — even though the relationship is that of son to a father — is shattered, as also the grim fatalism of a proverb that in effect denied the utility, let alone the rightness, of repentance (18:20). Marvellously, the truth that a refusal to submit to evil norms is not only right, but will attract the blessing of the Lord, will be set out in the next three verses.

3. The Lord does not rejoice in judgement (18:21-23)

18:21-23. '"'But as for the wicked person, if he turns from all his sins which he has committed and observes all my statutes and practises justice and righteousness — he will surely live; he will not die! None of all his transgressions that he has committed will be remembered against him — in the righteousness that he has practised, he will live! Do I delight in the death of the wicked?' declares the Lord Yahweh. 'Is it not when he turns from his ways — and lives?'"'

If the principle of common guilt leading to collective punishment applies (and Ezekiel 18 never denies this), how might a sinner distance himself from the judgement he would otherwise share with others? Having disposed of the popular misinterpretation of the law, Ezekiel addresses this critical issue. His message is that if a wicked man abandons his sinful way of life and honours Yahweh's commands, he will live. He will not die, since his previous misdeeds will not be charged to his account (18:21-22).

The Lord expresses this in the form of two questions, the first demanding a negative answer and the second, a positive: **'"Do I delight in the death of the wicked?" declares the Lord Yahweh. "Is it not when he turns from his ways — and lives?"'** That is, does God take a sadistic delight in condemnation and execution? Does he gloat when sinners are consigned to destruction? Never! Rather, does he not rejoice when he sees a sinner turning from his ways to find life? Nothing pleases him more. 'There is joy in the presence of the angels of God over one sinner who repents.'[320]

A delightful and essential logic permeates these verses. If Ezekiel demolishes the stale argument that because the sins of the fathers must be reckoned to their innocent children — a dogma which could only have generated moral lethargy among those who were duped by it — he must now encourage the sinful to repent in the awareness that it is the chief glory of God to forgive rather than to condemn.[321]

To repeat, we do not have here a doctrine of justification by works. Ezekiel's concern is with the direction of the heart rather than with a notional balancing of evil against good. Where a man's attitude to God is as it ought to be, **'he will surely live; he will not die!'** Further, **'None of all his transgressions that he has committed will be remembered against him — in the righteousness that he has practised, he will live!'** It is the will of God that men yield their obedience to him, thus fulfilling the design for which they were granted life. If a sinner does turn back to the Lord, the Lord will turn to him in mercy.

Shortly before the end of his life Moses had set before Israel 'life and good, death and evil' and 'life and death, blessing and cursing', urging his hearers and all who would follow them to 'choose life'.[322] Since that time the twelve tribes had shown themselves to be non-compliant, reducing the Sinai covenant to a dead letter. But, according to Ezekiel, Yahweh's promise still holds good: if an Israelite who abandons the covenant turns back to his God, he will be granted life, by which is meant the divine presence with all its attendant blessings. Life is God's creation, his pleasure, his desire and his gracious gift (18:23).[323]

4. Yahweh and Israel confront each other (18:24-29)

18:24-29. '"'And when a righteous man turns from his righteousness and commits iniquity, like all the abominations that a wicked man practises, will he do this and live? None of his righteous deeds that he has done will be remembered for the treachery that he has practised and for the sin that he has committed. He will die for them. Yet you are saying, "The way of the Lord is not measured."

'"'Hear, now, O house of Israel. Is my way not measured? Is it not your ways that are not measured? When a righteous person turns from his righteousness and commits iniquity, he dies for them; in the iniquity that he practises, he will die. And when a wicked person turns from his wickedness which he has done and practises justice and righteousness, he will preserve his life. For he has seen and has turned from all his transgressions that he committed — he shall live; he will not die. But the house of Israel is saying, "The way of the Lord is not measured." Is it my ways that are not measured, O house of Israel? Is it not your ways that are not measured?'"'

On the other hand, if a man's righteousness is hypocritical and temporary he will not live. Because he proves himself to be unfaithful he must die. The point is that the state of a man's heart determines his standing before God: if he is an apostate, an apparently holy lifestyle prior to his perversion cannot save him. Ezekiel does no more than repeat the axiom declared by 3:20: 'And when a righteous person turns from his righteousness and practises evil, and I set a stumbling block in front of him, he will die.'

Ezekiel has exploded two related perceptions. Firstly, he rebuts the belief that a man — any man — can accumulate a treasury of either sin or merit such that his status before God remains permanently fixed. Secondly, he refutes the notion that the spiritual status of a man will determine that of others, however near they may be to him. The only factor that is of overriding importance is the state of a man's heart when the time comes for him to undergo divine scrutiny. Then, if his attitude to Yahweh is right, he will live; if it is wrong, he must die (18:24).

When Ezekiel delivered this oracle he knew that it would not be well received. Like Paul in a later century and in another situation,[324] he anticipated the objections that perverse opponents would inevitably raise.

Such folk had committed themselves to the view that the God of Israel had dealt unfairly with them in that they did not merit the Babylonian invasion and subsequent exile: **'Yet you are saying, "The way of the Lord is not measured."'** 'Not measured' (*lô yittaken*, from a root meaning 'to determine')[325] shows that they considered the actions of God to have been capricious and unjust; they blamed him as well as their forefathers for their predicament.

The imputation is hurled back into the face of Ezekiel's critics, the prophet reiterating the assertion of 1 Samuel 2:3: 'For Yahweh is the God of knowledge; and by him actions are weighed.' If there is instability, it is not with God: **'Hear, now, O house of Israel. Is my way not measured? Is it not your ways that are not measured?'**

To reinforce this counteraccusation, Ezekiel reflects upon the statements of 18:21-24. The assertion of 18:27 that the repentant sinner **'will preserve his life'** does not mean that he can save himself by his own merit. Rather, as a rational being, the man is obliged to adopt a course of action that will lead to his salvation. Yet 18:29 suggests that Ezekiel was pessimistic, unsure that his message would be received: **'But the house of Israel is saying, "The way of the Lord is not measured." Is it my ways that are not measured, O house of Israel? Is it not your ways that are not measured?'** (18:25-29).

5. An encouragement (18:30-32)

18:30-32. '"'Therefore, I shall judge you, each man according to his ways, O house of Israel,' declares the Lord Yahweh. 'Repent and turn from all your transgressions, so that iniquity does not become a stumbling block for you. Cast all your transgressions, with which you have transgressed, from you and make for yourselves a new heart and a new spirit — and why should you die, O house of Israel? For I do not delight in the death of the dying,' declares the Lord Yahweh. 'So, repent and live.'"'

Ezekiel's message concludes with an exhortation to the **'house of Israel'** to **'repent and turn from all your transgressions'**, the reason being that Yahweh will **'judge you, each man according to his ways'**. Yet again, the criterion of Yahweh's assessment of a man is his attitude to the Lord at the occasion of judgement, whatever his previous life, or the sins of his forebears, may have been. **'Stumbling block'** repeats from 3:20: 'And when a righteous person turns from his righteousness and practises evil, and I set a stumbling block in front of him, he will die.' Yahweh allows those who are called by his name to be tempted by evil, although he never entices them to sin. But should they offend, their sins will precipitate a collapse (18:30).

Not only are the people of Israel commanded to **'cast all** [their] **transgressions'** away, they are to **'make for** [themselves] **a new heart and a new spirit'**. The **'new heart'** and the **'new spirit'** signify a fundamentally changed attitude towards God: remarkably, sinners are required to regenerate themselves. It is solely their responsibility, upon which depends their future. So let them ask themselves a pertinent question: **'Why should** [they] **die?'** If they do, they have only themselves to blame. There is no point to it, nothing to be gained by it, no rational explanation for it.

Given the fact that Jerusalem was currently under attack by the Chaldeans, this might have meant, inter alia, that those in the city, as well as the exiles, should have reconciled themselves to the fact that Yahweh had designed to bring about the collapse of the theocracy of Israel. According to Jeremiah 21:8-9, 'the way of life' meant surrendering to the enemy, and 'the way of death' holding out against the Babylonians. Genuine repentance, then, would have yielded the admission that Ezekiel's message to the exiles was true.

The present verse is remarkable for at least two reasons. Firstly, along with 18:30, the whole constituency of Israel is addressed as if it were apostate, as if (say) a zealous minister of a nominally evangelical church were to come to his congregation and urge them all to be converted. One can imagine the opprobrium that he might attract by so doing, even if he was right in his diagnosis of their spiritual condition.

Secondly, Ezekiel summons his people to regenerate themselves, fully aware that they would not and could not do the thing (18:31). As is admitted by 36:26 (cf. 11:19),[326] the new birth is essentially a gift from God. In any case, in the years following the occasion at Sinai when Israel had been summoned into a covenant relation with Yahweh, the twelve tribes had never shown any inclination to renew themselves spiritually and morally. Indeed, degeneration had always been the norm. So why the command? The simple yet elegant answer must be that what sinful men cannot and will not do nevertheless remains their duty. Original sin, with all its catastrophic effects, does not vitiate our obligation to turn to the living God. One can compare with Deuteronomy 10:16 and 30:6. In the former verse, Israel is commanded to 'circumcise the foreskin of' the 'heart', and in the latter it is predicted that Yahweh will one day perform this action so that Israel will be in a position to fulfil Deuteronomy 6:5, the greatest commandment.

To press home a truth that Israel needed to know, the final verse of the chapter repeats 18:23, but in a more emphatic form: Yahweh does not **'delight in the death of the dying'**. When the Lord perceives someone perishing for lack of repentance, he is unhappy even though the thing must be. God is never gleeful when a guilty person is lost. May it not be suggested that eternal destruction pains the Lord even though he ordains it to magnify his justice? **'So'**, let the exiles take courage: **'repent and live'** (18:32).

Ezekiel's immediate burden has been discharged. Let the people of Israel, whether those remaining in Jerusalem or those already carried into exile, face up to reality. Let the present generation of the family of Abraham accept that if they do not renounce the sins of their fathers they, too, must be judged. The promise of mercy and deliverance is held out even as Nebuchadnezzar busily invests Jerusalem. Sadly, however, the prophet has no expectation that his message will be heard.

Application

Nominal membership of a church, especially if it is evangelical in tradition, is inadequate: we need to turn to Christ personally before we seek to join a community of believers, rather than adhering to a church in order, hopefully, to be reconciled with God (as is the sacramental procedure). Ezekiel addresses Israel rather than the pagan world when he exhorts his hearers to repent.

Thankfully, there is always hope. Whatever our past and whatever our origins, if we seek the Lord he will receive us. It can never be too early to turn to the Lord, and it is never too late. But, having said this, we are not permitted to rest upon past experience. Paul commanded the baptized Corinthians to 'examine' themselves and only then to 'eat of that bread and drink of that cup'.[327]

Every Christian pulpit must tell out that because God is love he never delights to see any man wallowing in sin and unbelief, facing just condemnation. Let every preacher in every sermon insist that there is a heavenly welcome for all who turn to Christ.

Although a true conversion is an act of the freed will rather than of free will (so to speak), the unregenerate man has a positive responsibility to renew himself. Were this not so, the whole fabric of New Testament evangelism would collapse. It is because men are rational beings created in the image of God that they are required to repent and believe the gospel.[328] The fact that they are dead in sin does not cancel their duty to believe.[329]

The Bible teaches that, although in his grace God determines to save some, he does not purpose to save all.[330] And it also teaches that he never delights in seeing any man finally perish in sin. Therefore, if Scripture remains comfortable with what may appear to us to be an antinomy, we should be content to await the glory when, perhaps, we shall have access to more knowledge about God than is available now.

The (temporary) fall of the house of David (Ezekiel 19:1-14)

Chapter 19, a lamentation, brings to an end the long series of prophecies that commenced in about September 592 BC with Ezekiel's vision of idolatrous practices in Jerusalem (8:1). A new stage in his prophetic ministry will commence at 20:1, recording the visit of a deputation of elders to him in August 591 BC. This would mean that the content of the present chapter was given to Ezekiel about five years or so before the destruction of Jerusalem in 586 BC.

This lamentation concerns the imminent overthrow of the house of David, the tactic being to dissolve any lingering hopes that the throne might survive Nebuchadnezzar's onslaught.

In order to understand what Ezekiel says it might be helpful to recapitulate the events leading up to the final overthrow of Judah by the Chaldeans, and perhaps to look again at the genealogy outlined in the comments on chapter 17. An awareness of the background history to these chapters is essential if we want to appreciate the force of Ezekiel's words, and this may justify the repetition.

Godly King Josiah died in battle about 609 BC, having instituted a religious reformation in Judah. Jehoahaz, his twenty-three-year-old son, succeeded him. During his brief three-month reign the latter did evil prior to being deported to Egypt by Pharaoh Necho, where he died. He was replaced by his elder brother Eliakim, whose name was altered by the same pharaoh to Jehoiakim. This man reigned for eleven years and, like his fathers, sinned against Yahweh.

During Jehoiakim's reign the Egyptians were vanquished by the armies of Babylon at Carchemish in 605 BC. Nebuchadnezzar now cast his lurid shadow far and wide. Invading Judah, he made Jehoiakim his vassal. Three years later, the Jewish monarch rebelled.

His kingdom continued to be attacked by the Chaldeans and others as a punishment from God for the sins of Manasseh, grandfather of Josiah. After Jehoiakim's death, his eighteen-year-old son Jehoiachin succeeded him. This was in 597 BC. He reigned for just three months and, in a fashion typical of many, though not all, of his predecessors, 'did evil in the sight of Yahweh'. These words could be understood as virtually an epitaph for the last kings of Judah.

The assault on Jerusalem persisted, Jehoiachin surrendering to be deported to Babylon. It was at this time that the prophet-priest Ezekiel was removed to the same place. However, neither Jerusalem nor the temple was destroyed immediately. Jehoiachin's uncle, Mattaniah,[331] was installed as a puppet ruler by Nebuchadnezzar, who altered his name to Zedekiah.

Twenty-one years old when he became king, this man, concerning whom Jeremiah and Ezekiel have nothing good to say, reigned for eleven years. Nine years into his reign he resolved to turn against Nebuchadnezzar. The Chaldeans reacted violently, placing Jerusalem again under siege. This assault lasted for two to three years, after which the city was stormed and the temple destroyed. Zedekiah was blinded and taken prisoner to Babylon. But that was not the end of the matter: many years later Jehoiachin was released from captivity in Babylon, although he never went back to Judah.[332]

Chapter 19 divides into two parts. Firstly, the rulers of Judah are pictured as young, wild lions (19:1-9).

Secondly, the people are likened to a vine torn from the soil and transplanted elsewhere (19:10-14).

This lamentation is based upon Genesis 49:8-12, which records Jacob's prediction that within the family of Israel Judah would be granted a royal ascendancy and in time would give rise to 'Shiloh', probably meaning 'he whose it is',[333] the Messiah:

> Judah, you are he whom your brothers shall praise;
> Your hand shall be on the neck of your enemies;
> Your father's children shall bow down before you.
> Judah is a lion's whelp;
> From the prey, my son, you have gone up.
> He bows down, he lies down as a lion;
> And as a lion, who shall rouse him?
> The sceptre shall not depart from Judah,
> Nor a lawgiver from between his feet,
> Until Shiloh comes;
> And to him shall be the obedience of the people.
> Binding his donkey to the vine,
> And his donkey's colt to the choice vine,
> He [Judah] washed his garments in wine,
> And his clothes in the blood of grapes.
> His eyes are darker than wine
> And his teeth whiter than milk.[334]

In this passage not only is Judah said to be a 'lion's whelp', but mention is made of 'the sceptre', 'the vine' and 'blood'. A comparison of the Hebrew words in the two passages would seem to confirm that Ezekiel 19 draws upon Genesis 49.[335]

Surprisingly, perhaps, although 19:1 announces that Ezekiel is to **'take up a lamentation for the princes of Israel'**, it needs to be asked whether 19:1-14 is a purely an Old Testament-style lamentation or dirge of a type which frequently — although not here — commences with 'how' or 'alas'.[336] Furthermore, Old Testament lamentations focus upon past events, such as the lament of David over the defeat of Israel at Gilboa and the deaths of Jonathan and his father Saul.[337] There the subjects of such lamentations are unambiguous.

But Ezekiel's lamentation anticipates (presumably) the downfall of the house of David and the theocracy of Israel, leaving the reader to work out for himself the identity of the two lions, their mother and the vine that reaches to the clouds.

For these reasons the **'lamentation'** would appear to be a riddle in the style of the (interpreted) riddle of 17:1-10. Ezekiel's immediate hearers must have been puzzled — to say the least — about what they were being told, although the significance of the prophet's words would have been apparent a number of years later, when they received news of the destruction of Jerusalem.[338]

An analogy would be Isaiah 14:4-21, which parodied the king of Babylon a century and a half before the collapse of Babylon. In a similar fashion Ezekiel parodies the incumbents of the throne of David in Jerusalem *prior* to that throne being cast down, in apparent contradiction of the promise of Yahweh's everlasting covenant with David.[339]

And it is the predictive element and riddle-like mood alike that bring drama and vivacity to the 'lamentation'. Unlike so many of his fellow-exiles, not to mention those who were holding out in besieged Jerusalem, Ezekiel was convinced that the Chaldeans' punitive assault upon the city would lead inexorably to its destruction and the collapse of the Davidic monarchy. Therefore he issues a lamentation in advance of the event, expecting that in time its burden will become obvious.

1. The young lions (19:1-9)

19:1-9. 'And you, take up a lamentation for the princes of Israel, and you will say, "What was your mother? A lioness! She lay among the lions; among the young lions she reared her cubs. She brought up one of her cubs; he became a young lion. He learned to tear prey; he devoured men. Then the nations heard of him; he was caught in their pit and they brought him with hooks to the land of Egypt. And when she saw that she had been made to wait, that her hope was lost, then she took one of her cubs and made him a young lion. So he walked about among the lions and became a young lion — he learned to tear prey; he devoured men. Then he knew his widows and devastated their cities. The land and its fulness were appalled at the sound of his roaring.

'"Then the nations from the surrounding provinces attacked him. They spread their net over him; in their pit he was captured. Then they placed him in a cage with hooks and brought him to the king of Babylon. They brought him in hunting nets so that his voice should be heard no more on the mountains of Israel."'

Ezekiel was instructed to publish a **'lamentation for the princes of Israel'**. Unusually, there is no introduction, such as 'The word of Yahweh came to me, saying'.[340] Moreover, neither the incumbent of the throne of David, Zedekiah, is mentioned by name, nor any particular members of the royal family. This may be because Yahweh (and Ezekiel) held Zedekiah and his immediate family in very low esteem: Zedekiah may have been a prince of the blood, but he was no true king nor, in spirit, son of David. Zedekiah's fate was predicted in 12:1-16, and 17:1-24 focused upon Jehoiachin and Zedekiah. Now attention is given to the downfall of the whole princely family of David (19:1).

That Ezekiel propounds a lamentation in riddle form is indicated by the opening challenge: **'What was**

your mother?' rather than '*Who* was your mother?' She was, in fact, **'a lioness'**. That Ezekiel points to the nation of Israel as the corporate **'mother'** of the family of David is shown by 19:10: 'Your mother was like a vine full of shoots, planted by the waters.' The lion was a figure for Israel and probably for the family of David.[341]

'She lay among the lions; among the young lions she reared her cubs' (19:2). Does this mean that Israel had abandoned her high calling to descend to the low level of nations near and far, becoming one of them? Possibly so. But what of her cubs? The following verses will tell. At this early stage in the narrative Ezekiel's hearers must have been riveted to his words.

A litter of lions usually consists of between two and five cubs. Here, the lioness, Israel, singles out just one of her cubs which **'became a young lion'**. As such, **'he learned to tear prey; he devoured men'**. Although attacking men is not unusual for the species,[342] this young lion developed a singular craving for human flesh.

But vengeance caught up with the beast. Because it devoured men it was seized and taken **'to the land of Egypt'**. This helps to identify the young lion as Jehoahaz, who followed his immediate father Josiah upon the throne of David. 'He did evil in the sight of Yahweh, according to all that his fathers had done,' after which, as noted, Pharaoh Necho removed him.[343] In saying that he **'devoured men'**, perhaps Ezekiel knew more about Jehoahaz than is revealed by the terse comment in 2 Kings 23:31-33. The prophet's words suggest that he had been led captive by a rope attached to a hook piercing his lips (19:3-4).[344]

The lioness, Israel, realizing that the favoured young cub, Jehoahaz, had vanished and that **'she had been made to wait'**, selected another 'cub'. She raised it until it, too, grew up to be a **'young lion'** (19:5). But what was she waiting for? Perhaps that she might be like other lionesses in the pride — alias the surrounding nations — desiring to abandon her calling as Israel, the unique theocracy.

Passing over Jehoiakim, brother of Jehoahaz and his successor, the riddle/lamentation moves immediately to the former's son, Jehoiachin. When he ascended David's throne, Jerusalem was already being attacked because of Jehoiakim, appointed king by the pharaoh of the time and who had refused to pay tribute to Nebuchadnezzar.[345] This man 'did evil in the sight of Yahweh, according to all that his fathers had done'.[346] Although Nebuchadnezzar deported him to Babylon, he seems to have returned and to have died tragically in or near Jerusalem.[347]

As has already been noted, Jehoiachin, at the age of eighteen when he became king, reigned for a mere three months and also did evil.[348] It was a case of like father, like son, the record in 2 Kings being almost a commentary on Ezekiel 18.

But why does Ezekiel's riddle point neither to Jehoiakim nor to Zedekiah, king in Jerusalem when it was first issued? Perhaps Ezekiel looked upon Jehoahaz and Jehoiachin as representatives of the family of David rather than the former two men who were, respectively, a deceased puppet of Pharaoh and a still-living puppet of Nebuchadnezzar, and who were therefore not kings in the true sense of the term. References to them would probably have been deemed inappropriate.

The second cub's behaviour is given more attention than that of the first: **'So he walked about among the lions and became a young lion — he learned to tear prey; he devoured men.'** Seemingly, the youthful Jehoiachin sought to be the dominant male in the pride of lions, vainly desiring that his throne be on a par with those of other nations, and was eminently cruel (19:6). That **'he knew his widows'** may mean that, in the manner of Absalom, son of David,[349] he consorted with his predecessor's women in order to consolidate his throne.[350] Because, as a savage lion, he **'devastated'** the **'cities'** of Judah, the population — **'the land and its fulness'** — were terrified (19:7). Only three months were needed for Jehoiachin to wreak havoc.

Remarkably, **'the nations from the surrounding provinces'**, by which would be meant the component provinces of the empire of Babylon, stepped in to liberate **'the mountains of Israel'** so that **'his voice should be heard no more'**. Like Jehoahaz eleven or so years previously, this young lion was trapped and then deported **'in hunting nets'**, so to speak, but now **'to ... Babylon'**. The reader of this riddle / lamentation will recall that if Jehoiachin is the second young lion, Ezekiel was taken to Chaldea when Jehoiachin was captured. The prophet must have contemplated 19:9 ruefully, aware that Yahweh had employed a pagan sense of natural justice to bring about the temporary collapse of the house of David (19:8-9).

2. A transplanted vine (19:10-14)

19:10-14. '"Your mother was like a vine in your blood, planted by the waters. She was fruitful and full of branches because of the many waters. And the strong branches were for her sceptres of rulers, and her height was elevated among the clouds so that it was seen in its height in the multitude of its boughs. But it was rooted up in fury, it was cast down to the ground and the east wind caused her fruit to dry up. It was torn away and was dried up. As for its strong branch, fire devoured it. Thus, it is planted in the wilderness, in a dry and thirsty land. Fire has gone out from the branch of its shoots and has devoured its fruit — and there is no strong branch, a sceptre with which to rule, in it." This is a lamentation, and has become a lamentation.'

The figure changes dramatically. Now Israel is likened to a restful vine, and one not at all like the low, spreading vine of 17:6, nor even the charred vine of 15:1-6. The symbol of the vine was not new in Ezekiel's time, and would appear again.[351] As observed earlier, the link with Genesis 49:8-12 seems certain because both passages mention the **'vine'**, **'blood'** and **'sceptre'**.

'Your mother' would be Israel (cf. 19:2), and is likened to **'a vine'**. Unlike 19:1-9, which focuses upon the lioness's cubs, this element within the overall presentation concerns the mother herself. She was a vine 'full of shoots' and was **'fruitful and full of branches because of the many waters'**, meaning that initially Israel resembled a healthy, strong plant (19:10). **'In your blood'** is enigmatic and the Hebrew text has been the subject of emendation by some commentators. Yet, taken as it stands, it may mean, 'Your mother is like a vine living in the blood [that is, in the life] of her children,' which makes sense.[352]

Planted by the water, this vine put out **'strong branches'**, of which some were unusually sturdy, sufficiently rigid to become **'sceptres of rulers'**.[353] Because it attained to the **'clouds'**, a hyperbolical expression, all could see its many branches. But 'clouds' could mean 'branches' (*a'bôtim*; cf. 31:3,10,14), in which case there might be another play on words: these branches of David's line thought they were high and mighty (19:11).

Then came tragedy. An unnamed individual resented the vine and angrily pulled it out of the ground. **'Torn away'** and exposed to the searing heat of an **'east wind'**, and with no intake of water, it **'was dried up'**. The attacker would have been Yahweh himself (cf. 5:13), indignant because the vine of Israel had sought to become a lofty tree instead of a lowly vine content to produce grapes (cf. Assyria, the cedar, 31:3). Of course, Nebuchadnezzar was the immediate agent of destruction and transplantation. **'Its strong branch'** was **'devoured'** by **'fire'**, meaning that the throne of David was cast down (19:12).

Further, the vine's root — the pathetic remnant of Judah — was (presumably) seized by the marauder (again, Yahweh) and was **'planted in the wilderness, in a dry and thirsty land'**, where — when Ezekiel issued the riddle / lamentation — it remained. Babylonia was no pleasant place to which to be deported (19:13).

In the final verse attention is given to **'the branch of its shoots'**, meaning just one of the 'branches', alias 'sceptres', mentioned in 19:11. Instead of the fire of Yahweh's wrath consuming the vine, the branch burned what was left of **'its fruit'**. The reference is to Zedekiah and his duplicity in betraying his solemn covenant with Nebuchadnezzar: the flame of revolt led to the ruin of Jerusalem in that it triggered Nebuchadnezzar's final assault upon the city, its devastation and the fall of the throne of David.[354] In consequence, **'there is no strong branch, a sceptre with which to rule, in it'**. Who from the line of David will be in a position to assume the crown and govern with authority?

The dirge climaxes: **'This is a lamentation, and has become a lamentation.'** The holocaust, burning in Ezekiel's day, will be all-consuming (19:14).

Application

When Jacob prepared to leave this world he announced that Yahweh had decreed that Israel would eventually be a monarchy and that her kings would emanate from the tribe of Judah.[355] At a later time Yahweh revealed to Nathan the prophet that, far from David building a house for God, Yahweh would build David's house — that is, he would invest David's line with royal authority — and that his 'seed' would build the house of Yahweh. It was added that 'if his 'seed' offended, he would be 'chastened' 'with the rod of men' — that is, by punitive invasion. Yet, for all that, the throne of David would perpetuate.[356] Although this promise has fulfilled itself in the person of Jesus, the Messiah,[357] it applied to the royal line of David in the centuries preceding the incarnation. Unhappily, Jehoahaz, Jehoiakim, Jehoiachin and (particularly) Zedekiah, as well as numerous of their predecessors, chose to ignore the warning in Yahweh's word to Nathan, imagining that they were immune from judgement. Neglecting the stipulations of Deuteronomy 17:14-20, they were tragically wrong.

Not only does pride distort personality, it severs us from the mercies of God. Those who would be great in his kingdom must learn to serve their fellows as well as their God.[358]

Remarkably, 19:7-9 suggests that so appalling was the brief reign of Jehoiachin that Babylon determined to bring him down. The children of the world always scrutinize the churches and will never be slow to find fault. Sadly, they are sometimes justified in their criticisms.[359] If the 'salt of the earth' loses its savour, it must be discarded.[360] This is precisely what happened to Judah in the time of Ezekiel. If Christians do not live in holiness, who will?

3. The third series of prophecies

(Ezekiel 20:1 – 23:49)

It is now the seventh year, the fifth month and the tenth day since Jehoiachin was exiled. This translates to 9 August 591 BC.

Clearly, Ezekiel remembered the occasion well. Eleven months had passed since the commencement of the previous series of visions and oracles (8:1), and it was a little more than two years since Ezekiel had been called to the prophetic office (1:2). Now he issues a new series of prophecies that extend to the end of chapter 23. Following this, he will wait two years and five months before speaking again (see 24:1).

In this present series, which occurs about halfway through the initial phase of Ezekiel's ministry prior to the fall of Jerusalem, the prophet 'judges' the people: again he shows them their sins and predicts the consequences.

Israel's sad record (Ezekiel 20:1-44)

This chapter concerns itself with Israel's past, present and future (20:1-44), verses 45-49 really belonging to chapter 21. Unlike chapter 16, which covers the same ground, the present oracle is strictly non-allegorical. The immediate circumstances in which Ezekiel delivered his burden from Yahweh are disclosed in 20:1-3. In effect, chapters 20 – 23 enlarge upon the warnings of chapters 14 – 19, in which the principles of divine judgement were outlined (chapters 14; 15; 18) and in which the imminent collapse of the throne of David was predicted (chapters 17; 19). Yet Ezekiel shows that the prospects for Israel, though bleak in the short term, are far from hopeless, in that the promises of 20:32-44 have their foundation in the Messianic expectations of 11:17-20; 16:60-63 and 17:22-24.

What we find in chapter 20 is a report of Israel's past record of consistent rebellion against Yahweh, an account which, to Ezekiel's immediate audience, must have seemed revisionist in the extreme, even as, in a later century, was the address of the proto-martyr Stephen to the Sanhedrin.[1]

Several themes occur in this chapter: the rebelliousness of Israel in spite of Yahweh's mercies and in spite of his restraining his wrath; the journey in the wilderness, which demonstrated Israel's resolve to dishonour the covenant; and Yahweh's concern for the reputation of his own name, expressed by his determination to reconcile Israel to himself as a renewed people notwithstanding their evil ways.[2] In detail, this lengthy chapter may be said to divide into the following sections:

1. A preface (20:1-4)
2. Israel in Egypt (20:5-9)
3. The first wilderness generation (20:10-17)
4. The second wilderness generation (20:18-26)
5. Israel in the land of promise (20:27-29)
6. Israel in exile (20:30-31)
7. Israel in the desert of the peoples (20:32-38)
8. Israel residing on Yahweh's holy mountain (20:39-44).[3]

1. A preface (20:1-4)

20:1-4. And it was in the seventh year, in the fifth, on the tenth of the month, that men from the elders of Israel came to enquire of Yahweh and sat before me. And the word of Yahweh came to me, saying, 'Son of man, speak to the elders of Israel. You will say to them, "Thus says the Lord Yahweh: 'Are you coming to enquire of me? As I live, I shall not be enquired of by you,' declares the Lord Yahweh." Will you judge them? Will you judge, son of man? Make known to them their fathers' abominations.'

Ezekiel's stature as a prophet of Yahweh had now been established and, as in 14:1 (cf. 8:1), he was approached by **'men from the elders of Israel'** that he might **'enquire of Yahweh'** on their behalf. The date, as noted, is given precisely: **'in the seventh year, in the fifth** [month], **on the tenth of the month'**, which translates to 9 August 591 BC. It is possible that they came to him to receive some assurance that Jerusalem would not fall to the Chaldeans and that they might expect to return home in the not-too-distant future.

Was this a reaction to disappointment, in that Hananiah's prophecy of a return from exile in Zedekiah's sixth year (our 591 BC) was showing no signs of fulfilment? Or perhaps they had in mind Deuteronomy 4:29, which, anticipating Israelite apostasy and deportation from Canaan, had declared that 'from there [that is, in exile] you will seek Yahweh your God, and you will find him if you seek him with all your heart and all your soul'. They **'sat before'** Ezekiel, no doubt expecting a positive declaration from him (20:1).[4]

While we can imagine the scene, the Lord actually witnessed it. What is more, he responded: **'And the word of Yahweh came to me, saying'** (20:2). The divine rejoinder, much as that recorded in 14:3, was that the **'son of man'** should **'speak to the elders of Israel'** and **'say to them, "Thus says the Lord Yahweh: 'Are you coming to enquire of me? As I live, I shall not be enquired of by you.'"'** Yahweh **'declares'** this emphatically: he has nothing good to say about them (20:3). Whether they were aware of it or not, they were in the situation in which Saul found himself just before he died.[5]

Then a rhetorical question is addressed to Ezekiel. Although the prophet will transmit no word of comfort to the elders, he is asked, **'Will you judge them? Will you judge, son of man?'** (cf. 22:2; 23:36). In context, 'judge' means to bring to trial, and the question is really an affirmative. Ezekiel will accuse them![6]

In detail, he is to **'make known to them their fathers' abominations'**. The significance of this instruction is that the elders who sat before Ezekiel were in no frame of mind to qualify for the promise of Deuteronomy 4:29 because they had identified with the sins of previous generations. But what sins? According to Deuteronomy 18:9-12,[7] Israel, prohibited from adopting the 'abominations of those nations' who were then in occupation of Canaan, was (it is implied) to rely upon legitimate prophecy. The following verses tell that a 'prophet' like Moses — that is, the Christ — would eventually appear.[8]

Now, consistently with 5:6; 6:11; 8:6,9,17; 9:4; 12:16 and 16:47-58 and their contexts, Ezekiel must insist that his hearers are no better than the unclean nations ejected by Joshua at the time of the conquest. In effect, they had discarded all hope in Yahweh *and* in the future Messiah. Objectively, what we might understand as the unfolding plan of redemption had taken into its bosom a litany of ongoing Israelite sin, the dark background from which light would ultimately shine forth (20:4). As Eichrodt notes, 'There is only one parallel in the Bible to this declaration of judgment, Stephen's speech in Acts 7.'[9]

2. Rebellion: Israel in Egypt (20:5-9)

20:5-9. 'And you will say to them, "Thus says the Lord Yahweh: 'On the day when I chose Israel I raised my hand to the seed of the house of Jacob and made myself known to them in the land of Egypt, and raised my hand to them, saying, "I am Yahweh your God." On that day I raised my hand to them to bring them out from the land of Egypt to a land that I had spied out for them, flowing with milk and honey — it is the beauty of all the lands. Then I said to them, "Let each man throw away the detestable things of his eyes and do not defile yourselves with the idols of Egypt. I am Yahweh your God."

'"'But they rebelled against me and did not want to hear me; the men did not throw away the detestable things of their eyes, nor did they neglect the idols of Egypt. Then I declared that I would pour out my wrath upon them, to expend my anger among them in the midst of the land of Egypt. But I acted for the sake of my name — that it should not be profaned in the eyes of the nations in whose midst they were, in that I had made myself known to them in their sight to bring them out from the land of Egypt.'"'

Ezekiel was bidden to recall the more distant history of Israel, making his audience of elders aware of the evils perpetrated by their fathers.

He would remind these men that originally God had chosen Israel to be his own, which is why he made himself known to them in Egypt. There is a recall of Exodus 6:2-8, where Yahweh affirms the sovereign choice of Israel as his own unique people. In that the Lord **'raised** [the] **hand'**, a gesture accompanying the solemn words of an oath,[10] he bound himself to Israel. The expression is reiterated for emphasis as well as being repeated in the following verse. He placed himself under a most solemn oath to maintain **'the seed of the house of Jacob'**.[11]

Yet in fact the Lord had selected the family of Jacob as his own unique possession years before the departure from Egypt.[12] In the present verse, Ezekiel telescopes events immediately preceding and then soon following the Exodus: it was at that period that God made himself **'known to them in the land of Egypt'**.

Prior to the nation's departure, he revealed himself to Moses, and through Moses to Israel, as 'Yahweh'.[13] It was then that he declared himself to be **'Yahweh your God'**,[14] and it was then that the election of Israel became manifest: **'on the day when I chose Israel'**. From Ezekiel's perspective, the history of Israel as a nation chosen by God commenced with the appearance of Moses, and it is with this history that the prophet is concerned (20:5).

The solemn promise to Israel that Yahweh would be their God involved deliverance from Egyptian bondage followed by settlement in a land **'flowing with milk and honey ... the beauty of all the lands'**, which the Lord had, so to speak, personally **'spied out for them'**,[15] doing so in pursuance of his original promises to the patriarchs. Although the twelve spies reported that Canaan flowed with milk and honey,[16] Yahweh had already reached a similar conclusion (20:6).

Although Ezekiel records that the Lord had spoken to the children of Israel when they were still in Egypt, the Pentateuch gives no details, although Joshua was aware that the patriarchs had at one time embraced alien gods and that the twelve tribes had served the deities of Egypt when in that land.[17] And the incident of the golden calf suggests that the Israelites had been influenced heavily by Egyptian idolatry.[18]

This is given further support when we read between the lines of Exodus 20:1-17 and Deuteronomy 5:6-21, which insist that not only is Yahweh the only God, but that he must be revered as such to the exclusion of all other (non-existent) ethnic deities. Perhaps in the present verse Ezekiel offers a virtual paraphrase of the Decalogue's pronouncements. Speaking in the name of Yahweh, he insists that, at that early time, **'I said to them, "Let each man throw away the detestable things of his eyes and do not defile yourselves with the idols of Egypt. I am Yahweh your God."'** Yahweh reckoned the objects of idolatrous worship to be 'detestable' then, and Ezekiel's point is that the Lord still considered such objects to be disgusting (20:7).

Yahweh, through Ezekiel's lips, develops his complaint. Because **'they ... did not want to hear me'**, they did not reject **'the detestable things'** of their **'eyes'**. In that their gaze was fixed upon **'the idols of Egypt'**, nauseating in themselves, the children of Israel flaunted their perversity. Although Psalm 106:7 states that 'Our fathers in Egypt ... rebelled by the sea — the Red Sea', Ezekiel indicates that idolatry was not new when it appeared in the desert.

Apparently, even *before* the departure from Egypt Israel so offended Yahweh that he **'declared'** that he would **'pour out'** his **'wrath upon them'** and would

'expend' — that is, bring to completion — his **'anger among them in the midst of the land of Egypt'**. In that the direct words of Yahweh from the summit of Sinai to Israel expound his jealousy,[19] it would appear that his protectiveness had already been tested to the limit, and that already the Lord had in principle arrived at a decision to do away with the nation. Ezekiel makes the point so that his audience might realize that Israel had always been perverse (20:8).

'But' Yahweh restrained himself, acting instead **'for the sake of** [his] **name — that it should not be profaned in the eyes of the nations ... in that I had made myself known to them** [that is, to Israel] **in their sight** [that is, in the presence of the Egyptians and others] **to bring them out from the land of Egypt'** (20:9).

This was the basis of Moses' intercession for Israel when he knew that Yahweh purposed to destroy the whole nation because of its sins.[20] It was not so much that the Lord exercised mercy to his penitent people (for they were never really repentant), but that he might not be impugned as unfaithful to his covenant promises. Being **'known'** by Israel means that they (and, indeed, the Egyptians) understood that God had entered into a unique personal relationship with them and that, not withstanding their infidelity, his honour would be prejudiced were he to abandon them. Therefore the Sinai covenant had to remain in place in order to test the nation — although Moses anticipated (correctly) that Israel would remain faithless.

3. Rebellion: The first wilderness generation (20:10-17)

20:10-17. '"'So I took them out from the land of Egypt and brought them to the wilderness. And I gave them my statutes and made known to them my judgements, which if a man does them, he will live by them. And I also gave them my

Sabbaths to be a sign between them and me, to know that I am Yahweh who sanctifies them. But the house of Israel rebelled against me in the wilderness. They did not walk in my statutes and they rejected my judgements, which a man who does them will live by them, and they greatly profaned my Sabbaths. Then I declared that I would pour out my wrath upon them in the wilderness to make an end of them.

'"'Yet I acted for the sake of my name, so that it should not be profaned in the eyes of the nations before whose eyes I had brought them out. And in the wilderness I also raised my hand to them that I would not bring them to the land that I had granted, flowing with milk and honey — it is the beauty of all the lands — because they rejected my judgements, did not walk in my statutes and profaned my Sabbaths, for their heart was walking after their idols. But my eye spared them from destroying them and I did not make an end of them in the wilderness.'"'

Ezekiel looks back to Israel in the years immediately after the departure from Egypt. Then the people lived dangerously. Not only did the Egyptians loathe them,[21] but the Israelites as a whole were spiritually perverse. In the event, Yahweh graciously saw fit to preserve Jacob's family. Had he condemned Israel at the time of the Exodus, or later, a cynical world might have said that the God who had apparently committed himself to Israel was not only inconsistent but was incapable of saving them, thus causing his name to be blasphemed. **'So'** (the Hebrew connective, *vav*), he **'took them out from the land of Egypt and brought them to the wilderness.'** Their original election led to their redemption for the sake of the glory of God rather than for their own benefit, even though they were indeed benefited. The **'wilderness'** is mentioned rather than Sinai because it was there that, emancipated from ethnic slavery and in a new situation, Israel's obedience would be tested (20:10).

In the desert Yahweh **'gave'** Israel his **'statutes and made known to them** [his] **judgements, which if a man does them, he will live by them'** (20:11). Echoing 18:9,19,21-23, there would seem to be an allusion here to Leviticus 18:5: 'You shall therefore keep my statutes and my judgements, which if a man does, he shall live by them: I am Yahweh.'[22] The reference is, of course, to the totality of the Sinai legislation, held out by Deuteronomy 30:15-20 as 'the way to life and good'.

Gardiner's lengthy comment on the latter passage and on the function of Moses' law in general is worthy of repetition:

> It becomes plain ... that what was required was not a mere outward, technical, and perfunctory keeping of certain definite precepts, but a living and loving obedience to God's will from the heart. The same fundamental principle of life underlies the Old Testament as the New; yet the former is justly regarded, and frequently spoken of in the New Testament, as a covenant of works, because the people were not yet sufficiently educated spiritually to be able to receive the principle of faith [in Christ], and were therefore placed under a law of many definite precepts, that by keeping these with glad alacrity they might show their readiness and desire to do the Lord's will. It is in this sense that a man should live by doing the statutes of the law, and not on the ground of his thereby earning for himself salvation. But even thus, they [Israel] failed miserably under the test.[23]

And this explains why in the New Testament the rich young ruler knew that he did not possess eternal life, even though he (apparently) had never formally broken the commandments.[24] The problem with succeeding generations of Israelites up to and long after the time of Ezekiel was that most of them never cared to yield even outward obedience.

In the wilderness Yahweh **'gave them** [his] **Sabbaths'** so that Israel might **'know that I am Yahweh who sanctifies them'** (20:12). This is an allusion to Exodus 16:29 and to Exodus 31:13, the latter stating that 'Surely, my Sabbaths you shall keep, for it is a sign between me and you throughout your generations, that you may know that I am Yahweh who sanctifies you.'

The plural **'Sabbaths'** indicates that more than just the seventh day of the week is in mind, the term encapsulating holy days, sabbatical years and the year of jubilee.[25] These occasions, rather than the feasts of Israel, became a definitive token between Yahweh and Israel, reminding the latter of their unique status as the sanctified, elect nation. Furthermore, in Wright's words, the 'Sabbaths' had 'a vital role in the whole ethos of Israel's social life'.[26] And in later centuries this truth was never forgotten. Isaiah 56:2-6; Jeremiah 17:19-27 and Nehemiah 13:15-22, for instance, show that within the old dispensation Sabbath observance was the hallmark of Jewish fidelity to Yahweh.

'But', complains Yahweh, **'the house of Israel rebelled against me in the wilderness,'** thereby severing themselves from any hope of life. Although Ezekiel does not provide details, various passages from Moses' law would have been in his and in his hearers' minds.[27] The assertion that **'they greatly profaned my Sabbaths'** suggests that the record provided by Exodus through to Deuteronomy does not give a complete account of wilderness apostasy.

Such was the provocation that, as in Egypt (see 20:8), Yahweh **'declared'** that in his anger he would make an **'end'** of the nation (20:13). According to

Exodus 32:10 and Numbers 14:12, the declaration would have been made to Moses.

Yet, as in Egypt (cf. 20:9), Yahweh **'acted for the sake of** [his] **name'**, preserving Israel so that his **'name ... should not be profaned in the eyes of the nations'**. What would the world have said — and with some justice — had the deliverance of Israel from Egypt ground speedily to a halt? In the event, the Lord's reluctance was in the long-term interests of his own name, the name by which Israel was known (20:14).

Numbers 14 is now recalled. When Israel, poised to enter the promised land, endorsed the negative report of ten of the twelve spies and refused to take an initiative, Yahweh promised that, although he would preserve Israel, he would reject the generation that refused to advance into Canaan. The consequences were that all the men who were twenty years of age and over when they had left Egypt died in the desert and that the remainder survived.

Ezekiel, however, makes no mention of Israel's rejection of the recommendation of Caleb and Joshua that the nation should advance, attributing the failure to a characteristic rejection of the Lord's **'statutes'** and **'judgements'**, and a profanation of his **'Sabbaths'** (cf. 20:13). The verdict is that they were disobedient because **'their heart was walking after their idols'**. Although Numbers 14:11-12 does not state explicitly that Yahweh initially **'raised** [his] **hand'** to swear to Moses that he would renounce Israel, the declaration was of such a gravity in that 'as I live' occurs in Numbers 14:21,28. The elders listening to Ezekiel were being reminded that the land forfeited by their own rebellious generation and from which they had already been removed was, nevertheless, **'the beauty of all the lands'**. Their loss had been great (20:15-16).

Yet in earlier centuries Yahweh's **'eye spared'** Israel, and he **'did not make an end of them in the wilderness'** (20:17). The anthropomorphism is striking: when the Lord took a second look at the apostate people, he decided to preserve them in order to uphold his covenant obligations and his honour 'in the sight of the nations' (cf. 20:14). According to Psalm 78:38, mercy was exercised, divine sovereignty manifesting itself in the exercise of grace.

4. Rebellion: The second wilderness generation (20:18-26)

20:18-26. '"'And I said to their children in the wilderness, "Do not walk in your fathers' statutes, do not observe their judgements and do not defile yourselves with their idols. I am Yahweh your God. Walk in my statutes and observe my judgements, and practise them. And sanctify my Sabbaths, and they will be for a sign between me and you, to know that I am Yahweh your God."

'"'But the children rebelled against me. They did not walk in my statutes and they did not observe my statutes to practise them — which a man who does them will live by them. They profaned my Sabbaths. So I declared that I would pour out my wrath upon them, to expend my anger upon them in the wilderness. Yet I withdrew my hand and acted for the sake of my name so that it would not be profaned in the eyes of the nations, before whose eyes I had brought them out. Further, I myself raised my hand to them in the wilderness, to scatter them among the nations and to disperse them among the lands because they did not practise my judgements but rejected my statutes and profaned my Sabbaths, and their eyes were on their fathers' idols.

'"'Moreover, I myself gave them statutes that were not good and judgements by which they would not live, and I rendered them unclean through their gifts when they devoted every firstborn of the womb, so that I might desolate them, so that they might know that I am Yahweh.'"'

Ezekiel now recalls those second-generation Israelites who were born after the initial departure from Egypt, after the law had been given at Sinai, and who were raised in the desert. His words take the first person singular, **'I'**, since it is Yahweh who speaks through him. It is assumed here, as everywhere in chapter 20, that Israel before and after the Exodus typified all the generations down to Ezekiel's time.

Because the wilderness generation had never had any first-hand experience of Egyptian idolatry, they were told at that time to break with their **'fathers''** evil traditions. The immense stock of self-devised abominations handed down from parents to offspring at the time of quitting Egypt had to be forsworn in favour of obedience to the statutes, commandments and Sabbaths of their God. But repentance never occurred.

At the time prohibitions and imperatives abounded: **'Do not walk ... do not observe ... do not defile ... walk ... observe ... practise ... sanctify...'** In that the observance of the **'Sabbaths'** would lead Israel **'to know that I am Yahweh your God'**, the tone is more sombre than in earlier verses, Ezekiel's terse summary of Yahweh's approach to second-generation Israel giving the impression that the Lord had little confidence that the people would mend their ways.

The prophet's immediate point is that, because as yet they had done no more than inherit the evil Egyptian lifestyle adopted by their progenitors, they were relatively innocent. To this extent the future was still theirs. Yet because they did know what Yahweh had commanded at Sinai, they were ultimately without excuse when, as was almost invariably the case, they were disobedient (20:18-20).

Thus, second-generation Israel did not respond. Electing to reject the stipulations of the covenant, they **'rebelled against me'**. In so doing they were foolish: **'they did not observe my statutes to practise them**

— which a man who does them will live by them' (cf. 20:11). Principally, they **'profaned'** Yahweh's **'Sabbaths'**, which they were aware possessed a definitive status within the covenant arrangement. For a third time, no less (cf. 20:8,13), Yahweh determined that he would **'pour out** [his] **wrath upon them, to expend** [his] **anger upon them in the wilderness'** (20:21).

Yet for the third time the Lord resolved to contain his resentment (cf. 20:9,14), acting **'for the sake of** [his] **name so that it would not be profaned in the eyes of the nations'**, nations that were aware of Israel's triumphal exodus from Egypt (20:22).[28] But, not inert to the follies of the people, Yahweh **'raised** [his] **hand to them in the wilderness, to scatter them among the nations and to disperse them among the lands'**. In that the Exodus narratives do not mention any such event, Ezekiel's assertion is best understood as an allusion to such references as Leviticus 26:33; Deuteronomy 4:27; 28:64; 29:28; 30:1. These indicate that in the event of recalcitrance Israel must eventually be scattered — but only after time had gone by during which they would prove their inherent stubbornness. At the inception of the covenant relationship between Yahweh and Israel it was given to the latter to understand that, were they to prove bad tenants, they would eventually be evicted from their national home (20:23).

And it was anticipated correctly by the Lord that this would be the case, the people eventually being expelled **'because they did not practise my judgements but rejected my statutes and profaned my Sabbaths, and their eyes were on their fathers' idols'** (20:24). A systematic reading of the books of the Old Testament confirms that this is how it worked out. The present verse, then, would appear to reflect an ancient prediction as well as issuing a warning. Accordingly, up to the time of the Babylonian exile ancestral idolatry (**'their father's idols'**) was always the besetting sin of Israel, and idolatry, by definition, constituted a rejection of the Sinai covenant.

Moreover, Ezekiel insists that because of the perversity of parents and children alike, Yahweh had granted them **'statutes that were not good'** and judgements by which **'they would not live'** (20:25). Diametrically opposed to the Sinai legislation, full obedience to which would grant life (see 20:11,21), these traditions were probably the evil practices imported by Israel from the surrounding nations as well as those adopted from Egypt and from the banished Canaanites.

But how could it have been that Yahweh **'gave them'** such ordinances? Ezekiel's meaning might be that what the apostate Hebrews wanted, God allowed them as a disguised judgement: Yahweh surrendered his redeemed people that they might walk in their own sinful ways.

If so, the meaning is that, if men determine to be evil, it is possible that God will not restrain them. He is subtle as well as just in how he judges sinners. Firstly, he permits them to have what their wicked hearts desire; then, he leaves them to self-destruct with their own sins and with the righteous condemnation that their sins must attract. The following references might be consulted to establish the point: Exodus 9:16;[29] Psalm 81:12; Isaiah 6:10;[30] Isaiah 63:17; Acts 7:42-43, Romans 1:21-28; 2 Thessalonians 2:11-12.[31]

This is how it was when Israel journeyed in the wilderness between Egypt and the promised land. But in those early days there was a further purpose in Yahweh's lack of restraint: he abandoned them to their follies so that, if it were possible, the people might repent. Bringing themselves to the pit of misery, perhaps they would reflect before it was too late that Yahweh must be obeyed (20:25).

'Devoted' translates a Hebrew verb meaning 'to pass through', indicating that it was not unknown for Israelites to pass their children through the fire to Molech (cf. 16:21; 23:37, where, again, 'fire' is not supplied). The practice is so strongly condemned in the Old Testament that it may well have happened far more often than the occasions when it is specifically mentioned,[32] and this is suggested by the grim reference to the sacrifice of **'every firstborn of the womb'**. Does this point to a widespread perversion of the law of redemption for firstborn children?[33] Yahweh thereby **'rendered** [*Pi'ēl* of *tameh*] **them unclean'**, doing so **'that I might desolate them'**, yet, ultimately, **'that they might know that I am Yahweh'**. That is, these people were abandoned by God to their preferred iniquities so that they might in due course be desolated, and at a later time come to realize that Yahweh is the one who their Scriptures had claimed him to be (20:26).

5. Israel after the conquest of Canaan (20:27-29)

20:27-29. 'Therefore, speak to the house of Israel, son of man, and you will say to them, "Thus says the Lord Yahweh: 'Yet in this your fathers have reproached me by acting treacherously against me. When I brought them to the land concerning which I raised my hand to give it to them, then they saw every high hill and every leafy tree, and there they sacrificed their sacrifices and presented there the provocation of their offerings, and there they set out their soothing odours and there they poured out their libations. And I said to them, "What is the high place where you are going?" And its name was called "high place" until this day.'"'

The fourth period of the history of Israel is passed over by Ezekiel relatively briefly. In the name of Yahweh, the **'son of man'** tells out that the **'fathers'**, the more immediate precursors of his own generation, had **'reproached'** Yahweh. Purporting to be adherents to the Sinai arrangement, they dishonoured the Lord and brought him into international disrepute. To illustrate, when the Assyrian Rabshakeh had attempted to turn senior officials in Jerusalem against King Hezekiah by alleging that he had done away with Yahweh's high places and altars in favour of just one altar,[34] he may have been alluding to the practices of rulers such as Ahaz.[35] But it was men such as the latter who had acted **'treacherously against'** Yahweh (20:27).

Then, long after Yahweh had fulfilled his sworn promise to bring Israel to the promised land, the people abandoned themselves totally to idolatry (cf. 6:13; 16:24-25).[36] **'The provocation'** generated by their **'offerings'** may indicate that offerings *not* prescribed by Moses' law virtually became the norm, their **'soothing odours'** penetrating the inert nostrils of idols, representations of non-existent deities (20:28).

Although, as in the case of Samuel,[37] high places were initially not necessarily unlawful, because they came to be associated with idolatrous activities they were eventually condemned (cf. 6:3-7). It was to Solomon's shame that he erected high places for the gods of some of his wives,[38] and to Josiah's immense credit that he rendered them inoperative.[39]

As reported by Ezekiel, Yahweh challenged the perpetrators of such folly: **'I said to them, "What is the high place where you are going?"'** The Hebrew for 'high place' is *bamah*, and *ba*, in participle form, means 'going', while *mah* means 'what'. We have here a sardonic, assonantal and untranslatable play on words, meaning something like 'To what are you going?' An accurate response would be 'To nothing'. And it is implied that popular addiction to high places as sites for illicit worship had persisted until Ezekiel's time: **'And its name was called** [by Yahweh] **"high place" until this day.'** Here, *'bamah'* is probably a collective term standing for each and every elevated site where apostate Israel chose to worship the gods. 'What are these places?,' Ezekiel wants to know — and who told Israel to worship there? Yahweh had never issued such an instruction (20:29).

6. The present and the future (20:30-38)

20:30-38. 'Therefore, say to the house of Israel, "Thus says the Lord Yahweh: 'Will you defile yourselves in the way of your fathers and will you whore after their detestable practices? And in raising up your gifts by passing your children through the fire, you are defiling yourselves with all your idols until this day. And I, shall I let myself be enquired of for you, O house of Israel? As I live,' declares the Lord Yahweh, 'I shall not be enquired of for you. And what arises in your mind will never come about — that is, what you are saying: "We shall be like the nations, like the families of the lands, ministering to wood and stone."'

'"'As I live,' declares the Lord Yahweh, 'surely with a strong hand and an outstretched arm, and with poured-out wrath I shall be king over you. And I shall bring you out from the peoples and will gather you from the lands among which you have been scattered — with a strong hand and with an outstretched arm, and with wrath poured out. Then I shall bring you to the wilderness of the peoples and there will enter into judgement with you, face to face. Even as I entered into judgement with your fathers in the wilderness of the land of Egypt, so I shall enter into judgement with you,' declares the Lord Yahweh. 'And I shall make you pass under the staff and bring you into the bond of the covenant, and shall purge away from you the rebels and they who transgress against me. I shall bring them out from the land of their sojourning, but they will not come to the earth of Israel, and you will know that I am Yahweh.'"'

Now commences the final part of the review of Israel's infidelity, focusing upon Ezekiel's generation. Given the long record of national intransigence, the prophet is required to ask **'the house of Israel'** if they propose to continue to **'whore after'** the **'detestable practices'** of their **'fathers'**. Will they **'defile'** themselves in their **'way'**? (20:30). The questions are, of course, rhetorical. As previous chapters have shown, Ezekiel's constituency had no intention of surrendering their assimilation to heathen practices. Israel in exile stands accused and is in no position to blame the fathers for present afflictions.

The indictment unfolds, Ezekiel accusing his people of **'passing** [their] **children through the fire'** ('fire' is explicit here, unlike 20:26). They have been **'defiling'** themselves **'with all** [their] **idols until this day'**. The assertion is startling. Was child sacrifice being practised by the people of Jerusalem when their city lay under Nebuchadnezzar's shadow? Was this abomination known among the exiles in Babylonia? Apparently, yes! For this reason, will Yahweh permit himself to be **'enquired of for you, O house of Israel'**? May the elders who had approached Ezekiel expect any comforting word through him from their God? Yahweh **'declares'** by his own life that he will not permit himself to respond to a people who, in effect, despise him (20:31).

Centuries earlier, Israel's elders approached the prophet Samuel to request 'a king to judge us like all the nations', to 'go out before us and fight our battles', an arrangement which Samuel knew would lead to idolatry and the renunciation of the Sinai covenant.[40] And, as time passed, such desires persisted. Indeed, indicates Ezekiel, it was still arising **'in your mind'**.[41] Both the remnant in Jerusalem and the exilic community lacked any desire to be a people separated for Yahweh.[42]

But, retorts Yahweh, it **'will never come about'**. He will take action to ensure that, notwithstanding the declared aspirations of the people (**'what you are saying'**), post-exilic Israel will never finally succumb to heathen practices, **'ministering to wood and stone'**, and will never descend to being just one among many nations (20:32). Exactly how this is to be achieved is the theme of the following verses.

In short, Yahweh refuses to be other than King in Israel. Although a majority of the people seek to accommodate themselves to nations near and far which worship **'wood and stone'** (20:32), Ezekiel predicts that this state of affairs is to change dramatically and will come about by regeneration rather than by condemnation and the sword. By the gift of new spiritual life, rather than by consigning Israel to death, God intends to reclaim the throne.

The Lord swears — **'"As I live," declares the Lord Yahweh'** — that he will rule over Israel, doing so **'with a strong hand and an outstretched arm'** (20:33).

There is here more than may meet the eye. In addition to an unmistakeable recall of Yahweh's activity at the time of the exodus from Egypt,[43] it is promised that **'with poured-out wrath'** the Lord will **'be king over you'**. This expression has appeared already (7:8; 9:8; 14:19; 20:8,13,21) and will occur again in 22:22; 30:15 and 36:18. In that, apart from 30:15, all these refer to Yahweh's anger against *Israel*, Ezekiel declares that although there will be a new exodus, it will lead to discipline rather than mere deliverance: the anger that was manifested against the pharaoh of the time will, as in Jeremiah 21:5, now be directed towards the nominal people of God (20:33). As Block notes, 'The exodus in wrath leads to a face-to-face encounter with Yahweh in the desert, through which the cycle of rebellion and fury that determined every phase of the nation's past is finally broken.'[44]

Although the language of Exodus 6:6-8 concerning the removal from Egypt is employed in 20:33, the predicted departure **'from the peoples'** and a gathering **'from the lands among which you have been scattered'** cannot be a return of the exiles from Babylon to the land of Israel (20:34). This is because, repeating from 20:33, the anticipated restoration will be in some fashion an act of vengeance, **'with poured-out wrath'**, and because, according to 20:35, it will be an exodus into **'the wilderness'**. Under Moses' leadership Israel entered the wilderness of Sinai, but only in anticipation of the conquest under Joshua. It follows, then, that Yahweh will separate Israel in exile in a spiritual sense, not allowing them to continue to be, or to want to be, 'like the nations, like the families of the lands, ministering to wood and stone' (see 20:32). It would seem, then, that the predicted exodus towards some species of desert place is an act both of divine anger and mercy.

In the name of Yahweh, Ezekiel draws an analogy between **'the wilderness of the peoples'** and the **'wilderness of the land of Egypt'**. Even as Israel had spent forty years in the desert, Yahweh is to address Israel in exile when they remain absent from the promised land. There, undisturbed and with no interference, he will **'enter into judgement with you'**, just as he had **'entered into judgement with your fathers in the wilderness of the land of Egypt'** — that is, at Sinai. Moreover, he will treat with Israel, still in exile and far from home, **'face to face'**. This would be a direct allusion to Deuteronomy 5:4, where Moses recalls that 'Yahweh spoke with you face to face on the mountain from the midst of the fire', rather than to, say, Exodus 33:11 and Deuteronomy 34:10, which point to the direct 'face-to-face' encounters between Moses and Yahweh. Now there will be no mediator between Israel and the Lord in order to shield the former from the wrath of the latter.

'The wilderness of the peoples' cannot be any geographical desert, such as that of Sinai or the desert waste between Canaan and Babylonia, but the wilderness state of exiled Israel, still scattered among the nations. Then and there they are to be met by their God. Then and there he will terrify them by the revelation of his holiness, even as Israel had been terrified at Sinai.[45] When he confronts them they learn to fear. Yahweh **'declares'** that it shall be so.

Thus Ezekiel appears to anticipate a second departure of Israel from the world, a severance modelled centuries before by the exodus from Egypt. Then the nation was brought out to serve and worship,[46] to enter into a binding relationship with God and thereby entering into **'judgement'** (20:35-36).

The nature of this confrontation is explained. Just as a shepherd will pass his flock beneath his rod so that they can proceed through the entrance of the sheepfold where, counting and examining them, he can distinguish between the healthy and the sick,[47] so the Lord proposes to take Israel in exile into his special care. They will be brought **'into the bond of the covenant'**,[48] those who remain **'rebels and ... who transgress against'** Yahweh being removed. Even as an unbelieving generation perished in the desert many centuries ago, future apostates are to be eradicated from the nation.

So when Israel is reconstituted as the true people of God, Yahweh will **'bring them out from the land of their sojourning'** — that is, away from 'the wilderness of the peoples' (see 20:35) rather than from the land promised to Abraham's family,[49] to remain for an unspecified period beyond their homeland. Then they **'will know that I am Yahweh'**, accepting that he alone is the redeeming God of Israel. However, not yet will the original link between monarchy, land and divine presence, as enjoyed when Solomon's temple was consecrated, be restored (20:37-38).

7. The times of the Messiah (20:39-44)

The contrast in emphasis between the previous section and these verses is unmistakable. Whereas the former predicted a spiritual renewal of Israel, although not within the boundaries of the promised land, now we learn that a renewed Israel will serve God within that land.

20:39-44. '"'And as for you, O house of Israel,' thus says the Lord Yahweh: 'Each one of you, go, serve his idols; but afterwards, if you do not hear me — you will not profane my holy name any more with your gifts and with your idols. Because on my holy mountain, on the mountain of the height of Israel,' declares the Lord Yahweh, 'there the whole house of Israel shall serve me, all of them in the land. There I shall accept them and there I shall enquire about your contributions and the first of your tributes, with all your holy things. As a soothing odour I shall accept you when I bring you out from the peoples and gather you from the lands in which you have been scattered, and shall sanctify myself among you in the eyes of the nations.

'"'And you will know that I am Yahweh, when I bring you to the earth of Israel, to the land concerning which I raised my hand to grant it to your fathers. And there you will remember your ways and all your deeds with which you defiled yourselves, and to your face you will loathe yourselves for all the evil actions that you have done. Then you will know that I am Yahweh when I have dealt with you for the sake of my name, not according to your evil ways or because of your ruinous deeds, O house of Israel,' declares the Lord Yahweh."'

The promise of the previous section, 20:30-38, is now followed by an ironic, emotional and breathless exhortation, Ezekiel directing his words to **'the house of Israel'** rather than to the elders who (presumably) were still sitting before him to receive a word from Yahweh. He alludes to Deuteronomy 4:28, which predicts that an unrepentant Israel in exile will 'serve gods, the work of men's hands', and possibly to Joshua 24:15, where Joshua, anticipating that Israel will be faithless, challenges his generation to 'choose for yourselves this day whom you will serve, whether the gods whom your fathers served ... or the gods of the Amorites'.

The burden is that **'each one'** of those who refuse to repent may, if he so desires, serve his preferred idols, in that Yahweh is content to surrender him to his folly. And then, stating that if they **'do not hear'** the Lord, there is a break in syntax, as if Yahweh, in a state of emotional upheaval, loses his breath. But he recovers himself and asserts that such people will not be permitted to **'profane my holy name any more with your gifts and with your idols'**. No longer will Israel humiliate Yahweh in the eyes of the nations,[50] the reason being that, as the next verse shows, the work of spiritual renewal cannot be prejudiced because the house of Israel is destined to serve the Lord in the land of promise. The nation will include none who are infidel (20:39).

'My holy mountain' and **'the mountain of the height of Israel'** (20:40) reflect 17:23, 'on the high mountain of Israel'. Here, as there, the reference is to Canaan in general and to Jerusalem in particular. But Zion and Jerusalem are not now mentioned by name in that the elders listening to Ezekiel would have been confused, believing as they did that the city from which they had been deported must survive the Babylonian onslaught. Not so, Ezekiel has insisted, yet now pointing to a future age and a Jerusalem the like of which the elders had never envisaged.

At long last Yahweh will accept **'the whole house of Israel'**, **'all of them'**, when resident in their land, together with their sacrificial gifts. Moreover, there will be a divine interest: **'there I shall enquire about your contributions and the first of your tributes, with all your holy things'** (20:40). Whereas Yahweh had refused to respond to the enquiries of the elders who came to Ezekiel (20:1-3), the day must dawn when the Lord will want to know about Israel's gifts and choice offerings, now deemed to be holy. At long last the ancient pillars will be in place: Yahweh will accept a purified people, now gathered in the land granted to the fathers in perpetuity. Although the Davidic monarchy is not mentioned, the parallel reference in 17:22-23 allows the assumption that all this will come about through the agency of the Messiah.

Remarkably, in their renewed holiness the people of Israel, rather than their burnt offerings, will constitute **'a soothing odour'** which Yahweh will **'accept'**.[51] Formerly, the aromas ascending from offerings to false deities were an offence (20:28), but now a new situation supervenes. Language could not be more evocative: the relationship between Yahweh and Israel will be intimate and perfect.

And this will occur **'when'** Yahweh brings them out **'from the peoples'**, to **'gather'** them — presumably to the land of their fathers — **'from the lands in which you have been scattered'**. Ultimately, the motivation behind this act of grace will not be that of divine love for a chosen family, but that Yahweh's reputation **'in the eyes of the nations'** may be maintained. It is for this reason that he intends to **'sanctify'** himself **'among'** the people of Israel. Were he to fail here, his name would be profaned, even as it would have been in Egypt (see 20:9) and in the wilderness (see 20:14,22) had he not restrained himself from destroying Israel. Restored to the land of promise, Israel resides as a holy nation amid an unholy community of nations (20:41).

Thus Yahweh will show himself to be the God of the ancient covenant, the one who, long centuries before, had **'raised'** his **'hand'** in an oath **'to grant' 'the land'** to the **'fathers'**, by whom are meant Abraham and his posterity.[52] Honouring the original promise (mentioned in 20:5-6), a commitment provisionally rescinded during the wilderness journey and then after the settlement (see 20:15,23,28), in future time Yahweh will restore a spiritually renewed people to **'the earth of Israel'**, in consequence of which they will acknowledge, or **'know'**, that their God really *is* **'Yahweh'**, who has kept his original word (20:42).

'There', resettled in the promised land, the people will look back with disgust at **'all** [their] **deeds with which'** they had once **'defiled'** themselves. Indeed, their corporate **'face'** will be stamped with self-loathing. The principal sin for which they will upbraid themselves is idolatry, because the practice had constituted a renunciation of the covenant bond between Yahweh and the nation. Now they distance themselves from **'all'** their **'evil actions'** (20:43).

The prediction of 20:42 concerning a spiritually restored and geographically resettled Israel is repeated. Then, **'you will know that I am Yahweh'**. Whereas over the centuries their **'ways'** had been **'evil'** and their **'deeds'** had been **'ruinous'**, the covenant nation, having opted for a self-destruct mode, now knows that their God has vindicated his oath to the patriarchs and has protected the integrity of his **'name'**. Having committed himself to an elect people, Yahweh has not permitted himself to be dishonoured by being perceived to have given up on them, notwithstanding their sinfulness. Rather, he has sanctified them and made them the people that they ought to have made themselves, but would not and could not. Yahweh **'declares'** that it shall be so (20:44).

With this verse the immediate prophecy ends, as also the close of the chapter in the Hebrew text.

Application

In that Moses' law anticipated Christ, and in that godly Israelites were saved through faith because of the merits of the Christ yet to come, 20:1-4 implies that, like their predecessors and many of their descendants,[53] the elders who approached Ezekiel were in principle apostate.

During the wilderness journey, and long afterwards, Israel serially rejected the terms of the Sinai covenant. Yet this perversity had preceded Sinai, a rejection of Moses' law demonstrating what Israel had always been. Even so, Yahweh did not abandon his elect people, and this because he had set his name upon them. Although individual unbelievers perished,[54] Israel as a unique theocracy was never renounced. This is an important element within the overall message of the prophecy of Ezekiel.

Genesis 2:3 tells that on day seven God blessed and set apart, or sanctified, creation for his own lasting pleasure and so that corporate mankind, the zenith of his six-day activity, might worship him for ever. Essentially, the rationale for creation was a bipolar arrangement whereby God and man would enjoy a permanently harmonious relationship.

It would follow that Adam's sin was not only his personal rebellion, as well as that of the human race (see Rom. 5:12,19), it was a defamation and profanation of that which was initially holy and blessed. As Romans 8:22 and context remind us, creation 'groans', although not without hope.

This being so, I find it hard to see where in the New Testament Moses' institutionalized seventh day is transferred to the first day of the week and as such remains binding upon the churches and, presumably, upon all others.

Rather, one would take the view that the Mosaic Sabbath pointed retrospectively to day seven of the creation week and prospectively to the Messiah, in whom, according to Hebrews 4:9-11, we have perfect rest. Here, in verse 9, the writer of the letter employs the Greek *sabbatismos*, as unusual word, to represent the Hebrew *shabbat* in order to drive home his point: Christ, as the Sabbath's ultimate fulfilment, is by definition greater than this Old Testament shadow from which (amongst many such shadows) he emerges into the light of gospel day.

If it is supposed that the present tense inherent in 'remains' in Hebrews 4:9 suggests that this sabbatical 'rest' represents our heavenly future, it could be argued with reason that a one-in-seven Sabbath day is, indeed, still incumbent on believers. Yet such an exegesis is difficult in that verses 3 and 10-11 of this chapter tell out that entering into rest means reposing our souls upon Christ *now*. In the words of William Gadsby (1773–1844):

> The Sabbath was a day of rest;
> The day the Lord Jehovah blest;
>   A lively type of Christ;
> The labouring poor may venture here;
> The guilty banish all their fear,
>   And lean on Jesus' breast.[55]

All of which would mean that the desecration of the Sabbath by the Jews before and after Ezekiel's time was an anticipation of, and identification with, their posterity's ultimate rejection of Christ.

In passing, let it be said that the Lord's Day is vital as an occasion for worship, fellowship, service and rest when we celebrate our Lord's triumphal work for us. That is, since he personally is our New Testament 'Sabbath', the special task of day one will be to contemplate what he has done, is doing and will yet do for his people. Although he is our rest during all seven days of the week, on the 'lordly' or 'royal' day (see Rev. 1:10) we separate ourselves *if* essential secular duties allow. It would not be possible for the writer of this commentary to set too high a value on the importance of this day for his family and himself.

How is the last part of chapter 20 to be interpreted? Because there is no geographical datum it seems that it cannot point to the return from Babylonian exile. What is definite is that some (perhaps many?) but not all of the children of Israel will be embraced in a covenantal relationship with their God.

Perhaps 20:30-38 points to the Jewish sheep of 'this fold', mentioned by our Lord.[56] That is, following the Day of Pentecost large numbers of Jews were obedient to the faith although they did not (obviously) obtain possession of the land of Palestine.[57] If such an interpretation leads in the right direction, these verses are Messianic through and through: until the end of time there will be an accession of Jews to swell the ranks of the faithful.

So to what does 20:39-44 direct us? Whereas the previous section anticipated a renewal of Israel *beyond* the borders of the promised land, these verses appear to be adamant that a renewed Israel will be resettled *within* these borders, thus realizing the ideal of a complete relationship between God and his covenant people. The present commentator believes that this is the only way in which the section can properly be understood and that it anticipates chapters 34, 36 and 37. That is, a regenerated Israel will worship God through Christ within the land promised to Abraham and his seed. In being faithful to his own, the Lord will be faithful to himself. I believe that the apostle Paul anticipates this in Romans 11:25-29: 'For the gifts and calling of God are irrevocable.'[58]

The sword of Yahweh (Ezekiel 20:45 – 21:32)

In the Hebrew text, chapter 20 ends at the English Bible's verse 44, and chapter 21 and a new section commence at 20:45. In the Hebrew sequence, the parable of the blazing forest in 20:45-49 serves as an introduction to chapter 21.

Throughout the preceding chapters Ezekiel has predicted that the Chaldean invasion of Judah must lead to the destruction of Jerusalem, the fall of the Davidic monarchy and then national exile. But, so far, one name, that of the tyrant who would lead the onslaught, Nebuchadnezzar, who reigned from 605 to 562 BC, has not been mentioned, although, as in 17:12 and 19:9, he does appear as 'the king of Babylon' (so too, 21:19,21), and his name will occur in 26:7; 29:18,19; 30:10.

It is as if Yahweh, through the **'son of man'**, heightens the tension: it is *this* inhuman despot who will precipitate the downfall of the theocracy. For the Jerusalem of Ezekiel's generation there is no hope. The present oracle anticipates the catastrophe.

The prophecy may be said to divide into five sections: fire in the south, the enigmatic 'parable' of the sword (20:45-49); an elucidation of 20:45-49 (21:1-7); the song of the sword (21:8-17); the king of Babylon, the 'hand of Yahweh' (21:18-27); the sword turning against Ammon (21:28-29); and, finally, vengeance being taken upon the wielder of the sword (21:30-32). The staccato style of the Hebrew text reflects the intense emotion with which Ezekiel delivered this oracle: he was anything other than a dispassionate, unfeeling relay for the judgemental word of the Lord.

1. Fire in the south (20:45-49 [Hebrew text: 21:1-5])

20:45-49. Then the word of Yahweh came to me, saying, 'Son of man, set your face towards the way of the southland and let the word fall against the south, and prophesy against the forest of the field in the Negev. And you will say to the forest in the Negev, "Hear the word of Yahweh. Thus says the Lord Yahweh: 'Look, I am kindling a fire in you, and it will devour every fresh tree and every dry tree in you. The blazing flame will not be extinguished, and every face, from the Negev to the north, will be scorched by it. And all flesh will see that I, Yahweh, have burnt it — it will not be extinguished.'"' Then I said, 'Ah, Lord Yahweh, they are saying about me, "Is he not speaking parables?"'

Ezekiel records that the **'word of Yahweh'** came to him, instructing him to **'set** [his] **face towards the way of the southland'**. **'Southland'** translates *temanah*, a word related to the Hebrew *yamin*, 'right'. If facing towards the east, one's right hand would be to the south.

And the prophet would let his **'word fall against the south'**. **'Fall'**, or 'let drop',[59] suggests that, like driving rain penetrating the earth, the prophetic word is to drop on the **'south'**, the Hebrew behind this second word for south being *darôm*, a poetic term. As rain from the skies cannot be avoided, so Ezekiel's word will penetrate to the heart of Israel's situation.

More plainly, Yahweh commands Ezekiel to **'prophesy against the forest of the field in the Negev'**. Although **'Negev'**, a transliterated word, usually stands for the southern desert land, here it represents the land of Israel in general (as seen from Babylonia), and Jerusalem in particular (cf. 21:2,3,20,22).

We do not know exactly how Ezekiel was supposed to **'set** [his] **face'** towards the southland. Perhaps he turned his head to the south and west in the general direction of Jerusalem. If so, his action may have been clear to his audience. And, if **'forest'** stands for dry and inflammable brushwood, the acted metaphor would be that of a searing fire about to devour Jerusalem (20:45-46).

The prophet had to proclaim that Yahweh was in effect an enemy about to ignite a fire that would consume all vegetation, both green and arid. **'Every'** is now introduced no less than three times to give weight to the pronouncement, the trees representing men of every condition, both righteous and unrighteous. The **'blazing'**, searing **'flame'** cannot be put out; the whole forest, **'from the Negev to the north'**, perhaps from Beer-sheba to Dan, burns (20:47).

Consequently, it dawns upon **'all flesh'**, by which is meant the totality of the Jewish nation as well as others, that this holocaust can be nothing other than a judgement from Yahweh, the God of Israel who cannot allow the sinfulness of his nominal people to remain unrequited (20:48).

It appears that when faithful Ezekiel had delivered the message he found himself ridiculed for his pains, his hearers asking rhetorically, **'Is he not speaking parables?'** As far as they were concerned, of course he was. But the problem was that they had no desire to understand the meaning of his prophetic riddles.[60] Therefore, Ezekiel registers a prayerful complaint, perhaps asking for a plain interpretation of his words to give back to the people (20:49).

2. An elucidation of the parable (21:1-7 [Hebrew text: 21:6-12])

21:1-7. And the word of Yahweh came to me, saying, 'Son of man, set your face against Jerusalem and let the word fall against the sanctuaries, and prophesy against the earth of Israel. And you will say to the earth of Israel, "Thus says Yahweh: 'Look, I am against you and I shall draw my sword from its sheath and will cut off from you the righteous and the wicked. Because I shall cut off from you the righteous and the wicked, therefore my sword shall come out from its sheath against all flesh, from the Negev to the north. And all flesh will know that I, Yahweh, have brought out my sword from its sheath. It will not return again.'"

'And as for you, son of man, groan. Groan before their eyes with broken loins and in bitterness. And it shall be that when they say to you, "For what reason do you groan?" you will say, "For the report which is coming. Every heart will melt, all hands will sink down, every spirit will be faint and all knees will move as water. Look, it has come and has been realized," declares the Lord Yahweh.'

Yahweh, ever faithful to his beleaguered servant, responds. Despite popular scorn, the **'son of man'** is to **'set** [his] **face against Jerusalem'** and again to **'let the word fall'**, this time **'against the sanctuaries'**. He is to **'prophesy against the earth of Israel'**, the Negev forest mentioned in 20:46 (21:1-2). This could be divine irony because, as in 7:24, the holy places were probably unholy sanctuaries reserved for the false gods.

The earlier parable is given further clarification, the predicted fire being nothing other than military invasion. Yahweh bids Israel, both those who hold out against Babylon in Judah and those who have already been taken into exile, to **'look'**: the Lord proposes to **'draw** [his] **sword'** against the supposedly sacred

'earth of Israel' and **'cut off from'** that earth **'the righteous and the wicked'** — alias, as in 20:47, 'every fresh tree and every dry tree'. This is possibly a 'merism', two opposites — such as, say, 'from head to toe' — expressing totality (21:3).[61]

Ezekiel's immediate hearers must have been deeply offended by these words. At the time of Joshua's conquest of Canaan, the Angel of Yahweh had appeared to him with a drawn sword in his hand to fight on behalf of Israel.[62] But in Ezekiel's day, whereas his fellow-exiles reckoned that Yahweh would preserve his city, his people and the throne of David against the Chaldeans, the prophet insisted that the enemy was merely a sword in the hand of Yahweh, who was now Jerusalem's pledged and irresistible adversary. And, implies this verse, since the Lord can do no wrong, where does Israel stand?[63]

Concerning Ezekiel's theology, a superficial reading might suggest that he contradicts himself in that he has already declared that the righteous within Israel must be spared (see 9:4-6; 14:12-20; 18:1-32).[64] Perhaps part of the answer to this question might be discerned in what happened to Jeremiah and Baruch. Although they experienced the trauma of the Babylonian conquest, both were granted their lives.[65] Ezekiel's meaning, then, would be that although neither the righteous nor the wicked will be spared the horrors of war, the former will finally be delivered.

So, **'because'** he will **'cut off ... the righteous and the wicked'**, Yahweh intends to bring his **'sword'** out from its **'sheath'** against the land: from **'the Negev to the north'** there will be devastation, the prime target being Jerusalem, situated in the southern kingdom of Judah (21:4). This declaration corresponds to the condemnation of both the green and the dry trees in 20:47.

Nor can Yahweh's 'sword' **'return'** to its **'sheath'** until it completes its dreadful work. What Yahweh purposes to do shall be accomplished.[66] In consequence, **'all flesh will know that'** the God of Israel had precipitated the Chaldean descent upon Judah. With these words the Lord concludes his interpretation of the riddle of the fire (21:5).

Ezekiel is now commanded to **'groan'** in the presence of his hearers with an explosion of anguish, the symbolism of the action reflecting overwhelming emotion. In that the **'loins'** were regarded as the seat of strength (cf. 29:7),[67] the prophet is required to prostrate himself before his audience as if he was a **'broken'** man. Nor, in his **'bitterness'**, would the performance have been altogether feigned (21:6).

When asked to explain himself, he must acknowledge that he was anticipating the report from the homeland that was to be brought to the exiles. Yahweh expects that the attention of Ezekiel's hearers will be roused and that they will want to know why he displays such extreme emotional distress. His reply will be terse: **'For the report which is coming.'** Then, anticipating what he will hear, he predicts that others too will be in a state of collapse: **'Every heart will melt, all hands will sink down, every spirit will be faint and all knees will move as water.'** The final words may indicate involuntary urination (cf. 7:17). **'Look, it has come and has been realized.'**

But what is this **'report'** that is to generate so much terror? It might be Ezekiel's riddle of the fire (20:46-49), in which case the prophet urges his hearers to take his message seriously, or it could be the report of the final collapse of Jerusalem that he knew would eventually get through to the exiles (see 33:21). The former view seems better: the exiles should give heed to Ezekiel's words and rinse their minds of their unjustified belief in the immunity of Jerusalem. What Ezekiel had been predicting has potentially **'come'** and is as good as **'realized'**. Yahweh **'declares'** it to be so (21:7).

3. A song of the sword (21:8-13 [Hebrew text: 21:13-18])

21:8-13. And the word of Yahweh came to me, saying, 'Son of man, prophesy, and you will say, "Thus says the Lord Yahweh: Say, 'A sword! A sword sharpened and polished. It is sharpened to make a slaughter; it is polished to be lightning. Or shall we rejoice, the rod of my son, rejecting every tree? And he gave it for polishing — to grasp in the hand. It is a sharpened sword; it is polished, to give it to the hand of a slayer.'" Cry out and wail, son of man; for this has happened among my people, it is among all the princes of Israel. They have been thrown to the sword with my people — therefore, slap your thigh. For there is a testing, and what if even the rod which rejects shall be no more?' declares the Lord Yahweh.

The **'word of Yahweh'** came again to Ezekiel, requiring him to utter what turns out to be a frenzied ode in celebration of the sword, the weapon undoubtedly standing for Babylon. The prediction in 21:8-13 corresponds to 21:2-5, and that in 21:14-17 to 21:6-7.[68] It is almost as if the **'son of man'** finds the fascination of a flashing sword irresistible: **'Say, "A sword! A sword sharpened and polished."'** The feverish exclamations of the whole section seem designed to conjure up the image of a polished and sharpened sword flashing in every direction, creating a halo of light around the intended victim (21:8-9).

But why, it must be asked, an apparent celebration? War is cruel, and men who have seen action seldom take pleasure in reminiscing about their experiences. Here Ezekiel praises this particular sword because he knows that Yahweh is acting decisively to put an end to the waywardness of his erring people. The small print of the warnings of the Sinai covenant is being brought to light, and for this he is glad.

And this **'sword'** is **'sharpened to make a slaughter'** and **'polished to be lightning'**. It is a weapon ready for deployment against the enemies of Yahweh. Yet why? The last part of 21:10 is not easy to translate and interpret. Perhaps **'Or shall we rejoice, the rod of my son, rejecting every tree?'** may capture the sense. If so, it could be that Ezekiel's hearers, protesting against his denunciation of Judah, claimed that Jacob's prophecy of Genesis 49:9-10 concerning that tribe signified that it, and in later years all Israel as led by David, a man considered as Yahweh's 'son',[69] would be invulnerable, surviving every threat (cf. 19:11,14).

In a certain sense this may have been true, as chapters 38 – 39 will indicate, but Ezekiel's Jewish adversaries doubtless considered that what was meant was the survival of the state of Israel in their time, come what may. If so, they failed to discern the long-term Messianic content of the promise.[70]

But should Judah reject **'every** [other political] **tree'**? Should they despise the Babylonian sword that by the time this oracle was being delivered had already caused so much devastation within the Jewish homeland? No (21:10).

That Ezekiel had Jacob's prediction in his mind is shown by 21:27, where it is given an undoubted recall: 'Moreover, this will not be until he comes to whom the judgement is — and I shall grant it.'

Perhaps in order to heighten tension, the language is deliberately vague, as if Yahweh, through Ezekiel, cannot quite bring himself to gasp out the unthinkable — which is that it is none other than the Lord who causes the sword to be **'polished'** and **'sharpened'**, then delivering it to an agent, **'a slayer'**, for him to grasp. Ezekiel's point is that the God of Israel is mobilizing a killing machine to hurl against his own nominal people in the land that he had once granted to their forefathers. Judah is the intended victim (21:11).

And **'the son of man'** has to **'cry out and wail'** in order to reinforce the impact of his words, and to **'slap** [his] **thigh'**.[71] It is not just the land of Israel that comes under attack, but its **'people'** and the **'princes'** of Israel who have **'been thrown to the sword'**. The language is shockingly vivid, and Ezekiel's hearers would have been appalled by his performance. But his meaning is crystal clear: let the exiles not delude themselves by an appeal to a crass misinterpretation of the promises of Genesis 49:9-10 and 2 Samuel 7:14 (21:12).

'For there is a testing', declares Ezekiel. Although the verse is difficult, its burden may be that because the polished sword represents a military instrument already tested many times in war, Jerusalem's situation is hopeless. What, then, asks the Lord, if the arrogant **'rod ... shall be no more'**? This appears to be a rhetorical question: let Ezekiel's hearers imagine the unimaginable, the annihilation of Judah. **'The Lord Yahweh'** declares it (21:13).

4. Yahweh claps his hands (21:14-17 [Hebrew text: 21:19-22])

21:14-17. 'But you, son of man, prophesy and strike your hands together. Let the sword strike twice, thrice! It is the sword of the slain, the sword of a great slaughter surrounding them. So that hearts may melt and that there may be many who stumble at all their gates, I have set a slaughtering sword. Ah! It has been made for lightning, wrapped ready for slaughter. Be sharp; turn to the right; set yourself; go to the left — wherever your face is assigned. And I, even I, smite my hands together, and shall give rest to my wrath. I, Yahweh, have spoken.'

Ezekiel was instructed to **'prophesy'** and **'strike** [his] **hands together'**. In effect, he was to applaud the divine action. The content of his prophecy would have been a vocal summons, heard by his audience, to the **'sword'**, now a personification for Yahweh, to **'strike twice, thrice'** because it was **'the sword of the slain, the sword of a great slaughter surrounding them'**. It encircles those being slain within Jerusalem. The imagery is that of a burnished blade in the hand of an expert swordsman. Swinging to and fro with lethal accuracy, it fells each of its intended victims (21:14).[72]

This does not mean that in clapping his hands Ezekiel gloated over the fall of Jerusalem, but that he was reflecting the anger of the God who, fundamentally, does not desire the death of a sinner (see, 18:23). Compare with 21:17 and Balak's rage against Balaam in Numbers 24:10.

Ultimately, Yahweh's purpose is to create fear among his victims. **'So that their hearts may melt and that there may be many who stumble at all their gates'** signifies that the city gates, which in other circumstances could be avenues of escape, are where a fleeing populace will be judged.[73] The **'slaughtering sword'**, **'made for lightning'** and **'wrapped ready for slaughter'**, will execute Yahweh's sentence upon those who, like their forefathers, had rejected the terms of the Sinai covenant (21:15).[74]

Ezekiel's vocal summons to the personified sword of the Lord continues, instructing it to **'Be sharp; turn to the right; set yourself; go to the left — wherever your face is assigned'**.[75] Reading between the lines, enemy forces will be perfectly but unwittingly obedient to the God who ordains military action against his own people and his own city (21:16).

The prophecy now ends with a dramatic and (for Ezekiel's immediate hearers) a scandalous assertion: it is Yahweh, no less, who smites his **'hands together'** in anger not unmixed with satisfaction. The impending catastrophe is to be of such a magnitude that the divine rage will be slaked (cf. 5:13; 16:42; 24:13): **'I ... shall give rest to my wrath'** (21:17).

5. The king of Babylon, the 'hand of Yahweh' (21:18-27 [Hebrew text: 21:23-32])

21:18-27. Then the word of Yahweh came to me, saying, 'And you, son of man, set for yourself two ways for the sword of the king of Babylon to come — from one land the two of them will come out. Then fashion a hand; at the head of the way of the city fashion it. You will mark a way for the sword to come: "To Rabbah of the sons of Ammon" and "To Judah, in fortified Jerusalem". For the king of Babylon stands at the division of the way, at the head of the two ways, to practise divination. He shakes the arrows; he consults the household idols and looks at the liver. Into his right hand has come the divination "Jerusalem" — to set up battering rams, to open the mouth for murder and to lift up the voice with a war cry, to set battering rams against the gates, to cast up mounds, to build a siege wall.

'But it seemed to them like a false divination in their eyes: for them there were solemn oaths, but it will bring iniquity to remembrance, that they may be seized.

'Therefore, thus says the Lord Yahweh: "Because you have caused your iniquity to be remembered by uncovering your transgressions, by exposing your sins through all your deeds — because you have come to remembrance, you will be seized with the hand. And you, O profane, wicked one, the prince of Israel, whose day has come in the time of the punishment of the end, thus says the Lord Yahweh: 'Remove the turban and lift off the crown; this will no more be this. That which is low, make high, and that which is high, make low. I shall make it deformation, deformation, deformation. Moreover, this will not be until he comes to whom the judgement is, and I shall grant it.'"'

Again, the prophet tells that **'the word of Yahweh came'** to him, giving a further instruction based on the question of whose human hands would wield the sword of Yahweh, a horrific instrument of destruction. Ezekiel's message will tell out that **'the king of Babylon'** is the chosen instrument of death.

Firstly, Ezekiel was required to **'set for yourself two ways for the sword of the king of Babylon to come'**. This probably means that he had to sketch two lines in the sand, or earth, with his finger, or with a stick, the shape being like an inverted 'Y' (try to imagine it). Then he was to **'fashion a hand; at the head of the way of the city fashion it'**. The **'hand'** would have been a signpost,[76] and **'the head of the way of the city'** may have been at the centre of the inverted 'Y' (at Damascus, or perhaps at Babylon).[77] There the sign would have pointed travellers along the road leading to **'Rabbah of the sons of Ammon'** and also along that leading to **'Judah, in fortified Jerusalem'**. In that **'Rabbah'** means 'great', the issue concerned which of two powerful, defended cities might expect a Babylonian assault. Ezekiel would have inscribed the signpost in his sketch (21:18-20).

In 21:3-5 Yahweh's word to Ezekiel concerning 'the earth of Israel' had been that 'I am against you, and I shall draw *my sword* from its sheath ... *my sword* shall come out from its sheath against all flesh, from the Negev to the north ... and all flesh will know that I, Yahweh, have brought out *my sword* from its sheath.' The sovereignty of the God of Israel when his people were about to be ravaged by Nebuchadnezzar has been established: the Babylonian sword is actually that of God.

Nevertheless, Nebuchadnezzar the warlord remains blithely unaware that he serves the interests of the God of Israel. Instead, he resorts to **'divination'** to decide where he should advance. Standing **'at the division of the way'**, at the centre of the inverted 'Y', he inscribes two arrows. Upon one, 'Jerusalem' is marked; and upon the other, 'Rabbah'. Then he shakes the quiver and extracts at random one of the two arrows on the assumption that the gods, having predetermined his selection, will thereby reveal to him where he should go.

But can he be absolutely certain about this? To ensure that the arrows have not deceived him, he **'consults the household idols'**, domestic cult images.[78] Finally, to arrive at total certitude, he **'looks at the liver'**, by which is meant a scrutiny of the entrails of a sacrificed animal in order to ascertain the divine will (21:21).[79]

It is as if Ezekiel, beholding the Babylonian monarch indulging in this (for the prophet) foolish pantomime, silently mocks him (21:21).

Exactly how the arrows, the household gods and the liver yielded the requisite information is unknown. But what is important is that when Ezekiel beheld the heathen consultation, a single word had fallen, as it were, into the perplexed monarch's **'right hand'**: **'Jerusalem'** would be the target. The man's mind was now at rest because he believed his battle plan to have been determined by higher powers.

In the event, the consequences of the decision taken by Nebuchadnezzar, notionally obedient to his ancestral deities, and by Yahweh, the God of Israel, are terrifying: the Chaldeans intend **'to set up battering rams'**, **'open the mouth for murder'**, **'lift up the voice with a war cry'**, **'set battering rams against the gates'**, **'cast up mounds'** and construct **'a siege wall'**. The six infinitive phrases (in Hebrew) resonate with fury: total war is decreed against the besieged city of God, from which Zedekiah and his remaining forces will flee for refuge (21:22).

But although Nebuchadnezzar can never know it, the God of Israel has been in control all along, exercising his wisdom and power in requisitioning pagan superstitions (and, now, militarism) for his service. Of course, it had happened before, as witness Balaam and, perhaps, Pharaoh Necho. In later years, a demented Philippian girl would acknowledge Paul to be a servant of the Most High God.[80]

Ezekiel realized that, in spite of having assimilated themselves to alien cults, Zedekiah and his people must have been aware of Nebuchadnezzar's superstitious practice and would scoff at it as **'a false divination in their eyes'**. Therefore, the monarch and his satellites conclude that because Yahweh will never surrender Jerusalem they must be safe. But no! Ezekiel proceeds: **'for them there were solemn oaths, but it will bring iniquity to remembrance, that they may be seized'**.

This statement is difficult, but a comparison with 17:11-21 and 29:1-16 suggests that it points to the oath of allegiance to Nebuchadnezzar taken by Zedekiah,[81] or possibly to Zedekiah's broken amnesty for slaves.[82] Accordingly, Jerusalem's sin will lead to the downfall of the city at the hands of a man whom Yahweh directs by means of heathen divination. Ezekiel's words are ironic in the extreme (21:23).

He probes further. In that the people of Israel have deliberately uncovered their **'transgressions'** and have exposed their **'sins through all** [their] **deeds'**, they have caused their **'iniquity to be remembered'**. But in so doing they have flaunted their folly, and thus have **'come to remembrance'**. Yahweh decrees that because the nation is egregiously perverse, it **'will be seized with the hand'**, presumably by that of the king of Babylon (21:24). The Lord must repudiate those who repudiate him.

Within this whole sorry situation the chief culprit, Zedekiah, is addressed: **'O profane, wicked one, the prince of Israel'**. As in 12:10, he is not referred to as 'king', possibly because that term carried Messianic overtones, and Zedekiah, being the man that he was, in no sense prefigured the one who would come. Indeed, in that his own **'day'**,[83] the occasion of his demise, had virtually arrived, his opportunities for sin have come to their end. In that Zedekiah was exiled to Babylon rather than being put to death,[84] his impending deportation is construed by Ezekiel as **'the time of the punishment of the end'** (21:25).

The prophet must have been a brave man to have so castigated Zedekiah, even though at the time he was a long distance from Jerusalem. Other than (possibly) Elijah's terse rebuke to Ahab,[85] in the Old Testament there is no outburst so vehement.

Through Ezekiel, Zedekiah is commanded to **'remove the turban and lift off the crown'**. It does not matter that the king in distant Jerusalem may never have heard these words, the point being that the accredited servant of Yahweh declares in the name of his God that because Zedekiah is unfit to wear David's crown, he should abdicate the throne immediately. Although the Hebrew word behind **'turban'**, *mitznephet*, is employed elsewhere concerning the headgear of the high priest,[86] there is no evidence to suggest that Zedekiah imitated the folly of Uzziah in usurping the priestly office.[87]

Nor is Yahweh calling for a regime change only: in that **'this will no more be this'**, the kingdom of David as it had been known will cease to be. **'That which is low, make high, and that which is high, make low'** means, as in 1 Samuel 2:6-8 and Luke 1:51-53, a complete change in the existing state of things (21:26).

The immediate message concludes. Yahweh will ensure that the kingdom of David shall fall into ruin. **'Deformation, deformation, deformation'** tells out that everything will be twisted and disjointed, the triple repetition constituting a strong superlative.[88] And even the resultant state of collapse will be unstable, chaos generating further chaos.

Now comes another unmistakable allusion to Genesis 49:10 and its Messianic promise. Most commentators take the view that Ezekiel's words shine a ray of light into an otherwise impossibly dark situation. Accordingly, the prophet recalls Jacob's prediction that neither will the sceptre leave Judah, nor a commander's staff depart from between his feet, until there appears someone to whom such emblems rightly belong.

If so, Ezekiel declares that the crown of Judah will ultimately be given to one individual to whom belongs **'the judgement'**. A similar expression occurs in Deuteronomy 1:17: 'for the judgement is God's'.

The prophet's meaning would be that the one to come will be clothed with divine honour; indeed, that he will be God incarnate. In the person of the expected Christ, therefore, all ambiguity and uncertainty will end, Yahweh dwelling with and guiding his people.

However, Block suggests that the allusion to Genesis 49:10 generates a 'sinister' application.[89] Ezekiel predicts that, instead of the throne of David surviving the Babylonian holocaust, the one who **'comes to whom the judgement is'** is none other than the king of Babylon, to whom judgement *against* Israel will be granted by Yahweh. If so, an ancient Messianic promise thought by a majority to pledge political independence (see comments on 19:1-14) is distorted: instead of Judah ruling the world, the world in the person of Nebuchadnezzar will judge Judah. If this was Ezekiel's burden, he was attempting to jolt his hearers to surrender their belief in the short-term invulnerability of the throne of David and to accept that in the foreseeable future the God of Israel would hand the sceptre of Jewish dominion to a pagan rather than to someone of David's line.

Yet are we obliged to settle for an 'either / or' approach? In that Ezekiel must have been steeped in as many of the Scriptures of Israel as had been written by his time, might he not have wrenched Genesis 49:10 from its Messianic setting in order to shock his immediate constituency with an appalling but not inaccurate application, *and* to lay before them the golden truth that, notwithstanding the impending collapse of David's throne, the Messiah, the son of David, would eventually come?

The present writer would opt for this 'double' application of Genesis 49:10. Ultimately there will be a dawn — but not before thick darkness has supervened temporarily (21:27).

6. The sword turns against Ammon (21:28-29 [Hebrew text: 21:33-34])

21:28-29. 'And you, son of man, prophesy. So you will say, "Thus says the Lord Yahweh to the sons of Ammon and concerning their taunt: thus you will say, 'A sword, a sword! Loosed for slaughter, polished to consume, to be lightning — while they envision emptiness and divine falsehood for you — to lay you on the necks of the wicked who are slain, whose day has come in the time of the punishment of the end.'"'

Ammon, a nation whose territory lay on the east side of the river Jordan, had always been an inveterate enemy of Judah,[90] although, to judge by 21:20, it had taken part in a revolt against Nebuchadnezzar to which, in his perfidy, Zedekiah had contributed.

In that the condemnation issued by Ezekiel against Ammon in 25:1-7 was issued after the fall of Jerusalem, 21:28-32 may be predictive, anticipating the Ammonites' happiness in that, while Jerusalem was being attacked, they were being spared a Babylonian onslaught.[91] Therefore the prophet is to direct his words to this hostile nation, drawing upon the preceding song of the sword of Yahweh, a weapon which turns out to be none other than the sword of the king of Babylon: **'A sword, a sword! Loosed for slaughter, polished to consume, to be lightning'** (21:28).

Majestically, Ezekiel pronounces the sure word of Yahweh just at the time when **'they envision emptiness and divine falsehood for you'** — that is, for Ammon. But who were **'they'**? By comparing with 21:23, it may be that 'they' were the false prophets of Ammon: even as prophetic ministry in Jerusalem was asserting that that city could never be overwhelmed, soothsayers in Ammon were persuading their people that Nebuchadnezzar would never attack them.

But Ezekiel knew better. Because the sword must devastate Ammon, their warriors will fall dead **'on the necks of the wicked who are slain'** — that is, upon the corpses of those Jews already slain by the Chaldeans.

The language is hideously vivid, and Ezekiel requires the reader to exercise his imagination. Hence, although it is true that the Jewish state must suffer **'the time of the punishment of the end'** and that the Davidic monarchy must fall, this does not signify that the enemies of the throne of David will survive (21:29).

7. The destroyer destroyed (21:30-32 [Hebrew text: 21:35-37)

21:30-32. '"'Return it to its sheath. In the place where you were created, in the land of your origin, I shall judge you. Then I shall pour out my indignation upon you; with the fire of my fury I shall blow upon you and will give you into the hand of brutal men, skilled in destruction. You will be fuel for the fire; your blood will be in the midst of the land. You will not be remembered, for I, Yahweh, have spoken.'"'

The prophet now issues a command to the one who wields the sword. But who is being addressed, and whose sword is to be returned to its **'sheath'**? Not a few commentators take the view that Ezekiel summons the sword of Ammon to return to its scabbard, this people desisting from military adventures against Judah in order to return quietly to the land whence they derived,[92] there to await the judgement of Yahweh. To back this up, it is suggested that the Hebrew *feminine* singular behind the pronouns, **'in the place where *you* were created, in the land of *your* origin'**, shows that a man of war, Nebuchadnezzar, is not being addressed.

Another view is that the reference may be to Babylon addressed as a feminine entity. If this is so, the destinies of both Judah and Ammon recede into the background. Throughout this chapter Ezekiel has called upon the sword of Yahweh, alias Nebuchadnezzar, to devastate Judah. But would the king of Babylon be innocent? L. C. Allen suggests an answer to the question:

> Was Babylonian hegemony — for such the sword implies in the light of v. 24 (English, 21:19) ... to be Yahweh's last word? By no means. A voice offstage, as it were, gives an order for the sword to be replaced in its scabbard. Then the sword is addressed afresh, now as Yahweh's victim. Its work done, it is destined for destruction in its sheath.[93]

Men and nations who live by the sword die by it,[94] and Babylon can be no exception. I would opt for this view.

The metaphor of the sword now falls away, to be replaced by that of a searing wind from Yahweh. He will **'blow upon'** Babylon, a people now to be surrendered to **'the hand of brutal men, skilled in destruction'**, which subsequent history will identify as the Medes and the Persians. Nor will there be any post-war reconstruction, that 'bitter and hasty nation'[95] being consigned to total oblivion even as **'fuel'** is consumed by the flame that it generates. Its **'blood'**, all of it, will be poured away and its life will thereby be extinct. Yahweh 'declares' that it must be so. Nebuchadnezzar will accomplish his fell work — and then vanish. Ezekiel implies that the old must pass away so that the glories of a new age may appear. But they are not yet visible on a horizon that is so distant (21:31-32).

Application

When deliberately misinterpreted, the promises of God become the kiss of death. In Ezekiel's day, and since,[96] the people of Judah chose to believe that the Messianic prediction of Genesis 49:9-10 would render them immune to military conquest. But, as Ezekiel well knew, they were tragically wrong. There are multitudes of professing Christians who place their confidence in the institution of the church and its so-called 'sacraments' ('ordinances' is a better word) with a view to final salvation. But the Bible teaches another, exclusive, way — that of personal faith in Christ. Depending upon the attitude of your heart, this blessed route is either wondrously easy or intolerably difficult.

In truth, Nebuchadnezzar was the servant of Yahweh, but someone who sought to discern the mind of heaven by resorting to soothsaying and divination. Sometimes the Lord employs astonishing agents by whom to fulfil his purposes of redemption. Who would have supposed that we believers have cause to be thankful to our God for, say, men like Iscariot, Pilate and the anonymous soldiers who wielded whip, hammer and nails? Yet it would have been better for Iscariot had he never been born.[97]

As the Bible explains the matter, neither do God's purposes necessarily justify their means, nor may the Holy One of Israel be censured if he employs Nebuchadnezzar or Iscariot or, ultimately, even Satan himself.[98] Were the mind of the Lord not revealed to us in Scripture, who would comprehend it? Let us spend much time with this book.

The sins of Jerusalem and of Israel (Ezekiel 22:1-31)

Thus far in his prophecy Ezekiel has drawn attention to the grim fact that, because of the perversity of a people who in principle, although not formally, had thrown off the yoke of Moses' law, they must forfeit their tenure of the land of Canaan, are to be deprived of the throne of David and must suffer the loss of the temple of Yahweh in Jerusalem, the only place on earth where sacrifice to the one God could legitimately be made.

Moreover, Ezekiel has been at pains to show that by so doing Yahweh will be faithful to what we have termed the 'small print' of the Sinai covenant, in which the Lord forewarns of judgement in the anticipated event of Israel reneging on its commitment to him.[99]

The present chapter continues in similar vein, containing three distinct words from Yahweh, each commencing with **'Then the word of Yahweh came to me, saying'** (22:1,17,23), explaining why judgement was imminent rather than impending. It is as if the Lord was seeking to justify himself before his faithless people prior to triggering the destruction of Jerusalem. Because this God is personal, caring and concerned, and if the sword is to flash in temple, palace, avenue, street, workshop, school and home, bringing havoc to all, there must be a reason. There is, and Yahweh will declare it: although he is guiltless, the city is not, remaining without excuse for its sins.

The first word declares that these sins hasten the time when the city will become an object of universal scorn (22:1-16). The second predicts the purification of Israel under the metaphor of metal being refined in a furnace — although there is a twist to the figure of speech (22:17-22). The final word tells that because moral corruption pervades Israel, no one can escape judgement (22:23-31).

1. The city of blood (22:1-16)

Chapter 18 has shown that the Jews, both in Jerusalem and in exile, were indulging themselves in historical revisionism: whereas their forefathers had eaten sour grapes, the teeth of their descendants were being set on edge (18:2),[100] meaning that innocent offspring were suffering for their parents' errors. But those who said this were wide of the mark. Now the prophet will indict his people for specific transgressions. **'Blood'**, as shed in homicide, or by amoral and illegal activity, features largely in his recriminations (22:2,3,4,6,9,10,13).

22:1-16. Then the word of Yahweh came to me, saying, 'And you, son of man, will you judge? Will you judge the city of blood? But make known to her all her abominations. And you will say, "Thus says the Lord Yahweh: 'O city that pours out blood in her midst — so that her time may come — and that makes idols for herself for defilement. For your blood that you have poured out, you are guilty; and by your idols that you have made, you are defiled. So you have brought your days near and have come to your years. Therefore I have given you to be a reproach to the nations and a derision to all the lands. They who are near and they who are far from you will deride you, you of defiled name and abundant in tumult.

'"'Look, the princes of Israel! Each according to his strength has been in you in order to pour out blood. Father and mother among you they have treated with contempt. They have oppressed the alien in your midst. Orphan and widow in you they have maltreated. You have scorned my holy things and have profaned my Sabbaths. Slanderous men have been in you in order to pour out blood, and within you they have eaten on the mountains. They have committed lewdness in your midst. In you they have uncovered the nakedness of the father; they have humbled the defilement of the menstrual woman. And one man will commit abomination with the wife of his neighbour, and another will lewdly defile his daughter-in-law. And in you yet another will humble his sister, his father's daughter. In you they take bribes in order to pour out blood. You accept interest and profit, and by oppression you have injured your neighbour for profit, and have forgotten me,' declares the Lord Yahweh.

'"'Now, look, I clap my hand at your unjust gain that you have made and at your blood which is in your midst. Will your heart stand or will your hands be strong in the days in which I shall deal with you? I, Yahweh, have spoken, and I shall act. So I shall scatter you among the nations and shall disperse you in the lands, and I shall consume your uncleanness from you. Then you will profane yourself in the eyes of the nations, and you will know that I am Yahweh.'"'

In the same way that Yahweh questioned Ezekiel in 20:4, he again confronted the prophet with the danger of Israel's situation: **'Will you judge? Will you judge the city of blood?'** The Hebrew behind **'blood'** is in the plural — 'bloods', perhaps suggesting that there were bloodstains everywhere in the community. At the time of Ezekiel's ministry, Nineveh, 'the bloody city' (literally, 'city of bloods'; cf. 7:23; 9:9),[101] had already been overthrown. Perhaps Ezekiel likens Jerusalem to an eminent city that, for its sins, had attained its nemesis. The question **'Will you judge?'** is a masked imperative, meaning, 'you will judge'. Brown, Driver and Briggs comment that the Hebrew interrogative particle, as employed here twice, 'is used in questions which, by seeming to make doubtful what cannot be denied, have the force of an impassioned or indignant affirmation'.[102] Ezekiel was being challenged to fulfil his prophetic ministry at a critically difficult time. The **'abominations'** of Jerusalem that Ezekiel would **'make known'** associate bloodshed and idolatry, the two offences being considered as inseparable (22:1-2).

Thus far in this prophecy Ezekiel has recalled the detailed warnings of the Sinai covenant between Yahweh and Israel. Leviticus 18:24-30 insists, for example, that if (or when) Israel defiles herself with the abominations of neighbouring societies, she will defile the land that had been granted to her. Therefore, that land, by way of self-protection, will vomit her out. Ezekiel's point is that the anticipation of that and related passages has been realized, almost as if the children of Israel had sinned deliberately so that the **'time'** for the punishment of the city of Jerusalem **'may come'**.

Warned as they were both by the law of Moses and by subsequent prophets, Israel's idolatry, itself a blatant rejection of the terms of the covenant, now has the appearance of being a direct challenge to Yahweh: let him evict them if he dare! They test God[103] — a dangerous procedure (22:3).

Now Jerusalem is addressed directly, almost as if the city is being charged in a court, with Ezekiel the mouthpiece for the divine prosecutor, and yet with these differences: firstly, there is no jury because there is no need for such; secondly, the prosecutor is the judge, Yahweh himself. Since the nation's guilt has been established beyond all doubt by repetitive bloodshed and idolatry, and in that repentance is beyond them, they themselves — rather than Yahweh — **'have brought** [their] **days near'**. It is as though Jerusalem, representing the theocracy, is gripped by a death wish, offending deliberately in order to bring doom upon herself. The consequence is that Yahweh has decreed that **'the nations'** and **'the lands'** will have just cause to ridicule her. This does not mean that idolatrous peoples beyond the land of Israel exercise a moral and spiritual discernment superior to that of Israel. Rather, when the Jews have been deservedly cast out from their national home they will be mocked by those who still possess roofs over their heads (22:4). Few will love and protect the poor, particularly when the latter have wilfully brought destitution upon themselves.

The consequence of Israel's apostasy is given further delineation: whereas Jerusalem is **'of defiled name and abundant in tumult'**, the noise generated by oppression *within* the walls will cease, being replaced by **'derision'** from *without*. The prosecutor extends his accusing hand towards the guilty city — **'you'**. There is no answer; nor can there be (22:5).

Yahweh now presents evidence to justify the condemnation of Jerusalem. **'The princes of Israel'** without exception are held up as exponents of violence: **'each according to his strength'**, to the limit of his ability, **'has been in you** [that is, in Jerusalem] **in order to pour out blood'**. Although no specific instances are mentioned, one thinks of Manasseh and Jehoiakim.[104] Perhaps such men are termed **'princes'** because Yahweh never considered them to be kings in the true sense of the term (22:6).

Although we might think of murder as an infringement of what is sometimes termed 'natural law', Yahweh's indictment is based on Judah's rejection of the Mosaic covenant and, in particular, of the Decalogue and Leviticus 19 (22:6).

Thus **'they'**, the 'princes' in Jerusalem, have done their utmost to shed blood, violence being habitual. They have oppressed parents with children, have exploited strangers in distress and have doled out worse than rough justice to orphans and widows, the most vulnerable members of society (22:7).

Further, the **'holy things'** of God have been desecrated and his **'Sabbaths'** **'profaned'**, the plural indicating desecration not only of day seven in the week, but of sacred days and perhaps years (cf. 20:13,16,20,21,24).

The seven-day week and the sabbatical cycles were unknown in the world beyond Israel, first appearing as a central component of the Sinai covenant. The recurring seventh-day rests were ongoing reminders of Yahweh as both Creator and Saviour,[105] and the septennial sabbath years were designed to prove to the people their dependence upon Yahweh for all their material needs: they could rely upon him when resting on day seven and when not cultivating their land in year seven. In Ezekiel's time, Israel had long forgotten how to obey the commands and how to depend upon the promises of God (22:8).[106]

Given his priestly origins and his sensitivity to Judah's disregard for the demands of Moses' law, Ezekiel was exactly the right man to vocalize Yahweh's denunciation of Jerusalem.

Probably reflecting Leviticus 19:16, Ezekiel declares that there had been widespread employment of slander with a view to bloodshed, a sort of corporate agent-provocateur mechanism planned to destroy enemies by pseudo-legal process. And there were idolatry and **'lewdness'**, the latter contravening the stipulations of Leviticus 18 and 20. Historically, there had always been a link between pagan worship and immorality,[107] and one can only strain to imagine what was happening in Jerusalem when Ezekiel ministered far from home (22:9).

The 'city of blood' (22:2) continues to be addressed. Still reflecting upon Leviticus 18 and 20, Yahweh declares that sexual perversion was virtually the norm, innocent blood being exposed by means other than murder: non-consenting women, when ritually defiled because of the monthly cycle, were being humiliated (22:10). Adultery is termed an **'abomination'**. **'Yet another'** points to unmitigated licentiousness throughout the populace. Look where he would, Yahweh beheld the same sad spectacle (22:11).

Bribes were being taken by those in authority from those who sought the deaths of their adversaries, scaled-down reflections of Haman's bribery of Ahasuerus with a view to eliminating the Jews in the Persian Empire.[108] In that Haman contravened the law of conscience, evil-minded Jews in Jerusalem contravene that of the written law, which was far worse.[109] The requirement of Leviticus 25:35-37 that no Israelite should lend to a 'brother', a fellow-Israelite, at interest, had been put to one side.[110] Did Ezekiel know about Zedekiah's oppression of poor Hebrews who sold themselves into slavery, and of that king's violation of the law of release?[111] Neither was God feared nor men respected.

Accordingly, these appalling sins are declared to be no more than symptomatic: **'"You ... have forgotten me", declares the Lord Yahweh'** (22:12). Will not Yahweh, then, forget Jerusalem? Yes and no, as the following verses and chapters will tell.

Yahweh declares that he has clapped his hands in anger because of profiteering and bloodshed within Jerusalem (cf. 6:11). So, will the **'heart'** of the city and its **'hands'** be **'strong'** when smitten by those of the Lord? Because Yahweh has pronounced judgement, he will **'act'** as both judge and executioner. Nebuchadnezzar's armies are by implication the unwitting agents of destruction (22:13-14).

Thus, in fulfilment of Leviticus 26:33-39 and Deuteronomy 28:64-65, the people of Jerusalem are to be scattered among the nations, this being the only way to deal with the situation. In that Ezekiel addresses Jerusalem (cf. 22:2), the **'uncleanness'** to be consumed will be the populace, rather than their instruments of idolatry (22:15). According to Leviticus

26:43, which Ezekiel may have had in mind, 'The land also shall be left empty by *them*, and will enjoy its Sabbaths while it lies desolate without *them*.'

This first prophetic word closes with the prediction that, when the catastrophe is past, the dishonourable and dishonoured deportees will have abundant opportunity to **'profane'** themselves in the places where they are found, in fulfilment of Deuteronomy 4:27-28; 28:36-37,64. Eventually, when the prodigal people come to their senses, they **'will know that I am Yahweh'** (22:16). Nothing less than extreme suffering can lead to remorse.

2. Israel: refined in a furnace (22:17-22)

22:17-22. Then the word of Yahweh came to me, saying, 'Son of man, the house of Israel has become dross to me; all of them are copper, tin, lead and iron within a furnace; they have become the dross of silver. Therefore, thus says the Lord Yahweh: "Because all of you have become dross, therefore, look, I am gathering you in the midst of Jerusalem. Just as silver, copper, iron, lead and tin are gathered in the midst of a furnace to blow fire upon it for melting, thus I shall gather in my anger and in my wrath. I shall set you down and melt you. So, I shall collect you and will blow upon you with the fire of my fury, and you will be melted in its midst. As silver is melted in the midst of a furnace, just so will you be melted in its midst, and you will know that I, Yahweh, have poured out my wrath upon you."'

The **'word of Yahweh'** came again to the **'son of man'**. The figure of the refining of silver and other valuable metals was well known among the prophets, and Ezekiel would have been no exception.[112] Here he assumes that his hearers would also be acquainted with the technology of the separation of silver from crude ore.

Apparently, silver can occur in significant quantities, up to one per cent, in galena, a black mineral with a metallic appearance and consisting mainly of lead sulphide. To extract the silver the ore has to be melted, the floating slag oxidized and then skimmed off. What is left will retain the precious metal. But in the case of Jerusalem, what if there is no silver? What if **'the house of Israel has become dross to'** Yahweh? Here, the Lord informs Ezekiel that, far from being precious metal, the people of Jerusalem resemble worthless material that must be burnt away (22:17-18).

But what of those who had fled their homes to take refuge within the city walls? **'Therefore, thus says the Lord Yahweh: "Because all of you have become dross, therefore, look, I am gathering you in the midst of Jerusalem."'** Shockingly, their flight to the city is interpreted as having been devised by Yahweh, who assumes the role of a metal refiner. Jerusalem, the prime target of the Babylonian assault, becomes the crucible in which the fugitives, considered as **'dross'**, are to be consumed (22:19).[113]

Whereas **'silver, copper, iron, lead and tin are gathered in the midst of a furnace to blow fire upon it for melting'**, Jerusalem will experience meltdown (22:20). But, according to 22:18, no silver will be detected after the conflagration.

And it will be Yahweh himself who applies the heat of military conflict upon Jerusalem the crucible: **'I shall collect you ... and you will be melted in its midst'** (22:21). A consequence will be that those who survive will recognize that behind Nebuchadnezzar and his hordes had stood another, the God of Israel, and that he had honoured himself by honouring the covenantal warnings of Leviticus and Deuteronomy: **'and you will know that I, Yahweh, have poured out my wrath upon you'** (22:22).

Israel had always considered herself as having been redeemed from the furnace of Egypt.[114] But now there has to be a second purgation. So corrupt is the theocracy centred on Jerusalem that if there is to be a new beginning it cannot be in the heartland of Judah. All things must be new. This is why the word of God comes to his people from a prophet of the exile.

3. Judgement justified (22:23-31)

22:23-31. Then the word of Yahweh came to me, saying, 'Son of man, say to her, "You are a land which has not been cleansed or rained upon in the day of indignation. There is a conspiracy of her prophets in her midst, as a roaring lion tearing the prey. They devour life; they take wealth and costly things; they multiply her widows in her midst. Her priests have violated my law and have profaned my sacred things — they have not distinguished between the sacred and the profane and have not made known the difference between what is defiled and what is clean, and have hidden their eyes from my Sabbaths. And I have been profaned in their midst.

'"Her princes within her are like wolves tearing the prey, pouring out blood and destroying life for violent gain. And her prophets have smeared whitewash for them, envisioning vanity and divining falsehood for them, saying, 'Thus says the Lord Yahweh' — and Yahweh has not spoken. The people of the land have perpetrated oppression and have committed robbery. They have maltreated the needy and the poor, and they have oppressed the sojourner without justice.

'"Then I sought a man from them who would build up the enclosure and who would stand in the breach before me on behalf of the land so that it should not be destroyed — but I found none. Then I poured out my indignation upon them. In the fire of my fury I put an end to them. I have set their way upon their heads," declares the Lord Yahweh.'

The figure of washing replaces that of metallurgy, the focus of attention now being the land of Judah in general, rather than Jerusalem in particular. Perhaps Noah's Flood is in mind when Ezekiel confides that the **'word of Yahweh'** spoke to him, instructing him to inform the land that **'You are a land which has not been cleansed or rained upon in the day of indignation.'** Even as the world from which Noah escaped was scoured to remove human wickedness,[115] because the earth of Judah has been defiled it shall be purified. Already announced (13:11,13), the fulfilment is imminent.

The fact that Yahweh is said to be indignant shows that the impending catastrophe is merited by Israel and that when it comes it will not be unjust. Neither has the land been kept clean by its inhabitants, nor has it received rain from God. For these reasons it is barren and desolate. Before it can be commissioned again as a residence for the true people of God, the present generation — representative of all previous inhabitants — must be evicted (22:23-24).

Yahweh's word to Ezekiel explains why the land is to be purged. Firstly, the false prophets are said to be like lions devouring their prey, being nothing less than widow-makers. It is likely that Ezekiel alludes to Zephaniah 3:3-4, Zephaniah having ministered in Jerusalem during the time of Josiah:

> Her [Jerusalem's] princes in her midst are roaring lions;
> Her judges are evening wolves
> That leave not a bone till morning.
> Her prophets are insolent, treacherous people;
> Her priests have polluted the sanctuary;
> They have done violence to the law.[116]

If this is so, Yahweh, through Ezekiel, appeals to an indubitably faithful prophet of a previous generation, even as he has alluded already to the minutiae of the covenant stipulations. In this way, Ezekiel's ministry is given further authority and weight (22:25).

And the priests have violated the law by refusing to distinguish between the common and the sacred and by not making manifest the difference between cleanness and uncleanness.[117] One is reminded of Hophni and Phinehas, sons of Eli.[118] Specifically, they have averted their eyes from Yahweh's **'Sabbaths'** — collectively the definitive sign of the covenant relationship between Yahweh and Israel.[119] In sum, Yahweh has been **'profaned'** among them (22:26).[120]

Now, the **'princes within'** Jerusalem — probably the judiciary rather than the nobility[121] — are indicted. They are incarnate **'wolves'** tearing at their human **'prey'** for the sake of material gain, by which action is meant judicial murder (22:27).

And, as in 13:10, through their divinations and false visions the pseudo-prophets have assured their hearers in the name of Yahweh that they will prosper, thus obscuring the wretchedness of the situation. But Yahweh had never commissioned them to say anything in his name (22:28). Taylor notes that they were 'religious tranquillizers ... whitewashing their [that is, the judiciaries'] crimes with correct, but empty, formulae'.[122]

The tale of woe continues. **'The people of the land'**, the middle-class citizenry (cf. 7:27), are dishonest, ill-treating the destitute. The foreign resident is denied his rights (22:29). This statement reflects 18:12,18 and Jeremiah 22:13.

Recalling 3:17, anticipating 33:7 and borrowing from Jeremiah 5:1-6, it is declared that Yahweh has **'sought'** for someone to mend the broken walls, summoning the fallen theocracy to repentance and thus to avert a military occupation of Jerusalem. Yet all had been in vain: unlike Moses in his day,[123] no one had been found (cf. 13:5). Perhaps there is also an allusion to Genesis 18:22-32, where Abraham prays for the deliverance of righteous men, if any, living in Sodom. None among the royal family, the priests, the ruling classes, the magistracy, the official prophets or the citizenry were burdened for the degenerate state of Judah (22:30).

For this reason **'fire'** from the Lord is to burn until the populace of Jerusalem has vanished. The tenses inherent in **'poured out'**, **'put an end'** and **'have set their way'** are so-called 'prophetic perfects', meaning that Yahweh's retributive action is certain. In modern jargon, the thing is 'as good as done' (22:31).

Application

'The city of blood' (22:1) was the Jerusalem of Ezekiel's day. And yet more innocent blood would be shed there.[124] Just as the city was overthrown by Babylon, so it would be destroyed by the Romans. What, then, shall be the fate of those many regimes which systematically employ violence to maintain themselves? Eventually, they must fall.

The true leader should serve, not dictate (22:6-7).[125] To illustrate, the elders' advice to Rehoboam, son of Solomon, was that if he would serve his people they would serve him.[126] And at the level of the local church, although an elder must govern, he is never to be a tyrant.[127]

Nominal membership of a church is inadequate. Faith and love are all-important. As in Israel, so also in the churches: branches that do not bear fruit will inevitably be discarded.[128]

Those who lead are required to understand and then tell out God's truth, and this because we all live on the threshold of an eternity that embraces both heaven and hell.

For us, as for Ezekiel's people, the written Word of God is paramount, in that the Lord will always act in accordance with his stated promises, whether in blessing the penitent or judging the recalcitrant. He cannot deny himself.[129] Throughout the prophecy of Ezekiel, Yahweh shows himself determined to honour the warnings of Leviticus and Deuteronomy. Far from contradicting the original promises to the patriarchs concerning their tenancy of the land of Canaan (promises which commence at Genesis 12:7 and 15:7), the destruction of Jerusalem and the exile to Babylon are seen as a necessary preparative. Ezekiel looked forward to a time when the land would accommodate a renewed people delighting in the service of their God. The present chapter, therefore, anticipates the redundancy of the Sinai covenant and the dissolution of a nominal 'Israel' in favour of something new, an arrangement and a people based (as we must conclude in the light of the New Testament) upon the death and glorification of the Lord Jesus Christ.

Oholah and Oholibah (Ezekiel 23:1-49)

More than two years have passed since Ezekiel was called to the prophetic office (1:2). The present series of prophecies, which commenced with chapter 20, draws to its conclusion, the indictment against Judah approaching a climax. Condemnations have piled up and the mind of the reader recoils when trying to contemplate the spiritual and moral breakdown of Jerusalem, a collapse apparent to men of the calibre and sensitivity of Jeremiah, Daniel and Ezekiel, all of whom originated there.

A startlingly vivid allegory is employed: Samaria and Jerusalem, standing respectively for the two kingdoms of Israel and Judah, are likened to two promiscuous sisters who since the days of their youth had been habitually unclean.

The lengthy chapter 16 likened Judah to an impure girl who, when a grown woman, was far worse than her evil sisters. There the historic past of Israel was given recall in some detail. The procedure is the same here, to the extent that the picture given by Ezekiel hardly requires an elaborate exposition. Jeremiah 3:6-11 presents a similar metaphor, albeit in an abbreviated form. Yahweh is presented as the impassioned husband who bitterly resents being cuckolded, thus becoming an object of derision.

Nevertheless, there are significant differences in emphasis between chapters 16 and 23. In the former, the commencement of the nation's sinful career is traced back to Canaan; in the latter, to the residence of Jacob's expanding family in Egypt, suggesting that Yahweh's covenant partner had *always* been incipiently, if not actually, unfaithful. And, whereas in chapter 16 the focus is upon Israelite idolatry, in chapter 23 it falls upon military and political alliances that were symptomatic of spiritual apostasy. Further, if in chapter 16 Jerusalem is seen as the recipient of alien favours, in chapter 23 she pursues foreign lovers, her depravity knowing no bounds. And unlike 16:53-63, in chapter 23 there is no mention of a restoration of a penitent Israel to Yahweh's favour.[130]

1. One mother, two daughters (23:1-4)

23:1-4. Then the word of Yahweh came to me, saying, 'Son of man, there were two women, daughters of the one mother. And they committed whoredom in Egypt; in their youth they committed whoredom. There they let their breasts be pressed and there they handled their virgin nipples. And their names were Oholah, the elder, and Oholibah, her sister. Then they became mine and bore sons and daughters. And as for their names, Samaria is Oholah, and Jerusalem Oholibah.'

Throughout this chapter Yahweh narrates to Ezekiel the past history of Israel, rather than instructing him to transmit to the exiles in Babylonia what he hears. Perhaps the prophet had to enter into a yet deeper conviction concerning the necessity of the theocracy of Israel being brought to an end through the Chaldean invasion.

Accordingly, **'there were two women, daughters of the one mother'**. The children, who have yet to be identified, were full sisters with a common past and therefore possessing equal rights and responsibilities within their family unit (23:1-2).

It turns out that they also shared certain ruinous character traits: **'And they committed whoredom in Egypt; in their youth they committed whoredom'** (23:3). The second part of the present verse does not spare the details, its purpose being to show that when the children of Jacob entered into a formal covenant relationship with Yahweh they had no genuine desire to remain faithful to him. Exodus 14:12 records that, soon after the departure from Egypt, the Israelites were adamant that it would have been better for them 'to serve the Egyptians'.

The two sisters are entitled **'Oholah'** and **'Oholibah'**, names which are riddles proposed for Ezekiel's — and our — consideration. Although they represent **'Samaria'** and **'Jerusalem'**, the capitals of the two halves of the divided kingdom of Israel following Jeroboam's revolt,[131] the significance of their names is less certain. In that both incorporate a Hebrew word for 'tent', *ôhel*, **'Oholah'** might mean 'her tent' and **'Oholibah'**, 'my tent is with her'. If so, 'Oholah' could point to the northern kingdom, Israel, where Jeroboam I had instituted a pattern of worship designed to rival the legitimate system then centred at Jerusalem.[132] The illegitimate scheme endured until the Assyrians carried Israel into captivity.[133] And 'Oholibah' would allude to Judah, which in the earlier part of Ezekiel's ministry still contained Yahweh's authentic tabernacle, the temple constructed by Solomon. But, as Block points out,[134] the similarity of the two appellations stresses not only their relationship as full sisters, but also their common apostasy: the 'tent' of the former was sacrilegious from its inception, that of the latter being desecrated by many years of abuse.

It is stated by Yahweh that **'they became mine and bore sons and daughters'**, meaning that he entered into seemingly bigamous marriages with both women. Although Jacob married two sisters, Leah and Rachel,[135] at a later date Leviticus 18:18 prohibits the practice. Here, however, we are presented with an allegory reflecting the timeline from the division of Israel until the Babylonian exile, during which period Yahweh never relinquished suzerainty over either Samaria or Judah: both belonged to him as one in the most intimate of all relationships. *If* it appears that the Lord had two wives, it was they who were to be blamed for not maintaining the monogamous unity of Israel. The reference to an expanding family may point to the numerical increase of Israel both before and after the Egyptian captivity (23:4).[136]

2. Oholah and the Assyrians (23:5-10)

23:5-10. 'And Oholah played the harlot in place of me. She lusted over her lovers — after Assyria — who came near, clothed in purple, governors and prefects, all of them desirable young men, riders, horse charioteers. Then she bestowed her fornications upon them, all of them the choice of the sons of Assyria. And she defiled herself with all with whom she lusted, together with all their idols. And she did not abandon her fornications from her time in Egypt, for they had lain with her in her youth — they had handled her virgin nipples and poured out their fornications upon her. Therefore I gave her into the hand of her lovers, into the hand of the sons of Assyria after whom she lusted. They themselves revealed her nakedness: they took her sons and her daughters and slew her with the sword. So she became a name among women when they executed judgements in her midst.'

Yahweh now recounts certain principal features of the past history of Samaria and Jerusalem, commencing with the former. Following the departure from Egypt and subsequent settlement in Canaan, 'Oholah' continued to act in character, this time by forming a relationship with the Assyrians. Their nearness —

'lovers ... who came near' — possibly alludes to common affinities rather than to geographical proximity.[137] Here, the emphasis lies upon the Israelites pursuing aliens, rather than, as in chapter 16, foreign intrusions within Israel (23:5). The Black Obelisk of Shalmaneser III shows Jehu of Israel, or his ambassador, prostrating himself before the Assyrian, possibly to seek military aid against Hazael of Damascus,[138] and this might have been about 840 BC.[139] Or there may be an allusion to Menahem's approach to Tiglath-Pileser.[140]

In the event, Israel was dazzled by the brilliance, colour and prestige of the empire of Nineveh, and particularly by its aristocracy — individuals described as **'clothed in purple, governors and prefects'**. **'All'** were **'desirable young men, riders, horse charioteers'**. Although some of the Hebrew terms employed in the text might be foreign loanwords which at present cannot be translated accurately,[141] the point being made is that **'all'**, repeated three times for emphasis, were contemplated as objects of Israelite desire. And, since liaisons with foreign powers demanded Israelite deference to their cultures, the sister **'defiled herself with all with whom she lusted, together with all their idols'**.

Deuteronomy 17:16 had prohibited any Israelite king from acquiring large numbers of horses, a restriction implying that they were not to adopt a warlike posture. But the northern kingdom succumbed to materialism, thereby sealing her fate (23:5-7).[142]

Tragically, new times did not dissolve old memories, and the sins of Egypt were never forgotten. The girl's memory was long and imaginative, as witness the golden calves of Jeroboam, son of Nebat, which subsequent monarchs never removed.[143] Undoubtedly, they were a reflection both of Aaron's golden calf and of Egyptian practices.[144] Yahweh's words to Ezekiel are graphic and unpleasant in the extreme, yet necessarily so, given the shocking nature of Israel's apostasy (23:8).

The inevitable consequence was that Yahweh, now the outraged husband, handed 'Oholah', Samaria, over to her **'her lovers'**, **'the sons of Assyria'**, who soon came to despise her. They stripped her, abducted her children and killed her **'with the sword'**. To other **'women'** — that is, to other nations — she became a **'name'**, a byword for destruction.[145] Historically, all this had happened 130 years before the time of Ezekiel. The serial adulteress was publicly disgraced and then slain, the Assyrians having (unwittingly) **'executed judgements in her midst'** (23:9-10).

3. Oholibah, Assyria and Babylon (23:11-21)

23:11-21. Then her sister, Oholibah, saw, and made her lust more depraved than hers and her fornications more depraved than her sister's fornications. She lusted after the sons of Assyria, governors and prefects, who came near, clothed to perfection, riders, horse charioteers, all of them desirable young men. And I saw that she was defiled: one way for both of them! So she added to her fornications, and beheld men inscribed upon the wall: images of Chaldeans inscribed in vermilion, girded with belts on their loins and with flowing turbans on their heads. All had the appearance of officers, like the sons of Babylon, Chaldeans, in the land of their birth. Then she lusted after them — a sight for her eyes! — and sent messengers for them to Chaldea. So the sons of Babylon came to her for a bed of love and defiled her with their fornications. Then, when she had been defiled by them, her soul was disgusted with them. So she had uncovered her fornications and revealed her nakedness, and my soul was disgusted with her, even as my soul had been disgusted with her sister. Yet she multiplied her fornications, remembering the days of her youth when she had fornicated in the land of Egypt. For she lusted after their paramours whose flesh was the flesh of donkeys and whose ejaculations were the ejaculations of horses. And you gave thought to the lewdness of your youth, when they from Egypt handled your nipples because of your youthful breasts.'

Yahweh informs Ezekiel that Samaria's sister, **'Oholibah'**, was far worse than she in her indulgence of sinful intercourse. Within Jerusalem, Ahaz sacrificed to the gods of Damascus because he professed that they were more powerful than the God of Israel.[146] His pragmatic religion was based upon the fallacy that what seems to succeed must be right.

'Depraved' (23:11) translates a Hebrew root, *shachat*, which frequently signifies material or ecological destruction. But here, as in Genesis 6:12, the verb reflects an extreme moral decadence tantamount to self-destruction. In Jerusalem's case, the situation was aggravated in that Yahweh had chosen to establish his sanctuary within her bounds.

In turning her eyes upon **'the sons of Assyria'**, Judah was no less immoral than her sister, as indicated by a comparison between 23:12 and 23:5.[147] Like 'Oholah', 'Oholibah' became ensnared by their magnificence and overawed by their power, seeing their magnates as **'all of them desirable young men'**. Yahweh looked on, recognizing that there had been **'one way for both'** sisters (23:13).

After the Assyrians, the Babylonians. The reference to **'men inscribed upon the wall'** is easily understood, given the evidence of surviving monuments. Perhaps Jerusalem and Judah were fascinated by tales of brilliantly coloured imperial sculptures that must have attracted the attention of Hebrew emissaries to Babylon, as well as being bemused by the splendour of visitors from that land.[148] The exiles in Ezekiel's time would have been acquainted with the **'belts'** and **'flowing turbans'** mentioned here. Like the 'male images' referred to in 16:17, these portraitures would have been exclusively masculine. The sexual connotation is brought into relief, the Jews being dazzled by men who had **'the appearance of officers'** emanating from an omnipotent and militaristic nation, that of the **'Chaldeans'** (23:14-15).

Not unnaturally, the Chaldeans keenly grasped the opportunity for commerce offered by eager Judah. The foolish initiative of normally prudent Hezekiah in displaying his riches to messengers from Babylon comes to mind.[149] But, having been **'defiled by them, her soul was disgusted with them'**. **'Disgusted'**, from the verb *y'qa*, means dislocation or severance, as in the instance of Jacob's thigh.[150] Judah came to estrange herself emotionally from Babylon (23:16-17).

One consequence was that, even as Judah had rejected her Babylonian lovers, Yahweh alienated himself from her in the same way that he had separated himself from 'Oholah': **'and my soul was disgusted with her, even as my soul had been disgusted with her sister'** (23:18).

Babylonian attractions having waned, frustrated Judah turned in the opposite direction — to Egypt. This was the height of folly, as was pointed out at the time by Isaiah and then by Jeremiah.[151]

Although some commentators consider that there might be an allusion here to Josiah's confrontation with Pharaoh Necho at Megiddo in 609 BC,[152] the reality was that Judah had never ceased to reminisce over earlier, sinful days **'in the land of Egypt'**. Her bad blood showed itself many centuries later. Although partners changed, her waywardness was unrelenting (23:19).

The lustfulness of Judah is given vivid and shocking description, recalling the language of Jeremiah 5:8. If the word of Yahweh to Ezekiel appears to us as almost obscene, we need to consider the awfulness of Jerusalem's apostasy as seen by the eyes of heaven. What other metaphor would have been appropriate?

Judah's vacillations between the Chaldeans and the Egyptians were far more than exercises in realpolitik; the leaders in Jerusalem were, after all, no better than their distant ancestors in Egypt prior to the Exodus. This is why from verse 21 until verse 35 the Lord bypasses Ezekiel and addresses **'Oholibah'** directly: **'And you gave thought to the lewdness of your youth'** (23:20-21).

4. Love turns to hate (23:22-31)

23:22-31. 'Therefore, Oholibah, thus says the Lord Yahweh: "Look, I shall arouse your lovers against you, those from whom your soul was estranged, and I shall bring them against you from all around: the sons of Babylon and all the Chaldeans, Pekod and Shoa and Koa — all the sons of Assyria with them, desirable young men, all of them prefects and governors, officers and those who were summoned, all of them horse charioteers.

'"And they will come upon you with weapons and whirling wheels, and with an assembly of peoples, with body screen, shield and helmet. They will set themselves against you from all around and I shall place judgement before them, and they will sentence you with their judgements. Then I shall set my jealousy against you and they will deal with you in fury. They will remove your nose and your ears, and your posterity will fall by the sword. They will take away your sons and your daughters, and your posterity will be devoured by fire. Then they will strip away your clothes and take away your beautiful vessels.

'"So I shall make your lewdness cease from you, and your fornication since the land of Egypt, and you will not raise your eyes to them and will no more remember Egypt." For thus says the Lord Yahweh: "Look, I am giving you into the hand of those whom you hate, into the hand of those from whom you were alienated. And they will deal with you in hatred and will take away your hard-earned produce and will leave you naked and bare. Then the nakedness of your fornications will be uncovered — your lewdness and your fornications. I shall do these things to you because you fornicated after the nations in that you were defiled with their idols. You have walked in the way of your sister, and I shall give her cup into your hand."'

Because this was how it had been, Yahweh speaks to Ezekiel about Jerusalem, alias **'Oholibah'**, concerning the retribution about to fall on the city. His words make the careful reader shiver: **'I shall arouse your lovers against you ... and I shall bring them against you from all around.'** Verses 22, 28, 32 and 35 all lead with **'thus says the Lord Yahweh'**, each section (23:22-27; 23:28-31; 23:32-34; 23:35) being a distinct oracle signifying that the fate experienced by the woman's sister, Samaria, now stares her in the face. The vast array of her lovers again beat a track to her home, Jerusalem, but this time as hated aggressors. It will be the Lord's doing (23:22).

The men of **'Pekod and Shoa and Koa'** may have been rulers, rather than satellite tribes within the Chaldean empire. **'Shoa'** occurs in Isaiah 32:5 and Job 34:19 with the sense of a wealthy and liberal man. But although identification may be impossible, they are mentioned in order to lend dramatic effect to Yahweh's statement: none of her former lovers will be absent when the reckoning arrives at Jerusalem, all flocking to their one-time mistress to indulge in another, novel sport. Nor will the descendants of the Assyrians, earlier world rulers, miss out. They put aside their resplendent clothing and snatch up the apparatus of war. A comparison of verses 6, 12 and 23 would bring into relief the dimensions of the imminent tragedy.

Thus cavalry will encircle Jerusalem before the city is finally reduced (23:23). Whereas these despicable paramours had displayed themselves in their gorgeous robes, now they advance upon 'Oholibah' flaunting their excessive military might. Jerusalem's situation is utterly hopeless.

Worse, it is Yahweh who permits them to overcome the city, the aggressors treating it in accordance with their own ruthless code of war: **'and I shall place judgement before them, and they will sentence you with *their judgements*'**. Details may be imagined, and Ezekiel and his audience would have known exactly what was being said (23:24).

But how could the Lord, the redeeming God of Israel, do this thing? The only answer is that such had been the depravity of Jerusalem and Judah, along with the northern kingdom, that the land had to be scoured of its population.

Yahweh now outlines the atrocious details of the punishment to be meted out by the Chaldeans as the expression of his **'jealousy'**. Facial mutilation will destroy Oholibah's attractiveness, and those of her children not taken into captivity will be put to the sword or burnt (23:25). Ironically, whereas Jerusalem, considered as an immoral woman, had exposed herself to her lovers (23:18; cf. 16:25), she will now be stripped naked, will lose her finery (cf. 16:39) and be displayed to a mocking world (cf. 16:37).[153] Although Moses' law did not demand such degradation, it was a not unusual punishment for adultery in the lands surrounding Israel. The point being made by text and context is that if Jerusalem wishes to behave as an immoral non-Israelite woman, she will be dealt with as such by non-Israelites (23:26).

The object to be attained by such action will be to deliver such a shock to 'Oholibah' that never again will she **'raise'** her seductive **'eyes'** in invitation to **'them'** — that is, to the advocates of cultures such as those of Babylon and Assyria. Having been chastised by the world according to its own standards, the nominal people of God will never again desire to return to that world. Never again will Jerusalem act the nymphomaniac. She **'will no more remember'** her misdeeds in the land of **'Egypt'** (23:27).

A second denunciation commences. Judah's former lovers, now the objects of her hatred, from whom she alienated herself, will accept her into their **'hand'** from Yahweh himself, to do as they will. The present participle inherent in **'I am giving'** indicates that the process of judgement was happening when Ezekiel prophesied (23:28).

And they will recompense her hatred by seizing the fruits of her labour — her land, her cities and her fields — and abandon her. Exposed as she will be, all who behold her will consider that her fate was well deserved: **'the nakedness of your fornications will be uncovered — your lewdness and your fornications'** (23:29).

The picture appals, and it is meant to. What worse fate could there be for an unfaithful wife than to be branded as a prostitute by her husband and then paraded naked by him before the public? Yet this is what Yahweh purposes for once-favoured 'Oholibah'. All this is because Judah had followed other nations, polluting herself with their idolatries. **'I shall do'** follows the 'I am giving you' of 23:28: even when Ezekiel was delivering the oracle, Jerusalem had become the object of Yahweh's wrath and the target for Chaldean aggression (23:30).

Yahweh's judgement of 'Oholibah' is only a repeat of his treatment of 'Oholah'. In that Jerusalem **'walked in the way'** of her **'sister'**, she will drink from her sister's **'cup'** (23:31). Although what the 'cup' contains will be outlined in the following verses, perhaps Ezekiel's metaphor reflects Jeremiah 25:15-19, where Jeremiah tells that he had to hand the cup of Yahweh's wrath to various peoples, *including* 'Jerusalem and the cities of Judah'.[154]

5. Drinking her sister's cup (23:32-35)

23:32-35. 'Thus says the Lord Yahweh: "You will drink your sister's cup, which is deep and wide. It will cause laughter and derision — containing so much. You will be filled with drunkenness and grief — the cup of devastation and desolation, the cup of your sister, Samaria. So you will drink it and drain it, and you will gnaw its fragments and tear your breasts, for I have spoken," declares the Lord Yahweh.

'"Therefore," thus says the Lord Yahweh: "Because you have forgotten me and have cast me behind your back — so also you yourself will bear your own lewdness and your fornications."'

The third oracle, which ends with verse 34, commences: **'Thus says the Lord Yahweh'**. Lacking rhythm, it is a brief poem that seems disjointed, possibly to reflect the emotion of the God who authorized it and also that of the prophet who relayed it. The **'cup'** from which Judah drinks, and from which **'Samaria'** had drunk, is capacious, being both **'deep and wide'**. Because it contains **'so much'** it will **'cause laughter and derision'**, meaning that the nations will jeer because its contents, **'devastation and desolation'**, must be swallowed (23:32-33).

Compelled to raise the chalice to her lips and to gulp, Judah is overcome with unbearable misery and pain. In her agony, she smashes the drained cup and gnaws at a piece of the pottery so that, if at all possible, the agony might diminish. Writhing in torment, she tears her bosom with an earthenware fragment. The irony is shocking: the whore who had yielded her breasts to her lovers (23:21; cf. 23:3) now seeks to mutilate her bosom. And it must be, because **'"I have spoken," declares the Lord Yahweh'** (23:34).

The fourth and final oracle is brief, summarizing what has gone before. Because Jerusalem has **'forgotten'** her God and has **'cast'** him **'behind'** her

'back', she must bear the consequences. To cast something behind one's back means to proceed with no memory of recent events, whether good or bad, as when Hezekiah asserted that Yahweh had cast all the king's sins behind the divine back, or when Nehemiah lamented that Israel had cast the law of Yahweh behind her back.[155] Now Yahweh recalls centuries of infidelity, declaring that the price — eviction from the land of promise — must be paid (23:35).

6. The word of Yahweh is sure (23:36-45)

23:36-45. Then Yahweh said to me, 'Son of man, will you judge Oholah and Oholibah? So tell them their abominations. For they have committed adultery and there is blood on their hands. With their idols they have committed adultery, and they have even transferred their children whom they bore to me to them for food. Moreover, they have done this to me: they defiled my sanctuary on that day and profaned my Sabbaths. And when they had slaughtered their children for their idols, on that day they came to my sanctuary to profane it. And, look, thus they have done in the midst of my house.

'And, what is more, they sent for men who come from far away, to whom a messenger had been sent; and, look, they came, for whom you had bathed and painted your eyes and decorated yourself with ornaments. So you sat on a splendid couch with a table prepared before it, on which you placed my incense and my oil. And the noise of a company at ease was there, and along with men from the multitude of humanity were brought drunkards from the wilderness. Then they placed bracelets upon their hands and crowns of beauty on their heads.

'So I said to her who was worn out with adulteries, "Will they now fornicate with her fornications? And she …" And they come to her as one would come to a woman who is a whore. Thus they went in to Oholah and Oholibah, the lewd women. But righteous men — they will judge them with the judgement of adulteresses and with the judgement of those who pour out blood, because they are adulteresses, and blood is upon their hands.'

Again Yahweh addresses Ezekiel: **'Son of man, will you judge Oholah and Oholibah? So tell them their abominations'** (23:36). This recalls 20:4 and 22:2, indicating that the present section summarizes the prophecy beginning at 20:1: Ezekiel *will* judge these sisters through the medium of inspired prophecy. Although the northern kingdom of Israel had been wiped off the face of the map more than a century before Ezekiel's time, in the mind of God Israel and Judah remained one and must be arraigned together. What happened to the northern kingdom was only a precursor to, and anticipation of, the Chaldean reduction of Judah.

Firstly, Yahweh recapitulates what the two sisters had done over the years. 'Oholah' and 'Oholibah' committed multiple adulteries with other men, by which is meant that their idolatrous acts involved staining their hands with innocent blood and child sacrifice. They were guilty in that their immorality reflected a desire to dissolve their covenant bond with Yahweh.

As occasions offered, they committed **'adultery'** by sacrificing their **'children'**, who belonged to the Lord, to **'their idols ... for food'**. The spotlight, turning from pragmatic political-cum-religious alliances with Egypt, Assyria and Babylon, focuses upon the core of the matter: Israel's self-alienation from Yahweh (23:37).

Worse, in doing this they deliberately profaned Yahweh's **'sanctuary'**. Ezekiel reminds his hearers that when Jerusalem and Judah were satisfied with having offered their children to heathen gods, **'on that day'** — any one of the days when they committed such atrocities — they would enter the temple to worship, even if it was the Sabbath. They did not care to remember the strictures of Deuteronomy 32:21:

> They have provoked me to jealousy by what is not God;
> They have moved me to anger by their foolish idols.
> But I will provoke them to jealousy by those who are not a nation;
> I will move them to anger by a foolish nation.[156]

This was syncretism at its most blatant. In indignation, Yahweh tells Ezekiel to **'Look, thus they have done in the midst of my house.'** Their profanation of the covenant bond occurred not in a heathen temple, but within the building that had been erected by Solomon and which had been honoured by God's presence (23:38-39).[157]

Ezekiel continues to probe the past, **'what is more'** introducing fresh accusations. Displaying a naïve but misplaced optimism, Judah had sent emissaries to Babylon in order to persevere with her noisy, sinful lifestyle, blotting out any thought of a confrontation with her husband. Because she knew by experience how lewd men stare at women, she expected a favourable response. She bathed, painted her eyes and face and robed herself carefully.[158] She reclined on a bed before which was a table displaying the incense and oil once given to her by Yahweh, her husband and her God (cf. 16:18).[159] Hosea, who prophesied a century and a half earlier, employed the same figure.[160] 'Oholibah', putting her binding relationship behind her, knew that the apparatus of devotion would be useful — but not for its original purpose. The metaphor is about religious syncretism employed to cement political alliances (23:40-41).

Men came to her. Perversely, 'Oholibah' was by no means satisfied with their attentions. As she beckoned to **'drunkards'** from the world at large, such men travelled through **'the wilderness'** to arrive on the scene. They were permitted to place **'bracelets'** upon the arms of the two sisters, and tiaras, or **'crowns'**, upon their heads in prior payment for services yet to be rendered. Again, the northern kingdom and that of Judah are linked as partners in apostasy. Essentially, the prophet is concerned with an in-house, family matter, from which it follows that the timing of the stages of the judgement is unimportant. Will these creatures never weary? (23:42).

Ezekiel's Hebrew becomes difficult,[161] possibly because the first person singular may reflect a parenthesis, the prophet's own emotional distress coming to the fore as he contemplates the violence of the metaphor that Yahweh employs. In turmoil, he finds himself unable to complete his sentence: **'And she ...'** The Lord has witnessed everything and anticipates how fallen 'Oholibah', incorrigible even when **'worn out'** with her adulteries, will respond to further advances. Given the opportunity, she will seek out and welcome more custom (23:43).

Now it is Yahweh who speaks. Lustful men have come in to **'Oholah'** and **'Oholibah'**. In that each of the two is described as a **'whore'**, it is implied that these **'lewd women'** have abandoned their status as wives, offering themselves to their clients as if they were prostitutes. For their part, these men never consider that the sisters were, so to speak, married as one woman to Yahweh. The burden is that, because there is no more that the Lord can do to reclaim 'Oholibah', she must share the punishment of her guilty sister (23:44).

Even so, Yahweh, declining to regard the sisters as common prostitutes, does not forget that because they became his by marriage (see 23:4,5), they are **'adulteresses'** and must be judged as such. **'Righteous men'** will act as his executors in this respect, 'righteous' possibly because, unwittingly, they serve a just cause or because they are less sinful than Samaria and Jerusalem (cf. 16:47-52). Either way, these men are none other than the heathen Chaldeans. The description is striking in that Babylon was never other than pagan to the core and that Babylonians were among Jerusalem's lovers (23:45).[162]

7. Other women take fright (23:46-49)

23:46-49. 'For thus says the Lord Yahweh: "Bring up an assembly against them and give them over for terror and plunder. And the assembly will pelt them with stones and will cut them up with their swords. They will slay their sons and their daughters and will burn their houses with fire. So I shall cause lewdness to cease from the land, that all women may be warned not to act according to your lewdness. Then they will bring your lewdness upon you and you will bear the sins of your idols, and you will know that I am the Lord Yahweh."'

The oracles against 'Oholah' and 'Oholibah' draw to their conclusion, non-existent northern Israel yet again being linked with Jerusalem. But to whom does Yahweh speak when he says, **'Bring up an assembly** [an army] **against them and give them over for terror and plunder'**?[163] (23:46). Possibly he summons the nations, the identities of which are unspecified, to invest the apostate city. Or, as in Jeremiah 25:17-18, his own prophetic word will trigger the action.

A vast company will descend upon the sisters, now represented by Jerusalem, to **'pelt them with stones and ... cut them up with their swords'**. Here figure and reality are mixed in that, although stoning was the penalty for adultery,[164] the city must fall by the sword. Even the children will be killed and the city put to the torch (23:47).

In this way **'lewdness'** is eradicated from the land of Canaan; no longer will the sons of Israel surrender themselves to gross idolatry. Moreover, the destruction of Jerusalem will serve as a lasting reminder of the warnings in Leviticus 26 and Deuteronomy 28 – 29. **'They'**, the relatively 'righteous' assailants of 23:45, will requite the sisters for annulling the covenant between themselves and Yahweh. Because Israel as a whole must **'bear the sins'** of their **'idols'**, **'you'** — Jews both of Jerusalem and of the exile — will know that **'I am the Lord Yahweh'**. Possibly, the warning to **'all women'** not to imitate 'Oholah' and 'Oholibah' recalls 13:17-23 and 23:10, addressed to those Israelite women who had been deported to Babylon. They must take heed (23:48-49).

Application

Unlike chapter 16, which concerns itself both with the ingrained sinfulness of the people of Israel and with the promise of better times to come, chapter 23 does no more than develop the former theme, possibly because the final destruction of Jerusalem was on a somewhat nearer horizon. In that the apostasy of the northern kingdom of Israel and that of Judah, centred on Jerusalem, is likened to the sexual aberrations of depraved wives, two conclusions at least may be drawn.

Firstly, sexual uncleanness never satisfies. 'Oholibah', alias Jerusalem, eventually became disgusted with her lovers (23:17,22). In time, the abuse of the body induces regret. It is not for nothing that the Bible instructs Christians to 'flee fornication'.[165]

Secondly, in that Scripture presents monogamy as the ultimate pattern of the relationship between Christ and the church,[166] and marital infidelity as a picture of spiritual apostasy (as in chapter 23), those who are not united with Christ can never be at peace, either with God or with themselves. The Beatitudes insist that they alone are happy who live, and perhaps suffer, for the Lord.[167] If Wisdom 'calls aloud outside' and 'raises her voice in the open squares', there is also 'the seductress' who 'forgets the covenant of her God' — that is, her marriage vows — and whose 'house leads down to death'.[168]

4. The fourth series of prophecies

(Ezekiel 24:1 – 25:17)

Since the seventh year, the fifth month and the tenth day after Jehoiachin was exiled (see 20:1), translating to 9 August 591 BC,[1] the 'son of man' had issued a series of prophecies extending to the end of chapter 23. In these, he predicted that Jerusalem would be judged because Yahweh must honour the warnings inherent in Moses' law.[2] Now, when there is not much more that can be said to the erring city, Ezekiel speaks again (24:1). The hour has arrived. It is nemesis.

The date of the present oracle is given: it is the ninth year, the tenth month and the tenth day (the *terminus ad quem* being unspecified), the day when Nebuchadnezzar commenced his investment of Jerusalem (24:1-2). This would have been 15 January 588 BC.[3]

Firstly, by means of the parable of the pot, Ezekiel tells out the imminent fate of the city (24:3-14). Then the sudden death of his wife constitutes the widower a remarkable 'sign' to the exiles (24:15-24). The chapter ends with a promise from Yahweh to Ezekiel that the time will come when his mouth will, so to speak, be opened, and his ministry to Israel will recommence — but with a new dimension (24:25-27).

Chapter 25, which condemns Ammon, belongs to a group of prophecies addressed to the nations surrounding Israel (chapters 25 – 32).

Ezekiel loses his wife; Israel loses Jerusalem (Ezekiel 24:1-27)

1. Yahweh brings sad news to Ezekiel (24:1-2)

24:1-2. And the word of Yahweh came to me in the ninth year, in the tenth month, in the tenth of the month, saying, 'Son of man, write for yourself of the day, this selfsame day — the king of Babylon has invested Jerusalem on this selfsame day.'

Ezekiel's prophetic ministry commenced when he was thirty years old and in the fifth year of King Jehoiachin's exile, about 593 BC (1:1-2). Five and a half years have passed, and two years and five months since the beginning of the previous series of prophecies (20:1).

As observed earlier, Zedekiah, enthroned in Jerusalem in 597 BC, rebelled against Nebuchadnezzar. In the ninth year of Zedekiah's reign the armies of Babylon laid siege to Jerusalem. The city remained under blockade for eighteen months, after which enemy forces broke through the walls.

News of the initial assault upon Jerusalem may have taken several months to be relayed to the Jews already in Babylon. But Ezekiel knew immediately because the Lord revealed it to him. The timing of the divine revelation to and through Ezekiel proves that the siege of the city was not to be attributed to Babylonian military might, and even less to notional blind chance; the hand of God, rather than that of the

Chaldean superpower, was behind it all. Only God could have disclosed this to Ezekiel before the messengers reached Babylon with the tragic news (see 33:21).

Significantly, the notice of the date of this prophecy reflects that given by 2 Kings 25:1:

> Now it came to pass in the *ninth year* of his [that is, Zedekiah's] reign, in the *tenth month*, on the *tenth day of the month*, that Nebuchadnezzar king of Babylon and all his army came against Jerusalem and encamped against it; and they built a siege wall against it all around.[4]

Because elsewhere in his book Ezekiel dates his oracles with respect to his deportation from Jerusalem to Babylonia,[5] it must be asked why chapter 24 takes as its datum the regnal year of Zedekiah, when Ezekiel and others had already left the city.[6] The question cannot be avoided.

The reason for this exception to the rule may be that when the report of the siege of Jerusalem and, later, of the city's final destruction reached the exiles in Babylon, they would have recognized that our chapter 24, issued on the exact day when Nebuchadnezzar commenced his assault, had been a word from Yahweh. This explains why when the siege commenced the Lord revealed the actual day, month and year: **'Write for yourself of the day, this selfsame day — the king of Babylon has invested Jerusalem on this selfsame day.'**[7] Whereas thus far in his ministry Ezekiel had been the object of popular vilification, when the exiles learned that Jerusalem had been placed under siege on the precise date previously announced by him, he would have been accepted as a genuine prophet, unlike those who had predicted peace (see 13:8-16), and it would confirm that there could be no future for the Jewish state. From Ezekiel's perspective, he needed such authentication if he was to continue his ministry among people whose hopes had been dashed.

Furthermore, when they realized that the date in 24:1-2 was that given previously by 2 Kings 25:1 as well as by Jeremiah 39:1 and 52:4,[8] they would have been compelled to acknowledge that the acid test insisted upon by Deuteronomy 18:21-22 had been fulfilled in Ezekiel's case, and that they would have to give him their attention (24:1-2).

To illustrate, suppose that in AD 1063, about three years before the event occurred, someone predicted that on 14 October 1066 William of Normandy would overthrow Harold, King of England, in battle at Senlac Hill, about seven miles north of Hastings, and that then and there he would inaugurate his hegemony over the Saxons. When the sun went down on that fateful day both sides would have considered the man as something of a prophet.

2. The boiling pot (24:3-14)

24:3-14. 'And formulate a parable for the rebellious house, and say to them, "Thus says the Lord Yahweh: 'Put on the pot, put it on, and pour water into it. Gather its pieces into it — every good piece, thigh and shoulder. Fill with the most choice of the bones. Take the most choice of the flock and also a heap for the bones beneath it. Boil it vigorously and moreover boil its bones in its midst.'

'"Therefore, thus says the Lord Yahweh: 'Woe, city of blood, the cauldron whose corruption is in it, whose corruption has not gone out from it. Bring it out, piece by piece — no lot has fallen upon it. For her blood is in her midst; she has placed it upon the bare rock; she did not pour it out upon the earth to cover it with dust. In order to arouse wrath, to wreak vengeance, I have placed her blood upon the bare rock that it might not be covered.'

'"Therefore, thus says the Lord Yahweh: 'Woe, city of blood. Indeed, I myself will make the pile great. Heap on the wood, kindle the fire, put in all the flesh and mix in its spice, and let its bones be burned. Then stand it empty upon its coals so that it may scorch and its copper be hot and its defilement be poured out in its midst. Its corruption will be ended. He has exhausted his pains, and the greatness of her corruption has not gone out from her. Her corruption — into the fire! In your defilement there is lewdness. Because I would have cleansed you but you are not cleansed from your defilement, you will not be cleansed again until I have satisfied my wrath against you. I, Yahweh, have spoken — it is coming and I shall act. I shall not refrain, I shall not spare and I shall not relent: according to your ways and according to your deeds they will judge you,' declares the Lord Yahweh."'

The prophet was instructed to utter, or **'formulate'**, a **'parable'** for **'the rebellious house'**, for exiles who remained as much opposed to true prophetic ministry as they had been when Ezekiel was called to office (see 2:3-8; 3:9). Ezekiel must have been dismayed by this characterization of his people: Yahweh was reminding him that thus far all attempts to bring the exiles to their senses had failed.

Firstly, someone (Nebuchadnezzar?) is commanded to **'put on the pot, put it on, and pour water into it'**. Repetition of the imperative displays enthusiasm: Yahweh *wants* the worst to happen.

Some years earlier, the people of Jerusalem had likened their city to a cooking cauldron in which they would find security. It would insulate them, as it were, from the troubles of the world around (11:3-11). Although this false notion had been refuted, it persisted. The Jews could not get rid of the idea that because, as a race, they had been chosen by God, they remained invulnerable to attack. Ezekiel's immediate burden is that, if they insist upon the word-picture, let it stand:

Jerusalem *is* a cooking-pot. But what is to be 'cooked'? (24:3).

It transpires that the food to be prepared will be lavish and plenteous, untypical of a conventional domestic meal: **'Gather its pieces into it — every good piece, thigh and shoulder. Fill with the most choice of the bones'** (24:4). Further, the cook — whoever he may be — is to **'take the most choice of the flock and also a heap for the bones beneath it. Boil it vigorously and moreover boil its bones in its midst.'** Perhaps the repast will be in honour of Yahweh, and perhaps those who remain in Jerusalem after the deportation of 597 BC are to be the honoured participants. Or are they? (24:5). The following verses indicate that Ezekiel's hearers were in for a shock. Compare with Jehu's sacrifice to Baal.[9]

The explanation is now given. Far from being participants in a sacrificial meal in honour of the God of Israel, the people of Jerusalem are the sacrificial meat! Without specifying the crimes of which the people had been guilty, the Lord simply announces: **'Woe, city of blood, the cauldron whose corruption is in it.'** In that the 'cauldron' would probably have been made from copper or bronze (cf. 24:11), metals that do not rust, its 'corruption' (*chelatah*) would be the rotten meat within it. This Hebrew word occurs no less than five times in the context, although nowhere else in the Old Testament, and suggests sickness, impurity or filth.

So, far from being God's preserved people, the inhabitants of Jerusalem are regarded by Yahweh as corrupt. This rottenness has to be 'brought out' by a further deportation.[10] Whereas they believed that they were choice flesh, so to speak, concerning the pot (cf. 11:3) upon which the divine lot of acceptance had once fallen, **'no lot has fallen upon it'**. The populace were as much sinners as any, and perhaps more so, in that they had virtually rejected their adoption as God's people (24:6).

In preceding chapters Jerusalem had been charged with extreme violence (cf. 22:12-13; 23:37). Now the city is accused because of indifference to her crimes, not caring to cover the blood of the slain and allowing it to be exposed to the gaze of heaven. According to Moses' law, even animal blood, whether shed in sacrifice or for food, was to be poured on the ground so that it might be absorbed and thereby be put out of sight.[11] But uncovered blood was deemed to be crying for vengeance.[12] Moreover, it profaned the land that the Lord had given to Israel.[13] Therefore, because **'her blood is in her midst'** and because, flagrantly, **'she has placed it upon the bare rock'**, rock being unable to absorb fluid, Yahweh will act (24:7).

Strikingly, it is Yahweh himself who permits this spilt blood to remain exposed: **'I have placed her blood upon the bare rock that it might not be covered.'** The evils in which Jerusalem delights are left unpunished by God pending an inevitable retribution. In effect, Yahweh is justifying the exceptional severity of the action he proposes to take — **'to arouse wrath, to wreak vengeance'** (24:8).

In order to judge the **'city of blood'**, Yahweh appoints himself as the superintendent cook, making the heap of burning logs even larger: **'Indeed, I myself will make the pile great'** (24:9).[14] Then, either speaking to himself or to his subordinate agents, the Chaldeans, he requires a torch to be set to the fuel, thus to consume **'all the flesh'** in the pot. **'Spice'** might allude not to the addition of appetizing ingredients, but to the reduction of the meat and bones to broth, a concentrated soup-like essence. Then, when this has been boiled away, only the **'bones'** will remain to **'be burned'** (24:10).

And when the people (the broth) have been removed, the city (the cauldron) is to be purged by fire.

Numbers 31:23 states that contaminated metal implements needed to be cleansed by flame. The analogy is arresting: all residual **'corruption'** melts away in the red-hot, glowing **'copper'** cauldron. Because earlier and gentler efforts to purify the container had failed, more violent methods are to be employed. Previous attempts at cleansing would have been the ministries of the prophets, men who were almost always ridiculed.[15] The statement that **'he has exhausted his pains'**[16] renders a difficult Hebrew original, *t'ûnim*, occurring only here in the Old Testament and deriving from a root meaning 'pain'. So, let her **'corruption'** go **'into the fire'** (24:11-12).

Yahweh's incriminations reach their climax, Jerusalem being addressed directly rather than being referred to in the third person. Ezekiel declares that within the **'defilement'** of the city there is **'lewdness'** worthy of death. A comparison with Leviticus 18:17 and 20:14 suggests that this may point to gross immorality in addition to bloodshed. For these reasons, Yahweh does not desist, does not spare and refuses to relent. Because previous attempts by him to cleanse the city, short of destruction, had failed, he must employ this last resort. Perhaps Ezekiel alludes to Hezekiah's and Josiah's unavailing efforts to reform Judah,[17] ineffective in that they did not effect a nationwide spiritual regeneration. Only by employing the Chaldeans will the Lord be able to cause his **'wrath'** to rest, to be **'satisfied ... against you'** (24:13).

The oracle concludes. The might of Babylon reflects the rage of an angered God, **'I'** occurring four times for emphasis: **'It is coming and *I* shall act. *I* shall not refrain, *I* shall not spare and *I* shall not relent.'** And the action will be a just recompense for violating the covenant between Yahweh and Israel: **'according to your ways and according to your deeds'**. Finally, Nebuchadnezzar's hordes are given the role of a judge:

'they will judge you'. Yahweh has **'spoken'**; he **'declares'** it (24:14).

3. The Lord gives and the Lord takes away (24:15-24)

24:15-24. Then the word of Yahweh came to me, saying, 'Son of man, look. With a blow I am about to take from you the delight of your eyes. But you must not mourn and you must not weep, and your tears must not come. Groan silently for the dead; make no mourning. Bind your turban upon you and put your sandals on your feet. And you must not cover your moustache and must not eat the bread of men.' So I spoke to the people in the morning, and my wife died in the evening. And in the morning I did as I had been commanded.

Then the people said to me, 'Will you not tell us what these things that you do mean for us?' So I said to them, 'The word of Yahweh has come to me, saying, "Say to the house of Israel, thus says the Lord Yahweh: 'Look, I am profaning my sanctuary, the pride of your strength, the delight of your eyes and the object of your souls' compassion. And your sons and your daughters whom you have left behind will fall by the sword. And you will do as I have done: you will not veil your moustache and you will not eat the bread of men. Your turbans will be on your heads and your sandals upon your feet. You will not mourn and shall not weep, but you will rot in your iniquities and groan, each man to his brother. So Ezekiel will be a portent for you: just as he has done, you will do when it comes, and you will know that I am the Lord Yahweh.'"'

Before sunset on that momentous day, as indicated by 24:18, the day when Nebuchadnezzar's armies commenced their investment of Jerusalem, there was another startling revelation for the prophet. Ezekiel tells us that **'the word of Yahweh'** came to him announcing the imminent death of his wife. Remarkably, he was denied any opportunity to show his grief. Every proper emotion had to be bottled up and he was not permitted to display conventional signs of mourning: his **'tears must not come'**.

There can be no doubt that Ezekiel's marriage was idyllic, as shown by the Lord's reference to his wife as **'the delight** [or 'desire'] **of your eyes'**, meaning that he never looked at another woman. It seems that until that day she had not been ill and that her death was as unexpected as it was sudden, being a **'blow'**.[18] It might also seem that the Lord's word to Ezekiel was not shared by him with his wife so that she could prepare to meet her Maker, or with their children (if any), the prophet awaiting the fulfilment of what God had said to him. Nor would he have told anyone else. The tension must have been almost intolerable. Ezekiel does not disclose the physical cause of death (if he knew it) because the emphasis falls upon Yahweh's sovereign decision to terminate her life.

What a day that would have been! Ezekiel must have spent time with his wife knowing that they would have only a few fleeting hours left to them. At any rate, to judge by the flow of thought between 24:15-17 and 24:19-20, perhaps it was not until after his wife's death that the prophet understood why. Yet, given that in Judah the unthinkable disaster was already in motion, the announcement to him concerning his imminent bereavement would not have been totally incomprehensible. Even so, because his own feelings were irrelevant and the ministry to which he had been called was all-important, he makes no mention of them. Given his lacerated heart, his verbal reticence is a matter for wonder (24:15-16).

The Lord emphasized to Ezekiel that all evidences of personal grief were to be suppressed, even though, as both Yahweh and his servant knew well, priests were permitted to mourn for their loved ones.[19] Although he would (obviously) **'groan silently'**, there must be no outward **'mourning'**, such as (no doubt) donning sackcloth, baring the head, weeping, walking barefoot,[20] covering the lower part of the face as far as the nose (**'moustache'**)[21] and sprinkling the head with ashes.[22] Conversely, he would put on his **'turban'** and his **'sandals'**, yet declining **'the bread of men'** — that is, food sent by friends as an expression of sympathy.[23] The 'turban' (*pe'ér*) was the headdress of a priest when serving within the bounds of the tabernacle (cf. 44:18)[24] but could be worn by others as an expression of joy, or even luxury.[25]

Those who witnessed Ezekiel's apparently bizarre demeanour might have concluded that he had never cared for his wife. But the Lord knew better, which is why the prophet was permitted to grieve, albeit silently. (Could he have done any other?) Nevertheless, it must be asked: why the suppression of outward sorrow? (24:17).

Next morning, Ezekiel delivered the parable of the pot (24:3-14) but was silent about his wife. In the evening, about twenty-four hours after he had been advised that she would be taken from him, she did die. Burial would have followed almost immediately. Text and context intend us to admire the quiet dignity and immense self-restraint of the prophet as he recounts the event, telling us that **'in the morning I did as I had been commanded'** — that is, allowed himself to be seen as a man whose ministry had not been interrupted by bereavement.

Ezekiel reveals nothing of that agonizing night when, as a widower, he had just a few hours to take stock of what had happened, what Yahweh had said and what he, Ezekiel, would say. Nor did he break down when in the glare of a new day he remained master of his emotions. No one could see that his heart had been broken. Obedient to his Lord, he acted exactly as he **'had been commanded'** (24:18). But because he was a servant of God he must have known that his own loss was a little thing in contrast to events unfolding at Jerusalem.

The prophet had to explain. The exiles, unable to console Ezekiel, not unnaturally sought an explanation for conduct that they realized had significance for them: **'Will you not tell us what these things that you do mean *for us*?'** Ezekiel must share with them why his wife had died so suddenly and why he was spurning all forms of lamentation (24:19).

This was the not-to-be-missed opportunity that God had planned. The prophet did not give an immediate, direct answer, but informed **'the people'**, his fellow-Jews, that his strange behaviour was a coded message from God: **'The word of Yahweh has come to me, saying ...'** (24:20).

Now the exiles were to learn, although in an oblique fashion, why Ezekiel had lost his wife so tragically, acknowledging the obvious, which was that it was an act of God (cf. 24:16: '*I* am about to take from you the delight of your eyes'). Similarly, the children of Israel were about to lose the temple, which belonged both to their God and to them, a tragedy that they had refused to believe could ever happen. Not only so, but the Babylonian onslaught on Jerusalem would bring about the loss of so many lives: **'And your sons and your daughters whom you have left behind will fall by the sword.'**

But the destruction of the temple would also cause immeasurable grief to Yahweh: **'Look, *I* am profaning *my* sanctuary.'** If Ezekiel sorrowed because of his bereavement, and if Israel will sorrow because of the unexpected loss of the temple, **'the pride of your strength, the delight of your eyes and the object of your souls' compassion'**, he, the God of heaven, will be distressed because he had planned to deprive himself of his official residence (so to speak) in the heartland of Israel,[26] thus signalling his departure. It would be 'Ichabod' on a truly vast scale.[27]

Further, even as Ezekiel's wife had been an immense resource to her husband and the only woman ever to attract his desire and love, so had the temple been to Israel. Nevertheless, Yahweh will allow his and their house to be profaned by barbarous enemies, the text undoubtedly recalling Leviticus 26:19: 'I will break the pride of your power.' Contrary to every expectation, they will lose it (24:21). But they had been warned so often. For example, Jeremiah had told them, 'Do not trust in these lying words, saying, "The temple of Yahweh, the temple of Yahweh, the temple of Yahweh."'[28]

And now we come close to discovering why Ezekiel was bidden not to mourn when his wife died. Yahweh was telling the exiles that, when learning that the Jerusalem they had known and loved was no more, they would imitate Ezekiel. Yahweh's words are more a prediction than an imperative: **'you** [that is, collective Israel] **will not veil your moustache and you will not eat the bread of men'** (24:22). Further, **'Your turbans will be on your heads and your sandals upon your feet. You will not mourn and shall not weep, but you will rot in your iniquities and groan, each man to his brother.'** Here there is a deliberate recall of Leviticus 26:39, which anticipates the reaction of surviving deportees when they learn about the devastation of their homeland: 'And those of you who are left shall waste away in their iniquity in your enemies' lands; also in their fathers' iniquities, which are with them, they shall waste away.'[29] Compare with Ezekiel 4:17: '... so that bread and water may fail, and a man and his brother be desolated and be consumed by their iniquity'.

In his own person the prophet portrays the shock to be felt by his fellow-exiles when they learn from a messenger about the destruction of Jerusalem. This will be an unprecedented disaster, and one which they had imagined could never happen, given that Yahweh had honoured the temple in Solomon's time. It followed that no conventional sign of mourning could ever suffice to display the crushing sense of deprivation felt by the survivors, the formalities of bereavement appearing superfluous. Dumbfounded and speechless, they will waste away, groaning deeply in their hearts, just as Ezekiel had done in the aftershock of his bereavement (24:22-23).

This explains why the prophet, himself a grim **'portent'** for his people, did not mourn his wife openly: his grief was too intense, his loss too severe and his sorrow beyond expression. Conventional signs of bereavement would have been almost banal. He never thought that Yahweh would take away his wife — yet it happened. The exiles and those who at the time remained in Jerusalem never believed that God would deprive them of their city and its temple — but it was to be. Then, **'when it comes ... you will know that I am Yahweh'**. They might even realize that he, the God of Israel, could be their only hope (24:24).[30]

4. A new ministry (24:25-27)

24:25-27. 'And you, son of man, will it not be in the day when I take their fortress away from them, the joy of their glory, the delight of their eyes and the uplifting of their souls, their sons and their daughters — on that day a fugitive will come to you with information for your ears? On that day your mouth will be opened to the survivor and you will speak and will be no longer dumb. Then you will be a portent to them, and they will know that I am Yahweh.'

There is a sequel. Yahweh informed the **'son of man'** that he would learn about the fall of Jerusalem from the lips of an escapee from Judah. Does this indicate that Ezekiel had become a focus for communications between the exiles and those at home?

Up to now he had been permitted to proclaim only what Yahweh told him to say, at all other times remaining silent. From this point some three years would elapse until the destruction of Jerusalem and then the arrival of the not unexpected news (cf. 24:1 and 33:21). During this period of sorrowful anticipation Ezekiel would direct no further prophecies to Israel. Having declared what must happen to **'their fortress** [Jerusalem and its temple]**, the joy of their glory, the delight of their eyes and the uplifting of their souls, their sons and their daughters'**, he would quietly await the inevitable confirmation.

But what of the occasion when the appalling reality of judgement would be made known to the exiles? Then, established beyond doubt as a true prophet of Yahweh, Ezekiel's situation and ministry must change dramatically: his mouth is to be **'opened'** to the exiles who outlive the disaster. No longer will he be **'dumb'** — meaning that his future prophecies will concern the restoration and justification of Israel rather than her condemnation, even though there had already been some glimmers of hope (see 16:60-63; 17:22-24). He will continue to be a **'portent'** (cf. 24:24) in the sense that, even as his unexpected status as a widower had foreshadowed the fall of Jerusalem, his predictions concerning the corporate resurrection of Israel as the people of God will be no less credible and authoritative.

It is for this reason that Ezekiel's overall ministry may be said to divide into two phases, the former preceding and the latter following the arrival in Babylonia of the news of the downfall of Jerusalem. Each of these two phases had been planned by Yahweh to guide his erring people to a renewed faith in the only one who could, or would, ever help them. His condemnation and his comforts alike lead them to **'know that I am Yahweh'** (24:25-27).

Application

Until the occasion of his wife's death, Ezekiel had said much to his people. Nevertheless, in a sense he had been 'dumb'. After the reception of the sad news of the collapse of Jerusalem his mouth would be 'open' — meaning that henceforth he would have good news to bring to his people. Similarly, every preacher's mouth should be 'open' in the sense that the gospel is to be the sum and substance of his ministry. Let Christ in his fulness be proclaimed consistently to those who are sick with sin.

This is no idle plea. It may be suspected that too many preachers do not live up to their pulpit calling. To illustrate the point, John Bunyan (1628–88) tells us about his early ministry. His candour cannot fail to impress:

> In my preaching of the word, I took special notice of this one thing, namely, that the Lord did lead me to begin where His word begins with sinners; that is, to condemn all flesh, and to open and allege, that the curse of God by the law, doth belong to, and lay hold on all men as they come into the world... Thus I went on for the space of two years, crying out against men's sins, and their fearful state because of them.

Then follows a revealing disclosure:

> After which, the Lord came in upon my own soul, with some staid peace and comfort through Christ ... wherefore now I altered in my preaching (for still I preached what I saw and felt); now therefore I did much labour to hold forth Jesus Christ in all His offices, relations and benefits unto the world.[31]

And, if we find Ezekiel's pre-586 BC predictions of the destruction of Jerusalem as a divine judgement too harsh to bear ('How could a God of love ever have done that?', some might complain), turn to Acts 13:19. Paul, preaching the gospel in the synagogue at Antioch in Pisidia, refers to the destruction of 'seven nations in the land of Canaan'. Because that conquest was no less violent than that of Nebuchadnezzar nearly a thousand years later, and because Paul evidently had no qualms about referring to it, we might want to consider carefully how the Lord sometimes overthrows sinful societies.

The land of Israel was a delight alike to its people and to their God, as was Jerusalem and its temple. But because the Israelites had rejected the covenant between them and Yahweh, he turned against them. Without holiness, no man shall see the Lord.[32] We can only begin to be holy when we experience the second birth and receive the Holy Spirit, and we can only know this when we turn to Christ.[33]

Israel was God's 'prodigal son',[34] suffering in a far-off land. But the Lord was waiting for them to come to their senses and realize their need. Then he would show his grace. Thus it always is between God and repentant sinners.

Ezekiel's wife must have been a remarkable woman. Perhaps in earlier years she had looked forward to a tranquil life in Jerusalem as a priest's wife. Then came war when, among the deportees in Babylonia, she saw her husband as an object of popular ridicule. Her loneliness and sense of deprivation must have been great, relieved only by the love which he bore to her and she to him. Then she died, almost certainly not being aware that, in life and in death, she was a sign from her God to Israel. Her welcome in the glory must have been intense, and (who knows?) she may have much to disclose to us when we are there.

Ammon, Moab, Edom and the Philistines (Ezekiel 25:1-17)

During the period following the loss of his wife in which Ezekiel had nothing to say to his own people, he addressed the nations surrounding Israel, his burden being that they were not to exult over the anticipated downfall of Israel, but rather to humble themselves before Yahweh, the one who remained the Lord of all the earth and before whom they must fall.

In addition to the oracles against Ammon, Moab, Edom and the Philistines (25:1-17), Ezekiel predicts the ruin of three other peoples: Tyre and Sidon (chapters 26 – 28) and Egypt (chapters 29 – 32). Seven (four + three) may be significant, denoting completion.[35] Ezekiel's survey takes (roughly) a clockwise direction, indicating that, because of these nations' opposition to Israel, one by one they must collapse.

The insertion of these oracles at this point in the prophecy is dramatic, and the effect is not lost upon the modern reader. In Ezekiel's day, his silence during the three-year interval — between the ninth year, the tenth month and the tenth day of the month (24:1) and the twelfth year, the tenth month and the fifth day (33:21) — would have left his constituency in a state of apprehension. What, they must have asked themselves, would be the next word of Yahweh from Ezekiel to a people in exile who had been told that they would be effectively stateless, Jerusalem having been destroyed and Judah as a political entity wiped from the map? Some must have hoped that Ezekiel's predictions would turn out to be wrong and that Nebuchadnezzar would spare Zedekiah, Jerusalem and the temple.

Yet, as Ezekiel knew, any remaining hopes were to be dashed. In the meantime he spoke to the world of his day, a world that had never been other than hostile to Israel.

In trying to understand why these oracles are inserted here, Jeremiah 27:2-3 is relevant:

> Thus said Yahweh to me: 'Make for yourself bonds and yokes, and put them on your neck, and send them to the king of Edom, to the king of Moab, to the king of the sons of Ammon, to the king of Tyre and to the king of Sidon, by the hand of the messengers who came to Jerusalem to Zedekiah king of Judah.'

It would appear that when he rebelled against Babylonian suzerainty,[36] Zedekiah had sought the help of the nations mentioned in Jeremiah 27:2-3. In consequence, Jeremiah informed them that such a coalition must lead to disaster.[37]

Later, when the Babylonians were at the gates of Jerusalem, Yahweh through Ezekiel told his people that Israelite reliance on such nations for help had been misplaced in that they, too, were to be overrun by the Chaldeans.

Thirdly, Yahweh was granting comfort to Israel in anticipation of the sad day when the exiles would hear about the reduction of Jerusalem. Remaining the God of Israel, he would honour his covenant promise to his people.[38] This is why their opponents were his opponents.

Babylon is not mentioned in this list of condemned nations, possibly because Nebuchadnezzar was the appointed servant of the Lord. As observed by Gardiner, 'The effect of this [a reference to Babylon] would have been marred by the mention of her own ultimate punishment. For the present, all her enemies are to be overthrown, and she remains in strength.'[39] But compare with 21:30-32, verses that seem to point to the ultimate destruction of the Chaldean war machine.

The dates of the prophecies recorded in this section are not given, except that, according to 25:3,6,8, they may have been delivered after the final collapse of Jerusalem in 586 BC, or at some short time before when it was evident that the city was doomed. Yet, to judge by the position of these oracles in the complete book, the exiles had not yet learned about the loss of their city. Ezekiel provides light in a gathering darkness.

1. Against Ammon (25:1-7)

25:1-7. Then the word of Yahweh came to me, saying, 'Son of man, set your face towards the sons of Ammon and prophesy against them. And you will say to the sons of Ammon, "Hear the word of the Lord Yahweh. Thus says the Lord Yahweh: 'Because you have said "Aha!" against my sanctuary when it was profaned, and against the earth of Israel when it was desolated, and against the house of Judah when they went into exile, therefore, look, I am granting you to the sons of the east for a possession. And they will settle their encampments in you and make their dwellings among you. They themselves will eat your fruit and they will drink your milk. And I shall give Rabbah as a habitation of camels, and the sons of Ammon for a resting place for flocks, and you will know that I am Yahweh.' For thus says the Lord Yahweh: 'Because you have clapped your hand and have stamped with the foot, and have rejoiced with all your contempt, with your soul, against the earth of Israel, therefore, look, I have stretched out my hand against you and have given you as booty to the nations, and I shall cut you off from the peoples and shall make you to perish from the countries. I shall destroy you, and you will know that I am Yahweh.' " '

The **'son of man'** was to set his face towards **'the sons of Ammon'**. This does not mean that Ezekiel was physically to turn in the direction of Ammon when uttering his prophecy. The expression is an indication of hostility, both that of the Lord and of his servant, against this people.

Since the time of the Israelite judges, the Ammonites, descended from Lot's act of incest with his younger daughter,[40] had shown bitter enmity to Israel.[41] In his day, Solomon had imported their idolatrous practices.[42] After the fall of Jerusalem, their king, Baalis, seems to have encouraged a certain Ishmael to assassinate Gedaliah.[43] Prophets other than Ezekiel were not slow to condemn them.[44] This people must have gloated when they discovered that Nebuchadnezzar's sweep to the south and east would be directed against Jerusalem rather than their own territories, although Ezekiel indicates (see 21:18-29) that they would not escape completely (25:1-2).

Thus the **'sons of Ammon'** had witnessed the devastation of the sanctuary of Yahweh and of the land of Israel, and had ridiculed the miseries of deported Judah, crying out **'Aha!'** In particular, they rejoiced because the **'sanctuary'** of Yahweh had been **'profaned'**, because the **'earth of Israel'** had been ravaged by military invasion, and because **'the house of Judah'** had been led into exile. Because it seemed to them that the long-standing union of temple, land and people had fallen apart, the Ammonites believed that they had finally prevailed against their old enemy (25:3).

But they lacked perception, failing to realize that although the destruction of Judah was primarily an act of God rather than of Nebuchadnezzar, the Lord would never abandon his elect people. For this reason

Ezekiel was bidden to speak to the Ammonites in the name of Yahweh: **'Therefore, look, I am granting you to the sons of the east for a possession.'** The Lord would not permit those who despised his people, and therefore him, to prosper. Far from rejoicing over the loss of Judah, the Ammonites must forfeit their own territory to Arabian nomads, **'sons of the east'**,[45] who would **'themselves'** devour their wealth. Time must be when all will see it to be so (25:4).

Further, because the Ammonites have exulted over the fall of Jerusalem, their own chief city, **'Rabbah'**, will be a waste where **'camels'** lie down and feed. **'The sons of Ammon'** are to be **'a resting place for flocks'** — meaning that their lands will be taken over by aliens with their sheep and goats. Then the conquered will have reason to know **'that I am Yahweh'** (25:5).

Linked to 25:5, a new condemnation issues from the Lord. Tragedy confronts Ammon because the nation has **'clapped** [its] **hand'** and **'stamped** [its] **foot'** in glee (not in anger; cf. 6:11; 21:17), hopping up and down with malicious joy because of the misfortunes of Judah. Ammonite **'contempt'** has been from the **'soul'** and could not be more sincere (25:6).

Again, the people of Ammon are required to **'look'** (cf. 25:4). The Lord will see to it that the nation, being **'cut ... off'** from the society of other peoples, perishes. Ezekiel's parallelism emphasizes that this must happen. Repeating from 25:5, Ammon will realize that **'I am Yahweh'**, accepting that he had brought the nation down (25:7). Amos 1:13-15, from an earlier period, and Jeremiah 49:1-6 indicate that exile must be the punishment and the Chaldeans its executors. But whereas Jeremiah holds out some prospect for Ammon, Ezekiel, his contemporary, provides no hope. Taylor suggests that the apparent contradiction resolves itself if Jeremiah anticipates the Ammonites coming to know the true God.[46]

2. Against Moab (25:8-11)

25:8-11. '"Thus says the Lord Yahweh: 'Because Moab and Seir say, "Look, the house of Judah is like all the nations," therefore, look, I am opening up the flank of Moab from the cities, from its cities from its extremity — the beauty of the land of Beth-jeshimoth, Baal-maon and Kiriathaim — and I shall give it, along with the sons of Ammon, to the sons of the east for a possession, so that the sons of Ammon may not be remembered among the nations. Thus I shall execute judgements upon Moab, and they will know that I am Yahweh.'"'

Yahweh now denounces **'Moab'** and **'Seir'**. Seir was the area of land controlled by Edom, and by this token stands for the descendants of Esau. They cavorted with glee because Judah was now apparently like them — just another little nation bowing defenceless against the cruelty of warlords such as Nebuchadnezzar.

Moab owed its origin to the same dreadful incident that gave rise to Ammon[47] and, as already noted, as early as the time of Moses had been hostile to Israel.[48] Moses had enacted that no Ammonite or Moabite would ever be admitted to 'the assembly of Yahweh' because they had opposed Israel towards the conclusion of the wilderness journey.[49] In Ezekiel's day, Moabites had been included in the armies of Nebuchadnezzar that had assaulted Jerusalem.[50] It is true that Zedekiah introduced Moab as well as Ammon in an alliance against Babylon,[51] yet both peoples rejoiced when Jerusalem finally succumbed.[52]

Although Ezekiel is not explicit, it is likely that Edom laughed because Israel, now degraded by sin (as the Lord saw it) and humiliated by defeat, did not seem to be the elect people of God. The blessing granted by Isaac to Jacob centuries earlier now seemed to have fallen flat.[53] Were this not so, surely (they would have said) Israel could never have been permitted by the Almighty to suffer like certain other nations. To them it seemed obvious that Yahweh had hated Jacob but had loved Esau by preserving his posterity (25:8). The Old and the New Testaments, of course, take another view.[54]

The shoulder, or **'flank'**, of the land of Moab — that is, the western border — is to be opened up to enemy attack. Let Moab **'look'** at what she may expect. The cities named, **'Beth-jeshimoth'**, **'Baal-maon'** and **'Kiriathaim'**, had been occupied by Israel during Joshua's conquest of Canaan and were granted to the tribe of Reuben. Later they were seized by Moab.[55] Now **'the sons of the east'**, desert Bedouin, occupy Moab as well as Ammon. Moab, like many others, will in time acknowledge that Yahweh is, indeed, the true God (25:9-11).

As it happened, the Ammonites appear to have survived for many years, warring against the Jewish Judas Maccabaeus in the second century BC.[56] But the Moabites seem to have become extinct at a much earlier period, and are mentioned only in Ezra 9:1; Nehemiah 13:1 and Daniel 11:41.

3. Against Edom (25:12-14)

25:12-14. '"Thus says the Lord Yahweh: 'Because Edom has acted in taking vengeance against the house of Judah and has incurred severe guilt and avenged themselves upon them,' therefore, thus says the Lord Yahweh: 'Then I shall stretch my hand out upon Edom and shall cut off from her man and beast. And I shall give her for a wasteland; from Teman to Dedan they will fall by the sword. So I shall appoint my vengeance against Edom by the hand of my people Israel, and they will deal with Edom according to my anger and according to my fury, and they will know my vengeance,' declares the Lord Yahweh."'

Although Ammon and Moab had gloated cruelly at the downfall of Judah, the sin of Edom, to which people Ezekiel turns his attention once again, was more serious. When Israel was seen to be in dire straits, Esau's descendants pursued an unjustified and implacable feud, rejoicing when Jerusalem's fall was certain. The Old Testament shows that active hostility had been a characteristic of Edom from the first, an enmity traceable to the supremacy of Jacob, Esau's younger twin.[57] This hatred was always resented keenly by Israel.[58] According to Josephus, during the Babylonian captivity Edom took possession of many towns of Judah, including Hebron.[59]

Because this unjustified hatred had **'incurred severe guilt'** before Yahweh (25:12), the Lord proposes to **'stretch** [his] **hand'** upon them. **'Man and beast'** are to be removed from a land where there will be widespread devastation, **'from Teman to Dedan'**, meaning from one end of the country to the other. (Jeremiah 49:7,20 and Obadiah 9 offer Teman and Dedan as descriptive of the whole of Edom.) There will be nothing left by **'the sword'** (25:13).

Yet in this case the direct agent of destruction will be **'the hand of my people Israel'**: those who had enacted their malevolent vengeance upon the people of God will suffer Yahweh's just retribution through that same people. Perhaps the initial fulfilment of this prediction was the conquest of Edom by Judas Maccabaeus in the second century BC,[60] and later in the absorption of Idumea (Edom) by Judea in the time of Herod the Great, himself an Idumean.

Even so, Ezekiel's prediction might stretch out to the remote future, to a time yet to be, anticipating that Edom, the implacable foe of Israel, will ultimately be incorporated in the Messianic kingdom of God. It had long been believed, of course, that Edom would one day serve Israel,[61] and Ezekiel 35 assumes this. Although the present verse announces that the relationship between Yahweh and Israel will be restored (‘***my* people’**), it is not stated that Edom will also be favoured. But perhaps in context this does not need to be said, the emphasis upon the reinstatement of the covenant between Yahweh and Jacob at the expense of Esau being expounded in order to comfort the exiles (25:14).[62]

4. Against the Philistines (25:15-17)

25:15-17. ‘“Thus says the Lord Yahweh: ‘Because the Philistines have acted in revenge and have revenged themselves with contempt, and with their souls cause destruction with everlasting enmity,’ therefore thus says the Lord Yahweh: ‘Look, I am stretching out my hand upon the Philistines and shall cut off the Cherethites, and shall destroy the remnant of the shore of the sea. So I shall execute great vengeance among them, with wrathful rebuke, and they will know that I am Yahweh when I lay my vengeance among them.’”’

The Philistines are generally supposed to have been a sea people who colonized the south-western corner of the land of Canaan in the late second millennium BC. Although Amos 9:7 tells that they originated from the island of Caphtor, often identified as Crete,[63] Genesis 10:14 identifies them as Hamitic, implying a prior migration to Crete from Egypt. Later their coastal possession in Canaan was granted to Joshua but seems never to have been occupied by the Israelites.[64] They were always a menace to Israel until the time of David. Although on one occasion he found refuge in Philistine territory and he seems to have employed Philistine troops in his bodyguard,[65] his military operations eventually rendered that people relatively harmless.[66]

For all that, Philistine memories and aspirations lingered: **‘... and with their souls cause destruction**

with everlasting enmity'. They had resembled Edom and Ammon in their thirst for exacting vengeance from Israel and in rejoicing contemptuously over the collapse of Judah. Exactly how they **'acted in revenge'** is unclear, yet Yahweh responds (25:15).

Ezekiel predicts that this ancient enemy of Israel is to become extinct. Such a fate had been anticipated by Isaiah 14:31; Jeremiah 47:4 and Amos 1:8.

'Cherethites' may have been 'Cretans', native immigrants from Crete who settled in the southern areas of Philistine territory.[67] Because 'Cherethites' also resembles the Hebrew verb *karat*, 'cut off', a term signifying slaughter or even execution, there may be a play on words: the Lord proposes to 'cut off those who cut off', exacting personal retribution. Although the **'shore of the sea'** will remain, no longer will it grant them a livelihood because they will be gone (25:16).

In their final misery, the Philistines, like other peoples, will know that Yahweh, and none other, had brought them to ruin. Interestingly, Nehemiah 13:23-24 mentions that some post-exilic returnees to Jerusalem had married women from Ashdod, Ammon and Moab, and that some of their children spoke the dialect of Ashdod rather than Hebrew. In that Ashdod was one of the five cities of the Philistines,[68] it might seem that only that city remained, the Philistine power having been broken.

These words must have been an immense encouragement to those among Ezekiel's contemporaries who exercised discernment. Although Yahweh was bringing Jerusalem and its temple down to the dust, he still remained Israel's God (25:17).

Application

Throughout the Old Testament period the Lord often had harsh words to say to the people of Israel. And harsh words were sometimes backed up by harsh deeds, culminating in the Babylonian destruction of Jerusalem. Nevertheless, Yahweh never totally abandoned Israel, again and again coming to her defence and never allowing her enemies to gloat over her humiliations. Israel remained the apple of his eye.[69]

It is so with Christian people, who by definition belong to the 'commonwealth of Israel'.[70] Christ is with us, and we are always his, even until the end of the age, and then for evermore.[71] Further, those who contend with his people contend with him — and cannot prevail. This hope, when understood, will spur us on to holiness.[72]

5. The fifth series of prophecies

(Ezekiel 26:1 – 28:26)

1. Fortress Tyre — her rise and fall

It is now the eleventh year and the first day of the month, possibly 12 February 586 BC.[1] Although Jerusalem has not yet been taken, the end is certain. At the time, the fortress city of Tyre, situated a mere two hundred kilometres from Jerusalem, must have been aware of what was happening to a city she considered (falsely) to be her great rival, only a few days' away for her roving merchants. This is why she is condemned, although for a charge other than those directed to the nation-states mentioned in the preceding chapter. Because Tyre had been resentful of the commercial supremacy of the people of Israel, she, too, must be overthrown.

The name **'Tyre'** (*tsûr*) reflects the Hebrew word *tsôr*, 'rock', because the Phoenician city was built on a rocky offshore island. This explains 26:5; 27:4,32, which describe Tyre as set in the heart, or midst, of the sea.

The Greek historian Herodotus (born about 484 BC, a century or so after Ezekiel) tells that the city was established 2,400 years before his day. Although his dates may be apocryphal, it seems certain that the origin of Tyre is lost in the mists of time. Herodotus also relates that when he visited the city, he saw 'the holy temple of Heracles', which was 'richly equipped'.[2]

The city's affluence, although fading, was still considerable. Furthermore, archaeology suggests that Tyre was an established city protected by Egypt at least 1,500 years before Christ, about the time when Israel left Egypt to return to Canaan. And Joshua 19:29 mentions Tyre as a fortress.

The city was still powerful five hundred years after the conquest, in the period of King David, approximately 1000 BC.[3] Hiram, then its king, was friendly to both David and Solomon and provided materials and technical assistance with a view to building the temple. He also co-operated in commercial ventures in the east and the west.[4] Isaiah 23:12 describes the city as the 'virgin daughter of Sidon', and there was always a close association between the two.

In the ninth century BC, a later king of Tyre gave his daughter in marriage to Ahab of Israel to cement the alliance between their two peoples.[5] It was about then that emigrants from the city founded the North African city of Carthage. Tyre itself fell to Assyria around 722 BC, at the time of the dispersion of the northern kingdom of Israel.

Amos, who lived 150 years before Ezekiel, refers to the callous commercialism displayed by Tyre.[6] Hosea, a little later than Amos, mentions that Tyre had been 'planted in a pleasant meadow', God having allowed the merchants in the city to become opulent.[7]

With the decline of Assyrian supremacy in the late seventh century BC, Tyre regained something of her earlier independence and her flourishing sea trade. Zechariah, prophesying round about 500 BC, states that Tyre had heaped up silver and gold like the dust of the streets. But although she was the hugely wealthy mistress of the sea, the prophet of Israel expected that her power would vanish.[8]

According to Jeremiah 27:3, Tyre and Sidon supported a revolt against the Babylonians. Consequently, Nebuchadnezzar laid siege to the former city and captured it after thirteen years.[9] About three hundred years later, in 332 BC, Alexander the Great of Macedon besieged the island fortress for seven months when the city was standing alone against the European invader. Thousands died or were taken into slavery. Following that catastrophe, Tyre never regained its former glory, although in 126 BC it contrived to obtain a nominal independence, remaining a centre of commerce throughout the Roman period.

Jesus referred to Tyre, visited it and received travellers who came from there to hear him. Our Lord knew that Tyre had lost much of its previous greatness because of the judgements of God.[10] There were Christians in Tyre at an early date.[11] Conquered by the Arabs in AD 636, the city appears to have endured until the 1300s, when the Saracens razed it to the ground. Now the island fortress is no more. Isaiah 23, which predicts the collapse and then partial restoration of Tyre, is a relatively short-term prophecy, not stretching as far as the final destiny of the city.

Strictly speaking, there were probably two Tyres, one on the Phoenician mainland and the other on the aforementioned rock situated nearly two kilometres from the shore. Ezekiel addresses his prophecy to the island city to be attacked by Nebuchadnezzar and subsequently by Alexander.

2. The besetting sin of Tyre

The burden of Ezekiel's immediately preceding prophecies was that certain nations on the borders of Israel were doomed because of their hostility to Israel and their desire for territorial acquisition. Significantly, this accusation is not laid to the charge of Tyre. Rather, she is condemned because of her complete indifference to Israel's unique testimony to Yahweh, falling victim to an insatiable lust for material gain. Ezekiel's burden is that her love for money must lead to ruin. The interests of the kingdom of God had never been important for Tyre.

In earlier times, Amos had condemned the city for handing over Hebrew prisoners to Edom, and Joel refers to Tyre in connection with the transportation of Hebrew slaves to the Greeks.[12] The city stands out as the great Old Testament exemplar of the failure of men to ensure happiness and salvation when they abandon the true God. Godless because she wanted it so, Tyre fades away.

Chapter 26 threatens the destruction of Tyre; chapter 27 mourns its overthrow; and chapter 28 threatens the king of Tyre, then issuing a lament because of his ruin.

Ezekiel devotes as many as three chapters to the eventual fall of Tyre (and four chapters to that of Egypt, 29 – 32), possibly because Babylon was recognized by Ezekiel as Yahweh's engine of destruction, moving west and south towards the land of the Nile. Because at that time the only states that had not yet succumbed to Babylon were Tyre and Egypt, Ezekiel chooses to make them the targets of lengthy condemnations: how can they resist Yahweh?[13]

3. The divisions of the oracle against Tyre

Chapters 26 – 28 divide into five sections, each commencing with **'the word of Yahweh came to me'**: 26:1-21, the prediction of the destruction of Tyre; 27:1-36, a lamentation over the fall of Tyre, the city being likened to a magnificent merchant vessel overwhelmed by a tempest; 28:1-10, the downfall of the prince of Tyre; 28:11-19, a lament over the king of Tyre; and 28:20-26, a prophecy against Sidon.

Tyre must fall
(Ezekiel 26:1-21)

1. The announcement of the fall of Tyre (26:1-6)

26:1-6. And it was in the eleventh year, on the first of the month, that the word of Yahweh came to me, saying, 'Son of man, because Tyre has said concerning Jerusalem, "Aha! The gateway of the peoples is broken; she has been turned over to me. I shall be filled. She is laid waste" — therefore, thus says the Lord Yahweh: "Look, I am against you, Tyre, and I shall bring many nations against you, just as the sea brings up its waves. And they will destroy the walls of Tyre and break down her towers, and I shall scrape off her debris from her and make her a bare rock. She will be a spreading-place for nets in the midst of the sea, for I have spoken," declares the Lord Yahweh, "and she will be plunder for the nations. Then her daughters who are in the field will be slain by the sword, and they will know that I am Yahweh."'

The month in which Yahweh spoke to Ezekiel is not mentioned. He writes simply, **'in the eleventh year, on the first of the month'**. As already noted, the year was 586 BC. A possible explanation for the non-identification of the month could be that Ezekiel's prophecy against Tyre relates to the overthrow of Jerusalem in that year (26:2), a landmark event that occurred in the fourth month.[14] It might be that soon after, on the first day of the fifth month, the prophet responded to the taunt of the island-city (26:1).

Tyre has rejoiced because of the collapse of Jerusalem: **'The gateway of the peoples is broken; she has been turned over to me.'** Not only had Jerusalem been the spiritual centre of Israel, it was also a strategic hub of commerce, attracting lucrative business from nations near and far, as was certainly the case in Solomon's time.[15] Now Tyre expected to multiply her own revenues at the expense of Jerusalem. Because trade was a cut-throat matter, it was no time for sympathy, but for taking advantage.

Displaying neither religious animosity nor a desire for territorial gain at the expense of Israel (unlike Ammon, Moab, Edom and the Philistines), Tyre's besetting sin was the love of money. This had long since blotted out any lingering flicker of conscience concerning seeking the true God. **'Aha!'**, she cried, knowing that her time had come. Now that Jerusalem was virtually **'laid waste'**, her own revenues could be expected to soar. Traders from afar would stream in to swell her coffers (26:2).

So, because Tyre has calculated that **'many nations'** will gravitate to her, Yahweh promises that it will be so, although not in the way she hoped and expected. Perhaps looking far beyond Nebuchadnezzar's impending attack, Ezekiel predicts that other peoples will advance, **'just as the sea brings up its waves'**, hurling themselves against Tyre's sea defences. Because he is the Lord of all the nations and because he is **'against, you, Tyre'**, Yahweh can promise that it shall be so (26:3).

The **'walls'** and **'towers'** of the sea fortress are to vanish, as will the dust left by the initial destruction. The language is vivid in the extreme: Yahweh himself will **'scrape off her debris from her and make her a bare rock'**, an exposed surface hardly adequate for fishermen to spread out their nets. Taylor cites a traveller who visited Tyre in the 1800s and who wrote:

> The island, as such, is not more than a mile in length. The part that projects south beyond the isthmus is perhaps a quarter of a mile broad, and is rocky and uneven. It is now unoccupied except by fishermen, as 'a place to spread nets upon'.[16]

'The nations' will regard her as **'plunder'** (26:5).

In that Tyre must be the spoil of the nations rather than an international entrepreneur, **'her daughters'**, the mainland villages and towns dependent on her, will be devastated **'by the sword'**. Then they will acknowledge that Yahweh is truly God (26:6).

2. Nebuchadnezzar — the agent of destruction (26:7-14)

26:7-14. '"For thus says the Lord Yahweh: 'Look, I am bringing up from the north Nebuchadrezzar, the king of Babylon, the king of kings, with horses and chariots and cavalry, and an assembly, a vast people. He will slay your daughters in the field and will set up a siege wall against you, heap up a mound against you and raise a shield against you.

'"'Then he will direct the thrust of his attacking engine against your walls and will smash your towers with his axes. Because of the multitude of his horses their dust will cover you, and from the noise of cavalry, wheels and chariots, your walls will shake when he comes into your gates as they who come into a breached city. With the hooves of his horses he will trample all your streets. He will slaughter your people with the sword and bring to the earth the pillars of your strength.

'"'Then they will plunder your wealth, make booty of your merchandise, demolish your walls and tear down your desirable houses. They will lay your stones, your timbers and your dust in the midst of the waters. Thus I shall put an end to the abundance of your songs, and the sound of your harps will not be heard again. So I shall make you a bare rock. You will be a spreading-place for nets. You will not again be built, for I, Yahweh, have spoken,' declares the Lord Yahweh."'

The threat is expounded. Unwittingly led on by Yahweh, who insists that he is the prime mover, **'Nebuchadrezzar, the king of Babylon, the king of kings,'** will attack **'from the north'**. Although Babylon lay to the east and slightly to the south of Tyre, the invading war-machine, **'horses and chariots and cavalry, and an assembly, a vast people'**, will advance from the direction of Syria (26:7; cf. 1:4; 38:15).[17] In this verse, as in 29:18-19,[18] the tyrant, who is named for the first time, is **'Nebuchadrezzar'**, which transliterates the Babylonian *Nabu-kudurri-usur*, usually interpreted as 'O Nabu, protect my offspring'. Elsewhere, the name appears as the familiar 'Nebuchadnezzar', which is employed in this commentary.[19] In the Old Testament, the Hebrew consonant *nun*, corresponding to our 'n', may sometimes have been exchanged for *resh*, 'r', which could explain the alternatives.[20]

Equipped with all the *matériel* of war, battle-hardened armies **'will slay your daughters in the field'** — that is, Tyre's dependent communities on the mainland. Although Ezekiel would seem to address Tyre directly, he does no more than reflect Yahweh's condemnation (cf. 25:2) by, as it were, setting his face against the city. Nebuchadnezzar will spare no effort to reduce Tyre. Bereft of her satellites, she will stare at siege mounds and a ramp upon which assault troops will launch their attack against her walls and towers. The **'shield'** would probably have been something like the Roman 'testudo', a roof of shields like a tortoise shell held aloft by assailants for protection against incoming missiles (26:8-9).

And the invader will penetrate Tyre, a city to be smothered by **'dust'** raised by the Babylonian cavalry, ramparts quivering with the vibration of warhorses pounding through the breaches and surging into Tyre itself. Men must die, and the **'pillars of your strength'**, possibly memorials dedicated to the hereditary gods of Tyre,[21] collapse (26:10-11). If this is to be taken as a sign of judgement, it was not untypical, as witness the overthrow of Dagon and the prediction concerning Bel and the gods of Babylon.[22] In order to deploy his cavalry, perhaps Nebuchadnezzar built a mole to link Tyre to the mainland.

Wealth and merchandise are available in abundance for the spoilers. They do not stint themselves, walls being broken and palatial dwellings being smashed to the ground. Stone, timber and rubble are dumped into the sea. But this is only the beginning: in time, Tyre, now levelled flat, becomes a submerged ruin (26:12). In that Ezekiel refers to **'they'**, rather than to Nebuchadnezzar, he may be looking to the longer term, when Tyre will be devastated by a succession of invaders. This view is reinforced by 29:17-20, which indicates that the Babylonians were not totally satisfied with the outcome of their assault.

As with the destruction of Jerusalem,[23] Yahweh himself puts an end to the music of Tyre, the strains of her **'harps'** being heard no more. Unlike Jerusalem,[24] the **'sound'** of music **'will not be heard again'**. Tyre will never regain prominence (26:13).

Ezekiel repeats the prediction that she is to become an exposed rock where fishermen spread their nets (cf. 26:5). No one will build there. All this is because **'Yahweh'** has **'spoken'** (26:14).

3. An awful warning (26:15-21)

26:15-21. '"Thus says the Lord Yahweh to Tyre: 'Will not the coastlands quake at the sound of your fall — when the wounded groan, when the slain are slaughtered in your midst? Then all the princes of the sea will descend from their thrones and will remove their robes and strip off their embroidered garments. They will clothe themselves with trembling and will sit on the ground. They will tremble every moment and be desolated because of you. Then they will take up a dirge over you and say to you, "How have you perished, O inhabited one, from the seas — O renowned city, which was strong in the sea, she, and her inhabitants, who imposed her terror upon all her inhabitants. Now the coastlands will tremble on the day of your fall, and the coastlands which are by the sea will be terrified at your departure."'

'"For thus says the Lord Yahweh: 'When I make you a desolate city, like cities that are not inhabited, when I shall bring up the deep against you and the great waters cover you, then I shall bring you down to be with those who descend to the pit, to the people of antiquity, and shall make you to dwell in the earth beneath — like the places wasted from antiquity, with those who go down to the pit, so that you will not be inhabited — but I shall set beauty in the land of the living. I shall bring terrors upon you, and you will be no more. Then you will be sought for but will never be found again,' declares the Lord Yahweh."'

Verses 15-21 set forth the dismay felt by the rulers of neighbouring principalities, her dependencies and those who had developed commercial ties with Tyre. Because her overthrow threatens them, **'will not the coastlands quake at the sound of** [her] **fall'** when they learn of utter devastation in the **'midst'** of the city? (26:15).

The **'princes of the sea'**, all of them merchants whose accumulated wealth had elevated them to power as the nouveau riche,[25] will descend from their thrones and strip off their royal attire. Ezekiel's language is extraordinarily vivid: these folk wrap themselves, as it were, with trembling and now squat in humiliation on the ground, shivering moment by moment because of what has happened to Tyre. Their posture expresses profound lamentation and grief.[26]

They cry out: Tyre's demise could easily be theirs, and they are terrified (26:16).

As if seated around an occupied coffin or bier, they take up a dirge, addressing the corpse: **'they ... say to you'** [that is, to Tyre]**, "How have you perished ...?"'** Elsewhere, **'how'** introduced dirges over fallen cities[27] and here it expresses shock and horror: the unimaginable has occurred. Tyre is perceived as a formerly **'inhabited'** and **'renowned'** city **'from the seas'**, as if it was a rock covered by buildings and perceived to be rising majestically from the waves. She had **'imposed her terror upon all her inhabitants'**, possibly meaning that all who visited Tyre as temporary residents could do no other than revere the city for its opulence and apparent stability (26:17).

But **'now the coastlands will tremble'** and **'will be terrified at your departure'**. The commercial and political vacuum generated by the collapse of Tyre must have unforeseen and devastating consequences for all trading nations. The new links that they are compelled to forge will be difficult and uncertain (26:18).

Again Yahweh speaks. He, and none other, will make Tyre like earlier and now uninhabited cities. Ironically, the **'deep'** and the **'great waters'** that had conveyed wares to and fro will now engulf her. What had once happened to so many others must be her lot (26:19).[28] Joining those who in past times had descended to the nether regions, she receives from God her allotted place. Never again will she be a centre from which men gain their livelihoods.[29]

Having hurled Tyre into an eternal **'pit'**, where she meets other fallen nations, **'the people of antiquity'**, God now acts in **'the land of the living'**, where he will **'set beauty'**. The background Hebrew word for **'beauty'** (*tz'bi*) is found also in 20:6,15 and in Daniel 8:9; 11:16,41, referring to the beauty of the land of Israel. Here, the word would retain the same significance, Ezekiel predicting that when Yahweh has overthrown Tyre, the stereotype of godless materialism, he will establish his beautiful kingdom, within which a boastful Tyre can have no place.[30] The condemnation of the city does not lack a Messianic promise (26:20).

The **'terrors'** that Yahweh will **'bring'** upon Tyre are either the sensations of fear and shock felt by those who witness her collapse,[31] or, to judge by Job 18:14, by the miserable world of the dead. If the latter, Yahweh announces that Tyre, led away from the theatre of life, **'will be sought for but will never be found again'**: men will be looking in the wrong place. The Lord has declared it (26:21).

Application

The besetting sin of Tyre was the love of money, rather than, say, idolatry — although the love of money is a species of idolatry.[32] Religion, of whatever variety, was at best a secondary matter. Likewise, Demetrius, the Ephesian silversmith, complained about Paul's ministry to those among whom he made his fortune: not only was the gospel endangering his business, it was 'also' prejudicing the worship of 'Artemis', the goddess of the city.[33] 'Also' is revealing. For the entrepreneur, the deity came second.

If the believer will 'seek first the kingdom of God' and the 'righteousness' that the Lord ascribes to him, 'all these things' will be given in addition, as a sort of incidental spin-off.[34]

Neither Nebuchadnezzar, whose name has now appeared for the first time, nor Tyre feared Yahweh, even though Nebuchadnezzar would change his attitude in later days.[35] Yet Yahweh, the God of Israel, sends the former against the latter. He is the absolute Lord of heaven and earth. Not only so, but on earth he always acts in the interests of his people: Tyre would be reduced because the city held Jerusalem in contempt. Christ loves his church, be it ever so lowly.

Ezekiel laments the fall of Tyre (Ezekiel 27:1-36)

Ezekiel's second oracle against Tyre takes the form of a lamentation in which neither he nor Yahweh, his principal, displays personal sorrow or satisfaction over the collapse of the island city. Rather, there is a certain wistfulness, as if God and his servant witness the passing of a phenomenon majestic in its time but which held within itself the germ of its own destruction. None the less, sorrow is manifest — that of the spectators of the downfall of the great city who know that the source of their affluence has gone.[36]

Because the city was in effect an island surrounded by water, in this dirge it is likened to a magnificent galley, splendidly built and equipped, and with her great sail elevated to catch the wind. The merchantman and her convoys have voyaged everywhere in quest of wealth. And Ezekiel pictures this superb vessel being rowed far away from the shelter of the coast and into the ocean depths, a hazardous procedure because the ship is a single-sailed galley unsuited for the heavy seas that she meets far from land. So when the tempest strikes she founders without trace, leaving no survivors. When other mariners learn that she has sunk, they mourn because they might experience her fate.

The lament divides into several sections. Firstly, verses 1-11 outline the solid construction and magnificent equipment of the vessel, providing a poignant backdrop to the narrative of the disaster that would meet it. Ezekiel's words, issued at Yahweh's behest, display heavy irony. Secondly, verses 12-25 are a prose catalogue of the equipment of the fair ship. Thirdly, verses 26-36 expand the lament, reflecting the anguish of those sea peoples who witness the ruin of Tyre.

Unlike chapters 26 and 28, no obvious condemnation of the city is offered, and neither Yahweh nor the gods of the nations are mentioned. One explanation for what can only be a subtle and intentional void is that Tyre's great sin was that of materialism. Because the acquisition of wealth had been her driving ambition, she has passed into oblivion. Neither opposing nor supporting Israel and her God, and therefore a nonentity, she is removed from the only scene that she ever loved, the marketplace.

This analysis is supported by the lamentation's frequent references to commerce.[37] Although some of the terms mentioned are not found elsewhere in the Old Testament and are not easy to understand, their cumulative thrust is clear: Tyre had been a community dedicated to the pursuit of material wealth. By direct implication, this was her great sin. Because she desired everything, she must lose everything. Only those who profited financially by their association with her are said to cast dust on their heads and clothe themselves with sackcloth — but not because they loved her (27:30-31). No one cared.

Because the whole picture is vivid and clear, little explanation is necessary.

1. The glory of Tyre (27:1-11)

27:1-11. And the word of Yahweh came to me, saying, 'And you, son of man, take up a lamentation against Tyre. And you will say to Tyre, who dwells by the entrances to the sea, merchant of the peoples, to many coastlands, "Thus says the

Lord Yahweh: 'O Tyre, you have said, "I am the perfection of beauty." Your borders are in the heart of the sea; your builders perfected your beauty. With junipers from Senir they built for you all your planks; they took cedar from Lebanon to make a mast for you. Of oaks from Bashan they made your oars; they inlaid your boards of box trees with ivory from the islands of the Kittim. Your sail was of embroidered linen to be your banner; your awning was blue and purple from the islands of Elisha. The inhabitants of Sidon and Arvad were your rowers; your wise men, O Tyre, were with you — they were your seamen. The elders of Gebal and her wise men were with you, repairing your seams; all the ships of the sea and their sailors were with you to handle your merchandise. Paras and Lud and Put were in your army, your men of war. They hung shield and helmet on you; they gave you your glory. The sons of Arvad and your army were upon your walls, all around, and Gammadim were in your towers. They hung their armaments all around; they perfected your beauty.'"'

Ezekiel is instructed to utter a lamentation for Tyre, but without conveying any sense of divine wrath. The impression is given that Tyre has been considered insignificant in the scheme of things. **'The entrances to the sea'** may refer to the fact that the island city had two excellent harbours, facing north and south respectively, making her one of the principal gateways between mainland Phoenicia and the Mediterranean.

The lamentation takes for granted that Tyre had hitherto monopolized all maritime trade routes, extending her influence to **'many coastlands'**. The Hebrew *rôkelet*, underlying **'merchant'**, suggests someone who travels from one place to another to do business; evidently, Tyrian vessels were to be seen in every major port (27:1-3).

Ezekiel transmits Yahweh's word concerning the opulent city. The God of Israel had been listening to what she said concerning herself: **'O Tyre, you have**

said, "I am the perfection of beauty"' (cf. 28:12). Although this description was once applied properly to Jerusalem,[38] the Tyrians chose to deem themselves worthy of such gaudy language (27:3; cf. 27:4,11). Nor, it would appear, did Yahweh disagree.

Although Tyre is not described explicitly as a ship, the obvious metaphor now opens up in that she is situated **'in the heart of the sea'**. Her **'builders' 'perfected** [her] **beauty'**, ensuring that, Titanic-like, she could ride out any hazard (27:4).

For this reason no materials were spared. Her **'planks'**, meaning her decks and her hull, were apparently double (from a Hebrew dual noun), thus ensuring strength, and built from **'junipers'** imported from **'Senir'**, probably Lebanon.[39] Her single **'mast'** was perhaps of fir, again from **'Lebanon'** (27:5).

The vessel has been propelled not only by wind and sail, but principally by many rowers, whose **'oars'** were constructed from **'oaks from Bashan'**, tough enough to withstand continuous pressure. Her **'boards'**, or (perhaps) hull, were made of **'box trees'** from **'the islands of the Kittim'** (Cyprus), replete with **'ivory'** inlay. This wood is light, almost imperishable, immune to attack by sea-worms and therefore well suited for ship-construction. Confident because of her sturdiness and equipment, Tyre had rejoiced in every expectation of prosperity (27:6).

Not only was the good ship Tyre soundly constructed with a selection of the finest materials, she was magnificently adorned, her mainsail being of **'embroidered linen'**.[40] Her deck awnings were **'blue and purple from the islands of Elisha'**, displaying a pretended royalty. The purple dye may have been extracted from the murex, a marine mollusc, and **'Elisha'** appears in extra-biblical sources as 'Alashiya',[41] possibly in Cyprus (27:7).

The vessel also boasted a skilled crew, Phoenician **'inhabitants'** from **'Sidon'**, forty kilometres (or twenty-five miles) from Tyre, and from **'Arvad'**, an island 150 kilometres (over ninety miles) to the north.[42] The reference to **'your wise men, O Tyre'** who **'were your seamen'** points to those counsellors who determined to expand Tyre's commerce (27:8).

'Gebal', the modern Byblos, had sent her **'elders'** and **'wise men'** to maintain the ship's **'seams'**, keeping her seaworthy. That such prominent individuals served Tyre is an acknowledgement of the city's eminence.

Suddenly, the metaphor of the ship is dropped, albeit briefly, to bring into focus the immense resources of Tyre: **'all the ships of the sea and their sailors'** were to be found in her harbour **'to handle your merchandise'** (27:9).

But the figure of speech returns immediately, Tyre being likened to a trading vessel embarking a contingent of mercenaries for defence against marauders. Coloured shields were suspended from the sides of the vessel to display her **'glory'** and to warn pirates to steer clear.[43] **'Paras'** might have been Persia, although it could have been a region within Egypt.[44] **'Put'** was the modern Libya,[45] and **'Lud'** possibly the Lydians of Asia Minor.[46] The fact that men from **'Arvad'** as well as native Tyrians, **'your army'**,[47] were positioned on her **'walls'**, indicates that the vessel had resembled a fortified and defiant city. Who the **'Gammadim'** were is uncertain, but some have tentatively identified them as the Kumidi of the Amarna Tablets.[48] All **'perfected your beauty'** (27:10-11).

2. Tyre's patrons (27:12-25)

27:12-25. '"'Tarshish was your trader because of the abundance of all kinds of wealth; with silver, iron, tin and lead they offered your wares. Javan, Tubal and Meshech — they were your agents; with the lives of humans and copper utensils they bartered for your merchandise. From the house of Togarmah they gave horses, cavalry and mules for your wares.

'"'The sons of Dedan were your agents; many islands were your business agents. They brought back ivory tusks and ebony as your payment. Aram was your trader because of the abundance of your manufactures; they paid for your wares with turquoise, purple, embroidered work, linen, coral and rubies. Judah and the land of Israel — they were your agents; with the wheat of Minnith, cakes, honey and oil and balm, they bartered for your merchandise.

'"'Damascus was your trader because of the abundance of your manufactures, because of the abundance of all kinds of wealth — with the wine of Helbon and white wool. And casks of wine from Uzal they gave for your wares; smooth iron, cassia and cane were among your merchandise. Dedan was your agent for saddlecloths for riding. Arabia and all the princes of Kedar — they were your business agents: with lambs, rams and goats, they were your agents.

'"'Traders of Sheba and Raamah — they were your traders; with the most choice of all perfumes and with every precious stone and with gold they paid for your wares. Haran, Canneh and Eden, the traders of Sheba, Asshur and Kilmad were your traders. They were your traders in gorgeous materials, with cloaks of blue and embroidered cloth, chests of variegated cloth, with tightly wound cords in your trading place. The ships of Tarshish were your freighters for your merchandise. So you were filled and were heavily loaded in the heart of the seas.'"'

A list of nations with which Tyre maintained commercial ties is presented (27:12-23). The somewhat pedestrian, boring style could be deliberate, suggesting a trading ship's cargo inventory and thereby highlighting the city's manifold aspirations. In context, no less than six different terms deriving from the vocabulary of trade are employed, reflecting the fact that Tyre entertained widespread business ties.[49] The list suggests that her trading partners may have supplied her with raw materials and that she exported them as manufactured products. Tyre had become the exceedingly wealthy hub of an international market.

'Tarshish' could have been in the extreme west, and many have identified it with Tartessus, a Phoenician colony in western Spain.[50] From Tarshish, which possessed **'all kinds of wealth'**, Tyre obtained numerous metals from which she derived her **'wares'**. This word, employed in 27:14,16,19,22,33, translates *ize'bônaik*, the Hebrew root suggesting barter, something left in a purchaser's hand.

'Javan' would have been Ionia, or even Greece, and **'Tubal'**, the ancient tribe of the Tibareni. **'Meshech'**, the Moschi, was situated in central Anatolia between the Black Sea and the Caspian Sea. The three are associated in Genesis 10:2, as sons of Japheth,[51] and also in Isaiah 66:19. Joel 3:6 and Amos 1:9 suggest that both Tyre and these peoples were not unacquainted with slave trading. All are said to have been Tyre's **'agents'** (*rôklim*), from a root meaning (as said earlier) to travel about, whether for trade or (in other contexts) perhaps gossip (cf. 27:15,17,22,23): they sought out **'copper'**, or bronze, and defenceless **'humans'** on a wholesale basis, later to be retailed elsewhere by Tyre. **'Merchandise'** renders *ma'arab*, from a root meaning 'to exchange' or 'give in pledge' (cf. 27:17,19,25,27,34). The picture is once again that of acquisitive traders bartering in a marketplace (27:13).

'The house of Togarmah' might have been in Armenia in the remote north (see 38:6),[52] dealing in **'horses'** and **'mules'** as part of the international arms trade (27:14). **'Dedan'**, included among Tyre's **'business agents'**, may have been situated in the Persian Gulf, importing **'ivory tusks'** from India and **'ebony'** from Africa (27:15). **'Aram'**, which extended from

Mesopotamia to Damascus, conveyed manufactured wares from Tyre, paying for them **'with turquoise, purple, embroidered work, linen, coral and rubies'**. **'Turquoise'** is a conjectural translation, but the Hebrew *nôphek* occurs in the list of stones in the king of Tyre's pectoral, as in that of the Israelite high priest (cf. 28:13).[53] Tyre had become truly wealthy (27:16).

'Minnith', in Ammon, was rich in wheat.[54] Apparently, Tyre obtained Transjordanian products through Israelite traders. **'Cakes'** translates *pannag*, but this is conjectural. For the Tyrians it was yet more **'merchandise'**. With the mention of **'Judah'** and **'Israel'** we arrive at the literary and theological centre of the list of Tyre's trading partners (27:17; cf. 5:5): the nominal people of God were not reluctant to make money.[55] **'Damascus'** appears as another **'trader'**, taking advantage of the **'abundance'** of Tyrian **'manufactures'** and **'wealth' 'of all kinds'**. **'Helbon'**, modern Halbun, was situated about sixteen kilometres (ten miles) from Damascus and was known for its wines. These, along with **'white wool'**, were bartered with Tyre (27:18).

In verse 19, the Hebrew behind the usual translation, 'And Dan [the northernmost tribe of Israel?] ... and Javan [Ionia, Greece] ... from Uzal' seems to make little sense, in that diminutive Dan had long since been taken into captivity. And why would Dan be paired with Ionia? Some have suggested that *wedan* ('and Dan') is related to the Ugaritic *dn*, 'jar' or 'cask', and to the Akkadian *dannû*, a storage vat, and this proposition is adopted here: **'And casks of wine from Uzal they gave for your wares.' 'Uzal'**, though occurring in Genesis 10:27, may have been situated in Anatolia.[56] **'Smooth'**, or malleable, **'iron'** was imported, along with aromatic **'cassia'**,[57] the latter used for anointing priests, and **'cane'**, emanating from the distant East. Tyre had extended her trading links to remote places (27:19).

'Dedan', mentioned in 25:13 and 27:15, was a middleman for saddles. **'Arabia'**,[58] dwelling place of nomadic Bedouin, along with **'the princes of Kedar'**, descendants of Ishmael,[59] traded livestock (27:20-21).

'Sheba' and **'Raamah'**, possibly Hamites descended from Cush,[60] may have come from south-west Arabia to trade luxury goods with Tyre, benefiting from the overland and maritime trade routes to the East and to Africa. The expressions **'most choice of all perfumes'** and **'every precious stone'** are eloquent:[61] there was little with which Tyre did not fill her coffers (27:22).

The focus now turns to Mesopotamia. **'Haran'** is mentioned in the story of Abraham,[62] and **'Canneh'** might have been Calneh by the Tigris.[63] **'Eden'** (not the site of the Genesis garden) is mentioned in 2 Kings 19:12 and Isaiah 37:12. **'Asshur'** would have been Assyria, but **'Kilmad'** is apparently unknown. All these, too, were among Tyre's **'traders'** (27:23). As if to stress their importance, it is repeated that **'they were your traders'**, bartering with very costly textiles. Carefully bound and packed, such were to be seen in the appointed places of trade (27:24).

'Ships of Tarshish' may have been a technical term for large cargo vessels designed for ocean-going trade, and emanating from Phoenicia.[64] The first sentence of verse 25 presents Tyre purely as a commercial centre engaging **'freighters for your merchandise'**, while the second sentence resumes the metaphor, anticipating the saga of the shipwreck in verses 26-36: Tyre becomes a trading vessel par excellence. By manipulating the economy of the world, she had become the world's mistress.

In that Tyre had found herself **'filled'** and **'heavily loaded in the heart of the seas'**, surely only she could surpass her own splendour. Not only has Tyre dominated the oceans, she has hired other nations' bulk carriers to expand her business. The picture is of a splendour that, it was suspected, could never pass away (27:25).

This catalogue of near and distant trading partners is intended to show that the influence of Tyre reached to the north, south, east and west of Phoenicia, and that there were few who did not invest heavily in her trading enterprises. It was axiomatic that Tyre would provide an excellent security yielding a permanently high dividend, and that the bubble, if bubble there were, would never burst. When it did burst, as bubbles tend to do, the international business world was shaken to its core. Economies were at risk.

3. Disaster (27:26-36)

27:26-36. '"'Your rowers have brought you into great waters; the east wind has broken you in the heart of the seas. Your wealth and your wares and your merchandise, your sailors, your seamen, your repairmen, your dealers in merchandise and all your men of war who are in you, and all your company in your midst — they will fall into the heart of the seas in the day of your overthrow. At the sound of the cry of your seamen the suburbs will shake, and all who handle the oar will descend from their ships — the sailors and all seamen, they will stand on the land and will make their voice heard over you and cry bitterly. Then they will cast dust over their heads, roll themselves in ash, and will make themselves bald for you and gird themselves with sackcloth. So they will weep over you with bitterness of soul, with bitter mourning.

'"'So in their wailing they will raise a lamentation and will lament over you: "Who is like Tyre, she who is silent in the midst of the sea? When your wares went out from the seas you satisfied many peoples; with the abundance of your wealth and your merchandise you enriched the kings of the earth. Now that you are broken by the seas in the depths of the waters, your merchandise and all your company in your midst have fallen."

'"'All the inhabitants of the coastlands will be desolated because of you and their kings will bristle with horror — their faces are thunderous. The merchants among the people whistle over you — you have become a horror, and you will be no more.'"'

The magnificence of the good ship Tyre vanishes to be seen no more. As it is propelled by its oarsmen **'into great waters'**,[65] disaster strikes suddenly: **'the east wind'** breaks the vessel **'in the heart of the seas'**. In the eastern Mediterranean gusting winds can be lethal, and Ezekiel predicts that such a tempest is to overtake Tyre.[66] Engulfed by wind and waves, the vessel sinks (27:26).

Now the leading thought is that the catastrophe overtaking Tyre is total. In that her **'wealth'**, her **'wares'**, her **'merchandise'** and also the men who manned the vessel must perish, there is nothing left. Is it significant that the ship's cargo is mentioned first in the list, suggesting that all who were involved valued their affluence more than the lives of those being lost at sea? The language is dramatic: **'they will fall into the heart of the seas in the day of your overthrow'**: all who share Tyre's commerce and criteria of happiness go down with her (27:27).

'At the sound of' the cries of drowning **'seamen, the suburbs will shake'**. **'Suburbs'** translates *mig'r'shôt*, meaning 'open places' or 'common land' (cf. 45:2; 48:15).[67] Here, the word stands for those, whether at sea or on land, who witness Tyre foundering with the loss of all hands (27:28).

Oarsmen, and perhaps steersmen, disembark from smaller vessels — Tyrian dependencies — and **'stand on the land'**, giving vent to unprecedented sorrow. Because the unimaginable has happened, what will be their own fate? Although they **'weep over'** Tyre **'with bitterness of soul, with bitterness of mourning'**, it would be a mistake to interpret their sorrow as expressive of selfless pity (27:29-31).

Although the complete chapter was introduced as an expression of grief (see 27:2), here we are given an auxiliary lamentation (27:32, probably extending to 27:34) — that of the crews of other trading ships — over the late, great vessel Tyre. Does **'Who *is* like Tyre?'** allude to her past splendour, or to the awfulness of her ruin? To judge by **'she who *is* silent in the midst of the sea'**, the latter might be preferable, the lamentation confessing that such a tragedy is unique, without precedent in the annals of maritime loss (27:32).

The figure of shipwreck is temporarily dropped, the seafaring community being rocked by the overthrow of Tyre, the city that had **'satisfied many peoples'** and that had **'enriched the kings of the earth'**. They wonder whence they and their carriers will now derive their accustomed affluence (27:33).

Again the image of the wrecked ship appears: **'now that'** the vessel has been **'broken by the seas in the depths of the waters'**, her lavish cargoes and also all who worked the vessel **'have fallen'**. Nothing remains (27:34).

The text continues to oscillate between metaphor and reality. Now Ezekiel predicts the world's reaction when Tyre is known to have sunk without a trace. **'Kings ... bristle with horror'** and **'their faces are thunderous'** (27:35). **'Merchants ... whistle'**, hissing and crying in horror.[68] Lost in the depths of the sea, history rather than reality, Tyre **'will be no more'** (27:36).

Application

That upon which men dote and to which they addict themselves may well become the instrument of their destruction. Tyre gained her immense wealth from mercantile traffic, but in the metaphor it was the sea that eventually became her executioner and then her grave.

Consider the enormity of Tyre's sin. Notwithstanding an earlier time when a king of Tyre had blessed Yahweh, the God of Israel,[69] later generations chose to remain resolutely blind to the significance of the people of Israel. Tyre was jealous of Jerusalem, not because she was uniquely 'the valley of vision',[70] the only community on the face of the planet in which there was a true temple for God, but because for centuries she had matched, and possibly exceeded, Tyre's own wealth.[71] If you will allow a trivial comment, casual attendees at church may well be more interested in the size of the collection and how much the minister is paid than in what will be done with the money or what the minister preaches about. The inglorious principle is the same.

From verse 2 to the end of the chapter God is not mentioned. A superficial reading might, then, suggest that the downfall of Tyre, likened to the foundering of a mighty ship at sea, was the aftermath of military conquest. But such an interpretation would be mistaken because the chapter assumes that it is Yahweh who is in overall control of all terrestrial forces, whether natural or human. In that Tyre had boasted that she was perfectly beautiful (27:3), she was brought down.

Let him who thinks he stands take heed lest he falls.[72] Let God in Christ be our God.

The doom of the prince of Tyre and of Sidon; the establishment of Israel (Ezekiel 28:1-26)

Ezekiel's indictment of Tyre now culminates in a prosecution (28:1-19) levelled at the ruler of the city, who is referred to in 28:2 as **'the prince of Tyre'** and in 28:12 as the **'king of Tyre'** — this to be followed in 28:20-23 by a condemnation of neighbouring Sidon and in 28:24-26 by a prediction concerning the re-establishment of Israel.

Concerning the prince of Tyre, his arrogance is depicted in vivid terms (28:1-5) before his downfall is elaborated (28:6-10). Finally, the charge against him climaxes with a vivid lamentation (28:11-19).

The chapter presents certain problems, to which there may be no obvious answers. Why do there seem to be allusions in 28:12-19 to Genesis 1 – 3, and in particular to the positioning of the cherubim to the east of Eden,[73] and perhaps also to Exodus 28:15-30 and the jewels upon the garment of the high priest of Israel?

Then again, does the lamentation of 28:11-19 point obliquely to Satan, the angelic enemy of God and of men, and does the passage throw light upon his situation both before and after he fell? It would seem that in these verses Ezekiel has in mind someone far more powerful and insidious than a mere human king of an influential but localized and temporary city-state — and someone who is perceived as the model of which the latter had become a scaled-down version.

Furthermore, although Ezekiel denounces the king of Tyre, if this prince appears to be a shadow of Satan it might seem that the latter is actually the prime object of scrutiny. Perhaps, too, Isaiah 14:12-15, referring to the arrogance and eventual doom of the king of Babylon, the 'star of the morning, son of the dawn' ('Lucifer'), might be interpreted in rather the same way, giving weight to such an approach to Ezekiel 28.

The view taken here is that neither of the passages from Ezekiel and Isaiah refers *primarily* to the fall of Satan, but that Ezekiel, a captive in Babylon, wrote about the king of Tyre, just as in previous years Isaiah in Jerusalem was concerned with the king of Babylon. These prophets addressed potentates who rode roughshod over their fellows and who in one way or another despised the people of God.

This being said, it does appear to the present writer that there could be a secondary or background reference. Ezekiel might imply that the king of Tyre was like an anonymous cherub who in a previous era had ruined himself through his pride. If such an interpretation is not unreasonable, this angel could hardly be other than Satan.

As far as 28:11-19 is concerned, such an approach would suggest that Ezekiel takes up a known tradition concerning the fall of Satan in order to predict the overthrow of the king of Tyre. If so, a further question arises: was there such a tradition in Israel by the early sixth century BC, when Ezekiel exercised his ministry? And does the Old Testament exhibit a demonology preparative to that of the New Testament? Or, it may be asked, does it exhibit any demonology at all? Such questions will be addressed during the following exposition.

By way of anticipation, if it is accepted that 28:11-19 does recall the Genesis record (and perhaps Exod. 28), why should two men — the kings of Babylon (see Isa. 14) and Tyre — be held out as shadows or reflections of the Evil One, and why does the king of Tyre appear to be garbed in a high-priestly fashion? Part of the answer could be that in their arrogance each ruler was satanic, there being no degree of blasphemy to which each did not aspire. Their hearts showed that they were effectively children of the devil, even as Jesus told the Pharisees that their burning antagonism to him proved Satan to be their spiritual parent.[74]

1. The pride of the prince of Tyre (28:1-5)

28:1-5. Then the word of Yahweh came to me, saying, 'Son of man, say to the prince of Tyre, "Thus says the Lord Yahweh: 'Because your heart has become high and you have said, "I am a god and I dwell in the residence of the gods in the heart of the seas," yet you are a man and no god, and you have made your heart as the heart of the gods — Look, you are wiser than Daniel; no secret do they hold dark from you. By your wisdom and your understanding you have made wealth for yourself and have acquired silver and gold in your treasuries. By the abundance of your wisdom in your trading you have increased your wealth, and your heart has become high with your wealth.'"'

The **'son of man'** was instructed to address the **'prince of Tyre'** (28:1-2). **'Prince'** translates *nagid*, meaning a 'leader', 'one who goes before', and the monarch is possibly so called because he was the head of a mercantile state, rather than a sovereign who had gained his ascendancy by force of arms. In the Old Testament, whereas Yahweh is the 'King' of Israel, he is never described as *nagid*, a term applied only to some selected humans, which, again, could be why it is used here. After all, who was the king of Tyre? Compare Saul and David, neither of whom was recognized as an absolute monarch in the kingdom of God.[75]

Apparently, the man in question, whose patronymic was almost certainly 'Ethbaal' — perhaps meaning 'Baal is with him' — had laid claims to being close to his ethnic pantheon, or actually to be a deity, dwelling **'in the residence of the gods'** and **'in the heart of the seas'**. His assertion that **'I am a god'** contrasts with the prophecy's oft-repeated statement by the God of Israel that 'I am Yahweh'.[76] Further, he had claimed to exercise ultimate power in that he considered himself to be seated upon a virtual heavenly throne atop a mountain summit, which is what the island city of Tyre must have resembled.[77] Accordingly, he had asserted that he possessed divine wisdom: **'and you have made your heart as the heart of the gods'**. But the Lord states roundly that he is **'a man and no god'** (28:2). Of course, it would have been equally reasonable for Ethbaal to conclude (correctly) that the true God had given him his name and fame. But this would have made him feel small.

Sadly, Ethbaal was by no means the last man to exalt himself to the heavens. In Scripture, consider Sennacherib, Nebuchadnezzar, the pharaoh of Ezekiel's day, Herod Agrippa I, grandson of Herod the Great, and the yet-to-arrive 'man of lawlessness'.[78] Their doom is writ.

With heavy irony Yahweh seems to admit that the leader of Tyre was, indeed, **'wiser than Daniel'** and that **'no secret do they hold dark from you'**, which may be an acknowledgement that in his own field of expertise — that of amassing wealth — he was superlative and had nothing to learn.[79] Ethbaal did not bother as to whether or not he had been given an insight into spiritual realities, whatever (from his point of view) they might have been. For him, it was the market that mattered.

In his own way he had rivalled the statesman-prophet Daniel (cf. 14:14), who by this time had been in Babylon for perhaps more than twenty years and whose reputation must have reached Tyre.[80] The Lord does not criticize the ruler for being sagacious enough to accumulate wealth, but because he reckoned himself to be godlike (28:3). Yahweh, indeed, acknowledges that by his **'wisdom'** and **'understanding'** the man filled his **'treasuries'** with **'silver and gold'** (28:4).

Yet again, **'wisdom'** is mentioned. Ethbaal must have been supremely skilful in his management of the economy of Tyre, something for which he is not censured. But his **'heart'** had **'become high'** with all his **'wealth'**. Herein lay the certainty of downfall (28:5).

2. The imminent downfall of the prince (28:6-10)

28:6-10. 'Therefore, "Thus says the Lord Yahweh: 'Because you have made your heart like the heart of the gods, therefore, look, I am bringing upon you strangers, the ruthless of the nations, and they will draw their swords against the beauty of your wisdom and will profane your brightness. They will bring you down to the pit, and you will die the deaths of the slain in the heart of the seas. Will you still say, "I am a god," in the presence of your slayers — even though you are a man and not a god, in the hand of those who wound you? You will die the death of the uncircumcised by the hand of strangers, for I have spoken,' declares the Lord Yahweh."'

Yahweh, reiterating his accusation against the prince of Tyre, now proceeds to issue his verdict and sentence. In that the man had **'made** [his] **heart like the heart of the gods'** (or, 'of God'; cf. 28:2) and had arrogated to himself a status fitted only for the one

God (28:6), he is summoned to **'look'** at what Yahweh will do.

Firstly, God will bring upon the blasphemous prince **'strangers, the ruthless of the nations'**, by which are meant the Babylonians;[81] secondly, the invaders will destroy **'the beauty of your wisdom'**, meaning their reduction of a city made hugely rich by its prince's commercial acumen; thirdly, the Lord will **'profane'** the **'brightness'** of Tyre. In the Old Testament, **'brightness'**, deriving from a verb meaning 'to radiate', occurs only here and in 28:17 and is intended to inform the prince that the light and glory of what had become a quasi-throne for a god will be desecrated, becoming gloom and desolation (28:7).

And the invaders will **'bring'** the prince down into **'the pit',** where he will die the **'deaths'** of those killed **'in the heart of the seas'**. The plural **'deaths'** may mean that his painful end will resemble that of a man in his final agony who yearns for peace. He dies, as it were, many times over, yet cannot find release. Yahweh's announcement to the prince tells that, whereas he had exercised his dominion **'in the heart of the seas'** (cf. 28:2), there he will perish (28:8).

Yahweh mocks. Now in the 'pit', will the degraded prince be heard when he still claims (falsely) that he is **'a god'**? He will not, because if he were truly divine he would not have descended to the realm of his **'slayers'**, Babylonians, who **'wound'** him (28:9).

Thus the one who had claimed to be divine will not even die like a common man. He approaches his end as would **'uncircumcised'** persons, living and then perishing as an unclean, faithless barbarian in alienation from God's people. Much the same is said of Pharaoh in 31:18, as well as of Egypt, Elam, Meshech, Tubal, Edom and Sidon (32:19,21,24-32). Although for Israel circumcision was the appointed sign of covenant status,[82] it was not so for those other peoples in the region who apparently maintained the practice.

To be uncircumcised, therefore, signified inferiority because of personal impurity. Among the dead, the prince of Tyre will be compelled to identify with those whom in life he would have spurned. Yahweh **'declares'** that it must be so. He has **'spoken'** (28:10).

3. A final lamentation (28:11-19)

28:11-19. And the word of Yahweh came to me, saying, 'Son of man, raise a lamentation over the king of Tyre. And you will say to him, "Thus says the Lord Yahweh: 'You are the seal of perfection, full of wisdom and complete in beauty. You were in Eden, the garden of God; every precious stone was your covering: carnelian, topaz and moonstone; tarshish, onyx and jasper; lapis lazuli, carbuncle and emerald, and gold: the workmanship of your settings and of your sockets was in you. In the day that you were created they were established.

'"'You were the anointed cherub, he who covers, and I placed you in the holy mountain of God. You were in the midst of the stones of fire — you walked! You were perfect in your ways from the day when you were created until iniquity was found in you. In the abundance of your trade, all in your midst were filled with violence, and you sinned. So I banished you from the mountain of God and destroyed you, O covering cherub, from the midst of the stones of fire. Your heart became high in your beauty; you ruined your wisdom because of your brilliance. I threw you to the ground and made a spectacle of you for kings. Because of the multitude of your iniquities, in the injustice of your trade you have profaned your sanctuaries, and I have brought fire out from your midst; it has consumed you and I have given you as ash upon the ground in the sight of all who see you. All among the peoples who know you are desolated because of you; you have become a disaster and will be no more.'"'

In distant Babylon the **'son of man'** was instructed to **'raise a lamentation'** for **'the king of Tyre'**, doing so in the name of Yahweh. Yet unlike, say, David's lament over Saul and Jonathan,[83] no grief is expressed. Remarkably, here is a funeral dirge that, void of regret, insinuates joy that Tyre is gone. The ascription of kingship to Ethbaal may mean that Yahweh accuses him of aspiring to be more than a leader of men, and this would link with 28:2 (28:11-12).

Again employing heavy irony, Ezekiel announces that the king had been the **'seal of perfection'**. **'Seal'** represents a slight revocalization of the Masoretic *hôtém*, a participle form meaning 'he who seals'. **'Perfection'** (*toknit*; cf. 43:10) is from a verbal root suggesting plan and proportion, as in a building that is well designed and aesthetically pleasing.

Thus, **'seal'** may mean that the king of Tyre considered himself to be a crafted signet ring worn by deity, and by that token the authorized representative of God, or the gods.[84] As the divinely instituted personification of Tyre, the monarch had sealed his kingdom with the stamp of his **'wisdom'**, making it, as he thought, stable. Conversely, the **'beauty'** observable in the affluent community advertised the stature of its illustrious leader (28:12).

Although verses 13-19 seem to recall Genesis 2 and 3, thus linking the sin of pride of which both Adam and Tyre were guilty, it is not easy to discern the picture that Ezekiel offers his readers. But it does seem that the king of Tyre is likened to a guardian cherub, possibly a cherub in Eden and perhaps one of the cherubim covering and protecting the ark of the covenant.[85]

The created being of 28:13 appears to be the angelic personality mentioned in 28:14-15, the king of Tyre being considered solely in terms of a supernatural, holy yet created rational being who fell into sin. Arguably, Adam does not appear.

It follows that, however we care to view the passage, it may be that we find here the only explicit reference in the Bible to the *creation* of an angelic being. John 8:44, which refers to the original fall of Satan, would be no exception.[86]

The statement that **'every precious stone was your covering'** would indicate that the ruler garbed himself in gold and precious jewels. But is there also a recall of the pectoral of the high priest of Israel?[87] Both lists arrange the stones in triads, suggesting rows, and both commence (in Hebrew) with *ôdem* (possibly **'carnelian'**) and *pit'da* (possibly **'topaz'**).[88] Furthermore, the pre-Christian Greek Septuagint reshapes the Hebrew text of 28:13 by identifying twelve stones, plus silver and gold, to make explicit an allusion to Exodus 28.

Against this, a parallel between the king of Tyre, a **'cherub'** (see 28:14) and the Aaronic high priest would lead to a confused mixing of metaphors. Therefore the Septuagint's identification may be too imaginative and perhaps all that we are being told by the Hebrew text is that the king of Tyre had been gorgeously bejewelled and robed.

In the last part of the present verse (28:13), the monarch is said to have been **'created'**, as was also his regal apparel. Although this appears to be an allusion to the creation of Adam,[89] might it not point to the prior creation of the angelic being to whom the king is likened? Were the creation of Adam to be recalled just here, there would be another difficult mixing of metaphors, the monarch resembling Adam *and* a (fallen) cherub. Furthermore, the king is said to have been **'in Eden, the garden of God'**, which turns out in 28:14 to have been 'the holy mountain of God'.

Either way, the central point being made by the lamentation is that the king of Tyre had been established securely and with splendour in his fortress city by, presumably, Yahweh, the one God (28:13). This theme is continued in the next verse.

Now the monarch is identified as **'the anointed cherub, he who covers'**, who had been **'placed'** by Yahweh **'in the holy mountain of God'**, and not now 'within Eden, the garden of God' (cf. the previous verse). The definite article, **'the'**, followed by **'anointed'**, suggests that within the fraternity of the cherubim he had enjoyed a special status. Even as two representative cherubim covered the mercy seat within the tabernacle and later in Solomon's temple, so God had situated the king of Tyre in his castle as protector of the Lord's domain.

In the Old Testament, we read about:

1. A cherub being associated with the throne chariot of Yahweh;
2. Cherubim protecting the Garden of Eden (although they are not said to have been *in* it);
3. Cherubim as constituting the actual throne of the Lord of hosts;
4. The two cherubim of gold situated over the mercy seat in Moses' Holy of Holies;
5. Numerous representations of cherubim woven into the fabric of the inner curtains of the tabernacle and its veils;
6. The cherubim of Solomon's temple, also represented as the chariot of Yahweh;
7. Images of cherubim carved on the gold-plated planks within the temple, on the wooden doors and on the bases of the lavers;
8. The cherubim of Ezekiel's vision;
9. Cherubim carved upon the walls of Ezekiel's ideal temple.[90]

The closest parallel between any of these and the king considered as a cherub would seem to be that of the cherubim stationed at the eastern limit of the

Garden of Eden.[91] Yet although plural in number, they were (as already noted) not within the garden. Moreover, it is not said of either them or of any other cherubim that they were to be found **'in the holy mountain of God'**. Is this 'mountain' the flaming Mount Sinai, or does Ezekiel call attention to Mount Zion?[92] Perhaps, then, Taylor's remark is pertinent: 'It seems ... that Ezekiel's imagination wandered freely and drew on a wide variety of symbolical background all interwoven with his message of the fall of Tyre.'[93] If so, perhaps there is a threading of two strands of thought: the king of Tyre, considered as a cherub, was found beside Eden's garden as an anointed guardian; equally, in that he was in God's 'holy mountain', he enjoyed immediate access to deity.[94]

There, **'in the midst of the stones of fire'**, amid the incandescent brilliance of the dwelling place of God, he had **'walked'**, thus displaying his status. In the same fashion and with similar display, God in Eden, Abraham in Canaan and Satan in the heavenly court are, remarkably, said to have 'walked'.[95] But this monarch walks no more (28:14).

Apparently, there was a period following his creation (by God) during which the king of Tyre was blameless, or **'perfect'**.[96] Subsequently, **'iniquity'** was **'found'** in him. At this point the creation and the fall of Adam may be in mind unless — as this commentary would suggest — Ezekiel was considering not the apostasy of the first man but the prior fall of a very high-ranking cherub or archangel.[97] Similarly, the king of Tyre, set in a place of high honour by that same God, had allowed himself to be deluded by his material wealth and the power that accompanied it, and became his own deity (28:15).

The indictment of verse 15 is expanded, the person of the **'covering cherub'** now merging with that of the king of Tyre (**'in the abundance of your trade'**) and, indeed, with Tyre itself (**'all in your midst were filled**

with violence'). **'Banished'** stems from the *Pi'él* form of the root *chalal*, which would mean 'to render profane' (cf. 28:18) and thus become liable to exclusion (28:16).[98]

Concerning the parallel between the king of Tyre and a fallen cherub, Block remarks that 'the primary referent within the context is clearly the human king of Tyre', and that 'a detailed treatment of the origin of the demonic is not to be expected from the OT'.[99] Yet is this so? Is there not an obvious *secondary* referent — the fallen cherub? And if so, it might be asked whether Ezekiel employs a myth that originated beyond the sphere of Israelite belief and the Old Testament?

While the only adequate answer to the first question seems to be an affirmative, a response to the second would be that Genesis 1 – 3 does, indeed, provide much, but not complete material for the analogy. In that the creation record says nothing explicitly about any cherub who had fallen into sin, and in that Ezekiel arguably seems to employ the fact of such an apostasy to give emphasis to the enormity of the sin of the king of Tyre, it might be concluded that here, as in Isaiah 14:4-21, we are given an early revelation concerning the fall of Satan, a (created) personage who appears elsewhere in the Old Testament, as in Job 1:6-12; 2:1-7, as a supernatural, powerful and sinful being.

Further, if it is suggested that Ezekiel recruits elements from non-Israelite demonology, might it not be expected that archaeological research would by now have provided details? But Block observes that 'the efforts to relate this passage to the Ugaritic materials are ubiquitous',[100] meaning that in his view there is no demonstrable link. If so, it follows that Ezekiel does not employ myth. I would accept that this is the case.

Because the king's heart was elevated by a gratuitous sense of his glory, and because he **'ruined'** his **'wisdom'** through a vain contemplation of his **'brilliance'**, he must be hurled prostrate **'to the ground'** — 'ground' (*eretz*) possibly being synonymous with the 'pit' of 28:8 (cf. 26:19-20) — as a spectacle **'for'** other **'kings'**. Let them be warned (28:17).

The catalogue of the man's sins is not complete. The **'multitude'** of his **'iniquities'** and the **'injustice'** associated with his mercantile enterprises had driven him to pollute his **'sanctuaries'** — probably the temples that he believed had transmuted the island of Tyre into a holy place. But because he knew better, he ought to have followed the light given to him.[101]

This sin had become a fire issuing from the king, **'from your midst'**, consuming him in the process: Yahweh allows him to fall into ruin, reducing himself to ashes that remain scattered for a while upon the rock. The **'peoples'** who knew him as he used to be are devastated and appalled. His downfall is as final as it is terrible; he is no more (28:18-19).

4. Sidon (28:20-23)

28:20-23. And the word of Yahweh came to me, saying, 'Son of man, set your face towards Sidon and prophesy against her. And you will say, "Thus says the Lord Yahweh: 'Look, I am against you, Sidon, and I shall make myself glorious in your midst, and they will know that I am Yahweh when I execute judgements in her. So I shall be sanctified in her. And I shall send plague within her and blood in her streets. Then the slain will fall in her midst by the sword against her from all around, and they will know that I am Yahweh.'"'

Ezekiel turns his attention to Sidon, about forty kilometres north of Tyre. More ancient than Tyre but contributing to its wealth (27:8), Sidon and its idolatry had for centuries been a snare to Israel,[102] which may be the reason for Sidon's inclusion in the catalogue of the seven nations destined to fall under Nebuchadnezzar, the other six being Ammon, Moab, Edom, the Philistines, Tyre (25:1 — 28:19) and Egypt (29:1 – 32:32). And it may be that 28:24-26, in focusing upon the destiny of Israel and occurring in the centre of chapters 25 – 32, offers a symmetry between chapters 25:1 – 28:23 and chapters 29 – 32, which are of almost equal length.[103]

In that Sidon had allied herself with Zedekiah against Nebuchadnezzar,[104] it may be that, paradoxically, she opposed the true interests of Israel by resisting the world power destined to bring down the corrupt theocracy. In this way she compounded her own sin. Yet she had shown scorn when Jerusalem was in dire peril (see 28:24), and the Lord had taken note. Therefore, Yahweh requires the **'son of man'** to **'set** [his] **face towards Sidon'** and to **'prophesy against her'** (28:20-21).

Accordingly, Ezekiel is to declare that Yahweh is **'against'** Sidon and that he intends to **'make'** himself **'glorious in** [her] **midst'**.[105] There is a clear allusion here to Exodus 14:4,16-18 and to the departure of Israel from Egypt and their subsequent pursuit by Pharaoh within an area west of the Red Sea. Then Yahweh informed Moses that the Egyptians must soon realize that he, Yahweh, is God. This is how it will be with Sidon: Yahweh will show himself to be the holy God by delivering this city up to disease and bloodshed, the inevitable by-products of war, the sword from outside causing many to fall within the city. The predicted collapse of Sidon will demonstrate that Yahweh is the true God (28:22-23).

5. The regathering of Israel (28:24-26)

28:24-26. '"'And for the house of Israel there will be no more a pricking briar or a painful thorn from all who are round about them, who have despised them, and they will know that I am the Lord Yahweh.'

'"Thus says the Lord Yahweh: 'When I gather the house of Israel from the peoples among whom they have been scattered, then I shall be sanctified in them in the eyes of the nations. Then they will live on their own earth that I gave to my servant, to Jacob, and they will dwell on it securely: they will build houses and will plant vineyards. They will live in it securely when I execute judgements among all who despise them from round about them. Then they will know that I am Yahweh their God.'"'

Turning his gaze from Tyre, Ezekiel now looks to the future destiny of his own people, Israel, possibly alluding to Leviticus 13:51-52 and 14:44, which refer to malignant, **'pricking'**, leprosy, and to Numbers 33:55, which reads:

> But if you do not drive out the inhabitants of the land from before you, then it shall be that those whom you let remain shall be irritants in your eyes and thorns in your sides, and they shall harass you in the land where you dwell.[106]

This passage tells of the dire consequences for Israel if (or rather, when) the people fail to pursue the conquest of Canaan to its conclusion: remaining nations will become barbs in their eyes and thorns in their flesh. But Ezekiel declares that no more will the nations, ever contemptuous of Judah, be a **'pricking briar or a painful thorn'** to God's people. Then **'they** [antagonistic nations] **will know that I am the Lord Yahweh,'** the prediction of 28:22-23 being repeated for emphasis.

Could the recall of Numbers 33:55 be significant, implying that in time to come an obedient people will be settled safely within the land promised to Abraham and his family, and immune to the hostility of others? And it may be asked whether this happy situation fits nicely with the conditions that applied following the return from exile under Zerubbabel. Then the children of Israel found themselves in 'times of distress' and were less than careful about relationships.[107] Perhaps the present verses (28:23-24) point to the blessedness of a more remote future, thus anticipating verses 25-26. If so, Ezekiel anticipates events that, up to the early twenty-first century, have not yet happened.

Finally, Yahweh speaks through Ezekiel concerning the eventual regathering of Israel. As noted earlier, 28:24-26 seems to be a fulcrum around which revolve chapters 25:1 – 28:23 and chapters 29 — 32. Now the Lord announces that he will **'gather'** his people from the various places where they had been **'scattered'** and that he will **'be sanctified'** among them **'in the eyes of'** those peoples. Then Israel will dwell **'securely'** in the land that the Lord had promised to his **'servant ... Jacob'**, 'Jacob' standing for Israel considered as a coherent society.[108] Protected residents, they construct their **'houses'** and cultivate their **'vineyards'**. Beyond the borders of the land, Yahweh will move in repeated judgements against all the nations that had treated Israel with contempt. They must come to know that Yahweh is the God of Israel (28:25-26).

To repeat, because Ezekiel's expectations concerning the subjugation of the nations were not fulfilled at that distant time, we might suppose that this final, brief prediction concerning the return of Israel has not yet been realized. As we shall see, prophecies that Ezekiel has yet to declare appear to support this approach.

Application

It seems obvious that Ezekiel was aware of the early chapters of the book of Genesis and that he employed their record as a backdrop to his exposition of the Tyrian king's apostasy. And the rest of his prophecy shows that Ezekiel had an intimate knowledge of the law of Moses.

More generally, Ezekiel issues his condemnation of Judah in terms of the warnings in the books of Leviticus and Deuteronomy. In a sense, he was a disciple of Moses. This means that we shall never come to terms with Ezekiel or, for that matter, with the New Testament unless we take the first five books of the Old Testament at face value, accepting their implicit claim that they are historically accurate.

If 28:12-19 does *not* focus upon the creation and subsequent rebellion of an exalted cherub, we are faced with a problem in that the Old Testament presents us with the reality of Satan, yet fails to explain how he came into being. Perhaps it is simpler to interpret Ezekiel as paralleling the fall of the king of Tyre with that of the 'anointed cherub'.

It appears that Tyre is condemned partly because that city had allied itself with the renegade Zedekiah against Nebuchadnezzar,[109] thereby opposing the plan of God for his people. By analogy, may it not be that those who belong to and support Christian denominations that have largely abandoned evangelical truth are in a not dissimilar situation?

Verses 24-26 were good news to Ezekiel's generation — and are good news for us. There are times when we need to avert our gaze from the evils of this present world and consider the glory that shall be. Paul, in Romans 9:4, writes that to the Israelites 'belong' (note the present tense) 'the glory, the covenants, the giving of the law, the service and the promises', telling that Jacob's people remain within the plan of God for his church.

6. The sixth prophecy

(Ezekiel 29:1–16)

The date is 7 January 587. Ten years have passed since Ezekiel was deported from Jerusalem and one year since the commencement of the siege of Jerusalem (cf. 24:1-2). Although in this section the only indication of Egyptian lack of sympathy for Judah is expressed by 29:6, which states that Egypt had been **'a reed crutch to the house of Israel'** — alluding to the pharaoh's failed military expedition against the Babylonians in their siege of Jerusalem[1] — none the less the Lord has much to say to Egypt.

No less than four chapters (29 – 32) are devoted to the condemnation of this people. The pharaoh addressed in 29:2 was the impetuous Wahibra (in Hebrew transliteration, 'Hophra'), fourth king of the Twenty-Sixth Dynasty, who had become ruler of Egypt in 589 BC. Reigning until 570 BC, when he was slain by his successor, he was always keen to interfere in the affairs of Judah in order to enlarge his influence in the region.

Following his own accession, Zedekiah of Judah requested military assistance from the pharaoh, presumably against Nebuchadnezzar (cf. 17:11-21). In spite of the earlier defeat of one of his predecessors, Nekau II (in Hebrew transliteration, 'Necho'), by the Babylonians at Carchemish in 605 BC, Hophra advanced against Nebuchadnezzar at Jerusalem and sent a fleet to attack by sea.[2]

It was this Necho who had overcome Josiah of Judah at Megiddo when the latter attempted to repel Egyptian assistance for the Assyrians.[3] As already noted, Necho then removed Jehoahaz, installing his own puppet ruler, Eliakim, in Jerusalem and renaming him Jehoiakim.[4] Jehoiakim reigned for eleven years, to be followed by the youthful Jehoiachin, who held the throne for only three months, then being succeeded by Zedekiah. Hophra is mentioned explicitly in Jeremiah 44:30.

It will be recalled that it was about 593 BC that Ezekiel commenced his prophetic ministry. This was the fifth year of the captivity in Babylon of Jehoiachin. But a decade had passed since Ezekiel's deportation and, contrary to Jewish expectation, Jerusalem was facing destruction. Now Yahweh reveals his word to the prophet concerning mighty Egypt.

This dominant nation had survived every peril and remained a power to be reckoned with. Not unnaturally, hopes lingered for future greatness. But Ezekiel declares that it would not be, because God had decreed otherwise.

When the first of these prophecies against Egypt was issued, many Jews still looked upon the land of the Nile as their only significant ally in the struggle against Babylon. But in turning their gaze to the ancient enemy, the people of Yahweh were not looking to their God.

Of course, there was nothing novel about this. Since the occasion at Sinai when the Israelites had persuaded Aaron to supply them with a golden calf, they had always been inclined to look back to Africa.[5] And, unmoved by the more recent lessons of history, they put their trust in Egypt even after the fall of Jerusalem, when it should have been obvious that any intervention from Pharaoh, even if forthcoming, would be futile.[6]

Ezekiel's prophecies were designed both to rebuke arrogant Egypt and to warn Israel that reliance upon this nation must be a counsel of despair. Because Egypt was doomed,[7] Israel should not look to her for assistance in the evil hour.

To the modern reader, it may appear strange that four complete chapters, about one twelfth of the entire prophecy of Ezekiel, are devoted to an elaborate prediction of the reduction of Egypt from its status as a major international power. But the rationale seems clear: because Israel had been delivered from Egyptian bondage nearly one millennium before Ezekiel's time, why should they seek Egyptian aid? Like Jeremiah, Ezekiel saw Egypt, and all that that nation stood for, as a menace to the people of God.

Furthermore, Judah was regarded as at best a non-independent bargaining chip in the hands of any adjacent militaristic power — a political satellite, or even a platform from which to launch an attack elsewhere. But although the prophets knew that political and cultural isolation was the best policy, from the popular Jewish point of view an undoubted, though temporary, revival of Egyptian power after the fall of Assyria made an Egyptian alliance seem attractive. These four chapters, therefore, expound the futility of reliance upon the pharaohs.

More importantly, it was necessary for Ezekiel's generation to be reminded about who was in overall control of the nations. The prophet emphasizes that because Yahweh was operating at will within the international arena, as well as among his redeemed people, the Jews should not have feared, but should have assured themselves that their tiny nation would endure in order to present a Saviour to the world (as intimated by 29:21).

This series of prophecies against Egypt seems to have been delivered in chronological order, with the exception of the much later 29:17-21. Altogether, there are seven 'words' from Yahweh:

1. A prophecy against Pharaoh and Egypt (29:1-16). This was in the tenth year of Jehoiachin's exile, 587 BC.

2. A prediction of the conquest of Egypt by Nebuchadnezzar (29:17-21). It is dated to the twenty-seventh year of Jehoiachin's captivity, 570 BC. Jerusalem had fallen sixteen years previously. This prophecy would seem to have been the last uttered by Ezekiel.

3. An undated vision concerning the judgement that would explode soon upon Egypt and its allies (30:1-19). It might have been given in the period between the occasion of the preceding prophecy and that following, giving a date between about 586 and 570 BC, perhaps a short time before the fall of Jerusalem.

4. The destruction of the power of Egypt by Babylon (30:20-26). The date is the eleventh year of Jehoiachin's captivity, 586 BC.

5. Assyria is presented as a dire warning to Egypt and her satellites (31:1-18). This prophecy also dates to the eleventh year of Jehoiachin's captivity, 586 BC.

6. A lamentation over the king of Egypt (32:1-16), given towards the end of the twelfth year of Jehoiachin's captivity, 585 BC.

7. A second lamentation over the destruction of the imperial power of Egypt (32:17-32). Again, the year is the twelfth of Jehoiachin's captivity. As in 26:1, the month is not recorded, but it might have been the twelfth (cf. 32:1). This would mean that it was uttered two weeks after the preceding prophecy (the first and fifteenth days respectively).

1. The first 'word': Pharaoh, the great crocodile (29:1-9)

29:1-9. In the tenth year, in the tenth, on the twelfth day of the month, the word of Yahweh came to me, saying, 'Son of man, set your face against Pharaoh, king of Egypt, and prophesy against him and against Egypt — all of it. Speak, and you will say, "Thus says the Lord Yahweh: 'Look, I am against you, Pharaoh, king of Egypt, the great monster that lies in the midst of his rivers, who has said, "The river is mine, and I myself have made it for myself." But I shall place hooks in your jaws and shall make the fish of your rivers stick to your scales, and I shall bring you up from your rivers — and all the fish of your rivers that stick to your scales. Then I shall abandon you to the wilderness — you and all the fish of your rivers will fall upon the face of the field; you will not be collected and you will not be gathered: I have given you for food to the animals of the field and to the birds of the air. And all the inhabitants of Egypt will know that I am Yahweh because they have been a reed crutch to the house of Israel. When they took hold of you by the branches, you were crushed, and you pierced all their shoulders; and when they leaned on you, you broke, causing all their hips to stand out.'

'"'Therefore, thus says the Lord Yahweh: 'Look, I am bringing a sword against you, and I shall cut off man and beast from you. Then the land of Egypt will be a desolation and a wasteland, and they will know that I am Yahweh.'"'...

Jerusalem has been under siege for just over a year (cf. 24:1-2), and it will be two years before Ezekiel learns of the eventual fall of the city (see 33:21).[8] The occasion would have been the temporary withdrawal of the Chaldeans because of the advance of the Egyptian army under Pharaoh Hophra (29:1).[9] Although Jeremiah had predicted the futility of Egyptian help, the Jews in Chaldea no doubt clung to the hope that the incursion would be God's way of rescuing his city. Ezekiel knew otherwise, and says so.

The **'son of man'** is directed to **'set** [his] **face against Pharaoh, king of Egypt'**. Moreover, Yahweh himself is against **'Egypt — all of it'**, in that the solidarity between the king and his people is such that the offence of the former is that of the latter; they applaud Hophra in his pretensions (29:2).

Pharaoh, **'the great monster'** (*tannin*), almost certainly a crocodile, is said to have spread himself out languidly amid the tributaries of the Nile. The beast had claimed this river as his own, professing to believe that it, and therefore Egypt, which derived its fertility from the Nile, were his by right of creation — **'for myself'**.[10] The arrogance of the man was boundless, which is why Yahweh is antagonistic. *Tannin* may be employed because, according to Genesis 1:21, the 'great' *tanninim* were a part of the created order and subservient to Yahweh. Thus Pharaoh is indicted as an upstart doomed to perdition (29:3).

In ancient times, crocodiles were caught with large hooks. Just so for Egypt: Yahweh will, so to speak, drag this monster out of its waters with such an instrument. The fish clinging to its scales would be the numerous peoples of Egypt, and both they and the beast are to be cast by the Lord into **'the wilderness'**, even as a fisherman might heave his catch onto the riverbank. There they collapse in the open **'field'** where there is no rescuer. The crocodile and its attendant fish putrefy, to be devoured by scavenging animals and birds of prey (29:4-5).

The first part of 29:6, **'And all the inhabitants of Egypt will know that I am Yahweh'**, is really a conclusion to 29:1-5. The second part of the verse, **'because they have been a reed crutch to the house of Israel'**, leads into 29:7-12. Isaiah 36:6 claims that a century earlier, Egypt, a crushed reed upon which Judah leaned for support,[11] pierced the hand when weight was placed upon it. Ezekiel takes the picture further: its hollow, sharp leaves (**'branches'**) cracking under pressure, the broken end of the reed penetrates the shoulder. So, when a man rests upon it for support, it snaps. His hips, or loins, quiver and the body writhes (29:6-7).

The point of this condemnation is not that the Egyptians have again offered inadequate support to Judah, but that the military aid given to Zedekiah displayed a gross lack of perception: the Egyptians were interfering in a struggle in which they had no business. In allying himself with Zedekiah,[12] Hophra was resisting the God of Israel, who had decreed to overthrow Judah through the agency of Nebuchadnezzar.

The denunciation of the crocodile ends, **'the Lord Yahweh'** bringing **'a sword'** upon Pharaoh, who loses all his men and beasts of burden. Life grinds to a halt and Egypt becomes a waste. Because of their arrogance, **'they will know that I am Yahweh'** (29:8-9).

In that such a statement always concludes a train of thought, the division of these verses is unfortunate, and the section should end with the first part of 29:9.

2. The first word: Yahweh's imminent and long-term intentions (29:9-16)

29:9-16. ... '"'Because he has said, "The river is mine, and I made it," therefore, look, I am against you and against your rivers, and I shall make the land of Egypt a totally desolate wasteland from Migdol to Syene, and to the border of Cush. The foot of man will not cross it, and the foot of beast will not pass through it. It will not be inhabited for forty years. And I shall give the land of Egypt as a desolation in the midst of desolate lands, and her cities will be a desolation in the midst of wasted cities for forty years; I shall scatter Egypt among the nations and disperse them in the lands.'

'"For thus says the Lord Yahweh: 'At the end of forty years I shall gather Egypt out of the peoples among whom they were scattered and shall turn the captivity of Egypt and cause them to dwell in the land of Pathros, in the land of their origin, and there they will be a lowly kingdom. It will be the lowest of the kingdoms and will not lift itself up again over the nations; I shall make them so small that they will not govern among the nations. Never again will it be an object of confidence for the house of Israel, a reminder of iniquity when they turned after them, and they will know that I am the Lord Yahweh.'"'

This section commences with the second part of 29:9, Ezekiel repeating Pharaoh's blasphemous claim (see 29:3) that the river is his by right of creation. Yahweh displays profound disrespect for Pharaoh by refusing to address him by name. Now **'your rivers'** and **'the land of Egypt'** are to become **'a totally desolate wasteland[13] from Migdol to Syene, and to the border of Cush'**.

'Migdol', meaning 'tower', might have been the northern military station mentioned in Exodus 14:2, while **'Syene'** (the modern Aswan) was on the first cataract of the Nile, 700 kilometres (or 440 miles) to the south, a point from which **'Cush'**, lower Nubia (modern Ethiopia), could be attacked. Thus, the whole territory of Egypt will be ravaged (29:9-10).

There is worse to come, namely, **'forty years'** of desolation. Human commerce and agricultural activity must cease. **'Forty'** might be compared with 4:6, where the same figure is mentioned, although in a different context. Here, the number is almost certainly symbolic, possibly recalling Numbers 14:20-35 and representing an indeterminate time during which the Egyptians must suffer for their sins and then reflect upon their attempt to disrupt the plan of God for Judah (29:11). It is almost as if a glimmer of hope is being held out to Egypt.

Repeating the notice of a forty-year eviction, Yahweh announces that, even as Judah is to be scattered among the nations,[14] so, too, will Egypt. But there will be a difference: Egypt will be **'a desolation in the midst of desolate lands'**, meaning that her temporary destruction will be virtually complete (29:12). Jeremiah 43:8-13 and 44:30 had already announced that Nebuchadnezzar would be the instrument of divine wrath against the land of the Nile.

Yet whereas Pharaoh Hophra, the giant crocodile (29:5), will not be rescued, Egypt is to be recovered from this forty-year captivity and will be resettled at **'Pathros'**. This term transliterates the Egyptian for 'the south land', apparently the Thebaid, the region between the northern Nile delta and Cush, and representing the Egyptian homeland. But although the **'kingdom'** is to be restored, it will be **'lowly'**, a vassal regime eventually to become part of the empire of the Persians and, later, that of the Greeks and then the Romans.[15]

Yet it is Yahweh, rather than any world power, who reduces Egypt. He will not allow the blasphemous crocodile to straddle the Nile (29:13-14), for which reason Egypt will never regain her glory and must remain inferior to other kingdoms. No more will she lift herself up. Diminished by Yahweh, she is not sufficiently grand to be an ally for the people of Israel. At long last their temptation will vanish. For the third time Ezekiel predicts that when Egypt has been reduced, then they will **'know'** that Yahweh is God.

Since the time of Isaiah, Judah had been discouraged by the prophets from seeking help from Egypt when confronted by aggressors from the north and east.[16] Now, unlike some other nations, Egypt is not condemned for gloating over the destruction of Jerusalem. On the contrary, Hophra had dispatched an army to that city, albeit in an unenthusiastic and unsuccessful attempt to repel the Chaldeans. Because Zedekiah was utterly misguided in relying upon such aid, Yahweh needed only to relegate Egypt from a shortlist of the superior powers to a minor position:[17]

'Never again will it be an object of confidence for the house of Israel, a reminder of iniquity when they turned after them' (29:15-16).

And so it came to pass: 'The Egyptian kingdom was extinguished by the same fate that befell Babylon, the expansion of the Persian Empire, and Psamtek III was defeated at Pelusium by Cambyses in 525 BC.'[18]

Application

The Egyptian civilization was one of the greatest in the ancient world, enduring for more than three thousand years, from the inauguration of the first dynasty, *c.* 3100 BC, to at least the conclusion of the thirtieth in 343 BC. It has been said that most pharaohs could command resources beyond those of many modern nations. For instance, the Great Pyramid of Cheops at Giza, originally 146 metres (almost 480 feet) high, covering 5·3 hectares (thirteen acres) and erected about 2500 BC, was the tallest building in the world until the nineteenth century. Many hundreds of years after it was built, Abraham, Jacob, Joseph and Moses and the children of Israel would have gazed upon it, no doubt in awe. Its base area is so great that it can accommodate the cathedrals of Florence, Milan, St Paul's and Westminster Abbey in London, and St Peter's in Rome — and still have some space left over. The solid gold inner coffin of Tutankhamun, who reigned about one thousand years later than Cheops, is a priceless work of art, yet he was a relatively unimportant minor pharaoh.[19]

It is no wonder that over the generations the Egyptian pharaohs were haunted by dreams of imperial megalomania. And it is no wonder that spiritually insensitive Jewish kings, such as Zedekiah, should have looked to Egypt for help in times of crisis. But it was the God of tiny Israel who dominated the scene. (He still does!) In Ezekiel's day, not only would he brook no rival, least of all Egypt, the former slave-master of Israel, but all who stood in his path had to fall. This is why four chapters of the prophecy of Ezekiel are devoted to the diminution of Egyptian grandeur, and this is why Nebuchadnezzar, the incarnate sword of the Lord, was destined to deal the death blow. Yahweh removes Egypt from the scene in order to bring about the healing of his own people.

Empires come and go, but principles — and Israel — remain. The God of Israel, who is alike the Lord of history and of nations, has committed himself to the restoration and ultimate glorification of his people. This is why the prediction of the collapse of Egypt precedes Ezekiel's announcements concerning the final restoration of Israel. And this is why the final book of the Bible, that of the Revelation, anticipates the glorification of the church of Christ by taking up so much within Ezekiel's prophecy in announcing the final overthrow of all who oppose our Lord and his people.

In a world of gloom and doom, the Messiah of Israel remains the Victor.

7. The seventh series of prophecies

(Ezekiel 29:17 – 30:19)

It is the twenty-seventh year of Ezekiel's exile, and the first day of the first month. Through Ezekiel, the Lord utters his second word to Egypt.

1. Nebuchadnezzar's reward (29:17-21)

29:17-21. And it was in the twenty-seventh year, on the first, on the first of the month that the word of Yahweh came to me, saying, 'Son of man, Nebuchadnezzar, the king of Babylon, has made his army labour very hard against Tyre. Every head has been made bald and every shoulder has been chafed bare. But from Tyre there has been no recompense for him and for his army for the labour that he expended against it. Therefore, thus says the Lord Yahweh: "Look, I am giving the land of Egypt to Nebuchadnezzar, king of Babylon. And he will carry off her abundance and capture her spoil and plunder her loot, and it shall be a recompense for his army. I have given him the land of Egypt for his work which he laboured in her, which they did for me," declares the Lord Yahweh. "In that day I shall make a horn to sprout for the house of Israel, and to you I shall give an opening of mouth in their midst, and they will know that I am Yahweh."'

There is a problem of interpretation bound up in the recorded date of the oracle (29:17), and this must be considered before proceeding to chapter and verse.

It is to be noted that chapters 26 – 28, issued early in 586 BC, would appear to predict the complete overthrow of Tyre at the hands of Nebuchadnezzar (26:3-18; cf. 27:26-36; 28:18-19). Further, 29:17-21, issued in 571 BC, *sixteen or so years afterwards* and the latest of Ezekiel's dated prophecies — two years later than the temple vision of chapters 40 – 48 — suggests that Tyre had *not* yet been destroyed, but that the city would eventually be given into the hands of Nebuchadnezzar.

In fact, Nebuchadnezzar did lay siege to Tyre for thirteen years, from *c.* 587–574 BC, but did not destroy the city.[1] Subsequently, Tyre recognized Babylonian suzerainty, as witnessed by Babylonian contracts discovered by archaeology. The city still stood. Apparently, it was not until 332 BC that Tyre eventually fell under foreign conquest, being besieged by Alexander the Great.

Putting all this together, it would appear at first sight that the prediction of chapters 26 – 28 proved inaccurate, which would mean Ezekiel falling under the castigation of Deuteronomy 13:1-3 and rendering himself vulnerable to criticism by his fellow-exiles. How, then, is this problem to be resolved, if indeed there is a problem? There have arisen a number of solutions. Here are three.

Firstly, according to Clements, Ezekiel accepted that his earlier threats against Tyre had not worked out in a Babylonian victory and that some explanation needed to be given. Prophecy was never fixed but could be supplemented or amended as the divine purposes became clearer.[2] But chapters 26 – 28 are definite: Tyre would eventually be overthrown.

Secondly, Block proposes that chapters 26 – 28 are conditional, awaiting a change of attitude by the then ruler of Tyre. The argument is that because Tyre seems to have accepted vassal status under the Babylonians, it may be that Yahweh decreed that the threats of these chapters would be suspended.[3] In response, unlike Jonah's warning to Nineveh, which was uttered within the confines of the city and which was an ultimatum,[4] it is not certain that chapters 26 – 28 were intended to reach Tyre. There is no hint of direct challenge.

Finally, an older and now less fashionable approach is that Nebuchadnezzar attacked Tyre but failed to amass much spoil. The city was cowed but not destroyed. It appears that Jerome (*c.* AD 345–419) espoused this view, stating that the Babylonians attempted to seize the city by the same means used later by Alexander, by constructing a causeway from the mainland to the island. According to Josephus, who quotes from earlier writers, Nebuchadnezzar overran 'Syria and the whole of Phoenicia', a region which must have included Tyre.[5] The implication is that Ezekiel left 29:17-21 on record because he knew that, in full accordance with 26:1 – 28:19, Tyre would eventually be destroyed — as was the case.[6]

It seems to me that the third interpretation ought not to be disregarded. Accordingly, although Nebuchadnezzar did assault Tyre (cf. 26:11), chapter 26 does not predict that the city would *at that time* be destroyed. Ezekiel's burden, then, is that what the Babylonians had begun, others — to be specific, the armies of Alexander two centuries later — would complete.

This prophecy was uttered on the **'first'** day of the **'first'** month of the **'twenty-seventh year'**, translating to 26 April 571 BC, long after Jehoiachin had been taken into exile. The date is mentioned by Ezekiel for two reasons: firstly, as a matter of arrangement, to bring all the prophecies against Egypt together in a block; secondly, to identify the specific agent of the overthrow of Egypt following the more general prediction of judgement set out in 29:1-16 (cf. 26:7). Brief and to the point, the prophecy prepares the way for the more elaborate warnings against Egypt in chapters 30 – 32 (29:17).

It seems that the assault upon Tyre had been unsatisfactory as far as Nebuchadnezzar (605–562 BC) was concerned, the Babylonians failing to seize any great quantity of wealth after penetrating the city. **'No recompense'** suggests that Nebuchadnezzar and his armies had been pressed into service, the labour involved being arduous: **'Every head has been made bald and every shoulder has been chafed bare.'** Soldiers and slaves would have worn themselves out by bearing innumerable baskets of rubble to fill up the channel between the island and the mainland, thereby making a causeway for the attacking armies (29:18).

Remarkably, to compensate Nebuchadnezzar for his hard work in ravaging Tyre, Yahweh will grant him **'the land of Egypt'**, with the latter's **'abundance'**, **'spoil'** and **'loot'**. Albeit unwittingly, the Babylonian monarch has been the servant of Yahweh and therefore he will not be deprived of a just **'recompense'** for services rendered (29:19). Yahweh will be no man's debtor.

Although the Egyptians are permitted to remain where they are, Nebuchadnezzar will deprive them of their wealth. This is to be his payment (**'work'**, or wages, *p'ûllah*),[7] a just reward for what **'they did for'** the God of Israel. Yahweh **'declares'** solemnly that it will be so (29:20).

Anticipated by Jeremiah,[8] the campaign may have occurred in 568 BC, three years later than the present prophecy and not long after the death of Pharaoh Hophra in 570 BC.[9]

This is not the end of Ezekiel's prediction. Firstly, when Egypt falls prostrate before the might of Babylon, Yahweh **'will make a horn to sprout for the house of Israel'**. This promise may be compared with Psalm 132:17, in which Yahweh declares that in Zion he will 'cause a horn to sprout for David'. The wording is similar. As elsewhere in the Bible, a horn often stands as a symbol of power by which enemies are subdued.[10] Jacob shall triumph.

Is this an allusion to the coming Messiah? Indirectly, yes, in that the Lord declares that **'in that day'**, when Egypt will have fallen, the restoration of Israel will commence, issuing finally (as we now know) in the advent of the Christ from the line of David.

Further, Yahweh will **'give** [to Ezekiel] **an opening of mouth in their midst, and they will know that I am Yahweh'**. On the surface, this promise seems to be out of place since when it was issued Ezekiel's dumbness was a thing of the past (cf. 3:26-27; 24:26-27; 33:21-22). The probable meaning, therefore, is that not less than twenty-seven years since he was led into exile (see 29:17), Ezekiel and his fellow-Jews in Babylonia will learn of the downfall of Egypt, the ancient enemy. Thereby, his status as a true prophet of Yahweh will receive further confirmation and (possibly) the people will be encouraged in their hopes for a return from the land of captivity after seventy years of exile, as anticipated by Jeremiah.[11] And, when Egypt, representative of the might of the world, becomes impotent, the time of the Messiah will be seen to have come yet nearer (29:21). As Daniel 2:35 and the surrounding context tell, colossal worldly powers were already falling before the Christ of God.

2. The third word to Egypt (30:1-19)

This prophecy is undated but, as has been suggested, was probably delivered between the dates which precede (29:1) and which follow (30:20) — that is, at about the time when Jerusalem was being laid waste by the Babylonians and when Zedekiah and those who sympathized with him knew that there could be no further Egyptian intervention on their behalf.[12]

I. Howl in terror (30:1-12)

30:1-12. Then the word of Yahweh came to me, saying, 'Son of man, prophesy, and you will say, "Thus says the Lord Yahweh: 'Wail! Alas, O day! For the day is near, even a day for Yahweh is near — a day of clouds, a time of the nations it will be. And a sword will come upon Egypt, and there will be anguish in Cush when the slain fall in Egypt, and they will take away her abundance and her foundations will be torn down. Cush and Put and Lud and all the mingled folk, Chub and the sons of the land of the covenant will fall with them by the sword.'

'"Thus says Yahweh: 'And they who support Egypt will fall, and the pride of her strength will come down. From Migdol to Syene they will fall within her by the sword,' declares the Lord Yahweh. 'And they will be desolated in the midst of the desolated lands and her cities will be in the midst of wasted cities. Then they will know that I am Yahweh, when I put fire in Egypt and all her helpers are broken. In that day messengers will go out from my presence in ships to terrify secure Cush, and there will be anguish in them, like the day of Egypt — for, look, it comes.'

'"Thus says the Lord Yahweh: 'I shall also make the abundance of Egypt to cease by the hand of Nebuchadrezzar, king of Egypt. He and his people with him, the ruthless of the nations, will be brought in to ruin the land. So they will unsheathe their swords against Egypt and fill the land with slain. Moreover, I shall make the channels of the Nile dry and shall sell the land into the hands of evil men, and shall devastate the land and its fulness by the hand of strangers. I, Yahweh, have spoken.'"'

The section 30:1-19 divides into four parts, each opening with **'Thus says Yahweh'** (30:2,6,10,13). The first twelve verses concern the **'day'** of Yahweh and the last seven turn the reader's attention to the extent of Yahweh's judgements upon Egypt.

Ezekiel must summon men to howl in terror. Previously, the 'day' of Yahweh concerned the judgement of an apostate Israel (7:10); now the Egyptians are to **'wail'** and must address the day itself with a cry of woe: **'Alas, O day!'** (30:1-2).

'Day' now occurs no less than three times, as if to stress that a point in time has been reserved **'for'** the God of Israel — a point that will also be **'a time** [for] **the nations'**. Recalling the gloominess of Joel 1:15; 2:1-2 and Zephaniah 1:7-18,[13] it will be **'a day of clouds'**. It is not only Israel that must experience the wrath of Yahweh: Egypt and other peoples are to fall under his displeasure. Apparently, the overthrow of Egyptian power is just an initial step, leading to the collapse of every society and culture that chooses to oppose Yahweh (30:3).

'A sword' penetrates Egypt, shakes **'her foundations'** and destroys all the confederate nations. **'Cush'**, or Nubia (Ethiopia), is terrified. During the Egyptian Middle and New Kingdoms in the second millennium BC, large areas of Nubia had been annexed as Egyptian imperial possessions, but by now they had thrown off the yoke.[14] Consequently, Ethiopia suspects a domino effect: if Egypt collapses, losing her **'abundance'** — her wealth and prestige — will she be next? (30:4).

Yes, **'Cush'** will fall, as must **'Put'** and **'Lud'**. **'Put'** may have been within modern Libya on the North African coast, and **'Lud'** can be identified with Lydia in Asia Minor. The pharaohs hired mercenaries from far and wide, including **'all the mingled folk'** (*ereb*; not to be mistaken for Arabia).[15] **'Chub'** is an unknown name, which is why some versions, following the Septuagint, translate it as 'Libyans' (from a supposed *Lûb*),[16] but this emendation may be unnecessary. Allied to the Egyptians are **'the sons of the land of the covenant'**, who might have been apostate Israelites seeking refuge in Egypt, not identified by

Ezekiel with the 'mingled folk'.[17] None who associate in some way or other with the Egyptians can escape the sword (30:5).

Other hired men **'who support Egypt'** are now mentioned. Whoever they may be, they are destined to **'fall ... by the sword'** within the land of Egypt. Repeating 29:10, Ezekiel declares that from **'Migdol'** to **'Syene'**, from the far north to the extreme south of the kingdom, their strength must collapse. **'The Lord Yahweh'** has spoken (30:6). Recalling 29:12, their catastrophe is highlighted by a parallelism: desolation **'in the midst of the desolated lands'** and **'in the midst of wasted cities'** (30:7).

Then, when Yahweh sets Egypt ablaze in order to overthrow her every ally, they will know that **'I am Yahweh'** (30:8).

'In that day messengers' will travel southwards along the waterways of the Nile to **'Cush'** to spread the appalling news and, no doubt, to seek refuge. Without knowing it, they will have been sent from Yahweh (**'from my presence'**) because the Lord intends to create consternation. The emissaries will **'terrify'** a **'secure'** society by their report, and Egypt will become the ruination of all who are linked to her: her **'day'** is their day (30:9).

Now Yahweh announces his agent of destruction, **'Nebuchadrezzar'** (cf. the announcement against Tyre, 26:7). **'Abundance'** (*hamôn*), or 'tumult', probably does not refer to the teeming population of Egypt, but to the tumultuous fashion or exuberance with which they relished their national prestige. All was noise, excitement and emptiness — but only for a time. The artificial state of affairs must be brought to an end through the principal of the most **'ruthless of the nations'**.[18] The prospect appals: **'the land'** will be filled **'with slain'** (30:10-11).

Yet behind Babylon is Yahweh: **'I shall make the channels of the Nile dry.'**[19] The devastation of the rivers possibly means that all natural and economic resources fail in the aftermath of war. The Egyptians are to be sold by Yahweh to the **'evil'** Chaldeans, and **'strangers'** destroy the **'fulness'** of the land. **'I, Yahweh have spoken.'** It shall be (30:12).

II. The twilight of the gods (30:13-19)

30:13-19. '"Thus says the Lord Yahweh: 'Also, I have destroyed the idols and have caused the worthless gods to cease from Noph. Never again will there be a prince from the land of Egypt, and I shall grant fear in the land of Egypt. And I shall make Pathros desolate, shall give fire in Zoan and shall execute judgements in No. Then I shall pour out my wrath upon Sin, the stronghold of Egypt, and shall cut off the multitude of No. Then I shall grant fire in Egypt. Writhing, Sin will writhe and No will be breached. Then Noph — enemies by day! The young men of On and of Pi-beseth will fall by the sword, and, look, the women will go into captivity. And in Tehaphnehes the day will be dark when I break there the yokes of Egypt. Then the pride of her strength will cease in her. As for her, a cloud will cover her and her daughters shall go into captivity. So I shall execute judgements in Egypt, and they will know that I am Yahweh.'"'

Again Yahweh speaks, a horrendous prospect being given further description. Throughout 30:13-19, and in no apparent order, various localities are mentioned to accentuate the chaos that will supervene in Egypt.[20] Numerous violent actions are mentioned to emphasize the completeness of the destruction.

'Idols' will be destroyed and **'worthless gods'** — translating *elilim*, from a root meaning 'feeble' or 'poor'[21] — will be removed from **'Noph'** (Memphis). This city was just south of the Nile delta (cf. 30:16),[22] the main residence of the pharaohs during the Old Kingdom and the main cult centre of the god Ptah, a patron of arts and crafts and a creative force.[23] A colony of Jews lived there in Jeremiah's time.[24] It is appropriate that the prediction of Egypt's ruin should mention this city first.

But because there had always been an association between the pharaohs and the gods of Egypt, **'never again will there be a prince'** in that land. Ezekiel perceives the pharaoh of his day as a princeling who could and would be removed at will by Yahweh,[25] the true God who will cause this people to fear him rather than their ancestral deities (30:13).

Desolation spreads. As observed in the previous chapter, **'Pathros'** was upper Egypt, an extensive swathe of territory, while **'Zoan'**, possibly Tanis or Raamses,[26] more than a thousand kilometres to the north, was to the east of the Nile delta. **'No'**, or No-Amon ('The city of the god Amun'),[27] or Thebes, was situated on the sites of modern Luxor and Karnak (30:14). Jeremiah also pronounced judgement against its titular deity.[28]

There is no city that does not capitulate before a remorseless and cruel enemy, behind whom stands Yahweh. He proposes to **'pour out** [his] **wrath upon Sin, the stronghold of Egypt'**. 'Sin' (not 'sin' as in doing wrong), the Greek Pelusium, was by the Mediterranean coast, east of the Nile delta and a border fortress protecting Egypt from Asian invaders.[29] It is mentioned here as a national stronghold in order to indicate that the nation will be vulnerable to predators from the north and east. The buzzing **'multitude of No'** (cf. 30:10) will be **'cut off'**, or annihilated (30:15).

'Egypt' will be put to the torch. **'Writhing, Sin will writhe'** in agony. The Hebrew idiom, which the translation seeks to reflect, is vivid. Hostile forces will break through the defences of **'No'**, and as for **'Noph'**, **'enemies by day!'** The invader advances during the hours of sunlight because only limited forces are needed to crush a demoralized and defenceless city (30:16).

The youth of **'On'** (vocalized in Hebrew as *Aven* = 'iniquity') will **'fall by the sword'**, as will those of **'Pi-beseth'**. On would have been the Greek Heliopolis ('Sun city'),[30] a few miles north of Cairo, and Pi-beseth was 'the place of Pasht', from the cat-headed god Bubastis or Pasht, a city also situated north of Cairo. The **'women will go into captivity'**, possibly indicating the downfall of the female votaries of their feline deity. The reader is summoned to **'look'** at the tragic spectacle (30:17).

'Tehaphnehes', the Greek Daphnai and near the modern Suez Canal, was the frontier city to which Jeremiah was abducted after the assassination of Gedaliah.[31] There the **'yokes of Egypt'**, that nation's tyranny over other races, will be shattered. An ominous **'cloud'** covers the land, and the **'daughters'** of that community will be led away captive (30:18). According to Jeremiah 43:9-10, there was a royal palace in the city where Nebuchadnezzar was destined to erect his pavilion.

Afflicted by divine judgement, Egypt will have cause to despair — and, paradoxically, to hope: **'They will know that I am Yahweh.'** Knowing now that their gods were unable to save them in the evil hour, the Egyptians will acknowledge the sovereignty of the God of Israel (30:19). And who knows what blessings such an acknowledgement might draw in its train?

Application

Concerning 29:17-21, it might be asked why the Lord considered it needful to inform Ezekiel that Nebuchadnezzar, a man whose evil empire would eventually collapse,[32] must be remunerated for his attempt to reduce Tyre.

Prior to the fall of Jerusalem in 586 BC, many Jews, both in Judah and in Babylonia, refused to believe that Yahweh would allow the unthinkable to happen. And after Ezekiel and his fellow-exiles had learned the sad news (33:21), many would have remained in a state of consternation. Was it indeed the case that the God of Israel had sent Nebuchadnezzar against his own elect people, or was the war an aberrant freak of fate? Now, more than a decade after the calamity, Yahweh affirms that Nebuchadnezzar had (unwittingly) acted as his servant, for which service acknowledgement would be due. The grant of Egypt to Nebuchadnezzar, therefore, serves to authenticate Ezekiel as a true prophet of Yahweh and confirms that the warnings he had given prior to 586 BC were from God.

The apostle Paul declares that 'As many as may be the promises of God, in him [Christ] they are "yes"'[33] — as are also the divine warnings.[34] We need to pray for faith to rely upon the promises of the Bible and to protect ourselves from its warnings, especially when the world presses in upon us — as it always does.

With regard to 30:1-19, among the exiles in Babylon discerning souls must have been immensely relieved to hear this oracle. At long last, the capacity of Egypt to entice the people of God away from the proper object of their trust, Yahweh, will be a thing of the past. An ancient temptation will soon be lifted.

Further, it will be their God who does this, the first person singular, 'I', preponderating throughout the passage. Because God is love and God is great, in his wisdom he provides temptations — and in his faithfulness he removes them when they would seem to us to be intolerable.[35] Times change, but principles live on.

8. The eighth prophecy

(Ezekiel 30:20-26)

When Ezekiel began to issue his sombre predictions concerning Egypt, the prophet Jeremiah was being held in Tehaphnehes as an unwilling captive. There, he had much to say about that place, predicting that Nebuchadnezzar would erect his throne in this gateway to Egypt and that he would bring the nation, its ancestral gods and its temples to ruin.[1]

Similarly, Ezekiel must unburden his soul and declare that apostate Israel shall never be given cause to rely upon the African crocodile.

30:20-26. And it was that in the eleventh year, in the first, on the seventh day of the month, the word of Yahweh came to me, saying, 'Son of man, I have broken the arm of Pharaoh, the king of Egypt, and, look, it has not been bound up to give healing or wrapped for a bandage, to strengthen it to grasp a sword.

'Therefore, thus says the Lord Yahweh: "Look, I am against Pharaoh, the king of Egypt, and I shall break his arms, both the strong and the broken, and shall cause the sword to fall from his hand. So I shall scatter Egypt among the nations and shall disperse them in the lands. And I shall strengthen the arms of the king of Babylon and shall give my sword into his hand, and I shall break the arms of Pharaoh and he will groan before him with the groans of one who is pierced. And I shall strengthen the arms of the king of Babylon, but the arms of Pharaoh will fall. And they will know that I am Yahweh when I give my sword to the hand of the king of Babylon and he stretches it out against the land of Egypt. So I shall scatter Egypt among the nations and will disperse them in the lands, and they will know that I am Yahweh."'

It is now the eleventh year of Ezekiel's captivity in Babylonia, the seventh day of the first month. This corresponds to 29 April 587 BC, three months later than the prophecy recorded in 29:1-16, but before the final destruction of Jerusalem.[2] We are presented with Yahweh's fourth word to Egypt.

It is likely that 30:20-26 looks back to the temporary raising of the Chaldean siege of Jerusalem by the Egyptians under Pharaoh Hophra, and to his eventual retreat.[3] Yahweh will not allow his people to rely foolishly upon false hopes (30:20).

The Lord announces that he has already **'broken the arm of Pharaoh'** (30:21). This might refer both to the retreat of Pharaoh from Jerusalem and to the battle of Carchemish twenty years earlier.[4] Because Yahweh has nullified the power of Egypt, there can be no **'healing'** process, no **'bandage'** for the broken arm. Never again can Egypt **'grasp a sword'**. Indeed, the keywords in the section are **'arm'** and **'arms'**, which occur six times in 30:20-26. Behind the armies of Egypt and Babylon is Yahweh, the master strategist (30:21).

To complete the shambles, the second, still sound arm of Egypt must be broken: The tense switches from the past to the future: **'I shall break his arms, both the strong and the broken,'** Pharaoh's **'sword'** clattering uselessly to the ground (30:22). Although Hophra is not mentioned, this verse would seem to apply to him in that, as mentioned earlier, he was killed by one of his generals who supplanted him in 570 BC. So, when Egyptian military might is brought to nothing, Yahweh will **'scatter'** and **'disperse'** this people in other lands (30:23).

Conversely, Yahweh strengthens **'the arms** [the army] **of the king of Babylon'**, the one who wields the sword of the Lord. The God of Israel asserts his right and ability to dictate to the dictators. No longer shall Egypt be in a position to meddle in the affairs of Judah. Faced by the might of Babylon, Pharaoh **'will groan'** when run through by a blade (30:24). Again, does this refer to the assassination of Hophra?

While the 'arms of the king of Babylon' become progressively stronger, those **'of Pharaoh'** hang limply. When Yahweh proffers his **'sword'** to **'the king of Babylon'** in order to stretch it out **'against the land of Egypt'**, that nation will be scattered and in retrospect must admit that the Lord is the true and living God (30:25-26). Here and elsewhere this prediction runs like a refrain: whether in salvation or in judgement, men everywhere are unable to elude Israel's God; he compels them to acknowledge him as the absolute Lord of all.

Application

This section serves almost as a conclusion to 30:1-19, in which numerous Egyptian cities are mentioned by name. Twice (30:8,19) it was stated that the Egyptians would have cause to acknowledge Yahweh. So here (30:25,26). Egypt, reduced to impotence, must conclude that the God of Israel had granted his sword to Nebuchadnezzar.

All this is reminiscent of the events preceding the exodus of Israel from Egypt one millennium earlier. Then the pharaoh of the day and his people were compelled to admit that Yahweh was greater than their numerous gods.[5] Similarly, the ongoing struggle between the church and the world is a contest between the God of heaven and all the spiritual forces of evil.[6] One day, every knee shall bow to Christ.[7]

9. The ninth prophecy

(Ezekiel 31:1-18)

This prophecy divides into three parts: the poem of the splendid tree, to which Pharaoh Hophra is likened (31:2-9); its downfall (31:10-14); and its descent to Sheol, the realm of the departed (31:15-18). Apart from verses 1, 2 and 18, it is a parable that draws upon Assyria as a precedent for the predicted collapse of Egypt as an international power.

Two months have gone by since the previous declaration from Ezekiel. Jerusalem and the temple are still standing — but only just. Years earlier, the prophet Isaiah had likened Assyria to a great tree destined to be cut down in its pride.[1] Through Ezekiel, the Lord now warns that Assyria's doom is to be shared by Egypt. It is the fifth word to that nation.

The sting of this prophecy lies in the fact that the Babylonians had overrun Assyrian Nineveh not many years earlier, in 612 BC, and that in their time the Assyrians had controlled Egypt. So what hope can there be for Egypt of holding out against the empire that had vanquished her own conqueror? Yet there is a difference: whereas Assyria had been annihilated, Ezekiel has predicted already that Egypt will survive, albeit stripped of her former power (see 29:13-16).

Assyria had been, so to speak, a superbly beautiful and lofty cedar, but a tree brought to the ground by alien tyrants. When it happened, men stood aghast at the passing of Assyrian power from the international scene. Egypt, plus those in Israel who hitherto had trusted in her, are to learn a hard lesson from this example of misplaced imperial pride.

1. Assyria, a lofty cedar (31:1-9)

31:1-9. And it came about in the eleventh year, in the third, on the first of the month, that the word of Yahweh came to me, saying, 'Son of man, say to Pharaoh, king of Egypt, and to his multitude, "To whom are you like in your greatness? Look, Assyria! A cedar in Lebanon with beautiful branches and forest shade, and of great height, and its top among the clouds. Waters made it great; the deep made it high. It sent rivers around its planting bed and it issued its channels to all the trees of the field. Therefore its height was loftier than all the trees of the field. Its branches became numerous and its boughs long because of the many waters when the deep issued them. All the birds of the heavens nested in its branches. Beneath its boughs every animal of the field gave birth and in its shadow dwelt all the great nations.

'"So it was beautiful in its greatness, in the length of its branches, for its root was by many waters. Cedars could not eclipse it in the garden of God; cypresses could not compare with its branches, and plane trees were not as its boughs. No tree in the garden of God was like it in its beauty. I made it beautiful in the profusion of its branches, and all the trees of Eden were jealous of it that were in the garden of God."'

It is now **'the eleventh year'** and the **'first'** day of the **'third'** month since Ezekiel was taken into exile, and two months after the previous oracle (30:20). According to our calendar, this would have been 21 June 587 BC (31:1).

The prophecy is addressed to Pharaoh Hophra and his **'multitude'**. The Egyptians, having ventured their forces towards Jerusalem in a vain attempt to repulse Nebuchadnezzar, will have retired towards the safety of their own land.[2] Yet Hophra's pretensions to superiority in the international arena have not been dissolved. The interrogative, **'To whom are you like in your greatness?'**, is rhetorical: Yahweh searches about to identify an empire, the might of which matches that of Egypt. Only Assyria is an adequate role model, given Hophra's aspirations (31:2).

That this oracle was actually transmitted to the Egyptians is doubtful. Rather, it had Ezekiel's fellow-exiles as its target: they had not yet understood that Egypt was a broken reed.

Before the pharaoh can respond, Yahweh interjects: **'Look, Assyria!'** Because the Lord can read the mind of the Egyptian king, let the monarch consider the fate of that realm.[3] Yahweh now projects a metaphorical description: that empire had been **'a cedar in Lebanon with beautiful branches'**, offering extensive **'shade'**, **'of great height'** and with its **'top'** penetrating **'the clouds'**. This is a literary cartoon, the tree's extraordinary features being exaggerated in order to drive home a lesson (31:3). The allegory of a great people being likened to a cedar of Lebanon has appeared already in 17:1-10,22-24.[4]

Ezekiel's reader is expected to stand in awe of a tree made **'great'** by much water. The **'deep made it high'** and **'sent rivers'** to irrigate the site where it had been planted.[5] Moreover, irrigation **'channels'** were **'issued'** to nourish other peoples. With its influence extending everywhere, all the nations became client states of this vast empire (31:4).

Because there were **'many waters'**,[6] the tree became **'loftier'** than all other trees, and its **'branches'** and **'boughs'** more **'numerous'** and longer than those of the rest. Ezekiel's readers are expected to gape in astonishment and admiration (31:5).

'All the birds of the heavens' made their nests **'in its branches'** and all wild animals **'gave birth'** to their young beneath the protection of its leafy

'boughs'. **'Great nations'** lived within its protective **'shadow'** (31:6). In reality, the empire of Assyria was brutal in the extreme, as indicated, for example, by Rabshakeh's words to Hezekiah when Jerusalem was being invested.[7] Even as the Assyrians regarded themselves as benefactors, the Egyptians also reckoned that they, too, ruled in magnanimity and by divine right. This explains the slant of the verse.

The **'greatness'** and **'length'** of the Assyrian's branches made this particular cedar seem a lovely thing, beautiful because its **'root'** descended to an immense subterranean reservoir of water which would never cease to augment its stature (31:7). The Genesis record, which must have been known to Ezekiel and his hearers, is in the mind of Yahweh when he declares that **'Cedars could not eclipse it in the garden of God.'** Had the Assyrian cedar been planted in Eden, from whose ground the Lord 'caused to grow every tree that is pleasing to the sight and good for food',[8] it would have been pre-eminent, the most elegant of all (31:8).

Now the implication is that Yahweh, having established Assyria and made it an object of jealousy among **'all the trees of Eden'** and **'in the garden of God'**, eventually caused it to be uprooted. What hope, then, can there be for inferior Egypt? (31:9).

2. A cedar brought low (31:10-14)

31:10-14. '"Therefore, thus says the Lord Yahweh: 'Because you were high in your loftiness, and it set its tree top among the clouds, and its heart is exalted in its height, so I shall give it into the hand of a chief of the nations; he will assuredly deal with it. In its wickedness I have driven it away. Strangers, the ferocious of the nations, have cut it down and have abandoned it upon the mountains; its branches have fallen in all the valleys and its boughs have been broken in every ravine of the land. And all the peoples of the land have come down from its shade and have forsaken it. Upon its ruin all the birds of the heavens abide and on its boughs there are all the animals of the field, in order that all the trees by the waters might not be exalted in their loftiness, that they might not set their tops among the clouds and that their chiefs, all who are well-watered, may not stand in their height — for they have all been consigned to death, to the nether land amid the sons of men, with those who descend to the pit.'"'

Yahweh confronts the Assyrian tree directly, as if her fall, which in Ezekiel's day was an accomplished historical fact, has yet to occur. But the change in tense suggests a reorientation — a prediction of the future collapse of Egypt. The move from the second person to the third (**'you'** ... **'it'**) gives weight to the alteration in tone: hitherto, the Assyrian (alias the Egyptian) cedar has been viewed as a glorious thing, attracting the jealousy of others as well as being the product of a divine initiative. Now, the empire is said to have been **'high in your loftiness'** and **'exalted in its height'**, characterized by **'wickedness'**.

This being so, Yahweh, ever sovereign in the interactions of men and nations, reveals that he intends to **'give it into the hand of a chief of the nations'**, obviously Nebuchadnezzar, who will **'assuredly deal with it'**. Just as God expelled Adam from the Garden of Eden and just as Assyria was removed from the society of the nations, so Egypt will be cast out by him: **'I have driven it away.'** If Hophra entertains illusions of grandeur, let him consider the fall of Assyria as well as its rise (31:10-11).

The action now switches from the first person to the third, the Lord pointing to **'the ferocious of the nations'**, those who are to execute his sentence. What happened to Assyria will be the fate of Egypt, the two empires probably being considered in tandem. Woodsmen cut down the huge, magnificent tree, the prostrate trunk of which now straddles **'mountains'**, **'valleys'** and **'every ravine'**. In consequence, all dependent creatures scatter, meaning that peoples formerly in the thraldom of Assyria and currently beneath the shadow of Egypt travel elsewhere to survive as best they may. The verse is part of a surrealist verbal caricature, exhibiting a tree with grossly exaggerated features in order to drive home a truth (31:12). But very many (**'all'**, twice), having no place to go, remain **'upon its ruin'** and **'on its boughs'**. Horror-struck, they are destitute (31:13).

Verse 13 flows into its successor. The total destruction of the tree is not without purpose: **'... in order that all the trees by the waters might not be exalted in their loftiness'**. All men have **'been consigned to death'**, not excluding great leaders. All **'descend to the pit'**. After all, they are but **'the sons of men'**, frail humans ('men' translating *adam*).[9] Because pride is lethal, let not the trees **'set their tops among the clouds'** (31:14).

3. The world is amazed (31:15-18)

31:15-18. '"Thus says the Lord Yahweh: 'On the day when it went down to Sheol I caused lamentation; I covered it up with the deep and held back its rivers, and its mighty waters were shut up, and I made Lebanon dark on account of it and all the trees of the field swooned because of it. At the sound of its fall I caused nations to quake when I made it descend to Sheol with those who go down to the pit; all the trees of Eden, the choice and best of Lebanon, all that drink water, were comforted in the lower land. They also went down to Sheol with it, to those slain by the sword; and they who were its arm dwelt in its shadow amid the nations.

'"'To whom do you compare like this in glory and in height among the trees of Eden? Yet you will be brought down with the trees of Eden to the lower land. Amid the uncircumcised you will lie, with those who have been slain by the sword. This is Pharaoh and all his multitude,' declares the Lord Yahweh.'"

Again Yahweh speaks, describing the impression upon the surrounding nations caused by the downfall of the great tree. Everywhere there has been terrified lamentation because what happened to it could be their lot. Inferior monarchies sustained by Assyria and now Egypt retreat, reluctant to be seen to have been in league with a fallen empire. They swoon in terror.

Yet their sorrow has been induced by none other than Yahweh: **'*I* caused lamentation; *I* covered it up with the deep ... *I* made Lebanon dark on account of it.'** At the behest of the God of Israel, the **'mighty waters'** sustaining the Assyrian tree were **'shut up'**, its source of irrigation failing completely and thereby ensuring its death (31:15).

On earth, nations had been shaken at the demise of Assyria. But what of the **'pit'** pertaining to another world, **'Sheol'**, in which there are other formerly choice trees which once flourished in **'Eden'**? Even the most magnificent specimens of **'Lebanon'**, **'all that drink water'** like Assyria, comfort themselves because the latter now shares their fate.

The present verse offers a sensitive analysis of the emotions of fallen men. When they witness the collapse of the great, they fear lest they, too, might go the same way, yet are **'comforted'** in knowing that one whom they feared has at last been brought low.

The transliterated Hebrew term **'Sheol'** now appears in the book for the first time, Ezekiel expecting his readers to understand its meaning: the underworld, the abode of the dead, **'the lower land'** (31:16). Although some have considered that 'Sheol' is related to a Hebrew verb meaning 'to ask', suggesting a place of enquiry (alluding to necromancy),[10] this may be dubious. The etymology remains uncertain.

Other nations had been the unwilling **'arm'** of the Assyrians and had lived under the shadow of that empire. Fallen, they have descended to **'Sheol'** only to meet the erstwhile tyrant, the superpower having been struck down by the **'sword'**. They shed no tears (31:17).

In conclusion, Ezekiel repeats the question raised in 31:2. To whom are **'you'**, Pharaoh, like in your **'glory and ... height among the trees of Eden?'** With his tumultuous nation, Hophra and his empire are to be brought down to the world beneath. There he lies dead amid the lowliest denizens of the next world, **'uncircumcised'** (cf. 28:10), godless nations all **'slain by the sword'**. Yahweh **'declares'** that **'This is Pharaoh and all his multitude.'**

The argument is that if the Egyptian ruler entertains pretensions about rivalling the Assyrians in greatness, he may by all means do so. But let him also remember that the aftermath of pride is destruction, and that even as the Assyrian tree was felled, so must his own domain crash to the ground.

Ezekiel implies that those in Israel who were looking towards Egypt, a relatively minor tree, rather than to their God, for help needed to learn from this earlier example of blind arrogance. Their doom has been sealed (31:18).

Application

By introducing the theme of life beyond the grave, this chapter tells us that Yahweh, the God of Israel, determines our lot both in this world and in that to come, and that our conduct here and now will affect our situation when we are dead. In particular, men's pride and lust for power may well be their ruin in this world and will certainly devastate them when they pass into eternity. That is why we need to acknowledge Christ as Lord.

What Ezekiel 31 and other parts of the Old Testament tell out in shadow form is explained in fulness by the New Testament. Consider, for example, the parable in Luke 16:19-31 of the rich man, who — derisively — is unnamed but who was magnificently ‘buried’, and the poor man Lazarus (the name meaning ‘God is my helper’) who had no funeral. Which man was received into heaven, and why?

10. The tenth prophecy

(Ezekiel 32:1–16)

The sixth oracle takes the form of a contemptuous lamentation over Egypt and is dated to the twelfth year of the captivity of Jehoiachin. It is the twelfth month and the first day of the month, which would translate to 3 March 585 BC.

Because Nebuchadnezzar has proved to be unstoppable, the downfall of Egypt is impending. It is concerning this that the word of Yahweh comes to Ezekiel. Even though the geographical distance between Egypt and him is immense, Israel's God is not limited by space and time. It is Yahweh's sixth word to Egypt.

1. The monster is trapped (32:1-10)

32:1-10. And it came about that in the twelfth year, in the twelfth month, on the first of the month, that the word of Yahweh came to me, saying, 'Son of man, raise a dirge over Pharaoh, king of Egypt, and you will say to him, "You have likened yourself to a young lion of the nations, but you are as a monster in the seas. And you have burst forth in your rivers and have muddied the water with your feet and trampled their rivers."

'Thus says the Lord Yahweh: "So I shall spread my net over you with an assembly of many peoples, and they will lift you up in my dragnet. And I shall abandon you on the land — I shall hurl you upon the face of the field. Then I shall cause all the birds of the heavens to dwell upon you and shall satisfy the animals of all the earth with you. And I shall place your flesh on the mountains and shall fill the valleys with your heap. I shall irrigate the earth with your flow — with your blood — up to the mountains, and the ravines will be full of you. And with your snuffing out I shall cover the heavens and shall darken their stars. I shall cover the sun with cloud, and the moon will not radiate its light. I shall darken all the shining lights in the heavens over you and shall set darkness over your land," declares the Lord Yahweh.

'"Then I shall vex the heart of many peoples when I bring your shattered remains among the nations, upon nations which you have not known. I shall make many peoples desolate because of you, and their kings will bristle with horror because of you when I brandish my sword before their faces; and they will tremble every moment, each man for his life, on the day of your fall."'

Now, towards the end of 585 BC, almost two years have passed since the preceding oracle against Egypt (31:1), and it is nearly two months since a refugee from Judah had arrived in Babylon to announce the fall of Jerusalem (see 33:21). Now that the exiles know the worst, Yahweh speaks again to Ezekiel concerning Egypt (32:1).

The prophet is to **'raise a dirge over Pharaoh, king of Egypt'**. Hophra is still the reigning pharaoh and will endure for a further fifteen years until his assassination in 570 BC. But it may be that the present prophecy is addressed to the Egyptians as a whole, whoever may be the incumbent of the throne. Further, Ezekiel is speaking sideways, as it were, to his fellow-exiles to demonstrate that any residual hopes for Egyptian intervention in Judah on behalf of that people would be misplaced: there is no city left to be delivered!

Hophra has **'likened** [himself] **to a young lion of the nations'**, deceiving himself with the fantasy that he could manipulate the levers of power in the world at large.[1] In that the lion was an emblem of royalty in Egypt (thus the Sphinx), the allusion is apt.

But Pharaoh was mistaken in that, as seen by Yahweh, he was **'as a monster in the seas'** — 'monster' translating *tannim*. This would seem to connect with 29:3, which addresses Pharaoh as 'the great monster', or crocodile, 'that lies in the midst of his rivers'.[2] If so, the Nile and its tributaries are likened to **'seas'**, the waters of which the monarch has **'muddied'** and made foul. Not only so, he has **'trampled their rivers'**, suggesting that when the Egyptians ventured their armies into foreign lands, they created havoc (32:2).

Yahweh speaks authoritatively. Paralleling the assertion of 29:4-5, he will **'spread** [his] **net'** upon Pharaoh amid an **'assembly of many'** watching **'peoples'**. They employ Yahweh's **'dragnet'** to **'lift'** him up from his watery seclusion (32:3).[3]

Hurled upon **'the face of the field'**, Pharaoh is to be abandoned to the birds and the beasts of **'all the earth'**, as if mankind in its totality gathers to revel in the fall of Egypt. Nor will they be disappointed (32:4).

Pharaoh's **'flesh'** will be left **'on the mountains'** and his **'heap'** will **'fill the valleys'** (cf. the felling of the tree, 31:12-13). **'Heap'**, from *ramût*, might mean rottenness (cf. *rimmah*, 'worm'). If so, nothing other than corruption will be left (32:5).

Yahweh causes the earth to slake its thirst from the mountain-high discharge of Pharaoh's **'blood'** and other body fluids. The **'ravines'** are piled up with his remains, an illustration intended (successfully) to nauseate the reader. The downfall of Egypt is as complete as it is dishonourable (32:6).

Further, when Yahweh snuffs out Egypt, as a man might extinguish a lamp, he will **'cover the heavens and ... darken the stars'**. Neither the sun nor the moon, nor even the other lights of the night sky, shine. Darkness blankets Egypt. This is picture language, because natural phenomena did not cease when the power of pharaonic Egypt passed away. Developed from 30:18, the metaphor parallels Isaiah 13:10, which tells of the downfall of Chaldea.[4] It is as if there is universal darkness when Egypt is eclipsed. Shining, searching light cannot reveal this nation because its radiance has been transmuted at a stroke into impenetrable gloom. Or, there might be a recall of Exodus 10:21-23, which relates the ninth plague of Egypt. Even as a thousand years earlier Egypt had once fallen before the might of Yahweh, so again. There shall be **'darkness over your land'**. Yahweh **'declares'** it (32:7-8).

'Many peoples' formerly unknown to the Egyptians are agitated when they hear of the downfall of Pharaoh. **'Shattered remains'** translates *sheber*, which often means 'fracture' or 'crash', or even 'corn' or 'grain' (that which is crushed). Possibly, the idea here is that the broken remnants of Egypt are scattered by Yahweh among the nations so that they may fear.[5] Nursing their broken hearts, monarchs shudder and their hair stands on end. These great men of the earth realize at last that the **'sword'** of Yahweh has been brandished before their faces, and each will **'tremble ... for his life'** when he learns of the **'fall'** of Egypt. Whose turn will it be next? (32:9-10).

2. The sword of Babylon (32:11-16)

32:11-16. '"For thus says the Lord Yahweh: 'The sword of the king of Babylon will come to you. By the swords of the great ones I shall cause your multitude to fall — all of them are the ferocious of the nations. Then they will devastate the pride of Egypt, and all its multitude will be destroyed. And I shall cause all its cattle to perish from beside the many waters, and the feet of men will no longer muddy them, nor will the hooves of cattle muddy them. Then I shall cause their waters to settle down and make their rivers to stream like oil,' declares the Lord Yahweh.

'"'When I make the land of Egypt a desolation and the land is destitute of its fulness, when I smite all who dwell in it — they will know that I am Yahweh. This is a dirge, and they will chant it. And the daughters of the nations will chant it. Over Egypt and all its multitude they will chant it,' declares the Lord Yahweh."'

'The Lord Yahweh' speaks again. The metaphor of the crocodile hurled upon dry land fades and the realities of impending military disaster come into focus (cf. 21:9; 30:25): **'The sword of the king of Babylon will come to you'** — that is, to Pharaoh as the representative of Egypt. The theme of the sword of the Lord is not new to Ezekiel (cf. 30:4-5).

Thus the hand wielding the Babylonian weapon is that of Yahweh: **'By the swords of the great ones I shall cause your multitude to fall.'** Pitiless barbarians will devastate Pharaoh's proud multitudes. The reader is meant to be shocked: how can Yahweh do this thing? Yet he will do it so that none in Israel will turn to Egypt for aid in time of crisis (32:12).

According to 32:2, it was Pharaoh the monster, probably a crocodile, who had muddied the waters of Egypt and made them foul. Now the figure has a different orientation. Such will be the devastation that men and their cattle will no longer go down to the waters to drink, the reason being that they are dead. Possibly there is a recall of Exodus 9:3-4 and the fifth plague. Normal life will be put into suspension, Yahweh causing **'all its** [Egypt's] **cattle to perish from beside the many waters'**. Undisturbed, the waters will **'settle down'** and **'stream like oil'**. Again, the Lord **'declares'** that it shall be so (32:13-14).

None the less, following the Babylonian devastation of Egypt the nation will have a future of sorts, although its imperial grandeur will by then be a matter of history. In hindsight, those who remain will acknowledge that the God of Israel had overthrown the empire: **'they will know that I am Yahweh'** (32:15).

Even as Jeremiah had summoned female professional mourners to lament the downfall of Judah,[6] so Ezekiel's words are portrayed as **'a dirge'** to be sung by **'the daughters of the nations'**. It is as if the whole world rises up to demand a mocking lament over an empire that in its day had been universally loathed, equally by men and by God. All are happy that it is gone (32:16).

Application

When evil men and empires fade away, as they are bound to do, the world is not sorry. Thus, 'the daughters of the nations' contemptuously lament the passing of Egyptian grandeur (32:16). And with them stands Ezekiel (32:1-2), with the Lord behind him.

History can tell of nations and cultures that have passed from the scene without leaving anything of benefit to the world. Neither did the gods of Egypt bequeath any happy legacy to their devotees; nor do those faiths that are antagonistic to the Christ of the Bible benefit their adherents. Those who have eyes in their heads can see for themselves. It is not for nothing that our Lord said about his disciples that in principle they are 'the salt of the earth' and 'the light of the world'.[7]

11. The eleventh series of prophecies

(Ezekiel 32:17 – 33:20)

It is now the twelfth year and the fifteenth day of the month. The prophet issues a further lamentation, this time over the collapse of the imperial power of Egypt rather than Pharaoh in particular. Although the month is unmentioned (cf. 26:1), the implication is that this word from Yahweh came to Ezekiel two weeks after the previous prophecy.

One may speculate as to why these oracles against Egypt (chapter 29 through to chapter 32) were issued, so to speak, in instalments. Perhaps the Lord, aware that far too many exiles were reluctant to abandon lingering hopes for further Egyptian intervention in Judah, gives an ongoing tirade in order to dash their expectations. If so, here is the final salvo.

The seventh word to Egypt (Ezekiel 32:17-32)

This passage is effectively an elaboration of 31:14-18, which tells of the descent into 'Sheol' of the empire of Assyria and predicts a similar fate for Egypt, then on the cusp of extinction.[1] A spectacularly vivid song of lamentation, it may be said to fall into six sections. Its repetitive strain is designed to show that, notwithstanding the immense prestige bequeathed to Egypt by a long history of influence in international affairs, she is as weak as any of the other powers: they died; she dies. One might compare with the generations of Adam as recorded in Genesis. Although the first man and his descendants lived for many years, with the exception of Enoch they all perished: 'and he died' is repeated again and again in the list.[2] Terrestrial death springs from spiritual death.

1. The multitude has fallen (32:17-21)

32:17-21. And it was in the twelfth year, on the fifteenth day of the month, that the word of Yahweh came to me, saying, 'Son of man, wail for the multitude of Egypt and bring it down — you and the daughters of the splendid nations — to the land beneath, with those who go down to the pit. "Whom do you exceed in loveliness? Go down and be bedded with the uncircumcised. They will fall in the midst of those slain by the sword. A sword has been given: they have drawn her away, and all her multitudes. The strong among the mighty ones speak to him and to his helpers from the midst of Sheol. The uncircumcised, those slain by the sword, have descended; they have lain down."'

Jerusalem has fallen to the arms of Babylon, and Ezekiel and his fellow-exiles had learned about the tragedy two months earlier (cf. the date given by 33:21). Yet again, **'the word of Yahweh came'** to Ezekiel (32:17). It was 17 March 585 BC.

The **'son of man'** is to utter a dirge which will have the effect of precipitating **'the multitude of Egypt ... to the land beneath'**, to **'the pit'** (32:18). This is a vivid way of telling out that the prediction will most certainly be fulfilled. Although the English versions read that both Egypt and the **'daughters of the splendid nations'** will descend to the lower world, a slight yet perhaps not illegitimate alteration in the vocalization ('she' — Egypt — becoming **'you'**, second person, meaning Ezekiel) would indicate that the prophet and certain women will unite to mourn over Egypt.[3] Either these women are professional mourners from other nations, thus connecting with 32:16, or the allusion is epexegetic: 'daughters who are splendid nations', who turn out to be Assyria, Elam, Meshech-Tubal, Edom and Sidon (cf. 32:22-30).[4] This interpretation seems to give a better sense: peoples who anticipate the downfall of Egypt will eventually welcome her in Sheol.

Thus the nations, Ezekiel and Ezekiel's God taunt the Egyptians. Death being the great equalizer, Egypt will exceed none **'in loveliness'** in the society of the departed. Let this ancient and haughty empire descend and **'be bedded with the uncircumcised'**.

The insistence is surprising if it is remembered that the Egyptians practised circumcision. But Ezekiel prophesies on behalf of his own people, for whom uncircumcision was anathema. David lamented over the deaths of Saul and Jonathan, 'Proclaim it not ...

lest the daughters of the uncircumcised [Philistines] triumph.'[5] The sense, then, is that Egypt is deemed by heaven and the people of Israel, together with the world of the dead, to be unclean, fit only to lie with the uncircumcised (32:19).

Their common baseness is evident in that Pharaoh and his people lie prostrate along with nations **'slain by the sword'**. Comparing with 32:27, it appears that the dead are not soldiers who fell in battle, then to be buried with military honours, but those who were massacred or executed and who were granted no decent interment. The certainty of destruction is such that Ezekiel points to the executioners of Egypt: **'A sword has been given: they have drawn her** [Egypt] **away, and all her multitudes'** (32:20).

Fallen merchants of terror, **'the strong among the mighty ones'** chatter hoarsely about the tragedy and address Pharaoh along with **'his helpers'**. The latter are deemed to be among the **'uncircumcised'**, impure peoples who had been killed out of hand, who had **'descended'** and who had **'lain down'**. Egypt is finished (32:21).

2. A tour of Sheol: Assyria (32:22-23)

32:22-33. '"Assyria is there, with all her assembly; her graves are round about her. All of them are slain, they who have fallen by the sword, whose graves have been set in the recesses of the pit; and her company is round about her grave. All of them are slain, fallen by the sword — who had spread terror in the land of the living."'

As if to advertise the shameful end to which Egypt must come, Yahweh now grants Ezekiel and his readers a guided inspection of the denizens of Sheol. The first to be mentioned is **'Assyria ... with all her assembly'**, her **'graves'** surrounding her (32:22). In its day, this vicious empire had spread havoc far and wide, but (as noted earlier) was finally overcome at the battle of Carchemish in 605 BC. Not a few of Ezekiel's fellow-exiles would have been alive at the time.

Now the satellites of Assyria are all dead, **'fallen by the sword'**. Apparently, there are so many graves that they extend to the **'recesses of the pit'**, with Assyria occupying a place of macabre honour at the centre. Their miserable epitaph is that they **'had spread terror in the land of the living'** (32:23).

3. The tour continued: Elam (32:24-25)

32:24-25. '"Elam is there, and all her multitude round about her grave. All of them are slain, those who fell by the sword, who went down uncircumcised to the lower land, who had spread their terror in the land of the living. They have borne their disgrace with those who have gone down to the pit. In the midst of the slain they have made a bed for her, with all her multitude round about her. All of them are uncircumcised, slain by the sword, for they had spread their terror in the land of the living and have borne their disgrace with those who have gone down to the pit. They have been set in the midst of the slain."'

Similarly, **'Elam'** is to be seen in the pit, surrounded by **'all her multitude'**. Elam, situated within modern Iran, was one of the conquerors of Babylon, and Elamite archers served in the Assyrian army.[6] Its destruction had already been predicted.[7] Centuries later, Jews from Elam were present in Jerusalem at Pentecost.[8] Ezekiel's lamentation is similar to that for Assyria, the two references to the uncircumcised stressing the shame of Elam's downfall. The latter nation shares Assyria's appalling epitaph (32:24).

The degradation of Elam is complete, her **'bed'**, or bier, being placed amid the uncircumcised dead.

Again it is stated that **'in the land of the living'** the Elamites had **'spread their terror'**. And, repeating from 32:24, it is stated that they have **'borne their disgrace with those who have gone down to the pit'** (32:25). What hope, then, can there be for Egypt? None.

4. The tour extends: Meshech-Tubal (32:26-28)

32:26-28. '"Meshech-Tubal is there and all her multitude; round about her are her graves. All are uncircumcised, slain by the sword, for they had spread their terror in the land of the living. But they do not lie with the mighty ones, they who fall from the uncircumcised, who went down to Sheol with their weapons of war. They placed their swords beneath their heads, but the iniquity of these was upon their bones — though the terror of the mighty ones had been in the land of the living. But you — even you — will be broken in the midst of the uncircumcised and will lie with those slain by the sword."'

'Meshech-Tubal', to be identified as one entity, and **'her multitude'** are also in the pit, surrounded by the **'graves'** of her satellites. Perhaps it is not possible to identify this people accurately, although they were mentioned in 27:13 and will reappear in 38:2-3 and 39:1 as an element within a northern coalition bent on attacking a resettled Israel. They qualify for Assyria's appalling epitaph (**'they had spread their terror in the land of the living'**) because they had done exactly the same thing. **'Slain by the sword'**, they share the shame of the **'uncircumcised'** (32:26).

Yet their fate is even worse than that of the previously mentioned peoples. Although others who fell were buried with military honours, **'their swords beneath their heads'**, these miserable folk **'do not lie with the mighty ones, they who fall from the**

uncircumcised'. Who these **'mighty ones'** were is uncertain, although they would appear not to have been the Assyrians or Elam. Perhaps Ezekiel has in mind Genesis 6:4, which speaks of 'the mighty men who were of old, men of renown'. If so, the latter, evil in their time, are deemed to have been positively noble in contrast to Meshech-Tubal. A precedent for this type of interpretation may be found in 16:46-52, where the sins of Jerusalem are said to have made her earlier 'sisters', Samaria and Sodom, appear 'righteous'.

Lying in the pit, the **'iniquity'** of Meshech-Tubal rests **'on their bones'**, their dismembered skeletons proclaiming their just destruction. The shameful epitaph is repeated yet again. Because Pharaoh of Egypt is no better than they, he can expect to **'be broken'** and to **'lie'** down with other **'uncircumcised'** folk put to death by **'the sword'** (32:27-28).

5. And now, Edom and Sidon (32:29-30)

32:29-30. '"There is Edom, her kings and all her princes who with all their might have been placed with those slain by the sword. They will lie with the uncircumcised, with those who go down to the pit. The appointed princes of the north are there — all of them — and every Sidonian, who, in spite of their terror resulting from their might, in shame descended with the slain. So they lie uncircumcised with those who have been slain by the sword and bear their shame with those who go down to the pit."'

'Edom' and **'every Sidonian'**, plus local chiefs **'of the north'**, by which might be meant Syria and Phoenicia, appear. Whereas previous sections mentioned greater and more distant world powers, local and petty sources of aggravation must suffer as the others have suffered, even though the dreaded Assyrian epitaph is not ascribed to them. They, too, **'lie'** in the company of the **'uncircumcised'** who have been put to **'the sword'**, among whom they **'bear their shame'** (32:29-30). If Yahweh can cast down the small as well as the great, Egypt cannot escape.

6. Lastly, Pharaoh (32:31-32)

32:31-32. '"Pharaoh will see them and shall be comforted for all his multitude slain by the sword — Pharaoh and all his army," declares the Lord Yahweh. "For I have placed my terror in the land of the living, and he will be made to lie in the midst of the uncircumcised, with those slain by the sword — Pharaoh and all his multitude," declares the Lord Yahweh.'

The oracles against Egypt come to their close. **'Pharaoh and all his army'** will, like others, fall by **'the sword'** and will join the unlamented dead. Ezekiel indulges in heavy irony in that the Egyptian king and his minions will glean some small comfort when they discover that they are not alone in their ignominy. Whereas in 31:16 the inferior trees of Eden found some consolation when they beheld the vast Assyrian cedar joining them, here great Egypt, the oldest empire of them all, is relieved to find that it is not alone within the realm of the shameful dead. All who have terrorized their fellows will be terrorized by Yahweh **'in the land of the living'**, then to **'lie in the midst of the uncircumcised, with those slain by the sword'**. Yahweh **'declares'** that it shall be so (32:31-32).

Application

As we have travelled through chapters 29 – 32 it may have been noticed that although Babylon and its tyrannical king are often introduced as an instrument in the hand of Yahweh (29:18-20; 30:10,24-25; 31:12; 32:11-12), there is no mention of the eventual overthrow of Babylon (but cf. a possible allusion in 21:30-32). To this extent Ezekiel is unlike his contemporary Jeremiah, who had no hesitation in announcing the downfall of that great empire (see Jer. 50; 51).

There must be a reason for the omission. Some commentators suggest that, living as he did in Babylonia, Ezekiel refused to provoke his captors by writing about their demise, yet giving the impression that the downfall of some of Israel's enemies would be the downfall of all, the Chaldeans not excluded. In a subtle fashion, therefore, he offers hope to the exiles.[9]

Although this may be true, there could be a more fundamental reason for the exclusion. Throughout chapters 1 – 32 Ezekiel has focused upon the collapse of the theocracy of Israel, according to which the land, the people, the Davidic monarchy and the presence of Yahweh must part company, a tragedy in which the Chaldeans become the principal instrument. Then, from 33:1 onwards the prophet (as this commentary sees it) is concerned with the reinstitution of the theocracy, both in this world and in eternity. This polarization, which is *not* reflected by Jeremiah, fills the whole prophecy and is the burden of Ezekiel's heart and ministry. For him, an explicit condemnation of the Babylonians might even have been an unnecessary diversion.

All of which may teach us that because empires and personalities come and go, we need to stand back from time to time and gaze in awe at the wide sweep of the divine programme without peering too closely at the details upon the canvas. The Lord breaks down so that he may build up, and there are occasions when we should not expect to be granted an understanding of all the niceties. Thus we are not told in the Bible about what eventually happened to, say, Pontius Pilate. Clearly, the Lord deemed that we did not need to know.

Chapter 32 is concerned largely with the state of the wicked in the world to come, among whom are many from Egypt and from various other nations. 'Sheol', situated figuratively beneath the surface of the earth (32:18,24; cf. 31:18), is mentioned explicitly in verses 21 and 27 (cf. 31:15,16,17), as is 'the pit' in verses 18,24,25,29,30 (cf. 31:14). They bespeak an abode to which men descend, the verb *yarad*, 'to go down', occurring ten times in

32:17-32. And in the pit of Sheol they are conscious, fully aware of their common fate. Featured as being there physically, some, indeed, are said to have been granted a relatively honourable burial. The whole picture is metaphorical, offered to the reader in the interests of rhetoric. What we have here is a startling literary cartoon.

Whereas Ezekiel understood Sheol as the abode of the wicked, it would seem that, imperceptibly, the ground is being prepared for the fuller New Testament doctrine of an eschatological judgement involving bodily resurrection, both of the wicked and of the righteous.[10]

Nor in this matter does Ezekiel stand alone within the Old Testament canon. Indeed, Psalm 16, in declaring its writer's conviction that Yahweh will 'not leave my soul in Sheol, nor will ... allow your holy one to see corruption' (v. 10), is seen by the New Testament as having anticipated the resurrection of Christ. According to Acts 2:27,31 (Greek text), 'Hades', which translates 'Sheol', is a state in which the departed are abandoned permanently by God.[11] Neither was Christ permitted to remain physically dead, nor was he consigned by God to Sheol when, at the moment of death, his soul separated from his body. On the contrary, his soul escalated immediately to Paradise,[12] as must that of every dying believer when he meets his end. Ezekiel is telling us in a negative fashion that Sheol cannot be the prospect of those who belong to the God of Israel.

Ezekiel is still a watchman (Ezekiel 33:1-20)

The strain of waiting to learn of the outcome of the Chaldean assault on Jerusalem is nearly over. Very soon, sad news will reach Babylonia from Judah. The intervening series of condemnations against the foreign nations (chapters 25 – 32), uttered during and after the conquest of Jerusalem, is complete. Although there are to be other prophecies directed against alien peoples (chapters 35, 38 – 39), they are connected directly with promises to Israel rather than being unvarnished denunciations.

I. A phase of ministry ends; another begins

Thus the first phase of Ezekiel's ministry has concluded. Over a period of about seven and a half years he has predicted judgements of the utmost severity upon degenerate Israel and upon the adjacent nations. To the latter there is held out the certainty of annihilation or, at best, eclipse. Some shall fall never to rise again or, as in the case of Egypt, will never recover their glory.

Yet gracious promises have already been made to Israel. According to the interpretation offered by this commentary, Ezekiel has announced that the twelve tribes are to be regathered geographically and renewed spiritually (11:17-21; 14:11; 16:53-63). We recall that throughout these predictions there are unmistakable Messianic promises. Thus a cedar tree will grow in

Zion, arising from the most humble beginnings. When it is mature, birds of every species shelter in it (17:22-24). The Lord is Israel's God and they will regain their identity as his people (28:25-26; 29:21).

But nothing of this is to be fulfilled in the immediate future. Although Ezekiel has advised the exiles to contemplate an unspeakable disaster — the imminent destruction of Jerusalem and the temple — in a sense his mouth has remained closed (cf. 3:26-27; 24:27).

Now, when he receives from a fugitive the tragic news about the city, he commences a new phase in his ministry. He speaks!

And the time has almost arrived. The dire warnings of the law are to be replaced by good news. Now that all earthly, visible supports have been denied to Israel, the Jews in exile are to be informed in the most vivid fashion that their God remains the God of the covenant with Abraham. Not only shall he never discard them, he has decreed a blessed future for his people. About this Ezekiel will have much to say.

II. The call renewed

Firstly, the Lord addresses Ezekiel concerning his servant's situation. Before he can proceed, the call to prophetic ministry must be renewed. This is the burden of 33:1-20.[13] In order to understand these verses, it may be helpful to sketch the background.

This undated prophecy might have been uttered in the evening before the day when Ezekiel learned from an escapee that Jerusalem was no more (33:21-22). It could have been just then that the Lord opened Ezekiel's mouth. No longer would he be dumb. The rationale for this suggested timing is that there is no specific prophecy associated with the evening in question and because 33:1-20 is appropriate to the occasion.

The messenger has confirmed the exiles' worst fears and they realize now that Ezekiel's earlier predictions about Jerusalem had been accurate. About this the prophet, of course, was never in doubt. It is clear to all that he and his priestly colleagues will never return to Jerusalem to resume their functions, the temple having been destroyed.

From this it follows that the emphasis of Ezekiel's prophetic ministry must alter dramatically. It will be as if his mouth is open for the first time. This is because it is a season for consolation: all things will be new. The unimaginable having occurred, the exiles are to be told about the faithfulness and love of their covenant God. Judgement cannot remain for ever in the house of the Lord. It is time to build up.[14]

Nevertheless, Ezekiel knew well that most of those in Judah, not to mention the exiles, who had survived the holocaust were unrepentant. The horrors of the siege and the desolation of Jerusalem had not brought them to their senses. This is brought out by 33:17-20, which reveals their spiritual insensitivity, and by 33:26: 'You stand upon your swords; you commit abomination; and you each defile his neighbour's wife — and will you possess the land?'

Jeremiah had exposed the sad post-destruction state of affairs by pointing to the pernicious worship of 'the queen of heaven' by those Jews who fled to Egypt from Judah, their old abominations being transported by them wherever they went.[15] And Ezekiel knew that many who remained in Judah foolishly believed that their descent from Abraham meant that they were entitled to a permanent tenure of the land: 'We are many, and to us the land has been given for a possession' (33:24).[16]

In Babylonia, the exiles remained stolidly indifferent to the prophetic word. Although prepared to listen to Ezekiel and eager to display a formal deference, they refused to take him seriously. He was no better than a popular musician, among them for a brief time and then gone, interesting but irrelevant (33:32).

Because Ezekiel must still act as a watchman giving due warning to his constituency, the commission of chapter 3 is repeated: the holy God of Israel demands repentance. For Ezekiel, this principle was no less true now that Jerusalem was in ruins than it had been when city and temple were standing. He was convinced that, even if times had changed, truth would not.

And there was a further matter upon his agenda. Some of the exiles, professing to believe that God had treated them unjustly (33:17,20), remained perversely blind to the wisdom and justice of Yahweh, who — it was admitted by all — had brought suffering upon Israel. What was the point, they complained, in turning from sin and coming back to the Lord if they were destined to perish in a foreign land? (33:10-20).

To counter this fallacy, Ezekiel asserts that although the Lord can and must judge the impenitent, he delights to forgive if and when sinners repent, wherever they may be. Indeed, nothing pleases him more.

Because this was a lesson that had yet to be learned, the prophet repeats the burden of chapter 18 concerning the absolute necessity for a change of heart. Ezekiel has to explain to his fellow-exiles his duties as a watchman. This was God's way of preventing the prophet from being unnerved by the malice of the opposition: he will be able to justify his ministry by asserting that he had always been a man under authority, doing no more than seeking to honour his commission.

1. The duties of a watchman (33:1-9)

33:1-9. And the word of Yahweh came to me, saying, 'Son of man, speak to the sons of your people, and you will say to them, "A land upon which I bring a sword — and the people of the land take one man from their borders and make him a watchman for them, and he sees the sword coming upon the land and he gives a blast with the trumpet and warns the people. And he who hears the sound of the trumpet but does not take warning, and the sword comes and takes him away — his blood will be upon his head. He heard the sound of the trumpet but did not take warning: his blood will be upon him. Yet had he taken warning, he would have delivered his soul. But as for the watchman, if he sees the sword coming and does not give a blast with the trumpet and the people are not warned, so the sword will come and take a soul from them — he will be taken in his iniquity; but I shall seek his blood from the hand of the watchman."

'And you, son of man, I have appointed you a watchman to the house of Israel. So you hear a word from my mouth and will give them warning from me. When I say to the wicked person, "O wicked one, you will assuredly die," and you do not speak to warn the wicked person from his way, he — the wicked person — will die in his iniquity, but his blood I shall require from your hand. And you, if you have warned a wicked person from his way, to turn from it, and he does not turn from his way — he will die in his iniquity; but you will have recovered your soul.'

Ezekiel reports that **'the word of Yahweh came'** to him, instructing him to issue a parable, that of preparation for war, to the people. It is assumed that whenever war comes it is Yahweh who is the prime mover: **'A land upon which *I* bring a sword ...'** Then when invasion is impending, the people will quite properly appoint a **'watchman'**, one of their own, **'from their borders'**, meaning someone from within the extremities of their territory (33:1-2).

The first point brought home to Ezekiel and to be transmitted to his hearers is that if by sounding his **'trumpet'** the watchman warns his people of impending attack, any individual who disregards the caution will have only himself to blame when he is overcome.

'His blood will be upon his head' (33:3-4). It is emphasized that **'had he taken warning, he would have delivered his soul'**. He alone will be responsible for the ensuing tragedy (33:5).

But if an apathetic sentinel fails to sound his trumpet, individuals in the population will perish in their **'iniquity'**, yet the watchman must bear responsibility for their blood. This is because the guilty were not told what they had to do to avert the coming disaster. Had they listened, they might conceivably have protected themselves. The watchman's culpable silence is tantamount to murder by proxy. The consequence is that Yahweh will **'seek his blood from the hand of the watchman'** (33:6).

By now, Ezekiel's hearers might have been asking themselves about the point to which the prophet would no doubt come. Had they not already heard something like this, albeit years before? (Cf. 3:16-21). And if Ezekiel proposes to offer himself as a **'watchman'** to the exiled **'house of Israel'**, what is his burden? Even though they had not yet heard news of the downfall of Jerusalem (although Ezekiel had predicted it; cf. 24:15-27), was it not too late for repentance in order to turn back the sword of Yahweh? Surely, some would have suspected, Ezekiel's ministry as a watchman must have come to an end. Could he be credible when he asserts more than seven years after the commencement of his work among them (cf. 1:2) that Yahweh had now **'appointed'** him as such to the people'? What further word from the **'mouth'** of the Lord could he hold out in this time of tragedy? Unhappily, they did not comprehend their need (33:7).

The application of the parable of the sentinel does, indeed, recall 3:16-21, yet with something of a twist. Whereas in 3:16-21 Yahweh granted an initial commission to Ezekiel, in 33:1-9 the Lord reminds him that because his responsibility as a watchman has not been withdrawn, his future ministry will still involve warning the people. Although the anticipated peril will not be that of the sword of the Lord descending upon Judah (Jerusalem had fallen by now), those who persist in their wickedness must be informed that they may expect Yahweh to respond: **'he — the wicked person — will die in his iniquity'**. And if Ezekiel fails to give warning, **'his** [the sinner's] **blood I shall require from your hand'**. Conversely, if he remains faithful to his charge and warns the sinful, the prophet will have **'recovered'** his own **'soul'**.

All of which is an admonition both to Ezekiel and to the exiles that when the messenger of sad news arrives from Judah, none are to abandon themselves to despair, and thereby to sin.[17] Because there will be a new dawn bringing hope with it, they are to amend themselves (33:8-9).

2. Preaching to the helpless and hopeless (33:10-20)

Some of the exiles had exhibited a quality of despair that would appear to have been a manifestation of evil unbelief. Leviticus 26:39 anticipates the ultimate misfortunes of an apostate Israel: 'And those of you who are left shall waste away in their iniquity in your enemies' lands; also in their fathers' iniquities, which are with them, they shall waste away'.[18]

The exiles rightly believed that they were 'rotting away' (33:10). But they were mistaken in concluding that their situation was hopeless.

The section divides into two disputations between Ezekiel and the exiles: 33:10-16 and 33:17-20.

I. The promise of mercy (33:10-16)

33:10-16. 'And you, son of man, say to the house of Israel, "Thus you say, saying, 'For our transgressions and our sins are upon us, and we are rotting away in them. So how shall we live?'" Say to them, "As I live," declares the Lord Yahweh, "Surely I take no pleasure when the wicked dies, but when the wicked one turns from his way and lives. Turn, turn from your evil ways! For why should you die, O house of Israel?"

'And you, son of man, say to the sons of your people, "The righteousness of the righteous person will not deliver him in the day of his transgression, and as for the wickedness of the wicked person, he will not be tripped up by it in the day that he turns from his wickedness. But in the day that he sins, the righteous person will be unable to live. When I say to the righteous that he will surely live, and he relies upon his righteousness and commits iniquity, none of his righteousness will be remembered — and in his iniquity that he has committed, in it he shall die. But when I say to the wicked person, 'You will surely die,' and he turns from his sin and practises judgement and righteousness, the wicked person returns a pledge, restores what has been seized, walks in the statutes of life without practising iniquity — he will surely live; he will not die. None of the sins that he perpetrated will be remembered against him. He has practised judgement and righteousness — he will surely live."'

Ezekiel was required by Yahweh to cast in the faces of the exiles a saying that was already circulating among them. For the first time in the book we learn that Ezekiel's ministry appears to have had some effect (**'For our transgressions and our sins are upon us, and we are rotting away in them'**), but this is not surprising if by this time it had become obvious that Jerusalem must fall before the might of Babylon. Clearly, the exiles based their cry of despair on Leviticus 26:39 in that Israel had sinned and had lost so much. So, **'How shall we live?'** (33:10). It was Ezekiel's glorious task to inform them that the God of Israel is the God of hope. All was by no means lost.

Yahweh tells Ezekiel what he will say to despairing exiles who believed that they must perish in a foreign, unclean land. The promise of 18:20-32 is repeated with an emphasis upon verses 23 and 32. There, the Lord reminded a grossly erring community that it is never too late to turn to him. In the present context, Yahweh again declares that he takes **'no pleasure'** when he decides that an impenitent sinner must pay the price for the error of his ways. Positively, he does rejoice when an evil man finds life through repentance: **'Turn, turn from your evil ways! For why should you die, O house of Israel?'** (repeating the challenge of 18:31). The Lord is never gratified when he has to inflict pain (33:11).

Recalling 18:24,27-28, Ezekiel's words apply the assertion in 33:11 that Yahweh takes no delight in the death of any man. In fact, Ezekiel's constituency should have given attention to Leviticus 26:40-45. There Moses taught that when Israel in exile confesses her sins, Yahweh will take into account the primary covenant with Abraham, Isaac and Jacob. In saying this, Moses did not mean that the original agreement with the patriarchs was conditional, lapsing when broken by Abraham's family but capable of resurrection if the people cared to rethink their situation. The lawgiver knew that God in his goodness would never finally cast off Israel. Nor would the Lord allow them as a people finally to abandon him.[19] Moses meant that when Israelites show by their penitence that they are the believing children of Abraham, they will inherit the original promises of the covenant.

Although the English versions of Leviticus 26:40 invariably read something like, '*If* they confess their iniquity ...', suggesting that Israel might or might not attain to repentance, the Hebrew term underlying 'if' is a *vav*, a single consonant which acts as a demonstrative adjective or conjunction. It is normally translated as 'but', 'and', 'so', or even 'then' — but never 'if'.[20] Why, then, 'if' introduces Leviticus 26:40 is a matter for conjecture.

There is no question of chapter 33 supplying a crude doctrine of salvation by works, as if a surplus of good, however quantified, can make amends for evil, or as if a surplus of evil can dissolve a residue of good. The whole issue concerns the attitude of the heart: the man who repudiates sin and shows his love for the Lord by heeding his commandments **'will not be tripped up ... in the day that he turns from his wickedness'**. Conversely, **'the righteousness of the righteous person will not deliver him in the day of his transgression'**. Then, he will be **'unable'** to survive the breath of divine anger (33:12).

Continuing to speak for his God, Ezekiel is to inform his hearers that the attainment of divine favour does not rest in any notional excess of a man's good actions in comparison to those that are evil. That Yahweh felt urged to make this point so vividly speaks volumes for the exiles' superficial understanding of such matters. Notwithstanding any previous manifestation of righteousness, if a man is determined to remain **'in his iniquity that he has committed, in it he shall die'**. The emphasis rests upon **'in'**: the frame of mind to which a man chooses to commit himself will be the decisive factor. Equally, when Yahweh speaks personally to someone known to have delighted in sin, and that individual renounces evil in favour of **'judgement and righteousness'** and **'walks in the statutes of life'** — the latter being the commandments of Moses' law, at that time the final expression of the will of God for Israel[21] — **'he will surely live; he will not die'** (33:13-15). This promise is amplified: given a genuine change of heart, **'none of the sins'** of the offender **'will be remembered against him'**, meaning that he will not be charged. Having **'practised righteousness and judgement'** as a way of life, **'he will surely live'** (33:16).[22]

The exiles are challenged by exceedingly good news. Their future as a community is assured — provided that they respond positively to the word of Yahweh as relayed by his appointed watchman.

II. The complaint repeated (33:17-20)

33:17-20. 'But the sons of your people say, "The way of the Lord is not measured." Yet as for them — their way is not measured! When a righteous person turns from his righteousness and practises iniquity, then he will die in it. And when a wicked person turns from his wickedness and does judgement and righteousness — he himself will live by them. But you say, "The way of the Lord is not measured." I shall judge you, each according to his way, O house of Israel.'

The section closes with a repetition of the complaint of some of the exiles, **'the sons of your people'**, against Yahweh, and of the prophet's earlier reply (cf. 18:25-30): **'The way of Yahweh is not measured'** — that is, is not adjusted correctly. The people suspect that God is careless, inconsistent and unjust, and that they are the innocent victims of an ill-advised providence. But in reality the reverse is the case: **'Yet as for them — their way is not measured!'** It is not Yahweh who lacks balance (33:17).

To show where the one-sidedness is to be found, the Lord through Ezekiel clarifies the principles inherent in 33:10-16. The formerly righteous person who habitually **'practises iniquity ... will die in it'**. Equally, the penitent sinner who habitually **'does judgement and righteousness — he himself will live by them'**. Thus the charge of inconsistency is redirected to the exiles. Because inexorable rules governing the relationship between men and God have been laid down by Yahweh but ignored by the people, it is they who are devious (33:18-19).

In that the **'house of Israel'** is perverse, refusing to accept that **'the way of the Lord'** is other than **'measured'**, there is no point in disputing with them.

Yahweh concludes by stating that he will **'judge ... each** [man] **according to his way'**. Let them see who is to be the adjudicator (33:20).

Application

When the Lord Jesus spoke to the woman of Samaria, he gently broached the subject of her sinful manner of life, challenging her to place her trust in him. Yet she parried his invitation by seeking to argue about where true worship should be conducted: 'Our fathers worshipped on this mountain, and you [the Jews] say that in Jerusalem is the place where one ought to worship.'[23]

In later years, the apostle Paul wrote concerning some who persisted in querying his doctrine of justification and, indeed, that of election.[24] Experience and Scripture alike indicate that the hardened heart will never accept the word of God as it stands and will usually blame the Lord for its personal woes and for those of the world. Ezekiel's constituency was of a similar vein. When confronted by the demand for repentance, they ruffled themselves about alleged flaws in divine justice.

For those of us who cannot always interpret the ways of God, let Psalm 131 be our guide.

Lord, my heart is not haughty,
Nor my eyes lofty.
Neither do I concern myself with great matters,
Nor with things too profound for me.
Surely I have calmed and quieted my soul,
Like a weaned child with his mother;
Like a weaned child is my soul within me.
O Israel, hope in the LORD
From this time forth and for ever.[25]

Part 2:
From 'the twelfth year of our exile, on the tenth, on the fifth day of the month'

12. The twelfth series of prophecies

(Ezekiel 33:21 – 39:29)

Focus: concerning chapters 34 – 39

This commentary takes the view that chapters 34 – 39 are in substance an extended prediction and exposition of the ultimate renewal of ethnic Israel prior to the end of the world. As the writer sees it, they show that the blessedness of this people will come to fruition at what for us in the early twenty-first century is still a future time, and will be of a magnitude far greater than, say, that of Solomon's kingdom at its zenith. Trial, tribulation and redemption lead to glory.

In outline, Israel is to be delivered from those wicked shepherds — their kings and other leaders — who had ravaged the flock for their own selfish purposes. The Lord will care for his people through his servant David, the good shepherd whom he will send (34:1-31). Because Edom, the ancestral enemy, attacked Israel when she was unable to protect herself at the time of the Babylonian invasion, the land of Edom is to become a perpetual wilderness (35:1-15).

Accordingly, the time must be when the land of Israel shall prosper. The people, recalled from the nations, will be renewed in heart and multiplied numerically. They will delight in honouring the Lord's commandments and prosper in what will be a veritable Eden (36:1-38).

Previously, the sword had devastated the house of Israel, which resembled dead men's bones littering a field of battle. Now the dreadful scene is reversed. Restored to life, the people enjoy peace with God and peace among one another, dwelling in the land under the sovereignty of 'David'. The degree of harmony is such that internal division, typified by the ancient hostility between the northern and southern kingdoms, will be a thing of the past: Israel will be one nation under God.

Between Yahweh and Israel an eternal covenant of peace will operate, established in such a fashion that a formerly erring people will never repudiate it. The sanctuary of the Lord will remain among them (37:1-28).

But troublesome times are not past. After Israel has been restored both geographically and spiritually, Yahweh brings against them a tyrant identified as 'Gog'. A warrior from the land of 'Magog', he commits himself to the annihilation of Israel — yet fails in spectacular fashion. Along with his armies, he is destroyed supernaturally rather than by the outcome of human conflict.

The wisdom bringing this final catastrophe into play is that Israel is to be justified by the Lord her God in the presence of the whole world. In the light of what Yahweh had done in the past and has now done at the end time, all men realize that throughout the ages the one God had maintained a covenant relationship with Israel. They perceive that the sufferings of Jacob's family were inflicted by Yahweh on account of that family's numerous sins, and not because the Lord was incapable of defending them against other nations or had repudiated them finally. The latter are aware that God has renewed and upheld them, and acknowledge that there is no God like Yahweh (38:1 – 39:29).

In short, chapters 34 – 37 predict the spiritual and geographical restoration of Israel,[1] and chapters 38 –

39 promise that Israel will be vindicated as his own by Yahweh. All this will come about through their own sanctification *and* by the destruction of all who are hostile.

We shall comment on these chapters as they stand and then try to interpret them in the light of the New Testament and with particular reference to the last book of the Bible, the Revelation.

Earlier in this commentary it was observed that in Ezekiel's day many Jews relied upon their flawed understanding of the irrevocability of the unilateral covenant between Yahweh and Abraham (see 33:24). It is true, of course, that nearly a thousand years before the time of Ezekiel this covenant had led to the commitment of Israel and Yahweh to each other at Sinai, yet over the centuries a rebellious people had made a nonsense of this commitment.

The rupture led to the dismemberment and then to the destruction of the kingdom. Not only did the Jews forfeit their tenure of the land, and not only were they denied the throne of David, but the reduction of the temple signalled that the Lord had departed from his people. It must have seemed to those who lacked discernment that Yahweh, seemingly unfaithful to his promises and apparently impotent to repel the armies of Babylon, was therefore inferior to the gods of that cruel empire.

However, as chapters 1 – 33 have shown, the problem lay with the people rather than with their God. Moses' law stipulated that the presence and blessing of the Lord would remain with Israel only if they honoured their commitment to that law.[2] Further, it appears that Moses appreciated that the bilateral covenant, or agreement, between Yahweh and Israel at Sinai would eventually fall to the ground because of the people's intransigence. Indeed, Deuteronomy 31 – 32 anticipates this.

But what if Israel were to return in penitence to the Lord? Significantly, Moses allowed that this would happen rather than being an enchanting mirage.[3] His confidence was no less firm than that of Paul as expressed in Romans 11:15-29.

Paradoxically, therefore, the theology upon which pre-exilic Israel had depended was flawless. What was wrong was the recalcitrance and ignorance of a people who vainly believed that as a nation they would never be removed from their land, come what may. What they neglected to consider was the principle that without true holiness they could never see the good hand of the Lord upon them or know his presence among them.

In other words, a millennium of disobedience from Sinai until the deportation to Babylon proved, if proof were needed, that obedient love for Yahweh had never been an attribute of a people redeemed from Egypt by their covenant God. Therefore, the pillars upon which Israel was established — tenure of the land, the throne of David and the presence of Yahweh (as exemplified by the Jerusalem temple) — having been brought to nothing by divine judgement, would never be re-erected while Israelite hearts remained obdurate. Now, in the aftermath of the Babylonian holocaust, Ezekiel's message is that the pillars will again stand, in that Israel shall be deemed and shall be made holy, and thereby be eligible to inherit the promises to the fathers.[4]

But the reader of the prophecy of Ezekiel has every right to ask when this might happen. In response, it cannot be that the book anticipates the return under Zerubbabel in the mid-sixth century BC. So, does Ezekiel point to the inauguration of the new covenant in the first Christian century — a covenant in which, according to Galatians 3:28, in Christ 'there is neither Jew nor Greek'? Israel never regained statehood until 1948, and to this day the vast majority of Jews, whether resident in the homeland or within the Diaspora, do not accept Jesus as the Messiah. It follows that either Ezekiel's volume anticipates the present Christian dispensation in which we find ourselves, or it relates to events that to date have not occurred. I believe that Romans 11:11-36 points in the latter direction.[5]

It is of interest that concerning this important question some commentators tend to be diffident or even silent. For instance, in his magisterial commentary upon the prophecy of Ezekiel, D. I. Block has little to say and, to the present writer at least, his virtual silence is almost audible.[6]

But not all authors are so reticent. Those who hold that at his second coming Christ 'will inaugurate a visible kingdom of righteousness that will encompass the whole earth'[7] have few problems with chapters 34 – 39, nor, indeed, with 40 – 48, all of which, it is believed, point towards a millennial kingdom of Christ on earth.[8]

Yet others offer a somewhat shy insistence upon the future conversion of the children of Abraham. Thus J. B. Taylor writes concerning the 'good shepherd' of chapter 34 that 'the context is the consummation of the present age and the opening of the new age'.[9] But he does not opt explicitly for a premillennial approach.

Although the writer of the present commentary does not identify with premillennialism, he believes (to repeat) that towards the end of the present age, the age of the new covenant, itself the fulfilment of the covenant with Abraham, the spiritually renewed family of Israel will gather in the land of promise. There they will serve their Messiah, our Lord Jesus Christ, this occurring before, and not after, the return of the Lord. 'King David' will be with his people in the land of promise, although not physically and visibly. God, being able and willing to graft them in again to the true olive, the non-racial, cosmopolitan church, will see to it.[10]

Ezekiel's renewed ministry (Ezekiel 33:21-33)

We are now at the turning point of Ezekiel's ministry. He learns from a messenger that Jerusalem has been destroyed, which is what Yahweh had told him previously.

1. The fall of Jerusalem (33:21-22)

33:21-22. And it was in the twelfth year of our exile, on the tenth, on the fifth day of the month, that there came to me a fugitive from Jerusalem, saying, 'The city is smitten.' Now the hand of Yahweh had been upon me in the evening before the fugitive had come, and he had opened my mouth before he came to me in the morning. So my mouth was opened and I was no longer dumb.

It is now the twelfth year of Jehoiachin's captivity and of Ezekiel's exile, the tenth month and the fifth day. This translates to 8 January 585 BC. Almost exactly three years earlier the Lord had informed the prophet that Nebuchadnezzar was commencing the siege of Jerusalem: 'And the word of Yahweh came to me in the ninth year, in the tenth month, in the tenth of the month, saying, "Son of man, write for yourself of the day, this selfsame day — the king of Babylon has invested Jerusalem on this selfsame day"', which itself translates to 15 January 588 BC.[11]

Therefore he entertained no doubts about the outcome of the Chaldean assault. Even as his wife would die suddenly, Jerusalem would unexpectedly (from the perspective of the exiles) fall (see 24:16,21). Suddenly, Ezekiel's predictions, and thereby his prophetic office, are vindicated. It will now be recognized by the exiles that the God whom he purports to represent has justified him.

Babylonian forces penetrated Jerusalem in the fifth month of the nineteenth year of Nebuchadnezzar, in 586 BC.[12] Ezekiel received the news of the final collapse on **'the morning'** of the **'fifth day'** of **'the tenth month'** of the **'twelfth year'** of his exile, that is, 8 January 585 BC, seventeen months later. Perhaps it is not surprising that a refugee from Jerusalem took such a considerable time to reach Mesopotamia.[13] Years later, when peace reigned, returning exiles took no less than four months in journeying from Babylon to Jerusalem.[14]

Late on the previous day the Lord had spoken to Ezekiel: **'the hand of Yahweh had been upon me in the evening before the fugitive had come'**. Apparently, it was then that the Lord **'opened** [his] **mouth'**, **'before he** [the messenger, possibly one of a new wave of deportees to Babylon] **came to me in the morning'**.[15] Now that the exiles were in receipt of irrefutable evidence that Jerusalem had been taken, Ezekiel was **'no longer dumb'**.

One can imagine the shock waves that must have reverberated throughout the Jewish community. For them, two words (in Hebrew) said it all: **'The city is smitten.'** Yet the focus rested upon Ezekiel rather than upon the people. We can almost visualize the sense of utter relief entertained by him. When matters are at their worst, the Lord is at his best, and the prophet could commence a new, positive ministry of hope (33:21-22).

2. The need for true repentance (33:23-29)

33:23-29. Then the word of Yahweh came to me, saying, 'Son of man, they who dwell in these wastes on the earth of Israel are saying, "Abraham was one, and he possessed the land. We are many, and to us the land has been given for a possession."

'Therefore, say to them, "Thus says the Lord Yahweh: 'You eat with blood in it and raise your eyes to your idols, and you pour out blood — and will you possess the land? You stand upon your swords, you commit abomination and you each defile his neighbour's wife — and will you possess the land?' Thus you will say to them, "Thus says the Lord Yahweh: 'As I live, whoever is in the waste places will fall by the sword, and whoever is upon the face of the field I shall give to animals for food, and they in the strongholds and the caves will die of plague. So I shall make the land desolate and a desolation, and the pride of her power will cease, and the mountains of Israel will be desolate so that none shall pass through. Then they will know that I am Yahweh, when I make the land desolate and a desolation because of all the abominations which they have committed.'"'

Yet even now, since the publication of the news concerning the destruction of Jerusalem, all was far from well. Both the ones who survived in Judah (33:23-29) and the exiles (33:30-33) were for the most part recalcitrant; they had no genuine desire to hear and to respond to true prophecy.

Concerning those left behind in Judah, they imagined that they would remain in possession of the land by virtue of some sort of mechanical fulfilment of the promise given to Abraham, of whom they deemed themselves to be worthy descendants. They considered that their survival since the Babylonian invasion demonstrated the good hand of the Lord upon them. It followed that, even if the temple had been consigned to the flames, it was inconceivable that God would permit the land of promise to be bereft of his people. Therefore, those who were left, for the most part agricultural labourers and not numbering more than a few thousands, must remain in possession.[16]

As we try to project ourselves into the situation in Judah two and a half millennia ago, it seems likely that, with none to resist them, such people were seizing unoccupied properties, considering that they had squatters' rights and that possession was at least nine tenths of the law.

Their spurious theology of inheritance, for them the icing on the cake, was based upon the undoubted fact that whereas **'Abraham was one'**, a solitary man, they, his natural children and allegedly his heirs,[17] were relatively many. This being so, they would be in a position to overcome any hazards that might come their way. The rationale for this fallacy was that the Lord was obligated to honour them because of their virtuous father: **'We are many, and to us the land has been given for a possession.' 'The word of Yahweh'** informed Ezekiel in Babylonia about what the survivors were **'saying'** so confidently (33:23-24).

Their empty claim was astonishing, given that Judah had been ravaged time and again by marauders and that it had now fallen under military occupation. One is reminded of the Pharisees who bragged to Jesus that because they were the seed of Abraham they had never been enslaved to anyone.[18] Yet at the time they and their land were under the Roman boot.

The Lord responded, and Ezekiel was summoned to speak **'to them'**, to the survivors in Judah. Whether or not his words were transmitted westwards is unknown, but among the exiles the impact of his warning must have been considerable.

Ezekiel had to make clear that although Abraham was a man of faith,[19] the inhabitants of Judah were of a different calibre, persisting in their sinful ways and knowing nothing of repentance and faith. They **'eat**

with blood in it',[20] meaning that they consumed butchered flesh that had not been drained.[21] Moreover, they chose to **'raise** [their] **eyes to** [their] **idols, and ... pour out** [innocent] **blood'**. Murder and idolatry went hand in hand. Would they **'possess the land?'** By no means (33:25).

And they had stood **'upon** [their] **swords'**, meaning that they were criminally violent. The assassination of Gedaliah and a further deportation by Nebuzaradan,[22] presumably because of Jewish unrest, illuminate Yahweh's word. Adultery was not unusual, together with a general rejection of common decency. In that such sins had brought judgement upon Jerusalem (cf. 18:10-13; 22:6-12), again the cry rings out: **'Will you possess the land?'** (33:26). The answer must have been obvious.

Yahweh swears by himself — **'as I live'** — that those who inhabit already desolated areas must **'fall by the sword'**. Here there may be a play on two Hebrew words, standing respectively for **'waste places'** and for **'sword'**, both deriving from the root *hrb*. Because the two are spelt and pronounced almost identically, there is a suggestion that the wilderness *is* effectively a devouring sword. Those who remain on **'the face of the field'** — by which is meant the open countryside — will be ravaged by beasts, and those who hide in **'caves'** and rocky **'strongholds'** must perish from disease. Nor was the threat of wild animals new.[23] The arrogance of these people must come to an end and the land be desolated. Having failed to learn from the destruction of Jerusalem, they will come to know by sad experience that Yahweh is truly the **'Lord'** (33:27).

One might suspect that Nebuchadnezzar's invasion of Judah had brought desolation enough. But apparently not: what that tyrant had commenced, other, unnamed predators will complete. Given the hardness of heart of the Jewish survivors, their land will be depopulated in that **'none shall pass through'**. Their boast that they descended from Abraham will prove to be in vain. The **'land'** that they were claiming as their own by right of inheritance will be **'desolate and a desolation because of all the abominations which they have committed'** (33:28-29).

To the extent that Ezekiel does no more than announce the fulfilment of the warnings of Moses' law, his predictions do not refer to his time only. They would apply to any future apostasy. The conclusion cannot be avoided that the historic destruction of Jerusalem and the consequent scattering of the Jews in AD 70 were the principal and (perhaps) final example. Then the Jews rejected the Messiah of whom Moses had spoken so eloquently.

3. Ezekiel the minstrel (33:30-33)

33:30-33. 'And you, son of man, the sons of your people are speaking to one another about you by the walls and by the entrances of the houses, and one speaks to another, each man to his brother, saying, "Come, now, and hear what word is coming forth from Yahweh." So they come to you as people will come, and my people sit before you and hear your words — but they do not do them, for they act with lustfulness in their mouths; their heart goes after their gain. And, look, you are to them like a sensual song of one who has a beautiful voice and who plays well; for they hear your words but they are not practising them. So when it comes (look, it is coming), then they will know that a prophet was in their midst.'

There can be little doubt that by now Ezekiel had acquired a certain status among his fellow-exiles. Time was when they had not been pleased to hear him and when the prophet had to strengthen himself against their opposition (3:7-9), even though during the first phase of his ministry he was approached by the elders and others and had communicated with them (8:1; 11:25; 12:21-28; 14:1-3; 20:1). Now they have been compelled to accept that his predictions concerning the fall of Jerusalem had been fulfilled and that he was a prophet sent from Yahweh. Accepting condescendingly that he was a man not entirely unworthy of their attention, they were graciously allocating him some of their time, acknowledging that the Lord continued to speak through him now that Jerusalem was no more. There was a show of faith.

The Lord warns his servant to be on his guard, in that the respect granted to him by his hearers was contrived. Although Ezekiel might well have been a topic for discussion both at home and in public, the people enjoyed rather than appreciated his eloquence and bizarre deeds (remember the acted signs of chapters 4; 5; 12; 24), the messenger being far more interesting than the message. **'By the walls and by the entrances of the houses'** suggests that he never lacked a congregation. Their crude sarcasm is evident: **'Come, now, and hear what word is coming forth from Yahweh'** (33:30).

Apparently, they were granted admission to Ezekiel's house, where they sat together in his presence as if they really were the people of God, **'as people will come'**, giving every appearance of being engrossed. But it was a sham.

The Lord informs Ezekiel that appearances had been deceptive in that his ministry was falling upon closed ears and because these people will refuse to act upon what he tells them. What they do want to discuss seriously is the acquisition of further material profit: **'their heart goes after their gain'** (33:31). By comparing this passage with 22:13,27, it is obvious that they were no better than those rulers in Jerusalem who had been swept away by the tide of war.

At best Ezekiel is like a singer of **'a sensual song'** (literally, 'song of loves'), gifted with a pleasant voice and with the ability to handle an instrument **'well'**. Nowadays, pop singers tend to celebrate one theme only, and normally in a debased manner. It seems that his hearers estimated Ezekiel in this fashion, switching off when he had hard things to say and treating him as no more than an entertainment.[24] When the performance was over, and when their ears had been tickled pleasurably, they would disperse and return to normal business. The picture is vivid, and we can readily understand it: although music and lyrics are core entertainment for the masses, they are never taken seriously, the top tune and its singer being soon forgotten because they are only a temporary diversion. Ezekiel was a passing voice that men of sense would not allow to affect their lives (33:32).

How embarrassing for the prophet! Yet he is assured by Yahweh that his warnings cannot be in vain, for which reason Ezekiel must persist in his ministry. One day **'it'** will come, and then men will appreciate fully that he was a prophet (33:33; cf. 2:5).

But what would 'it' be? Because Jerusalem was no more, what further affliction could the exiles expect? In that up to this point Leviticus 26 has played such a large part in Ezekiel's ministry, perhaps there is a veiled allusion to Leviticus 26:36-39, which anticipates that impenitent Israelite exiles will rot away in the lands of their enemies.

This penetrating word of the Lord to Ezekiel concerning his people was sad yet realistic. It served as an introduction to what this commentary will argue are the largely unfulfilled prophecies of chapters 34 – 39.

There is one further point. Yahweh was good to Ezekiel in that he reminded him about the sullen unbelief of the congregation. This meant that the prophet would be able to count the cost of his future ministry beforehand instead of embarking on a fool's errand, hoping for revival when it would probably never come. In Babylonia, as in the homeland, the Jews refused to read the signs of the times. Ezekiel still had to contend with an apostate people.

Application

As in chapter 18, it is asserted that the Lord never rejoices in the death of the sinner (33:11). This principle reverberates throughout the Bible: it is the chief glory of God to forgive. Christ was born to save, and for this he died and was triumphant. Let every pulpit tell out that the living Christ receives sinners.

Salvation is by grace through faith.[25] God does not, and we should not, base our prospects in the world to come by constructing a balance sheet in which a surplus of alleged good deeds are weighed against what we know to be wrong in our lives. The whole issue rests upon the desires and attitude of the heart. If we want to fear and serve God and show this by turning to his Son, we shall be saved — even if our sins are as scarlet.[26]

Although the person who has godly parents has much for which to be thankful, he must never think that he will be saved because of them, or because, say, he had been surrounded by a church in his earlier years. Ezekiel tells us that not all the natural children of Abraham are the children of God (33:24-29).[27] We must be born again, an ultimate experience in which family background and a track record of notional good deeds are irrelevant.[28]

It is possible for godly ministers to attract to themselves superficially appreciative hearers who remain in unbelief. Let pastoral and pulpit success be estimated privately in terms of faithfulness to the ministerial commission. In his initial call to the prophetic ministry, Ezekiel was warned about opposition (2:1-8); now he is warned about popularity. The one is as dangerous as the other.

From the point of view of the pew, those who place themselves under a faithful ministry owe it to their minister, to themselves, and ultimately to the Lord, to respond positively to what they hear, even if it means conversion and baptism. To illustrate: the writer of this commentary was once informed by a group of young Jews in

Jerusalem that they wanted to come to church to listen to him, but that they would *never* be baptized! They did, in fact, turn up — but that was all. Yahweh's sad diagnosis of the people in 2:3 – 3:15 remained valid until after the destruction of Jerusalem at a later time (cf. 33:30-33). Apparently, over the years many who were pleased to hear Ezekiel never turned to his God. But, for all that, he was no failure.

The good shepherd (Ezekiel 34:1-31)

This prediction builds on Jeremiah 23:1-6, a somewhat earlier prophecy which seems to have been before Ezekiel's eyes when he considered the theme of the good shepherd. Compare also Isaiah 11:1-2 and the later Zechariah 3:8 and 6:12. The point that needs to be made is that Ezekiel, a link in a chain of predictive prophecy, amplifies and does not innovate.

Jeremiah looked forward to the advent of 'a righteous branch', a scion of the house of David, someone altogether unlike the faithless shepherds of Israel. He would govern wisely, grant safety and would be considered as 'Yahweh our righteousness'.[29]

When mulling over the words of his near-contemporary, Ezekiel divided chapter 34 into three distinct sections.

Firstly, 34:1-10 denounces the wicked shepherds from whose rapacious hands the Lord rescues the flock.

Secondly, 34:11-22 tells that Yahweh himself intends to pastor his own sheep, these being Jews settled within the land of Israel: Yahweh will be to them what the evil shepherds never were.

Thirdly, 34:23-31 announces that the good shepherd is to be manifested in the person of 'David', the servant and agent of Yahweh. He cares for them, and they, the sheep of Yahweh's pasture, live safely in a fruitful and pleasant land.

1. The evil shepherds (34:1-10)

34:1-10. Then the word of Yahweh came to me, saying, 'Son of man, prophesy against the shepherds of Israel. Prophesy, and you will say to them, to the shepherds, "Thus says the Lord Yahweh, 'Ho, shepherds of Israel who tend themselves — should not the shepherds tend the flock? You eat the fat and clothe yourselves with the wool; you slaughter the fat sheep; you do not tend the flock. You have not strengthened the weak, and the sick you have not healed; you have not bound up the injured and have not brought back the stray, nor have sought the lost. But with force you have dominated them, and with harshness. So they have been scattered for lack of a shepherd, and they came to be food for every animal of the field, and they have been scattered. My flock goes astray through all the mountains and on every high hill, and my flock is scattered on all the face of the earth, and none seeks for them and none enquires for them.'

'"'Therefore, shepherds, hear the word of Yahweh. 'As I live,' declares the Lord Yahweh, 'surely because my flock has become a prey and my flock has come to be food for every animal of the field for lack of a shepherd, and my shepherds did not seek my flock, but the shepherds tended themselves and did not tend my flock — therefore, shepherds, hear the word of Yahweh.' Thus says the Lord Yahweh: 'Look, I am against the shepherds and shall seek my flock from their hand and shall stop them from tending the flock. So the shepherds will no longer tend them, and I shall deliver my flock from their mouth so that they will no longer be to them for food.'"'

Yet again, **'the word of Yahweh'** came to the **'son of man'**. Notwithstanding a long and faithful ministry that had been validated in every way, he was still a weak, frail man — and was not allowed to forget it. Although these words are undated, they may follow 33:21 chronologically.

Ezekiel is instructed to **'prophesy against the shepherds of Israel'**, undoubtedly the kings of Judah and the civil authorities, as distinct from the prophets and priests.[30] According to Jeremiah 23:1-6, the David yet-to-be, by implication the shepherd of his nation, will be a king rather than a prophet or priest, and the one whom Ezekiel predicts will be their prince as well as their shepherd (see 34:24). Clearly, Jeremiah and Ezekiel point to the same individual.

Thus Ezekiel is required to summon the attention of those who **'tend themselves'**. Should they not **'tend the flock'**? Although conventional shepherds do not lack in that sheep provide for humans, these metaphorical 'shepherds' ought to labour for the sake of their sheep. The kings of Judah had forgotten this principle. As noted by M. C. Lind, 'Ezekiel uses his opened mouth to begin his renewed ministry with a saying on liberation — a liberation not from Israel's traditional enemies but from Israel's kings!' (34:1-2).[31]

The indictment of selfishness is expanded. The false shepherds **'eat the fat'** (or 'milk', consonantal *hlb* meaning both), **'clothe'** themselves with **'the wool'** and kill **'the fat sheep'**. This could be coded language: over the years an impoverished people had been inflicted by judicial murder (34:3).

Negatively, the shepherds had shown no concern for the needs of the flock. The **'weak'** were not **'strengthened'**; the **'sick'** had not been **'healed'**; the **'injured'** had not been tended; and those who were **'stray'**, or even **'lost'**, had not been recovered. They had been governed **'with harshness'** (34:4). The books of the Kings expound the tragedy.

The disastrous consequences are outlined. **'Scattered'** occurs three times to indicate that Israel had become easy prey **'for every animal of the field'**, by which is meant the hostile nations surrounding the twelve tribes. Worse, in that the people were not simply sheep but were **'my flock'**, the rulers outraged

Yahweh, who had seen fit to establish the throne of David.[32] Not only did they not care, displaying a cruelty towards poor Israelites prohibited by Leviticus 25:43,46, but no one else could help (34:5-6).

The assertion that Israel is **'my flock'** resonates throughout the passage (six times in verses 6-8). Because the welfare of Israel is Yahweh's responsibility, he must react — and he will. Therefore the rulers, **'my** [i.e. Yahweh's] **shepherds'**, are compelled to hear his **'word'**. Since his sheep have become a **'prey'** and **'food for every animal of the field'**, in that they received no pastoral care, but have suffered under gross misgovernment,[33] Yahweh places himself under oath — **'as I live'** introducing a statement of intent (34:7-8).

Again, the **'shepherds'** are required to **'hear the word of Yahweh'**. Since Zedekiah and Jehoiachin had been deported to Babylon,[34] it must have seemed to the Jews of the time that the throne of David could never be restored and that it was the end for the monarchy. Or would it be? In that the kings of Judah had transformed themselves from shepherds to predators devouring Yahweh's **'flock'**, the tragic experience must never be repeated. It is implied that the demolition of 586 BC was nothing other than an essential groundwork for a new beginning. David's line will not vanish for ever (34:9-10).

2. The Lord recovers the lost sheep (34:11-15)

34:11-15. '"For thus says the Lord Yahweh: 'Look, it is I, and I shall seek my flock and shall look for them. Just as a shepherd inspects his drove on the day when he is among his dispersed flock, thus I shall inspect my flock and shall rescue them from all the places where they have been scattered in a day of cloud and dark gloom. And I shall bring them out from the peoples, shall gather them from the lands and shall bring them to their own land, and I shall tend them upon the mountains of Israel, in the valleys and in all the inhabited places of the land. I shall tend them in a good pasture and their habitation will be on the mountain heights of Israel. There they will lie down in a good habitation and will feed in a lush pasture, upon the mountains of Israel. I myself shall tend my flock and I shall make them to lie down,' declares the Lord Yahweh."'

Considered under the figure of a flock of sheep, Israel still needs someone to lead and guide. Yahweh introduces himself as that person: **'Look, it is I.'** In that the wicked shepherds have not protected the Lord's flock, Yahweh will assume the responsibility because he cares. In the Hebrew text the first person singular, **'I'** and **'my'**, occurs fourteen times in verses 11-15, occasionally in emphatic form, as in verse 15, **'I myself'**, in order to highlight the divine initiative. The Lord will **'look for'** his **'flock'**, possibly in the manner that a priest would examine a leper,[35] or like the harlot of 1 Kings 3:21 who examined her child. The good shepherd will want to ascertain the state of his sheep and then come to their aid (34:11).[36]

Displaying intense concern for the sheep's welfare, he retrieves **'his drove'**[37] from where, vulnerable to hostile nations, they had been dispersed in a **'day of cloud and dark gloom'**, possibly the period of deportation to Babylon (34:12).

Yahweh brings his forlorn people out **'from the lands'** to **'their own land'**. There, **'upon the mountains of Israel'**, he proposes to **'tend them ... in the valleys and in all the inhabited places'**.

Three of the four pillars of an ideal Israel are being put back into place: the land, the people and the presence of the sovereign and compassionate Yahweh. Only the throne of David remains unmentioned (34:13).

All the needs of the sheep are to be met by the Lord personally: **'I shall tend them.'** Within the land **'of Israel'**, their situation will be most comfortable. The employment of the first person singular is intended to show that because the former shepherds had routinely failed to serve their God in not caring for his sheep, they had been removed (34:14).

The section ends with a delightful promise: **'I myself shall tend my flock and I shall make them to lie down.'** It is as if the Lord pacifies each sheep in the flock in such a way that, relieved from anxiety, it lies down peacefully. **'The Lord Yahweh'** declares that it shall be so (34:15).

3. Justice (34:16-22)

34:16-22. '"'I shall seek the lost and shall bring back the stray; I shall bind up the wounded and shall strengthen the sick. But the fat and the strong I shall destroy: I shall shepherd them with judgement. But as for you, my flock,' thus says the Lord Yahweh: 'Look, I judge between one sheep and another, between the rams and the he-goats. Is it too small a thing for you that you graze on the good pasture and the rest of your pastures you trample with your feet? Or that you drink from the clear waters and the rest you foul with your feet? And as for my flock, they feed on what your feet have trampled and drink from what your feet have fouled.'

'"Therefore, thus says the Lord Yahweh to them: 'Look, I, even I, shall judge between the fat sheep and the lean sheep. Because you push with the flank and the shoulder and you gore all the sick with your horns until you have scattered them abroad, I shall save my flock, and they will no longer be for a prey; and I shall judge between one sheep and another.'"'

What the earlier shepherds, alias the rulers of Judah, had not done (34:4), Yahweh will himself do. **'The**

lost' will be sought; the **'stray'** will be recovered; **'the wounded'** will be tended; and **'the sick'** will be made strong. Further, if some of the sheep turn out to be **'fat'** and **'strong'**, they are to be destroyed (34:16). Here fatness and strength would denote aggression and cupidity, possibly among the nobility and within the commercial sector. The love of Yahweh is discerning, yoked inextricably with justice. Righteousness will reign along with mercy.

Addressing the flock directly, Yahweh announces that he will **'judge'** among the sheep and the goats. Although it would be easy to conclude that Jesus' words in Matthew 25:32-33, concerning the final separation of the sheep and the goats, are an allusion to the passage, this is almost certainly not the case. Ezekiel's meaning seems to be that among the restored flock of Yahweh, cruelty and injustice are not to be permitted. The prophet is not referring to a terminal, eschatological judgement.

There had been much cruelty in Israel in days when the rulers' misconduct was imitated by their wealthy cronies. But in a restored Israel matters will be different: overweight sheep will be unable to victimize sickly animals within the pasture (34:17).

Not content with satisfying their own needs, the bullies in the flock had carelessly downtrodden the poor and defenceless. **'Is it too small a thing for you'** to **'trample'** the **'pastures'** of others and **'foul'** their **'waters ... with your feet'**? Yahweh cannot but respond in indignation (34:18).

And these others were Yahweh's **'flock'**, compelled to feed from **'trampled'** pastures and to drink from contaminated water. The present tenses **'feed'** and **'drink'** indicate that it was still so, presumably in post-destruction Judah (34:19).

Yahweh's verdict is followed up by personal intervention: **'Look, I, even I, shall judge between the fat sheep and the lean sheep.'** This does not mean that the Lord will examine these issues in court. Rather, because he knows where guilt lies he will remove the oppressors (34:20).

The flock of Yahweh had been afflicted by bad leaders (the kings) and by evil members (the nobility and merchant classes). All shared joint responsibility for the destruction of the theocracy of Judah and had **'scattered'** the people **'abroad'** to Babylon. Therefore Yahweh, who cannot abdicate his responsibility, intends to **'save** [his] **flock'**. They will be restored to the land promised to the fathers, will be invulnerable to attack from without their borders and will be at peace among themselves (34:21-22).

At this point we arrive at what might seem to be an anomaly. The complete section, 34:1-22, implies that Yahweh himself will pastor the people of Israel. Nevertheless, neither in this prophecy nor in the parallel Jeremiah 23:1-6 is the Lord described explicitly as the shepherd, even though he leads his flock and acts as a responsible pastor would (see 34:12,15). The tension demands a resolution, and we are given it in the following verses.

4. David: the good shepherd (34:23-31)

34:23-31. '"'Then I shall raise up a single shepherd over them and he will tend them — even my servant David. He will tend them and he will be a shepherd for them. And I, Yahweh, shall be God to them and my servant David will be prince in their midst. I, Yahweh, have spoken. Then I shall cut a covenant of peace for them and shall eliminate the evil beast from the land, and they will dwell securely in the wilderness and sleep in the forests. And I shall set them and the places around my hill a blessing, and shall send down the shower in its season — they will be showers of blessing.

'"'Also, the tree of the field will give its fruit and the land will give its produce, and they will be secure upon their earth and will know that I am Yahweh when I break the bars of their yoke and deliver them from the hand of those who enslave them. Then they will no longer be a prey for the nations, and the animals of the land will not devour them. So they will dwell securely with none causing terror.

'"'Then I shall establish for them a renowned planting-place, and they will not again be drawn away for famine in the land and will not again bear the reproach of the nations. So they will know that I am Yahweh their God with them, and that they are my people — the house of Israel,' declares the Lord Yahweh. 'And you are my flock, the sheep of my pasture — you are men; I, your God,' declares the Lord Yahweh."'

The flow of thought tells us that when resettling the people of God, his 'flock', Yahweh will **'raise up a single shepherd over them and he will tend them — even my servant David'**. We are told much about him.

Firstly, Israel will be a true theocracy, controlled by Yahweh through the ministry of his servant.

Secondly, **'servant'** points to an individual rather than being a collective term. The sometimes very rapid succession of kings, both in the northern kingdom of Israel and in that of Judah to the south, will be no more. Nor, by implication, will there be any internal political division. It will be as in the time when David ruled the united twelve tribes.

Thirdly, the shepherd-to-come will be **'David'**.[38] In his person he will embody the promise to the son of Jesse that his throne would endure.[39]

Fourthly, the future 'David' will be the **'servant'** of Yahweh, an assertion intended to mark him off from those failed 'shepherds' of the Lord (cf. 34:8).

Fifthly, **'my servant David will be prince'**. It is likely that the term 'king' is not used, and for both of two reasons: to recall 1 Kings 11:34, which states that Solomon had been appointed a 'prince' for the sake of his father David, and in order to create space between the new 'David' and the degenerate kings of Israel and Judah.

Sixthly, the prince will embody the presence of God among his people, **'in their midst'**.[40] Their God will not be an inaccessible tyrant like Ahasuerus.[41]

Thus the covenants with Abraham and with David will not be forgotten, in that the people, the land, the presence of Yahweh and David's princely offspring will be components within the new settlement.[42]

The effect of these words upon Ezekiel's immediate hearers must have been dramatic. They had learned of the fall of the house of David, had known that an implacable enemy was devouring their land and were aware that there was no legitimate temple for their God anywhere upon the face of the earth. Now a prophet whose credentials have been abundantly verified by the fulfilment of his earlier predictions tells them that a good shepherd will occupy David's throne and will care for the family of Israel (34:23-24).

'Then', when Yahweh establishes 'David' the shepherd, he will **'cut a covenant of peace for them'** — that is, for the flock over which 'David' presides. The two events will be synchronous.

The expression **'covenant of peace**' occurs in Numbers 25:12, which narrates the award of such a covenant to Phinehas and his descendants in consideration of that priest's activity in atoning for the sin of Israel. And Isaiah 54:1-10 announces that Yahweh will never again remove his 'covenant of peace' from Israel.[43] The common factor appears to be that, no longer being wrathful, Yahweh purposes to maintain his favour towards the objects of his pleasure.[44]

Verses 25-30 recall Leviticus 26:3-13, which tells of the blessings that the people will receive in their land 'if' they are obedient to Yahweh. It would appear that Ezekiel had this passage much in his mind. But there is an important difference. Now Yahweh establishes his 'covenant of peace' unilaterally, not waiting for the people to fulfil the condition of obedience, the 'if' of Leviticus 26:3 not being reflected.

The certain inference is that at this stage in its national existence Israel will already be a regenerate nation, by definition qualifying for the benefits promised by Leviticus 26:3-13. Were the people disobedient, they would not be favoured with the divine covenant. As it is, the Lord will **'eliminate the evil beast from the land, and they will dwell securely in the wilderness and sleep in the forests'** (34:25). All this is a résumé of the blessings consequent upon obedience listed in Leviticus 26.

The **'hill'** of Yahweh, around which there will be **'blessing'**, is the land of promise rather than Mount Zion.[45] Since the curses of Leviticus 26:19-20 and Deuteronomy 28:23-24 are no more, God, nature and the people are in happy equilibrium (34:26).

Israel dwells safely in a fruitful land, realizing with delight and thankfulness that Yahweh is their God in that he breaks **'the bars of their yoke'** of servitude to other nations and has delivered them from violent hands. There is a direct allusion here to Leviticus 26:13 and the deliverance of Israel from Egypt. Now there is to be a new exodus, after which neither the pharaohs nor any other potentates will oppress the people of God in their own happy land (34:27).

It is implied that Israel had at one time been surrendered to the power of the nations because of the infidelity and cruelty of the evil shepherds of David's family. But never again. The people **'will dwell securely with none causing terror'** (34:28).

And the Lord will **'establish for them a renowned planting-place'** (literally 'a plantation for a name'),[46] meaning that Yahweh will make the land so fertile that those who work it will be renowned. **'Famine'**, which would attract the **'reproach'** of surrounding **'nations'**, will be unknown (34:29). Ezekiel appears to recall

Deuteronomy 26:19, which, like Leviticus 26:3-6, promises the blessings of God in the event of Israel's full obedience.

And by grace they *are* obedient. The Lord expounds the intimacy of the anticipated relationship between the people and him. They will **'know'** that he is **'their God'** and that they are his **'people'**, his **'flock'** in his **'pasture'**. Yet in his proximity God remains transcendent: **'you are men; I, your God'**.[47] Yahweh proclaims that it shall be so (34:30-31).

Application

The principal theme of this chapter is the faithfulness of Israel's God in honouring the promises to Abraham and his family, in fulfilling the ideals of Leviticus 26:1-13,44-45 and Deuteronomy 4:6-8; 28:1-14, and in raising up a shepherd from the family of David to lead the flock. The links between the Lord, the land and the people of Israel had been sundered because of their sin and by Babylonian invasion, but they shall be restored. Moreover, Israel will be spiritually renewed within the land, being the beneficiary of a covenant other than and prior to that of Sinai.

Gentile believers already participate in that covenant of peace, as do believing Jews.[48] But the present author believes that there will be a new dawn for the natural family of Abraham, a people residing within their own inherited land, who own Jesus as the Messiah, and who will prove to be of incalculable benefit to the world at large.[49]

The condemnation of Edom and blessing for Israel (Ezekiel 35:1 – 36:38)

Chapters 35:1 – 36:38 form one interconnected prophecy, including a condemnation of the mountains of Edom (35:1-15) and a promise of blessings upon the mountains of Israel (36:1-38). The link between the two sections is shown by Ezekiel's statements that **'the word of Yahweh'** came to him to prophesy **'towards'**, or against, **'Mount Seir'** (35:2) and then to prophesy in favour of **'the mountains of Israel'** (36:1).

Like the prophet Obadiah more than two centuries earlier, Ezekiel has already predicted, albeit briefly, the fall of Edom, the territory of Esau, the brother and enemy of Jacob who lived in the land of Seir (25:12-14).[50] But now Ezekiel has more to say: the destruction of Edom is presented as a foil intended to bring into bold relief the ultimate prosperity of Israel.[51]

The prophet tells that the devastation of the family of Edom is essential if Israel is to rise: the collapse of the former is intertwined with the resurgence of the latter, the victory of the one presuming the defeat of the other. When restored and renewed, Israel will know that Yahweh is the God of the covenant (34:30), and Edom will accept that it is so. This will be achieved not by the salvation of Edom, but through the just retribution executed by the Lord upon that people (35:15).

Throughout this commentary note has been taken of the many occasions when Yahweh predicts that he will bless his true people and curse those who are their, and therefore his, opponents, whether they stem from within Israel or from the surrounding nations. Again and again it is stated by Ezekiel that salvation and condemnation alike will lead men to know that Yahweh is. The repetitive formula is that 'you [or 'they'] will know that I am Yahweh'.

The grand strategy to be accomplished by the twin processes of salvation and judgement is that Yahweh is shown to be the God who chose his people and who would never abandon them. Because no man can finally evade the reality of Israel's God, the whole book is a challenge to its reader to reconcile himself to Yahweh.

Edom, then, is offered as the representative of the world's undying hostility to the Lord and his people. This would appear to be borne out by 36:5, where Edom is paralleled with the **'rest of the nations'**. Corroboration is given by Isaiah 34 and 63:1-6, which consider Edom in a similar fashion.

This race had always hated Israel. The psalmist begs the Lord to remember what the Edomites did on the day when Jerusalem fell to Nebuchadnezzar.[52] Amos 1:11-12 is indignant: 'Thus says Yahweh: "For three transgressions of Edom, and for four, I shall not turn away its punishment, because he pursued his brother with the sword."'

Ezekiel's doctrine is that all who oppose God's kingdom must fall, thus demonstrating that the purposes of Yahweh cannot be frustrated. Not even a family as closely related to Israel as Edom is an exception.

1. Yahweh is against Seir (35:1-15)

Ezekiel is instructed to turn his face **'towards'** Mount Seir, a region situated east of the Arabah and the rift valley extending south from the Dead Sea, and to prophesy **'against'** it. 'Against', which signifies hostility, is duplicated for emphasis (35:2,3). These people are indicted, firstly, because they attacked Judah when facing destruction (35:5); secondly, because they hoped to seize Israelite territory (35:10); and, thirdly, because they rejoiced over the desolation of Jerusalem (35:12-15). But they had forgotten that Jacob and his family were tenants and that Yahweh had never surrendered freehold ownership (35:10).[53]

I. The Lord is indignant (35:1-9)

35:1-9. Then the word of Yahweh came to me, saying, 'Son of man, set your face towards Mount Seir and prophesy against it. And you will say to it, "Thus says the Lord Yahweh: 'Look, I am against you, Mount Seir, and I shall stretch out my hand and I shall appoint you a desolation and a devastation. I shall make your cities a waste and you will be a desolation; then you will know that I am Yahweh.

'"'Because you have everlasting enmity and dragged away the sons of Israel to the hand of the sword at the time of their calamity, at the time of the end punishment, therefore, as I live,' declares the Lord Yahweh, 'I shall give you over to blood, and blood will pursue you. Because you hated blood, so blood will pursue you. So I shall appoint Mount Seir a desolation and a devastation and shall cut off him who comes and goes. And I shall fill its mountains with its slain; your hills and your valleys and all your ravines — those slain by the sword will fall in them. I shall make you an everlasting desolation and your cities will not be inhabited, and you will know that I am Yahweh.'"'

The **'son of man'**, instructed to **'set** [his] **face towards Mount Seir'**, must **'prophesy against it'**. The people of Edom are designated by the land they inhabit,[54] territory granted to Esau by Yahweh.[55] The Lord stretches his **'hand'** out upon them. Together with its cities, the area is to be desolate. Edom will then **'know that I am Yahweh'** (35:1-4). Why Yahweh is hostile to people living within their allocated borders will be revealed in the following verses.

In fact, divine antagonism derived from the age-old enmity entertained by Edom against Israel (literally, 'enmity of eternity'; cf. that of the Philistines, 25:15).[56] Ingrained hostility had driven them to stand by maliciously at the **'time of their calamity'**, at **'the end punishment'** (literally, 'the time of the final iniquity'), when the sins of Jerusalem brought the Chaldeans against that city. But although Israel had been commanded to treat the Edomites with respect because they were cousins,[57] Yahweh never purposed to maintain the family of Esau.[58] For this reason the Edomites will endure a just judgement (35:5).

It appears that they had been uneasy about the tragic spectacle of the destruction of Judah, suggesting to them that eventually they might not escape and that perhaps their own blood might flow. Ezekiel tells that their suspicions were not in vain: **'blood'** (Hebrew, *dam*), which they **'hated'**, will **'pursue'** them.[59] There is an ironic play on words here in that because 'Edom' means 'red', the punishment will fit the case (35:6).

Every inhabitant, as well as the traveller who **'comes and goes'**, will fade away. Nomadic tribes ferrying goods between Egypt and the East will be **'cut off'** to be seen no more. The land is to be **'a desolation and a devastation'** (35:7).

The entire region, **'mountains'**, **'hills'**, **'valleys'** and **'ravines'**, will be filled with the corpses of those who are **'slain by the sword'**. The prospect is frightful.

Edom becomes an **'everlasting desolation'** and its **'cities'** are no longer **'inhabited'**. When it is too late, this unfortunate people will acknowledge that Yahweh is truly God (35:8-9).

II. Greed cannot succeed (35:10-15)

35:10-15. '"'Because you have said, "The two nations and the two lands will belong to me and we shall possess it", even though Yahweh is there, therefore, as I live', declares the Lord Yahweh, 'I shall do according to your anger and according to your envy with which you acted in your hatred against them. So I shall make myself known among them even when I judge you.

'"'Then you will know that I, Yahweh, have heard all your insults which you have uttered against the mountains of Israel saying, "They are desolate; they have been granted to us for food." And you have magnified yourselves against me with your mouths and have multiplied your words against me — I have heard!'

'"'Thus says the Lord Yahweh: 'When all the land rejoices, I shall make you a desolation. As you rejoiced for the inheritance of the house of Israel because it was a desolation, thus I shall deal with you. You will be a desolation, Mount Seir and all Edom — all of it — and they will know that I am Yahweh.'"'

The prophet introduces further justification for the destruction of Edom: their intense longing to possess the land inherited by the formerly united kingdom of Israel, a territory more extensive than theirs, extending from Dan to Beer Sheba.

This insatiable desire persisted in spite of the fact that Edom always knew that **'Yahweh'** was **'there'** — that is, in Canaan (cf. 28:25; 37:25). That this territory had never been granted to Edom was never appreciated, even though the Lord had given the family of Jacob's brother the land of Seir.[60] Nor did they care to reflect that, although Yahweh had turned the land of Israel over to Nebuchadnezzar's sword, he had never given permission for any people to disinherit Jacob's descendants. On the contrary, if Yahweh has remonstrated with Jewish land-grabbers (cf. 11:15; 33:24), will he not resist Edomite efforts to take over what had never been theirs? In the event, hatred had prevailed over wisdom and, when the opportunity arose to smite brother Jacob, it was not lost. The ancient enmity was implacable (35:10).

Ezekiel's burden is that the Lord will execute a proportional judgement, **'according to your anger and according to your envy with which you acted in your hatred against them'**, making himself **'known among them'** — that is, among Israel — in the act of striking Edom. Then Israel will discover that their God does not allow his property and his people to be attacked with impunity (35:11).

And Edom will learn that Yahweh had overheard their **'insults'** when they claimed that the **'desolate'** land would at last become their bread basket. Yahweh's quotation of Edom's taunt suggests that this people had arrogated to themselves the right of primogeniture, reckoning the God of Isaac to have displaced Jacob as the firstborn:[61] **'the mountains of Israel ... have been granted** [by Yahweh] **to us for food'**. They could not have been more wrong (35:12).

Again, the Lord declares that he has **'heard'** what Edom had been saying. In deriding the people of Israel and the land, they were mocking the latter's divine benefactor: **'you ... have multiplied your words against me'**. Perhaps they thought that they would introduce their own deities as patrons of the land, forcing Yahweh to retreat in shame (35:13).

But the tables will be turned (cf. 35:11). **'When all the land rejoices,'** declares the Lord, **'I shall make you a desolation.' 'All the land'** might indicate either the land of Israel or the whole earth. Either way, all will witness the devastation of every enemy of Yahweh and of his people and their territory (35:14).

There is a final word for Edom. Eventually, **'Mount Seir and all Edom'** will be **'a desolation'**, a just recompense for those who **'rejoiced'** that **'the inheritance of the house of Israel'** had come to ruin. **'They will know that I am Yahweh'** (35:15).

2. Restoration: on Planet Earth, a transformed land and a renewed people (36:1-38)

This chapter seems to fall into four principal divisions. Firstly, verses 1-7 tell that, because surrounding nations, and pre-eminently Edom, had reproached Israel, so those nations must endure reproach.

Secondly, verses 8-15 expound the future prosperity of **'the mountains of Israel'** in that they are to be resettled by Yahweh's people.

Thirdly, verses 16-21 recall the past devastation of the land because of the sinfulness of its tenants, yet state that the freeholder, Yahweh, had never ceased to care for the land and its dispossessed people.

Finally, verses 22-38 declare that Yahweh will repopulate a renewed land in order to uphold the honour of his name in the presence of the nations and before his own restored people.

Promises of a new beginning for Israel were introduced in chapter 34 with the presentation of Yahweh as the good shepherd and of his 'servant David' as his agent. Chapter 35 was almost a parenthesis, demonstrating that the exaltation of the people of God must be accompanied by the downfall of their enemies.

Now Ezekiel anticipates the complete reorganization of the pillars of the Israelite theocracy — the people, the land and, above all else, the presence of Yahweh among his restored people.

I. The nations endure reproach (36:1-7)

36:1-7. 'And you, son of man, prophesy to the mountains of Israel. And you will say, "Mountains of Israel, hear the word of Yahweh. Thus says the Lord Yahweh: 'Because the enemy has said against you, "Aha! The everlasting heights have become our possession,"'" therefore prophesy. And you will say, "Thus says the Lord Yahweh: 'Because they have devastated and crushed you from all around so that you should be a possession for the rest of the nations, and that you have been taken up by the moving tongue and with the defamation of the people, therefore, mountains of Israel, hear the word of the Lord Yahweh.'

'"Thus says the Lord Yahweh to the mountains and to the hills, to the ravines and to the valleys, to the desolated wastes and to the abandoned cities that were for prey and for a derision to the rest of the nations that are round about.

'"Therefore, thus says the Lord Yahweh: 'Surely, with the fire of my jealousy I have spoken against the rest of the nations and against all Edom, they who appropriated my land for themselves for a possession with wholehearted joy and with soulful scorn, so that her territory might be for booty.'"

'Therefore, prophesy concerning the earth of Israel. And you will say to the mountains, to the hills, to the ravines and to the valleys, "Thus says the Lord Yahweh: 'Look, it is I. In my jealousy and in my wrath I have spoken because you have borne the ignominy of the nations.'" Therefore, "Thus says the Lord Yahweh: 'I myself have raised my hand that surely the nations which are around you — they will bear their ignominy.'"'

Ezekiel has already been summoned to address **'the mountains of Israel'** in order to announce their devastation by the Babylonian hordes in pursuance of ancient warnings (see 6:2). The plural **'mountains'** is employed because, unlike Seir, the topography of Canaan includes several ranges of hills. Now, he is instructed to do so again, but this time to tell them of the blessedness that will be theirs, unlike the devastation that will come upon 'Mount Seir' (36:1; cf. 35:2,7,15). The whole section is poignant, **'therefore'** occurring no less than five times, as if to stress the Lord's determined response to dramatically changed circumstances.

Israel's enemies had claimed that **'the everlasting heights'** would be theirs, possibly alluding to the blessing of Jacob in Genesis 49:26 and that of Moses in Deuteronomy 33:15, according to which Israel would for ever occupy the high ground. But the descendants of Esau, Jacob's elder brother, could not shake off the belief that they should, and therefore would, take possession (cf. 35:10). When Jerusalem had been destroyed they imagined that their time had come. Perhaps other nations had entertained similar delusions (36:2).

Thus Ezekiel is commanded to **'prophesy'**. **'Because'** is emphatic,[62] the background being that **'the rest of the nations'** surrounding Judah had sought to trample upon a land already ravaged by war. Therefore there must be a rejoinder from Yahweh. **'Defamation'** (*dibba*) means a bad report.[63] Superstitiously, aliens had asserted that the land was inherently evil, unable to sustain its Hebrew residents. But why, then, one might ask, were they so determined to enter into possession? In effect, they had calumniated the relationship between Yahweh, his people and his land, and therefore the veracity of Israel's God: in possession, they imagined they would fare better (36:3).

Yahweh responds most graciously to **'the mountains ... the hills ... the ravines and ... the valleys'** — by which is designated the complete territory of Israel. The Lord purposes to reverse the judgement announced by 6:3 in that he will not allow the land granted to the family of Jacob to remain **'a derision to the rest of the nations that are round about'** (36:4).

Ezekiel's vehemence continues. Because of the malignant and blasphemous hostility of the nations, the land and the people are to be justified by their God. Yahweh has spoken with **'the fire of my jealousy against the rest of the nations and against all Edom'**, nations which had sought **'with wholehearted joy'** to appropriate **'my land for themselves'**. Theirs was no matter of mere territorial expansion. Personified by Edom and not unaware of the ancient covenant between Yahweh and Israel, in effect they challenged God himself, their actions being a blustering claim that, as they saw it, he had never had any right to the land of Canaan. In this way the world has compelled Yahweh to safeguard his good name by honouring his original promises (36:5).

Because Israel's territory had borne the contempt of these nations, Yahweh conveys good news: **'Look, it is I.'** Every valley, every hill, every glade and every meadow will have cause to realize that the Lord now looks upon them with favour. Time was when he permitted the land to be ravaged because of its evil residents (cf. chapter 6), but no more. In his **'jealousy'** and **'wrath'** against **'the nations'**, he intends to justify **'the earth of Israel'** in the presence of those who have cast shame upon it (36:6). The language is affecting in the extreme.

He has **'raised** [his] **hand'** to confirm that alien aggressors must **'bear'** their own **'ignominy'**. Perhaps there is an allusion here to 20:6, which draws attention to the time when Yahweh raised his hand in confirmation that he would lead Israel out of Egypt to a land 'flowing with milk and honey'. What the enemies' future will be is not stated because for now it is enough for the land of Israel to know that it will not be abandoned for ever to an unbelieving world (36:7).

II. The resettlement of 'the mountains of Israel' (36:8-15)

36:8-15. '"'But you, mountains of Israel, you will send forth your branches and will bear your fruit for my people Israel, for they are about to come. For, look, I am for you and I shall turn to you, and you will be cultivated and sown. And I shall multiply people on you — the whole house of Israel, all of it — and the cities will be settled and the waste places will be built. Then I shall multiply men and cattle, and they will increase and be fruitful, and I shall settle you as in your former times and shall do good, more than in your beginning, and you will know that I am Yahweh. Then I shall cause men, even my people Israel, to walk on you. So they will possess you and you will be their inheritance and never again make them childless.'

'"Thus says the Lord Yahweh: 'Because they are saying to you, "You are a devourer of men and you have made your nation childless," therefore you will no more devour men and will never again make it childless,' declares the Lord Yahweh. 'And I shall never again cause the disrepute of the nations to be heard against you, and you will never again bear the reproach of the peoples. You will not again make your nation childless,' declares the Lord Yahweh."'

Averting his gaze from the surrounding nations, Yahweh focuses upon the glorious future that awaits the **'mountains of Israel'**, by which is meant the territory promised to Abraham: **'you will send forth your branches and will bear your fruit'**. This promise recalls Leviticus 26:1-13 and Deuteronomy 28:1-14, which anticipate blessings upon the land of Israel in the event of Israel's obedience to the Lord. Now Yahweh states that the region will be tenanted by **'my people Israel'**, by which is meant a spiritually renewed and loyal people at long last acknowledged by him (hence, **'my'**). Because they **'are about to come'** to resume their residence, the land must, so to speak, be patient. This does not mean that reoccupation would occur, say, in Ezekiel's lifetime or at the end of the exilic seventy-year Sabbath rest,[64] but that the realization of the promise is certain (36:8). Similarly, in Philippians 4:5 Paul writes that 'the Lord is near'.

No longer antagonistic to the land, Yahweh states that he is **'for you'** and **'shall turn to you'**. Because he and the people will both be there, it is to be **'cultivated and sown'** to support the house of Israel (36:9). **'Cities'** are to be inhabited and **'waste places will be built'**. In that **'the whole house of Israel, all of it'**, will settle in the land, it seems clear that the reference cannot be to the partial restoration which took place from 539 BC onwards, when the number of returnees was no more than about 42,000, with many remaining behind in Babylonia.[65] Nor can it be imagined that Ezekiel predicts the return of the Jews to the land of Israel during the twentieth century AD. At the time of writing of this commentary, there are very many expatriate Jews besides the population of the state of Israel, and it not easy to see that this imbalance will be reversed in the foreseeable future. **'You'**, the mountains or highlands (cf. 36:8), will accept and sustain a rapidly increasing population (36:10).

That the resettlement of the land will be without precedent is indicated by the promise that Yahweh will **'multiply men and cattle'** and that they **'will increase and be fruitful'**. If Genesis 1:22,28 are being recalled, Ezekiel predicts that the fruitfulness of Eden will be the only adequate model for a renewed Israel (36:11). The prosperity of the era of David and Solomon will be far exceeded. To date, this has not happened.

Never again will the land be possessed by alien nations in that those who reside there will be **'my people Israel'**. The territory, the people and Yahweh will rest in peaceful equilibrium. Ezekiel possibly alludes to Numbers 13:32, where most of the spies are said to have declared that the land of Canaan 'devours its inhabitants', this in turn possibly reflecting upon the ever-present threat of famine, wild animals, plague and invasion (cf. 5:17). In the new order, the mountains of Israel will be **'their inheritance'** and will be benign. Yahweh himself will **'cause'** this to be so, justifying himself before Israel and the nations (36:12).

God himself had overheard the calumnies uttered by surrounding nations: **'they'** declared that the land of Israel was like some sort of rapacious beast devouring all who come near. But it had been forgotten that if the people of Israel were afflicted when settled in their own land, it was because they were disobedient to Yahweh.[66] Now, in that Yahweh acknowledges resettled Israel as his people (cf. 36:8,12), an acknowledgement that can only presume their spiritual and moral renewal, the land will not be hostile. Families will flourish (36:13-14).[67]

Addressing the land as if it has maternal attributes, Ezekiel anticipates: **'You will not again make your nation childless.'** This means that the nations will have no further excuse to slander it. Gazing at resident Israel with an admiration possibly tinged with envy, the world admits that the twelve tribes live safely in a happy land (36:15). That this is the correct interpretation is shown by what follows.

So far (35:1 – 36:15), because this prophecy mentions Edom (35:15; 36:5) as a nation that had rejoiced in the apparently permanent downfall of Israel, some have argued that a literal fulfilment is not anticipated in that Edom has long since disappeared. Therefore, it has been concluded that the complete prophecy — concerning the downfall of Edom and the resurgence of Israel — must have been fulfilled long ago.[68]

But is this necessarily so? Chapter 35 focuses upon 'Mount Seir', and chapter 36 addresses 'the mountains of Israel'. Might it not be that Yahweh points Ezekiel and his readers to the situations of those who in a time yet to come will occupy these regions? This would tie up neatly with chapters 38 – 39, which point to the ultimate confrontation between a resettled Israel and hostile invaders.

III. Israel had been like an unclean woman (36:16-21)

36:16-21. Then the word of Yahweh came to me, saying, 'Son of man, when the house of Israel were residing on their own earth then they defiled it with their ways and their deeds — their way before me was like the defilement of menstruation. So I poured out my wrath upon them for the blood that they had poured out upon the land, for they had defiled it with their idols. Then I scattered them among the nations and they were dispersed throughout the lands; I judged them according to their ways and according to their deeds. But when they came to the nations wherever they went, then they profaned my holy name, when it was said concerning them, "These are the people of Yahweh, but they have come out from his land." Then I had compassion for my holy name which the house of Israel profaned among the nations to which they had come.'

Edom drops from view, the Lord speaking to his own family. The burden of these verses is that Yahweh determines to be honoured both by a restored Israel and by the surrounding world. Because God will be seen to be God, his promises to the patriarchs must be fulfilled.[69] The fact that in times past the people of Israel betrayed the commitment they had made with Yahweh at Sinai, and had by implication shown themselves not to be of Abraham's calibre (36:16-20), will be no obstruction to the long-term purpose of Yahweh. A renewed and resettled Israel will seek to serve him (36:21-32). Equally, nations that once derided Israel, and therefore her God, will be given cause to reconsider, as will the people of Israel themselves (36:33-38).

So it was that **'the word of Yahweh'** came again to Ezekiel, for the moment the prophet not being considered as a medium for communication to his people but as a confidant: the Lord shares with him what he intends to do.[70] First, however, Yahweh employs a shockingly vivid metaphor to tell Ezekiel why Israel had been compelled to quit Canaan. The neglect shown by them to their means of livelihood, **'their own earth'**, resembled the way in which a slovenly woman might stain her clothes and her surroundings. Menstruation was a form of ritual impurity,[71] and Isaiah 64:6 likens men's supposed righteous deeds to stained sanitary clothing. Similarly, the land of Israel had been defiled. Worse, gross idolatry accompanied habitual bloodletting. The conditions stipulated by, say, Leviticus 20:22-26; Numbers 35:33 and Deuteronomy 18:9-12 had been disregarded (36:16-17).

In just retaliation, Yahweh had vented his anger upon Israel because of **'the blood that they had poured out upon the land'** and because of **'their idols'** that **'defiled it'**. As ever, false religion and amoral conduct had gone hand in hand (cf. 23:37). In accordance with the warnings of the Sinai covenant,[72] the people had been **'scattered'** so that they could practise their abominations in idolatrous **'lands'** *and* ultimately recognize the folly of their ways.[73] Perhaps there is an allusion here to the seven-day purification of a haemorrhagic woman and the seventy-year sabbatical rest granted to earth that had been stained with blood.[74] Certainly, the exile is regarded as a means to a glorious end, that the prodigal nation might in time see the error of its ways (36:18-19).

The Lord continues to discuss the past. Following the deportation there was a predictable consequence: in exile **'they'** — Israel — had **'profaned'** the **'name'** of Yahweh. This does not mean that their misconduct had shocked those among whom they lived.[75] Rather, it had been asked, why should **'the people of Yahweh'** have been removed from **'his land'**? Moses' great fear, according to Exodus 32:12, that Yahweh would be thought by Israel's enemies to be malicious (cf. 8:12; 9:9) or, as noted by Numbers 14:16, that he was unable to deliver his promises, had apparently been realized. In slipshod modern jargon, the God of Israel was considered a 'loser'[76] (36:20). The next verse leads into a refutation of the slander.

A subtle yet profound truth is being thrust to the fore. Exile, although a God-given judgement because of Israel's degradation of Canaan, is seen as itself a profanation of the **'name'** of Yahweh which had been brought into ill repute in the world arena.[77]

For this reason Yahweh intends to have **'compassion'** for his **'holy name'** so that the world will be denied any excuse, however lame, to charge him with inertia or impotence (36:21).

IV. Because the Lord is concerned for his own honour, he will restore Israel (36:22-38)

36:22-38. 'Therefore, say to the house of Israel, "Thus says the Lord Yahweh: 'It is not for your sake that I shall act, O house of Israel, but rather for my holy name which you have profaned among the nations to which you came. And I shall sanctify my great name, which has been profaned among the nations — which you profaned in their midst — and the nations will know that I am Yahweh,' declares the Lord Yahweh, 'when in their eyes I sanctify myself among you. Then I shall take you from the nations and shall gather you from all the lands, and shall bring you to your own earth. And I shall sprinkle pure water, and you will be clean; I shall cleanse you from all your defilements and from all your idols.

'"'So I shall give you a new heart and shall set a new spirit within you, and shall remove the heart of stone from your flesh, and give you a heart of flesh. And I shall place my Spirit within you and shall act so that you walk in my statutes and observe and practise my judgements. So you will dwell in the land that I gave to your fathers and you will be to me for a people and I shall be God for you.

'"'Then I shall save you from all your defilements; and I shall call to the grain and shall multiply it and shall not bring a famine upon you. And I shall multiply the fruit of the tree and the produce of the field so that you may never again receive the taunt of famine among the nations. Then you will remember your evil ways and your deeds that were not good, and you will loathe yourselves in your own sight because of your iniquities and because of your abominations. It is not for your sake that I am acting,' declares the Lord Yahweh, '— let it be known to you. Be ashamed and be humiliated because of your ways, O house of Israel.'"

'"Thus says the Lord Yahweh: 'In the day that I cleanse you from all your iniquities I shall cause the cities to be settled and the waste places will be built. Then the desolated land will be cultivated instead of being a desolation in the eyes of every passer-by. So they will say, "This desolate land has become like the Garden of Eden, and they inhabit as fortified places those that were desolate and torn down." And the nations that remain around them know that I, Yahweh, have built the ruined places and have planted that which was desolate. I, Yahweh, have spoken it and I have done it.'"

'"Thus says the Lord Yahweh: 'Furthermore, I shall let myself be sought by the house of Israel to act for them; I shall multiply them as a flock — of men! As the flock for consecrated places, as the flock of Jerusalem at her appointed seasons, thus will the devastated cities be filled with flocks of men , and they will know that I am Yahweh.'"'

Thus far the Lord has spoken privately to Ezekiel concerning the profanation of the divine name by Israel in exile. Now the prophet is charged to communicate good news to **'the house of Israel'**.

Yahweh's thesis is not that Israel had merited her sufferings (which, in fact, she had), but that the **'name'** — by which is meant the integrity — of the

Lord had been brought into apparent disrepute. In that his people had lost their homeland to alien intruders, Yahweh appeared to have been unable to maintain Israel.

To redress the calumny, God will **'act'** so that all concerned, both within and beyond the boundaries of Israel, shall have cause to acknowledge that his original commitment to the patriarchs has been honoured. The surrounding nations are to realize that there had always been a binding relationship between God and Israel. That this people had been temporarily scattered was because Yahweh brought it about and not because he was unable to secure their safety or did not care for them (36:22).

Not present in Yahweh's message is any statement that Israel is to be restored because he has loved them and is concerned for them in their misery. The figure of the good shepherd (cf. 34:7-31) apparently fades from view. But to conclude, as do some commentators,[78] that Yahweh is concerned more for himself than for Israel would be to miss the latent point, which is that he must act because centuries previously he had committed himself to this elect people, doing so on the basis of his love for them.[79] Negatively, unless Israel is restored, Yahweh will never be seen to be the God who keeps his promises; positively, the restoration of Israel must lead to the sanctification of his **'great name'** both by Israel and the peoples of the world.[80] The **'eyes'** of the nations will have cause to stare in astonishment, knowing that Yahweh is the powerful and faithful God of Israel (36:23).

How this divine self-sanctification will be effected is now stated, there being a definite allusion to Deuteronomy 30:1-5.[81] In context, Moses teaches that when, as would be inevitable, Israel denies her allegiance to Yahweh and is expelled from the land, the people will eventually 'return to Yahweh' with all their 'heart' and 'soul'. Then, the Lord will 'take' them 'back from captivity ... and gather' them 'again'. He will 'bring' them 'to the land' which the 'fathers possessed' and they 'shall possess it', and this because he will have 'compassion' on them. Indeed, 36:24 employs the same verbs as Deuteronomy 30:3-5.[82] Restored, Israel is told that they are to be settled on **'your own earth'**. By means of the recall of Deuteronomy 30:1-5, Yahweh acknowledges that self-interest does not exclude love for his people; rather, it presupposes it (36:24).

Although restoration to the land has been mentioned and will be mentioned again, it has now become a major theme.[83] For God to be seen as the God of Israel, there *must* be a return to the land.[84]

But by itself this enormous act will never be sufficient. How can the Lord deny his holiness by readmitting a defiled people to a land from which they had been expelled because of their sinfulness? The fantasy is as impossible as it is abhorrent. A holy logic demands that repossession of the land must be accompanied by the spiritual renewal of those who live there. By ensuring that Jacob's family become his true people, Yahweh will exhibit himself to the world as the covenant Lord of Israel.

Thus, **'I shall sprinkle pure water, and you will be clean; I shall cleanse you from all your defilements and from all your idols.'** The cleansing process is mentioned three times for emphasis, the application of water denoting the removal of defilement, in this case idolatry (36:25).[85]

It has been noted that 36:24 recalls Deuteronomy 30:1-5. This allusion is confirmed by the promise that Yahweh will **'give you** [Israel] **a new heart and shall set a new spirit within you, and shall remove the heart of stone from your flesh, and give you a heart of flesh'**. Here Deuteronomy 30:6 must have been in Ezekiel's mind: 'And Yahweh your God will circumcise your heart and the heart of your descendants, to love Yahweh your God with all your heart and with all your soul, that you may live.' Virtually repeating 11:19, which in context promises the restoration of a renewed community to the land of Israel, Yahweh amplifies the passage in Deuteronomy: circumcision of the heart is replaced by a transplant. Such had been the recalcitrance of Israel over the centuries that only an action as radical as this will suffice. **'Heart'** and **'spirit'** represent the centre of human emotion and will.[86]

The point being made in the present verse is that Moses' anticipation that Israel would apostatize, would be evicted from the land, yet would eventually be spiritually renewed and then brought home, is to be fulfilled. The covenant with Abraham will be honoured by Yahweh's unilateral activity (36:26).

How Israel's radical change of 'heart' and renewal of 'spirit' will come about is explained: **'And I shall place my Spirit within you and shall act so that you walk in my statutes and observe and practise my judgements.'** Although Ezekiel does not mention a 'new covenant', it is clear that he reflects Jeremiah 31:31-34, which looks forward to the covenant instituted by Christ.[87] Accordingly, Jesus promised that the Spirit would be 'in' (not 'with') the disciples.[88] Because, left to their own devices, the people of Israel would never voluntarily obey their God ('a stiff-necked people'),[89] the Lord will cause them to submit to him, doing so as free (or freed) agents (36:27).

Looking back in hindsight, we may conclude that the era of the new covenant and the age of the Spirit,[90] instituted two millennia ago, will climax in the spiritual renewal of the natural family of Abraham and in their restoration to the land promised to him. Appendix C considers the matter.

In consequence of Yahweh's initiative, the relationship between the people, the land and God will be restored. Although the 'covenant' with Abraham is not mentioned, it must have been in Ezekiel's mind in that he writes that Israel will **'dwell in the land that I gave to your fathers'**.[91] The people and their God will be mutually reconciled, thus fulfilling the expectation of the intermediary Sinai arrangement.[92] The situation of Israel will be complete (36:28).

Moreover, the Lord intends to **'save'** them from their multiple **'defilements'**. These people have been reconciled to God even though, apparently, they are not yet completely free from the taint of sin (36:29).

The residual sinfulness of renewed and rehabilitated Israel may be paralleled by the awareness of the godly Christian man, for whom abiding sin is a matter for profound regret.[93] The present verse assumes that the prosperity of the land depends upon the spiritual and moral health of its tenants, which, apart from a divine saving activity, would be, to say the least, precarious. This is why Yahweh will save the people from themselves.[94] Only then will he feel free to **'call to the grain'**, to **'multiply it'** and **'not bring a famine upon you'**.

The impression given by text and context is that Ezekiel anticipates a family of believers who are the spiritual as well as the natural children of Abraham.[95] The promise of Romans 11:26 will at long last be realized: 'The Deliverer will come out of Zion, and he will turn away ungodliness from Jacob.'[96] Ezekiel would seem to anticipate the final stages of the Messianic era, the era in which we now find ourselves. Because the curse of judgement will have been removed, the land will be fruitful. Never again will aliens be in a position to ridicule the bond between Yahweh, Israel and their inheritance (36:30).

Then, resident in the land, this sanctified people will never cease to remember the **'evil ways'**, the **'deeds that were not good'**, the **'iniquities'** and the **'abominations'** of their forefathers, whom they consider themselves obliged to acknowledge (hence, **'your'**, five times). The sins of previous generations disgust them. A similar prediction is found in 20:43. They hang their heads in shame (36:31).

That Yahweh restores and renews Israel is not because they are worthy. Let them know that **'it is not for your sake that I am acting'**. This is why the solidarity between the Israel of Ezekiel's time and that of the distant future — sixth-century BC exiles and (from the perspective of the early twenty-first-century AD commentator) a generation yet to be — is given prominence. In anticipation of future blessing, the whole family, of whatever time and throughout time, is commanded to **'be ashamed and be humiliated because of your ways, O house of Israel'**. The motor for the agenda of redemption is to be found in Leviticus 26:40-45 and Deuteronomy 30:1-10: because Yahweh entered into a covenant relationship with Abraham and his family, at a later time imposing conditions at Sinai, he would dishonour himself were he to reject them permanently, even if acceptance by him necessitates his initiative in bringing about their voluntary repentance (36:32).

Yahweh now focuses upon the bonds between, on the one hand, himself and, on the other, his restored people and the land in which they will dwell. Were this to remain in a state of devastation, and were the city sites to be uninhabited, surrounding nations would still be able to rake up an excuse for slandering the integrity of the God of Israel. Therefore, when he cleanses his people **'from all your iniquities'**, he will **'cause the cities to be settled'** and the **'waste places'** to be **'built'** (36:33). **'Then'** it will be obvious to **'every passer-by'** that Yahweh has vindicated his people and by so doing has justified himself. Israel's God will be seen to be God (36:34).

Whereas those who witnessed the eviction of Israel from their ancestral habitat had perceived that there was a hiatus in the relationship between Yahweh and that people (cf. 36:20), now it will be said that the land resembles **'the Garden of Eden'** (as far as that land can be imagined!). They observe that since it was God rather than man who planted that garden,[97] the restoration of Israel must be the sovereign work of Yahweh rather than the product of an Israelite self-help programme (36:35).

The section closes with a typical prophetic figure of speech, the future being presented as a reality accomplished long ago. The **'nations'** who witness the prosperity of Abraham's family acknowledge that Yahweh had brought it about and recognize that he has been faithful to his promises to the patriarchs.[98] Therefore, if Yahweh is pleased to declare his intention, it must come to pass (36:36).

So sinful was the Israel of Ezekiel's day that the Lord refused to hear the people's prayers (see 14:3,4; 20:3; cf. 8:18). In these concluding verses of chapter 36 the situation is entirely different: Israel has been renewed and for this reason will be heard by Yahweh. Settled in their land, the residents petition their God, possibly for numerical enlargement, since a reduced population would not be a true fulfilment of the promise to Abraham (36:37).[99] J. D. Currid remarks that:

> The last two sections of Leviticus 26 are a pointer to the future history of Israel. The sequence,
>
> Rebellion → exile → repentance → restoration
>
> summarizes the unfolding nature of Israel's existence.[100]

The Lord multiplies their numbers to the extent that they are as numerous as the many thousands of animals — oxen, sheep and goats — once brought to the Jerusalem altar on the appointed feast days. **'Devastated cities'** will be replete with **'flocks of**

men'. To appreciate the force of the metaphor, compare with Josiah's extraordinary donations of sacrificial animals.[101] These latter-day human sheep will be living sacrifices, devoted to the Lord. The end of the matter will be that all **'know that I am Yahweh'** (36:38).

Application

Like so many within Israel in Ezekiel's day, Edom did not realize that Yahweh, for them no more than the titular God of Israel, was not to be compared with fictitious, and therefore impotent, gods. They did not recognize that the devastation of the northern tribes by the Assyrians, and then that of Judah by the Babylonians, was a unitary act of judgement inflicted by Yahweh upon his erring people, and that his abandonment of the twelve tribes and their lands would not be permanent. Lacking spiritual discernment, they viewed the overthrow of the monarchy of Israel as a phenomenon that could never be reversed, or so they hoped.

Similarly, many often mock when they behold the apparent weakness of Christian churches, not excluding those of Europe. The false conclusion that large numbers seem to draw is that the Christian gospel is irrelevant and therefore doomed to oblivion.

But because the God of Bible-believing Christians is God, when his true people are weak, then they are strong. Wisdom will always be justified by her newborn children. The light shines and there must always be conversions.[102]

The Edomites had planned to seize Judah for themselves, forgetting that Yahweh remained 'there' (see 35:10), albeit without a temple in which he could be worshipped and without the throne of David. Yet as the Bible reader travels from the prophecy of Ezekiel towards the later books of the Old Testament and then into the depths of the New, he will ask himself if the God who promised the land to Abraham has ever rescinded his commitment.[103] If he understands the thrust of chapters 35 – 36, he may conclude that the only possible answer is negative, from which he will infer that an inhabited 'beautiful land' (20:6,15)[104] will yet feature in the plan of God for the natural family of Abraham and for the worldwide influence of the gospel of our Lord Jesus Christ.

Chapter 36 does not mention the promised descendant of David, or the nature of his work, or how the Spirit of God will be given to Israel. But there is a good reason for these omissions. At this point the emphasis falls upon the renewal of the people, upon their return to Abrahamic territory and upon Yahweh's self-vindication through the fulfilment of the promises to Abraham and later to Israel at the inception of the Sinai covenant. Hebrews 1:1 reminds us that in the Old Testament there is no single place in which we may discover a comprehensive exposition of the plan of God for his people.

Christians everywhere have reason to look ahead with glad anticipation. The best is yet to be.[105]

The valley of the dry bones and the united sticks (Ezekiel 37:1-28)

Two connected revelations are given to Ezekiel to complement the prophecy of the good shepherd (chapter 34) and that of the restoration of the land of Israel (chapter 36).

Firstly, the **'son of man'** is shown that Israel as a people will rise into new life, and (remarkably) is commanded to prophesy in order to make it happen (37:1-14). Then he is instructed to perform and subsequently explain a symbolic action to predict the future reunion of Israel under the benign government of an individual shepherd-king. The latter is identified as **'David'**, the **'servant'** of Yahweh (37:15-28).

The intention of the complete chapter is to show that in time to come, and against all expectations, the theocracy will be re-established in unprecedented splendour. Although this has already been intimated, now we are granted a fuller exposition: the people of Israel are to rise again, spiritually renewed and united, dwelling in the land vouchsafed by Yahweh to Abraham and his family. Yahweh will acknowledge them to be his people and himself to be their God. This blessed state will be witnessed by the nations of the world.

Those who first heard Ezekiel deliver these prophecies must have been astonished, yet not more so than we if, two and a half millennia later, we realize their implications.

1. A resurrected nation (37:1-14)

37:1-14. And the hand of Yahweh was upon me and he brought me out by the Spirit of Yahweh and caused me to rest in the midst of the plain, and it was full of bones. Then he made me pass among them round about, and, look, there were very many upon the surface of the plain, and, look, they were very dry. And he said to me, 'Son of man, will these bones live?' And I said, 'Lord Yahweh, you know.' Then he said to me, 'Prophesy over these bones, and you will say to them, "Dry bones, hear the word of Yahweh. Thus says the Lord Yahweh to these bones: 'Look, I am bringing breath into you and you will live. And I shall put sinews on you and shall bring flesh upon you and shall cover you over with skin and shall place breath within you, and you will live. Then you will know that I am Yahweh.'"'

So I prophesied just as I had been commanded, and there was a sound as I prophesied, and, look, a quaking, and the bones came together, bone to its bone. And I saw, and, look, there were sinews upon them, and flesh came up, and above this a skin covered them — but there was no breath in them. Then he said to me, 'Prophesy to the breath. Prophesy, son of man, and you will say to the breath, "Thus says the Lord Yahweh: 'Come, O breath, from the four winds, and blow within these who are slaughtered, and they will live.'"' So I prophesied just as he had commanded me, and the breath came among them and they lived and stood upon their feet, a very, very great army.

Then he said to me, 'Son of man, these bones — they are all the house of Israel. Look, they are saying, "Our bones are dried up and our expectation has perished. As for ourselves, we are cut off." Therefore prophesy, and you will say to them, "Thus says the Lord Yahweh: 'Look, I am opening your graves and shall bring you out from your graves, O my people, and shall bring you to the earth of Israel. Then you will know that I am Yahweh when I open your graves and when I raise you up from your graves, O my people. Then I shall put my Spirit within you and you will live, and I shall cause you to rest upon your own earth, and you will know that I, Yahweh, have spoken and have done it,'" declares Yahweh.'

The vision of the valley of dry bones is not difficult to interpret as far as the obvious explanation of the words is concerned. **'The hand of Yahweh'** came upon Ezekiel, who was led by **'the Spirit of Yahweh'** to the middle of **'the plain'**. There he rested. The definite article, **'the'**, seems to suggest that this was where Ezekiel had received his first revelation concerning Jerusalem and its inhabitants (cf. 3:22; 8:4).

Scattered everywhere in the valley were dead men's bones. The area was **'full'** of them, as if it had been a battle zone where none had buried the dead; they decomposed where they fell (37:1).

The Lord prompted Ezekiel to walk **'among'** the bones and look around the site in order to take stock. He observed that the bones were **'very many'**, that there were no graves and that the bones had been bleached under the sun (**'very dry'**). Apparently, these innumerable skeletal fragments were the remains of a society that had perished a long time previously. As a priest not unacquainted with war, Ezekiel would have been deeply offended at the sight, knowing that these unburied dead, now fully decomposed, would have defiled the land where they lay (cf. 39:12). Not only were they accursed,[106] nobody had cared for them, or for the land (37:2).

The Lord asked Ezekiel if these **'bones** [will] **live'**, a question posed in the knowledge that the dead cannot resurrect themselves and that living persons are unable to perform such a service.

Because Ezekiel must have known that on very rare occasions the dead had been revivified and that nothing is impossible for God,[107] he is cautious: **'Lord Yahweh, you know.'**[108] In effect, he acknowledges that the Lord can make it happen. As the prophet saw the situation, it was not hopeless (37:3).

Having given a not unsatisfactory reply, Ezekiel was instructed to **'prophesy'** to the **'dry bones'** as if they were living persons rather than ossified remains. They were to **'hear the word of Yahweh'**. Here, to prophesy implies command rather than prediction. The fact that the prophet's duty appears absurd heightens the reader's anticipation (37:4).

The good news for the bones is that God will convey **'breath'** to them and that they will live. 'Breath' translates the Hebrew *rûach*, a word which occurs also in 37:1, 'the *Spirit* of Yahweh'; in 37:6,8, 'breath'; in 37:9, 'wind' and 'breath'; and in 37:14, the divine 'Spirit'. In each case the context must determine which English word is to be used.[109] Here, if there is an allusion to Genesis 2:7 and its mention of 'Yahweh God' (cf. **'Lord Yahweh'**), 'breath' is appropriate: the Lord will infuse the breath of life into lifeless bodies. These bones shall **'live'** (37:5).

The process is outlined. Yahweh intends to re-articulate these dismembered skeletons with **'sinews'**, to cover them with **'flesh'**, to spread **'skin'** over the flesh and finally to grant **'breath'** (37:6). But the object of the exercise is not that bleached, long-dead bones might live again. Rather, this as yet unnamed society will **'know that I am Yahweh'**, from which it can be inferred that the reference is to Israel (cf. 34:30; 36:11,38). The covenant relationship between Yahweh and Israel will be renewed.

Ezekiel records that he was obedient to Yahweh's instruction. Remarkably, even as he was prophesying, there was **'a sound'** and **'a quaking'** generated by the movements of innumerable bones clicking together as intact skeletons. And not only was the action immediate, nothing was random or inexact, in that **'the bones came together, bone to its bone'**. Then, as always, God was precise. The hip bone, for example, would have been connected to the knee rather than to the elbow (37:7).

At this point Ezekiel was surprised. He relates that he **'saw'**, and summons his readers to **'look'** in their imaginations at the rearticulated bones, now perfected skeletons, which were equipped with **'sinews'**, **'flesh'** and, finally, **'skin'**. Yet they were no more than inanimate bodies, lying helpless on the surface of the earth. **'There was** [as yet] **no breath in them.'**[110] A divine initiative is anticipated (37:8).

Now the level of excitement is raised considerably. It transpires that the erstwhile bones were those of people who had been **'slaughtered'**, presumably in war. Nor had they been given decent burial, their bodies being left in the open to putrefy. The picture is that of Israel, devastated, scattered and abandoned by both God and man.

In the light of Ezekiel's frequent recalls of Leviticus and Deuteronomy, it is reasonable to assume that here he alludes to Deuteronomy 28:25-26, in which Yahweh informs a potentially apostate Israel that if they do not repent they will eventually be overthrown by their enemies, their unburied dead being food for scavenging beasts and birds. If so, Ezekiel sees the aftermath of the covenant curse upon his own renegade people.[111] This inference is given confirmation by verse 11.

Significantly, the **'son of man'** (for Ezekiel is only a man, and must remember it) was to **'prophesy'** and **'say to the breath'**, commanding it to **'come ... from the four winds'** and **'blow within'** the innumerable casualties of war scattered across the plain. Perhaps the winds from every part of the earth stand for irresistible force, symbolizing the focused power of Yahweh in granting life in a hopeless situation. The wind, as in John 3:8, represents the Spirit of God.

That the divine inbreathing did not occur automatically after the reformation of the bodies of the slain, but had to be invoked by prophecy, would signify that, even as Moses publicized the curse of the covenant, so Ezekiel, the prophet of the exile, announces that the curse is about to be lifted. It is almost as if he encourages the Spirit of God to fulfil his commission: **'blow ... and they will live'**. Genesis 2:7 must lie behind this promise (37:9).

Obedient to the heavenly summons, Ezekiel could scarcely conceal his surprise at what happened next: each inanimate body was infused by **'breath'** — that is, by the Spirit — and stood on its **'feet'**. Then, the prophet beheld **'a very, very great army'** (37:10).[112] Israel, liberated from the covenant curse, is virtually innumerable and irresistibly powerful.

Yahweh spoke again to the **'son of man'** to clarify the meaning of a vision in which Ezekiel has had such a significant role. The bones represent **'all the house of Israel'**, by which is meant the complete nation, and not just those who perished as a result of the Babylonian offensive (cf. 36:10). And there is a stated reason for the disclosure: the prophet is bidden to **'look'** and take note that his people had, apparently, given up all hope for the future of the nation: **'we are cut off'**. Since the time of the Assyrian invasion a century earlier, Israel had lost everything. Surely, they concluded, Yahweh had abandoned his covenant people (37:11).

Because of this prevailing (and unjustified) sense of hopelessness, Ezekiel must **'prophesy'**. The metaphor moves abruptly from that of the articulation of scattered bones to that of bodily resurrection: **'I ... shall bring you out from your graves.'** In that the language is obviously figurative, Yahweh does not tell Ezekiel that Israel is to experience a literal resurrection of the dead. As Taylor observes, 'The figures of speech do not have validity in their own right.'[113] The meaning is that in time to come the nation of Israel, accepted at long last by Yahweh as **'my people'**, will be revivified as a cohesive unit and be brought back **'to the earth of Israel'** — that is, the land promised to the fathers. The **'opening'** of their **'graves'**, an action that in other contexts would be sinister, bespeaks the power of God. Only he can do this thing, and he will do it (37:12).

'Then', when it happens, **'you'**, the people of Israel, **'will know that I am Yahweh.'** He is the God who had never ignored his covenant commitment. For their part, the people belong to him. In due time the Lord himself will open the national grave, exhume the corpse, revive it and cause the body politic to stand up in full vigour (37:13).

The section concludes. Indwelt by the **'Spirit'** of Yahweh (cf. 36:27), the people of Israel will **'rest'** on their **'own earth'**. Then they will have abundant reason to accept that what Yahweh had **'spoken'** by way of promise, he had delivered. The Lord **'declares'** that it shall be so (37:14).

2. A reunited people (37:15-28)

37:15-28. Then the word of Yahweh came to me, saying, 'And you, son of man, take for yourself a single stick and write on it, "For Judah and for the sons of Israel, his companions." Then take a single stick and write on it, "For Joseph, the stick of Ephraim and all the house of Israel, his companions." And join them, one to one, for yourself for a single stick, that they may be a single entity in your hand. And even as the sons of your people are speaking to you, saying, "Will you not tell us what these things are to you?", speak to them, "Thus says the Lord Yahweh: 'Look, I am taking the stick of Joseph, which is in the hand of Ephraim, and the tribes of Israel, his companions, and I shall place them on it, upon the house of Judah, and shall make them a single stick, and they will be one in my hand.'"

'And the sticks upon which you write will be in your hand before their eyes. And say to them, "Thus says the Lord Yahweh: 'Look, I am taking the sons of Israel from among the nations where they have gone and I shall gather them from around and bring them to their own earth. Then I shall make them into one nation in the land, on the mountains of Israel; and one king will be king for all of them; and they will no longer be two nations and will no longer be divided into two kingdoms. They will no longer defile themselves with their idols and with their detestable things and with all their transgressions, but I shall save them from all their dwelling places in which they sinned and shall cleanse them. Then they will be to me for a people and I shall be to them for God.

'"'And my servant David will be king over them and there will be one shepherd for them all. Then they will walk in my judgements and will observe my statutes and do them. So they will dwell upon the land that I gave to my servant, to Jacob, in which your fathers lived, and they will dwell upon it — they and their sons and their sons' sons for ever, and David my servant will be their prince for ever. And I shall cut a covenant of peace for them — an eternal covenant with them, and shall establish them, multiply them and shall set my sanctuary in their midst for ever. So my dwelling place will be above them, and I shall be to them for God, and they will be to me for a people. Then the nations will know that I am Yahweh who sanctifies Israel, when my sanctuary is in their midst for ever.'"'

Following his inauguration to the prophetic ministry, Ezekiel had been required to perform various sign-actions.[114] Now, **'the word of Yahweh'** comes to him with another such instruction (37:15).

The prophet must procure two pieces of wood and inscribe on one of them, **'For Judah and for the sons of Israel, his companions'**, and on the other, **'For Joseph, the stick of Ephraim and all the house of Israel, his companions'** (37:16). Not necessarily wooden rods or staves,[115] they would have been shaped in such a way that they could conveniently fit together and be held in one hand.

Judah had remained loyal to the throne of David after the secession of the northern tribes in the time of Rehoboam, while the name of Ephraim, the younger son of Joseph, became the appellation of those who seceded.[116] It is possible that Joseph is mentioned because the ten tribes had been apostate since the time of the division of the kingdom of Solomon, and the burden of the sign-action is to indicate the eventual unity of a regenerate Israel.

Having written upon the two pieces of wood, Ezekiel will join them together **'that they may be a single entity in your hand'**. How they are to be attached is not mentioned. That the two are now one is the point being made (37:17).

It may be significant that the Lord identifies Ezekiel's observers as **'the sons of *your* people'**, implying that currently they were not *Yahweh's* people.[117] Even as Ezekiel inscribes and then joins the pieces of wood, the bystanders are puzzled, not for the first time,[118] demanding that he explains himself. **'Will you not tell us ...?'** may suggest that they believed that he had a duty to do so if he did not wish to be considered a fool. They were arrogant (37:18).

Yahweh condescends to their limitations. Ezekiel is to speak and act in the name of the Lord, who will reunite the separated kingdoms of Ephraim and Judah so that they remain permanently in his **'hand'** — that is, under his control. That **'the stick of Joseph'**, representing northern Ephraim, is to be placed above that representing **'the house of Judah'** may suggest Judah's superiority as the foundational tribe. How, when and for what reason this will happen is not stated (37:19). When the prophet raises the sticks, now joined to each other, and then (probably) carries them about with him, those who stare will take note (37:20).

As they gaze, his words and actions tell out the message of the regrouping by Yahweh of **'the sons of Israel from among the nations'**. The reference to the children of Jacob, or Israel,[119] rather than to Joseph and Judah, emphasizes the origins of the nation, a people to be brought back **'from around'** — that is, from every place to which they had been dispersed — to their **'own earth'** (37:21; cf. 36:24).

Further, they will be united, as in the time of David and Solomon, under **'one king'**. Political division as a consequence of royal abuse of power will be unknown.[120] Yet there will be no democracy: the **'one nation'** settled **'in the land'** and **'on the mountains of Israel'** will be in the care of an absolute monarchy (37:22).

It seems evident that Ezekiel predicts three distinct but inseparable acts of divine grace. Firstly, there will be the gathering of dispersed Israel from other lands; secondly, their spiritual reunion under one king; thirdly, their settlement in the land of their fathers. But there is more.

Resident in their own land, the people of Israel do not defile themselves with idolatry and associated evils. They are to be saved by Yahweh from **'all their dwelling places'**,[121] formerly idolatrous sites within the land that recall the evils perpetrated there. In this way the covenant relationship between Yahweh and Israel will be restored. Not only are evil desires absent from the hearts of the settlers, the welcoming environment is clean (37:23).

In a development of 34:23-24, the identity of the absolute monarch is brought into focus: **'David'** is not only the **'servant'** of Yahweh and 'prince' and **'shepherd'** to Israel, he will be **'king over them'**. Moreover, this realm is to be a theocracy: God himself legislates for a people whose sole desire is to **'walk in** [his] **judgements'** and **'observe** [his] **statutes'**, terminology that recalls the demands of the Sinai covenant.[122]

It is assumed that such is the unanimity between Yahweh and 'David' that the requirements of the one are the requirements of the other, and that the people's allegiance to the one will be tantamount to obedience to the other: the two are one (37:24).

At this point Ezekiel introduces a new factor, not mentioned in the parallels in chapters 34 and 36. He predicts that the new arrangement is to be eternal: Israel will **'dwell ... for ever'** in the land granted originally to Jacob and where their **'fathers'** had lived.[123] And **'David'**, the **'servant'** of Yahweh, **'will be their prince for ever'** (37:25).

The **'covenant'** that Yahweh will **'cut'** with them is equally **'of peace'** and **'eternal'** (cf. 16:60-63). The Lord will place his **'sanctuary'** among them in perpetuity in fulfilment of the anticipation of Leviticus 26:9,11. He will be their God, and they will be his own obedient people. Restoration and reconciliation are complete and permanent. This covenant, not the provisional arrangement of Sinai, can be none other than a fulfilment of that established with Abraham and, later, of that with David.[124]

The **'dwelling place'** (*mishkan*) of the Lord will remain **'above'**, or 'over' (not 'with') Israel. This probably means that, even as Yahweh's glory dwelt over the tabernacle,[125] and as Solomon's temple once dominated the Jerusalem skyline, so Yahweh overshadows and protects his own (37:26-27).

Now other nations know that Yahweh has set Israel apart when he places his **'sanctuary ... in their midst for ever'** (37:28). Compare this with Psalm 68:29, which literally reads, 'Because of your temple above Jerusalem, kings will bring you gifts.' Not only does the Lord dwell above them for their protection, he places himself at their centre as the sole object of their worship. In vindicating Israel as his people, the Lord has justified himself. He is acknowledged by all to be the promise-keeping God.

Application

At first sight it may seem strange that the person and work of the Messiah, alias 'David', are not given detailed attention, as they are in, say, the 'Servant Songs' of Isaiah. But were this the case, Ezekiel 37 would be overloaded. In context, the purpose of this crowning chapter is to show that at long last the theocracy of Israel must be established in the land of promise. Although how this will come about, and when, are matters of enormous interest to us, as they must have been to Ezekiel's generation, they are not unfolded within the present agenda.[126]

For all that, the chapter centres upon Christ. The presence of 'David' is indispensable because he, the 'servant' of Yahweh, is alike the people's 'king', 'shepherd and 'prince'. Without him there must be a separation between Yahweh, Israel and the land.

We need to read this chapter through the lens of the New Testament.

Focus: the interpretation of Ezekiel 34 – 48

From 34:1 until the end of the book Ezekiel's prophecy looks to a future in which the relationship between the God of Israel and his people is undisturbed by their sin and, in consequence, by his wrath. Peace reigns. Because, as intimated in 'Introductory matters', interpretations of these chapters vary enormously, it might be helpful to attempt an overview of what 34 – 48 have to say before delving into 38:1 onwards.

1. A recapitulation of chapters 34 – 37

The major emphases of chapters 34 – 37 would seem to be that at some time in the future Israel is to be resettled in the land promised by Yahweh to Abraham and his posterity, the land from which, up to Ezekiel's time, the twelve tribes had been evicted by the Assyrians and the Babylonians. They will dwell in this land peacefully. For an unspecified period other nations will be restrained from molesting them.

The Lord justifies Israel. In terms of the Levitical procedure, the people are sprinkled with pure water, so to speak, to become a reconciled, worshipping community. Within this new arrangement none lacks a new heart and a new spirit, and all desire to obey their Lord. They are regenerate.

Although justified and sanctified, Israel continues to experience daily forgiveness for daily sins. The people surrender themselves happily to the dominion of the good shepherd, someone who stems from the family of David.

We are not told when this will happen, or for how long Israel will dwell peacefully in the land. Apparently, Ezekiel expects his readers to wait and see.

In that there is no mention, either explicit or implicit, of any employment of the Levitical sacrificial system, the apparatus of Old Testament temple worship gives every impression of being redundant.

In brief, the situation seems to be a realization of the godly realm projected by Leviticus 26:1-13. What degenerate Israel never was, but should have been, Israel regathered will be. Further, the people experience Yahweh's earthly and material blessings in this world rather than in the heavenly scene.

2. The shepherd and the sheep: Christ with Israel — but how?

There is no need to assume that the presence of the Davidic shepherd-prince-king among his subjects is to be physical and visible, in the way that it was, of course, in the time of our Lord's earthly ministry. It could just as well be spiritual and invisible, none other than what we know as the communion of the Holy Spirit and the presence of Christ within every believer and in every true church.[127]

3. Israel regathered before Christ returns

Yet the family of Israel are said to be resident in their land, for which reason they are untypical of the Gentile Christian situation in which most of us now find ourselves. But where they are and what they are does not logically preclude Gentile churches elsewhere.

About this Ezekiel appears to have nothing explicit to say, and his silence must be taken into account.

If it is suggested that the scene presented by the prophet refers to what some might consider a millennial, post-advent situation, we would be travelling beyond the evidence of the prophecy. This being so, the interpretation cannot be ruled out that Ezekiel looks towards, but not beyond, the final appearance of the Messiah. Otherwise expressed, between chapters 34 and 37 inclusive (and, indeed, onwards into chapters 38 and 39) Ezekiel's vision is restricted to the terrestrial destiny of the family of Abraham. This is the interpretation being offered here.[128]

4. No condemnation

Chapters 34 – 37 outline a reversal of the condemnation expounded so terribly and graphically by the earlier part of the prophecy. In detail, Ezekiel's interest was not with matters that occupied, say, Jeremiah 31, concerning the establishment of the new covenant.

Rather, being aware of Jeremiah's prediction, he assumes the new covenant to be operative among the children of Israel. His distinctive ministry points to the destiny of this people after what we now know to be the passage of many centuries, revealing that towards the end ethnic Israel will become the obedient people anticipated by Moses.

5. A literal return to the promised land

The intended implication of chapters 34 – 37 would seem to be that the regrouping and spiritual renewal of Israel are to be understood as future historical events. Even as disobedient Israel fell by the wayside (thus incurring the judgements predicted by Leviticus and Deuteronomy — plague, famine, wild beast and sword), by contrast an obedient family will arise to inherit the covenant blessings.

Chapter 37 has brought this out powerfully. Even as the living nation was reduced to an accumulation of the bones of a multitude of men slain by the sword, so these bones are refashioned into a vibrant, peaceful and large community. Whereas the elect people were degenerate, collapsing into sin and judgement, they are to be renewed to serve the Lord. An inference would seem to be that their spiritual and moral regeneration will be as actual and historic as was the former debacle.

To repeat, Ezekiel is not concerned with the more closely defined Messianic predictions given by, say, Isaiah, Jeremiah, Amos, Hosea, Micah, or even Daniel. Ezekiel lived at a time when the judgements of Moses' law were being realized, yet was given to understand that the covenant between Yahweh and Abraham's family must be fulfilled. Accordingly, they inherit the land because they satisfy the necessary conditions of inheritance laid down by Moses.

One might draw a comparison with 1 Corinthians 15:50, which states that 'flesh and blood are not able to inherit the kingdom of God' and that 'corruption' cannot 'inherit incorruptibility'. This being so, there *must* be a glorious resurrection if the saints are to enter the glory, as they shall.[129] Paul's reasoning is akin to that of Ezekiel.

It was that prophet's great concern to tell out that the sovereign grace of God would lead Israel to repentance and faith. Much of the complex and delicate apparatus of the coming Messianic salvation had been outlined already by other prophets, as well as by Moses, and would be expounded further in later years by men such as Zechariah, Haggai and Malachi. Ezekiel built upon past prophecy, but also anticipated future revelations. In essence, his presentation of a spiritually and geographically restored Israel presumes the prior incarnation and work of the shepherd-prince of Israel, the Messianic God-man. Ezekiel looks ahead to a time long after Bethlehem but prior to the glorious, public and final appearance of the Lord Jesus Christ.

6. Ezekiel and Daniel

There is even a certain parallel between Ezekiel and Daniel. The latter prophet lived through the tragic events of 586 BC, when Jerusalem fell, and at least until 539 BC, when the decree for the reconstruction of the temple came into effect.

Daniel knew that a second temple in Jerusalem would eventually be destroyed, and was informed that a man far worse than the shadow Antichrist, Antiochus Epiphanes, who died in 164 BC, must emerge to threaten the existence of the people of God.[130] He unfolded the future, both near and remote, in contours drawn from his dispensation — that of the temple and the Aaronic priesthood. Could it have been otherwise?

In much the same fashion, by referring to a system that had been ordained by God, abused by the people but not in his day redundant, Ezekiel outlines the ultimate destiny of Israel. It is because of this that chapters 34 – 39 concern events that have not taken place — yet! Romans 11 and the book of the Revelation appear to confirm this view. The reader of this commentary might like to scan through Revelation, chapter 20, and compare with chapters 38 – 39 of Ezekiel.

7. Chapters 40 – 48

If all this is so, it might follow that chapters 40 – 48 unfold the eternal state of Israel in terms of an idealized temple. Again, this would extend and realize the typology of Moses' administration. The ultimate glory is pictured as a perfected kingdom where active worship is the sole exercise.

8. Deuteronomy and Leviticus

To sum up, it may be suggested that the prophecy of Ezekiel is founded largely upon the books of Leviticus and Deuteronomy. The principal references would be Leviticus 26:1-13 and Deuteronomy 28:1-14, which predict the Lord's blessing upon obedient Israel resident in the land of promise, and Leviticus 26:40-45 and Deuteronomy 30:1-10, which promise mercy to penitent Israel in exile. Ezekiel tells that the yearnings of Moses' heart will come to pass. A godly people are to dwell at long last in their own land — but only until the time arrives for the ultimate conflict between Israel and the nations. Then the Lord will champion his own. Afterwards, beyond the horizon of this world, the Lord remains in Jerusalem for ever.

The destruction of Gog and Magog (Ezekiel 38:1 – 39:29)

Chapters 38 – 39 form one continuous oracle divided into four main parts. Each begins with an instruction to Ezekiel to speak, initially to Gog (38:2,14; 39:1) and then to all the birds and animals (39:17).

The scene is the resettled land of Israel in what for Ezekiel would have been the remote future. The Abrahamic servants of God dwell at peace with the Lord, among themselves and with all others. But the world is not at peace with them.

In the same way that Babylon had attacked Israel, Gog from the land of Magog is also permitted to strike the people in their heartland. But between the incursions of Nebuchadnezzar and Gog there is a profound difference in emphasis. Whereas Babylon functioned as the punitive sword of Yahweh appointed to afflict Israel for her sins, unrighteous Gog and the people of Magog, although sent by Yahweh, are to be vanquished. Righteous Israel will be assailed at home, in a land that again becomes a field of conflict, yet for a different reason. Non-combatant, Jacob's family behold at close quarters the ultimate overthrow of the enemy by weaponry more powerful than that of men under arms.

That this will be a penultimate event, occurring immediately before the end of the present age, is indicated by Revelation 20:7-9, where we read that 'Satan ... will go out to deceive the nations which are in the four corners of the earth, Gog and Magog, to gather them together for battle.'[131]

But why should all this be now that Israel is settled happily in the land bequeathed to Abraham and his family? Already, 'the nations ... know that I am Yahweh who sanctifies Israel, when my sanctuary is in their midst for ever' (37:28). What else remains to be done?

What remains to be done is that action must be taken to show that the world can never again overwhelm Yahweh's people by destruction and by deportation, and that godly Israel shall inherit the earth. The God of Abraham will have the last word. Chapter 37 leaves us with the suspicion that another trauma could just happen. After all, the fact that mankind realizes that the Lord and his own people are reconciled does not inhibit a renewal of tribulation. This possibility remains so long as Israel is in the world although not of it. A final resolution is necessary.

To express it another way, this commentary would propose that chapters 38 and 39 are essential for the following reason: to respond to a criticism of the God of Israel, as venerable as it had been unjust. The rationale for this approach draws its strength from 38:23, **'And I shall magnify myself and shall be sanctified, and shall be known in the sight of many nations, and they will know that I am Yahweh'**, and from 39:28: **'Then they** [Israel] **will know that I am Yahweh their God when, having exiled them among the nations, I shall assemble them on their own earth, and never again shall I leave any of them there'** — that is, in exile.

Since the time of Sinai, when Abraham's family entered into a formal commitment to serve Yahweh, Israel had suffered repeatedly at the hands of surrounding peoples. This, of course, was punitive justice because of Israel's repeated violation of the covenant mediated by Moses.[132] Yet during those weary centuries most of the people did not see it like that. Many chose to profess that their God had appeared unable, and perhaps unwilling, to honour his side of the covenant agreement. And idolatrous nations that had shown inveterate hostility to Israel never knew an occasion when Israel's God had repelled all invaders once and for all. That Israel had returned to live peacefully in Abraham's land was no final proof that, yet again, predators might not achieve what the Assyrians and Nebuchadnezzar, among others, had done in their day. It had yet to be seen that Yahweh was truly the covenant God of the family of Abraham, the God who had the power to render his obedient people invulnerable to an antagonistic world. The suspicion still lurked that Yahweh was a subordinate member of a pantheon, inferior (say) to Bel and Nebo.[133]

This would seem to explain the divine strategy underlying chapters 38 and 39. According to 38:4,8 and 39:2, Yahweh actually introduces a seemingly invincible oppressor to a territory variously described as **'the mountains of Israel'**, **'the land of Israel'** and, remarkably, Yahweh's own **'land'**.[134]

Further, it appears that this final confrontation between Yahweh and the world involves not only the downfall of Gog and his numerous confederates within the land of Israel, but also the reduction of his own territory, Magog (see 39:6). Can we take this to mean that a hostile world will never again attack God's people, Israel, because that world will have vanished, the only surviving terrain being the land vouchsafed to Abraham?[135] Essentially, when we read chapters 38 and 39 we find ourselves on the cusp of eternity. This would explain why these two chapters are an appropriate, and arguably an essential, introduction to chapters 40 – 48.[136]

The section 38:1-13 is built upon one of the great mysteries of the Bible: that God employs sinful men to fulfil his own holy purposes, yet reckons such men guilty because of their evil deeds even when they serve the interests of the Lord's people and ultimately his own glory. Here, although it is Yahweh who leads Gog against Israel, Gog, rather than God, is held responsible for the unwarranted aggression.

1. Yahweh is sovereign (38:1-9)

38:1-9. Then the word of Yahweh came to me, saying, 'Son of man, set your face towards Gog, of the land of Magog, the prince of Rosh, Meshech and Tubal, and prophesy against him. And you will say, "Thus says the Lord Yahweh: 'Look, I am against you, Gog, prince of Rosh, Meshech and Tubal.

'"'And I shall turn you around and place hooks in your jaws; and I shall bring you out, and all your army, with horses and cavalry, all of them robed in perfection, a vast assembly, with shield and buckler; all of them grasping swords: Persia, Cush and Put with them, all of them with buckler and helmet; Gomer and all its troops; Beth-Togarmah, the remote parts of the north, and all its troops — many peoples with you.

'"'Be prepared, and prepare yourself, you and all your companies who have been assembled about you, for you will be a guard for them. After many days you will be summoned; in the latter years you will come to a land recovered from the sword and gathered from many peoples, to the mountains of Israel, which had been a continual waste. But they have been brought out from many peoples and they dwell securely — all of them. Then you will come up like a devastating storm, you will come like a cloud to cover the land — you and all your troops, and many peoples with you.'"'

Yahweh's **'word'** again came to Ezekiel, who was commanded to set his face **'towards Gog, of the land of Magog'** and to **'prophesy against him'**. Because Gog is not mentioned elsewhere in the Old Testament, his identity remains uncertain. The most likely identification would seem to be that the name derives from the seventh-century BC Gyges, a king of Lydia, an Anatolian territory not far from the Ephesus of the New Testament. Perhaps, by 'giving the name of a powerful king from the previous century to the northern enemy, Ezekiel admits the dangers associated with a northern attack, although his ultimate purpose in this account is consolatory for Israel'.[137] Or, 'Gyges' may have been a dynastic title, like 'Caesar'. Either way, although identification may not be possible, what seems important is that this (to us) obscure monarch represents the leader of a remote and powerful people 'from the far North, the immemorial home of mystery and peril', distant from the borders of Israel.[138]

The text does not predict that Gog in person is to be resurrected at the end of time in order to confront Israel. As with Antiochus IV ('Epiphanes'), the Greek Seleucid king who reigned from 175 until 164 BC and who features in Daniel 11:21-35 as a type of the ultimate Antichrist, Gog foreshadows this arch opponent of the people of God.[139]

Within Scripture, the latter's name and person are never identified. None other than the 'man of lawlessness' predicted by 2 Thessalonians 2:3,7, we can assume that his identity is to be revealed when he eventually strides upon the stage of history.

'Magog' occurs in Genesis 10:2 as a descendant of Japheth, and has sometimes been understood collectively as a people living in Scythia. Or, it may be a contraction of an original term meaning 'land of Gog', which would be the aforesaid Lydia.[140]

It follows that in chapters 38 and 39 Gog is almost undoubtedly an individual, alias **'the prince of Rosh, Meshech and Tubal'**, these apparently being races or countries in Anatolia, a considerable distance from Canaan.[141] Alternatively, in that the Hebrew *rôsh* (translated here as 'Rosh') means 'head' or 'chief', Gog may be identified as a chief of Meshech and Tubal, a prince among the leaders of nations. Either way, in his brutality Gog foreshadows the final human adversary of a regathered Israel. Ezekiel looks far beyond those nearer foes such as Babylon and Assyria who had already ravaged his people. The scene takes on cosmic proportions (38:1-2).[142]

Ezekiel is to summon Gog to **'look'** at what is happening. Whatever his pretensions, the individual must be aware that none other than Yahweh is **'against'** him, he who is a distant warlord (38:3).

Remarkably, Yahweh will **'turn'** Gog **'around'**, meaning that Gog will be diverted from his current pursuits to be led, like a prisoner, with **'hooks'** in his **'jaws'**. Compare with the judgement of Pharaoh (29:4), and that of Sennacherib.[143]

Superficially, it is implied that Gog is like a wild beast compelled to obey God strictly against his will. Yet, unlike Sennacherib, who was to be led by God *away* from Judah, Gog, eager for the fray, will be marched **'out'** from his own remote territory and, as noted by 38:8, *towards* 'the mountains of Israel'.

Furthermore, Yahweh will drag behind him **'all your army ... a vast assembly'** replete with **'swords'**. Whereas a defeated army does not retain its weapons, this host, in principle subjugated already to the God of Israel, will be **'robed in perfection'** and impatient for conflict. The verse sets out to astonish its readers, and is not unsuccessful (38:4).

Having summoned various nations from the north, Yahweh turns his attention to the east (**'Persia'**),[144] the south and west (**'Cush'**, or Ethiopia; and **'Put'**, possibly Libya; cf. 27:10; 30:5). **'Gomer'** is often identified as the Cimmerians of Greek literature, a people resident in an area north and west of the Black Sea.[145] **'Beth-togarmah'**, in **'the remote parts of the north'**, was a trading partner of Tyre, possibly in Armenia (cf. 27:14).

Like Gog, his allies are remote from the immediate world in which Israel found herself.[146] In that they stream in from all points of the compass, the impression is given that Yahweh is stirring up a worldwide, universal conspiracy against innocent Israel (38:5-6). But it is Yahweh who is in overall control, the aggressors being the intended victims.

Accordingly, Yahweh's tactic is that Israel's foe shall invade the land. The Lord, requiring them for his own ultimate purpose, directs that Gog must **'prepare'** himself, together with **'all** [his] **companies'**, and be **'prepared'** for action. Gog will be **'a guard'** for those who rally to his cause, possibly meaning that he will lead them out to war (38:7).

But these things are not to come to fruition just yet; time must pass. **'After many days'** the evil potentate will be **'summoned'** and will descend upon **'the mountains of Israel'**, a land long since **'recovered from the sword and gathered from many peoples'**, whose population dwell **'securely'** because now they honour their covenant relationship with Yahweh (38:8).[147] It is as if the warrior must remain inert in his distant land until the call comes to attack. The sense of drama intensifies.

It is assumed that Gog will not only receive the divine summons but, with his confederate armies, will be obedient: **'Then you will come up like a devastating storm'** to **'cover the land'** like a storm cloud. Peaceful Israel will be at his mercy (38:9). Yahweh, the master strategist, summons invincible hordes into action against a defenceless foe. Yet these armies are *his* foes, and the intended victims of their unjust and cruel aggression are those to whom he is bound intimately, his own people whom he has resettled on the land that he granted to them long ago.

2. God uses, but never excuses, the sins of men (38:10-13)

38:10-13. '"Thus says the Lord Yahweh: 'And it shall be in that day that matters will arise in your heart and you will devise an evil scheme. Then you will say, "I shall go up to a land of villages; I shall come upon those who are quiet, they who dwell securely, all of them dwelling with no wall and with no bar and gates, to capture spoil and to seize plunder" — to turn your hand against the waste places now inhabited and to a people withdrawn from the nations, who have acquired livestock and possessions, who dwell upon the height of the land. Sheba and Dedan and the merchants of Tarshish and all its young lions will say to you, "Have you come to capture spoil? Is it to seize plunder that you assemble your company? To lift away silver and gold, to take livestock and possessions, to capture great spoil?"'"'

In this section the God of Israel informs Gog that although it is predetermined that he shall attack Israel, the tyrant nevertheless does so willingly. Divine sovereignty ordains, predicts — and will harness — human villainy, yet the villain in question remains solely accountable for his evil machinations. Because he, and he alone, aspires to annihilate the people of God, Gog will be no automaton, a nerveless puppet on a string: **'in that day ... matters will arise in your heart and you will devise an evil scheme'** (38:10).

At that time Gog will contemplate a descent upon the people of Israel, those who live quietly and (apparently) with no suspicion that Yahweh will allow an assault upon them. This would seem to be why they reside in **'villages'**,[148] rural dwellings lacking conventional fortifications. For his part, seemingly unaware that the God of Israel is provoking him to war, the aggressor decides to strike (38:11). The idyllic pastoral lifestyle of Israel is depicted graphically. Formerly, their land had been **'waste'**; now it is **'inhabited'**. Formerly, the people had found themselves among

'the nations'; now they live **'upon the height** [*tabbûr*] **of the land'** (38:12). The meaning of *tabbûr* may be indicated by Judges 9:37, in which this word alludes to the highlands of Israel, locations not requiring artificial defences.

Whereas the coalition against Israel emanates from the remote north and also from the south, merchant peoples from the east (**'Sheba'** and **'Dedan'**) and the west (**'Tarshish'**) are eager to profit from the venture.[149] **'Capture'**, **'seize'**, **'lift away'** and **'take'** reflect their motives. It is as if the whole world to its farthest ends seeks the downfall of Israel (38:13).

3. Yahweh's strategy (38:14-16)

38:14-16. 'Therefore, prophesy, son of man, and you will say to Gog, "Thus says the Lord Yahweh: 'Will it not be on that day, when my people Israel dwell securely, that you will know? Then you will come from your place, from the extremities of the north — you and many peoples with you, all of them riding upon horses, a great assembly and a vast army — and you will come upon my people Israel like a cloud to cover the land. In the latter days it will be, and I shall bring you upon my land so that the nations may know me when I am sanctified through you before their eyes, O Gog.'"'

Ezekiel must continue to address Gog. Israel is described by Yahweh as **'my people'**, indicating that any attack on them displays hostility to God himself, a hazardous procedure. After all, by now the nations are not unaware that the Lord is with his people. However, **'on that day'** Gog **'will know'**, which probably means that the aggressor will perceive the opportune time to launch his armies upon a tranquil people (38:14).

He elects to advance from his **'place, from the extremities of the north'**. Accompanied by numerous confederates, a multitude **'all ... riding upon horses'**, he will engage in blitzkrieg against Israel,[150] looking for a decisive knockout blow (38:15).

Again, **'Israel'** is described by Yahweh as **'my people'**. In the remote future, **'the latter days'**, numberless enemies will **'cover the land' 'like a cloud'** (cf. 38:9). Yet although the latter-day Gog may plan this, he should be aware that Yahweh has appointed him as his instrument so that in the humiliation of his total defeat **'the nations may know me when I am sanctified through you before their eyes'**.[151] In defending innocent Israel against an attack from virtually the whole world, the Lord defends his own name and reputation. The downfall of Gog will prove that Yahweh cares for his own. The verse ends in defiance — **'O Gog'** — and the pathos is obvious. Gog is given due notice, rendering his aggression completely inexcusable (38:16).

4. Yahweh wages total war (38:17-23)

38:17-23. '"Thus says the Lord Yahweh: 'Are you he concerning whom I spoke in the earlier days by the hand of my servants the prophets of Israel, who prophesied in those days that over the years I should bring you upon them?' 'And it will be on that day, in the day when Gog comes up on the earth of Israel,' declares the Lord Yahweh, 'that my wrath shall come up in my anger. And in my jealousy, in the fire of my fury, I have spoken: surely, on that day there will be a great earthquake on the earth of Israel. The fish of the sea and the birds of the heavens and the animals of the field, and every creeping thing that creeps on the earth, and every man who is on the face of the earth will quake, and the mountains will be thrown down, and the steep places will fall, and every wall will collapse. Then I shall summon a sword against him in all my mountains,' declares the Lord Yahweh.

'"'Each man's sword will be against his brother. So I shall enter into judgement against him with plague and with blood; and I shall rain upon him and upon his troops with driving rain and hailstones, fire and sulphur, and upon the many peoples who are with him. And I shall magnify myself and shall be sanctified, and shall be known in the sight of many nations; and they will know that I am Yahweh.'"'

Again the Lord addresses Gog. Will he not admit that he is the individual who had been mentioned by Yahweh in previous times? Had not the Lord spoken about him through earlier **'prophets'** in Israel? The question is rhetorical: Gog *had* been the subject of previous prophecy. Yet is there a problem here, in that neither Isaiah nor Jeremiah, nor any other prophet, mentions Gog and Magog explicitly?

It may be that the present verse indicates that the dynamic of a universal and ongoing hostility to Israel had always been appreciated and had often been expressed by the prophets. Thus Gog's incursion had been anticipated, even if somewhat obscurely.[152] The meaning of 38:17, then, might be that prophecies contained in the Old Testament indicate that a terminal assault of unprecedented magnitude will burst upon Israel. Gog and Magog do not innovate in that they bring to a climax the world's hatred levelled against the Lord and his people, and precipitate a final manifestation of the love of God for his own. It is Gog who will perish, rather than they.

Alternatively, the expected reply to the question, **'Are you he concerning whom I spoke in the earlier days?'** (38:17), may be 'No'. One reason for this interpretation would be that, whereas previous invasions were judgements upon Israel, Gog's descent upon Israel will exhibit the faithfulness of Yahweh in defending his own people. Because Gog is *not* to consider that he acts on behalf of the God of Israel, he must abandon any notion that he follows in the footsteps of, say, Nebuchadnezzar. He is to beware.[153] If he trespasses upon the land of promise, he will have only himself to blame for his destruction. I tend to opt for this approach.

In the name of **'the Lord Yahweh'**, Ezekiel expounds Yahweh's anger against Gog. When the latter **'comes up on the earth of Israel'**, the **'wrath'** of God will **'come up in'** his own **'anger'**. Unjust action provokes a righteous and commensurate reaction (38:18).

Enraged at the assault and the insult, the Lord speaks. Compare with 21:31, where God pours out his indignation against Ammon, and 22:21, where Yahweh declares that he will heat up the cauldron that is Jerusalem. When Gog invades there is to be **'a great earthquake'**, or trembling, **'on the earth of Israel'** (38:19).

The **'mountains'** are to be destroyed; the **'steep places'**, terraces on the hillsides,[154] will crumble, and every **'wall'** is to crash to the ground. Animate creation will tremble (38:20). The picture is similar to those given in less detail in Joel 3:16; Haggai 2:6-7 and Zechariah 14:4-5, which recall the shaking of Sinai when the Lord met Israel.[155]The final collapse of all things, both natural and man-made, is an act of judgement, although not directed against the land, admittedly the epicentre of the cataclysm.

Because the wrath of Yahweh has been aroused by Gog, the Lord will **'summon a sword against him in all my mountains'**. Yet the weapon will not be wielded by Israel but, remarkably, by the armies of Gog which turn upon one another.[156] Worse, the destruction of the enemy is accelerated by the forces of nature.[157] Put to the final test, Yahweh allows himself to be vindicated by an ordeal of strength against Gog and all his allies, the instruments being **'plague'**, **'blood'**, **'rain'**, **'hailstones'**, **'fire'** and **'sulphur'** hurled down upon Gog and his many adherents. A direct comparison with Sodom and Gomorrah is intended.[158] Perhaps Ezekiel anticipates both seismic and volcanic activity. Every possible weapon of vengeance shall be deployed (38:21-22).

The fall of Gog and his confederates will demonstrate to **'many nations'** that Yahweh has now shown himself to be great. He will have **'sanctified'** himself (cf. 36:23; 38:16). All now accept that previous dispersions of Israel were punitive and not because their God could not have come to their aid. Now, **'they ... know that I am Yahweh'** (38:23).

5. The annihilation of Gog (39:1-8)

39:1-8. 'And you, son of man, prophesy against Gog; and you will say, "Thus says the Lord Yahweh: 'Look, I am against you, Gog, prince of Rosh, Meshech and Tubal. And I shall turn you around, shall lead you on and bring you up from the remote parts of the north, and shall bring you against the mountains of Israel. Then I shall strike your bow from your left hand and make your arrows fall from your right hand.

'"'You will fall upon the mountains of Israel — you and all your troops and the peoples who are with you. I shall give you for food to every kind of bird of prey and to the animals of the field. You will fall upon the face of the field, for I have spoken,' declares the Lord Yahweh. 'And I shall send fire against Magog and against the inhabitants of the coasts who are secure, and the nations will know that I am Yahweh.

'"'So I shall make my holy name to be known in the midst of my people Israel and shall not again profane my holy name, and the nations will know that I am Yahweh, the Holy One in Israel. Look, it is coming, and it will happen,' declares the Lord Yahweh. 'That is the day about which I have spoken.'"'

The prediction of the invasion of the land of Israel by Gog and his destruction is retold, but with greater emphasis upon his overthrow. The repetition highlights the truth that Yahweh determines to be recognized by the world as the faithful God of a resettled and spiritually renewed people.

It is important to note that, although chapters 38 and 39 look forward to events that are to occur in the (as yet) future, the two chapters do not unfold consecutive actions. Rather, chapter 39 recapitulates chapter 38. If this is not appreciated, the interpreter will tie himself up in knots.

Recalling 38:2-4, Yahweh commands Ezekiel to announce that he is **'against Gog'** and his client states, and that the Lord predicts that he will **'turn** [him] **around'**, presumably from his normal routine, and send him on a special mission. Although the intensive Hebrew verb behind **'lead ... on'** is unique in the Old Testament, hopefully the translation offered here brings out the sense.[159] The Lord brings him up from **'the remote parts of the north'** to **'the mountains of Israel'**. The scene is set (39:1-2).

We learn from 38:15 that the armies of Gog will 'all' be mounted. Now it transpires that these cavalry hordes will be armed with bow and arrow, skilled warriors able to shoot accurately from horseback without grasping the reins of their steeds. In the highlands of Israel the Lord will strike the **'bow'** from the **'left hand'** of Gog and cause his **'arrows'** to fall from his **'right hand'**. There is no mention made of military resistance being offered by Israel because it is Yahweh who intervenes victoriously (39:3).

The disarmed warrior is rendered helpless and harmless. Together with all his **'troops'**, he collapses prostrate upon **'the mountains of Israel'** where Yahweh offers him as **'food'** to all species of scavenging birds and beasts. That Gog and his allies will **'fall'** is repeated in order to drive the lesson home. The dynamic behind his unexpected yet sudden death in the open **'field'** is Yahweh's infallible declaration (39:4-5).

And **'fire'** will be hurled **'against Magog'**, as upon the seemingly secure **'inhabitants of the coasts'**, or 'islands'.[160] By comparing this passage with Amos 1:4,7,10; 2:2,5 and Hosea 8:14,[161] it appears that in some unspecified manner the Lord will overthrow his enemies' territories. Not even the avaricious merchants mentioned by 38:13 are to be spared.

In that Revelation 20:8 identifies 'Magog' as representing 'the four corners of the earth', it would appear that the end of the world as we know it is being predicted. Then, at the last moment, **'the** [ruined] **nations'** will **'know'** that Yahweh is the God who keeps covenant with Israel (39:6).

In this manner the Lord causes his **'holy name to be known in the midst of** [his] **people'**. In that the undiscerning had reckoned that Yahweh was unable or unwilling (or both) to rescue Israel from the ravages of war (cf. 36:3,15,20), they profaned his **'holy name'**. At last the nations realize that Yahweh remains **'the Holy One in Israel'**.

The key word here is **'holy'**: both the Lord's people and all others will be aware that God, ever immanent in human affairs, remains transcendent and is faithful both to his promises and his warnings (39:7).

But why had the world at large ridiculed Israel's God? The answer would be that because men reckoned that evil was of no great consequence, defeat in battle convinced them that the amoral gods of vanquished nations were not sufficiently powerful to protect their devotees. Might was right, and divine justice did not enter into the matter. This is how Yahweh was regarded.

To illustrate, the king of Syria was informed that the 'gods' of Israel were mountain deities, the armies of which could be overthrown in the plain.[162] Ezekiel's message is that this shallow analysis had never actually applied to Yahweh and Israel: at no time had the Lord lost control. For this reason Gog and all others must **'look'**, realizing that the catastrophe, the event about which Yahweh has had much to say in chapter 38, **'is coming, and it will happen'**. To emphasize the certainty, Yahweh adds, **'That is the day about which I have spoken'** (39:8).

6. War will be no more (39:9-10)

39:9-10. '"'Then they who inhabit the cities of Israel will go out and burn and make fires of weaponry, buckler and shield, of bow and arrows, clubs and spears, and they will make fires of them for seven years. And they will not carry wood from the field nor hew from the forests, because they will make fires with the weaponry and will spoil those who despoiled them and plunder those who plundered them,' declares the Lord Yahweh."'

Verses 1-8 are saturated with the first person singular, emphasizing that the overthrow of Gog and his armies will be a direct act of God, rather than the consequence of successful resistance by Israel. Now attention is directed to those **'who inhabit the cities of Israel'** in the immediate aftermath of the conflict. Apparently unharmed by the invaders and the event of war, they **'go out'** in order to rid their land of all munitions of battle.

That seven types of weaponry are mentioned may indicate the totality of the cleansing process. Because God has appeared on behalf of his people, war is no more.[163]

Moreover, Gog's munitions will provide fuel for the population of Israel for a period of **'seven years'**. Extending Isaiah's picture of the detritus of war being burned as fuel,[164] perhaps this suggests a species of Sabbath rest for both land and people in that the former will not be denuded of timber by the latter (39:9-10).

Overall, within the borders of their own land the people of Israel **'will spoil those who despoiled them and plunder those who plundered them'**, parallelism lending emphasis to the assertion.[165] But there is no mention of the victors taking the battle back to the land of Magog. Apparently, that land has been devastated already (cf. 39:6).

Although the language is clearly that of imagery, a literal interpretation being nonsensical, it seems no less obvious that text and context insist that in the distant future the people and land of Israel are to be attacked by a worldwide coalition. **'The Lord Yahweh' 'declares'** that when it happens Israel shall triumph (39:10).

7. The burial of Gog and the cleansing of the land (39:11-16)

39:11-16. '"'And it will be on that day that I shall give Gog a burial place there — in Israel, the valley of those who pass by, east of the sea, and it will block off the passers-by. So there they will bury Gog and all his multitude and will call it "the Valley of the Multitude of Gog". Then for seven months the house of Israel will bury them in order to cleanse the land. And all the people of the land will bury, and they will have a name for themselves on the day when I glorify myself,' declares the Lord Yahweh.

'"'So they will set apart men who pass permanently through the land burying the passers-by, they who remain on the face of the land, to cleanse it. At the end of seven months they will search; and when they who pass through cross over the land and someone sees a human bone, then he will erect a signpost beside it until the buriers inter it in "the Valley of the Multitude of Gog". And the name of the city is "Multitude", and they will cleanse the land.'"'

One can only speculate about the means employed by Yahweh to overthrow Gog within the land of Israel (but compare with 38:19-22). Yet in the aftermath of war and at the commencement of the seven-year period during which redundant enemy munitions will be put out of commission, the enemy's slain multitudes lie unburied, contaminating the ground and also any who might come into physical contact with them.[166] For this reason, Yahweh will personally allocate **'a burial place'** for **'Gog'** where he and **'all his multitude'** are to be interred.

Given the vast numbers of the slain, there will have to be a mass burial, the site being known as **'the valley of those who pass by'**, meaning 'valley of the travellers'. The significance of this designation is uncertain unless it is wordplay, **'pass by'** meaning 'pass on', the macabre valley being devoted to the dead who have passed on to another world.[167]

Its location will be **'east of the sea'**, the sea in question being of necessity either the Mediterranean or the Dead Sea. But because a reference to dry land to the east of the Mediterranean would be superfluous, it would seem that the valley is to be to the east, as against the west, of the Dead Sea. Indicating, then, that the slain will not be buried within the borders of sacred Israelite territory (cf. 47:18), the setting seems appropriate.

The heap of corpses in the mass grave will be so vast that **'it will block off the passers-by'**,[168] this being mentioned to give the reader some notion of the immensity of the slaughter. No more will the valley be a thoroughfare. In consequence, Israelites (**'they'**) will name the place **'the Valley of the Multitude of Gog'**, in Hebrew *gé h'môn Gôg*, a possible play on *gé hinnôm*, 'the Valley of Hinnom', or Gehenna (39:11).

Notwithstanding the overthrow of Gog, the earth of Israel had been contaminated by alien incursion, as also by the unburied enemy slain: invasion *is* defilement.[169] Whereas according to Numbers 19:19, purification from contact with the dead would take seven days, this act of cleansing will require **'seven months'**, so many are there to be interred. No mention is made of personal defilement, the essential point being that all are eager **'to cleanse the land'** because they cannot tolerate anything that will offend the holiness of Yahweh and the sanctity of Israel (39:12).

Yahweh continues to address Gog (cf. 39:1), informing him that after his certain overthrow within the land of Israel an exultant people will be of one heart and one mind in their enthusiasm to rid their land of every vestige of his incursion: **'all the people of the land will bury'**. And in so doing they will **'have a name for themselves'**, meaning that the surrounding world will observe that Israel is consumed by an intelligent zeal for the Lord. Yet Yahweh had appointed enemy action and Israelite reaction with a view to self-glorification rather than for the exaltation of his people. He **'declares'** that it shall be so.

Because this evil world would seem to be drawing to its end when Israel buries the dead (cf. 39:6), how, then, can peoples other than a holy Israel survive to gaze at the seven-month burial process? The anomaly suggests that the language employed here must be figurative (39:13).

Taking into account the dimensions of the task, text and context anticipate that some corpses might remain unburied. As a precaution against defilement, when the seven months mentioned in 39:12 come to an end some individuals are to seek out what may be left. There appears to be another deliberate play on the verb 'pass', or 'pass by'. Verse 11 refers to 'the valley of those who pass by' and to 'the passers-by', while now the appointees will **'pass permanently through the land'** to bury **'the passers-by'** — transients, now dead, whose corpses disfigure **'the face of**

the land'. The dual object of the exercise is the removal of all defilement *and* an energetic return to the status quo prior to Gog's invasion. Until that is accomplished there will be much activity (39:14).

The quest for cleanliness will be scrupulous, so much so that if the burial squads come across even a single **'human bone'**, a **'signpost'** is placed beside it so that it will be seen and subsequently removed for burial in **'the Valley of the Multitude of Gog'** (39:15).

It would appear that although the site for the interment of the dead will be a valley beyond the eastern border of Israel (cf. 39:11),[170] the vast numbers of the slain will constitute a virtual necropolis, a city of the dead. Accordingly, it will be dubbed with the name **'Multitude'** (*hamônah*), no doubt as a memorial to the downfall of the enemy hosts.

The section ends tersely: **'and they** [those who gather and inter the fallen] **will cleanse the land'** (39:16). That the enemy dead should be granted a decent burial is not even a subordinate consideration.

8. The great banquet (39:17-20)

39:17-20. 'And you, son of man, thus says the Lord Yahweh: "Say to every kind of bird and to all the animals of the field, 'Assemble yourselves and come; gather yourselves from all around for my sacrifice which I am sacrificing for you — a great sacrifice upon the mountains of Israel. And you will eat flesh and drink blood. You will eat the flesh of mighty men and will drink the blood of the princes of the land: rams, lambs and goats, and bulls — all of them the fatlings of Bashan. So you will eat fat until you are satisfied and drink blood until you are drunk, from my sacrifice that I am sacrificing for you. Then you will be satisfied at my table with horse and chariot, with the mighty man and every man of war,' declares the Lord Yahweh."'

The **'son of man'** is to trigger the prediction of 39:4 by summoning **'every kind of bird'** and **'all the animals of the field'** to **'a great sacrifice'** which Yahweh **'is sacrificing'** just for them **'upon the mountains of Israel'**. According to Moses, worshippers would sacrifice animals and birds in honour of Yahweh; now, Yahweh provides an immense sacrifice of human remains for the benefit of natural scavengers **'from all around'**, eager to gorge themselves upon **'flesh'** and **'blood'**.

How can this be if, as the context appears to show, the dead had already been properly buried beyond the borders of Israel?

As noted earlier, it would seem that Ezekiel's message must be figurative. Having been defeated by Yahweh, buried by Israel and any remnant now devoured by birds and animals, Gog's rejection and destruction are complete (39:17).[171]

The menu is outlined, birds and animals being summoned to devour **'mighty men'** and to **'drink the blood of the princes of the land'**, **'land'** (*eretz*) probably standing for the world. **'Rams'**, **'lambs'**, **'goats'**, **'bulls'** and **'fatlings of Bashan'** designate the nobility of the world at large (39:18). Further, the **'sacrifice'** provided by Yahweh will be abundant: **'you will eat ... until you are satisfied ... and drink ... until you are drunk.'** Whereas in conventional Israelite sacrifices the consumption of **'fat'** and **'blood'** was prohibited,[172] now the Lord offers such a **'sacrifice'** to bird and beast, perhaps to indicate the insignificance of Gog and his minions (39:19).

The imagery is shocking, and even repugnant, but designedly so: Gog is being warned that should he attack Israel, he will do so at his peril. At Yahweh's **'table'** the participants **'will be satisfied'**, having eaten their fill of **'horse and chariot'** and of **'the mighty man and every man of war'**. Nothing will remain of the immense host sent to destroy Israel.

'The Lord Yahweh' declares that it shall be so (39:20).

9. Now the nations understand (39:21-24)

39:21-24. '"'And I shall set my glory among the nations, and all the nations will see my justice which I have executed, and my hand which I have laid on them. Then the house of Israel will know that I am Yahweh their God from that day onward. And the nations will know that for their iniquity the house of Israel went into exile. Because they acted treacherously against me I hid my face from them and gave them into the hand of their adversaries, and they fell by the sword — all of them. I dealt with them according to their defilement and according to their transgressions.'"'

The remainder of the prophecy against Gog concerns the dual effect of his overthrow within the land of Israel. Firstly, Yahweh **'will set** [his] **glory among the nations'** when they see his punitive **'justice'**[173] and the **'hand'** that he had made to rest upon the adversary (39:21).

Furthermore, **'from that day onward'** — that is, perpetually — the **'house of Israel'** will accept that **'Yahweh'** is **'their God'** (39:22).

Herein may lie a problem of interpretation. This commentary has suggested that the war between Yahweh and Gog is an eschatological event.[174] But how can we contemplate a godly Israel living at peace in this world alongside nations that have already been devoured, as it were, in the sacrificial meal, and now acquiescing gladly? Block, for example, insists that the war 'does not occur at the end of time'.[175]

Perhaps a resolution may be discovered in the fact that we are dealing with imagery, the complete section being, as has been suggested, figurative and not to be considered literally. In the manner of a kaleidoscope, pictures flash before the eyes. Maybe the kernel of the oracle is that the nations' universal recognition of the lordship of Yahweh and of his care for Israel would endure were time to continue.

Further, if the invasion by Gog does *not* occur at the end of time, would there not be yet more problems of interpretation? For example, are we to believe that Magog, the land whence Gog came and which was attacked by fire (see 39:6), is to survive along with a triumphant Israel? If the former is not obedient to Yahweh (for which obedience there is no evidence in Ezekiel), there would be an enduring hostility (39:22).

In any event, these verses are essentially theocentric: witnessing the restoration of Israel, the **'nations'** will be fully aware that Yahweh had never been powerless to deliver his people when attacked by, say, Nebuchadnezzar. They will accept that the exile to Babylon was on account of Israel's repudiation of their covenant with their God, for which they were justly deprived of their homeland. It will be seen that they had been guilty of **'iniquity'**, had **'acted treacherously'**, had indulged in **'defilement'** and had repeatedly defied the requirements of the law (**'transgressions'**). Yahweh **'dealt with them'** accordingly. This is why he **'hid** [his] **face from them'**, abandoning them to a hostile world.[176]

Ezekiel's words are remarkable. Apparently, men everywhere will accept that there had always been a solemn covenant and a binding relationship between God and this diminutive people. It will acknowledge at long last that, about 2000 BC, the Lord had entered into a bond with a non-Jew called Abraham, that about 1500 BC he had refined and defined this bond by means of a subordinate and provisional covenant ratified at Sinai, and that, millennia later, he had caused an errant Israel to conform to his will and thus be readmitted to the land of promise (39:23-24).

10. Peace (39:25-29)

39:25-29. 'Therefore, "Thus says the Lord Yahweh: 'Now I shall turn back the captivity of Jacob and shall have compassion on the whole house of Israel, and shall be jealous for my holy name. And they will bear their shame and all the treachery that they perpetrated against me, when they dwell securely on their own earth with no one to frighten. When I bring them back from the peoples and gather them from the lands of their enemies, then I shall sanctify myself through them in the eyes of many nations. Then they will know that I am Yahweh their God when, having exiled them among the nations, I shall assemble them on their own earth, and never again shall I leave any of them there. And I shall not hide my face from them again, because I shall have poured out my Spirit on the house of Israel,' declares the Lord Yahweh."'

In that shame and exile had been the just deserts of rebellious Israel, **'the Lord Yahweh'** now declares that he will **'turn back the captivity of Jacob'**. This is virtually a technical term, elsewhere denoting the restoration of favour to a nation or an individual.[177]

And the underlying rationale is that the unhappy situation of this family is to be reversed because the Lord is **'jealous'** for his **'holy name'**. Having bound himself to Israel long ago, Yahweh cannot abandon this people unless he is prepared to be justly maligned by the world. But, given his fundamental commitment, the exercise of **'compassion'** is a virtual necessity (39:25).

Consequently, the whole family of Israel will be disgusted when they contemplate their past history (cf. 16:54,61-63; 36:31). In addition, their happy residence **'on their own earth with no one to frighten'** will cause them to ponder the love of the God who summoned their remote ancestors to faith and obedience, whose rejection of Israel was temporary, who at the end of the age had renewed them spiritually and had restored them geographically, and who, finally, had defended them from aggression so that no more will they have cause to fear. They will know that grace has reigned (39:26).

So, by restoring them **'from the lands of their enemies'**, Yahweh will **'sanctify** [himself] **through them in the eyes of many nations'** (cf. 28:25).[178] This means that it will be accepted generally that there is one God, that he is personal, that he is inherently holy, that he is graciously willing to relate with and to redeem sinful men, that in time past he had chosen Israel exclusively to be his own people, and that he has dealt righteously in honouring all his warnings and promises to them (39:27).

Commencing at 34:1, the glorious message of ultimate restoration, having occupied six chapters, now concludes. It is as if the world is shut out, the doors are closed and the people of Israel contemplate their own blessed situation. Now, after centuries of exile **'among the nations'**, the complete family has been brought back to the ancient homeland and is convinced that **'never again'** will there be a dispersion. They see that **'Yahweh'** is in truth **'their God'** and that he has done this thing (39:28).

Finally, a promise: **'I shall not hide my face from them ... because'** Yahweh has **'poured out** [his] **Spirit on the house of Israel'**.[179] The Lord **'declares'** that it shall be so. This grant of the Spirit of God to Israel had occurred before Gog's incursion (cf. 36:27), and is now described as an outpouring because, drenched, so to speak, by this divine fluid,[180] the people are aware that they are in relationship with their God.[181] They know that he is within them rather than simply among them.[182] Geographical restoration, although an evidence of Yahweh's power and grace, would never have been a sufficient confirmation.

Application

The apostle Paul tells us that God 'has shone in our hearts to give the light of the knowledge of the glory of God in the face of Jesus Christ'.[183] Among other great truths, this means that the God of love glorifies himself when he saves. Although he can and does condemn guilty sinners, he has no 'pleasure in the death of the wicked' (18:23). 'Why will you die?' (33:11).

This being so, when Yahweh declares in 39:21 that he will 'set my glory among the nations; and all the nations will see my justice which I have executed, and my hand which I have laid on them', the meaning is that because of the covenant imposed graciously and unilaterally upon Abraham,[184] the Lord has bound himself to uphold his chosen people. Historically, this commitment manifested itself in the preservation of Abraham's family until and after Jacob's emigration to Egypt, and then in the bilateral covenant between Yahweh and Israel at Sinai. But even when Israel broke that covenant, effectively placing themselves among the nations as one of them, the Lord never declared that he had finally surrendered his love for them. Indeed, in anticipating Israelite apostasy, Yahweh also anticipated the people's future conversion and a renewed association with them.[185] The Lord keeps those whom he calls, nothing being able to tear them from his powerful hand.[186]

Ezekiel's prediction of the regathering of the family of Jacob within the borders of their own land, their spiritual renewal, an attack by Gog and confederate forces, and the latter's overthrow at the end of time makes no mention whatever of the ingathering of the Gentiles, a theme that is so prominent in the New Testament. So, what of these 'other sheep'?[187]

One answer to such a question might be that the revelation of the mystery of Gentile inclusion within the 'commonwealth of Israel' was not placed by the Lord high upon Ezekiel's agenda.[188] It was the prophet's allotted task to convince Israel, a people ravaged by war and shamed by eviction from their land, that God was faithful to the original covenant and that there would be a glorious future for them.

Assuming that the majority of today's readers of the prophecy of Ezekiel are non-Jews, it is incumbent on us to pray continually for 'the peace of Jerusalem'.[189] If we are among the very many small dogs privileged to lick the crumbs from beneath the Master's Jewish table,[190] let us never forget that Israel has never been denied a permanent place at that table. We need to stand with Simeon and Anna and identify with the prediction of Romans 11:23-29.[191] There Paul does not dream, but writes about what shall be because it must be.

Part 3:
From 'the twenty-fifth year of our exile, in the beginning of the year, on the tenth of the month, in the fourteenth year after the city had been smitten'

13. The thirteenth, and final, series of prophecies

(Ezekiel 40:1 – 48:35)

Focus: the progression from chapter 39 to chapters 40 – 48

1. Israel, and Israel alone

The final nine chapters of the prophecy of Ezekiel focus upon believing Israel to the exclusion of all other nations. In detail, when we read onwards from chapter 40 we sense immediately that we are in a situation other than that presented by chapters 34 – 39, which concern themselves with a regenerate Israel this side of eternity. It is as if we are precipitated into an environment where the drab features of a fallen and perishing world are absent. Sin and discord within Israel are no more; divine wrath is exhausted; conflict does not exist between Israel and other peoples; and God and his own are reconciled. We are given the impression that the journey of Israel has now reached its appointed end and that we gaze upon a habitat not of this familiar scene.

Over the centuries, the apostate people of Israel had rejected Yahweh and for their sins were evicted from the land originally promised to Abraham and his family. Formally yet not truly the people of God, they learned by sad experience that Yahweh honours his covenant warnings as well as his promises.

The nations of the world, ever antagonistic to Israel and her God, have also been judged. Like the pharaoh of the Exodus, they have come to know that Yahweh is who he had always claimed to be. Regenerate Israel has finally been returned to the land of their inheritance. Now, willingly obedient to God, they are secure in their tenancy, unlike their disobedient forefathers. Vindicated by Yahweh, they know that he has remained faithful to his pledged word.

Like Nebuchadnezzar, Gog from Magog had been brought by Yahweh into the land of Israel. But unlike the Babylonian tyrant, Gog became the object of divine wrath in an apocalyptic judgement rather than God's instrument of chastisement. The man and his minions were overthrown, although not by human hands.

Along with Israel, the nations have witnessed Yahweh act as he did centuries before at the Red Sea. Both in judgement and in mercy he is recognized as the one who has defended his people, and thereby his own name, by overthrowing their enemies. Now, hostility gone, Israel remains a prince with God.

2. History at an end

In short, when we consider the movement of the prophecy from chapter 39 to chapter 40 onwards we are driven to a remarkable conclusion. Prior to the scene outlined in chapters 40 – 48, history appears to have come to an end. We do not sense that Israel has any further mission to the world.

3. The ocean of eternity

The impression is conveyed that we have arrived at an estuary where the river of time flows into the ocean of eternity. The glory of God in redemption and judgement has been manifested to all men. The vehicle of salvation has arrived at its terminus, and time as we comprehend it is no more.

Moreover, the conclusion that chapters 40 – 48 have to do with the ultimate glory is given corroboration in that they provide so much foundational material for Revelation 21 and 22, chapters concerned exclusively with the post-resurrection world to come.

Over the years, Ezekiel had ministered to an apostate people to warn them of impending judgement. Then, when Jerusalem was overrun by barbarian hordes, he encouraged the remnant. Now, as chapter 40 opens, he gazes beyond the terrestrial horizon to another world and towards a new Jerusalem. He writes in chapters 40 – 48 of the realms of the blessed, doing so in the only way possible for him, harnessing the concepts and terminology of his priestly vocation.

4. Now the Lord has no need to make his name known

I would suggest that it is of the greatest possible significance that nowhere in this final part of his book does Ezekiel tell out that men, whether in Israel or elsewhere, come to know that Yahweh is. Nor, within these chapters, does the Lord take action to convince friend and foe alike that 'I am Yahweh'. This is because all have come to know it already, one way or the other. Now the prophet leads his readers up to and within the gates of the celestial city, having been instructed to reveal everything he sees (see 40:4).

This he does with characteristic faithfulness, ending his ministry with the statement that the beloved city, which can be none other than Jerusalem, has a new and everlasting name, a name spelling out the mercies of a covenant-keeping God: 'Yahweh is there' (48:35). In Ezekiel's day, the glory of Yahweh had departed from the temple (see 10:18). Now this glory returns, never to leave.

Focus: the ultimate destiny of Israel (Ezekiel 40:1 – 48:35)

1. Continuity yet change

As observed, the final nine chapters of the prophecy stand apart from all that comes before. Yet they do not lie in isolation, guillotined from the main body of the book. The fundamental theme of chapters 34 – 39, the residence of the people of God in the land of promise, persists, albeit in a highly developed form.

From chapter 40 onwards the prophet records his vision of a new matrix for the priestly worship of God and a revised division of Canaan among the tribes of Israel. An explicit continuity with the past is maintained, yet a continuity that is self-qualifying. Gloriously, the blessedness of this permanently settled people is of a quality far superior to that which Israel had ever known during her long terrestrial history.

It may also be concluded that Ezekiel's outline is not that of an ultimate settlement in this world. As Ellison observes caustically, 'The suggestions of supersonic aircraft bringing pilgrims to Jerusalem and of others sharing in the temple services by television are tragic-comic.'[1] I shall argue that such a literal interpretation is impossible, mainly because the dimensions of Ezekiel's city, temple and tribal allotments do not fit the topography of the region. This section of the prophecy must be apocalyptic.[2]

2. The Law and the Prophets

It may be supposed, then, that Ezekiel offers us a metaphor, both colossal and magnificent, stimulating our imagination rather than relaying some sort of revised legislation for terrestrial Israel. For example, consider the instruction in 40:4: 'Declare to the house of Israel all that you see.' Here the prophet does not assume the role of a second Moses required to specify the particulars of a modified system of temple worship. What he does is give the broad outline of an idealized arrangement, an outline that is meant to be pondered.

It needs to be borne in mind that Ezekiel saw 'visions of God' (40:2; cf. 1:1; 8:3; 43:3). Although both the Old and the New Testament give commands that bind the Lord's people, law was never prescribed through the medium of prophetic visions.

According to Numbers 12:6-8, which contrasts Moses with all other prophets, the former is said to have received his revelations directly and face to face rather than through visions and dreams. Because Ezekiel beheld visions of a system of temple worship in many details differing markedly from, yet not opposed to, that prescribed by Moses, it follows that the prophet did not reckon himself to be a legislator.

3. Alternative interpretations

Although the temple seen in this final vision is nowhere said explicitly to be Jerusalem, it is described as a city situated within a restored Israel (see 40:2). The implication is obvious. Yet this arrangement cannot represent some sort of geographical reconstruction of the Jerusalem temple complex. For one thing, the description of the temple is no three-dimensional plan;[3] for another, building materials are not specified. Were he to consult these chapters in order to build such a temple, a contractor would be at a loss. And, as Block observes, 'The man with a measuring line takes Ezekiel on a tour of an existing structure already made.'[4] Either the prophet predicts in symbol form the present worldwide church, or he is concerned with eschatological realities.

This commentary would suggest that the former alternative is impossible. Nowhere in the New Testament is the worship of the Christian churches and their organization expounded in any way in terms of the rituals of temple worship. For example, there is no separated order of priests. Nor is the offering of our Lord as the fulfilment of Old Testament shadows a contradiction.[5]

We know that the churches are not intended by Christ to hobble backwards towards the 'weak and beggarly elements' of outmoded Jewish legislation.[6] It follows that chapters 40 – 48 are not a symbolic exposition of the present gospel dispensation. Arguably, what we have here points to an unending blessedness in another, better world. There, no Gog and Magog can intrude and no residual sins molest.[7]

Chapters 34 – 39 encouraged Israel in exile. Now chapters 40 – 48 go further, picturing the initial covenant with Abraham, Isaac and Jacob as fulfilled in the age to be, an age which the New Testament would pinpoint as following the Second Coming and the general resurrection. In taking up so much material from Ezekiel 40 – 48, Revelation 21:9 – 22:5 virtually proves this to be the only valid interpretation. This point has been made, but bears repetition.

4. Is there to be another temple in Jerusalem?

Perhaps there are those who hold that chapters 40 – 48 predict a rebuilding of the temple after the Second

Coming. But does not the death of Jesus fulfil, and therefore end, all previous typological sacrifices?[8]

That is, there is no hint in the New Testament that the priestly offerings will ever be reintroduced as a retrospective commemoration of Calvary. But Scripture does tell us that the Lord's Table is the one appointed method by which Christians together are to remember the death of Jesus.[9] In this world, we shall never need anything else.

Further, the notion of another temple in Jerusalem seems altogether inappropriate. Does the Bible anticipate a historical resurrection of the tribe of Levi and of the priestly family of Aaron appointed to go within a torn veil desecrated by the Lord himself?[10]

And in so far as the ceremonial worship enacted by Moses was an integral and inseparable element of his total legislation, a reintroduction of the temple ritual would necessitate the subjection of all believers to the form of worship operative under the old covenant and thereby subjection to Mosaic law in its completeness. Surely, the thing cannot be.

5. Ezekiel, a man for his day

Why, then, are the shadows of the old dispensation pressed into service by Ezekiel to depict what would appear to be the heavenly scene?

Perhaps the answer is not elusive if we bear in mind that Ezekiel the priest lived through the devastation of Jerusalem, in an alien land ministering to deportees to assure them that the Lord would in time establish a renewed Israel within the land of promise. But I believe that he anticipated, too, that this present habitat would yield to and shade into another where the family of God would worship and rest for ever.

If some of the exiles understood this, what a wonderful encouragement chapters 40 – 48 must have been to them!

It may be supposed that the heavenly realm is pictured in a manner that would have been comprehensible to pious Jews in Ezekiel's time, and since. Indeed, there could have been no finer and, for that matter, no other appropriate vehicle of expression. The saints of the old dispensation were being promised that their yearnings would at last be realized in a new and better world. Reinforced by such a splendid assurance, they were to wait patiently for the ultimate consolation of Israel and for the redemption of Jerusalem. When our Lord was born, Simeon and Anna, among others, were doing just this.[11]

6. The future in terms of the past

These final chapters of the prophecy of Ezekiel share an important principle of interpretation in common with some earlier visions recorded in the book, where past events are recalled in order to sketch future happenings. For instance, in chapter 4 the judgements to fall upon Israel and Judah are portrayed in terms of the years spent by Israel in Egypt and in the wilderness.

But no literal repetition of the events surrounding the Exodus is expected. Ezekiel's representation of the king of Tyre projects him as a guardian angel who had fallen into sin, yet without demanding that the reader should consider the haughty monarch as a fallen angel incarnate (28:1-19). Egypt, which made itself out as some sort of quasi-god in its dealings with Israel, must experience the forty-year sufferings of Israel in the desert and a scattering among the people (29:1-16). But Egypt is no Israel.

In short, Ezekiel saw history as supplying shadow outlines and anticipations for the future. The prophet beheld the past turning in full circle, although never repeating itself in precise detail. He knew that the Lord is uniform in his dealings with men, and appreciated that earlier experiences sometimes typified impending, and at other times more distant events. Nor are Christians ignorant of this principle in that we know that the typology of the Old Testament is the key to the New Testament. For example, Christ is equally the lamb and the lion.[12]

Is it not like this with the new city-temple that Ezekiel saw, yet with a vital qualification? His description incorporates modifications of the past ritual which demonstrate that the splendour of the new situation will far exceed that of the forms prescribed by Moses.[13] This principle becomes an essential help when we try to grapple with Ezekiel 40 – 48.

To illustrate, the highest ideas that we can conceive about the church's ultimate glory are sometimes foreshadowed by everyday life here and now. Who can understand what Paul means by the 'spiritual body' that the believer is to assume when he rises from the dead?[14] But the apostle's doctrine is that there *is* to be such a body, freed from the limitations of our present natural frame. Perhaps we can come to terms with this.

Again, what will be the nature of the ultimate wedding banquet?[15] We cannot tell, except that the meeting between our Lord and his own is typified by the exhilaration characteristic of a wedding. Here is something to bite on.

Ezekiel's visions were the pledge of blessings promised to God's people, a pledge outlined in a manner appropriate for a priest-prophet and those who were steeped in temple ritual. He announces that the Lord will be worshipped in the eternal temple. Similarly,

Isaiah 60, written a century before Ezekiel, tells out the same message.

7. Why the detail?

On the face of it, the wealth of detail in Ezekiel's outline of the sanctuary and its ceremonies is bewildering. We want to know why the Lord gave so many exact measurements for gates, walls, apartments, guard rooms, courts, doors and windows. Why were there eight tables rather than, say, six for killing the animal sacrifices? (40:41). Why was the altar of burnt offering described precisely with its various recesses and ledges? (43:13-17). Do these and other details embrace truths for which scholars have to search diligently to obtain more light from God's Word? Is there here a half-hidden symbolism that awaits our investigation before it yields all its spiritual treasures?

Perhaps the answer to this question could be more simple — and profound — than we might imagine. Let's remember that the tabernacle that Moses constructed in the wilderness was built in strict accordance with the pattern given to him by the Lord.[16] In its way it was no less detailed than the sanctuary seen by Ezekiel. Essentially, it was a place of worship designed and instituted by God alone. Moses' task was to relay instructions, neither he nor any other man being permitted to innovate.[17]

To illustrate the principle, the prime fault of Ahaz of Judah in the eighth century BC was that he introduced to the temple an alternative altar, Assyrian in origin, which the Lord had not commanded.[18] In effect, Yahweh was being informed that he must be content with imported forms of worship. His sovereignty was being usurped.

In brief, the unusual wealth of detail both in Moses' tabernacle and much later in that sanctuary seen by

Ezekiel appears to have served one interest alone: the pattern of worship to be offered by the congregation was defined by God, rather than some arrangement concocted by the sinful wit of men. Salvation was seen to be of the Lord. Perhaps we need look no further for the answer to our question.

Nor should we interpret literally. In his vision Ezekiel had beheld the departure of the divine glory from the temple (10:1-19), demonstrating that for a time at least Yahweh had abandoned Israel. Similarly, the visionary restitution of temple worship and the return of God's presence on a permanent basis signify reconciliation between Yahweh and Israel. It would be a mistake to interpret the visions of chapter 10 and chapters 40 – 48 as literal predictions.

8. Almost the end of a ministry

This prophecy was Ezekiel's penultimate revelation. His last word, recorded in 29:17 – 30:26 concerning Nebuchadnezzar and Egypt, was issued two years later, about 571 BC. Nebuchadnezzar would reign in Babylon for nine more years. Daniel was possibly at the height of his influence, although Jeremiah's ministry had ceased. Another thirty years would pass until Cyrus the Persian authorized the rebuilding of the temple in Jerusalem.[19] Men and matters were on the move. As far as he was concerned, before he concluded his life's work Ezekiel was required to point the people to the ultimate glory of Israel.

The importance of the collective vision of chapters 40 – 48 is highlighted by the fact that Ezekiel gives the year: 'in the twenty-fifth year of our exile' (40:1). As noted at the beginning of this commentary, the qualifier 'of our exile' is found elsewhere only in 33:21, while the opening of Ezekiel's prophetic ministry is dated to the fifth year of Jehoiachin's 'exile' (1:2).

Taken together, these dates mark the commencement of Ezekiel's ministry of warning to sinful Jerusalem and then that of his ministry of encouragement.

This tends to confirm our analysis of the essentially triple division of the book. Ezekiel, it may be believed, was concerned initially with the judgement of God upon degenerate Israel, then with the vindication of a regenerate Israel living in Canaan, and, finally, with an eschatological, otherworldly, scene.

The vision of the temple (Ezekiel 40:1 – 42:20)

It is now the twenty-fifth year of Ezekiel's exile, the first month of the religious year, Nisan, or Abib, and the tenth day. This may have been 28 April 573 BC. According to Exodus 12:3, the day would have been the beginning of Passover, and it could be that Ezekiel the priest had that in mind (cf. 45:21-24). Perhaps text and context are concerned with the exodus of Israel towards a homeland not of this world.

This last series of visions is also said to commence fourteen years after the Chaldeans had destroyed Jerusalem (**'the city'**, 40:1) in 586 BC. The dates fit.

1. Ezekiel meets the angelic surveyor (40:1-4)

40:1-4. In the twenty-fifth year of our exile, in the beginning of the year, on the tenth of the month, in the fourteenth year after the city had been smitten, on this selfsame day the hand of Yahweh was upon me and he brought me there. In the visions of God he brought me to the land of Israel and set me down upon a very high mountain; and on it to the south there was like the structure of a city. So he brought me there, and, look, a man. His appearance was as the appearance of bronze, and a cord of linen was in his hand, and a measuring reed, and he was standing in the gate. Then the man spoke to me: 'Son of man, see with your eyes and hear with your ears, and set your heart to all that I am about to show you, for you have been brought here in order to show you. Tell all that you see to the house of Israel.'

As in 1:3 and 37:1, **'the hand of Yahweh'** came upon Ezekiel. In his renewed vision he was sent back to the site where Jerusalem had once stood. Although it was twenty-five years since his own deportation in 597 BC and fourteen years since the city had been destroyed, for the prophet the place was still sacred, **'there'** equating with **'the city'**. 'City' is poignant in that for Ezekiel there could be only one city, which is why the name is not mentioned (40:1). Similarly, in his Gospel Matthew would direct his readers' attention to 'the holy city'.[20]

But what Ezekiel beheld **'in the visions of God'** was not the remnant of a city ravaged by war. Rather, he tells that he was aware that he found himself within the borders of **'the land of Israel'** where he was **'set ... down upon a very high mountain'**. **'And on it to the south'** would mean that, having been conveyed in vision from Babylonia — that is, from the north — he looked southwards towards the elevation, on the exact summit of which (cf. 43:12) he beheld something **'like the structure of a city'**.

This would have been a compact, integrated area unlike the derelict Jerusalem of his time. Height implies security and prosperity, the extreme elevation being in pointed contrast to terrestrial Jerusalem, which, although situated in the highlands of Judaea, did not, and does not, lie on top of a lofty mountain range. Metaphorically, Zion was always considered to be exalted above the tops of all other mountains.[21]

Yet the earthly Jerusalem was, none the less, reckoned to be an elevation, which is why Daniel, who was contemporary with Ezekiel and also an exile in Babylonia, would refer to the city as the 'holy mountain' of Yahweh.[22] At this point, continuity between the two Jerusalems — earthly and celestial — is implied.

Although **'like'** indicates that Ezekiel did not literally see with his naked eyes,[23] the reader is supposed to bear in mind that (as noted above) although unnamed, the city *was* Jerusalem. As it turned out, it was actually a temple complex, a concept that is typically that of the Old Testament.[24]

In that the focus switches almost imperceptibly from the city in the previous verse towards the land of Israel, we are being given notice that the present burden is Israel's unchallengeable and permanent settlement within the land of the fathers (40:2).

The prophet informs us that, **'look,'** he beheld **'a man'** whose appearance resembled **'bronze'**, radiating light (cf. 1:7), but who, although an angel, in all probability was not the angel of the Lord, contrary to the 'man' mentioned in 43:6.

In his hand were a **'cord of linen'** and a **'measuring reed'**, the former probably to be used for the longer and the latter for the shorter measurements that he would take.[25] He stood in a **'gate'**, which would almost certainly have been a gate in the wall surrounding the temple area. Again it is to be concluded that, as in Revelation 21:22, the city and the temple were coextensive (40:3).

The enigmatic individual addressed Ezekiel as the **'son of man'**. Although this is the first occasion when, apparently, someone other than Yahweh spoke to Ezekiel, even this representative of the heavenly host regarded the prophet as but weak and fallible, with no strength of his own. Do the angels in heaven look upon us with compassion?

He commanded Ezekiel to **'see'**, **'hear'** and **'set** [his] **heart'** upon **'all'** that he would be shown, and then to tell all **'to the house of Israel'**. Years after his deportation to Babylonia and his call to the prophetic office (cf. 40:1; 1:2), he still had a ministry to his own people. He must hold nothing back (40:4).

2. The outer gate in the middle of the east perimeter wall (40:5-16)

40:5-16. And, look, there was a wall outside the house, all around, and in the hand of the man a measuring reed, six cubits, by a cubit and a handbreadth; and he measured the width of the structure — one reed, and the height one reed. Then he came to the gate, the face of which was in the way of the east, and he went up by its steps and measured the threshold of the gate, one reed broad; and the other threshold, one reed broad. And the recess was one reed long and one reed wide, and between the recesses were five cubits. And the threshold of the gate beside the porch of the gate on the inside was one reed. Then he measured the porch of the gate on the inside, one reed.

And he measured the porch of the gate, eight cubits, and its side pillars two cubits. Now the porch of the gate was on the inside. And the recesses of the gate facing east were three on this side and three on that side; there was one measure for the three of them and one measure for the side posts on this side and on that side.

Then he measured the width of the entrance of the gate, ten cubits. The length of the gate was thirteen cubits. And there was a barrier in front of the recesses, one cubit, and a barrier of one cubit on the other side, and the recess was six cubits on this side and six cubits on that side.

Then he measured the gate from the roof of one recess to the roof of the other, the width being twenty-five cubits, entrance opposite entrance. And he determined the side pillars, sixty cubits; and to the side pillar of the court the gate was round about. And from the front of the entrance gate to the front of the porch of the inner gate, fifty cubits. And there were closed windows for the recesses and for their side pillars within the gate, round about, and likewise for the thresholds; and the windows were all around on the interior, and upon each side pillar were palm trees.

THE EAST GATEWAY

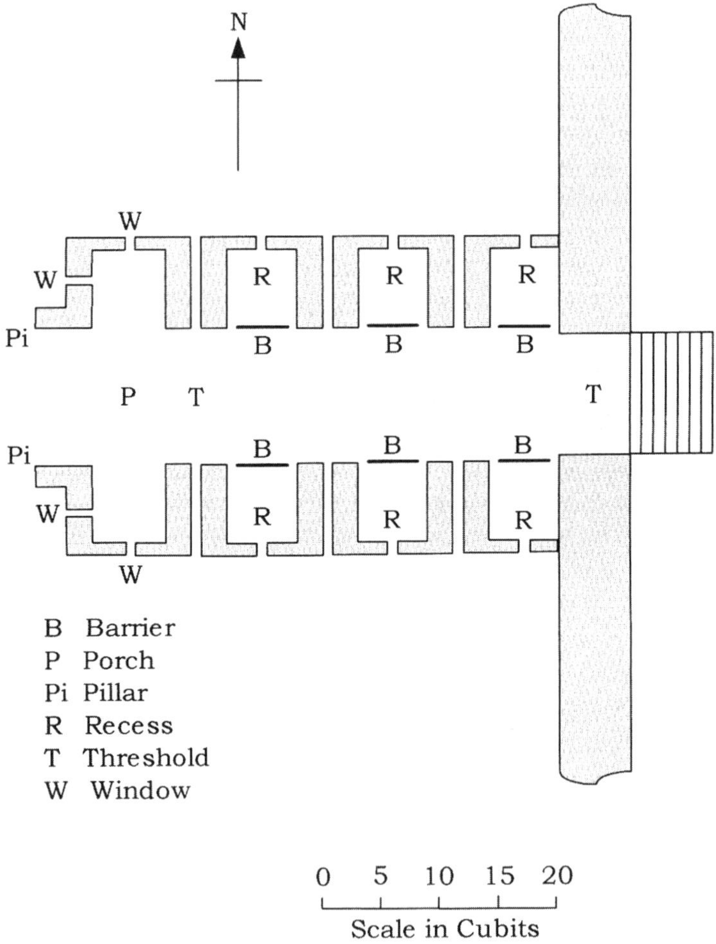

Firstly, Ezekiel saw **'a wall'** surrounding **'the house'** — that is, the city-temple. In the guide's hand was a **'measuring reed, six cubits'** long. The length of each cubit was that of a conventional cubit plus a **'hand-**

breadth' (cf. the specification given by 43:13). It might follow that the man's measuring reed was 3.34 metres (just under 11 feet) in length.[26] He **'measured the 'width'** and **'the height'** of the **'structure'**, by which is meant the perimeter wall of the outer court. Both measurements were **'one reed'**, the square cross-sectional area of the wall being substantial. Trespassers, if any, would have been deterred (40:5).

The angelic surveyor was then seen to advance to the **'east' 'gate'** of the wall. Ascending the external **'steps'**, seven in number (cf. 40:22,26), he measured **'the threshold of the gate, one reed broad'** (east-west), the same width as the surrounding wall. Considerably more than a simple two-dimensional entrance, the complete gate was a small building facing east-west. **'The other threshold'**, situated towards the western end of the gate, was also **'one reed broad'**. The height is not given (40:6).

Apparently, Ezekiel followed his guide inside the gate, where he saw a square **'recess'**, with sides of **'one reed'** (east-west; or, 40:12, six cubits). And there were others, separated at intervals of **'five cubits'** (nearly 3 metres, or a little over 9 feet). According to 40:10, there were six such recesses, three on each side of the gate. The function of the recesses is not revealed, but they would almost certainly have been guardrooms.[27]

Expanding from the previous verse, Ezekiel states that within the western end of the gate there was a **'threshold'** similar to that facing east on the **'inside'**, **'beside the porch of the gate'**, **'one reed'**, (east-west) in width. Its length, north to south, is not given, but it might have been greater than the five cubits between the recesses. It seems to have separated these guardrooms from a **'porch'**, or antechamber, on the west side of the building. This, too, was **'one reed'**, presumably east-west (40:7-8).

The man was then seen to measure **'the porch of the gate'** at its western end (40:9). The recorded **'eight cubits'** (about 4·4 metres, or 14 feet 6 inches) might point to the measurement referred to in 40:8, but is now the external rather than the internal length.[28] If so, the porch, although **'on the inside'**, or within the main edifice of the gate, could have been an adjunct with return walls on the west, one cubit thick. **'Side pillars'**, mentioned in 40:9,14, were each **'two cubits'** in plan (slightly more than 1 metre, or about 3 feet 8) and square in cross-section.

Ezekiel refocuses upon the **'recesses'** or guard-rooms, of which there were six, **'three'** on each **'side'**, north and south of the east-west line of entrance. He tells that they were of uniform dimension. On the northern and southern sides of the western end of the porch were the aforesaid **'side posts'**, one on the north and the other on the south side of the gate. Similar to each other, they were probably integral to the west wall (40:10).

The surveyor returned to the front of the **'gate'**, presumably to the steps in front of the threshold, in order to measure **'the width of the entrance'** from north to south. This amounted to **'ten cubits'** (just over 5·5 metres, or 18 feet). But the complete gate, again north to south, was **'thirteen cubits'** in width. In order to reconcile this with the one reed for the breadth of the threshold, perhaps it included that part of the gate that was roofed over (cf. 40:13), including the threshold. Within the edifice of the gate was a **'barrier'** one cubit wide running east-west in front of three **'recesses'**, or guardrooms, and a parallel barrier in front of the three facing them (40:11-12).

A measurement was then taken across **'the gate'** from north to south. The **'width'** of **'twenty-five cubits'** (nearly 14 metres, or 45 feet 6 inches) would have incorporated ten cubits for the central passage, six for each guardroom, and (say) a cubit and a half for the outer wall [10 + 2 x (6+ 1½) = 25] (40:13).

'The side pillars' mentioned in 40:9-10 and standing at the west face of the gate were **'determined'**, or estimated, to be **'sixty cubits'** in height, higher by ten cubits than the complete length of the gate (40:14). The guide did not climb them to take a vertical measure with a plumb line. Given that the cross-sectional area of each was a diminutive two cubits by two cubits, this was an enormous figure,[29] perhaps, as suggested, the pillars being integral with the west walls in order to gain stability. Apparently, they towered over the temple complex so that worshippers would recognize the entrances from afar.

The second part of 40:14 is difficult, and may mean that the gate structure projected inwards from the eastern section of the boundary wall of the city-temple and terminated in the side pillars.[30]

Then the surveyor measured the external length of the **'gate'**, now designated as **'the entrance'** (to the outer temple court). It was **'fifty cubits'** (nearly 28 metres, or just over 91 feet) in an east-west direction, extending to **'the porch'** at the west end. Twice as long as it was wide (cf. 40:13), it would have been made up by the outer (east) threshold (6 cubits), three recesses (each 6 cubits → 18 cubits), two intervals between these (each 5 cubits → 10 cubits), the inner (west) threshold (6 cubits), the porch (8 cubits) and the side pillars (2 cubits), giving 6 + 18 + 10 + 6 + 8 + 2 = 50 cubits (40:15).

The edifice was equipped with **'closed'**, or latticed, **'windows'**,[31] apparently above the **'recesses'**, or guardrooms, and facing inwards.[32] The latter's **'side pillars'** — possibly the spaces between the guardrooms (cf. 41:3) — would have been other than the two 'side pillars', or high columns, at the western end of the gate (cf. 40:9,14). Upon these were inscribed **'palm trees'** to adorn the western exit (40:16).[33]

3. The arrangement of the outer court (40:17-19)

40:17-19. Then he brought me to the outer court, and, look, rooms and a pavement made for the court round about. There were thirty rooms for the pavement. And the pavement by the flank of the gates, by the length of the gates — this was the lower pavement. Then he measured the width from in front of the lower gate in front of the inner court facing the outside, a hundred cubits on the east and on the north.

Ezekiel was then conducted through the east gate into the **'outer court'** of the temple. On the outside edge of this court, and adjacent to the inside of the perimeter wall, were **'a pavement'** — possibly a mosaic — and a total of **'thirty rooms'** (or pillared porticoes; cf. 42:6) built into the wall and set apart for the use of the people during festivals. Their size is not mentioned (40:17). Such gates had also been situated within Solomon's temple.[34]

It is possible that ten rooms were situated respectively on the inner faces of the north, south and east sides of the perimeter wall, sides otherwise unoccupied.[35] Because gates similar to the east gate were placed in the north and south sides of the surrounding wall, it is reasonable to assume that five rooms would have been set on either side of each of the three gates.[36]

The **'pavement'** was necessarily adjacent to the rooms and seems to have been slightly **'lower'** than the main area of the outer court. This means that the approach to the heart of the complex incorporated a gentle ascent (40:18).

The guide then **'measured the width'** of **'the inner court'**, starting from the western end of the outer east gate and finishing at the **'front'** of **'the inner court facing the outside'** — that is, at the eastern extremity of the east gate leading into the inner court (see 40:23,27). The distance was **'a hundred cubits'**, about 56 metres (or 182 feet 6 inches). It was so, too, on the **'north'** side of the outer court (40:19).

4. The north and south perimeter gates (40:20-27)

40:20-27. And as for the gate of the outer court, the face of which was to the north, he measured its length and its width. And its recesses — there were three on this side and three on that side, and its side pillars and threshold were as the measure of the first gate: its length was fifty cubits, and the width twenty-five, by cubits. And its windows and its threshold and its palm trees were as the measure of the gate the face of which was towards the way of the east; and by seven steps they would go up, and its threshold was before them.

And the gate of the inner court was opposite the gate to the north, like the gate to the east, and he measured from gate to gate — a hundred cubits. Then he brought me to the way of the south, and, look, the gate of the way of the south; and he measured its side pillars and its threshold, the same as these measurements. And it and its threshold had windows all around, like these windows. The length was fifty cubits, and the width twenty-five cubits. And seven steps led up to it, and its threshold was in front of them. And it had palm trees, one on this side and one on that side, on its side pillars. And there was a gate to the inner court on the way of the south, and he measured from gate to gate, the way of the south — a hundred cubits.

'The gate' situated on the north side of the perimeter wall was then **'measured'**. Its dimensions in plan duplicated those of the east gate. Moreover, it too was **'one hundred cubits'** from **'the gate to the north'** of the inner court. We are now informed that there were **'seven steps'** in front of the northern end of the north gate, and it may be assumed that this was so at the southern end of the south gate, as, of course, at the east end of that to the east (40:20-23).

Ezekiel's guide then conducted him **'to the way of the south'**, meaning the southern side of the square perimeter wall. We are invited to **'look'** and notice that not only was there a **'gate'** in the wall, but that it was similar to the north and east gates. It was **'a hundred cubits'** distant from the southern gate leading to **'the inner court'** (40:24-27).

5. The gates to the inner court (40:28-37)

40:28-37. Then he brought me to the inner court by the south gate, and he measured the south gate according to these measurements. And its recesses and its side pillars and its threshold were as these measurements, and it and its threshold had windows round about — fifty cubits was the length, and the width twenty-five cubits. And there were porches round about, twenty-five cubits long, and the width five cubits. And its threshold faced the outer court, and there were palm trees on its side pillars. Its stairway had eight steps.

Then he brought me to the inner court on the way of the east and measured the gate according to these measurements. And its recesses, its side pillars and its threshold were as these measurements, and it and its threshold had windows round about. The length was fifty cubits, and the width twenty-five cubits. Its threshold was towards the outer court, and palm trees were on its side pillars on this side and on that side. Its stairway had eight steps. So he brought me to the north gate and measured according to these measurements, its recesses, its side pillars and its threshold. And it had windows round about. The length was fifty cubits, and the width twenty-five cubits. Its side pillars were towards the outer court, and palm trees were on its side pillars, on this side and on that side. Its stairway had eight steps.

Ezekiel relates that, after being shown the perimeter gates, he was conducted through the inner **'south**

gate' into **'the inner court'**. Although we are not told that there was a boundary separating the inner and outer courts, its existence may be inferred in that the aforementioned three gates (east, north and south, 40:19,23,27) led into the former. I have also assumed that within the outer court there was a line or border connecting the outer entrances to the inner gates, and this is shown on the sketch of the temple courts (see pages 640-41). However, this line (if it existed) would not have subdivided the outer court into two parts.

The dimensions of the south gate and the east and north gates of the inner court were, with two differences, the same as those of the perimeter gates giving access to the outer court. The first difference was that **'eight'**, rather than seven, **'steps'** led up to each inner gate (40:31,34,37), giving a higher elevation to the inner court. This suggests that the rising approach to the heart of the sanctuary proclaimed an intensifying degree of holiness.

Secondly, the porches of these inner courts faced outward, towards those of the inward-pointing corresponding outer gates, rather like mirror images. Everywhere there was precision and symmetry. Verse 30 is difficult, and I have accepted a variation in the Masoretic vocalization, whereby 'threshold' becomes **'porch'**.[37] Being relatively independent of the main gate, it may be that these measurements were taken in a direction other than those of the gate itself.

Throughout this section (40:28-37) vertical dimensions are never given, again suggesting that what we have here could not have been intended as a three-dimensional plan for a new, terrestrial temple.

6. Rooms for preparing sacrifices (40:38-43)

40:38-43. And a cell and its entrance were by the side pillars, at the gates. There they rinse the burnt offering. And by the threshold of the gate there were two tables on this side and two tables on that side, to slaughter upon them the burnt offering, the sin offering and the guilt offering.

And to the side, on the outside, as one goes up to the entrance of the north gate, two tables, and at the other side of the threshold of the gate two tables. Four tables on this side and four tables on that side flanking the gate — eight tables upon which they slaughter. And the four tables for the burnt offering were of hewn stone: of length one and a half cubits, and width one and a half cubits, and height one cubit. On them they lay the utensils with which they slaughter the burnt offering and the sacrifice. And hooks, of one handbreadth, were fixed in the house round about, and upon the tables the flesh offering.

Ezekiel, having been shown the gate situated on the northern side of the inner wall (40:35-37), tells that there was **'a cell and its entrance ... by the side pillars, at the gates'**. Although the plural, 'gates', might indicate that there were such cells at the north, south and east gates, this commentary assumes that the reference is to the north gate alone. There animals appointed as 'burnt offerings' would be washed, or 'rinsed', prior to slaughter.[38] The routine of sacrifice demanded cleanliness (40:38).

According to Moses, it was required that burnt, sin and guilt offerings were to be killed by their offerers within the court at the north side of the altar.[39] Furthermore, offerers were required to lay their hands upon the living animals prior to slaughtering them in order 'to make atonement'.[40] The principle of identification comes to the fore in the ritual for the Day of Atonement, when Aaron was to rest both hands upon the scapegoat so that it would 'bear on itself all their [i.e. Israel's] iniquities to an uninhabited land'.[41]

However, according to 44:11, now the sacrificial beasts are to be slaughtered by the Levites. This being so, it would have been desirable that the killing should take place in the presence of the original offerer and the people, and thus of necessity in the outer court. To this extent the prescription is understandable.

But perhaps there is more to the procedure than meets the eye. Ezekiel the priest must have been aware that in a sense the principle of representative sacrifice was *not* being perpetuated exactly by the new system: no longer do animal sacrifices tell out that sinful men must identify with them by means of physical contact. Because the previously essential symbolism of touch is no more, is this visionary sketch of a new temple and its ritual to be interpreted literally? Surely, text and context anticipate a scene in which, at long last, 'there is no longer an offering for sin'.[42] May it not be that in the sixth century BC, chapters 40 – 48 looked forward to a time when type would have yielded to antitype? Are not text and context Messianic?

Ezekiel then noticed that by the gate's **'threshold'** were **'two tables'** on each side, upon which were to be killed **'the burnt offering, the sin offering and the guilt offering'** (40:39). Burnt offerings, the typical Hebrew sacrifice, were intended to propitiate an offended God ('a sweet aroma'), sin offerings to purify their offerers, and guilt offerings to afford restitution.[43]

Additional **'tables'** were now seen, **'two'** on each side of **'the entrance of the north gate'** by the inner perimeter of the outer court (40:40). Opinions differ concerning their exact location, but it seems that the animals were killed on eight tables, four on each side of the north gate of the inner court, but essentially within the area of the outer court (40:41).[44]

Apparently, in addition to the eight tables mentioned in 40:39-41, there were four more, each one-and-a-half cubits long and wide, and one cubit high, on which slaughtering tools were laid (40:42).

By now, Ezekiel's reader will be somewhat confused, imagining the porch to the north inner gate to be cramped by no less than twelve tables. Again it is to be doubted that we have here a blueprint for an actual construction.

Finally, it was noted that **'hooks'**, each as wide as a hand, were fastened around the walls of **'the house'**, by which might be meant the porch of the north inner gate (40:43).

7. Rooms for officiating priests and singers (40:44-46)

40:44-46. And from the outside to the inner gate were the singers' rooms in the inner court by the side of the north gate, one with its front towards the south and one at the side of the east gate facing towards the north. Then he spoke to me: 'This, the room that faces towards the south, is for the priests who hold the guard duty of the house. And the room, the face of which is to the way of the north, is for the priests who hold the guard duty of the altar — they are the sons of Zadok who from the sons of Levi approach Yahweh to minister to him.'

Having been conducted through the north gate of the inner wall to the inner court where the holy place was situated, Ezekiel beheld **'rooms'**, or chambers (or 'cells'; cf. 40:38), **'one'** facing the south and dedicated to **'the singers'**, and the other by the northern side of the east gate (40:44). The layout is not easy to visualize. The reference to **'singers'** has become a matter for discussion, one reason being that elsewhere in the Old Testament the Levitical temple musicians are distinguished from the priesthood.[45] Thus, it is reasoned that since the accommodation for the singers was within the inner court, they must have been priests.[46] But if the ritual has already been modified in one important respect (the slaughter of sacrificial animals by the priests, 40:38-39), perhaps the singers were other than priests.

Ezekiel recounts that the guide explained to him the function of **'the room that faces towards the south'**: the cell adjacent to the south corner of the inner north gate was for **'the priests who hold the guard duty of the house'**. They were required to protect the holy place from desecration by unauthorized visitors (40:45).

Moreover, **'the room'** adjacent to the north side of the inner east gate was reserved **'for the priests who hold the guard duty of the altar'**. On the basis of Numbers 18:5, it may be that 'house' (40:45) and 'altar' are epexegetic, one describing the other.[47] If this were not so we would be compelled to differentiate between two orders of priests, and this would clash with the assertion that all the officiating priests would be of **'the sons of Zadok'**.

Whereas according to Moses all the sons of Aaron were entitled to act as priests, in Ezekiel's vision only the sons of Zadok retain the privilege (cf. 43:19; 44:15; 48:11). 1 Samuel 2:30-36 tells that the high priesthood was to be withdrawn from the family of Eli as a punishment (again, cf. 44:15). Furthermore, when Adonijah rebelled against his father David, Zadok remained faithful to the king, and his loyalty was honoured when Solomon dismissed Abiathar.[48] Here the principle being established is that only priests of proven fidelity may **'approach Yahweh to minister to him'** (40:46).

8. The dimensions of the porch leading into the temple (40:47-49)

40:47-49. So he measured the court: the length a hundred cubits, and the width a hundred cubits, foursquare; and the altar was in front of the house. Then he brought me to the porch of the house and he measured the side pillars of the porch: five cubits on this side and five cubits on that side, and the width of the gate was three cubits on this side and three cubits on that side. The length of the porch was twenty cubits and the width twelve cubits, and by the steps by which they would ascend to it were columns by the side pillars, one on this side and one on that side.

Ezekiel was then shown **'the court'**, which was **'a hundred cubits'** square (each side about 56 metres, or 182 feet 6 inches, in length). That it would have had a boundary wall separating it from the outer court may, as noted earlier, be assumed. An **'altar'** was **'in front of the house'**, or temple,[49] and was situated at the absolute centre of the whole complex. This being so, it would have been visible through the north and south outer and inner gates of the temple site, if open, the east outer gate, according to 44:2, being permanently closed (40:47).

Now, at last, Ezekiel was escorted by his guide **'to the porch of the house'**, which was measured. In attempting to understand the layout, one would sympathize with Keil when he observes that 'the measurements in [verses] 48 and 49 ... are apparently irreconcilable with one another', whence he infers that, centuries ago, the same problem had 'led the Septuagint to the adoption of arbitrary interpolations and conjectures in [verse] 49'.[50]

Nevertheless, here is an attempt to interpret the vocalized Hebrew text as it stands. There were **'side pillars'**, or jambs, each **'five cubits'** wide (east-west) and each standing **'three cubits'** (north-south) proud of its side wall. The distance between the side pillars is unspecified, although, by taking into account other north-south measurements, it may have been fourteen cubits (40:48).

The interior measure, or **'length'** (i.e. the longer measurement, north-south), **'of the porch'** was **'twenty cubits'** (about 11 metres, or just under 37 feet). Its east-west **'width'** was, according to the

Septuagint, **'twelve cubits'**.[51] Two **'columns'** stood in front of, or perhaps within, the entrance, probably corresponding to Solomon's pillars, Jachin and Boaz.[52] The height of these is not given. An unspecified number of **'steps'** led up to the porch (40:49).[53]

9. The dimensions of the temple (41:1-4)

41:1-4. Then he brought me to the temple and measured the side pillars: six cubits wide on this side and six cubits wide on that side, the width of the tent. And the width of the entrance was ten cubits, and the sides of the entrance were five cubits on this side and five cubits on that side; and he measured its length, forty cubits, and the width twenty cubits.

Then he went inside and measured the side pillar of the entrance, two cubits; and the entrance was six cubits, and the width of the entrance was seven cubits. And he measured the length, twenty cubits; and the width twenty cubits at the front of the temple. And he said to me, 'This is the holy of holies.'

Ezekiel was led through the porch to **'the temple'** proper. The Hebrew *hékal* (cf. 8:16) behind 'temple' means a palace for a monarch.[54] Here, it designates the place where the Lord Yahweh would normally reside. **'The side pillars'** were **'six cubits wide'** (east-west) on each side, yet incorporated into **'the width of the tent'**, 'tent' implying continuity with Moses' tabernacle (41:1).[55] The interior **'width'** (north-south) **'of the entrance'** to the holy place was **'ten cubits'**, presumably less than the width of the entrance to the porch. The internal length of the nave between the porch and the holy of holies was **'forty cubits'** (about 22 metres, or 73 feet, east-west), and its internal width **'twenty cubits'** (north-south). As yet we are

THE TEMPLE

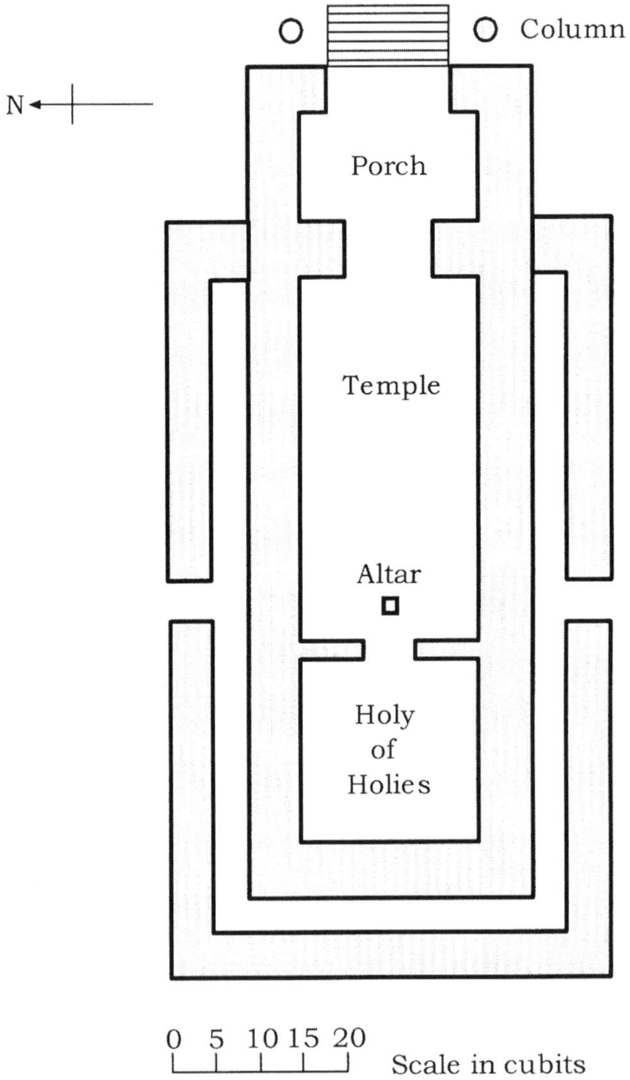
Column
N
Porch
Temple
Altar
Holy
of
Holies
0 5 10 15 20
Scale in cubits

not told the thickness of the surrounding walls (but cf. 41:5). The ground area was the same as that of the nave within Solomon's temple, although, unlike that of the temple,[56] the height is not given (41:2).[57]

The guide went in to the inner sanctuary, the holy of holies. Because Ezekiel was not the high priest, he did not enter.[58] Two 'side pillars', one on each side of the entrance, were **'two cubits'** wide (east-west). **'The entrance'** was measured at **'seven cubits'**, this probably being the north-south width of each of the side pillars. Consistent with this, **'six cubits'** indicates the total width between the side pillars, north to south, of the double doors leading into the sanctuary (cf. 41:23). It should be noticed that the diminishing lateral dimensions of the entrances to the porch, the holy place and now the holy of holies (14, 10 and 6 cubits respectively) tell out the absolute sanctity of the dwelling place of Yahweh (41:3).

Ezekiel relates that the internal measurement of the space beyond the entrance was in plan a square of **'twenty cubits'** (again, about 11 x 11 metres, or 37 x 37 feet), exactly half the area of that of the holy place and the same as that of the innermost sanctuary in Solomon's temple.[59] The guide informed the prophet that **'This is the holy of holies'** (41:4).

10. The wall of the house (41:5-11)

41:5-11. Then he measured the wall of the house, six cubits, and the width of a side chamber four cubits, all around the house — all around. And the side chambers were one upon another, in three storeys, with thirty in each and entering into the wall of the house for the side chambers all around so that they might be fastened, but not be fastened in the wall of the house.

And there was a spiral incline widening out for the side chambers because the surrounding of the house went upward and upward all around the house. Therefore there was a broad upward way around the house, and thus the lower would ascend to the highest through the middle storey.

Then I saw that there was a raised platform all around — the foundations of the side chambers — a full reed, six cubits was the space. The width of the wall for the side chamber on the outside was five cubits, and so also was what was left for the house of side chambers belonging to the house.

And between the rooms there was a width of twenty cubits, all around the house — on every side. And the entrance of the side chamber for the free area: one entrance was on the way of the north, and one entrance for the south. And the width of the place for the free area was five cubits all around.

The wall of the house was a substantial **'six cubits'** thick (over 3 metres, or just under 11 feet), lending stability and security to the building. **'All around'** the external **'wall'**, although presumably not on the east side, the side of entry, were side chambers (*tzela*, 'rib' or 'side'),[60] individually measured at **'four cubits'** in width (41:5). Because this figure implies relative slenderness, perhaps the chambers were integral with the sanctuary's external peripheral wall.

Apparently, the **'side chambers'** were arranged **'in three storeys'**, or levels, **'one upon another'**. This was repeated **'thirty'** times, giving a total of ninety chambers (possibly for each storey twelve on the north and south sides respectively, and six at the west end). Although not unlike the chambers surrounding Solomon's temple,[61] they were one cubit narrower. It is assumed here that the construction reflected that mentioned by 1 Kings 6:6, the thickness of the temple wall reducing with each of the three storeys so as to leave a ledge on which horizontal supporting beams would rest.

Although **'fastened'**, or attached, the beams were **'not ... fastened** [perhaps dovetailed] **in the wall of**

the house', the reason being to preserve the integrity of the temple as a separated holy place (41:6).

The Hebrew of 41:7 is difficult, and the best way to interpret it may be by considering 1 Kings 6:6-8. In Solomon's temple not only did the width of each storey increase by the same measure as the width of the temple wall decreased, the two upper storeys were reached by interior winding stairs. Perhaps there were two such staircases in Ezekiel's temple, one on the north side and the other on the south, although this information is lacking.

Nevertheless, the description in 1 Kings 6 does not provide a precedent for what we now read. It would seem that, because it was entered by a flight of steps (40:49), Ezekiel's temple, as well as **'the side chambers'**, rested on **'a raised platform'**, a **'full reed'** in height (over 3 metres or about 11 feet) above the level of the inner court.

This constituted **'the foundations'** for the complete edifice (41:8). In the diagram of the temple courts (see pages 640-41) I have named it as the 'raised platform' ('RP'), showing it as in plan extending slightly beyond the north, south and west sides of the temple, although this is conjectural in that it might interfere with the 'width of twenty cubits' mentioned by verse 10. On the other hand, perhaps it corresponds to the elevated five-cubit width within the twenty-cubit separate place ('SP', as shown in the diagram of the temple courts), or 'free area' (so, 41:11), and situated next to the temple's outer wall, as mentioned by verse 11.

The outer walls are stated to have been **'five cubits'** thick. Further, there was a remaining space, **'what was left'** (cf. 41:11), unoccupied by the temple and its adjacent **'side chambers'**. But all belonged to the central **'house'**, or temple (41:9).

Between the foundation on which the temple and the side **'rooms'** stood and the wall of the inner court was an open area **'twenty cubits'** wide, **'on every**

side', by which is meant the north, south and west sides.

From the information thus given it seems possible to calculate the north-south width of the temple, excluding the surrounding free space. The thickness of the outer walls (5 x 2) + the width of the side chambers (4 x 2) + the base of the temple walls (6 x 2) + the internal north-south width of the temple (20) amounts to fifty cubits.

Given that the east-west length was 100 cubits (see 41:13), it transpires that in plan the temple complex was a rectangle, twice as long as it was broad (41:10).[62]

Ezekiel notes that there were two exits to the side chambers, both facing **'the free area'** (again, marked as 'separate place' on the plan) surrounding the outer wall of the temple. One was on the north side of the complex and the other on the south side. Within the twenty-cubit width of the free area there seems to have been a distinct five-cubit width, perhaps elevated and paved, and lying next to the outer wall (41:11).

11. The building behind and to the west of the temple (41:12-14)

41:12-14. And the building that faced the separate place on the west side was seventy cubits wide; and the wall of the building was five cubits thick all around, and its length was ninety cubits. Then he measured the house: the length was one hundred cubits. And the separate place and the building and its walls were one hundred cubits long. Also, the width of the front of the temple and of the separate place towards the east was one hundred cubits.

We are introduced to a **'building'** situated behind the temple on its west side. Internally, it was **'seventy cubits wide'** (apparently, east-west) and **'ninety**

cubits' long (apparently, north-south), its walls being **'five cubits thick'**. Its external dimensions would therefore have been 80 x 100 cubits.

This switch in orientation will be confusing unless it is remembered that the greater dimension is by convention the length, and the shorter, the width. My diagram assumes that the thickness of the wall at its west side was in addition to that of the western boundary wall.

Between the building and the temple's foundation platform there was a **'separate place'** (part of the 'free area' — see 41:11). Although its function is not stated, the building might have been employed for storage purposes. Alternatively, if we draw a parallel with 43:21 perhaps it was 'the appointed place of the house' where the remains of sacrifices and other refuse were burnt (41:12).

Ezekiel's guide then **'measured the house'** — that is, the temple. Externally and in an east-west direction it was **'one hundred cubits'** in **'length'**. **'The separate place and the building'** were also **'one hundred cubits long'**, east to west (41:13).

If the sketch of the plan of the temple complex is compared with these measurements, it will be seen that on the diagram the east-west length of the separate place plus the building amounts to a little less than the stipulated 100 cubits. This does not imply that Ezekiel's dimensions are inaccurate, but simply that I have found it less than easy to reconcile all the data.

The next verse is somewhat difficult, but perhaps the **'east'** was the east side of the separated place, adjacent to the west end of the temple. If so, the overall meaning might be that the width, north-south, of the face of the temple at its west end, and including the separated area on its eastern side, was 100 cubits (41:14).

THE TEMPLE COURTS

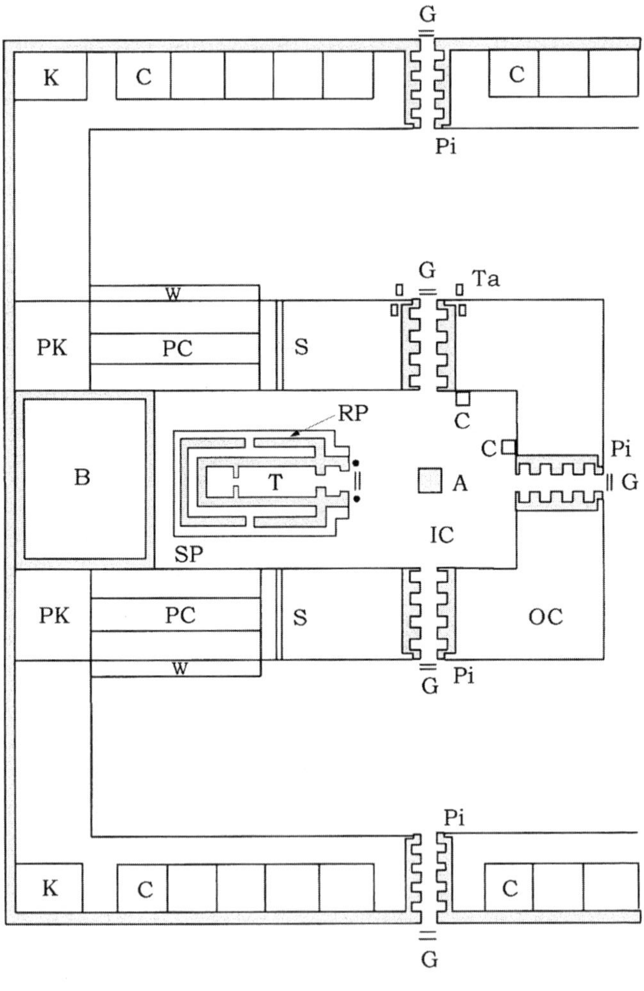

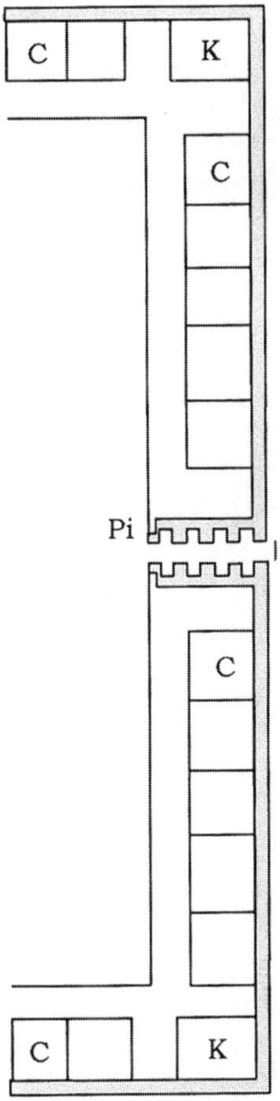

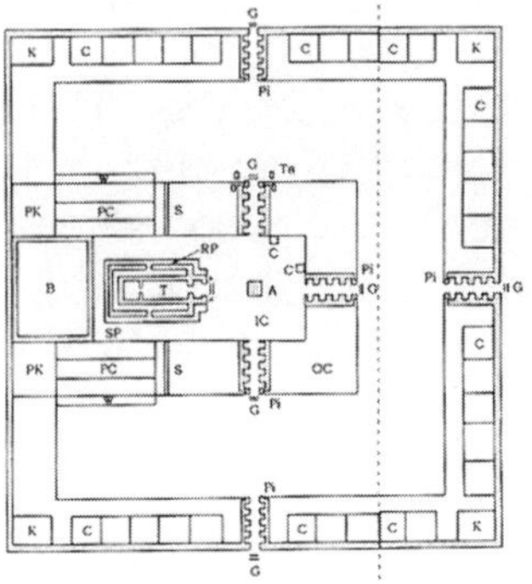

A Altar
B Building
C Chambers
G Gates
IC Inner court
K Kitchen
OC Outer court
PC Priests' chambers
Pi Pillars
PK Priests' kitchens
RP Raised platform
S Screen
SP Separate place
T Temple
Ta Tables
W Walkway

N

0 200

Scale in cubits

12. The galleries of the rear, western building (41:15-17)

41:15-17. So he had measured the length of the building facing the separate place behind it, with its galleries on both sides — a hundred cubits; and also the inner temple and the porches of the court. The thresholds and the closed windows and the galleries around the three, opposite the threshold, were overlaid with wood all around, and from the ground to the windows (but the windows were covered); from above the entrance to the inner house, and on the outside, and on all the wall, all around, on the inside and on the outside, by measurement.

The remainder of the chapter summarizes measurements already given, adding some new details. Taking up from 41:12, the north-south length of **'the building'** to the west of the temple was **'one hundred cubits'** (90 + 5 + 5). Now we learn that it possessed **'galleries** [*attiqeha*, derivation unknown; cf. 41:16; 42:3,5] **on both sides'**. These may have been galleries or porches covering the entrances to the building. Because their location is uncertain, they are not indicated on the plan.

Ezekiel also notes that the guide had already measured **'the inner temple'**, or the holy place within the temple as viewed from the interior, and the **'porches of the** [boundary wall of the inner] **court'** (41:15), their **'thresholds'** (cf. 40:6-7), their **'closed windows'** (cf. 40:16) and — a new detail — the **'galleries'** (again, balconies?) pertaining to these **'three'**. All were panelled internally with **'wood'** from the floor up as far as the latticed **'windows'** (41:16).

Ezekiel stresses that everything was examined **'by measurement'**. The impression conveyed by this apparently bewildering wealth of detail is that of a building where everything was in place, where all was order and calm, and where disharmony was inconceivable (41:17).

13. The ornamentation of the holy and most holy places (41:18-26)

41:18-26. And it was made of cherubim and palm trees, and a palm tree between cherub and cherub, and two faces for each cherub: the face of a man towards a palm tree on the one side, and the face of a lion towards the palm tree on the other side — thus it was carved for all the house all around. The cherubim and the palm trees were constructed from the ground to above the entrance, and on the wall of the temple.

As for the temple, the doorposts were square, and the front of the holy place; the form of the one was as the form of the other. The altar was of wood, three cubits high, and its length two cubits; it had corners, and its length and its walls were of wood. Then he spoke to me: 'This is the table that is before Yahweh.'

And there were two double doors for the temple and for the holy place, and there were two leaves for the double doors: two revolving leaves, two for the one door and two leaves for the other. And carved upon them, on the doors of the temple, were cherubim and palm trees, just as they had been made for the walls. And there was a wooden railing to the front of the porch outside; and closed windows and palm trees on one side and on the other, on the sides of the porch, on the side walls of the house, and the railings.

Verses 18-21 describe the ornamentation of the inner walls of the sanctuary, which was not unlike that of Solomon's temple.[63] Apparently, the **'cherubim'** and **'palm trees'** were carved everywhere upon the wooden panelling. Whereas the three-dimensional cherubim in chapters 1 and 10 each had four faces, the present two-dimensional cherubim had only **'two'**, that of a **'man'** and that of a **'lion'**.

The significance of what is obviously symbolic may proclaim strength (the lions), fruitfulness (the date palms) and protection (the cherubim). The carvings covered every part of **'the wall'** and perhaps the ceiling **'above the entrance'** (41:18-20). Unlike the description in 1 Kings 6, we are not told that they were overlaid with gold.

'The doorposts', the frames upon which the entrance doors were hung, **'were square'**. Moreover, the frames leading from the eastern porch into **'the temple'**, or nave, were similar to those giving admission to **'the holy place'**, by which is meant the holy of holies (41:21).

Ezekiel tells that within the nave in front of the holy of holies was **'the altar ... of wood'**. Whereas elsewhere the table of shewbread is never described as an altar, an altar is occasionally considered as a table (see 44:16),[64] whence it appears that the prophet may have beheld the altar of incense, albeit with larger dimensions.[65] As if to dispel any uncertainties that Ezekiel might have had, the guide informed him that **'This is the table that is before Yahweh'**, essentially belonging to the holy of holies although not within it (41:22).[66]

As had been the case in the temple of Solomon,[67] a set of wooden **'double doors'** gave admission to **'the temple'**, or nave, and another set to **'the holy place'**, the holy of holies (41:23). Each door was in two parts and was attached to pivots by the doorposts. Moreover, each part consisted of **'two leaves'**, giving four leaves for each of the two entrances. This would have granted economy of space and minimal disturbance when opened (41:24).

As on the interior **'walls'**, **'cherubim and palm trees'** were carved on the doors. Ezekiel's attention returning to **'the porch'** leading into the nave, he observes that **'there was a wooden railing'** in front of it. What this **'railing'** (*ab*; cf. 41:26) was is uncertain,[68] although it may have been a wooden moulding (41:25).

Upon both **'sides of the porch'** and **'the side walls of the house'** (the nave) were **'closed'** or latticed **'windows'**, as well as **'palm trees'** carved in the wood. These also featured on the aforementioned **'railings'** (41:26). Apparently, carvings of guardian cherubim were reserved for the holy place and for the holy of holies.

Compared with Moses' tabernacle and Solomon's temple, within this complex there were important omissions and modifications.

Remarkably, neither the table of shewbread nor the seven-branched lamp is mentioned. There is no mention of any gold overlay similar to the furnishings of Solomon's temple.[69] The ark of the covenant, 'that climax of Israel's symbolic worship', as Gardiner expresses it,[70] was almost certainly absent. Its presence and dimensions would, surely, have been mentioned had it been there. Though present, the altar of incense was of plain wood. All this must have given Ezekiel the priest much food for thought. An explanation is called for.

Was what Ezekiel saw a vision of that future age predicted by Jeremiah 3:16-17, to the effect that in time to come the symbolic ark of the covenant would not be missed because Jerusalem, rather than a separated building within the city, would be the throne of Yahweh?

But be this as it may, there is continuity in format between the prophet's visionary temple and Moses' tabernacle (cf. 41:1), as well as the temple of Solomon. Ezekiel's vision extends to an era in which the divisions and separations within the largely two-dimensional plan of his temple proclaim that the Lord, although the transcendent Lord of heaven, dwells among his own people with none to disturb the relationship.[71]

14. The north and south apartment blocks (42:1-12)

42:1-12. Then he brought me out to the outer court, the way towards the north, and he conducted me to the chamber opposite the separated space opposite the building towards the north.

Facing the length, which was one hundred cubits, was the north entrance, and the width was fifty cubits. Opposite the twenty that were for the inner court and opposite the pavement belonging to the outer court was gallery against gallery, in threes.

And in front of the chambers was a walkway, ten cubits wide, on the inside, a way of one hundred cubits, and their entrances were towards the north. And the upper chambers were shortened because the galleries took space from them more than from the lower and the middle ones of the building. Because they were a three and had no pillars like the pillars of the courts, therefore they were set back from the ground more than the lower and the middle.

And there was an enclosing wall on the outside parallel to the chambers, along the way of the outer court, facing the chambers. Its length was fifty cubits because the length of the chambers towards the outer court was fifty cubits, and, look, that facing the temple was one hundred cubits. And from beneath it were these chambers. There was an entrance from the east, as one goes into them from the outer court. In the thickness of the enclosing wall of the court facing east, facing the separate area and facing the building, were chambers.

And a walkway in front of them was like the appearance of the chambers towards the walkway of the north: as their length, so their width; and all their exits were according to their arrangements and their entrances. And according to the entrances of the chambers that were for the way of the south there was an entrance at the head of the way, a way facing the enclosing wall corresponding to the east way, as one enters.

Now follows a description of rooms for the officiating priests, rooms unknown in Moses' tabernacle and in Solomon's temple. Ezekiel's guide conducted him **'out'** of the temple **'to the outer court'** on its **'north'** side. He found himself **'opposite'**, on the **'north'** side of the **'building'** and of the **'separated space'** situated behind the temple at the latter's west end (42:1).

From his vantage point he saw an apartment block on the north side of, and running parallel (east-west) to, the building to the west of the holy place and to the holy place itself. Adjacent to the inner court, although within the outer court and (apparently) abutting the inner wall, its external measurements were **'one hundred cubits'** east-west, and **'fifty cubits'** north-south. Its **'entrance'** was necessarily on the **'north'** side leading to the outer court (42:2).

If we compare this data with 46:19, there seems to be a problem. How could the priests' chambers (see 42:13) and their counterparts to the south of the temple have been sited to the west of the inner court, abutting the outer walls, if (open?) spaces reserved for cooking were situated there? One solution may be that the latter were deemed to be an integral part of the priests' accommodation. In the diagram of the temple courts I have sited the cooking places, each one about 50 x 40 cubits and slightly larger than the people's kitchens (46:21-22), to the west of the priests' chambers.

Immediately to the south of this chamber, parallel to it and to the west of the temple, was the aforesaid interval of **'twenty'** cubits wide, running east-west. On the other side of the chamber and to its north there was a stone **'pavement'** running east-west and parallel to it. Was this the 'walkway' mentioned in 42:4? Apparently, the chamber consisted of three galleries, or arcades, with roofs at different levels, the middle **'gallery'** parallel to that to the south (the highest?) and to that (the lowest?) to the north (42:3).

The Hebrew of 42:4 is difficult, and the following suggestions are capable of challenge. **'In front of'**, to the north of the component **'chambers'** of the apartment block, itself situated to the north of the inner court, was **'a walkway, ten cubits wide'** giving access to **'their entrances'** which were facing **'the north'**. The reference to 'one cubit' (as given by the Hebrew text) is far from easy to interpret, and this commentary would accept the proposal that by switching two of the three letters in the Hebrew for 'cubit' to give 'hundred', the text will state that the walkway (or, the 'pavement' of 42:3?) was **'one hundred cubits'** in length, east-west.[72]

Verses 5-6 expand 42:3. The **'building'** to the north of the temple comprised, as has been stated, three distinct levels. These resembled terraces, the uppermost being to the south of the other two, and that in the centre being higher than that on the north.[73] Because **'they'**, the **'upper chambers'**, **'had no pillars'** to support them, along with the other two levels they comprised **'a three'**, a tripartite freestanding building. Apparently, there were pillars or porches in both the inner and outer **'courts'**.

A screening **'wall'**, **'fifty cubits'** long and running north-south, was sited to the east of the cell-block, possibly to give privacy to its occupants (42:7).[74]

The reason for this wall's fifty-cubit length was that the **'length of the chambers towards the outer court'** — that is, facing east — was the same. Instead of **'length'** we might read 'width'. Yet the longer dimension, or length, east to west, of the same complex of chambers (or 'the chamber'; cf. 42:1) was **'one hundred cubits'** (42:8; cf. 42:2).

Again, the Hebrew text is difficult, and it may be that we are dealing with architectural terms of which we possess insufficient knowledge. **'And from beneath'** the screening wall **'were these chambers'**, possibly meaning that as one looked at the building from the east it appeared to arise out of the wall.[75] Then a new clause begins: **'There was an entrance from the east.'** This could mean that although the entrance to **'them'**, to the integrated chambers, was from the north yet from a walkway running east-west (see 42:4), access to the walkway was from the east, possibly from the north porch of the gate to the inner court (42:9).

A corresponding block of apartments to the south of the sanctuary is described briefly. The **'wall'** was the dividing partition between the inner and outer courts, and the building was adjacent to the inner court's southern side as the wall extended towards the **'east'**. Because the dimensions and entrances of the block were **'according to'** those of its twin on the north side, the details are not given.

The last part of 42:12 is not easy, probably paralleling 42:7, but describes a screen running in front of the east, narrower side of the building. Obviously, the whole complex was symmetrical (42:10-12).

15. The function of these apartments (42:13-14)

42:13-14. Then he said to me, 'The north chambers and the south chambers that face the separate place, they are the holy chambers where the priests who approach Yahweh eat the most holy offerings. There they lay the most holy offerings — the meal offering and the sin offering and the guilt offering — because the place is holy.

'When they, the priests, enter they will not go out from the holy place to the outer court, but there they will lay their garments with which they minister, because they are holy. They will put on other garments and will approach that which is for the people.'

The examination of these apartment blocks concludes. Because neither Moses' tabernacle nor Solomon's temple offers any parallels, these **'north chambers and the south chambers that face the separate place'** are an innovation. Yet again the guide offered Ezekiel an explanation (cf. 40:45-46; 41:4,22), informing him that they were **'holy'** and that there the priests who approach Yahweh would set down and then **'eat the most holy offerings'** — that is, the **'meal offering'**, the **'sin offering'** and the **'guilt offering'**. The edible portions would be the elements of the sacrifices that had not been burned upon the altar,[76] being cooked in another room to the west (cf. 46:19-20).

It was stipulated by Moses that the priests should wear their robes only when on duty and that ordinary garments were to be donned when leaving the tent.[77] This formality is repeated in the temple seen by Ezekiel. Perhaps the prophet refers to the disrobing of the priests before they transferred from the altar to the apartment blocks. Apparently, the public were not to see them moving in their official attire. It is likely that the blocks were so large that some interior apartments would have been employed for robing and yet others for eating (42:13-14).

16. The outer space surrounding the house (42:15-20)

42:15-20. Then he concluded the measurements of the inner house and brought me out through the way of the gate facing the way of the east, and he measured it all around.

He measured the east side with the measuring reed — 500 reeds by the measuring reed, around. He measured the north side — 500 reeds by the measuring reed, around. He measured the south side — 500 reeds by the measuring reed.

He turned to the western side and measured 500 reeds by the measuring reed. He measured it on the four sides. It

THE TEMPLE AND ITS SURROUND

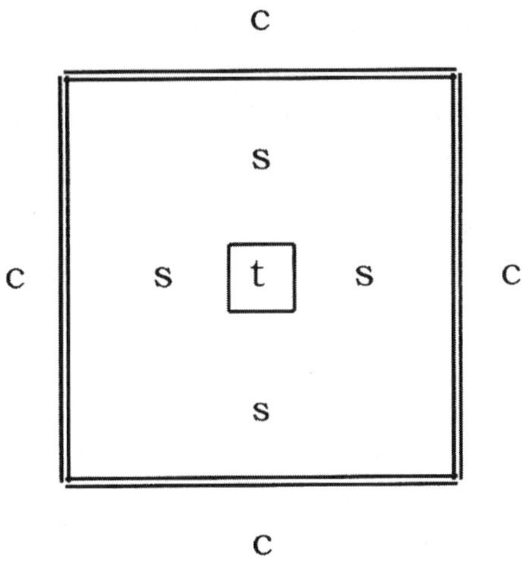

c: Circuit of 50 cubits width (nearly 28 metres, or approximately 91 feet) around the surrounding space (see 45:2)

s: Space surrounding the temple and its courts, 500 reeds square (nearly 3 square kilometres, or a little over a square mile, in area)

t: The temple and its courts, 500 cubits square (about 0·08 square kilometres, or 0.03 square miles, in area)

The ratio between the area of the space surrounding the temple complex and the area of that complex is about 36:1.

had a wall all around, the length 500 and the width 500 — in order to separate between the holy and the common.

Having completed his measurement of **'the inner house'**, the guide **'brought'** Ezekiel **'out'** by the east way. By **'inner house'** is meant everything contained *within* the outer perimeter wall: the temple, the rear (western) building, the priests' apartments (north and south), the inner court, the wall separating the inner and outer courts and the outer court with its walls and their gates (42:15).

Then the guide **'measured the east side ... five hundred reeds'**,[78] as were the **'north'**, **'south'** and **'western'** sides of a very large space in which was situated the complete temple complex (42:16-19). To judge by 40:5, five hundred reeds would have been 1·67 kilometres. That reeds, as specified by the text, are, indeed, reeds is argued by Appendix 'A'. There is no need to emend.

Surrounding this space was **'a wall'**, not a separation barrier like that mentioned in 42:7, but of a magnitude perhaps not dissimilar to the wall referred to in 40:5. Its stated purpose was to **'separate between the holy and the common'** (42:20).

Application

Until and unless the reader of chapters 40 – 42 attempts to saturate himself with their contents and also with the layouts and procedures of Moses' tabernacle and the temple of Solomon, he will possibly be mystified. Yet if we try to gaze at the vision through Ezekiel's experienced eyes, shadows may to some extent be dispelled.

It seems that the prophet beheld an elaborate and for the most part a two-dimensional plan of an ideal temple complex that could never be erected in this world. What he tells out is a message of expectation, hope, comfort and encouragement for the godly remnant among his people Israel. We may assume that those who lacked spiritual sensitivity would have made nothing of it. And so it would be today.

Along with many of his fellow-countrymen, the prophet had lived through the Babylonian holocaust. But, unlike too many Jews, he knew exactly why Israel had been expelled from the land granted to the fathers, why the Jerusalem temple had been destroyed, why the throne of David had been cast to the ground and why, for seventy years, there would be no place for legitimate sacrifice to Yahweh anywhere. He knew why the nominal people of God had been scattered in such a way that for some considerable time they could not be a united worshipping community.

Now he knows that in a happier age Israel will be reconvened to worship within the land of promise and at the holy mountain of Jerusalem. Yet although the vision tells that the principles enshrined in the Sinai tabernacle and then in Solomon's temple will never falter, in some respects the situation will be remarkably different. The revelation is pure typology, yet even in its own eyes a typology that in time to come will have been fulfilled and must therefore become redundant. Of this, Ezekiel would have had some comprehension.[79]

That is, his temple anticipates not just the coming Messianic era, but predicts in the only way possible, given Ezekiel's background and situation, the lasting glory to be shared by the Messiah and his people, a glory reaching beyond time. All is tranquillity, decorum and equilibrium. In short, at this late stage in his ministry the prophet was occupied not with the return from Babylonian exile, nor with the inauguration of the gospel dispensation in (as we now know) the first century of the Christian era, or even its progress throughout the millennia, but the everlasting consequence: there will be for ever a land, a temple and a worshipping people.

But in the same way that there will be no enduring ark of the covenant, there will be no three-dimensional temple within and distinct from a terrestrial Jerusalem. Nor will worshippers lay their hands on their sacrificial sheep, oxen and goats. Faintly, yet, as I see it, how eloquently and unmistakeably, the vision tells of a time of absolute fulfilment in a world other than this, beyond the horizon which separates time from eternity. This, I believe, is the essential message of these chapters.

Would you allow me a personal observation? I sketched my diagram of Ezekiel's temple and its courts on A3 graph paper, assuming that it would be scaled down to a relatively diminutive size of something like A5, for the purposes of this book — which is what happened.

Although I do not profess that my effort is anything like 100-per-cent accurate, like most line drawings that attempt to portray Ezekiel's vision, it might give some idea of what the prophet would have seen.

My point is that my prototype sketch impressed me deeply with its (dim) reflection of the symmetry and elegance of the temple courts and with the implication of the orderliness and precision of temple ritual. Gone is the confusion of the centuries during which worship was centred upon the temple in Jerusalem. Nor does the plan foreshadow the long pilgrimage of the Christian churches, beset as they are by turbulence within and opposition without. I find it hard to comprehend chapters 40 – 48 of Ezekiel's prophecy as anything other than a glimpse through the veil into an age yet to come, an age not of this world.

I think that I ought to state that I have reached this conclusion partly by a process of (for me) the reasonable elimination of other interpretations and partly by trying to give careful thought to what Ezekiel seems to be saying.

Although I have anticipated the following comment already in this book, perhaps it needs to be spelled out again: if one could discover in the New Testament any passages that obviously, or even by implication, employ chapters 40 – 48 in connection with the life of the churches here and now, a principal thesis of this commentary would fail immediately. But because I reckon that I have been unsuccessful in making any such discovery, it appears to me that this popular interpretation should be discarded.

Further, it seems to me that a transition from this world to eternity bespoken by the leap from chapters 1 – 39 to 40 – 48 is perfectly understandable, given the life and times of Ezekiel. How else was an Old Testament prophet to minister to his people about the world to come than by doing so in terms of the familiar temple and its ritual service? He could only communicate within the frames of reference of his constituency.

Indeed, I would go far as to request that, if chapters 40 – 48 concern the establishment and the progress of the Christian church *prior* to the Second Coming, could someone please demonstrate by dint of careful exegesis and by comparison with the New Testament data how he can arrive at such a conclusion? My own strong suspicion is that the thing cannot be done.

The Lord comes to a new temple (Ezekiel 43:1-12)

Nineteen years earlier Ezekiel had witnessed in a vision the departure of Yahweh from the temple in Jerusalem (cf. 8:1; 10:18; 11:22-24).

Now the new sanctuary, with its dimensions and arrangements, has been revealed to the prophet. In that Moses' tabernacle and Solomon's temple were blessed by the manifestation of the divine presence,[80] it is to be expected that the present structure should be so honoured. But does Yahweh wish to reside there? If so, upon what terms? The present chapter addresses the matter.

1. The chariot of fire (43:1-5)

43:1-5. Then he brought me to the gate, the gate that faced the east way. And, look, the glory of the God of Israel came from the way of the east, and its sound was as the sound of many waters; and the earth lit up with his glory. And it was like the sight of the vision that I had seen, like the vision that I had seen when I came to destroy the city, and visions like the sight that I had seen by the Chebar canal; and I fell on my face. Then the glory of Yahweh came to the house by way of the gate that faced the way of the east. And the Spirit raised me up and brought me to the inner court, and, look, the glory of Yahweh filled the house.

Ezekiel tells that the man with the measuring reed conducted him to the east **'gate'** on the outer perimeter. It was here that he had found himself before witnessing the measurement of the vast boundary space surrounding the temple (42:15-20). And it was from the east, outer, gate of Solomon's temple that the glory of Yahweh had departed nineteen years earlier (10:18-19; 11:1,23). The Lord will return by the same route (43:1).

Here Ezekiel saw the glory of Yahweh approaching from **'the way of the east'**. So remarkable was the sight that the prophet invites his readers to **'look'** — that is, to try to imagine the scene. The **'sound'** accompanying the vision was like that of **'many waters'** (cf. Ezekiel's initial vision, 1:24), and **'the earth'** was illuminated by the **'glory'** of God (43:2).[81] What Ezekiel witnessed was nothing less than the restoration of the covenant relationship between Yahweh and Israel.

'The vision' was like those that the prophet had seen **'by the Chebar canal'** and when he had predicted in advance the destruction of Jerusalem.[82] The statement that it was similar to what Ezekiel saw **'when I came to destroy the city'** (cf. 9:1-11) means that that oracle had been the judicial sentence of God upon Jerusalem.[83] Nebuchadnezzar was no more than the executioner. Now all is changed. Ezekiel prostrated himself (43:3).

'The glory of Yahweh' came in **'to the house'** through the main entrance, the outer **'east'** gate, the Lord being determined to travel speedily and directly through the east inner gate and then through the gate of the temple to the inner sanctuary. Evidently, he intended to return to his home (43:4).

When Ezekiel beheld for the first time the vision of the enthroned Yahweh he had fallen upon his face, only to be raised to his feet by the Spirit of God in order to hear what the Lord had to say to him (see 2:2). Now he is again **'raised'** by **'the Spirit'**, but in order to behold rather than hear. Transported **'to the inner court'**, to which, as a priest, he had right of access, he was evidently surprised by what he saw.

Again, he invites his readers to exercise their imagination: **'look, the glory of Yahweh filled the house'**, the **'house'** being the outer sanctuary and the holy of holies (43:5).

2. A man speaks to Ezekiel (43:6-12)

43:6-12. Then I heard someone speaking to me from the house, and a man was standing next to me. And he said to me, 'Son of man, this is the place of my throne and the place for the soles of my feet. There I shall dwell for ever in the midst of the sons of Israel, and the house of Israel will never again defile my holy name — neither they nor their kings, with their fornications and with the corpses of their kings on their high places. In setting their threshold by my threshold and their doorpost by my doorpost with only a wall between them and me, then they defiled my holy name with their abominations which they did. So I have consumed them in my anger. Now they will remove their fornication and the corpses of their kings away from me, and I shall dwell among them for ever.

'You, son of man, describe the house to the house of Israel, and let them be ashamed of their iniquities and let them measure the pattern. And if they are ashamed of all that they have done, make known to them the fashion of the house and its pattern, its exits and its entrances, all its forms, all its statutes, all its fashions and all its laws. Write in their sight so that they might observe all its form and all its statutes and do them. This is the law of the house: upon the top of the mountain, all its border, all around, is most holy. Look, this is the law of the house.'

Within the court of the priests Ezekiel heard **'someone speaking'** to him **'from'** within **'the house'**, and saw **'a man ... standing'** by him. Although some suggest that he was the prophet's guide,[84] a better interpretation would be that the God who addressed Ezekiel from the temple did so through the medium of someone who, as God's mouthpiece, would have been the divine angel of the Lord. This interpretation is consistent with 1:26 and 44:2,5,9.

From this point the angel with the measuring reed does not reappear until 47:3, withdrawing temporarily in favour of the angel who describes the altar and expounds the mode of its decontamination (43:6).

The prophet tells that he was informed that here would be **'the place'** of God's **'throne'**, where Yahweh would set **'the soles'** of his **'feet'**. The temple has again become the footstool of God, who intends to manifest his presence there permanently.[85]

At the same time, Israel and its princes no longer defile the holy name of Yahweh with **'their fornications'** — meaning their idolatrous practices — and with the **'corpses'** of their **'kings'** (43:7). Although some consider that these corpses may have been those of certain of the kings of Judah who had been interred within the temple area, there is no evidence that there were any such burials. Perhaps the present verse recalls Leviticus 26:30, which reads literally, 'I shall place your corpses upon the corpses of your idols.' Manasseh and others had introduced idols, inert as dead bodies, into the temple.[86]

That temple had never been surrounded by open ground to separate it from the city of Jerusalem, and it is probable that some of the kings of Judah had set their idols not only within the temple but adjacent to it. Consequently, the thresholds and doorposts of holy and unholy buildings would have been adjacent, there being no more than **'a wall'** between the defilements of the city and the dwelling-place of the Lord — **'between them and me'**. Impurity triumphed and the sanctity of God was outraged. Because of this desecration, Yahweh had **'consumed'** Israel in his **'anger'** (43:8).

Most versions give, 'Now let them remove their fornication ...', as if to issue a challenging imperative. But the Lord is predicting what shall be (cf. 43:7); hence the suggested translation: **'they will remove...'** No more will **'corpses'**, lifeless idols, desecrate the house of Yahweh (43:9).

Ezekiel reveals that he was instructed to **'describe the house to the house of Israel'** so that they might **'be ashamed of their iniquities'**. To this end, they are to **'measure the pattern'**, contemplating the dimensions of the temple complex (43:10).[87]

This must have given both comfort and anguish to those of the prophet's fellow-exiles who exercised discernment: comfort, in that they were told that the destruction of the temple of Solomon had not been the end; anguish, in that the dignified symmetry and essential purity of Ezekiel's structure stood in vivid contrast to the chaos that, thanks to the follies of Judah and many of its kings, had supervened within the Jerusalem temple.

The burden of 43:10 is expanded, although in a contingent form: **'if they are ashamed of all that they have done'**, Ezekiel will **'make known to them'** all that he had seen, summed up as the **'laws'** of the new temple, so that the people might **'do'**, or honour, them.

This does not mean that a generation of Israelites yet to be born would reconstruct a temple in accordance with Ezekiel's blueprint (supposing, for the sake of the argument, that it *was* a blueprint). What Yahweh promises obliquely is that although he purposes to return to dwell among his people (see 43:1-5), he will do so only if they are repentant. **'If'** is the key word at this point: Yahweh is gracious only to those who bow themselves with a consciousness of sin and guilt. Vainglory is abhorrent. The Lord gives his people a not-to-be-missed opportunity to show their sincerity by enthusing over the exactness of the system of worship that he prescribes (43:11). A terse statement sums up the rationale for repentance: the principle, or **'law'**, governing the construction and the use of the temple is that, set as it is **'upon the top of the mountain'** (cf. 40:2), in its entirety it **'is most holy'**. **'Look,'** says Yahweh to Ezekiel and to his readers, as if to imprint the lesson on their hearts, **'this is the law of the house'** (43:12). Those who remain impure will never see their God.[88]

Application

The description of idols as 'corpses' is telling. We live in a syncretistic world in which political correctness seems to reign and in which the absolute uniqueness of the religion of the Bible is ridiculed or downplayed, or even denied.

Yet without the true and living God, who by means of the Jerusalem temple prefigured his self-revelation and programme of redemption, there is no life worth living. If men will turn to fictitious deities, they do so at their peril.

Thankfully, the message of Ezekiel's great prophecy is that, one way or another, through salvation or condemnation, all men will come to know that the Lord is. Almighty God will not permit himself to be permanently ignored.

The altar and its ordinances (Ezekiel 43:13-27)

Ezekiel's visions now enter a new phase in which he is shown the ritual ordinances of the new sanctuary. The revelation begins appropriately with a description of the altar of burnt offering, the locus of reconciliation. It had been mentioned in passing in 40:47 to indicate that it was situated 'in front of the house' — that is, east of the entrance to the central sanctuary. A consideration of chapters 40 – 44 indicates that it was sited at the exact centre of the complete temple complex.

Nowhere is there any suggestion that this description is the draft of an altar to be erected in the temple site within a terrestrial Jerusalem. Although three-dimensional measurements are given, materials are not specified.

1. The measurements of the altar (43:13-17)

43:13-17. 'And these are the measurements of the altar by cubits (a cubit being a cubit and a handbreadth): the hollow, one cubit, and one cubit wide, with a rim of a single span all around its edge. This is the base of the altar. And from the hollow in the earth to the lower ledge, two cubits; and the width, one cubit; and from the smaller ledge to the greater ledge, four cubits; and the width, one cubit. The altar hearth is four cubits, and from the altar hearth the four horns extend upwards. And the altar hearth, twelve cubits long by twelve cubits wide, is square in its four sides. The ledge is fourteen cubits long by fourteen wide on its four sides. And the rim around is of half a cubit; its hollow, a cubit all around; and its steps face the east.'

The measurement of the altar is based upon Ezekiel's cubit: a conventional cubit plus the width of a hand (cf. 40:5). Although we may obtain a general picture of the altar, some of the details are obscure, which is why the diagram and the following exposition are tentative.[89]

THE ALTAR OF BURNT OFFERING

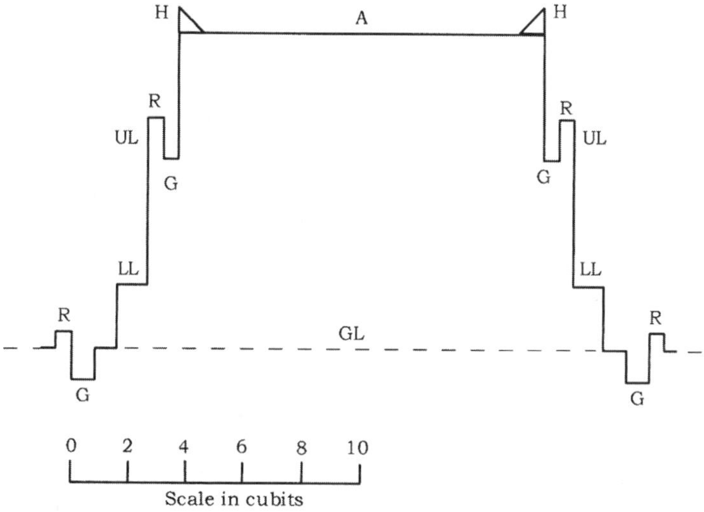

A Altar hearth
G Gutter, or Hollow
GL Ground level
H Horns
LL Lower ledge
R Rim
UL Upper ledge

A **'hollow'** (*hēq*), perhaps a gutter or shallow trench, one cubit deep and one cubit wide, surrounded the base of the altar. This Hebrew word, often translated as 'bosom' and occasionally signifying the fold of a garment at the breast,[90] occurs also in 1 Kings 22:35 with reference to the blood of Ahab trickling into the possibly concave 'floor' of his chariot. Such references may help to explain Ezekiel's description.

Outside the gutter and at ground level there was a surrounding border, or **'rim'**, a handbreadth in height (and width?). The gutter and its rim might have been intended to prevent the blood of animal sacrifices from spilling onto, and thereby desecrating, the surrounding earth. Ezekiel tells that the gutter and its rim constituted the borders of **'the base'** platform **'of the altar'** (43:13).[91]

Unusually, we are given vertical measurements. The lower section of the altar was situated **'one cubit'** horizontally within **'the** [square] **hollow of the earth'**. From this it might be deduced that the trench was cut into the ground. The height of this section from ground level **'to the lower ledge'**, alias **'the smaller ledge'**, was **'two cubits'**.

'From', or 'above', the smaller or lower ledge, and **'one cubit'** horizontally within its border, was a further section of elevation **'four cubits'**, terminating at what is termed **'the greater ledge'** (43:14).

These two sections, one upon the other, provided a base for **'the altar hearth'** (*ar'ēl* or *ari'ēl*; 43:16). These two Hebrew words are enigmatic. As they stand, *ar'ēl* signifies 'mountain of God', and *ari'ēl*, 'lion of God'.[92] But in the present verse these meanings may be unlikely, the two possibly being orthographic variations of one word. Dating from the ninth century BC, the celebrated Mesha inscription, lines 12 and 17, mentions that Mesha, one-time king of Moab, had carried away the 'ariels', perhaps altars, of Yahweh and of David.[93] If so, Ezekiel outlines an elevated altar upon which sacrifice would be offered. Upon this structure were **'four horns'** extending **'upwards'**. As such, they were not an innovation. Presumably, sacrificial blood would have been smeared on them (cf. 43:18,20), although 40:42 indicates that in Ezekiel's temple the animals were to be killed elsewhere.[94] It is emphasized that the *ari'él* was exactly **'twelve cubits'** square (43:15-16).

At the foot of the hearth of the altar and its surrounding was a **'ledge'** projecting **'one cubit'** in each direction, the base upon which the altar stood being a square of **'fourteen cubits'**. Integral to the ledge there were a **'rim'** and a **'hollow'**, the former **'half a cubit'** wide and the latter **'one cubit'** deep. They would have served the same purpose as those at the bottom of the whole structure.

The altar in Moses' court of meeting had been five cubits square and three cubits high, without any steps, and that of Solomon's temple was twenty cubits square and ten cubits high.[95] By comparing with 43:13-17, it follows that the altar seen by Ezekiel was higher than these and with a ground area greater than that within Solomon's temple, the latter being measured in old cubits. **'Steps'** leading to Ezekiel's altar were on the **'east'** side, the complete structure being symmetrical.

Questions arise. Why is this massive altar outlined in three dimensions? Why was it apparently situated at the exact centre of the temple complex? And why could it be seen through the inner and outer porches to the east, north and south (were they to be opened), thereby being unavoidably visible?

There would appear to be one answer, and only one, to these questions. Although Yahweh desires to reside among his people and although the people of Israel are presumably penitent (cf. 43:10-11), there can be no *rapprochement* without an acceptable sacrifice. Firstly, divine righteousness requires the vicarious shedding of blood; secondly, repentant sinners must assent to this principle; thirdly, grace supplies an offering acceptable to the Lord.[96]

Imagine a two-dimensional board upon which is inscribed in detail the square ground plan of Ezekiel's temple. Apart from the vertical columns at the outer gates (40:14), the board is flat except for the centre point, upon which rises an almost perfect cube of which each side is about four per cent of the length of each side of the surrounding complex. Even in relative terms it is not tiny. By its very nature, this projection — nothing other than the altar of offering — is, as it were, almost aggressive, demanding to be noticed (43:17).

In short, the size, centrality and intentional visibility of the place of offering speak with a united voice. Not for the first time (cf. 43:10-11), Ezekiel's readers are expected to ponder carefully.

2. The duties of the family of Zadok (43:18-27)

43:18-27. And he said to me, 'Son of man, thus says the Lord Yahweh: "These are the statutes of the altar on the day when it is constructed, to offer up burnt offerings on it and for throwing blood upon it.

'"And you will give for the priests, the Levites, who are from the seed of Zadok, who draw near to me to minister to me," declares the Lord Yahweh, "a young bull of the cattle for a sin offering. Then you will take some of its blood and place it upon its four horns, on the four corners of the ledge and upon the surrounding rim; thus you will de-sin it and will make atonement for it. Then you will take the young bull for the sin offering and burn it in the appointed place of the house, outside the holy place. Then on the second day you will bring near a perfect kid of the goats for a sin offering and they will de-sin the altar just as they de-sinned it with the young bull. When you have finished de-sinning, you will bring near a perfect young bull of the cattle and a perfect ram from the flock. And when you bring them near before Yahweh, the priests will cast salt on them and will offer them up as a burnt offering to Yahweh.

'"Every day for seven days you will prepare a goat for a sin offering, and they will prepare a young bull of the cattle and a ram from the flock, both being perfect. For seven days they will make atonement for the altar and will cleanse it and fill its hands. Then, when they have completed the days, from the eighth day onward the priests will render your burnt offerings and your peace offerings upon the altar, and I shall accept you," declares the Lord Yahweh.'

The man, apparently none other than the angel of the Lord, spoke in the name of **'the Lord Yahweh'**, explaining to Ezekiel **'the statutes of the altar on the day'** when it would be **'constructed'**. It is implied that there must be no delay between the erection of the altar and the commencement of a seven-day process of purification, carried out upon the precedent of the procedure of Exodus 29:36-37, where Moses is instructed to initiate the decontamination of the altar of burnt offering. Only then will it be deemed to be (literally) 'a holy of holies', or most holy. Now Ezekiel learns that what he sees is a matter for the future as expounded in terms of the past: following the altar's consecration, the **'blood'** of sacrificed animals will be applied to it (43:18).

'You' (singular) — that is, Ezekiel — must **'give'** the priests **'from the seed of Zadok'**, who alone may **'draw near ... to minister'** to Yahweh (cf. 40:46; 44:15-16), **'a young bull ... for a sin offering'**. This would be on the first day of the seven-day ritual. By comparing with Exodus 29:36-37, it looks as if Ezekiel assumes the role of a second Moses. If so, it can only be in the sense that chapters 40 – 48 predict the Messianic future of Israel in terms of Mosaic typology. It is almost as if the priest-prophet issues a God-breathed 'let there be', laying down guidelines for times ahead.

Whereas, through no fault of its own, Moses' administration had collapsed, the new arrangement, announced by Ezekiel and based on exactly similar principles, will not fail. Furthermore, even as the Mosaic dispensation was itself an anticipation of the person and work of Christ,[97] so too Ezekiel's temple and its ministry cannot be other than Christ-centred. If this is understood, text (43:19) and context make sense.

When the Zadokite priests have slaughtered the sin offering, **'blood'**, emblematic of life that has been destroyed violently and as a propitiation, will be placed by Ezekiel on the four horns of the altar, on the four corners of (apparently) the upper **'ledge'** and on the upper **'rim'**. By so doing, the prophet will **'de-sin it and will make atonement for it'**. I have employed 'de-sin', meaning to purify or decontaminate, because it translates the *Pi'él* (active-intensive) form of a common Hebrew verb meaning 'to sin' or 'to miss a mark', and as such occurs in Exodus 29:36, which forms the background to this passage.[98] To illustrate, in English the verb 'to bone', when accompanied by a direct object, means to 'debone', to remove bones from meat or fish before cooking.[99]

'Make atonement' translates the verb from which is derived *kippûr*, as in 'Day of Atonement'. It is not that the altar will be forgiven its sins (which would be absurd), but that it is cleansed of all defilement incurred by human contact. Apparently, unlike the ritual prescribed by Moses for the purification of the altar within the tabernacle,[100] hands are not laid upon the victim, perhaps because the animal is deemed impure even without a ritual transfer of guilt (43:20).

During the first day of decontamination and following the application of blood, Ezekiel is to **'take'** the carcase of the **'bull'** of the **'sin offering'** and **'burn it**

in the appointed place'. Of course, he never did any such thing, nor did he expect to. The point is that by an association with the Mosaic rite of consecration, he does no more than anticipate a future age when ongoing worship will be untainted.

'The appointed place' for the incineration of the sin offering may have been the building behind the west end of the holy of holies, as described in 41:12. According to Moses, a bullock, when killed as a sin offering for the high priest or for the congregation, had to be burned outside the camp.[101] Similarly, Ezekiel's sin offering covers the transgressions of either the high priest or the whole community, or both, the altar having being contaminated by human contact (43:21).

On the second day Ezekiel is to bring to **'the altar'** a physically **'perfect'** young goat for a **'sin offering'**, the sacrifice prescribed for a ruler in Israel.[102] Employing the same ritual as on the previous day, the Zadokite priests continue the process of decontamination (43:22).

Upon completing the task allocated for the second day, Ezekiel is to **'bring near'** to Yahweh a faultless **'young bull'** and a similarly **'perfect ram'** for **'a** [joint] **burnt offering'**. After slaughter, the priests are to throw a copious amount of salt on the carcasses and burn them for Yahweh (43:23-24). Compare with Leviticus 2:13, where a somewhat smaller quantity of salt is implied. Salt was, and is, a preservative and, as in Numbers 18:19 and 2 Chronicles 13:5, symbolizes a lasting relationship between the worshipper and God. Much salt proclaims a glorious truth.

The sin and burnt offerings are to be repeated on each of seven consecutive days. The former will be goats, to be provided by Ezekiel, and the latter bulls and rams, provided by the Zadokite priests. All are to be **'perfect'** (43:25).

Thus the decontamination process will extend over **'seven days'**, during which time the priests **'make**

atonement for the altar' that had (presumably) been defiled by human contact.

The Hebrew language possesses a number of vivid anthropomorphisms, and one such occurs here: to 'fill the hand(s)', meaning consecration or even ordination.[103] Following its purification, **'the altar'** will always be supplied with sacrificial gifts, **'its hands'**, so to speak, never being empty, implying unceasing worship. This is the only occasion in the Old Testament in which we read of the ordination of, and service undertaken by, an inanimate, albeit sacred, object. It is as if everything associated with worship offers itself unreservedly to the high task (43:26).

After the conclusion of the unique seven-day period of consecration of the altar and from the eighth day onwards, **'the priests'** officiate at **'the altar'** to ensure the acceptance of the congregation by Yahweh. According to Leviticus 9:1, the inauguration of the family of Aaron continued into an eighth day. The extension is omitted here, possibly because it is assumed that they had been consecrated long ago.

The people's **'burnt offerings'** would symbolize glad commitment to Yahweh, and their **'peace offerings'** their joyfulness in the presence of God. Now, all is well between Yahweh and Israel: he is pleased with them and accepts them (43:27).

Application

The highly unusual three-dimensional measurement of the altar of burnt offering, its unprecedented size and its position at the heart of Ezekiel's temple complex bespeak its indispensability. If Yahweh and Israel are to be in relationship, God cannot be reconciled to the people and they, notwithstanding their holy desires, have no claim upon him unless there is adequate objective sacrifice.

Moreover, if the description of the altar that has been suggested here is not inaccurate, it is seen as so stained by sacrificial blood that, unlike Moses' altar, it was designed with gutters or 'hollows' at two levels to allow the blood to be conducted away. 'Blood' seems to be the pre-eminent keyword.

Worship, then, depends upon blood shed in sacrifice and subsequently smeared, or poured, or sprinkled, upon the altar. In the Old Testament 'blood' symbolizes violent death and, when sprinkled, denotes a covering for sin and ceremonial purification leading to access to God.[104]

Because he had no other medium of expression, Ezekiel harnessed the typical sacrifices of Moses' dispensation to anticipate the perfect efficacy and the absolute centrality of the death of the Messiah. Through faith, his blood avails, and God takes pleasure in his people.[105] Both sides participate in an everlasting covenant of salt.

Princely and priestly duties (Ezekiel 44:1-31)

Although the altar of burnt offering has been consecrated and the way opened up for Israel to worship Yahweh, provision must be made for ensuring the ongoing sanctity of the people. Prior to the Babylonian captivity Israel had been degraded largely through the misconduct of princes, priests and Levites. Because this must never happen again, directions are given concerning the prince (44:1-3), the admission of foreigners, the appointment of priests and Levites (44:4-16) and, finally, the conditions and privileges of the priestly office (44:17-31).

1. The prince (44:1-3)

44:1-3. Then he brought me back by way of the outer gate of the sanctuary, facing east, but it was closed. And Yahweh said to me, 'This gate will be closed. It will not be opened and no man will come through it because Yahweh, the God of Israel, has come through it; therefore it will be closed. But as for the prince, he — the prince — will sit in it to eat bread before Yahweh; he will enter by way of the porch of the gate and will go out by the same way.'

From the inner court where he had been standing (43:5), Ezekiel was led back to the east **'outer gate'** of the **'sanctuary'** (cf. 40:6), by which is meant the complete temple complex, and found it **'closed'**. This verb occurs three times in verses 1-2, implying emphasis on the part of the Lord and perhaps surprise on the part of the prophet (44:1).

Although the speaker may have been Ezekiel's guide, what the prophet heard was effectively the word of **'Yahweh'** (cf. 43:6). He was informed that henceforth the entrance would be prohibited to worshippers because **'Yahweh, the God of Israel'**, had entered it already (cf. 43:2). Effectively, and in fulfilment of 43:7,9, the Lord, having gone in to his sanctuary (cf. 43:2), had shut the door behind him with no intention of departing through it (cf. 11:23). He had come to stay. Therefore, if he will never use it again, no mortal man may employ it for transit (44:2). According to 46:9, worshippers would enter by means of the north and south gates.

Nevertheless, **'the prince'** may **'sit in it to eat bread before Yahweh'**, the gate serving as a site for princely fellowship with Yahweh. The act of eating compares with the experiences of Jacob and Laban, of Jethro, and of Aaron and the elders who ate in the presence of God.[106]

'The prince', who is mentioned for the first time in the complete prophecy and whose presence is presupposed rather than announced, may be no more than a typical prince of the house of David, taking his place in an idealized kingdom. If so, future, long-term realities are being pictured in terms of earlier conditions. Alternatively, he could be the Messianic David of 34:24 and 37:24-25. In this case, none other than the Messiah may sit in the gate and eat in the presence of Yahweh.

Some clarification may be given by what follows. That **'he** [the prince] **will enter by way of the porch of the gate and will go out by the same way'** could indicate that he will do no more than enter from the east to eat and leave when he has finished. Therefore, he does not enjoy a status equal to that of the Levites and the Zadokite priests, who are permitted to minister within the inner court (cf. 42:13-14; 43:19).

Because of these restrictions, perhaps the first view (the 'typical prince' interpretation) is better. During the troubled years of the monarchy, the descendants of David had often corrupted the people's worship.[107] In this final state the prince of the time, whoever he might be, leads Israel in holy worship. His identity does not matter. What is important is that his presence, status and activity signify a break with the sinful past. Therefore, the verse is non-Messianic (44:3).

2. Foreigners, priests and Levites (44:4-16)

44:4-16. Then he brought me by way of the north gate to the front of the house; and I saw, and, look, the glory of Yahweh filled the house of Yahweh, and I fell on my face. And Yahweh said to me, 'Son of man, fix your heart and see with your eyes and hear with your ears all that I am telling you concerning all the statutes of the house of Yahweh and all its laws; and set your heart to the entrance of the house, with all the exits of the sanctuary.

'And you will say to the rebellious ones, to the house of Israel, "Thus says the Lord Yahweh: 'For you, enough of all your abominations, O house of Israel. When you brought the sons of the foreigner, uncircumcised in heart and uncircumcised in the flesh, to be in my sanctuary, to profane my house, when you brought near my food — fat and blood — then they annulled my covenant with all their abominations. And you have not kept the observance of my holy things but have appointed others for you as keepers of my observance in my sanctuary.'

'"Thus says the Lord Yahweh: 'No son of a foreigner, uncircumcised in heart and uncircumcised in flesh, will enter my sanctuary — no foreigner who is amid the sons of Israel. Yet the Levites who distanced themselves from me when

Israel went astray, when they went astray from me after their idols — they will bear their iniquities. But they will be in my sanctuary, ministering the oversight at the gates of the house and ministering to the house; they will slaughter the burnt offering and the sacrifice for the people, and they will stand before them to minister to them. Because they used to minister to them before their idols and were to the house of Israel a stumbling block of iniquity, therefore I have raised my hand against them,' declares the Lord Yahweh, 'and they will bear their iniquity. And they will not draw near to me to act as priests nor come near to any of my holy things — to the most holy things — but they will bear their disgrace and their abominations that they have committed. But I have appointed them as keepers of the observance of the house, for all its work and for all that is done in it.

'"'But as for the priests, the Levites, the sons of Zadok who kept the observance of my sanctuary when the sons of Israel went astray from me — they will come near to me to minister to me, and will stand before me to offer me fat and blood,' declares the Lord Yahweh. 'It is they who will enter my sanctuary and it is they who will come near my table to minister to me, and they will keep my observance.'"'

The prophet was escorted through **'the north gate'** — probably that on the boundary of the inner court — where he could see **'the front of the house'**, the central sanctuary. **'The glory of Yahweh filled'** it. As in 43:3, which recounts the glory of the Lord entering the outer court from the east, Ezekiel fell prostrate. To judge by his interjectory **'and, look'**, he was filled with awe. That the Lord should, after Israel's long and sad history, reside in **'the house of Yahweh'** astonished him. The splendour of the occupied temple rendered it unapproachable (44:4).

44:5 may be compared with the first part of 2:8: 'And you, son of man, hear what I am telling you.' There Ezekiel was being commissioned to proclaim the imminent doom of Israel; now he is to tell out that, although there is a glorious long-term future for Israel, the people must be scrupulous in their obedience to directions concerning who may and who may not enter the temple via **'the entrance'** and **'all the exits'**.[108] The passage is almost a reflection of Psalms 15 and 24:3-6.[109] But before Ezekiel goes to his constituency, what Yahweh will be **'telling'** him must be **'set'** upon his **'heart'**: he is to strain sight and hearing to digest the regulations governing the house and is to give strict attention to the temple entrances and exits. This means that reverence and order must characterize entrance to and departure from the place of worship.

The recall of 2:8 and Ezekiel's first commission to go to an obstinate people now comes to the fore.[110] Yet although the exiles are still potentially **'rebellious'**, **'the house of Israel'** may expect a blessed future. For this reason, past **'abominations'** are **'enough'** and must cease, declares **'the Lord Yahweh'** (44:6).

In earlier times, Israel had practised all manner of abominations, including the introduction of **'the foreigner'**,[111] uncircumcised both in heart and in flesh, into the holy place. While aliens were sometimes allowed to offer sacrifice,[112] the reference here is to those who had had absolutely no desire to seek the God of Israel. Although names are not mentioned, such had been permitted to consume Yahweh's **'food'**, by which is meant sacrificial offerings, and associated **'fat and blood'**.[113] This and other malicious activities effectively nullified Yahweh's **'covenant'**, ratified at Sinai, between Israel and himself (44:7). Compare with 16:58-59.

Worse, profane foreigners had been appointed **'as keepers'**, or temple servants, in place of, or in addition to, the Levites.[114] This had infringed Yahweh's **'observance'** in his **'sanctuary'**, and he was outraged (44:8).

To guard against a repetition of the evil, a specific precaution is to be taken: **'no son of a foreigner'**, **'uncircumcised'** both in the **'flesh'** and in his **'heart'** in that he refuses to identify with the people of Israel, may enter the **'sanctuary'**. The prohibition of Exodus 12:43-51 concerning admission to the Passover is given a clear allusion.

But the double disqualification of the uncircumcised in flesh and in heart seems to presume that the foreigner who *is* circumcised in his heart is welcome, being reckoned to have the same standing as a native-born godly Israelite (cf. 47:22-23). Ezekiel appears to come near to the New Testament's approach to Gentile believers (44:9).[115]

As a further protection against the profanation of the sanctuary, **'Levites'**, who now appear in the prophecy for the first time, will be appointed as its servants. In spite of having **'distanced themselves'** from Yahweh, they will now be allowed to serve (cf. 44:15-16).

Descendants of Levi, a son of Jacob by Leah, the Levites assumed the role of those males in Israel who by virtue of their primogeniture belonged to the Lord. Responsible for serving within the tabernacle, they were never allocated tribal land, but possessed cities within territories belonging to the other tribes. In earlier times they were notable for their allegiance to Yahweh, but their first love is not now remembered.[116]

In what fashion, and when, the Levites had apostatized is not specified. After the division of Israel into the northern and the southern kingdoms, many of them remained loyal to Yahweh but in later years had succumbed to popular idolatry (as suggested by 8:11).[117] That they **'will bear their iniquities'** is a direct recall of Numbers 18:23, which tells that the Levites had to protect the sanctity of the tabernacle, possibly on pain of death.[118] The present verse, then, tells out that the Levitical guards will exercise extreme diligence in their ministry (44:10).

Their duties comprise **'the oversight'** of the temple **'gates'**, possibly involving crowd-control, killing the sacrifices elsewhere (cf. 40:39) and assisting in the kitchens (cf. 46:24). While the priests stand before Yahweh (44:15), the Levites (cf. 44:13) **'stand'** before the worshippers **'to minister to them'**. Their reduced status is essentially that of priests with physical disabilities, who, according to Leviticus 21:17-23, would not be permitted to approach the Lord (44:11).

The Mosaic system is modified in that worshippers within the new temple will not kill their own sacrifices. A reason for this is suggested in the comments on 40:38.[119]

'Because' in the past the Levites had connived in a general apostasy, abusing their position of responsibility to lead and to teach, the Lord raises his **'hand'** in confirmation that demotion shall be their lot. No more will they stand before Yahweh to bless the people in his name.[120] In terms of Numbers 18:23, in that **'they will bear their iniquity'** they will honour their new assignment lest they suffer (44:12).

Levites may not approach the Lord **'to act as priests'** and may not touch or handle either sacrifices or holy objects: **'they will bear their disgrace.'**[121] Their past failures and **'abominations'** having been forgiven, their shame flows from a sense of remorse (44:13).

In spite of this, they are not denied an **'appointed'** ministry, that of supervising all that occurs in **'the house'**, including its maintenance and the slaughter of animal sacrifices. Their labour will be as prominent as it will be essential (44:14).

But **'the sons of Zadok'** are to serve Yahweh in his **'sanctuary'** because they were faithful **'when the sons of Israel went astray from me'**. (The comments on 40:46 seek to give the background.) Perhaps this means that priests faithful to their calling in later times of apostasy are considered to be in principle sons of Zadok even though they might not be members of his immediate family. Only such may **'come near'** to Yahweh, may **'stand before'** him to **'offer'** his sacrifices, may enter the holy place and may approach his **'table'**, by which is meant the altar (44:15-16).

3. The priestly office (44:17-31)

44:17-31. '"'And it shall be that whenever they come within the gates of the inner court they will put on linen garments; no wool will come upon them when they minister within the gates of the inner court and in the house. Linen turbans will be upon their heads and linen undergarments will be upon their loins; they will not clothe themselves with anything that causes perspiration. And when they go out to the outer court, to the outer court to the people, they will put off the clothes in which they ministered, will lay them down in the holy apartments and will clothe themselves with other garments; they will not sanctify the people with their garments.

'"'Nor will they shave their heads nor let their locks grow long; they will assuredly trim their heads. And the priests shall drink no wine when they come to the inner court. They will not take a widow or a divorced woman for a wife, but take virgins from the seed of Israel or the widow who is a widow of a priest. And they will teach my people the difference between the sacred and the common, and make them know the difference between defilement and uncleanness. And in a dispute they will stand to judge according to my judgements and will judge it, and will observe my laws and my statutes in all my appointed meetings, and they will sanctify my Sabbaths.

'"'They will not approach a dead person so as to be defiled. Yet for a father or a mother, a son or a daughter, a brother, or a sister who had no husband, they may defile themselves. And after his cleansing they will count out seven days for him. And on the day when he comes to the holy place, to the inner court, to minister in the holy place, he will bring near his sin offering,' declares the Lord Yahweh."

'"'Thus it will be to them for an inheritance — I am their inheritance. And you will grant them no possession in Israel — I am their possession. As for the grain offering, the sin offering and the guilt offering, they will eat them; and every devoted thing in Israel will be theirs. The first of all the first fruits of everything and every offering of all, from all your offerings, will be for the priests. And the first of your dough you will give to the priest to cause a blessing to rest upon your house. The priests will not eat any carcass or torn thing, whether of bird or beast.'"'

The remainder of chapter 44 concerns the clothing and conduct of the Zadokite priests. The manner in which those who guide worship cover and comport themselves reflects the state of their hearts.

When entering the inner court the priests must wear **'garments'**, **'turbans'** and **'undergarments'** woven from flax-linen.[122] Clothing made from **'wool'** is prohibited because bodily warmth generated by hair fabric might cause them to perspire, rendering them unclean and uncomfortable.[123] Moreover, they will only wear their official garments when they **'minister within the gates of the inner court and in the house'** (44:17-18).

Although the requirement that the priests don their official dress exclusively when on duty, discarding it when leaving the inner court, is implied by Exodus and Leviticus,[124] here it becomes explicit: the priests are not to **'sanctify the people with their garments'** (cf. 46:20). A reasonable explanation of this injunction is that the congregation's physical contact with priestly garments would contaminate the priestly office. This means that, were they allowed to brush against the priests, the crowds would be under the impossible obligation of avoiding all ritual defilement in their daily routine in order to sustain the sanctity of the priests. As a result of inadvertent contact between the sacred and the unclean, sanctity would be degraded by uncleanness rather than uncleanness being purged by holiness. Haggai 2:10-13 expounds the principle. To pre-empt this, when not in use the garments are to be reserved in the **'holy apartments'** mentioned in 42:1-14 (44:19).[125]

The priests are not permitted to **'shave their heads'** or to leave their hair uncut; rather, their hair must be trimmed neatly,[126] possibly because in past times such practices had been associated with mourning or pagan rituals (44:20).

Nor are they to consume **'wine'** when about to enter **'the inner court'**, no doubt because alcohol has a deadening effect on the mind (44:21).[127]

And the priests may not marry widows, other than widows of priests, or divorced women.[128] Moses had stipulated that although a priest could marry a widow, the high priest was barred from union with a widow or a divorcee. Nor could a harlot be considered (44:22). Although Ezekiel does not explain, his restrictions would seek to preserve the purity of the priestly line.[129] Also, although Moses' legislation permitted divorce, the practice was never approved.[130] In short, it is implied that the priests will have the unmixed blood of Aaron in their veins.

Alluding to Leviticus 10:10-11, one of the principal duties of the priests within this new arrangement is to show **'my people the difference between the sacred and the common'** and **'between defilement and uncleanness'**. Their lives are to be sermons (44:23).

In fulfilment of Moses' prediction concerning the tribe of Levi,[131] the Zadokite priests will act as judges within Israel. This constitutes a break with one monarchical tradition, whereby according to popular request the king was to administer justice.[132] Yet the priests will be careful to reflect the revealed will of Yahweh, **'my'** in connection with the Lord's requirements occurring no less than five times for emphasis. Particular importance is accorded to Yahweh's **'Sabbaths'**, reflecting 20:12-24. He is King (44:24).

An individual priest must not **'approach a dead person'**, other than **'a father or a mother'** or **'a son or a daughter'** or **'a brother'** or an unmarried **'sister'**. The prohibition reflects Leviticus 21:1-4 and would refer to mourning in time of bereavement, priests of God not reacting to death, itself an effect of sin.[133] But even permitted involvement in the funerals of such near relatives would incur defilement, for which cleansing is essential (44:25).

Thus, in the event of a priest incurring ritual uncleanness because of the loss of a loved one, the procedure laid down by Numbers 19:11-19 will be followed. Accordingly, water of purification is to be sprinkled upon the individual on the third and seventh days of a seven-day period. Yet the contaminated priest in Ezekiel's temple will travel beyond this ritual in that after an additional seven days he must render a **'sin offering'** when resuming his duties **'in the holy place'** (44:26-27).

The grammar of 44:28 is puzzling in that, although **'it will be'** is feminine, there is no feminine antecedent.[134] Possibly the meaning is that 'there will be no [tribal] allocation for them'.

Positively, because Yahweh is equally the **'inheritance'** and the **'possession'** of the priests, they will be granted no distinct territories throughout Israel. In practical terms this means that, as in earlier times, the priests are to be supported by tithes, sacrifices and first fruits given by the congregation to the Lord.[135] And, if individuals are generous to the priests, the Lord will **'cause a blessing to rest upon'** the **'house'** of each contributor. The command of Leviticus 17:15 not to eat the flesh of anything that had died naturally or had been killed by predators is repeated (44:28-31).[136]

But there is one important modification to Moses' arrangement. The allocation of towns to the priests does not obtain here because, according to 45:4, they now reside near the central sanctuary.

Application

Neither within this chapter nor elsewhere does Ezekiel, himself a priest, refer explicitly to the Aaronic high priesthood — an eloquent silence. Nor is there any mention of the Day of Atonement[137] or of the ark of the covenant. Perhaps the prophet signifies that in principle the services of a succession of high priests within an earthly tabernacle or temple are now redundant. Perhaps Ezekiel anticipates a time when the once-for-all sacrifice of Christ will be an accomplished reality. Perhaps he describes the eternal future in the only way possible for him, in terms of the shadows of the past — yet in such a fashion as to make it clear that these shadows are not to be reintroduced. This is how the writer of this commentary would see it.

With their past failures and 'abominations' forgiven (44:13), the Levites' shame flows from a deep sense of remorse. In God's harvest field, ripe corn hangs its head.

Because they have come to know the grace of God and exercise a teaching ministry, the priests are to exemplify the holiness required of a worshipping community (44:23). Similarly, a truly holy Christian is by that token a teacher of the gospel. Salt and light may lack lips yet can say so much.[138]

Whereas the priests are not to contract defilement by approaching the dead (44:25), our Lord deliberately touched the bier of a dead man, giving him back his life.[139] When confronted by Christ, death and corruption die. But he cannot be tainted.

According to 44:30, the people are to maintain the priesthood with their offerings and thereby experience the blessing of God. Similarly, Christians are given the promise that if they give it shall be given to them.[140] And when, as in the case of the Zadokite priests (44:28), the Lord bestows himself, no needful thing will be lacking.[141]

All in all, chapter 44 gives the impression of a prevailing state of order among the people when they approach the God who is among them. Nothing that defiles can enter in because sin has been banished permanently. Worship is presented as the sole activity in this city-temple. It would seem that Ezekiel takes us beyond the horizon of the world as we know it and anticipates Revelation 21:10,22 and the surrounding context.

The sacred portions of the land, offerings and regulations (Ezekiel 45:1-17)

Israel's duty to maintain the priesthood is now expounded. An immense area of land is to be reserved for the priests' use as well as for the central sanctuary and for the Levites. The presentation is remarkable for two reasons. Firstly, such an allocation was unknown in Israel; secondly, it would appear that Ezekiel's division of the land shows him to be concerned with a heavenly vision rather than with a practical, this-worldly, possibility. This is not a picture of the family of Israel resettled happily in a terrestrial Canaan.

1. The central allotment (45:1-8)

45:1-8. '"'And when you allot the land by inheritance, you will offer an offering to Yahweh. It will be from the land, holy. The length: 25,000 in length; and the width: 10,000. It will be holy in all its border round about. From this there will be for the holy place a square area, 500 by 500 round about, and an open space for it, fifty cubits round about. And from this measure you will measure 25,000 by length and 10,000 by width, and in it will be the sanctuary — the holy of holies. It is holy, set off from the land, for the priests who minister in the sanctuary, they who draw near to minister to Yahweh; and it will be for them a place for houses and a sacred area for the sanctuary.

'"'And 25,000 in length and 10,000 in width will be for the Levites, the ministers of the house, as a possession: their cities to live in. And you will appoint as the property of the city 5,000 by width and by length, 25,000 adjacent to the holy offering; it will be for all the house of Israel. And for the prince, on one side and on the other of the holy offering and the possession of the city, facing the holy offering and the possession of the city — from the west side, westward, and from the east side, eastward. And the length will be adjacent to one of the divisions from the west border to the east border. The land will be his possession in Israel; and my princes will no longer oppress my people, but shall give the land to the house of Israel according to their tribes.'"'

Restored to the land of promise, Israel divides the land and is to **'offer'** some of it as **'an offering'**, by which is meant territory deemed to be **'holy'**. The background Hebrew for **'offering'**, *t'rûmah*, signifies that it is to be lifted up to Yahweh, although (in this case) not literally:[142] the people are glad to hold high before the Lord what they have received. A fuller description of this territorial gift occurs in 48:8-22.

To **'allot the land'** is an ellipsis for 'when you cast the lot for the land', alluding to Numbers 26:53-56 and Joshua 18:6-10.[143] Yet now the division is not according to providential disposition, the tribal allocations being specified in advance by Yahweh.

The Hebrew text, which I have attempted to translate literally, does not define the unit of measurement of the land offering. I would suggest that the measuring reed (cf. 40:5) is to be assumed, and this for both of two reasons: firstly, to fit with the suggested dimensions of the temple complex (42:16-20); and, secondly, because 45:2 mentions cubits with reference to an **'open space'** surrounding **'the holy place'**, implying that the standard of measure in other cases is different (45:2,3,5,6).[144]

According to 40:5, the measuring reed was 'six cubits, by a cubit and a handbreadth', each cubit being an ordinary cubit plus the span of a hand. As noted earlier,[145] it may be supposed that the length of one reed was about 3·34 metres, or just under 11 feet. This calculation is most important because the reed is the basic unit of measure for the allocation of the territory.

Here, the **'holy'** portion of land would be 25,000 reeds long and 10,000 wide, approximately 84 by 34 kilometres, or 52 by 21 miles (45:1).[146] Within this sacred reservation, and presumably at its centre, there is to be **'a square area'**, designated as **'the holy place'**, with each side **'500'** (reeds) long, about 1·7 kilometres, or just over a mile. Mentioned in 42:16-20, it will be surrounded by a narrow strip **'fifty cubits'** wide, about 28 metres, or 93 feet (45:2).

Assuming that 45:1 refers to an area 25,000 reeds long (east-west) and 10,000 wide (north-south),[147] verse 3 reflects upon these measurements in order to show that the central **'sanctuary'**, **'the holy of holies'** will be situated within it.

And this band of territory will also be granted to **'the priests'** who **'draw near ... to Yahweh'**, and who will not have far to travel to **'minister in the** [central] **sanctuary'**. Here they will possess their **'houses'**. This allocation is vastly greater than the thirteen cities granted to the priests by Moses[148] and is much larger than that given to any one of the tribes within the new arrangement (see chapter 48). Worship is the sole activity of the reconvened nation (45:4).

A further allotment of land, 25,000 reeds long (east-west) and 10,000 wide (north-south), apparently parallel to that of the priests, is to be dedicated to **'the Levites'** as their **'possession'**. Unlike the requirement of Moses' dispensation,[149] they will not be scattered throughout the land. The Hebrew of the last part of

45:5 is not easy and might mean that the area is 'for cities for them to live in'.[150]

A third parallel space, **'the property of the city'**, is designated: 5,000 reeds wide (north-south) and 25,000 long (east-west) — about 17 by 84 kilometres, or 10½ by 52 miles. Accessible to **'all the house of Israel'**, perhaps it is designed to serve as a stopover for those travelling from a distance to worship at the central sanctuary. Whether it is north or south of the central area will be disclosed by 48:18-19.

We must visualize, therefore, a central square with sides each 25,000 reeds (84 kilometres, or 52 miles) long, yet divided into three parallel bands, each running east-west. One section is for the Levites, another for the priests and the sanctuary, and a third, only half the north-south width of the other two, for the **'city'**. Although it is true that the temple is described as a 'city' in 40:2, it is to be distinguished from this city, now mentioned for the first time (45:6). This point is important, and we shall return to it.

On the west (Mediterranean) and east (Jordan) sides of this immense square, territory is allocated to **'the prince'**. The northern and southern borders of each of the two sectors of his land run parallel to the inheritances of two of the tribes, as yet unspecified (but see 48:22).

Historically, the kings of Israel were not permitted to be landowners. But because many of them were degenerate, extortion was always more than a possibility. Moses anticipated this; Samuel feared it; Saul may have contemplated it; and Ahab practised it.[151] Now there shall be neither opportunity nor incentive for royal tyranny because the family of David possesses its own ample lands. That there will be no injustice anywhere is the point being demonstrated by this elaborate division (45:7).

The reference to **'my princes'** is not intended to indicate that succeeding generations of David's family will perpetuate the dynasty. The future situation of Ezekiel's people is outlined typically in terms of David's court and a benign administration (45:8). The prophet was aware that there would be just one Messianic king in Israel (see 34:23-24; 37:24-25). Isaiah 32:1 is similar in its anticipation of the kingdom of God in Christ.

2. The duties of the princes (45:9-17)

45:9-17. '"Thus says the Lord Yahweh: 'It is enough for you, princes of Israel. Remove violence and oppression and practise righteousness and judgement. Lift away your evictions from my people,' declares the Lord Yahweh. 'You will have just balances, a just ephah and a just bath. The ephah and the bath will be of the same capacity, so that the bath may contain a tenth of a homer, and the ephah a tenth of a homer. Their measurement will be according to the homer. And the shekel will be twenty gerahs: twenty shekels, twenty-five shekels, fifteen shekels will be your maneh.

'"'This is the offering which you will offer: a sixth of an ephah from a homer of wheat, and you will give one sixth part of an ephah from a homer of barley. And the statute of oil — the bath, the oil — a tenth of a bath from a cor, which is ten baths, a homer, for ten baths are a homer. And one sheep from the flock, from two hundred, from the watering places of Israel, for a grain offering and a burnt offering and for peace offerings, to make atonement for them,' declares the Lord Yahweh.

'"'And this offering for the prince in Israel will be the care of all the people of the land. And it will be for the prince to provide the burnt offerings, the grain offering and the libations at the feasts, the new moons, at the Sabbaths, in all the appointed seasons of the house of Israel. He will prepare the sin offering and the grain offering, the burnt offering and the peace offerings, to make atonement on behalf of the house of Israel.'"'

Following on from 45:8, the Lord addresses the **'princes'** of Israel. Even as the Levites and priests must repudiate uncleanness (see 44:10-31), the princes are to reject social injustice, of which there had been **'enough'**. Dedicated to righteousness, no longer will they expel landowners. When Samuel was moved by popular demand to inaugurate a monarchy, he was not reluctant to predict the characteristic behaviour of the typical Israelite king. And he anticipated that Yahweh would allow degenerates to occupy the throne of David.[152] The incident of Ahab and Naboth was, it seems, not unusual.[153] **'The Lord Yahweh'** declares that it (i.e. commitment to righteousness) must be so (45:9).

The princes are to take a lead in employing **'just balances, a just ephah and a just bath'**.[154] The ephah was a dry measure of capacity, about 22 litres, and equivalent to the bath, probably a liquid measure. Both are defined here as one-tenth the capacity of **'a homer'**, the definitive measure. D. J. Wiseman observes that ancient balances had a margin of error of up to 6% and that no two Hebrew weights of the same denomination yet found are of identical weight. Such variations underpin the significance of the present verses (45:10-11).[155]

The unit of money is **'the shekel'**, containing **'twenty gerahs'**, about ten grams, or just over ⅓ ounce.[156] According to 1 Kings 10:17 and 2 Chronicles 9:16, it might be that a **'*maneh*'**, a unit possibly of foreign origin, was equivalent to about fifty shekels.[157] The difficult statement that **'twenty shekels, twenty-five shekels, and fifteen shekels will be your *maneh*'** could mean that in Ezekiel's time there were three different values for the *maneh* (for which there is no extra-biblical evidence), or, better, that a single *maneh* was 20 + 25 + 15 = 60 shekels (45:12).[158]

Verses 13-16 provide for a fixed and regular contribution to be made by the people to the prince of the time to enable him to provide the required offering at the sanctuary. **'Offering'** implies something lifted up to the Lord as a gift, and occurs also in 45:1 to describe the offering of the land by the people, and in 44:30 with regard to offerings for the priests. From every **'homer'** of **'wheat'** and of **'barley',** an **'ephah'** (one tenth) will be separated, and from each ephah **'one sixth'** is to be extracted. That is, one part in sixty of the produce of the land will be committed as offerings within the temple (45:13).

The proper measure of olive **'oil'** will be one **'tenth of a bath'** (two litres), the bath being one tenth of a **'cor'**, and the cor the same as a **'homer'** (45:14).[159]

Of the **'sheep'**, one from every **'two hundred'** which had been fed upon **'the watering places of Israel'**[160] is to be given for **'grain'**, **'burnt'** and **'peace'** offerings, sacrifices designed to atone for the people. **'Yahweh' 'declares'** that it shall be so (45:15).

'All the people of the land' bear the responsibility of contributing the **'offering for the prince in Israel'** (45:16). And to him, as one of the principal agents of the nation's sacrificial worship, falls the duty of furnishing **'the burnt offerings, the grain offering and the libations'**, or liquid offerings. Perhaps Ezekiel considered the latter to consist of oil, in that wine is nowhere mentioned.[161] Such sacrifices are required for **'the new moons'**, for **'the Sabbaths'** and for **'all the appointed seasons of the house of Israel'**. The prince provides animals and food given to him by the people in order to **'to make atonement'** for them (45:17).

This arrangement is novel in that Moses never specified the sources from which the priests must bring animals and the fruits of the earth for sacrifice. Now the contributions are involuntary: the people shall give. It is assumed that within this new regime no one will wish to hinder the service of Yahweh; gifts flow in continuously.

Application

These verses proclaim a perfect harmony between the prince of the day and his people, to the extent that they willingly convey to him the material of sacrifice so that he may transfer it to the Zadokite priests. What is more, it is he who initiates sacrificial atonement for the complete house of Israel.

We are shown here a picture of the heart of a people devoted to the worship of Yahweh, the land being allocated in such a way that the sanctuary is geographically central. Communion with God binds the nation together.[162]

The Gentile who reads this chapter superficially may make little sense of it. But if we are steeped in the unhappy history of Israel and Judah from the institution of the monarchy in the time of Samuel until the Babylonian exile, much may become clear. The pillars that should have undergirded the theocracy of Israel — the Davidic monarchy, a protected land, a godly people and the central sanctuary — now coexist in delightful equilibrium. This is Yahweh's promise and this is Ezekiel's gospel.

Sacrifices
(Ezekiel 45:18 – 46:24)

Ezekiel specifies the animals and other gifts that he, the prophet, will personally present for sacrifice at the altar and the times when such sacrifices are to be made. Yet again, the command to Ezekiel to act on certain occasions (**'you'**, singular, 45:18,20) does not indicate what Israel ought to do at some future time, but predicts the typical state that shall supervene. Prophecy defines and determines the future.

1. Special occasions (45:18-25)

45:18-35. '"Thus says the Lord Yahweh: 'In the first, on the first day of the month, you shall take a perfect bull from the herd and will de-sin the sanctuary. And the priest will take of the blood and will place it upon the doorpost of the house, on the four corners of the ledge of the altar and on the doorpost of the gate of the inner court.

'"'You will do this on the seventh of the month for the person who sins inadvertently or in naivety, and you will make atonement for the house. In the first, on the fourteenth day of the month, there shall be the Passover for you, a feast of seven days. Unleavened bread will be eaten. And on that day the prince will provide a bull for a sin offering for himself and for all the people of the land. For the seven days of the feast he will provide a burnt offering for Yahweh: seven perfect bulls and seven perfect rams each day for the seven days; and a sin offering, a kid of the goats. He will also provide a grain offering: an ephah for a bull and an ephah for a ram, and a hin of oil for an ephah. In the seventh, on the fifteenth day of the month at the feast he will do likewise for seven days, according to the sin offering, the burnt offering, the grain offering and the oil.'"'

Sacrifices are to be offered on specified occasions. The deviations from Moses' legislation are obvious, as is the omission of references to the Feast of Weeks,[163] the Day of Trumpets[164] and the Day of Atonement, the latter held on the tenth day of the seventh month.[165] Because Ezekiel was a priest, it follows that these omissions must be intentional. It should be emphasized that, like the divisions of the land, the system presented here is ideal. Historically, Jews have never attempted to apply the scheme.

On the first day of the first month an unblemished young ox is to be taken by Ezekiel (**'you** [singular] **shall take ...'**) to **'de-sin the sanctuary'** (45:18). The priest places some of the blood of this sin offering **'upon the doorpost of the house'**, **'on the four corners of the ledge of the altar'** and **'on the doorpost of the gate of the inner court'**, by which is meant either the east gate or all three gates considered collectively (45:19). The procedure is repeated on the seventh day of the month to **'make atonement for the house'** because of the errors, mistakes and follies of the worshippers (45:20).

All this is dissimilar to the procedure given by Moses. He had prescribed a he-goat for the first day of every month, in addition to burnt and meal offerings, and for the tenth day of the seventh month, when two such animals were to be offered. Nor did the law specify the sprinkling of the blood of the sin offerings on the first day of each month, probably because this was included in the normal procedure. Only in the case of the high priest or of the whole congregation was blood introduced to the holy place itself, sprinkled before the veil and applied to the horns of the altar of incense. On the Day of Atonement, blood was brought into the holy of holies and sprinkled before the mercy seat.[166] All this vanishes, being replaced, it would seem, by a less elaborate ritual, yet fulfilling the intention of Leviticus 16:16 in cleansing the holy place from the sins of the people.[167]

'The Passover' is to be observed by **'you'** (plural: the nation and not Ezekiel as an individual) **'on the fourteenth day'** of **'the first'**, by which is meant the first month. As in Exodus 34:25, it is described as a **'feast'** (45:21). Yet, unlike the procedure laid down by Moses, **'the prince'**, rather than the head of each house, takes charge,[168] providing a young ox as a sin offering both for himself and for all others (45:22). Perhaps this is reminiscent of the actions of those reforming kings of Judah, Hezekiah and Josiah,[169] who summoned their people to Jerusalem to celebrate the Passover.

On each of **'the seven days of the feast'**, **'seven'** unblemished **'bulls'** and **'seven'** unblemished **'rams'** for **'a burnt offering'** and a young he-goat as **'a sin offering'** are to be provided by the prince (45:23). The **'grain offering'** is to be **'one ephah for a bull'**, **'an ephah for a ram'**, **'and a hin'** (almost 4 litres) **'of oil'** for each ephah (again, about 22 litres). No mention is made of the Passover lamb, but perhaps this may be assumed. The sacrifices are much richer and more numerous than those prescribed by Moses (45:24).[170]

Whereas the original Passover was designed to avert the wrath of Yahweh, and whereas subsequent Passovers were memorials of that first, great event,[171] with its inclusion of sin offerings Ezekiel's Passover is also intended to effect propitiation for a redeemed people who, nevertheless, are deemed to be not without residual sin.

In the **'seventh'** month and **'on the fifteenth day'** the procedure will be repeated. This event corresponds to the Feast of Tabernacles, although this is not mentioned, perhaps because the custom of living in booths is to be discontinued. Moses' regulations are simplified and the procedure for the eighth day of the feast is omitted (45:25).[172]

As observed, no mention has been made of Pentecost, the Day of Atonement and the Day of Trumpets (the first day of the seventh month). Moreover, the routines for Passover and Tabernacles are greatly modified, harmony between prince and people and the absolute need for holiness now coming to the fore.

2. The prince and his sacrifices (46:1-15)

46:1-15. '"Thus says the Lord Yahweh: 'The gate of the inner court that faces east will be closed for the six days of activity, but on the Sabbath it will be opened, and on the day of the new moon it shall be opened. And the prince will enter by way of the vestibule of the gate from the outside and will stand by the doorpost of the gate. Then the priests will prepare his burnt offering and his peace offerings, and he will worship by the threshold of the gate and will go out, but the gate will not be closed until the evening. And the people of the land will worship at the entrance of that gate before Yahweh on the Sabbaths and on the new moons.

'"'The burnt offering that the prince will bring near to Yahweh on the Sabbath will be six perfect lambs and a perfect ram. And the grain offering will be an ephah for a ram, and a grain offering for the lambs — the gift of his hand. Of oil, a hin for an ephah. Then, on the day of the new moon a perfect bull from the herd, six lambs and a ram. They shall be perfect. And he will provide a grain offering — an ephah for a bull and an ephah for a ram, and for the lambs whatever his hand can secure. And of oil, a hin for an ephah.

'"'Then, when the prince goes in, he will enter by way of the vestibule of the gate, and by that way he will go out. And when the people of the land come before Yahweh at the appointed times, he who enters by way of the north gate in order to worship will go out by way of the south gate, and he who enters by way of the south gate will go out by way of the north gate; he will not return by way of the gate through which he entered, but will go out through its opposite. And the prince will enter among them when they enter, and when they go out he will go out. Then, at the feasts and at the appointed times, the grain offering will be an ephah for a bull and an ephah for a ram, and the lambs — the gift of his hand. Of oil, a hin for an ephah.

'"'And when the prince provides a voluntary gift, a burnt offering or peace offerings voluntarily to Yahweh, then someone will open for him the gate which faces east and he will provide his burnt offering and his peace offerings, just as he does on the Sabbath day. Then he will go out and someone will close the gate after he has departed.

'"'And you will provide a perfect lamb, one year old, for a burnt offering each day for Yahweh; morning by morning you will provide it. Also you will provide a grain offering for it morning by morning, a sixth of an ephah, and of oil, a third of a hin, to moisten the fine flour. It is a continual grain offering for Yahweh, a perpetual statute. And you shall provide the lamb, the grain offering and the oil, morning by morning, a continual burnt offering.'"'

In these verses, which continue the theme of chapter 45, the Lord gives prescriptions for the festivals to be observed by Israel and highlights the prominent role to be taken by the prince.

The east gate of the outer court remains shut following the entrance of Yahweh to his house, never to leave it again (see 43:4; 44:2-3). Yet the east gate of the inner court, closed for **'the six days of activity'**, by which are meant the six working days of each week, is to be **'opened'** on **'the Sabbath'** and on the first day of each month, **'the day of the new moon'**. The emphasis is upon the sanctity of the place rather than of the day: people streaming in by way of the north and south gates (see 46:9) will not be permitted to profane the house (46:1).[173]

Nevertheless, even as **'the prince'** is permitted to sit and eat within the precincts of the closed outer east gate (44:3), so he may enter **'the vestibule'** of the inner east **'gate'** when it is open. Presumably, he will have entered the outer court through the north or south outer gates, as suggested by 46:10. Advancing as far as the **'doorpost'** of the inner gate, yet without passing through, he may behold what happens in the inner court. When **'the priests'** make ready and present the prince's burnt and peace offerings, he will **'worship'**, probably by adopting a kneeling posture or by prostrating himself **'by the threshold'**. From there he will exit (cf. 44:3; 46:8), no doubt before **'the evening'**, when the gate will be closed. His stay will have been brief (46:2).

Similarly, **'the people of the land'**, the whole population other than the prince, the priests and the Levites,[174] will **'worship at the entrance of that** [inner east] **gate ... on the Sabbaths and on the** [monthly] **new moons'**. Everything is done in the presence of, or **'before Yahweh'** (46:3).

The **'burnt offering'** to be brought by **'the prince'**, **'six perfect lambs and a perfect ram'**, greatly exceeds the two lambs (no rams) prescribed by Numbers 28:9, and the same applies to the **'grain offering'** and the **'oil'** (46:4-5; cf. 45:24).

On **'the day of the new moon'**, the first of the month, the prince will offer **'a perfect bull'**, **'six lambs and a ram'**, plus the statutory grain offering of **'an ephah'** for each animal. According to Numbers 28:11-15, the offerings, rendered by the people as a whole, were two bulls, one ram and seven male lambs with their grain offerings, and a he-goat for a sin offering (omitted here). Ezekiel's programme does no more than maintain what, at least as early as the time of Samuel, had become an established festival in

Israel.[175] Unlike Moses' requirement, wine is not added (46:6-7).

Now Yahweh commands that **'the prince'** must **'enter by way of the vestibule of the gate'** and **'by that way he will go out'**. This means that he may not proceed from the outer court into the inner court, to exit by another inner gate back to the outer court, thus entering the inner court, an area reserved for the priests (46:8).

Although unspecified, **'the appointed times'** would be the solemn feasts, the appointed Sabbaths and the new moons. According to Moses, the men of Israel had to appear before the Lord on the three great feasts of Passover, Pentecost and Tabernacles,[176] and now the requirement perpetuates. What we read here is probably a direction for crowd-control, given the very large numbers of worshippers massing in a limited space: those who enter the outer court by **'the south gate'** will proceed directly to **'the north gate'**, and vice versa, thus obviating congestion caused by turning, in that the entrance and the exit will be opposite each other (46:9). As stated by 44:2, the east gate remains closed.

Yet on the occasion of the annual feasts, **'the prince'** must **'enter'** and **'go out'** together with his subjects and worship among them. Although he provides sacrificial animals for the people as well as for himself (see 45:17) and is, in a sense, Israel's patron, he nevertheless remains one with them. Never again will the princes of Israel lord it over the nation (46:10).

Repeating 45:24 and 46:5-7, rules are given for grain offerings, probably in order to emphasize the required order and regularity of the sacrificial system **'at the feasts and at the appointed times'** (46:11).

Whenever **'the prince'** wishes to offer a **'voluntary'** sacrifice, whether **'a burnt offering'** or **'peace offerings'**, he may do so, the stipulation of 46:1 being waived. On such occasions he may enter — but never pass through — the inner **'east' 'gate'**, which will be opened for him. Then, after he has departed, it is to be closed rather than remaining open until sunset (46:12).

As in Numbers 28:3-5, there is to be a daily sacrifice. Yet unlike the procedure in the tabernacle and in the temple in later times, the routine will demand a single **'perfect lamb, one year old'**. The triple repetition of **'morning by morning'**, with no reference to an evening sacrifice, suggests that the latter is omitted deliberately. Although there will be no wine, the quantities of meal and oil are increased slightly, from Moses' one tenth of an ephah to **'a sixth'**, and from a quarter of a hin of oil to **'a third'**. **'And you shall provide'** in verse 15 is plural and imperative, as if to remind the priests that it is their duty to ensure that the **'perpetual statute'** is honoured (46:13-15). An explanation for this dramatic revision of Moses' daily sacrifice will be suggested in the next 'Application' section.

3. The prince and his lands (46:16-18)

46:16-18. '"Thus says the Lord Yahweh: 'If the prince bestows a grant to any of his sons, and it is his inheritance, it will be for his sons; it is their possession by inheritance. And if he bestows a grant from his inheritance to someone from his servants, then it will belong to him until the year of liberty, when it will return to the prince. But with regard to his sons, his inheritance will be theirs. And the prince will not take from the inheritance of the people, to evict them from their possession; he will cause his sons to inherit from his own possession so that my people may not be scattered, any man from his own possession.'"'

Verses 16-18 should be considered in the light of Deuteronomy 17:14-20 and 1 Samuel 8:10-18, to which reference has already been made. In the former passage Moses predicts that Israel in possession of the land will desire a monarchy, and gives definitive guidelines concerning any future king of Israel. In the latter, Samuel, faced by a popular demand for the immediate institution of a monarchy, seeks to persuade Israel that such a step will be a disaster. The subsequent history of the divided kingdoms of Israel and Judah is a sad confirmation of what both men knew would happen.

Now matters will be different. Complementing 45:7-9, regulations are given in 46:16-18 concerning the right of the prince to bequeath or give away his land, territory that will be ample for him and his family. The underlying rationale is that the land had been given leasehold by God to the children of Israel, Yahweh remaining, so to speak, the freeholder.

If a prince elects to convey some of his land **'to any of his sons'**, it becomes the hereditary possession of that son. In short, if he may not seize the people's land (the case of Naboth's vineyard, 1 Kings 21, again comes to mind), the prince is not permitted to grant any portion of his land to the people. It is inalienable, remaining within the control of the royal family: **'it is their possession by inheritance'** (46:16).

Yet if the prince wishes to make a grant **'to someone from his servants'**, he may do so, but on the strict condition that the land reverts to him in **'the year of liberty'**, the fiftieth year, that of jubilee. According to Moses, although land could be consecrated to Yahweh, there is no mention of the possibility of it being sold off in order to discharge a debt. And if a debtor sold himself to his creditor, his servitude had to terminate in the year of jubilee. Nor could land be given away.[177] Here Ezekiel insists that royal land must never be alienated. Even so, repeating from the previous verse, there may be a permanent transfer of land among the members of the princely house (46:17).

Significantly, 'the people of the land' (46:3) are termed **'my** [i.e. Yahweh's] **people'**. Although the prince is allotted his own land and needs no more, the Lord's overall concern is for the welfare of the whole nation. The appalling state of affairs outlined by 34:1-19 will never be repeated. For the third time in three verses it is stressed that the prince of the day may do no more than transfer his own land to his immediate family, implying that he may not seize from others to benefit his children. Eviction will be consigned to history (46:18).

4. Sacrificial food (46:19-24)

46:19-24. Then he brought me by the entrance by the side of the gate into the holy apartments of the priests facing north, and, look, there was a place at their far side, to the west. And he said to me, 'This is the place where the priests will boil the guilt offering and the sin offering, where they bake the grain offering, so as not to bring them out to the outer court to sanctify the people.'

Then he brought me to the outer court and led me to the four corners of the court, and, look, there was a court in a corner of the court, a court within a corner of the court. In the four corners of the court were enclosed courts, forty by length and thirty by width. There was one measure for the four of them on the corners. And around each there was a row, around the four of them, and boiling places were made under the rows round about. Then he said to me, 'These are the boiling places where the ministers of the house boil the sacrifice of the people.'

Now that detailed regulations for offerings and sacrifices have been given, Ezekiel's guided tour of the temple complex, which paused at 42:20, is resumed. In verses 19-24 the prophet tells that he was shown the kitchens used by the priests on behalf of the people and themselves.

The prophet was conducted, presumably by the angelic surveyor who was introduced in 40:3, along the path mentioned in 42:4, a way that led from the steps of the north **'gate'** of the inner court towards the priests' **'apartments'**, but which was just within the outer court. Apparently, he entered. The ensuing description complements 42:1-14. Behind the priests' rooms and to the extreme rear (west) of the central sanctuary, on the north side, Ezekiel saw **'a place'** where the priests were to cook those parts of the flesh and grain offerings that they would afterwards eat in their official capacity (46:19). It can be assumed that because of the symmetry of the temple there must have been a corresponding kitchen on the south side of the inner court, and also at its west end.

Ezekiel's guide now informed him that the location of these kitchens behind the priests' apartments meant that there would be no need for the priests to bring the sacrifices into the outer court to prepare them there. Were they to do so, the contact would **'sanctify the people'**, this ritual sanctification disturbing the routine of life. The comments covering 44:19 seek to explain the matter. In the confusion, priestly sanctity would disintegrate. As in Moses' law, all sacrificial flesh, except that of the Passover, is to be boiled, and bloodless offerings are to be baked (46:20).

Now the prophet relates that he was led **'to the outer court'**, properly so called. In each of its **'four corners'** — to the north-east, south-east, south-west and north-west — was seen a relatively small **'enclosed'** courtyard, **'forty'** by **'thirty'**, the unit of measurement presumably being the cubit (46:21-22).

Around the internal walls of each of these courtyards there was **'a row'**, which might have been a brick or stone shelf beneath which was a cooking hearth or oven. Ezekiel was informed that here **'the ministers of the house'**, probably Levites (cf. 44:10-14), would **'boil the sacrifice of the people'**. Although 2 Chronicles 35:11-13 tells that on the occasion of Josiah's Passover, Levites and (apparently) priests cooked the people's offerings, that seems to have been a unique event, not anticipated by Moses' law. Now such service will be the norm (46:23-24).

Application

The application of 45:1-17 could be repeated at this point, with few additions. In the ideal theocracy projected by 45:18 – 46:24, the prince, whose relations with his people are unruffled, is not to be considered as the expected Messiah, the ultimate shepherd from the family of David (34:23). Rather, he typifies the calibre of monarchy that should have pertained from the time of David onwards. He is essentially one with the people and one of them (46:10), something that could not have been said even of Solomon in all his glory.

Further, Ezekiel's sacrificial system is based upon that of Moses' law, yet — as with a morning offering each day instead of daily morning and evening sacrifices (46:13-15) — there are significant differences. The tentative interpretation offered here is that Ezekiel, who could do no other than paint an imaginative picture of the glorious future of Israel with materials supplied to him by Moses' administration, within which he found himself, intimates that in time this system will be phased out in favour of another, that of the new covenant anticipated by his contemporary Jeremiah.[178] Not tampering with the law, he looks forward to its demise.[179]

Crowd-control within the temple precincts (46:9) shows that the worship of God is to be the preoccupation of his people and that it must be conducted in an orderly, calm fashion.[180] Because in eternity all will be tranquil and calm, it ought to be so in our churches.

The distribution of the land (Ezekiel 47:1 – 48:35)

The son of man has witnessed the return of the glory of the Lord to the temple. In his presence, the sanctuary has been subjected to meticulous examination. Further, he has been shown a dramatically revised liturgical system. This commentary has suggested why this was so. In the remainder of the prophecy Ezekiel writes about a river flowing from the temple, about the boundaries of the holy land and about the gates and the name of the city.

1. The river of life (47:1-12)

47:1-12. Then he brought me back to the door of the house; and, look, waters were coming out from underneath the threshold of the house, towards the east, because the front of the house was towards the east. And the waters were flowing from underneath, from the right side of the house, from the south of the altar. And he brought me out by way of the north gate and led me around by the outside way, by the way that faces east, and, look, waters were trickling from the south side.

When the man went out to the east with a line in his hand, he measured a thousand cubits. Then he caused me to pass through the waters: the waters were up to my ankles. Then he measured a thousand and caused me to pass through the waters: they were up to my knees. And he measured a thousand and caused me to pass through: the waters were up to my loins. Then he measured a thousand: it was a river that I was not able to cross because the waters had risen up, waters for swimming, a river that could not be crossed. And he said to me, 'Did you see, son of man?' Then he brought me and returned me to the bank of the river. When I had returned, look, by the bank of the river were very many trees, on one side and the other.

Then he said to me, 'These waters go out towards the eastern region, go down to the Arabah and come to the sea. Being made to go out to the sea, its waters are healed. And it will be that every living creature that swarms wherever the rivers come will live, and there will be very many fish because these waters go there, and they are healed; and wherever the river goes everything will live.

'And it will be that fishermen will stand by it from En-gedi to En-eglaim; there will be places for spreading nets. Their fish will be according to their kind, like the fish of the Great Sea — very many. Its swamps and its marshes — they will not be healed; they will be given over for salt. And along the river, on its bank, on one side and the other, will grow every kind of food-bearing tree. Their leaves will not fade and their fruit will never end. Every month they will bear their fruit early because their waters come out from the sanctuary. Their fruit will be for food and their leaves for healing.'

The angelic guide conducted Ezekiel from the outer court (see 46:21) back **'to the door of the house'**. This entrance was neither the east gate of the outer perimeter wall nor the east gate leading into the inner court, but the porch within the latter giving access to the sanctuary.[181]

From his vantage point he could see **'waters'** emanating from beneath **'the threshold'**, the base of the door of the sanctuary, and flowing towards the east. Moreover, they came **'from underneath, from the right side of the house, from the south of the altar'**. Here, **'right'** would mean 'south': although the general course of the flow was eastward, the stream had to be deflected at its start in order to avoid the sanctuary's porch, the altar and the inner and outer eastern gateways (47:1).

Because the outer east gate was closed (see 44:1-2), Ezekiel was escorted through the outer **'north gate'** and beyond the limits of the city-temple towards the east gate. Again, he instructs his readers to **'look'**, or imagine the sight; evidently, he was surprised to behold the **'trickling'** of water **'from the south side'**, or to the right of the east gate. **'Trickling'**, from *pakak*, occurs only here in the Old Testament but is related to the Hebrew *pak*, a phial or flask used for anointing.[182] Ezekiel beheld an insistent and irrepressible stream (47:2).

'The man', Ezekiel's guide, apparently the angelic being who retreated from view in 43:6 in favour of the divine angel, was seen to have **'a line in his hand'**, an instrument apparently other than the measuring reed employed earlier (see 40:5). Presumably commencing from the outer east gate, he proceeded for a measured distance of **'a thousand cubits'** (about 550 metres, or just over 600 yards). The prophet, conducted through the flowing stream so that he might be impressed by its surge and increasing depth, found himself ankle-deep in water (47:3).

The procedure was repeated three times: another **'thousand'** cubits further, and the water reached the prophet's **'knees'**; and yet another **'thousand'**, and the torrent came up to Ezekiel's **'loins'**. Finally, after another **'thousand'**, the waters were so deep that Ezekiel was unable to wade. He would have had to swim a virtual **'river'** in order to cross.[183]

All this means that the prophet found himself out of his depth when the measured length of the river from its temple source had attained 4,000 cubits, more than 2 kilometres, or 1.4 miles. There would have been a corresponding increase in width. The essential point is that this flow was not that of a conventional river, which, even at a considerably greater distance from its source, would remain no more than a modest stream. What Ezekiel beheld was a cascade fed neither by tributaries nor interrupted in its eastward course by elevations such as today's Mount of Olives or by the ridges between that elevation and the River Jordan. It follows that the vision cannot reasonably be interpreted as a *literal* presentation of the blessedness yet to be (47:4-5).

The surveyor summoned Ezekiel's attention to the river and then brought him along its bank: **'Did you see, son of man?'** Since the prophet *had* seen it, the man was telling him that the sight merited the closest attention. Led out of the water to the bank where he had been standing, Ezekiel was astounded: **'look, by the bank of the river were very many trees, on one side and the other'** (47:6-7).[184]

He was then informed that the waters advanced into **'the eastern region'** (or, literally, 'circle'),[185] the area between Jerusalem and the Jordan, and north of the Dead Sea.[186] Thence the stream progressed into **'the Arabah'**,[187] or desert, the rift valley just north of the **'the sea'**, the Dead Sea, into which the river then flowed and the **'waters'** of which were **'healed'** (47:8).

The symbolism is vivid. It is well known that the salty and poisonous waters of the Dead Sea cannot sustain life. There is no natural outlet, and evaporation removes more water than is supplied by the Jordan. But in the vision this sterile lake had been transformed. The Hebrew behind **'rivers'** may indicate that Ezekiel saw this urgent current dividing into numerous tributaries. The healing process occurred because fresh water gushed copiously into the Dead Sea, the toxicity of which was cancelled so that wherever the streams reached life would teem. There was renewal rather than replacement. The guide predicted that immense numbers of **'fish'** would be the living proof (47:9).

The variety and abundance of fish are said to rival those of the Mediterranean, the **'Great Sea'**. **'En-gedi'** was, and is, situated midway on the west shore of the Dead Sea, opposite the River Arnon in what once was Moab. The location of **'En-eglaim'** is unknown, but might have been on the east side.[188] If so, the imagery is that of a colossal soup of toxic salts transformed into a very large freshwater lake. Thus, **'fishermen'** will be at every point on the shores to spread out their **'nets'**. **'According to their kind'** evokes the fruitfulness of Genesis 1:20-22 (47:10).

Perhaps surprisingly, the inland sea does not lack a stagnant area: **'Its swamps and ... marshes ... will not be healed; they will be given over for salt'** (47:11). Over the centuries the southern part of the Dead Sea has remained exceedingly shallow, beyond which there is flat land lying almost at the level of the salt water. When the Jordan comes into flood this area is inundated, the waters subsiding only when the level of the river goes down. Then dry or slushy salt is left on the ground. The annual cycle occurs because there is no outflow.

Some commentators suggest that the residual salt water in Ezekiel's vision shows that where the flow from the temple did not penetrate, there was death. If so, this verse provides a warning to its readers. Alternatively, what we may have here is, in Taylor's words, 'a touch of practical realism'.[189] That is, the southern tip of the sea would provide Israel with necessary salt. The present commentary inclines to this view.

Ezekiel's guide informed him that there would be **'food-bearing'** or fruit trees of every conceivable variety **'along'** each **'bank'** of the **'river'**. Moreover, every month of the year would be a season for fresh fruit. Genesis 2:9,16 comes to mind immediately. **'Leaves'** will not wither because there is no alternation between rainy periods and long, hot summers. Indeed, rain is unnecessary because the trees are irrigated continuously by fresh water emanating **'from the sanctuary'**. Moreover, the 'leaves' of the trees are medicinal (47:12).

In Ezekiel's vision, the river gushing from the temple irrigates the Dead Sea, but apparently for the benefit of Israel only. According to Revelation 22:2, the leaves of the trees are said to be 'for the healing of the nations', from which it may be inferred that the ultimate Israel includes Gentiles. As 47:22-23 will indicate and as 16:53-63 has anticipated, this development is not absent from Ezekiel's prophecy.

And if, as I believe, chapters 40 – 48 point beyond the horizon of time as we know it, we begin to perceive that for the people of God heaven will be a veritable Eden.

2. Equality among the twelve tribes (47:13-14)

47:13-14. 'Thus says the Lord Yahweh: "This is the boundary by which you will inherit for yourselves the land, for the twelve tribes of Israel. For Joseph, two parts. And you will give it for an inheritance, each one as his brother; for I raised my hand to give it to your fathers, and this land will fall to you by inheritance."'

Now Ezekiel's angelic guide is heard no more. **'The Lord Yahweh'** speaks and, to judge by the second-person plural verb, **'you will inherit'**, he addresses not the prophet in particular but all Israel.

The Lord personally defines the external boundaries, or even the outlying territories,[190] of **'the twelve tribes of Israel'**, one united family whose members retain their own tribal identities (cf. 36:24-38; 37:19). Joseph inherits two of the twelve internal divisions for his sons Ephraim and Manasseh.[191] It is assumed that the tribe of Levi is to retain its inheritance within the central sacred area (47:13).

The rationale for this final disposition of the land is the original oath made by Yahweh to the effect that the patriarchs and their seed would ultimately inherit Canaan: **'for I raised my hand to give it to your fathers'**.[192] In the fulfilment of this promise the tribes are to share the land **'each one as his brother'** — that is, on equal terms.

There is a significant difference between this allocation and the original partition of Canaan in the time of Joshua. Then lots were cast to determine land ownership, even though the Lord overruled in the matter;[193] now Yahweh, having decreed who shall live where, announces his prior decision (47:14).

3. The details (47:15-23)

47:15-23. '"And this is the border of the land on the north side: from the Great Sea, the road to Hethlon, to the entrance of Zedad; Hamath, Berothah, Sibraim, which is between the border of Damascus and the border of Hamath; Hazer-hatticon, which is by the border of Hauran.

'"And the boundary will be from the sea to Hazar-enan, the border of Damascus; and north, northward is the border of Hamath. This is the north side. And the east side: from between Hauran and Damascus, and from between Gilead and the land of Israel, along the Jordan; you shall measure from the border to the eastern sea. This is the east side. And the Negev side, towards the south: from Tamar to the waters of Meribot-kadesh, to the brook, to the Great Sea. This is the south side, towards the Negev. And the west side: the Great Sea, from the border to opposite the border of Hamath. This is the west side.

'"Thus you will divide this land for yourselves, according to the tribes of Israel. And it shall be that you will cause it to fall by inheritance for yourselves and for the dwellers who sojourn in your midst, who bring forth children in your midst. And they will be to you as native-born among the children of

Israel. With you they will allot by inheritance, in the midst of the tribes of Israel. And it shall be that in the tribe with whom the resident sojourns, there you will grant his inheritance," declares the Lord Yahweh.'

Before details are revealed concerning the distribution of the land (chapter 48), the external frontiers of Israel are identified. In general, they reflect those of Numbers 34:1-15, where, however, the presentation is south → west → north → east. This anticipates Joshua's invasion of Canaan from the south, from the direction of the Sinai, even though he launched his assault from across the Jordan.[194] Now a return of the exiles from the north is in mind.

In Joshua's time, the intended eastern border of the land was the Jordan, the addition of land to the east of that river being a modification. According to Ezekiel's allocation, Reuben, Gad and all Manasseh are settled to the west of the Jordan.

The northern limits of the inheritance are defined first. They extend from somewhere on the coast of **'the Great Sea'** (the Mediterranean) by way of the otherwise unknown **'Hethlon'** (cf. 48:1) on the route to **'Zedad'** (47:15). Mentioned in Numbers 34:8, this was a northern border city of Israel.

Other border areas will be **'Hamath'**, about fifty kilometres (a little over 30 miles) north of Damascus; **'Berothah'**, mentioned in 2 Samuel 8:8 and possibly north-north-west of Damascus; **'Sibraim'**, otherwise unknown but stated to be between **'Damascus'** and **'the border of Hamath'**; and **'Hazer-hatticon'**, also unknown but not far from **'Hauran'**, possibly an area between Gilead and Damascus. Thus Ezekiel's Israel absorbs much of the modern state of Lebanon (47:16).

This northern boundary, about fifty kilometres wide, extends from the Mediterranean and ends at **'Hazar-enan'** ('Court of the Springs'; Numbers 34:9,10), adjacent to **'the border of Damascus'** and to **'the border of Hamath'** at the north-east corner of the territory.

Although it not possible to identify this frontier with precision, it must be substantially the same as in Numbers 34. In that only David and Jeroboam II of Israel extended the northern borders of Israel towards Hamath,[195] thus reclaiming the territory specified by Numbers 34:8, Ezekiel's boundary indicates the total restoration of the land of promise to Israel (47:17).

The eastern boundary is described much as in Numbers 34, but without giving details about the region north of Lake Gennesaret. Running southwards from **'between Hauran and Damascus'**, although (as in Numbers 34) not actually embracing Damascus, **'and from between Gilead and the land of Israel'**, although apparently not absorbing Gilead, it proceeds along the Jordan to **'the eastern sea'**, the Dead Sea (47:18).[196]

From the **'Negev'**, or southern point of the Dead Sea, the boundary continues to the south-east corner of the inheritance at **'Tamar'**, which would have been to the south and west of the Dead Sea. Thence it extends **'to the waters of Meribot-Kadesh'**, in Moses' day known as 'the waters of strife', and presumably to Kadesh-barnea.[197] From there, it proceeds **'to the brook'**, the modern Wadi el-arish, and thence **'to the Great Sea'**, the western border, and northward along the coast and back full circle to **'the border of Hamath'** (47:19-20).

Summing up 47:13-20, the Lord states that within these boundaries land is to be shared among the twelve **'tribes of Israel'** (47:21), territory being allotted also to **'the dwellers who sojourn in your midst, who bring forth children in your midst'**. Such are to be regarded as **'native-born'**.

Moses stipulated that, although foreigners resident in Israel were to be treated with kindness,[198] they could not acquire land. Nor could a poverty-stricken

Israelite sell himself permanently to an alien creditor living in Israel.[199]

Now these provisos are modified. Although there is no question of land transfer, or slavery in order to settle debts, the foreigner desirous of settling permanently in Israel, albeit without (apparently) receiving circumcision, is welcome to share in the land division. Indeed, he may select the tribal territory in which he wishes to put down his roots and there be granted **'his inheritance'**. Yahweh **'declares'** that it shall be so.

The resident alien's right to land indicates far more than racial and social impartiality. Like Ruth, such a person indicates a desire to worship and serve Israel's God.[200] Essentially, the barrier between Jew and Gentile has collapsed and the glorious prediction of Isaiah 56:3-8 will have been fulfilled (47:22-23).

4. The northern tribal divisions (48:1-7)

As with the delineation of the national borders (47:15), that of the tribal lands commences from the north, in which region seven tribes are allocated their territories. Immediately to their south lies the central area reserved for the sanctuary, the city, the priests' region and that of the Levites, and (on either side, west and east) that of the prince. To the south of this central block are lands granted to the five remaining tribes.

48:1-7. '"And these are the names of the tribes: from the northern extremity, beside the way of Hethlon to the entrance of Hamath, to Hazar-enan, the border of Damascus northward, in the direction of Hamath from the east side to the west: for Dan, one. And by the border of Dan, from the east side to the westward side: for Asher, one. And by the border of Asher, from the eastward side to the westward side: for Naphtali, one. And by the border of Naphtali, from the eastward side to the westward border: for Manasseh, one. And by the border of Manasseh, from the eastward side to the westward side: for Ephraim, one. And by the border of Ephraim, from the east side to the westward side: for Reuben, one. And by the border of Reuben, from the east side to the westward side: for Judah, one."'

The tribal divisions extend uniformly and in parallel from the eastern boundary westwards to the Great Sea, giving an approximately equal area of land for each tribe, quite unlike Joshua's arrangement. In this new situation the twelve tribes are settled in Canaan only, between, on the one hand, the line of longitude marked out roughly by the Jordan and, on the other, that of the Mediterranean Sea.

In Joshua's time, the tribes of Gad and Reuben and the half-tribe of Manasseh were settled east of the Jordan.[201] Now the tribes are geographically united. Never again will any one of them wish to be separated from the others.

On average, the territory falling to each tribe is less than in the first administration. This is because of the size of the central section, which amounts to about one fifth of the land. One may contrast this disposition with that of the first settlement.[202]

Although it may not be possible to discern any principle governing the positioning of the tribes, a comparison of the order of birth of the sons of Jacob and the allocation of territory may be significant:

Ezekiel's north-to-south allocation

Dan (5th son, by Bilhah of Rachel)
Asher (8th son, by Zilpah of Leah)
Naphtali (6th son, by Bilhah of Rachel)
Manasseh (= 11th son, of Rachel via Joseph)
Ephraim (= 11th son, of Rachel via Joseph)
Reuben (1st son, of Leah)
Judah (4th son, of Leah)

THE DIVISION OF THE LAND AMONG THE TRIBES

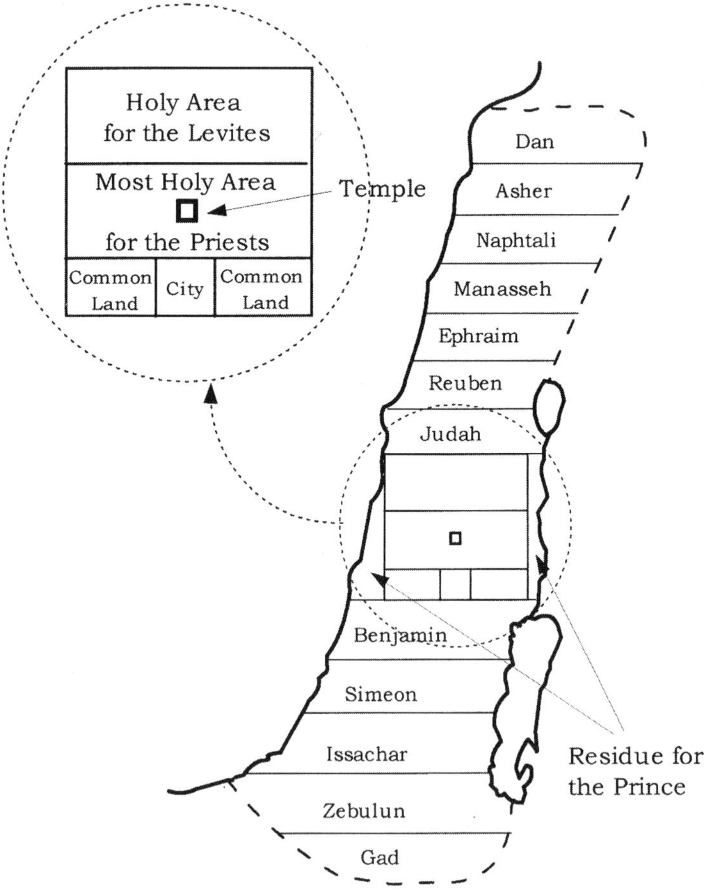

Central reservation (Levi, 3rd son, of Leah)
Benjamin (12th son, of Rachel)
Simeon (2nd son, of Leah)
Issachar (9th son, of Leah)
Zebulun (10th son, of Leah)
Gad (7th son, by Zilpah of Leah)

The tribes represented by the four children of the handmaids Zilpah and Bilhah are situated towards the northern and southern borders, whilst those descending from the wives Rachel and Leah are placed towards the centre. Is this meant to suggest that, ideally, Jacob should not have been offered, and should not have accepted, Zilpah and Bilhah?

Ephraim and Manasseh are adjacent, possibly because they stem from Joseph. Further, Judah and Benjamin are both adjacent to the central section, although with reversed positions (Benjamin now to the south of Judah), even as after Joshua's settlement they embraced Jerusalem. Judah was the tribe from which the Messiah would come,[203] and Benjamin was Jacob's favourite son, Joseph being supposedly dead.[204] Now no tribe, other than that of priestly Levi, is in the centre, thus obviating the possibility of tribal dominance.

5. The central allotment (48:8-22)

Immediately to the south of Judah's territory lies the sacred offering of land. This extends a distance of 25,000 unspecified units southwards as far as the border of Benjamin and the northern extremity of the southern tribal block (48:8,22).

I. The unit of measurement (48:8)

48:8. '"And by the border of Judah, from the east side to the westward side will be the offering that you shall offer: 25,000 in width (and the length as one of the divisions) from the eastward side to the westward side. And the sanctuary will be at its centre."'

This commentary takes the view that the linear measure employed here is almost certainly not the cubit. Admittedly, nowhere in the immediate context does the Hebrew text define explicitly the unit of measure as either the cubit or the reed. Nor, indeed, does the pre-Christian Greek Septuagint.

However, in chapters 40 – 42, wherever the cubit *is* the unit of measurement, this is stated. But in 45:1-6, where cubits are not mentioned, it seems safe to infer that the reed is the intended unit. The reader is referred to the comments on those verses and to Appendix A.

It appears to be the same here, the Hebrew text implying the measuring reed. If so, and because the reed was more than three metres long (or between 10 and 11 feet), the distance from the east to the west of the central allotment would be about 84 kilometres (or 52 miles).

This figure is approximately the north-south distance between the Sea of Galilee and the Dead Sea, and the furthest distance east-west between the Jordan and the Mediterranean. Ezekiel projects an enormous square of land.

It follows that if the cubit is the assumed standard, the central reservation becomes a relatively meagre square with its sides each about 14 kilometres (8·7 miles) long and with a considerable area of land on either side reserved for the prince. From this it would seem that the city called 'Yahweh is there' (48:30-35) is a square with its sides no more than a scanty 2·5 kilometres (or 1½ miles) in length — no larger than a small town, or even a large village. Appendix B argues against this.

As with our discussion of the linear dimensions of the sanctuary's boundary (42:16-20), this question is not academic. If the reed is the standard, the proportions of the central reservation could not fit into the topography of the land of Israel as we now know it.

There is happy irony inherent in this verse, in that **'you'** — plural, the people of Israel — are to **'offer'** back to Yahweh what he had already granted them. The east-west **'width'** will be **'25,000'** reeds and, in what we might deem to be a parenthetical statement, its north-south extent will, it seems, be 10,000 reeds in **'length'** (see 48:9-10), corresponding to that of one of the **'divisions'** allocated to each of the twelve tribes.[205] This allotment will be situated between the southern border of Judah's territory and the northern border of Benjamin. So, between these boundaries and at the **'centre'** of **'the offering'** will lie **'the sanctuary'**.

II. The site of the central sanctuary (48:9-12)

48:9-12. '"The offering that you will offer to Yahweh: the length, twenty-five thousand; and the width, ten thousand. And to these — the priests — will belong the holy offering: northward 25,000; and westward 10,000 in width; and eastward, 10,000 in width; and southward, 25,000 in length; and the sanctuary of Yahweh will be at its centre. It will be for the priests who are sanctified, from the sons of Zadok who kept my observance, who did not go astray when the children of Israel went astray, as the Levites went astray. And it will be an offering for them, from the offering of the land, most holy, by the border of the Levites."'

In the overall context, **'offering'** is employed in three senses: firstly, the complete central section, a square of 25,000 (reeds) (48:20); secondly, the portion of this square set apart for the Levites (48:13; cf. 45:5); thirdly, the fraction of the total square reserved for the priests and the temple (48:10-12; cf. 45:1-4). The last is now mentioned rather than the other two because it is **'most holy'** (see 48:12), of primary importance.

This rectangle offered **'to Yahweh'** will be 25,000 (reeds) from east to west and 10,000 (reeds) from north to south, about 84 by 33 kilometres (52 by 20½ miles). Here **'the priests'** will reside, with **'the sanctuary of Yahweh ... at its centre'** (48:9-10). This is a studied contrast to 10:18, which tells of the departure of the glory of the Lord from the Jerusalem temple.

And **'the priests'** will be those who **'are sanctified'** — that is, recruited from **'the sons of Zadok'** who remained faithful to Yahweh during the years of general apostasy (48:11).[206]

This strip, Israel's **'offering'** to the priests **'from the offering of the land'** (the 25,000-reed square) and **'most holy'**, will be adjacent to **'the border of the Levites'** (48:12).

III. Land for the Levites (48:13-14)

48:13-14. '"Then for the Levites: opposite the border of the priests, 25,000 in length; and the width, 10,000. And they will not sell or exchange any of it, nor will they transfer this best of the land, for it is holy to Yahweh."'

The rectangular strip of land reserved for the priests abuts, and is parallel to, another rectangle of similar size granted to **'the Levites'**. Whether this land committed to the Levites is north or south of that belonging to the priests cannot be ascertained from the immediate context. Because **'it is holy to Yahweh'**, although not most holy, as in the case of the priests' territory, the Levites may neither **'sell'** nor **'exchange'** nor **'transfer'** any of it to other people.

According to Moses, houses within the cities granted to the Levites could be sold on condition that they would be redeemed in the year of jubilee. Yet Levite land could never be alienated, even temporarily.[207] In the new arrangement there is not even a temporary loss of any part of the inheritance of the tribe of Levi. Their property is a block of land, rather than scattered areas occupied by distinct communities, and cannot be split up. It all belongs to the Lord, the divine freeholder (48:13-14).

IV. Land for the city and for the workers (48:15-20)

48:15-20. '"The 5,000 that remain in the width, facing the 25,000, will be common for the city, for residence and for open land; and the city will be in its centre. And these are its measurements: the north side, 4,500; the south side, 4,500; and from the east side, 4,500; and the west side, 4,500. The open land for the city will be: to the north, 250; southward, 250; eastward, 250; and westward, 250.

'"And the rest of the length, next to the holy offering, will be 10,000 eastward and 10,000 westward, and it will be adjacent to the holy offering. Its produce will be for food for the workers of the city. And the city's workforce, from all the tribes of Israel, will cultivate it. The whole offering will be a square, 25,000 by 25,000; you shall offer the holy offering with the possession of the city."'

The rectangles of land belonging to the priests and the Levites are each 10,000 (reeds) in width from north to south, giving a total of 20,000 (reeds). Now a further rectangular strip, 25,000 (reeds) long from east to west, and 5,000 (reeds) wide from north to south, is mentioned. It is **'common'** land — that is, unconsecrated and accessible to 'the whole house of Israel' (see 45:6), rather than being separated specifically for the service of Yahweh. The **'city'** is situated at the **'centre'** of this allocation. **'For residence and for**

open land' may suggest that the strip will provide temporary accommodation for worshippers from the tribal territories and perhaps for cultivation (48:15).

The dimensions of the city are those of a square, the sides facing **'north'**, **'south'**, **'east'** and **'west'**, and each being 4,500 (reeds) long, about 15 kilometres, or a little over 9 miles (48:16).

Surrounding and adjacent to the sides of **'the city'** there is **'open land'** 250 (reeds) wide, perhaps for pasture.[208] In sum, these measurements show that the city and its suburbs constitute a square, each side being 5,000 (reeds), about 17 kilometres, or 10½ miles, and therefore the exact north-south length of the band of territory in which the city is situated (48:17).

To the east and west sides of the city, **'the holy offering'**, there remain, respectively, two areas, each 10,000 (reeds) in length running east to west, and 5,000 (reeds) wide from north to south. The function of these residual areas is to provide land where food can be produced **'for the workers of the city'**. These people, **'the city's workforce'**, who would be other than visiting worshippers, emanate **'from all the** [twelve] **tribes of Israel'**, to whom the city belongs on an equal basis rather than being monopolized by any particular tribe (48:18-19).

The overall dimensions of the tripartite sacred reservation of land, **'the whole offering'**, are summarized: the whole is exactly **'25,000'** (reeds) square. In that the complete nation — **'you'** (plural) — **'shall offer the holy offering with the possession of the city'**, Ezekiel signals that the time will come when Israel will worship Yahweh gladly and in perfect harmony (48:20).

V. The prince's land (48:21-22)

48:21-22. '"And the rest will be for the prince, on one side and the other of the holy offering and of the city's possession, facing the 25,000 of the offering as far as the eastern border, and westward facing the 25,000 up to the westward border, adjacent to the divisions. It will be for the prince. It will be the holy offering, and the sanctuary of the house will be at its centre. And, excepting the possession of the Levites and the possession of the city in the centre of what is for the prince, what is between the border of Judah and the border of Benjamin will be for the prince."'

The land belonging to **'the prince'** is now defined, this individual almost certainly not being the Messiah and his identity being irrelevant (see the comments on 44:3). His significance is that he appears as an element within the developed metaphor of the ideal theocracy, a society indwelt by Yahweh.

The prince's territory lies both to the east and to the west of the holy offering of land, and extends 25,000 (reeds) from the north to the south, from land belonging to Judah to that pertaining to Benjamin.

We have noted already that 25,000 reeds, about 84 kilometres or 52 miles, is approximately the distance from Galilee to the Dead Sea and also from the Jordan to the Mediterranean. This suggests that if the historical geography of Israel is assumed and if we are dealing with a this-worldly disposition of territory, there could be practically no land available for the prince in that **'the holy offering'** and **'the sanctuary of the house'** would take up virtually all the space available. But if the picture given by Ezekiel 48 is ideal, not to be taken literally, the problem vanishes.

Verses 21-22 refer concisely to the three parallel bands of territory given respectively to the priests, the Levites and to the city, all within the bounds of the central 25,000-reed square. Even though their north-south order is not explicit, it is possible to infer the sequence. Because the narrower belt of land for the city (not the central sanctuary) is said to be sandwiched between the priests' territory (**'the holy offering'**, 45:6; 48:18) and, apparently, land belonging to Benjamin (see 48:23), it follows that the north-south arrangement is, firstly, the Levites' land; then, secondly, the central holy portion for the priests, including the sanctuary; and, thirdly, common land including the city (48:21-22).

VI. The southern tribal divisions (48:23-29)

48:23-29. '"And the rest of the tribes, from the eastward side to the westward side: for Benjamin, one. And by the border of Benjamin, from the eastward side to the westward side: for Simeon, one. And by the border of Simeon, from the eastward side to the westward side: for Issachar, one. And by the border of Issachar, from the eastward side to the westward side: for Zebulun, one. And by the border of Zebulun, from the eastward side to the westward side: for Gad, one. And by the border of Gad to the side of the Negev, towards the south, the border will be from Tamar to the waters of Meribot-kadesh, to the brook, to the Great Sea. This is the land which you will allocate from the inheritance to the tribes of Israel, and these are their divisions," declares the Lord Yahweh.'

'The rest of the tribes' are now granted their allocations. That of **'Benjamin'** lies immediately to the south of the central offering. Then, in order, **'Simeon'**, **'Issachar'**, **'Zebulun'** and **'Gad'**, extending to the southern limits of Israel, **'the Negev'**, a distribution unlike that of the first settlement.[209] The complete area, from Dan in the north to Gad in the south, is said to be the land which **'you'** (plural), apparently the twelve tribes rather than Ezekiel, are to divide as an inheritance. So **'declares the Lord Yahweh'** (48:23-29).

VII. The gates of the city (48:30-35)

48:30-35. '"And these are the exits of the city. From the north side, 4,500 by measure (and the gates of the city will have the names of the tribes of Israel), three to the north: one gate for Reuben, one gate for Judah and one gate for Levi. And to the eastward side, 4,500, and three gates: one gate for Joseph, one gate for Benjamin and one gate for Dan. And the southward side, 4,500 by measure, and three gates: one gate for Simeon, one gate for Issachar and one gate for Zebulun. The westward side, 4,500, and their three gates: one gate for Gad, one gate for Asher and one gate for Naphtali. All the way round will be 18,000, and the name of the city from that day on: 'Yahweh is there.'"'

The dimensions of the city boundaries are repeated in order to specify the locations and names of the gates. That the four sides are of equal length, 4,500 (reeds) has been mentioned in 48:16-17. The linear dimensions emphasize the perfect symmetry of the city and its gates.[210] Given these measurements, the perimeter of the city, excluding the open space, is 18,000 (reeds), or about 60 kilometres (37 miles).

On each side there are three gates. Ezekiel does not state whether or not the naming of the gates rotates in a clockwise or an anticlockwise direction, although the clockwise description of the borders of Israel (47:15-20), may argue for the former. Nor is there a parallel with the east → south → west → north locations of the encamped tribes as given by Numbers 2, Levi now being included and Ephraim and Manasseh excluded in favour of Joseph.

Numbers 2

	Dan, Asher, Naphtali	
Ephraim, Manasseh, Benjamin		Judah, Issachar, Zebulun
	Reuben, Simeon, Gad	

48:30-34 (assuming a clockwise rotation)

Reuben, Judah, Levi

Gad, Asher, Naphtali | Joseph, Benjamin, Dan

Simeon, Issachar, Zebulun

Why Jacob's children by the handmaids Bilhah and Zilpah (Dan, Naphtali, Gad and Asher) are situated on the east and west sides, with Rachel's sons Joseph and Benjamin to the east, and his children by his wife Leah (Reuben, Simeon, Levi, Judah, Issachar and Zebulun) to the north and south, is unclear. Yet the balanced proportions of the plan might suggest ease of access to the city and effective crowd control if each Israelite enters and leaves through his own tribal gate.

What does stir the reader is that now, at long last, the people of Israel are united and that internal distinctions and tensions are past and gone.

Significantly, the **'gates'** are termed **'exits'**, and walls as such are not mentioned.[211] The impression is given that this **'city'** lacks fortifications because it will never be attacked and that it makes itself, so to speak, willingly accessible to all who wish to enter and leave.

In their brevity, the closing words of the prophecy are marvellously eloquent. **'The name of the city from that day on: "Yahweh is there."'** Unlike the cities of this world, all of which tend to vanish with the passage of time, or have their names altered by new occupants, the theocracy endures.

But why, it may be asked, is the city — unlike the 'Jerusalem' of Revelation 21:2,10 — not given its ancient name? An answer may be that not only was 'Jerusalem' originally a Canaanite city, during the long years following its capture by David and identification by Yahweh as the site for his temple, it had been desecrated by its kings and its people. Therefore — and this is the theme of chapters 1 – 33 — Yahweh abandoned it, refusing to grace the city with his presence. Now, he has returned, and the ancient city of peace is once again 'the city of God', 'the city of the Great King' and 'the city of Yahweh, the Zion of the Holy One of Israel'.[212] Never again will he depart (48:30-35).

Application

We have now come to the end of Ezekiel's story. In order to understand it, we must imagine ourselves in Ezekiel's situation, a priest summoned to the prophetic ministry when an exile in Babylonia six hundred years before the time of our Lord.

Prior to the destruction of Jerusalem in 586 BC, this saintly man, who had suffered along with his people, understood exactly why the temple of the Lord in Jerusalem would soon be demolished, why Israel must be scattered to the winds, why the throne of David would be cast to the ground, and why (as it seemed to many who lacked discernment) the Lord had renounced his commitment to Israel. Yet he knew that the promises of God to Abraham and his family would retain an eternal validity.

Following the holocaust of 586 BC, Ezekiel's mouth was opened and he predicted to a ruined church that there would in time be a twofold restoration of Israel: firstly, a spiritually renewed people would be resettled in the land of promise and would be saved from the ultimate menace of an antagonistic world ('Gog' and 'Magog'); secondly, that the restored relationship between Yahweh and Israel would endure for ever, extending beyond the horizons of this world and into what today's Christian would term 'eternity'.

Chapters 47 – 48 complete the vision. Here we are shown a united people settled happily and permanently in the land vouchsafed to Abraham, and whose sole reason for existence is to worship the God who resides in their midst and who is accessible to all — but accessible only because at the heart of the land there is a temple with an altar, telling that without propitiation there can be no lasting reconciliation.

In his own priestly fashion — for, as a son of Aaron, he could be no other than a priest — Ezekiel preaches to today's churches of 'the blessed hope and appearing of our great God and Saviour, Christ Jesus' and of the glory that shall ensue for all who believe.[213] And, although he possibly did not realize this, he challenges Gentile dogs such as we who crouch beneath the Master's table to pray earnestly for the conversion of the natural family of Abraham.[214]

Appendix A

42:16-20 and chapters 45 and 48: the reed or the cubit?

1. 42:16-20 — 500 cubits or 500 reeds?

Interpretations of the temple wall and of the figure of 500 tend to vary. Many modern commentators take the view that what was measured was each side of the perimeter wall of the entire temple complex, and that each was found to be five hundred *cubits*.[1]

And not only commentators, but some Bible versions also. For example, the English Standard Version offers '500 cubits' no less than six times, with no marginal indication that this must involve a textual emendation.[2]

It has to be admitted that if this was what Ezekiel's guide measured, he might not be deemed inaccurate because 40:20-27 implies that 500 cubits was the probable length of each side of the temple.[3]

But the measurements indicated by 42:16-20 may *not* have been those of the perimeter of the temple complex, but those of the boundary of a very much larger space. This is the sense given by the Authorized (or King James) Version and by the New American Standard Bible,[4] and which is accepted here.

In making a decision, much depends upon an examination of the background Hebrew text of 42:16-20 and of the respective Hebrew words for 'cubit' and 'hundred', the consonants of which are not entirely dissimilar ('cubit' = *amah*; 'hundred' = *meah*), and of the process of textual transmission.

The relevance of the question is that the view that 500 reeds, rather than 500 cubits, are indicated makes all the difference to whether or not Ezekiel's visionary temple is or is not to be understood as a predicted reality for this world. As mentioned in the body of the commentary, the argument is not academic.

I. A case for 500 reeds

In Solomon's temple, the outer court was adjacent to land occupied by the city. This meant that the defilement of the land because of the sins of the people could penetrate, so to speak, through to the sanctuary of Yahweh, no space being available to insulate the temple.

But matters are different in this new arrangement. Now a vast separated area prevents defilement. The temple complex, 500 cubits square, lies in sanctified isolation at the centre of an otherwise vacant 500-reed square space.

If the measuring angel did no more than measure the perimeter wall of the immediate temple complex, there would remain the distinct possibility of moral contamination by the urban environment. Reason demands that because this was not to be the case, the guide measured something other than the temple area. This, I believe, is favoured by the preserved Hebrew text of 42:16-20, where reeds rather than cubits are mentioned explicitly.

This commentary, then, would dissent from the view that, as articulated by Taylor:

> The Hebrew has *five hundred reeds* (AV) for the measurements of the four sides of the temple area (16-19), but this is obviously wrong: we

> must understand *five hundred cubits* (RSV), which corresponds with all the measurements previously given, unless we are to suppose that the reference here is to a previously unmentioned outer wall forming a square of 3,000 cubits each way ... but this is most unlikely.[5]

II. Ezekiel's temple and Mount Moriah

If accepted, these figures lead us to a startling conclusion. It should be borne in mind that the measuring reed employed by Ezekiel's guide was six cubits, well over three metres, or between ten and eleven feet, long (see comments on 40:5).

It follows that each side of this square was nearly 1,700 metres, or more than 1½ kilometres (just over a mile), in length (see comments on 42:16-19). Therefore its ground area, almost three kilometres square, was vastly larger than that of the relatively diminutive temple complex in Jerusalem which the young Ezekiel had seen with his own eyes.

Remarkably, this figure works out at over twenty times the ground area of the enormous temple that Herod the Great commenced in 19 BC. Taking about eighty years to complete, it was soon destroyed by the Romans.[6]

The point being made here is that the sanctuary seen by Ezekiel takes up so much ground space that it could not be situated within an earthly Jerusalem. The task of construction would be like trying to squash an international airport, with its full-length runways, into a sports stadium around which there is no vacant space. So, *if* we accept the Hebrew text as it stands, it follows that the vision is figurative and must relate to a situation not of this present world.[7]

2. Chapters 45 and 48

As has been remarked, with the exception of 45:2 the unit of measurement in the background Hebrew of chapters 45 and 48 is not stated explicitly. In this, the Septuagint agrees with the Masoretic text. Yet at least one version, the New American Standard Bible, gives 'cubits' in italics, assuming without proof positive that the prophet took this as the unit.[8] The English Standard Version goes further, giving '25,000 cubits' throughout without indicating that 'cubits' is a translator's insertion, and thereby implying that there is no problem. Without offering any discussion, explanatory footnotes inform the reader that 'A *cubit* was about 18 inches or 45 centimetres.'[9]

But perhaps the matter is not so simple. When we take into account 42:16-20, where the house is said to be within a square with sides each 500 reeds in length, and when we consider the specific reference in 45:2 to the fifty-cubit width of the open space surrounding the holy place, the suppressed but implied unit in chapters 45 and 48 would seem to be the reed rather than the cubit.

The crux of the issue is as follows. Why should Ezekiel in 45:2 specify the cubit for a relatively minute margin of land, yet not do so both for the central allotment and for the distribution of the promised land among the tribes? The sensible conclusion is that he did *not* have the cubit in mind. This commentary would propose that because the cubit is not mentioned as the unit of length of the central allotment, the measuring reed, over six times as long, is Ezekiel's assumed unit.

If in chapters 45 and 48 the linear unit is the cubit rather than the measuring reed, the dimensions given might possibly accommodate to the present topography of the region. From this it could be argued that Ezekiel predicts the erection of a restored temple at some future time and in this present world, before the end. Those who accept a doctrine of the premillennial return of Christ might favour such an interpretation, whereas those who do not could enhance their case by arguing for the (non-literal) measuring reed rather than for the (literal) cubit. This is the position adopted here.

Appendix B
Ezekiel's city

Did Ezekiel consider the city-temple that he saw descending from heaven (40:2) to be the city named 'Yahweh is there'? (45:2; 48:15-19,30-35). Formally, no; in principle, yes.

1. The sanctuary, the city and the sacred offering of land

It is to be remembered that the city within the southern strip held by the common folk is, like the complete offering of land (25,000 x 25,000 reeds), also a square, but with sides only 5,000 reeds in length. This means that it occupies a relatively small area, four parts in a hundred of the offering.

But when compared with the city, the ground area of the temple at the heart of the priests' allocation is much smaller. A tiny square of 500 cubits bordered by a relatively large square with sides each 500 reeds (42:16-19), the total complex occupies no more than four parts in ten thousand of the whole offering of land, and is just one part in a hundred of the area of the southern city. (It should be noted that the diagram on page 716, 'The division of land among the tribes', does not attempt to reflect the scale. If it tried to do so, the temple would appear as a minute dot.)

Given these considerations, plus the fact that the city and the sanctuary are situated in different parts of the central offering of land, are they identical? To repeat: formally, no.

2. A city that has no sanctuary, and a sanctuary that stands apart

But perhaps we can travel further. The temple, outlined in considerable detail in 40:1 – 43:17, is said to have been 'like a city' (40:2). This description is unique because the temple is nowhere else described in this fashion. In the remainder of the prophecy it is invariably presented as the sanctuary, or the house of Yahweh, rather than a metropolis.

Furthermore, the city within the southern strip is dissimilar in function as well as in its proportions. Firstly, no Levites or priests are present, apparently, remaining within their own allotted territories. Secondly (and to repeat), the ground-area is much larger than that of the temple. Thirdly, this city is situated in a different band of territory. Fourthly, it is separated from the sanctuary by a distance of 5,000 reeds, nearly 17 kilometres, or 10½ miles.

Historically, the temple of Yahweh had always been situated within Jerusalem, probably in the oldest part of the city.[1] In the early first century AD the sanctuary and its courts might have taken up more than ten per cent of the area of the city. In a real sense Jerusalem *was* the temple. The Acts of the Apostles records that the Ethiopian eunuch travelled far to be in Jerusalem to worship at the sanctuary,[2] and he was typical of thousands who regarded the city in this light.

But the conclusion to Ezekiel's prophecy looks elsewhere. Not only has the temple no immediate geographical connection with the city, the city lacks a sanctuary and displays every appearance of being, at the most, a quasi-secular location where non-Levites work (see 48:18-19).

When we come to the end of Ezekiel's prophecy, we are given further detailed information about 'the city' (48:30-35) — not the temple. Remarkably, the sanctuary is mentioned neither explicitly nor by implication. Enlarging upon 48:16, the final verses show that each side of the city is 4,500 reeds in length. It is almost as if the text wants us to understand that the walled-off sanctuary on a mountain top, only 500 reeds square, is most definitely *not* under consideration.

In each boundary wall of the square city there are three gates, twelve in all, each named after one of the twelve tribes, including (as noted) Levi and excluding Ephraim and Manasseh. The name of the city is 'Yahweh is there'. Such details are lacking in Ezekiel's exposition of the house of Yahweh (40:1 – 46:24). In this extended metaphor of Israel-to-be the two cannot be the same.

3. Why the separation of city and sanctuary?

It would appear that the southern city represents the ultimate Jerusalem, but a Jerusalem that lacks a temple. How can this be, given that the Lord is there and given the parallel fact that the presence of God apparently remains exclusively in the sanctuary, seventeen kilometres (10½ miles) distant to the north, and from which the river of life flows? (See 43:2-7; 47:1-12).

Perhaps the only way to reconcile this apparent anomaly is to suppose that what Ezekiel saw was a breathtaking vision of the age to come. To interpret these details as part of a literal blueprint for Jerusalem and the Holy Land prior to the end of the world would tie us up hopelessly in knots.

We might put this in a rather more down-to-earth fashion. Are we to imagine that at some future time converted Jews are to build a new temple somewhere in Judea, then relocating Jerusalem a considerable distance towards the southern Negev? Chapters 40 – 48 tell against the notion.

4. Ezekiel distinguished; John combines

Revelation 21:1-27 would seem to resolve our difficulties. Here, Ezekiel's city and Ezekiel's sanctuary are fused together. The southern-belt city and the middle-belt temple descend as one from heaven to rest on a mountain summit. The parallel with Ezekiel 40:2, referring to the sanctuary, is explicit and unmistakable.

John's 'holy city', the 'new Jerusalem', is perceived to lack a temple.[3] That it is Ezekiel's southern, sanctuary-less city is certain. Revelation 21:12 shows that its twelve gates, three on each side, are each named after a tribe of Israel. Yet this new Jerusalem is more than a city: it is said to be the tabernacle, or tent, of God in which rests the glory of God, transforming the metropolis into a huge sanctuary, a gigantic glistening cube with sides each 12,000 stadia (about 2,220 kilometres, or 1,370 miles).

That this city is nothing other than Ezekiel's sanctuary is proved beyond all doubt by Revelation 22:1-2. The river of the water of life is said to have its source at the throne of God and of the Lamb within the city. Just like Ezekiel's river, it gives life wherever it goes.

If we consider John's city in terms of Ezekiel's measuring reeds, we find that the new Jerusalem, which appears to be the prophet's city and temple combined, has a ground area about 18,000 times that of the land taken up by Ezekiel's city.[4] These immense numbers are hugely disproportionate. It follows that the revelation to Ezekiel, as well as, of course, that to John is not to be taken literally.

5. The New Testament is in the Old concealed; the Old is in the New revealed

In short, when a prisoner on the island of Patmos, John saw a vast city that had no temple, but which was nothing other than a temple site. He saw a sanctuary that was not a city, yet was nothing but a city. John beheld both the city and the sanctuary of Ezekiel merged together in one eternal and indivisible unity.

Why, then, did the Lord grant to Ezekiel a revelation of the everlasting future (according to the view taken by the present commentary) of the people of God in terms of a non-literal temple and a geographically distinct, non-literal city? Perhaps his purpose was to show that the dimensions were to be interpreted symbolically. Ezekiel, after all, must have been aware that the God-fearing Israelite could no more imagine Jerusalem without a temple than he could conceive of a temple planted beyond the walls of that city. It follows that Ezekiel's picture is just that, a picture, and would have been seen in this light by all thinking readers.

If prophecy is history foretold, albeit in shadow form rather than proleptically, history is prophecy fulfilled. When Christ comes we shall experience the realities set forth in vision form by Ezekiel and, six centuries later, by John.

Appendix C

Romans 11:25-26

This commentary supposes that Ezekiel anticipated that, following the collapse of the theocracy of Israel in his day, there would in time be a permanent restoration extending from this world into eternity, 'Israel' signifying the now spiritually renewed twelve tribes issuing from Jacob.

1. 'All Israel'

Should it be asked whether the New Testament gives support to this interpretation, Romans 11:25-26 and context come immediately to mind.[1] In these verses, Paul reveals what he terms **'this mystery'** to his **'brothers'**, for the most part Gentile members of the church at Rome. They should know that **'a hardening in part has happened to Israel until the fulness of the nations** [i.e. Gentiles] **comes in; and so all Israel shall be saved'**.

There are not a few able commentators who consider that **'all Israel'** refers to the full number of the elect from the natural family of Israel and also from the world, and is an analogue to **'the fulness of the nations'**, there being just one 'olive tree', as indicated by Romans 11:17-24. Otherwise expressed, until the end of time the predetermined number of Jews and Gentiles will be brought to saving faith, all constituting the true 'Israel'. It is suggested that because throughout the Roman letter the apostle has emphasized that natural descent from Abraham, Isaac and Jacob is not what matters primarily in the sight of God, Paul would not contradict himself by predicting that Jacob's natural family must be restored to their original covenant relationship with their God.[2]

In disagreeing with this type of approach, one would take the view that Paul anticipates that in time to come a large majority of Jews — in fact, the overwhelming mass of ethnic Israel — will convert to faith in Jesus the Messiah.

2. The flow of argument in Romans 11:1-27

Firstly, the apostle affirms that, although the nation of Israel had always shown itself apostate, God graciously saw fit to preserve an elect remnant, of which he, Paul, was one (Rom. 11:1-10).

Secondly, although the people of Israel had stumbled, they never fell completely or permanently. That is, their rejection of Jesus Christ was a reflex of God's rejection of them. Yet it was a mutual rejection that would not endure for ever.

In detail, had Israel not delivered Jesus to the Roman authority to be crucified, there could be no salvation for either Jew or Gentile. Moreover, Paul claims that the fact that so many Gentiles come to believe in the Lord provokes the Jews to jealousy, stimulating some of their number to emulate non-Jewish believers by turning to Christ. Thus, in time the historic **'failure'** or 'defeat', or even 'loss', of Israel, beginning in the first century AD (see the first part of Rom. 11:12), will precipitate the **'fulfilment'**, or 'completion', of the nation, meaning that most Jews living at the time, although not all, will convert to Christ (the second part of Rom. 11:12). Paul adds that if their rejection by their God has led to **'the reconciliation of the world'**, their **'acceptance'** by the Lord as converted Christians must be what is termed **'life from the dead'** for the world (Rom. 11:15). 'Life from the dead' would denote, in the words of J. Murray, not the ultimate resurrection of the dead, but 'an unprecedented quickening for the world in the expansion and success of the gospel'.[3]

Thirdly, employing two metaphors, that of dough, probably taken from Numbers 15:17-21, and that of a cultivated olive into which is grafted a branch from a wild olive, the apostle shows that, eventually, unbelieving Israel, considered as a people, will embrace the Messianic hope of their fathers to unite with believing Gentiles in a common salvation. He writes this to warn Gentile Christian readers against considering themselves innately superior to Jewish unbelievers (Rom. 11:16-24).

To recapitulate, it is important to note that Paul has predicted the mass conversion of most of the nation of Israel and their acceptance by God, this to be followed by a period of unparalleled blessing for the Gentiles, to whom (presumably) a believing Jewish people will be conveying the gospel. Although Paul writes as a prophet of the new dispensation, he does not state that his words thus far are a revelation.

But now the temperature escalates. For the first time in the letter the apostle discloses what he conceives to be **'this mystery'** (Rom. 11:25). In the New Testament, whatever requires a divine revelation to become an object of human knowledge is deemed a 'mystery', this word being employed with regard to the doctrines of the gospel that are matters of revelation rather than truths accessible by reason.[4]

Paul indicates that the **'hardening'** of Israel since Christ was first rejected by his people is neither total nor permanent. That is, not all in Israel were hardened in unbelief, and at some future time the stubborn and persistent ethnic rejection of Jesus as the Messiah will be a thing of the past. The revelation, which he does *not* expound in Romans 11:1-24, is that the (predicted) mass conversion of the Jews will occur *after* what he terms **'the fulness of the Gentiles'** (Rom. 11:25). **'So, all Israel will be saved'** (Rom. 11:26).

If it is argued that the Greek *houtôs* behind **'so'** in this verse means 'thus', rather than 'then', suggesting that the ingathering of the full number of the Gentiles is in itself a component of the redemption of 'all Israel', it may be suggested that the word can sometimes possess a temporal sense.[5] But even if this is denied, the overall thrust remains: the disobedience of Israel leads in time to the 'fulness' of the Gentiles so that, eventually, ethnic Israel may turn back to the Lord.

3. A seeming problem — and a response

If, as this commentary supposes, by **'Israel'** is meant the natural descendants of Abraham at a future time when most of them accept Christ and in turn are accepted back by the Lord (Rom. 11:15), it may appear superficially that Paul is confused.

That is, he indicates that the failure of Israel to accept the Messiah has led to **'riches'** for the Gentiles, this in turn leading to the latter's **'fulness'** (Rom. 11:12,25), otherwise termed **'the reconciliation of the world'** (Rom. 11:15). This, Paul asserts, will precipitate the **'fulness'** and **'acceptance'** of Israel, leading to **'life from the dead'** (again, Rom. 11:12,15). Apparently, both *before* and *after* the conversion of the majority of the people of Israel, the Gentile world will, by means of respectively, first, an unyielding and then, secondly, an obedient Israel, be granted the blessings of the gospel leading to very many conversions. But how, it may be asked, can the 'fulness' of the Gentiles prior to the conversion of Israel become, so to speak, even fuller after Israel's renewal?

William Hendriksen is scathing. He asks if the advocates of this approach have forgotten that:

> ... according to the interpretation of Rom. 11:25,26, favoured by them and/or by their friends, there will be no more Gentiles left to become candidates for conversion, since, as these exegetes see it, it is only *after* the totality of Gentile believers has been gathered into God's fold that Israel will finally be saved.[6]

Two points at least may be made in response. In the words of J. Murray:

> 'The fulness of the Gentiles' [prior to the conversion of Israel, Romans 11:25] denotes unprecedented blessing for them [the Gentiles] but does not exclude even greater blessing to follow. It is to this subsequent blessing [again, for the Gentiles] that the restoration of Israel contributes.[7]

More importantly, the overarching theme of Romans 11 is that, both in initial and continuing unbelief and, finally, in obedience, the family of Abraham has been and will be used by God to bring gospel benefits to the world at large.

Undoubtedly, here is the core of **'this mystery'** (Rom. 11:25). Paul's thesis is that if unregenerate Israel induced the means (the cross and all that followed) by which multitudes of Gentiles would be saved, this same people, when eventually regenerate, will of necessity be the agent of unprecedented blessing for the Gentiles.

For these two reasons, as distinct as they are inseparable, supercilious Gentile Christians at Rome (and elsewhere, and since Paul's day) need to guard themselves against conceit (see Rom. 11:20). Rather, the Jews, as the chosen instrument for the salvation of the world, should attract their profound respect — and prayers. We might suppose that a criticism such as that of Hendriksen fails to understand the content, the grandeur and, indeed, the pastoral application of the apostle's prediction.

4. Does Romans 11 fit with Ezekiel?

This commentary has suggested that in chapters 34 and 36 – 39 Ezekiel predicts the return of the people of Israel to the land of promise, there to be attacked by Gog and Magog, and that these enemies will be overthrown by supernatural means.

The common factor shared by these chapters and Romans 11 is that, in what we now know to be a future far distant from the time of Ezekiel and, indeed, from that of Paul, the family of Israel will be spiritually renewed. Yahweh's 'servant David' will be 'their shepherd' (34:23) and the 'fulfilment' of Israel will be the negation of their stumbling, their transgression and their defeat (Rom. 11:11-12).

Yet Ezekiel 34 – 39 makes no mention of the influx of the Gentiles, and Romans 11 is silent about Israel's possession of the promised land. It may be asked, then, whether Ezekiel and Paul look towards the same programme of events.

I would argue in the affirmative. In Ezekiel's day, Gentile inclusion in the Israel of God was an unrevealed mystery, not understood clearly by the prophets of the old covenant. This is indicated, for example, by Ephesians 3:3-9. Ezekiel's task was to show that the warnings of Leviticus 26 and Deuteronomy 28 must soon be fulfilled, *and* that the relationship between Yahweh and Abraham's family would never fade. We could even say that the rhetorical question of Romans 11:11, 'They did not stumble so that they might fall, did they?', sums up the burden of Ezekiel's ministry.

Even though we may assume that Paul understood and applauded Ezekiel's burden, Romans 11 projects a different emphasis. In order to secure Gentile Christian respect for the people of Israel in general and for converted Jews in particular, the apostle needed only to insist that in their historic apostasy, in their persistent and continuing unbelief and subsequently in their future conversion, Jacob's family could be none other than a blessing to the world. The resettlement of the twelve tribes in Canaan and the traumas and triumph of the end time were not upon his agenda.

For example, F. F. Bruce states that 'in all that Paul says about the restoration of Israel to God, he says nothing about the restoration of an earthly Davidic kingdom, nothing about national reinstatement in the land of Israel. What he envisaged for his people was something infinitely better.'[8]

But might not such comments miss the point? Within Romans 11 could there not be a latent 'both/and' (i.e. renewal *and* resettlement) theology that the apostle saw no need to elaborate? Could not Paul have assumed relocation as a platform for renewal? Two thousand years since the apostolic age, may we not suspect that the regeneration of the family of Abraham might occur more easily and more appropriately within, as well as beyond, the boundaries of their promised land rather than in a purely Diaspora situation? Keil and Delitzsch's view of Deuteronomy 30:4-5, to the effect that Moses did not have a geographical resettlement of the land of Israel in mind because 'Palestine will never furnish room enough for a nation multiplied like this' seems to the present writer to be more speculative than realistic.[9]

Can we not therefore conclude that Romans 11 is consistent with the eschatology of the prophet Ezekiel?

5. Israel and the law of Moses

If, as this commentary supposes, the overwhelming majority of the people of Israel will one day turn to Jesus Messiah, the question arises as to what extent, if any, they will submit themselves to the law of Moses, the ancestral Torah.

Although this is by no means an academic question, I would suggest that a detailed answer lies beyond the limits of this commentary. Yet we might suppose (and prayerfully trust) that the people of Israel will reflect the position taken by the apostle Paul, who in his day knew that the 'old covenant' was swiftly becoming redundant (see 2 Cor. 3:14 and context) and that he found himself 'within the law of Christ' (1 Cor. 9:21 and context). The law of Moses obligatory upon Jewish Christians was at that time being replaced once and for all (see Heb. 7:12; 8:13).

6. Postscript

This appendix has not considered the identities of Gog and Magog in Revelation 20, nor the Lord's promise that the gospel of the grace of God must be proclaimed to all nations,[10] nor the identity of the Antichrist.[11] Of course, together with Romans 11, such matters must enter into our thinking concerning the 'Where?', 'When?', 'Who?' and 'How?' of the events of the end: we peer into the future because we desire to know. Yet we need to keep our feet solidly on terra firma, agreeing with two recent commentators who have remarked jointly that the prophecy of Ezekiel tells that, notwithstanding 'gross infidelity, Israel's future is one *with* God rather than *without* God. For the prophet, God is sovereign but bound to Israel by an inexplicable love.' Again, they say, 'This is a stunning assertion coming from someone living in exile. It is a testament to faith. The writers of the NT, particularly Paul, will ask for that same faith from those who believed in Christ.'[12]

So these pages would not speculate upon such questions as 'Where?', 'When?', 'Who?' and 'How?' Philip Doddridge (1702–51) wrote in his interleaved New Testament, 'Never let me enter into long Schemes about *future* Events, but in the general refer myself to GOD's Care.'[13] May it be so for us.

Suffice it to say that in his time Ezekiel knew that vast tectonic plates had moved, were moving and would continue to move beneath the surface of world history. These unseen — and perhaps by many Christians, unsuspected — forces are still operative. One day, yet before the Second Coming, they will generate seismic shocks such as men have never witnessed and that most of us do not expect. We await the future.

Notes

Preface

1. Exod. 3:14,16.

Introductory matters

1. So D. I. Block, *The Book of Ezekiel,* NICOT series (Grand Rapids: Eerdmans, 2 vols, 1997), vol. 1, p.41, referring to *Biblia Hebraica Stuttgartensia,* edited by A. Alt and others (Stuttgart: Bibelgesellschaft, first published 1967/77).
2. So G. A. Cooke, *A Critical and Exegetical Commentary on the Book of Ezekiel,* International Critical Commentary series (Edinburgh: T. & T. Clark, 1985 edition), p.xx.
3. L. C. Allen, *Ezekiel,* Word Biblical Commentary (Dallas: Word Books, vols. 28, 29, 1990–94), vol. 28, p.xxvi. Cf. W. Eichrodt, *Ezekiel: A Commentary,* translated by C. Quinn (London: SCM Press, 1970), p.24. Yet fashions change with the years. Thus R. L. Kohn writes, 'In the early part of the century [i.e. the twentieth], much of the book was attributed to late editors; most recent studies, however, have reassigned the majority to the prophet himself' ('A New Heart and a New Soul: Ezekiel, the Exile and the Torah', *Journal for the Study of the Old Testament, Supplement Series 358*, London: Sheffield Academic Press, 2002, p.1).

One would tend to identify with J. Job, who writes that 'we may limit the editor's work to *at most* filling in a picture already sketched out firmly and in some detail by Ezekiel himself' (*Watchman in Babylon: A Study Guide to Ezekiel,* Achimoto, Ghana: Africa Christian Press; Exeter: Paternoster, 1983, p.99). Yet perhaps his '*at most*' is somewhat generous.

It should be noted that Josephus reported concerning the fall of Jerusalem that 'the prophet Ezekiel ... left behind two books which he was the first to write about these matters' (*Antiquities* 10.5.1). These volumes *may* have been chapters 1 – 32 and 33 – 48 (desolation followed by consolation), according to E. J. Young, *An Introduction to the Old Testament* (London: The Tyndale Press, revised edition, 1960), p.256.

4. Cf. Haggai and Zechariah.
5. R. E. Clements, *Ezekiel,* Westminster Bible Companion series (Louisville: Westminster John Knox Press,1996), p.179. This has

been a fairly common approach. Thus, for example, J. D. Levenson writes, 'After the return from Exile, some elements of Israel, probably influenced by this vision, sought to rebuild the Temple and to reinstitute its liturgy, chief among them the prophets Haggai and Zechariah' (*Theology of the Program of Restoration of Ezekiel 40 – 48*, Missoula, Mont.: Scholars Press, 1976, p.162). And C. R. Biggs says, 'The final major part of the book of Ezekiel ... provided a structure for the life of the returned and restored people' (*The Book of Ezekiel,* London: Epworth Press, 1996, p.128). Long ago, E. W. Hengstenberg commented concerning these chapters that their 'fulfilment ... belongs to the times immediately after the return from the Chaldean exile. So must every one of its first hearers have understood it' (*The Prophecies of the Prophet Ezekiel Elucidated,* translated by A. C. Murphy and J. G. Murphy, Edinburgh: T. & T. Clark, 1869, p.352).

6. See J. B. Taylor, *Ezekiel: An Introduction and Commentary,* Tyndale Old Testament Commentary series (Leicester, U.K. & Downer's Grove, U.S.A.: IVP, 1969), p.251.

7. Taylor, *Ezekiel,* p.252.

8. L. E. Cooper, *Ezekiel,* The New American Commentary, vol. 17 (Broadman & Holman, 1994), pp.351-2.

9. Recently, C. J. H. Wright, *The Message of Ezekiel,* The Bible Speaks Today: Old Testament Series (Leicester: Inter-Varsity Press 2004 reprint [first published 2001]), pp.340-4, 358-9; D. Thomas, *God Strengthens: Ezekiel simply explained* (Darlington: Evangelical Press, 1993), p.264.

10. P. Fairbairn, *An Exposition of Ezekiel* (Indiana: Sovereign Grace Publishers, 1960), p.435.

11. W. Greenhill, *An exposition of Ezekiel,* Geneva series (Edinburgh: Banner of Truth, 1994 [first published 1654–1667]), p.774.

12. Taylor, *Ezekiel,* p.252.

13. Fairbairn, *Ezekiel,* pp.435, 445. Not a few writers are ambiguous. So, P. C. Craigie states that 'Ezekiel had transcended the negative and empirical evidence of his time to grasp the better world beyond' (*Ezekiel,* Edinburgh: St Andrews Press and Philadelphia: Westminster Press, 1983, p.321), without identifying Ezekiel's 'when', 'where' and 'how' of this 'better world'. Years ago, H. D. M. Spence and J. S. Exell suggested that chapters 40 – 48 concern 'the Israel of Messianic times' and that 'the Holy Spirit had some such design is at least an idea which one might be pardoned for entertaining' (*Ezekiel,* London and New York: Funk & Wagnalls, 2 vols, 1906, vol. 2, p.320). They were unsure.

14. Cooper, *Ezekiel,* p.353.

15. *Ibid.,* p.381. So, too, C. L. Feinberg, *The Prophecy of Ezekiel: The Glory of the Lord* (Chicago: Moody Press, 1969), p.276. He states that 'The final chapter of this surpassingly important

prophecy concerns the distribution of the promised land for the millennial age.'
16. Gal. 4:3,9; Col. 2:8,20.
17. See F. Gardiner, *Ezekiel,* A Bible Commentary for English Readers, ed. C. J. Ellicott (London: Cassell & Co., undated, 8 vols), vol. 5 (pp.199-352), p.316. I own a considerable indebtedness to this little-known commentator for the lucidity of his remarks.
18. So Gardiner, *Ezekiel,* p.314.
19. See Appendix A.
20. See the sketch on page 716.
21. Gardiner, *Ezekiel,* p.314.
22. Num. 35:9-15.
23. See Gardiner, *Ezekiel,* p.316.
24. John 14:2.
25. 2 Tim. 4:18.
26. Rev. 21:3.
27. C. F. Keil, *Ezekiel* (C. F. Keil and F. Delitzsch, *Commentary on the Old Testament*, translated by J. Martin, Grand Rapids: Eerdmans, 1976, 10 vols.), vol. 9, p.421.
28. Block, *Ezekiel,* vol. 1, p.57.
29. So Block, *Ezekiel,* vol. 1, p.55. E. Lucas discounts (1) a premillennial interpretation, (2) the view that Ezekiel wrote to encourage Haggai and Zechariah and their fellow-returnees, and (3) that chapters 40 – 48 anticipate the Christian church (*Ezekiel: the People's Bible Commentary,* Oxford: The Bible Reading Fellowship, 2002, p.193). Yet, in opting for what he terms a 'symbolic apocalyptic view', he remains indefinite, simply stating in general terms that 'The visions in chapters 40 – 48 fill out the promise in 37:27-28 that God will once again dwell with his people' (p.229). Such ambiguity is not uncommon.
30. So Wright, *The Message of Ezekiel,* p.35.
31. Gen. 15:13.
32. Exod. 2:23-25.
33. Exod. 5:1-21.
34. Exod. 3:14-16; 5:22 – 6:5.
35. Exod. 6:6-9.
36. Exod. 7:5,17; 8:10,22; 9:14,29; 10:2; 14:4,18.
37. Exod. 16:6,12; 29:46; 31:13; Deut. 29:6.
38. 2 Kings 19:19; Isa. 37:20.
39. 5:13; 6:7,10,13,14; 7:4,9,27; 11:10,12; 12:15,16,20; 13:9,14,21,23; 14:8; 15:7; 17:21; 20:26,48; 21:5; 22:16; 29:16.
40. Cf. Exod. 31:13. See the 'Application' on pages 311-13, at the end of the comments on Ezekiel 20.
41. 16:62; 20:42,44; 29:21; 34:30; 36:38; 37:6,13,14; 39:28.
42. Cf. 1 Kings 19:18; Rom. 11:1-6.
43. Cf. Isa. 11:4; 2 Thess. 2:8; Rev.19:15.
44. Cf. John 19:26; 20:19-23; Acts 3:1 – 4:4.

45. Block, *Ezekiel,* vol. 1, p.8.
46. Gen. 15:1-21.
47. Rev. 22:2.
48. Matt. 8:11.
49. So Wright, *The Message of Ezekiel,* p.42.
50. Exod. 20:4; Lev. 26:1; Deut. 5:8-9.
51. Cf. Josh. 24:14.
52. 1 Kings 11:1-10.
53. 1 Kings 11:31-40.
54. Jer. 1:1.
55. 2 Kings 22:8-10; 2 Chr. 34:8-18.
56. 2 Kings 24:1,12-14; 2 Chr. 36:5-7; Dan. 1:1-2; 2:1; 4:8.
57. 2 Chr. 36:22-23; Ezra 1:1-4.
58. Num. 22 – 24.
59. 2 Peter 1:21.
60. Rev. 1:9.
61. The links between the prophecy of Ezekiel and the book of Revelation have often exercised commentators. For example, S. Bøe observes that 'It seems ... appropriate to speak of a "prophecy" in Ezekiel 38 – 39 which John expected to be "fulfilled" in the way he describes the last battle in Rev 20,7-10. The problem is, however, that John alludes to Ezekiel 38 – 39 in Rev 19,17-21 also, and it is not very satisfactory to speak of a "double" or "multiple fulfilment"' (*Gog and Magog: Ezekiel 38–39 as Pre-text for Revelation 19,17-21 and 20,7-10*, Tübingen: Mohr Siebeck, 2001), p.388. Yet may not this dilemma be resolved if John's Revelation is internally 'cyclic', the central theme — the progress of the Christ and his church until the advent of glory — being expounded repetitively, yet on different levels and with different emphases in a series of seven sections (chapters 1 – 3; 4 – 7; 8 – 11; 12 – 14; 15 – 16; 17 – 19; 20 – 22)? If so, Rev. 20:7-10 is a reiteration of Rev. 19:17-21.
62. Jer. 46:2.
63. 2 Kings 21:1-18; 24:3-4; 2 Chr. 33:10-20.
64. 2 Kings 23; 2 Chr. 34.
65. 2 Kings 23:29; 2 Chr. 35:20-24. The Babylonian Chronicle, a reliable account of the annals of the Babylonian Empire from 626 to 539 BC, reveals that Egypt was seeking to aid Assyria against Babylon (cf. 2 Kings 23:29). Perhaps Josiah attacked Pharaoh Necho because he preferred the possibility of Babylonian dominance to an actual Egyptian hegemony. See Taylor, *Ezekiel,* p.30, n.1.
66. 2 Kings 23:33-34; 2 Chr. 36:3-4.
67. Jer. 22:13-19.
68. 2 Kings 24:2,6; 2 Chr. 36:6; Jer. 35:11; 36:30. See comments on 19:1-9 (pp. 273-80) and chapter 2, note 347 below.
69. Jer. 22:24,28; 1 Chr. 3:16.

70. 2 Kings 24:7.
71. 2 Kings 24:11-16; 2 Chr. 36:10.
72. 2 Kings 25:27-30.
73. Jer. 37 – 38.
74. Jer. 37:5.
75. 2 Kings 25:7; Jer. 39:6-7; 52:10-11.
76. 2 Kings 25:9; 2 Chr. 36:19; Jer. 52:13.
77. This chronology is adapted from that offered by Taylor, *Ezekiel*, p.36.

1. The first series of prophecies (1:1 – 7:27)

1. Cf. Rev. 1:1-3, verses that introduce the first chapter of that book.
2. An explanation as old as Origen (AD 185–254).
3. Num. 4:3,30; 8:24; 1 Chr. 23:24-25; 2 Chr. 31:17; Ezra 3:8; cf. Jesus, Luke 3:23.
4. So Taylor, *Ezekiel,* p.53.
5. Eichrodt, *Ezekiel,* p.52.
6. Cf. Isa. 66:1; Acts 7:48; 17:24.
7. Exod. 33:20; cf. Ezek. 8:3; 40:2.
8. **'Canal'**, as elsewhere in this commentary, translates *nahar*, which means 'stream' or 'river' (cf. 31:4,15; 32:2).
9. 2 Kings 24:8-12; 2 Chr. 36:9-10.
10. Again, 2 Chr. 36:9.
11. Following the collapse of Jerusalem, Jehoiachin was regarded as the true king of Judah (see 2 Kings 25:27-30; Jer. 52:31-34)According to J. B. Pritchard (ed.), *Ancient Near Eastern Texts Relating to the Old Testament* (Princeton: Princeton University Press, 1950), 'From administrative documents found in Babylon, some information concerning the fate of Jehoiachin, king of Judah, can be gathered' (p.308). Thus from text Babylon 28186, reverse ii 13-18, rations for the king of Judah and his five sons are mentioned (cf. 2 Kings 24:17; 2 Chr. 36:10).
12. Again, cf. 2 Kings 24:17; 2 Chr. 36:10.
13. The fourth year of Zedekiah's reign (Jer. 51:59) may have been the fifth year of Jehoiachin's exile (1:2), if Zedekiah's first year was the first full year after accession. See Block, *Ezekiel,* vol. 1, p.87, n.48.
14. Cf. 3:22; 8:1; 33:22; 37:1; 40:1; 1 Kings 18:46; Dan. 8:18; 10:10; Rev. 1:17. **'Chaldeans'** represents the underlying Hebrew *casdim*. 'Chaldaea' is employed by Ezekiel to cover all the Babylonian dominions. From D. J. Wiseman, 'Chaldaea, Chaldeans', in J. D. Douglas (ed.), *The New Bible Dictionary* (London: The Inter-Varsity Fellowship, 1962), pp.203-4.
15. Jer. 51:59.
16. Eph. 3:20.
17. 2 Kings 22 – 23; 2 Chr. 34 – 35.

18. 2 Cor. 12:10.
19. Jer. 1:14,15; 4:6; 6:1.
20. Cf. Exod. 19:9-16.
21. Septuagint: 'electrum', a gold-silver alloy, or amber, or even brass. G. R. Driver argues in favour of 'brass', in that the smelting of brass has been detected in Palestinian remains dating to *c.* 1400–1000 BC ('Ezekiel's Inaugural Vision', *Vetus Testamentum* I, 1951, pp.60-62).
22. Gardiner, *Ezekiel,* p.204.
23. *Calvin's Old Testament Commentaries,* vol. 18: *Ezekiel I (chapters 1 – 12),* translated by D. Foxgrover and D. Martin (Grand Rapids: Eerdmans; Carlisle: Paternoster, 1994), p.24.
24. Gen. 3:24; Exod. 25:17-22; 37:7-9; cf. Ezek. 41:18-20. For the agility of calves, cf. Ps. 29:6; Mal. 4:2.
25. 1 Kings 6:27; cf. Exod. 37:9.
26. Luke 2:34.
27. Luke 2:1; 23:24.
28. Eph. 1:22.
29. NKJV.
30. So Gardiner, *Ezekiel,* p.206.
31. Isa. 46:1.
32. Exod. 20:4; Deut. 5:8.
33. E.g. Gen. 1:6.
34. E.g. Gen. 31:40.
35. Isa. 6:2.
36. Exod. 25:10-22.
37. So Block, *Ezekiel,* vol. 1, p.105.
38. Cf. 1 Sam. 4.
39. So Jer. 3:16.
40. With acknowledgements to Wright, *The Message of Ezekiel,* p.52.
41. Cf. John 4:23; cf. Dan. 7:2.
42. Gen. 1:26-27.
43. So Taylor, *Ezekiel,* p.59.
44. Gen. 9:12-17.
45. Judg. 6:22; 13.
46. Greenhill, *Ezekiel,* p.60; Gardiner, *Ezekiel,* p.207.
47. Rev. 4:2,9,10; 5:1,7,13; 6:16; 7:10,15; 19:4; 21:5.
48. Isa. 7:14; Matt. 1:23; John 14:11.
49. Cf. 2 Cor. 4:6.
50. 1 Peter 1:12 (NKJV).
51. John 1:17.
52. Lev. 8:33 – 9:4.
53. So Gardiner, *Ezekiel,* p.208.
54. Isa. 6:5-7; Dan. 8:18; 10:15-19; Rev. 1:17; cf. Luke 5:10.
55. Cf. Isa. 5:1; Jonah 4:10; Luke 10:6.

56. R. W. Klein, *Ezekiel: The Prophet and His Message* (Columbia, SC: University of South Carolina, 1988), pp.3-4. Cf. Num. 23:19; Job 25:6; Ps. 8:4; Isa. 51:12; 56:2; Dan. 8:17; cf. Dan. 7:13.
57. Cf. Heb. 5:7-9.
58. 2 Kings 17; cf. Ezra 2:2; 3:1; Acts 26:7.
59. Gen. 32:28; cf. Amos 5:5; Hosea 4:15; 5:8; 10:5.
60. Cf. 'hard of neck', or 'stiff-necked', Exod. 32:9; 33:3,5; 34:9; Deut. 9:6,13; 31:27; Isa. 48:4.
61. Isa. 6:9-10.
62. Exod. 3:11 – 4:17; Jer. 1:6; Jonah 1:3.
63. 2 Cor. 2:15-16.
64. Cf. 4:14; Acts 10:14.
65. Cf. Ps. 19:10; 119:103; Jer. 15:16; John 6:53-58; Rev. 10:9-10.
66. Probably papyrus. See Block, *Ezekiel,* vol. 1, p.124.
67. T. J. Betts, *Ezekiel the Priest: A Custodian of Tôrâ* (New York: Peter Lang Publishing, 2005), p.60. Cf. Rev. 5:1.
68. Col. 3:2.
69. 1 Tim. 4:13.
70. Acts 13:15,42,44-48.
71. J. L. Berquist, *Surprises by the River: The Prophecy of Ezekiel* (St Louis, Mo: Chalice Press, 1993), p.32. See Jer. 15:16; Rev. 10:9-10; cf. Ps. 19:10; 119:103.
72. Jer. 20:9; cf. Acts 4:20; 1 Cor. 9:16.
73. Cf. Zech. 7:12.
74. Deut. 6:8; 11:18.
75. Isa. 48:4; cf. Jer. 3:3. John 15:20-21.
76. Cf. Exod. 4:25; Josh. 5:2-3.
77. Isa. 50:7, Jer. 1:18; 15:20.
78. Exod. 32:7, italics added; cf. Dan. 9:24; 10:14.
79. Cf. 8:3; 11:1,24; Acts 8:39.
80. So Taylor, *Ezekiel,* p.67; Block, *Ezekiel,* vol. 1, p.134.
81. Cf. Isa. 6; Rev. 4.
82. Amos 3:8 (NKJV); cf. Jer. 20:8-9.
83. Block, *Ezekiel,* vol. 1, p.135; Eichrodt, *Ezekiel,* p.67.
84. Cf. Job 2:13; also Ezra 9:3; Dan. 4:19.
85. Lev. 8.
86. Cf. 2 Sam. 18:24; 2 Kings 9:17.
87. Hab. 2:1.
88. Jer. 6:17; cf. Isa. 56:10; Hosea 9:8.
89. Exod. 20 – 24.
90. Cf. Gen. 9:5-6; 2 Sam. 12:9.
91. Cf. Matt. 4:1-11; Mark 1:12-13; Luke 4:1-13; James 1:13.
92. Isa. 8:14; cf. Rom. 9:32-33; 1 Cor. 1:23; 1 Peter 2:8.
93. Luke 1:6.
94. With acknowledgements to Gardiner, *Ezekiel,* p.212.
95. Jer. 37:21; 38:6.

96. Conceivably, the restraint might have been the resentment shown to Ezekiel by his hearers, or even a form of house arrest (cf. Jeremiah's experiences: Jer. 20:1-2; 29:26-28; 36:5-19; 37 – 38).
97. Taylor, *Ezekiel*, p.74.
98. Acts 20:26-27.
99. 1 Cor. 9:16.
100. Ezekiel was by no means the only prophet who employed acted signs: cf. Ahijah (1 Kings 11:30); Zedekiah (1 Kings 22:11); Elisha (2 Kings 13:15-19); Isaiah (Isa. 20:2-4); Jeremiah (Jer. 13:1-14; 19:1-13); Agabus (Acts 21:10-11).
101. Cf. Jer. 27 – 29.
102. The Hebrew calendar year was comprised of lunar months, which began when the thin crescent moon was first visible at sunset. The month would consist of twenty-nine/thirty days, with 354 days for the lunar year. The fourteen months or 413 days between 1:2 and 8:1 would therefore be (7 x 30) + (7 x 29). See Taylor, *Ezekiel*, p.79.
103. With acknowledgements to Gardiner, *Ezekiel*, p.348.
104. The Qumran *Damascus Rule* 1:5-11 interprets the 390 years as the infliction of wrath after the destruction of Jerusalem. C. Rabin (ed.), *The Zadokite Documents* (Oxford: OUP, 1954), p.1; and G. Vermes, *The Dead Sea Scrolls in English* (London: Penguin Books, 1987 [first published 1962]), p.83.
105. Cf. the explanations in Exod. 28:38; Num. 18:1.
106. So Deut. 26:6-8; Hosea 2:14; 8:13; 9:3; 11:5.
107. Again, Exod. 12:40-41; cf. Gal. 3:17.
108. The relevant Old Testament references and possible dates are:

References

1 Kings 2:11; 1 Chronicles 29:27 — David reigned seven years over Judah and thirty-three years over Israel.
1 Kings 6:1 — 480 years after the Exodus, and in the fourth year of Solomon's reign, the second month, the construction of the temple commenced.
2 Chronicles 3:2 — construction began on the second day of the second month of the fourth year of his reign.
1 Kings 6:38 — in the eleventh year of Solomon's reign, the eighth month, the temple was finished (i.e. it was seven and a half years in building).
2 Chronicles 8:1 — Solomon took twenty years to build the temple and his palace.
1 Kings 11:42; 2 Chronicles 9:30 — Solomon reigned for forty years.

Possible dates

1876 BC — descent of Jacob into Egypt, leading to a 430-year sojourn.
1446 BC — the departure of Israel from Egypt, 480 years before the construction of the temple.
1010 BC — accession of David to the throne of Judah.
1003 BC — accession of David to the united throne of Israel.
970 BC — accession of Solomon to the united throne of Israel.
966 BC — commencement of the construction of the temple (480 years after the Exodus; or 440 years after the initial exodus, after another forty years in the wilderness, allowing five years for the initial conquest — Josh. 14:10 — totalling 485 years).
959 BC — the completion of the temple.
930 BC — accession of Rehoboam.
586 BC — the destruction of the temple, 380 years after its construction had begun.

109. 2 Kings 17.
110. Cf. 18:19-20; 23:35; Lev. 19:8; Num. 14:33-34; Isa. 53:11, which refer to bearing the consequences of sin.
111. So 2:3-5; 3:4,5,7,9,17,26,27; cf. 4:3,4,13; 5:4; 6:11; 8:6,10,12 etc. A good concordance will confirm the assertion. I am indebted to Wright, *The Message of Ezekiel,* pp.78-9, for his exposition.
112. Cf. 15:7; 20:46; Lev. 17:10; 20:3,5,6; 26:17; 2 Chr. 20:3.
113. Cf. Isa. 52:10.
114. Dan. 1:8; 1 Cor. 8 – 10.
115. So, Block, *Ezekiel,* vol. 1, p.185.
116. Deut. 23:11-13; Josh. 22:19; Amos 7:17.
117. Acts 10:14.
118. Lev. 17:11-16; Deut. 12:16.
119. Lev. 7:18; 19:7.
120. Isa. 65:4.
121. Job 1:20; Isa. 22:12; Jer. 7:29; Micah 1:16; Num. 6:18.
122. Lev. 19:27; Deut. 14:1.
123. Cf. 2 Sam. 10:4.
124. Lev. 21:5; Ezek. 44:20.
125. Cf. Hag. 2:12.
126. It has been argued by some that this fire was a fire of purification rather than of judgement. But this makes **'fire'** mean two different things, which does not fit the context.
127. With acknowledgements to Block, *Ezekiel,* vol. 1, p.195.
128. Rom. 2:12, cf. Isa. 22:1-14.
129. Cf. Rom. 2:14.
130. Gardiner, *Ezekiel,* p.350.
131. NKJV; cf. Rom. 7:5.
132. Cf. Isa. 2:2-5; Micah 4:1-5; Amos 3:2.
133. Cf., too, Gen. 27:42 and Isa. 1:24 for the language of revenge.

134. Deut. 32:15-18.
135. Lev. 26:29; Deut. 28:53-57; cf. 2 Kings 6:28-29; Isa. 9:19-21; Jer. 19:9; Zech. 11:9.
136. 1 Thess. 2:13-16; cf. Heb. 8:13.
137. Cf. Deut. 7:16; 13:8; 19:13,21; 25:12.
138. As narrated by 2 Kings 25:1-21; 2 Chr. 36:17-21; Jer. 39:1-18.
139. Cf. Gen. 27:42; Isa. 1:24; Deut. 28:63.
140. Gen. 12:3; 18:18; 22:18; 26:4; 28:14; cf. Acts 3:25; Gal. 3:8.
141. Deut. 26:19; 28:1-14.
142. Lev. 26:22,31-33; Deut. 29:23-28.
143. Block, *Ezekiel,* vol. 1, pp.218-19, gives unmistakable parallels.
144. Cf. Deut. 28:1-14; 28:15-68.
145. Deut. 32:5; cf. Matt. 17:17; Acts 2:40; Phil. 2:15.
146. Exod. 19:8; 24:3,7; 32:1-35.
147. Cf. Deut. 12:2-3; 2 Kings 17:10-11; Jer. 2:20; 3:6; Hosea 4:13.
148. 1 Sam. 9:14; 1 Kings 3:2,4.
149. 2 Kings 18:4; 23:4-20; 2 Chr. 31:1.
150. 2 Kings 21:3; 2 Chr. 33:3.
151. Gen. 31:21; 1 Kings 2:15.
152. Cf. 13:17; 21:2; 25:2; 28:21; 38:2.
153. Cf. Dan. 6:10.
154. With acknowledgements to Block, *Ezekiel,* vol. 1, p.222.
155. Cf. 2 Chr. 34:4. See Block, *Ezekiel,* vol. 1, p.225.
156. Cf. Num. 9:6-10; 2 Kings 23:14,16.
157. Taylor, *Ezekiel,* p.91, among others.
158. Judg. 6:31.
159. 2 Kings 23:20; Ps. 53:5; 141:7; Jer. 8:1-2.
160. Exod. 17:14.
161. 2 Kings 21:13; cf. Gen. 6:7; 7:4.
162. NKJV; cf. Jer. 7:33.
163. Cf. 21:14,17; 22:13; 25:6; Num. 24:10.
164. Gen. 35:8; 1 Chr. 10:12.
165. Cf. Gen. 8:20-21; Exod. 29:18,25,41; and frequently in Leviticus.
166. Cf. 1 Sam. 23:14,15,24; 25:1.
167. 2 Kings 19:32; 2 Chr. 32:1-23; Isa. 37:33.
168. As noted by Taylor, *Ezekiel,* p.92.
169. Amos 5:18-20.
170. Isa. 13:1-16; Zeph. 1:7-18.
171. As also 11:17; 12:19,22; 13:9; 18:2; 20:38,42; 21:2,3; 25:3,6; 33:24; 36:6; 37:12; 38:18,19.
172. Cf. Isa. 11:12; Rev. 7:1.
173. Amos 8:2.
174. Cf. 14:19; 28:23; Exod. 15:7; Ps. 78:49.
175. Luke 15:11-32.

176. Cf. Nahum 1:9.
177. Cf. Amos 8:2.
178. But cf. Isa. 16:10 for a related noun.
179. Gen. 22:14; Exod. 17:15.
180. Taylor, *Ezekiel,* p.93.
181. Cf. Israelite arrogance in Jer. 50:31-32.
182. But compare with a related word in Exod. 15:2; Jer. 6:2.
183. So Taylor, *Ezekiel,* p.94.
184. Lev. 25:14,27-28.
185. Cf. Gen. 14:10; 19:17,19; Josh. 2:16,22; Judg. 6:2; 1 Sam. 13:6; 23:14; Matt. 24:16; Mark 13:14 for mountains as refuges.
186. For baldness as a mark of shame, cf. Isa. 3:24; 15:2; Jer. 7:29; 16:6; Micah 1:16.
187. As did Manasseh, 2 Kings 21:7; 2 Chr. 33:2-9.
188. Cf. Ps. 75:8; 101:8; 119:119.
189. Cf. Nahum 3:10; Eccles. 12:6; Isa. 40:19.
190. Cf. Deut. 28:49-50.
191. Cf. Luke 21:26.
192. Cf. 1 Sam. 28:15; Prov. 1:28.
193. Cf. 1 Sam. 3:1.
194. Jer. 18:18 (NKJV).
195. 1 Chr. 22:1.
196. NKJV.
197. Matt. 5:24.
198. Acts 17:6.
199. 1 Cor. 10:13.
200. Heb. 4:16.
201. Rev. 20:13.
202. Exod. 19:5-6 (NKJV); cf. 1 Peter 2:9.
203. See Jer. 31; cf. Heb. 8:7-13.
204. NKJV.
205. Matt. 16:18; cf. Matt. 28:18.
206 Dan. 11:38.
207. Ps. 91:4.

2 — The second series of prophecies (8:1 – 19:14)
1. Wright, *The Message of Ezekiel,* p.97.
2. Jer. 28:2.
3. So Block, *Ezekiel,* vol. 1, p.278.
4. Cf. Exod. 33:20.
5. Cf. 2 Kings 21:4-7; 2 Chr. 33:7,15.
6. So Wright, *The Message of Ezekiel,* p.99.
7. 2 Kings 16:14.
8. 2 Kings 21:7; 2 Chr. 33:15.
9. Jer. 7:17-19; 44:18-19.
10. Lev. 1:11.
11. Cf. 1 Kings 6:5.

12. 2 Kings 24:12-16.
13. 2 Kings 22:3,14; Jer. 29:3; 36:10; 39:14.
14. Jer. 26:24.
15. With acknowledgements to Taylor, *Ezekiel,* p.99.
16. Num. 16; 2 Chr. 26:16-21.
17. Cf. the seventy mentioned in Exod. 24:1-14; Num. 11:16; see also 1 Kings 12:31.
18. Cf. Ps. 10:11; 94:7.
19. Cf. Num. 33:52.
20. Cf. Jer. 7:10.
21. See Block, *Ezekiel,* vol. 1, p.295. D. J. Halperin observes that '... the roots of the cult are tangled and complex. The prototype of Tammuz, the Sumerian Dumuzzi, was perhaps originally a historical person, a king of the first dynasty of Uruk ... but he was also perceived as a vegetation god or numen of some sort' (*Seeking Ezekiel: Text and Psychology,* Pennsylvania State University Press, 1993, p.122).
22. 1 Chr. 24:5-18; 2 Chr. 36:14.
23. Deut. 4:19; 17:3; cf. 2 Kings 23:5,11.
24. Joel 2:17.
25. So Block, *Ezekiel,* vol. 1, p.297, n.76.
26. Cf. Prov. 1:24-28; Matt. 7:22-23.
27. Exod. 32:1-6.
28. Exod. 32:10-13; cf. Num. 14:12-19.
29. Exod. 33:12-23.
30. 1 Kings 18.
31. 1 Kings 19:1-13.
32. Gen. 15:7.
33. Matt. 1:1-17.
34. NKJV.
35. Cf. Rom. 9:15-16.
36. Rom. 9:17.
37. Thomas, *God Strengthens,* p.76.
38. Reading 'approach' (*qr'bû*) as a *Pi'él* imperative rather than as a *Qal* perfect, which would yield, 'they have come near'.
39. Cf. Gen. 18:1-2; Josh. 5:13; Judg. 13:11; Dan. 8:16.
40. Cf. Jer. 1:15.
41. Cf. Exod. 28:31-43; Lev. 16:4; Dan. 10:5.
42. From *qeset hasôpér*, *qeset* apparently being an Egyptian loan-word.
43. 2 Chr. 4:1; 2 Kings 16:14.
44. Exod. 25:18-22; 37:7-9; cf. Num. 7:89.
45. Taylor, *Ezekiel,* p.102.
46. Cf. Rev. 7:3; 9:4; 14:1.
47. Cf. the high priest's apparel, Exod. 28:36-38.
48. Cf. the blood of Passover smeared on the doorposts and lintels of Hebrew houses, Exod. 12:7.

49. Cf. Job 31:35.
50. Exod. 12:12-13.
51. Cf. 1 Peter 4:17.
52. Gen. 19:22-25; 2 Peter 2:6-8.
53. Num. 19:11; cf. 1 Kings 13:2; 2 Kings 23:16.
54. 1 Kings 2:28-34.
55. Gen. 18:22-32; Amos 7:1-6.
56. 2 Kings 15:29; 17:1-6; 24:1-20.
57. 2 Sam. 24:16; 1 Chr. 21:15.
58. Gen. 6:8-9,12.
59. Cf. Rom. 5:12,19-20.
60. Cf. Acts 2:40; 1 Peter 1:18.
61. So Taylor, *Ezekiel,* p.106.
62. 1 Kings 6:29,35; 7:29,36.
63. For Yahweh seated above the cherubim, cf. 1 Sam. 4:4; 2 Sam. 6:2; 2 Kings 19:15; 1 Chr. 13:6; Ps. 80:1; 99:1.
64. So Block, *Ezekiel,* vol. 1, p.321.
65. Gen. 19:24.
66. Deut. 4:24; cf. Heb. 12:29.
67. There is a measure of supposition in my interpretation of the movement of the divine glory. Commentators such as J. W. Wevers, *Ezekiel* (New Century Bible Commentary, Eerdmans, Grand Rapids, and Marshall, Morgan & Scott, London, 1982 [first published, 1969]), p.73, and Cooke, *A Critical and Exegetical Commentary on ... Ezekiel,* p.114, see a problem here. But not if one assumes a pluperfect sense, as suggested in this commentary.
68. Cf. Gen. 3:24.
69. Block, *Ezekiel,* vol. 1, p.324.
70. 2 Cor. 2:16.
71. Matt. 21:43 (NKJV).
72. Wevers, *Ezekiel,* pp.75-6.
73. As shown by Block, *Ezekiel,* vol. 1, p.329.
74. Cf. Jer. 26:10.
75. Cf. 1 Chr. 27:1-22.
76. Taylor, *Ezekiel,* p.108, n.2.
77. Jer. 35:3.
78. 2 Kings 25:23; Jer. 40:8; 42:1.
79. Jer. 21:8-10.
80. M. Luther, *A Commentary on St Paul's Epistle to the Galatians* (London: James Clarke & Co. Ltd., 1961 [based on the 'Middleton' edition of the English version, 1575]), p.418.
81. Cf. Jer. 11:20; 12:3; 17:10; Ps. 26:2; 139:1-6,23.
82. Micah 3:1-3.
83. Cf. Jer. 39:4-7; 52:7-11.
84. 1 Sam. 8:5.
85. See 1 Sam. 8:8.
86. So Block, *Ezekiel,* vol. 1, p.338.

87. Cf. Deut. 18:22.
88. Lev. 25:23-34,47-55; Num. 35:19-28; Ruth 3:6-13; 4:1-12; cf. Jer. 32:7-8.
89. Cf. David's lament, 1 Sam. 26:19.
90. Cf. the perception of Naaman the Syrian, 2 Kings 5:15-19.
91. So Block, *Ezekiel,* vol. 1, p.349.
92. Cf. John 2:19-22; 4:21; cf. Acts 7:48; 17:24.
93. Gen. 12:7; 13:14-15; 15:18; 17:8.
94. Num. 14:3-4.
95. Cf. Acts 2:40; 1 Peter 1:18.
96. Cf. 1 Chr. 12:33; Ps. 12:2; 86:11.
97. Jer. 24:7; 31:33; 32:39; cf. Ps. 51:10; Acts 4:32.
98. Cf. Exod. 19:4-6; Lev. 26:12; Deut. 29:13; 2 Cor. 6:16; 1 Peter 2:9; Rev. 21:3.
99. Cf. Heb. 8:8-13; 10:16-18.
100. Cf. Luke 22:20; 1 Cor. 11:25.
101. 1 Kings 19:18; cf. Rom. 11:4-5.
102. Cf. Matt. 24:1-3; Luke 19:37-44; cf. Luke 24:50-51; Acts 1:9,12.
103. Lev. 26; Deut. 28; and also Deut. 17:14-20, which anticipated that Israel, when settled, would desire a king 'like all the nations' round about.
104. Cf. Matt. 6:33; 7:26.
105. So Taylor, *Ezekiel,* p.110.
106. 2 Chr. 36:22-23; Ezra 2:1-70.
107. Ezra 10:1-44; Neh. 13:23-31.
108. Contrary, for example, to Cooke, *A Critical and Exegetical Commentary on ... Ezekiel,* p.125.
109. The following, among others, are silent as to when 11:16-17 may be fulfilled: G. Beasley-Murray, 'Ezekiel', in The *New Bible Commentary, Revised,* eds. D. Guthrie and others (London: Inter-Varsity Press, 1970), pp.664-87 (see p.671); Block, *Ezekiel,* vol. 1, pp.349-54; Clements, *Ezekiel,* p.49; Gardiner, *Ezekiel,* p.231; Wevers, *Ezekiel,* p.79; Wright, *The Message of Ezekiel,* p.124.

Cooper, writing from a premillennial point of view, asserts that the realization will occur 'in a future Messianic age' (*Ezekiel,* p.144). Yet do we not find ourselves *now* in the Messianic age?
110. Rom. 11:5.
111. Cf. Isa. 6:9; 65:2; Jer. 5:21; Matt. 13:14-15; Mark 4:12; 8:18; Luke 8:10; John 9:39; 12:40; Acts 28:26-27; Rom. 10:21.
112. Cf. Jer. 27:16; 28:1-4; 29:8,10,21-23,31-32.
113. Cf. Exod. 12:11,33; and Jer. 46:19, where Egypt is summoned to prepare for exile.
114. Taylor, *Ezekiel,* p.115.
115. So Block, *Ezekiel,* vol. 1, p.370.
116. Cf. Jer. 39:2.
117. For **'dusk'**, cf. 12:7; Gen. 15:17.

118. 2 Kings 25:4-7; Jer. 39:4-7; 52:7-11.
119. Cf. the experience of Shallum, son of Josiah, Jer. 22:11-12.
120. Cf. Hosea 7:12; Lam. 1:13.
121. Block suggests that the land which Zedekiah will not see is his homeland, rather than Babylon (*Ezekiel,* vol. 1, p.378). But as **'Babylon'** is the nearest antecedent to **'it'**, the usual interpretation might stand.
122. Cf. the allies of Ben-hadad, 1 Kings 20:16; see also 1 Chr. 12:1.
123. Cf. Jer. 41:16 – 43:7.
124. Exod. 32:12.
125. Cf. Jer. 22:8-9.
126. Cf. 7:27; 22:29; 33:2; 39:13; 45:16,22; 46:3,9.
127. NKJV.
128. Cf. 1 Kings 13:4; 18:4,13,16-46; 22; 2 Kings 2:23-25; 17:13-14; 2 Chr. 24:20-22; Isa. 28:7-13; Jer. 20:1-6; 36; Dan. 9:10; Amos 7:10-17; Micah 2:11; 3:5-7; Matt. 23:29-32; Acts 7:52; 13:40-41; 28:23-27.
129. Cf. Jer. 5:12-13; 17:15,18.
130. Cf. Isa. 1:1; 2:1; Amos 1:1; Obad. 1; Micah 1:1. The prophets 'saw' the divine word.
131. False prophecy was, it appears, almost endemic in the early churches (cf. 1 Thess. 5:20-21; 2 Thess. 2:1-3; 1 John 2:18-23; 4:1-3).
132. Cf. Eccles. 8:11; Amos 6:3; Matt. 24:43; Luke 12:39-40; 1 Thess. 5:3; Rev. 3:3; 16:15.
133. Cf. Num. 23:19; Isa. 55:11.
134. Matt. 25:13.
135. Jer. 23; cf. Jer. 14:13-18; 27:1 – 28:17.
136. Jer. 29:8-9,21.
137. Jer. 29:10; cf. Jer. 25:12.
138. Cf. 1 Kings 19:10,14.
139. Cf. Jer. 23:16; cf. Num. 16:28; 1 Kings 12:33.
140. Taylor, *Ezekiel,* p.120; cf. Ps. 14:1; 74:18; 1 Sam. 25:3,25; Isa. 32:6.
141, NKJV.
142. Cf. Lam. 5:18.
143. Eichrodt, *Ezekiel,* p.163.
144. There are two rare Hebrew verb-forms in 13:6: the *Pi'éls* of *yhl* and of *qûm,* telling that the false prophets chose to believe that their utterances were self-fulfilling.
145. With acknowledgements to Block, *Ezekiel,* vol. 1, p.404. For the **'hand'** of Yahweh being **'against'** his adversaries, cf. 6:14; 14:9.13; 16:27; 25:7,13,16; 35:3.
146. Cf. Jer. 23:18,22.
147. Cf. Exod. 32:32-33; Ps. 69:28; Isa. 4:3; Dan. 12:1.
148. Cf. Jer. 23:17; Micah 3:5.

149. Cf. 22:28; Jer. 23:13; Lam. 2:14.
150. Acts 23:3; cf. Matt. 23:27.
151. Block, *Ezekiel*, vol. 1, p.407.
152. This commentary stays with the Masoretic Text, which is vocative, addressing the hail.
153. Cf. Matt. 7:24-27; Luke 6:48-49.
154. Cf. Micah 1:6.
155. Cf. Noadiah (Neh. 6:14), and Rev. 2:20, which mentions a false prophetess, 'Jezebel', at Thyatira. That Yahweh did speak through the lips of inspired women is certain. Cf. Exod. 15:20; Judg. 4:4; 2 Kings 22:14; 2 Chr. 34:22; Isa. 8:3; Luke 2:36; Acts 21:9; 1 Cor. 11:5.
156. Cf. Exod. 32:7.
157. Cf. the witch of En-dor, 1 Sam. 28:3-25.
158. 'My hands' (*yaday*) may be an anomalous plural form. So Block, *Ezekiel*, vol. 1, p.410, n.4, p.414.
159. Cf. 13:9,10,19,21,23; 14:8,9.
160. Block, *Ezekiel*, vol. 1, p.416.
161. Cf. 1 Sam. 9:7-8; 1 Kings 14:3; Micah 3:5.
162. The Hebrew *l'phôrchôt* could mean that the victims were being hunted 'as birds' or, better, that they would be delivered by Yahweh so that they could fly away as freed birds.
163. 'Discourage' is from the *Hiph'il* of *ka'ah*, unique in the Old Testament: 'because you have caused the heart of the righteous to be despondent'.
164. 2 Peter 1:20-21 (NKJV).
165. Cf. Isa. 40:8; 1 Peter 1:24-25.
166. 1 Cor. 11:19.
167. Jude 3.
168. Acts 19:19 (NKJV).
169. 2 Tim. 4:3.
170. Gen. 19:26; Luke 17:31-32.
171. E. Kautsch, *Gesenius' Hebrew Grammar*, translated by A. E. Cowley (Oxford: Clarendon Press, 2nd edition, 1966 [first published 1910]), p.136.
172. Num. 22:20.
173. 1 Kings 22:15-28.
174. Cf. Eph. 5:5; Col. 3:5; 1 John 5:21.
175. Jer. 31:33.
176. Intransitive *Qal* once; intransitive *Hiph'il* once; transitive *Hiph'il* once. The assonance is striking.
177. Cf. Esth. 8:17.
178. Cf. Lev. 17:10; 20:3,5,6; Ps. 34:16; Jer. 44:11. With acknowledgements to Block, *Ezekiel*, vol. 1, p.430.
179. Cf. Num. 17:10.
180. Cf. Balaam, Num. 31:8; Micaiah, 1 Kings 22:18-28; see also Jer. 4:10; 20:7; 23:16-17.

181. Cf. 2 Thess. 2:11-12.
182. Cf. Lev. 7:18; 20:17; Num. 5:31; 9:13; 30:15.
183. Taylor, *Ezekiel,* p.128.
184. Gen. 18:23-32.
185. Cf. Josh. 6:18-19; 22:20.
186. See 15:8; 17:20; 18:24; 20:27; 39:23,26.
187. E.g. Exod. 3:8; 5:23; 6:6; 18:8-10; Judg. 6:9; 1 Sam. 10:18.
188. Dan. 1:8-9; 9:23; 10:11-12; Ezek. 28:3. Not a few commentators hold that the 'Daniel' mentioned by Ezekiel was not the biblical Daniel but was probably someone named 'Dan'el' who occurs in an ancient Canaanite epic discovered in 1930 at Ras Shamra, the ancient Ugarit, on the north Syrian coast, dating from about 1400 BC (e.g. Taylor, *Ezekiel,* p.129; Eichrodt, *Ezekiel,* p.189). The present commentary takes the view that when he spoke to Ezekiel, Yahweh was pointing to the biblical Daniel. More than two millennia have passed since the time of Ezekiel, during which, according to the 'Dan'el' hypothesis, multitudes must have been mistaken in their identification of Daniel. Is this likely?
189. Job 1:1 (NKJV); cf. Job 1:8; 2:3; 42:7.
190. Gen. 6:18; Job 42:8-10.
191. Dan. 1:8-20.
192. For **'judgements'**, cf. 5:10,15; 11:9; 16:41; 25:11; 28:22,26; 30:14,19.
193. So Cooke, *A Critical and Exegetical Commentary on ... Ezekiel,* p.154. For **'deeds'**, cf. 14:23; 20:43-44; 24:14; 36:17,19; Jer. 4:18; 7:3,5.
194. Cf. 2 Tim. 2:13.
195. Cf. Rom. 9:6.
196. 2 Chr. 16:12.
197. Matt. 11:23.
198. With acknowledgements to Taylor, *Ezekiel,* p.128.
199. Contrary to the versions, **'what becomes of the wood of the vine...?'** leads into what is probably not a contrast between the wood of the vine and other trees. Cf. Gen. 37:20; Judg. 13:12; 1 Kings 14:3; Eccles. 6:12; 11:2. With acknowledgements to Block, *Ezekiel,* vol. 1, p.456.
200. See Ps. 80:8-13; Isa. 5:1-7; Jer. 2:21; Hosea 10:1; cf. John 15:1-8.
201. For a metaphorical use of the wooden peg, see Isa. 22:23-25.
202. So Gen. 12:7 onwards.
203. John 15:6.
204. Rom. 11:17-24.
205. Gal. 5:19-22.
206. So Wright, *The Message of Ezekiel,* p.128.
207. Hosea 2:1 – 3:5.
208. Cf. Lev. 26:40-44; Deut. 30:1-10.

209. This presents a problem for both a translator and commentator. Are they to dilute Ezekiel's language to avoid offending the modern reader, or should they seek to reflect the shock that must have been felt by Ezekiel's initial hearers, people who would have known exactly what he meant?
210. Cf. Deut. 7:1-5.
211. Josh. 18:28; Judg. 19:10-11; 2 Sam. 5:6; 24:16-25; 1 Chr. 11:4-5; 21:15-28.
212. See Block, *Ezekiel,* vol. 1, p.474.
213. Deut. 26:5.
214. The Hebrew behind the proposed **'smooth'**, *l'mishi*, occurs only here and is unknown beyond the Old Testament. The translation is, therefore, possible although conjectural. See F. Brown, S. R. Driver and C. A. Briggs, *A Hebrew and English Lexicon of the Old Testament* (Oxford; Clarendon Press, 1959 [first published, 1907]), p.1044.
215. W. H. Brownlee quotes E. W. G. Masterman, who wrote in 1918 concerning 'the Palestinian custom', 'As soon as the navel is cut the midwife rubs the child all over with salt, water, and oil, and tightly swathes it in clothes [cloths?] for seven days; at the end of that time she removes the dirty clothes [cloths?], washes the child and anoints it, and then wraps it up again for seven days — and so on till the fortieth day' (W. H. Brownlee, *Ezekiel 1-19,* Word Biblical Commentary, vol. 28, Waco: Word Books, 1986, p.223).
216. Cf. Ps. 105:16-24.
217. Gen. 15:13; Exod. 12:40.
218. Cf. Exod. 19:5-6; 24:8; Deut. 5:2.
219. Prov. 2:17; Mal. 2:14.
220. Cf. Ruth 3:9.
221. See Deut. 22:13-21.
222. Cf. Ruth 3:3.
223. Cf. Exod. 25:5; Num. 4:6.
224. Cf. Gen. 24:22.
225. Gen. 24:47; Isa. 3:21; Hosea 2:13.
226. Cf. Isa. 62:3; 7:15.
227. Cf. Solomon, 1 Kings 10:23; 2 Chr. 9; Matt. 6:29.
228. Cf. Deut. 32:15; 6:10-12.
229. Cf. Prov. 7:16-17.
230. 1 Kings 11:1-13; 13:1-2.
231. Cf. Hosea 2:2-13; Exod. 32:2-4; Judg. 8:24-27.
232. 2 Kings 16:3; 17:17; 21:6; 23:10; 2 Chr. 28:3; 33:6; Jer. 32:35; cf. Lev. 18:21; 20:2.
233. Cf. Prov. 26:11; 2 Peter 2:22.
234. 2 Chr. 28:24-25.
235 Cf. Isa. 20:5-6; 30:1-5; 31:1; Hosea 7:8-11.
236. Respectively, Exod. 32; 1 Kings 12:28-32; 1 Kings 3:1.

237. **'Flesh'** stands for the male reproductive organ in 23:20; 44:7,9; Gen. 17:11,14,23,24,25; Exod. 28:42.
238. Exod. 12:12.
239. Jer. 37:5-10.
240. See 25:15-16; 2 Chr. 26:7; 28:18; Jer. 25:20; 47:1-7; Zech. 9:6.
241. 2 Kings 16:7-18; 20:12-15; 2 Chr. 32:31; Isa. 39:1-8.
242. See also Isa. 23:8; Hosea 12:7: Zeph. 1:11.
243. See Deut. 23:18; Isa. 23:17-18; Hosea 9:1; Micah 1:7.
244. English versions usually identify *n'hûshtek*, translated here as **'your discharge'**, as 'brass' a contemptuous term for money. But see Block, *Ezekiel*, vol. 1, p.500, who argues that the term is related to an Akkadian verb meaning 'to overflow'. Brown, Driver and Briggs also hint at this interpretation (*A Hebrew Lexicon*, p.639), which is adopted in the present commentary.
245. D. L. Smith-Christopher notes that '... it was the circumstances and practices of warfare by the Mesopotamian imperial states of the first millennium BCE that suggested the imagery of stripping, and not a generally practised punishment of adulterous women in Israelite society' ('Ezekiel in Abu Ghraib: rereading Ezekiel 16:37-39', in *Ezekiel's Hierarchical World: Wrestling with a Tired Reality,* eds. S. L. Cook and C. L. Patton, Atlanta, Ga.: Society of Biblical Literature, 2004, p.153). This would give a terrifying substance to Ezekiel's words.
246. For stoning see Lev. 20:2; cf. John 8:5; for the sword see Deut. 13:15.
247. Lev. 20:14; 21:9; cf. Deut. 13:16; Josh. 7:25.
248. R. V. G. Tasker, *The Biblical Doctrine of the Wrath of God*, p.v, as cited by Taylor, *Ezekiel*, p.140.
249 J. Galambush, *Jerusalem in the Book of Ezekiel: The City as Jahweh's Wife* (Atlanta, Ga.: Scholars Press, 1992), p.159.
250. Cf. Neh. 13:23-29.
251. Gen. 19:1-29.
252. Taylor, *Ezekiel,* p.141.
253. Matt. 11:23.
254. See Gen. 19:14-15.
255. 1 Kings 12:28.
256. 2 Kings 17:3-23.
257. Cf. Jer. 3:11.
258. Brown, Driver and Briggs, *A Hebrew Lexicon,* p.813. Cf. Gen. 48:11 for a similar construction: Jacob never expected to see Joseph's face.
259. 25:15; 2 Kings 15:37; 16:6; 24:2, 2 Chr. 28:18-19.
260. Lev. 26:42,45.
261. See especially Jer. 29:14; 30:3,18; 31:23; 32:44; 33:7,11,26; Lam. 2:14. With acknowledgements to Block, *Ezekiel*, vol. 2, p.513.

262. Cf. Deut. 30:1-10; Jer. 33:6-9.
263. Gen. 12:7 onwards.
264. See Isa. 1:9-10; 3:9; 13:19; Jer. 49:18; 50:40; Amos 4:11.
265. Some commentators read 'Edom' for **'Aram'**, although the Septuagint gives 'Syria', presupposing a Hebrew *aram*.
266. Exod. 32.
267. Cf. Rom. 7:7.
268. Gen. 15:12-21; Exod. 2:24; 3:1-6; 24:1-11; Deut. 4:36-37; Gal. 3:18-19.
269. Deut. 18:15,18; 2 Sam. 7:5-16.
270. Isa. 55:3.
271. Cf. Heb. 8:8-12; 10:16-17. See my comments covering 33:12 and the endnote.

In my opinion, H. L. Ellison's comments regarding chapters 36 and 37 are valuable:

> It is beyond any cavil or question that what the Lord promises Israel, 36:24-27; Jer. 31:31-34, is what He has done to us in Jesus Christ. The fulfilment for Israel can neither be greater nor less nor other than for us. Yet it is noteworthy that the former passage is not quoted in the New Testament, and though the latter lies behind Mark 14:24 and parallels, and is quoted in Heb. 8:8-12 and 10:16f., it is given in terms of description rather than fulfilment, by which I mean that there is no suggestion that the promise has been exhausted in the Church's enjoyment of it (*Ezekiel: The Man and his Message,* London: Paternoster, 1956, p.129).

272. Cf. 2 Cor. 4:6 and context.
273. Cf. Rom. 1:16.
274. Eph. 5:23-27.
275. 2 Kings 24:8-20; 2 Chr. 36:1-21; Jer. 37; 52.
276. Judg. 14:10-20.
277. Matt. 13:11-13.
278. Cf. Isa. 23:8; Hosea 12:7; Zeph. 1:11.
279. Cf. Jer. 48:40; 49:22 for a similar picture.
280. 2 Kings 24:6-17.
281. 2 Kings 24:17. Or, his brother, according to 2 Chr. 36:10.
282. It is grammatically possible that **'lift himself up'** should be translated 'might not lift itself [i.e. the kingdom] up'. But the former might be better in that the burden of the passage is upon Zedekiah's treachery.
283. 2 Kings 24:19.
284. Jer. 51:59.
285. D. A. Horovitz, ed., *An Introduction to the Language of Scripture* (Jerusalem: The Hebrew University, 1971), p.27.

286. 'To act for him in war' translates a Hebrew idiom which elsewhere can mean 'to act against in war' (see 7:27; 16:59; 22:14; 23:25,29; 39:24). But cf. 20:44, which *must* be translated with 'for' rather than 'against'.
287. See Josh. 9:15; 2 Sam. 21:1-2.
288. Isa. 11:1; cf. 2 Sam. 3:39; 1 Chr. 22:5; 29:1; Isa. 53:2.
289. Jer. 23:5; 33:15.
290. Cf. Ps. 78:67-72; 132:10-18; see also Ps. 2:6; Isa. 2:2-4; Micah 4:1-2.
291. Cf. 1 Sam. 2:1-10; Luke 1:52-55.
292. Cf. John 18:36.
293. Cf. 2 Sam. 7.
294. Cf. Acts 17:27.
295. NKJV.
296. NKJV.
297. Cf. Exod. 34:7; Deut. 5:9.
298. Wright, *The Message of Ezekiel,* p.181.
299. Exod. 20:5; Deut. 5:9.
300. Exod. 32:1-6; 34:7.
301. Jer. 32:18.
302. Jer. 15:4.
303. Matt. 23:34-36 (NKJV).
304. 2 Kings 14:6; cf. the sons of Korah, Num. 26:11. One can contrast with the Code of Hammurabi, ruler of Babylon possibly *c.* 1792–1750 BC. For example, Laws 209 and 210 state that 'If a man strike a free-born woman so that she lose her unborn child, he shall pay ten shekels for her loss. If the woman die, *his* daughter shall be put to death' (emphasis added). Exodus 21:22-23, referring to a similar situation, does not transfer the death penalty to an innocent relative. From W. J. Martin, 'Hammurabi', in *The New Bible Dictionary.*
305. Deut. 6:5; cf. Exod. 20:5; 34:7; Deut. 5:9; Jer. 32:18-19; Lam. 5:7; Matt. 23:35-36.
306. Acts 2:40; cf. 1 Peter 1:18.
307. Cf. Isa. 22:13; 1 Cor. 15:32.
308. Jer. 31:29.
309. Wright, *The Message of Ezekiel,* p.184.
310. Cf. Eph. 2:1,5.
311. Insofar as it is possible to employ black-and-white categories such as 'evil' and 'righteous'.
312. Ps. 33:5; 89:14; 97:2; Jer. 9:24 (cf. 1 Cor. 1:31; 2 Cor. 10:17).
313. Taylor, *Ezekiel,* p.45.
314. Cf. Exod. 20:14; Lev. 15:24; 18:6-23; 20:10-21; Deut. 4:19; 5:18; 12:2-3; 22:22.
315. Cf. Exod. 22:21-27; Lev. 19:33; 25:14,17,35-37; Deut. 24:6,10-13; Ps. 15:5.
316. Cf. John 1:12-13.

317. Cf. James 2:10.
318. Cf. Deut. 24:14-15; Mal. 3:5.
319. Cf. Mal. 2:10.
320. Luke 15:10 (NKJV).
321. Cf. 2 Cor. 4:6.
322. Deut. 30:15-20.
323. Wright, *The Message of Ezekiel,* p.203.
324. E.g. Rom. 6:1,15.
325. Cf. 33:17,20; Prov. 16:2; 21:2; 24:12.
326. Cf. John 3:6; 1 Peter 1:23.
327. 1 Cor. 11:28-29.
328. Cf. Acts 17:27-30.
329. Cf. Eph. 2:1,5.
330. Among many relevant texts, cf. John 6:37-39; 1 Peter 1:2.
331. The relationship is defined by 2 Kings 24:17 and 2 Chronicles 36:10. In the latter verse, the Hebrew for 'brother' might signify a less close relation, perhaps a 'kinsman' (cf. Gen. 11:26-27; 13:8; 14:14-16). This might reconcile the two references.
332. Jer. 52:31-34.
333. So Brown, Driver and Briggs, *A Hebrew Lexicon,* p.1010.
334. NKJV.
335. As shown by Block, *Ezekiel,* vol. 1, p.603.
336. Cf. 26:17; 2 Sam. 1:19; 1 Kings 13:30; Isa. 1:21; Jer. 9:19; 22:18; 48:17; 50:23; 51:41; Lam. 1:1; 2:1; 4:1-2; Micah 2:4.
337. 2 Sam. 1:17-27.
338. One might note the anointing of Jesus by Mary, which, as our Lord explained at the time, anticipated a future event (John 12:3,7; cf. Luke 22:19; 1 Cor. 11:24-25). Thus, in a sense, with Ezekiel's 'lamentation'.
339. 2 Sam. 7:8-17.
340. Cf., thus far in the prophecy, 1:3; 6:1; 7:1; 12:1; 13:1; 14:2; 15:1; 16:1; 17:1; 18:1.
341. See Gen. 49:9-10; Num. 23:24; 24:9; 1 Kings 10:19; Micah 5:8.
342. For man-eating lions, cf. 1 Kings 13:24-28; 20:35-36; 2 Kings 17:25-26; cf. 1 Sam. 17:37.
343. See 2 Kings 23:31-33; 2 Chr. 36:1-4.
344. Cf. 2 Kings 19:28; Isa. 37:29; Job 40:24.
345. 2 Kings 23:34.
346. 2 Kings 23:37; 24:1.
347. 2 Chr. 36:6-7; 2 Kings 24:6; cf. Jer. 22:18-19. It is for this reason that the present commentary does not identify Jehoiakim as the second young lion in the lamentation. That he was actually taken to Babylon seems to be suggested by the Chronicler, who records that Nebuchadnezzar '*also* carried off some of the articles from the house of Yahweh to Babylon', 'also' (Hebrew, *vav*) implying their removal in addition to that of Jehoiakim. After his return

from deportation he possibly fell in battle against the Chaldean armies prior to the siege of Jerusalem when his enemies were advancing against the city. Did he remain unburied? (See Jer. 22:19). The fact that he 'slept with his fathers' (2 Kings 24:6) does not necessarily imply a peaceful death (cf. that of Ahab, 1 Kings 22:40). 19:9 insists that the second lion was brought to 'the king of Babylon', presumably in Babylon.
348. 2 Kings 24:8-9; cf. 2 Chr. 36:9.
349. 2 Sam. 16:22. Cf. Adonijah, 1 Kings 2:17.
350. There is no need to emend **'widows'** to 'palaces', involving the alteration of just one Hebrew consonant, as is advocated by many commentators.
351. Isa. 5:1-7; 27:2-6; Ps. 80:8-16; cf. Matt. 21:33-41; John 15:1-8.
352. Gardiner, *Ezekiel,* p.254. The Masoretic, **'Your mother was like a vine in your blood,'** has been emended via an alteration in the word division in the Hebrew text to give something like 'Your mother was like a vine full of shoots'.
353. Cf. Gen. 49:10.
354. 2 Kings 24:18 – 25:17; 2 Chr. 36:11-21.
355. Gen. 49:8-12.
356. 2 Sam. 7:5,11-16.
357. Heb. 1:5.
358. Luke 22:24-30.
359. E.g. 1 Cor. 5:1.
360. Matt. 5:13; cf. Rev. 2:5.

3. The third series of prophecies (20:1 – 23:49)
1. Acts 7:2-53; cf. Ezra 9; Neh. 9; Ps. 78; 106; Dan. 9:1-19.
2. With acknowledgements to Taylor, *Ezekiel,* p.155.
3. With acknowledgements to Block, *Ezekiel,* vol. 1, p.617.
4. See Block, *Ezekiel,* vol. 1, pp.618-19.
5. 1 Sam. 28:6,15.
6. See Brown, Driver and Briggs, *A Hebrew Lexicon,* p.210. Cf. Gen. 27:36.
7. Cf. 1 Kings 14:23-24; 2 Kings 16:3; 21:2; 2 Chr. 28:3; 33:2.
8. See Deut. 18:15-22; cf. Acts 3:22; 7:37; John 1:29,45; 6:14.
9. Eichrodt, *Ezekiel,* p.263.
10. Cf. 20:15,22,23,28,42; 36:7; 44:12; 47:14; Exod. 6:8; Num. 14:30; Deut. 32:40; Neh. 9:15; Dan. 12:7.
11. Cf. Deut. 7:6-8.
12. Cf. Gen. 35:10-12.
13. Exod. 3:14-15; 6:2-8.
14. Exod. 6:7.
15. Cf. Num. 10:33; Deut. 1:33.
16. Num. 13:27; cf. Josh. 24:13; Jer. 3:19.
17. Josh. 24:2,14.

18. Exod. 32.
19. Exod. 20:3-5; cf. Deut. 5:7-9; 6:15.
20. Exod. 32:12; Num. 14:11-19; Deut. 9:28; 32:27-28.
21. See Gen. 43:32.
22. Cf. Rom. 10:5; Gal. 3:12.
23. Gardiner, *Ezekiel,* p.256.
24. Mark 10:17.
25. Cf. Exod. 20:8-11; 31:13-17; 34:21; 35:2-3; Lev. 19:3,30; 23:3,38; 25:1-55; Deut. 5:12-15; 2 Kings 4:23; Isa. 1:13; Hosea 2:11; Amos 8:5. In that the seventh day is implied by 20:12 to be only one in a family of several Sabbath occurrences during the fifty-year cycle, albeit the most frequent, and in that God 'gave' all of them to Israel just prior to, and then at the time of, Sinai (cf. Exod. 16:29), it can be argued reasonably that neither Abraham's continuing family nor any other ethnic group was aware of any species of Sabbath obligation before the events mentioned in Exodus 16.
26. Wright, *The Message of Ezekiel,* p.159.
27. Cf. Exod. 16:25-28; 32:1-6; Num. 11:1-6; 12:1-15; 13:31-33; 14:1-4; 15:32; 16; 20:2-5; 25:1-3; Deut. 1:26-46; 9:8; 32:5-6,28-33.
28. Cf. Josh. 2:10; 9:9.
29. Cf. Rom. 9:17.
30. Cf. Mark 4:11-12; John 12:40; Acts 28:26-27.
31. Block suggests that the evil statutes given to Israel by Yahweh were the sword, famine, plague and bloodshed 'as expressions of his wrath' (*Ezekiel,* vol. 1, p.640). The present writer finds this unconvincing since these 'expressions' were instruments rather than ordinances by which Israel dishonoured Yahweh.
32. Cf. Lev. 20:1-5; 2 Kings 17:17; 21:6; 23:10; 2 Chr. 28:3; Jer. 7:31; 32:35; cf. Acts 7:43. See Taylor, *Ezekiel,* p.159.
33. Exod. 22:29; Num. 18:15-16.
34. 2 Kings 18:22.
35. 2 Kings 16:3-4.
36. Cf. 1 Kings 14:23; 2 Kings 17:10.
37. 1 Sam. 9:12-14.
38. 1 Kings 11:7-8.
39. 2 Kings 23:8; 2 Chr. 34:3.
40. 1 Sam. 8:5,8,20.
41. Cf. 11:5 for a similar expression.
42. Exod. 19:5-6.
43. Cf. Exod. 3:20; 6:6; Deut., 4:34; 5:15; 7:19; 11:2; 26:8; Ps. 136:12.
44. Block, *Ezekiel,* vol. 1, p. 650.
45. Exod. 20:19; Heb. 12:19-21.
46. See Exod. 3:12,18; 4:23; 5:1,3; 7:16; 8:27,29.
47. Cf. Lev. 27:32-33; Jer. 33:13; Micah 7:14.

48. Block, noting that the statement, **'I shall ... bring you into the bond of the covenant'**, has perplexed commentators over the centuries, suggests that the Vulgate provides the 'most hopeful reading': *in vinculis foederis*, 'in the bond of the covenant' (*Ezekiel*, vol. 1, p.652).
49. Gen. 17:8; 28:4; 36:7; 37:1; Exod. 6:4.
50. For profanation of Yahweh, or of the name of Yahweh, cf. 13:19; 22:26; Lev. 18:21; 19:12; 20:3; 21:6; 22:2,32; Jer. 34:16; Amos 2:7; Mal. 1:12.
51. Cf. Rom. 15:16; 2 Cor. 2:14-16; Eph. 5:2; 2 Tim. 4:6, although it may be questioned whether Paul extracts his metaphors from 20:41.
52. See Gen. 15:7 and following references.
53. Cf. John 5:39-40.
54. See Num. 14:23.
55. W. Gadsby, *A Selection of Hymns for Public Worship* (London: Gospel Standard Publications, 1965), p.483 (hymn no. 636).
56. John 10:16.
57. See Acts 2:41,47; 4:4; 6:1; 21:20.
58. See Appendix C, concerning Rom. 11:25-26.
59. Cf. Amos 7:16; Micah 2:6,11.
60. Matt. 13:10.
61. See Wright, *The Message of Ezekiel*, p.114, n.59.
62. Josh. 5:13-15.
63. Cf. Rev. 2:12-17.
64. Cf. Gen. 18:25.
65. Jer. 40:1-6; 45:1-5.
66. Cf. 2 Sam. 1:22; Isa. 55:11.
67. Job 40:16; cf. Ps. 66:11; 69:23; Isa. 21:3; Nahum 2:10.
68. So Gardiner, *Ezekiel*, p.261.
69. Cf. 2 Sam. 7:14.
70. Cf. Acts 1:6.
71. Cf. Jer. 31:19.
72. Cf. Jer. 9:22.
73. E.g. Ruth 4:1; Amos 5:12,15.
74. **'Slaughtering sword'** reflects the Septuagint's reading; the Hebrew is not easy.
75. Block ascribes these words to Yahweh rather than to Ezekiel (*Ezekiel*, vol. 1, p.680). But is not the prophet bidden to 'prophesy' (21:9) — that is, to address the sword in the name of the Lord?
76. Cf.1 Sam. 15:12; 2 Sam. 18:18; 1 Chr. 18:3; Isa. 56:5.
77. For the illustration of the inverted 'Y', see Taylor, *Ezekiel*, p.163. Block prefers Damascus for the site of the signpost (*Ezekiel*, vol. 1, p.684).
78. Cf. Gen. 31:19,30,35; 1 Sam. 15:23; 2 Kings 23:24.
79. Block notes that 'numerous clay models (presumably used in the training of diviners) have been discovered. One of these from

2nd-millennium-BC Babylon is mapped into more than fifty sections and punctuated by special interpretative marks' (*Ezekiel,* vol. 1, p.687).
80. Num. 22 – 24; 2 Chr. 35:21; Acts 16:16-17.
81. 2 Chr. 36:10,13; Jer. 52:3.
82. Jer. 34:8-22.
83. Cf. 30:9; Job 18:5-21; Ps. 137:7; Isa. 9:4; Jer. 50:27,31; Hosea 1:11 for similar terminology.
84. 2 Kings 25:7; Jer. 39:7.
85. 1 Kings 18:18.
86. Exod. 28:4,37,39; 29:6; 39:28,31; Lev. 8:9; 16:4.
87. 2 Chr. 26:16-20.
88. Cf. Isa. 6:3; Jer. 7:4.
89. Block, *Ezekiel,* vol. 1, p.692.
90. Cf. Judg. 11:4-33; Jer. 49:1-6; Amos 1:13-15; Zeph. 2:8-11.
91. Ammon was not the only enemy eager to taunt Judah in the latter's distress: cf. 16:57; 35:15; Ps. 137:7; Obad. 12; Zeph. 2:8.
92. Gen. 19:30-38.
93. Allen, *Ezekiel,* p.28. As with Assyria, so with Babylon; cf. Isa. 10:5-19; 13 – 14; 37:21-38; 47; Jer. 50:1 – 51:64; Micah 5:4-6; Hab. 1:6 – 2:20.
94. Gen. 9:6; Matt. 26:52.
95. Hab. 1:6.
96. See John 8:33; Acts 1:6.
97. Matt. 26:24; Mark 14:21.
98. Cf. John 12:31; 13:2-3; 1 Cor. 2:8.
99. See Lev. 26; Deut. 28 – 29.
100. Cf. Jer. 31:29-30.
101. See also Nahum 3:1.
102. Brown, Driver and Briggs, *A Hebrew Lexicon,* p.310. Cf. Gen. 27:36; 1 Sam. 2:27; 1 Kings 20:13.
103. Cf. Deut. 6:16; Matt. 4:7.
104. 2 Kings 21:16; 24:4; 2 Chr. 33:1-9; 36:5.
105. Cf. Exod. 16:23; 20:11; Deut. 5:15.
106. So Block, *Ezekiel,* vol. 1, p.709.
107. See Num. 25:1-18.
108. Esth. 3:9.
109. Exod. 23:8; Deut. 10:17; 16:19; 27:25; cf. 1 Sam. 8:3; Isa. 1:23; 5:23; Amos 5:12; Micah 3:11.
110. Cf. Lev. 19:13.
111. Jer. 34:8-22.
112. See Isa. 1:22,25; 48:10; Jer. 6:27-30; 9:7; Zech. 13:9; Mal. 3:2-4.
113. Cf. Jer. 35:11,18-19. Because the refugee sons of Jonadab refused to consume anything emanating from the vine, they were assured that the Lord would grant them their lives.
114. E.g. Deut. 4:20; 1 Kings 8:51; Jer. 11:4.

115. Gen. 6:13,17; cf. 1 Peter 3:20-21.
116. NKJV.
117. For the difference between the common and the sacred, see Zeph. 3:4 (cf. Lev. 10:10). For the difference between cleanness and uncleanness, see Lev. 10:9-11.
118. 1 Sam. 2:12-17.
119. Cf. Neh. 13:22.
120. Cf. 13:19; Isa. 52:5; Mal. 2:5-9; Rom. 2:24.
121. Cf. Zeph. 3:3.
122. Taylor, *Ezekiel,* p.169.
123. Cf. Ps. 106:23.
124. Matt. 23:25-39; Luke 11:46-52.
125. Cf. Deut. 17:14-20.
126. 1 Kings 12:7; 2 Chr. 10:7.
127. Cf. 1 Peter 5:3.
128. John 15:1-11.
129. 2 Tim. 2:13.
130. With acknowledgements to Block, *Ezekiel,* vol. 1, p.729.
131. Cf. 1 Kings 12; 2 Chr. 10.
132. 1 Kings 12:26-33; 2 Chr. 11:14-15.
133. 1 Kings 12:26-33; 2 Kings 17:21-23.
134. Block, *Ezekiel,* vol. 1, p.736.
135. Gen. 29.
136. Exod. 1:7; 2 Sam. 24:9; 1 Chr. 21:5.
137. Cf. Hosea 5:13; 7:11; 8:9; 12:1. But **'near'** (*q'rôbim*) might allude to Assyrian warriors in that there is a Hebrew word, *q'rb,* for 'battle' or 'combat'.
138. Cf. 2 Kings 10:32-33.
139. So Taylor, *Ezekiel,* p.172.
140. 2 Kings 15:19-20,29.
141. E.g. 2 Kings 18:24; Isa. 36:9; Jer. 51:23,28,57; Esth. 3:12.
142. As 2 Kings 15:19-20 implies.
143. 1 Kings 12:28-29.
144. Exod. 32:4.
145. See 2 Kings 15:29 and, in detail, in 2 Kings 17.
146. As intimated by 2 Kings 16:7-18 and 2 Chr. 28:16-25.
147. Cf. Ahaz's alliance with Tiglath-Pileser of Assyria against the Syrians and the northern kingdom of Israel (2 Kings 16:5-10).
148. Cf. 2 Kings 20:13; Jer. 29:3.
149. 2 Kings 20:12-15; Isa. 39; cf. 2 Chr. 32:25.
150. Gen. 32:25.
151. Isa. 19:1-15; 20:3-6; 31:1-3; Jer. 37:5; 41:17; 44:8-14.
152. 2 Kings 23:29-30.
153. See also Jer. 13:22; Hosea 2:10; Nahum 3:5.
154. For the cup of divine wrath, see Ps. 60:3; 75:8; Isa. 51:17,22; Jer. 49:12; Lam. 4:21; Matt. 20:22; 26:39; Rev. 14:10.
155. Isa. 38:17; Neh. 9:26.

156. NKJV; cf. 1 Cor. 10:21-22.
157. 1 Kings 8:10-12; 2 Chr. 6:12-14; 7:1-3.
158. Cf. 2 Kings 9:30; Jer. 4:30.
159. Cf. Exod. 30:37-38; Prov. 7:16-18.
160. Hosea 2:8.
161. Block observes that 'This verse is so disjointed that many do not even attempt an interpretation' (*Ezekiel,* vol. 1, p.761). But why not?
162. Cf. Hab. 1:5-11.
163. Block interprets **'bring up'** as an infinitive absolute, rather than an imperative, standing possibly for a third-person future (so Keil and Delitzsch, *Ezekiel,* p.338), meaning 'one will bring up' (*Ezekiel,* vol. 1, p.762, n.192). But the vocalization suggests an imperative.
164. Lev. 20:10; Deut. 22:21-25; cf. John 8:5.
165. 1 Cor. 6:18.
166. See Eph. 5:22-33.
167. Matt. 5:2-12.
168. Prov. 1:20; 2:16-18.

4. The fourth series of prophecies (24:1 – 25:17)
1. See 'Introductory matters'.
2. See Lev. 26; Deut. 28 – 29.
3. Again, see 'Introductory matters'.
4. NKJV, emphasis added; cf. Jer. 39:1; 52:4.
5. 1:2; 8:1; 20:1; 26:1; 29:1; 30:20; 31:1; 32:1; 33:21; 40:1.
6. 2 Kings 24:12,17; 2 Chr. 36:9-11.
7. A report that Jerusalem was under siege would have taken some months to reach Babylonia (cf. Ezra 7:9).
8. Cf. Zech. 8:19.
9. 2 Kings 10:18-28.
10. Cf. 2 Kings 25:11.
11. Lev. 4:7; 16:15; 17:13; Deut. 12:16,24; 15:23.
12. Gen. 4:10; Job 16:18; Isa. 26:21.
13. Num. 35:33.
14. Cf. Isa. 30:33.
15. 2 Chr. 36:15-16.
16. So Keil and Delitzsch, *Ezekiel,* p.341.
17. 2 Kings 18:4; 22 – 23; 2 Chr. 31.
18. Cf. Num. 14:37; 17:13.
19. Lev. 21:2-3.
20. 2 Sam. 15:30; Isa. 20:2.
21. Cf. Micah 3:7.
22. Cf. 2 Sam. 15:30; Isa. 20:2; 61:3; Jer. 14:3; Micah 3:7.
23. Cf. Deut. 26:14; 2 Sam. 3:35; Jer. 16:7; Hosea 9:4.
24. See also Exod. 39:28; Lev. 6:10-11.
25. Isa. 3:20; 61:10.

26. Yet the Lord had never actually promised to dwell within the temple. In his prayer of consecration, Solomon repeated the truth that God remains in heaven, his dwelling place (1 Kings 8:27,30,32,34,36,39,43,45,49; cf. 2 Chr. 6).
27. See 1 Sam. 4:21.
28. Jer. 7:4.
29. NKJV.
30. According to A. A. Bonar, the command to Ezekiel not to mourn draws upon Leviticus 10:4-7, in which Aaron and his surviving sons, Eleazar and Ithamar, are instructed not to mourn openly for the loss of Nadab and Abihu 'lest you die, and lest wrath come upon all the people'. That is, even as Aaron and his sons represented to their people Jehovah's just verdict on the sin of Nadab and Abihu, so the prophet's silence would reflect his acquiescence in the divine overthrow of Jerusalem, as typified by his wife's death. Hence, any expressions of lamentation or regret would have been tantamount to Ezekiel's disapproval of the divine judgement (*A Commentary on the Book of Leviticus: Expository and Practical,* London: James Nisbet & Co, 1861, p.199). Although there may be force in this, I think that the interpretation offered in the body of the commentary is more obvious.
31. J. Bunyan, *Grace Abounding to the Chief of Sinners* (London: the Religious Tract Society, undated), pp.152-3.
32. Matt. 5:8.
33. See 1 Peter 1:2-3.
34. See Luke 15:11-32.
35. Cf. Gen. 1.
36. 2 Chr. 36:13.
37. Jer. 27:4-8.
38. Cf. Lev. 26:40-45.
39. Gardiner, *Ezekiel,* p.273.
40. Gen. 19:35-38.
41. Cf. Judg. 3:13; 10:6 – 11:33; 1 Sam. 11; 2 Sam. 10; 2 Kings 24:2; 2 Chr. 20:1-25; 26:8; 27:5; Ps. 83:7; Jer. 49:1.
42. 1 Kings 11:7.
43. Jer. 40:14.
44. Cf. Isa. 11:14; Jer. 49:1-6; Amos 1:13-15; Zeph. 2:8-11.
45. Cf. Judg. 6:3; Job 1:3.
46. Taylor, *Ezekiel,* p.187.
47. Gen. 19:30-38.
48. See Num. 22 – 24.
49. Deut. 23:3-4.
50. 2 Kings 24:2.
51. Jer. 27:3.
52. Jer. 48:27-35; Zeph. 2:8-9
53. Gen. 27:26-29.
54. Mal. 1:2; Rom. 9:13.

55. Num. 21:13,26; 32:37-38; Josh. 13:19-21; 2 Kings 3:4-7; Isa. 15 – 16; Jer. 48:1-47.
56. According to the apocryphal 1 Macc. 5:6-7.
57. Gen. 25:23.
58. See 35:5; Num. 20:18-21; 24:18-19; 2 Chr. 28:17; Ps. 137:7; Isa. 11:14; Jer. 49:7-13; Joel 3:19; Amos 1:11-12; Obad. 1-21.
59. Josephus, *Antiquities,* 12.8.6; *Wars of the Jews,* 4.9.7.
60. 1 Macc. 5:65.
61. Gen. 27:29,40; Num. 24:18; Amos 9:12; Obad. 17-18.
62. Gen. 25:23.
63. Cf. 1 Chr. 1:12.
64. Josh. 13:2-3.
65. 1 Sam. 27; 2 Sam. 8:18; 15:18; 20:23.
66. 2 Sam. 5:17-25.
67. Cf. 1 Sam. 30:14; Zeph. 2:5.
68. Cf. Judg. 16; 1 Sam. 5:1 – 6:18.
69. Deut. 32:10; Zech. 2:8.
70. Eph. 2:12.
71. Matt. 28:20.
72. Cf. 1 John 3:3.

5. The fifth series of prophecies (26:1 – 28:26)
1. See 'Introductory matters'.
2. Herodotus, *Book 2,* 44.
3. 2 Sam. 24:7.
4. 2 Sam. 5:11; 1 Kings 5:1-12; 7:13-14; 9:10-14,27-28; 1 Chr. 14:1; 2 Chr. 2:3-16.
5. 1 Kings 16:31.
6. Amos 1:9-10.
7. Hosea 9:13.
8. Zech. 9:2-4.
9. Josephus, *Against Apion,* 1.154-8; *Antiquities,* 10.228.
10. Matt. 11:21-22; 15:21; Mark 3:8; 7:24; Luke 6:17; 10:13-14.
11. Acts 21:3-6.
12. Amos 1:9; Joel 3:4-6.
13. So Block, *Ezekiel,* vol. 2, p.32.
14. 2 Kings 25:3; Jer. 39:2; 52:6.
15. 1 Kings 10; 2 Chr. 9.
16. Taylor, *Ezekiel,* p.190, n.2.
17. See also Jer. 1:13-15.
18. Cf. Jer. 21:2,7.
19. Cf. 2 Kings 24:1; 25:1 etc.
20. Block, *Ezekiel,* vol. 2, p.40, gives details.
21. Herodotus mentions that he had seen two pillars, one of gold and the other of emerald, within the Tyrian temple of Heracles (*Book 2,* 44).
22. 1 Sam. 5:3; Isa. 21:9; 46:1.

23. Cf. Jer. 7:34; 16:9; 25:10; Lam. 5:14-15; Amos 5:23.
24. Cf. Jer. 33:11.
25. Cf. Isa. 23:8.
26. Cf. Job 2:12-13.
27. Isa. 1:21; Lam. 1:1; 2:1; 4:1.
28. See Gen. 6 – 8.
29. Cf. the fate of Egypt (31:14-18; 32:13-32) and that of Babylon (Isa. 14:4-21).
30 Block suggests that the Hebrew behind 'I will set glory' should be translated as 'you will not radiate splendour', the verb being an archaic second-person feminine form (cf. 16:50). See Block, *Ezekiel,* vol. 2, p.47.
31. For the same word, cf. 27:36; 28:19; Job 18:11; 24:17; 27:20; 30:15; Ps. 73:19; Isa. 17:14.
32. Eph. 5:5; Col. 3:5.
33. Acts 19:27.
34. Matt. 6:33.
35. Dan. 4:34-37.
36. Cf., again, Acts 19:27.
37. **'Merchant'**, 27:3; **'merchandise'**, 27:9; **'trader'** and **'wares'**, 27:12; **'agents'** and **'merchandise'**, 27:13; **'agents'**, **'business agents'** and **'payment'**, 27:15; **'trader'**, **'manufactures'** and **'wares'**, 27:16; **'agents'** and **'merchandise'**, 27:17; **'trader'** and **'manufactures'**, 27:18; **'wares'** and **'merchandise'**, 27:19; **'agent'**, 27:20; **'business agents'**, **'agents'**, 27:21; **'traders'** and **'your wares'**, 27:22; **'traders'** (twice), 27:23; **'traders'**, 27:24; **'freighters'** and **'merchandise'**, 27:25; **'wares'**, **'merchandise'** (twice), 27:27; **'wares'**, **'wealth'** and **'merchandise'**, 27:33; **'merchandise'**, 27:34; **'merchants'**, 27:36.
38. Lam. 2:15.
39. Cf. Deut. 3:9.
40. For **'linen'**, cf. 16:10.
41. Cf. Gen. 10:4; 1 Chr. 1:7.
42. Cf. Gen. 10:18.
43. Cf. S. of S. 4:4.
44. So Block, *Ezekiel,* vol. 2, p.64.
45. Cf. Gen. 10:6.
46. Cf. Gen. 10:13.
47. Because **'your army'** translates *chelek*, it has been suggested that Cilicia, in south-east Asia, is meant.
48. So Taylor, *Ezekiel,* p.193.
49. Block gives details (*Ezekiel,* vol. 2, pp.68-9).
50. Cf. Gen. 10:4; 1 Chr. 1:7; Jonah 1:3.
51. Cf. 1 Chr. 1:5.
52. Cf. Gen. 10:3.
53. Exod. 28:18; 39:11.
54. Judg. 11:33; 2 Chr. 27:5.

55. So Wright, *The Message of Ezekiel,* p.242.
56. Block provides bibliographic details in support of this translation (*Ezekiel,* vol. 2, p.76, n.138).
57. Cf. Exod. 30:23-24; Isa. 43:24; Jer. 6:20.
58. Cf. 1 Kings 10:15.
59. Cf. Gen. 25:13; Isa. 60:7.
60. Gen. 10:7. Block disputes this genealogy (*Ezekiel,* vol. 2, p.78, n.159).
61. Cf. 1 Kings 10:10.
62. Gen. 11:31-32; 12:4; 27:43.
63. Gen. 10:10.
64. Cf. 1 Kings 10:22; 22:48; Isa. 2:16; 23:1.
65. Gardiner suggests that at that time the art of sailing in all weathers was 'imperfectly understood' (*Ezekiel,* p.282).
66. Cf. Jonah 1:4; Acts 27:14.
67. See also Num. 35:4; Josh. 14:4; 21:2.
68. For **'whistle'** (from *sharaq*, 'to hiss'), cf. Isa. 5:26; 7:18; Zech. 10:8.
69. 2 Chr. 2:12-16.
70. Isa. 22:1.
71. Cf. 2 Chr. 9.
72. 1 Cor. 10:12.
73. Gen. 3:24.
74. John 8:44.
75. 1 Sam. 10:1; 2 Sam. 7:8. Yet *nagid* is associated with *melek* in Ps. 76:12.
76. Cf. Hosea 11:9.
77. Cf. Ps. 48:1-2; Isa. 2:2-3.
78. 2 Kings 18:33-35; Dan. 3:15; 4:30; cf. Dan. 7:25; 11:36-37; Ezek. 29:3; Acts 12:21-23; 2 Thess. 2:3-4.
79. I have translated thus because whereas **'secret'** is singular, **'they hold dark ...'** is (obviously) plural.
80. Cf. Dan. 1:20; 2:48; 4:18; 5:11-12; 6:3.
81. For the term, cf. 30:11; 31:12; 32:12; Hab. 1:6-7.
82. Gen. 17:9-27.
83. 2 Sam. 1:17-27.
84. For the concept of representation, cf. Gen. 41:42; Esth. 3:10; 8:8-10.
85. Gen. 2:7-8; 3:6,24; Exod. 25:20-21; 1 Kings 8:7; 2 Chr. 5:8.
86. Cf. 2 Peter 2:4; Jude 6.
87. Exod. 28:17-20; 39:10-13.
88. With acknowledgements to Block, *Ezekiel,* vol. 2, p.106.
89. Gen. 1:26-28; 2:7.
90. (1) 2 Sam. 22:11; Ps. 18:10; (2) Gen. 3:24; (3) 1 Sam. 4:4; 2 Sam. 6:2; 2 Kings 19:15; 1 Chr. 13:6; Ps. 80:1; 99:1; Isa. 37:16; (4) Exod. 25:18-22; 37:7-9; Num. 7:89; (5) Exod. 26:1,31; 36:8,35; (6) 1 Kings 6:23-28; 8:6-7; 1 Chr. 28:18; (7) 1 Kings 6:29-35;

2 Chr. 3:7; 1 Kings 7:29-36; (8) 1:5-28; 9:3; 10:1-22; 11:22; (9) 41:18-25.
91. Gen. 3:24.
92. For Sinai see Exod. 3:1; 18:5; 19:2-3,18; 24:13. For Zion see Ps. 48:1-2; Isa. 14:13.
93. Taylor, *Ezekiel*, p.197.
94. So Block, *Ezekiel*, vol. 2, p.114.
95. Gen. 3:8; 13:17; Job 1:7 respectively.
96. *Tamim*; cf. Job, among others: Job 1:1,8; 2:3.
97. Gen. 2 – 3; cf. 2 Peter 2:4; Jude 6.
98. So Brown, Driver and Briggs, *A Hebrew Lexicon*, p.320.
99. Block, *Ezekiel*, vol. 2, p.119.
100. Block, *Ezekiel*, vol. 2, p.119, n.142. He quotes Calvin on Isaiah 14, the Reformer noting that 'the exposition of this passage, which some have given, as if it referred to Satan, has arisen from ignorance' (*Ezekiel*, vol. 2, p.119, n.139), and suggests that what Calvin claimed about Isaiah 14 applies to Ezekiel 28. The problem is that this does not dismiss the possibility of an angelic secondary referent.
101. Cf. Rom. 1:21.
102. Judg. 10:6,12; 1 Kings 11:33; 16:31.
103. So Block, *Ezekiel*, vol. 2, p.123.
104. Jer. 27:3.
105. Taking the *Niph'al nikbadti* as reflexive rather than as passive. Cf. 39:13.
106. NKJV; cf. 5:12; 6:12; 7:15; 12:16; 14:12-22; Deut. 28:22.
107. Dan. 9:25; Neh. 13:23-27.
108. Cf. Isa. 44:1,2; 45:4; 48:20; Jer. 30:10; 46:27-28.
109 Jer. 27:3.

6. The sixth prophecy (29:1–16)
1. Jer. 37:5-7.
2. Jer. 37:5,11; 47:1. Herodotus says that Hophra 'was more fortunate than any former king (save only his father Psammetichus) during his rule of twenty-five years, in which he sent an army against Sidon and did battle by sea with the king of Tyre' (*Book 2*, 161).
3. 2 Kings 23:29; 2 Chr. 35:20-24.
4. See 2 Kings 23:29-30,34; 2 Chr. 35:20-24; 36:3-4.
5. Exod. 32:1-8.
6. Jer. 41:16 – 43:13; cf. Isa. 30:1 – 31:9.
7. Cf. Jer. 44:30. According to Josephus, Nebuchadnezzar 'invaded Egypt in order to subdue it, and, having killed the king who was then reigning, and appointed another, he again took captive the Jews who were in the country and carried them to Babylon' (*Antiquities*, 10.9.7).
8. See also 2 Kings 25:1; Jer. 29:1.

9. Jer. 37:5,11.
10. Taking the pronominal suffix here as a dative (see Block, *Ezekiel,* vol. 2, p.135). Herodotus states that their land was 'given' to the Egyptians 'by the river' (*Book 2,* 5).
11. Cf. 2 Kings 18:21.
12. Cf. Jer. 37:5-11.
13. Or, more literally, 'wastes, waste and a desolation'. For the expression, cf. Isa. 61:4; Jer. 49:13.
14. Cf. 11:16; 12:15; 20:23; 22:15; 36:19.
15. Cf. 17:14, in which Zedekiah's kingdom is said to be 'lowly', subservient to Babylon.
16. See Isa. 20:5-6; 30:6-8; 36:6-9; Jer. 37:5-10; 43:8-13; 44:29-30; 46:25-26.
17. So Block, *Ezekiel,* vol. 2, p.145.
18. According to *The British Museum Book of Ancient Egypt,* eds. S. Quirke and J. Spencer (London: British Museum Press, 5th impression, 1997), p.49.
19. From P. A. Clayton, *Chronicles of the Pharaohs: The reign-by-reign record of the rulers and dynasties of ancient Egypt* (London: Thames & Hudson, 1994), p.6.

7. The seventh series of prophecies (29:17 – 30:19)
1. According to Josephus, 'Under King Ithobaal, Nabuchodonosor besieged Tyre for thirteen years... For it was in the seventh year of his reign that Nabuchodonosor began the siege of Tyre ...' (*Against Apion,* 1.156,159; cf. *Antiquities,* 10.11.1).
2. So Clements, *Ezekiel,* p.134.
3. Block, *Ezekiel,* vol. 2, p.149. Also Wright, *The Message of Ezekiel,* p.249.
4. Jonah 3:1-10.
5. Josephus, *Against Apion,* 1.144; Gardiner, *Ezekiel,* p.288.
6. So Cooke, *A Critical and Exegetical Commentary on ... Ezekiel,* p.329.
7. Cf. Lev. 19:13; Isa. 40:10; 62:11.
8. Jer. 43:8-13; 46:1-26.
9. A fragmentary cuneiform text dated to Nebuchadnezzar's thirty-seventh year (568 BC) refers to his assault upon Egypt. See Block, *Ezekiel,* vol. 2, p.151.
10. E.g. Deut. 33:17; 2 Sam. 22:3. There are many such references.
11. Cf. 2 Chr. 36:21; Jer. 25:11-12; 29:10.
12. Cf. Jer. 37:5.
13. Cf. Isa. 13:6,9; Amos 5:18-20; Obad. 15.
14. *The British Museum Book of Ancient Egypt,* p.202.
15. Cf. Jer. 25:20; 50:37.
16. Cf. Nahum 3:9.
17. Cf. Jer. 24:8; 42:16-18; 44:1.

18. Cf. 28:7; 31:12; 32:12; Isa. 25:3,5.
19. Cf. Sennacherib's boast, Isa. 37:25.
20. Cf. Isa. 10:27-32; Micah 1:10-15; Zeph. 2:4.
21. Brown, Driver and Briggs, *A Hebrew Lexicon,* p.47.
22. Cf. Hosea 9:6.
23. So *The British Museum Book of Ancient Egypt,* pp.13,62.
24. Jer. 44:1.
25. With acknowledgements to Block, *Ezekiel,* vol. 2, p.168.
26. Cf. Exod. 1:11.
27. Cf. Nahum 3:8; Exod. 12:12; Num. 33:4.
28. Jer. 46:25.
29. Cf. Exod. 13:17.
30. Cf. Gen. 41:45,50; Jer. 43:13.
31. Jer. 43:7; 44:1.
32. Cf. Jer. 51:62-64.
33. 2 Cor. 1:20.
34. Cf. 2 Tim. 2:12-13.
35. 1 Cor. 10:13.

8. The eighth prophecy (30:20-26)
1. Jer. 43:8-13.
2. Cf. 2 Kings 25:8; Jer. 39:2; 52:6.
3. Cf. Jer. 37:5-11.
4. Jer. 46:2.
5. Exod. 7:5; 14:18.
6. Eph. 6:12; Rev. 12:1-9.
7. Phil. 2:10-11.

9. The ninth prophecy (31:1-18)
1. Cf. 17:1-10,22-24; Ps. 1; Dan. 4:1-27 for the metaphor.
2. Jer. 37:5.
3. Many commentators (e.g. Taylor, *Ezekiel,* p.205) do not accept that there is a reference to Assyria, and amend **'Assyria'** to read 'cypress [tree]', the Hebrew words being similar. But the reference to Assyria is appropriate.
4. Cf. 19:10-14; Isa. 14:4-21; Dan. 4:1-12,19-27; Matt. 13:31-32.
5. The Hebrew text is complicated, and I have taken **'the deep'** to be the subject of the verbs in this verse.
6. The translation of this verse presumes 'deep' (31:4) as the subject of the verb.
7. 2 Kings 18:19-35.
8. Gen. 2:9.
9. Cf. Gen. 2:7.
10. Brown, Driver and Briggs, *A Hebrew Lexicon,* p.982.

10. The tenth prophecy (32:1–16)
1. Isa. 10:33-34. **'Likened'** translates the *Niph'al* of *dama*, 'to be like'. Grammatically, it could mean 'you have destroyed yourself', but this would not fit the context.
2. Some, e.g. Taylor, *Ezekiel*, p.209, suggest that the reference is to both the Egyptian crocodile and a mythological monster of the chaos, Tiamat, which was killed by the god Marduk. But does not such an approach overload the text?
3. **'Net'** translates *reshet*, and **'dragnet'**, *herem*, a fisherman's net.
4. Cf. Isa. 14:12; Joel 2:10; 3:15; Acts 2:20.
5. Cf. Judg. 19:29; 1 Sam. 11:7. So Block, *Ezekiel*, vol. 2, p.207.
6. Jer. 9:17-20.
7. Matt. 5:13-14.

11. The eleventh series of prophecies (32:17 – 33:20)
1. Cf. Isa. 14:4-23.
2. Gen. 5:3-31.
3. Block explains the technicalities of the matter (*Ezekiel*, vol. 2, p.215, n.12).
4. With acknowledgements to Block, *Ezekiel*, vol. 2, p.217.
5. 2 Sam. 1:20.
6. Cf. Isa. 21:2; 22:6; Dan. 8:2.
7. Jer. 49:34-39.
8. Acts 2:9.
9. So Taylor, *Ezekiel*, p.212.
10. Cf. Ps. 9:17; 31:17; Isa. 14:4-21; 2 Peter 2:4; Jude 6; John 5:29.
11. Cf. Acts 13:35.
12. Luke 23:43.
13. If this chapter is read in context it may be interpreted as a recommissioning in the light of the news of the fall of Jerusalem and the exiles' changed circumstances.
14. Cf. Jer. 1:10.
15. Jer. 44:17-19.
16. Cf. John 8:33-47.
17. Cf. Isa. 22:13; 1 Cor. 15:32.
18. NKJV.
19. Cf. Rom. 11:1-6.
20. Brown, Driver and Briggs, *A Hebrew Lexicon*, pp.251-5; Kautsch, *Gesenius' Hebrew Grammar*, p.458. Compare 1 Kings 8:46-48; 2 Chr. 6:36-39; Neh. 1:9 for exactly similar constructions. In each of these passages it is not easy to recognize conditionality: in exile, the people *will* turn to the Lord.
21. Cf. Lev. 18:5.
22. Cf. Gal. 5:6; James 2:17.
23. John 4:1-26.
24. Rom. 6:1; 9:19.
25. NKJV.

12. The twelfth series of prophecies (33:21 – 39:29)
1. With acknowledgements to Wright, *The Message of Ezekiel,* p.273.
2. See Lev. 26:1-39; Deut. 4:1-40; 27 – 28.
3. See Lev. 26:40-45.
4. With acknowledgements to Clements, *Ezekiel,* p.155.
5. See Appendix C: Romans 11:25-26.
6. In his *Ezekiel* (vol. 2, pp.268-309), Block, expounding chapter 34, insists upon the fulfilment of the divine promises to Israel. He goes so far as to say that 'these covenant hopes will all be fulfilled in the Messianic age ... when Yahweh's people live securely in their land, are ruled by a divinely appointed David, and enjoy the *shalom* of God's presence and grace' (p.308). But the matter seems to be almost marginalized. Pulling his punches, he does not venture an opinion as to *when* this will be.
7. Cooper, *Ezekiel,* p.45.
8. So Cooper, *Ezekiel,* pp.298-9.
9. Taylor, *Ezekiel,* p.222.
10. Rom. 11:23-24.
11. 24:1-2.
12. 2 Kings 25:8 mentions the seventh day of the month, and Jeremiah 52:12 the tenth.
13. Keil and Delitzsch suggest that, although the actual siege lasted for one and a half years (cf. 2 Kings 25:1,8-9; Jer. 39:1; 52:4-7), another one and a half years were needed for the news to reach Ezekiel, given 'the fearful confusion which followed the catastrophe' (*Ezekiel,* p.71). But, surely, Nebuzaradan (2 Kings 25:8-9) would have communicated the matter as soon as possible.

Another approach is to suggest that, although Ezekiel normally dates his oracles with respect to his deportation from Jerusalem to Babylonia, in 24:1-2 he points to Zedekiah's first full year as king in order to give subtle notice to the exiles that he is a true prophet of Yahweh (see the comments on 24:1-2).
14. Ezra 7:8-9.
15. 2 Kings 25:11.
16. Cf. 2 Kings 25:12; Jer. 52:16.
17. Cf. Luke 3:8; John 8:37.
18. John 8:33.
19. Gen. 15:6; 2 Chr. 20:7; Neh. 9:8; Isa. 41:8.
20. Literally, 'you eat upon blood'.
21. Cf. 24:7; Gen. 9:4; Lev. 3:17; 7:26; 17:10-14; 19:26; Deut. 12:16; 1 Sam. 14:32-33; cf. Acts 15:20.
22. 2 Kings 25:25; Jer. 41; 52:30.
23. Cf. Exod. 23:29; Lev. 26:22; 2 Kings 17:25.
24. Cf. Herod, Mark 6:20.
25. Eph. 2:8.
26. Rom. 10:9; Isa. 1:18.

27. Cf. John 8:39-40.
28. Cf. John 1:13-14; 3:7.
29. Jer. 23:5-6.
30. Cf. Num. 27:17; 2 Sam. 5:2; Ps. 78:70-72.
31. M. C. Lind, *Ezekiel* (Scottdale, Penn. and Waterloo, Ont.: Herald Press, 1996), p.273.
32. Cf. Isa. 56:9-10; Jer. 12:9.
33. Cf. 1 Kings 22:17; Matt. 9:36.
34. 2 Kings 24:15; 25:7.
35. Lev. 13:36.
36. Cf. Luke 15:4-7.
37. **'Drove'** is employed because it reflects the Hebrew *éder*, and not the usual *tzôn*, 'flock'.
38. Cf. 37:24-25; Isa. 9:6-7; 11:1; 55:3; Jer. 23:5; 30:8-10; 33:17,20-21,25-26; Hosea 3:5; Amos 9:11.
39. 2 Sam. 7:8-16; 1 Chr. 17:7-14; Ps. 89:35-37; cf. Isa. 40:11. In the New Testament, cf. Matt. 15:24; 18:11-14; Mark 6:34; Luke 15:1-7; John 10:1-18; Heb. 13:20; 1 Peter 2:25; 5:4.
40. For the belief that the Lord would dwell among his own people, cf. Gen. 17:7; Exod. 29:45-46; Lev. 26:12-13; Isa. 7:14; Mal. 3:1.
41. Esth. 4:11.
42. Cf. Deut. 4:31. At this point I am indebted to Block's exposition of 34:23-24 (*Ezekiel,* vol. 2, pp.297-301).
43. Isa. 54:10.
44. Cf. Gen. 9:8-17.
45. Cf. Deut. 28:1-14.
46. Some commentators would emend the Hebrew behind 'for a name' to give 'plantations of peace', or 'prosperity'. But this is surely unnecessary.
47. Some versions omit **'men'**, but this commentary would follow the Masoretic Text.
48. Cf. Rom. 11:1.
49. Rom. 11:15.
50. Cf. Gen. 25:22-26; 27:41; 36:8-9. But, as Taylor observes, the fault was not always on one side (*Ezekiel,* p.225); cf. 2 Sam. 8:14; 2 Kings 14:7.
51. There is a similar contrast in Isa. 34 – 35. Ezekiel does not innovate. With acknowledgements to Gardiner, *Ezekiel,* p.301.
52. Ps. 137:7.
53. Cf. 2 Kings 17:24-28.
54. Cf. Gen. 36:8,9; Deut. 2:1,5; Josh. 15:10; 1 Chr. 4:42.
55. Deut. 2:5.
56. Cf. Gen. 25:22-23; 27:41-45; 32:4-22; 33:1-16.
57. Deut. 23:7.
58. Mal. 1:3; Rom. 9:13.

59. Block considers the Masoretic Text's **'you hated blood'** to be meaningless' (*Ezekiel,* vol. 2, p.312, n.11). This commentary considers that it is meaningful.
60. Deut. 2:1-7.
61. Cf. Gen. 25:23,32; 27:29.
62. So Brown, Driver and Briggs, *A Hebrew Lexicon,* p.775; cf. Lev. 26:43.
63. Gen. 37:2; Num. 14:36.
64. 2 Chr. 36:21. I would, with respect, disagree with Thomas when he asserts that 'It is a mistake to think that these passages teach a restoration of the Jews to their land that goes beyond what happened during the days of Ezra and Nehemiah' (*God Strengthens,* p.230).
65. Ezra 2:64; Neh. 7:66.
66. Cf. Lev. 26:14-33; Deut. 28:15-68.
67. In verses 14,15 the Masoretic Text reads, 'and you will not make them again to stumble', from *kashal.* This may be a transcriptional error in that, consistent with verses 12,13, the original could have been, 'you will not make childless', from *shakal.* See Block, *Ezekiel,* vol. 2, p.332, n.53. My translation and commentary accept the emendation.
68. So Gardiner, *Ezekiel,* p.304.
69. Cf. Deut. 9:5.
70. Cf. Gen. 18:17; Exod. 33:12-13; John 15:15. With acknowledgements to Block, *Ezekiel,* vol. 2, p.344, n.41.
71. Lev. 15:19.
72. See Deut. 4:27-28; 28:64; cf. Amos 7:17.
73. Cf. Deut. 4:29-31.
74. Lev. 15:19-30; 2 Chr. 36:21. So Block, *Ezekiel,* vol. 2, p.347.
75. Cf. Isa. 52:5; Rom. 2:24.
76. With acknowledgements to Wright, *The Message of Ezekiel,* p.290.
77. Cf. Num. 14:15-16; Jer. 33:23-26.
78. Block comments that 'Yahweh looks like a stuffy egotistical monarch' (*Ezekiel,* vol. 2, p.352).
79. See Deut. 4:37; 23:5.
80. Cf. Matt. 6:9.
81. Cf. Exod. 6:7-8.
82. Common to both 36:24 and Deut. 30:3-5 are **'bring'**, **'gather'** and **'take'**. There can be no coincidence.
83. 11:17; 20:34-35,41-42; 28:25; 34:13; 37:12,21; 39:27.
84. Wright states that 'The text is referring, of course, to the expectation of restoration from exile, which historically took place in the following generation' (*The Message of Ezekiel,* p.293, n.58). But why the 'of course'? Ezra and Nehemiah tell that the generality of the returnees were far from regenerate.

85. Cf. Exod. 19:10; 29:4; 30:17-21; Lev. 14:5-9,52; 16:4,24,26; Num. 8:7; 19:11-19; Ps. 51:2,7; Isa. 1:15-16; 4:3-5; Jer. 4:14.
86. Cf. 2 Cor. 3:3, although it cannot be proved that Paul draws upon 36:26-27.
87. Cf. Matt. 26:28; Luke 22:20; Rom. 11:27; 1 Cor. 11:25; 2 Cor. 3:3,6; Heb. 8:8-13; 10:16-17.
88. John 14:17.
89. Deut. 9:6.
90. Cf. Isa. 42:1; 44:3; 59:21; Joel 2:28; John 16:7-15; Acts 2:17-21; 2 Cor. 3:17 and context; Gal. 3:2; 4:6.
91. Cf. Gen. 15:7; 17:8 etc.
92. Cf. Exod. 19:5-6.
93. Cf. Rom. 7:14-25; 1 John 1:8-10.
94. Cf. Matt. 1:21.
95. Cf. John 8:56 and context; Gal. 3:29.
96. NKJV; cf. Isa. 59:20.
97. Gen. 2:8.
98. Cf. Lev. 26:40-45; Deut. 30:1-9.
99. Cf. Gen. 17:2; Lev. 26:9.
100. J. D. Currid, *A Study Commentary on Leviticus* (Darlington: Evangelical Press, 2004), p.359. Yet one would respectfully disagree with this author when he claims in the same book concerning 'the lavish promises of blessing given to Israel in this passage [i.e. Lev. 26:1-13]', that 'the later prophets predicted that these promises would not be fulfilled until the eschaton' (p.348). One of the theses of the present commentary is that 'these promises' will be honoured *prior* to the Second Coming of our Lord.
101. 2 Chr. 35:7.
102. Matt. 11:19; Luke 7:35; John 1:5.
103 Gen. 15:7.
104. Jer. 3:19; Dan. 8:9; 11:16,41.
105. Concerning the fulfilment of the covenantal promises to Abraham and then to Israel (Gen. 17; Lev. 26), Block writes that 'How these prophetic promises will be fulfilled remains an open question. Nevertheless, to reduce these oracles to symbolic language and to restrict their fulfilment to the NT church is to annul the hope that the prophet was attempting to restore' (*Ezekiel,* vol. 2, p.367). As the reader of the present commentary might have noted, I have endeavoured to be more specific.
106. Deut. 28:25-26; cf. Jer. 34:17-20.
107. Cf. 1 Kings 17:21-23; 2 Kings 4:35; 13:21.
108. Cf. Rev. 7:14.
109. Cf. John 3:5-8.
110. Cf. Gen. 2:7.
111. Cf. Jer. 34:17-20; 2 Sam. 21:9-10.
112. For the translation **'army'**, cf. 17:17; 27:10.

113. Taylor, *Ezekiel*, p.236. This vision has little or nothing to do with the New Testament insistence that the dead in Christ will rise (see 1 Cor. 15). As noted by M. Greenberg, 'The vividness of these metaphors was so great as to mislead later interpreters into taking them literally' (*Ezekiel 21–37,* New York: Doubleday, 1997, p.747).
114. 4:1,9; 5:1; 12:3,18; 24:17.
115. Cf. Num. 17:2; Zech. 11:7. Block suggests that the two pieces of wood were flat writing tablets (*Ezekiel,* vol. 2, p.399). This is plausible.
116. Cf. 1 Kings 12:1-20; 2 Chr. 10:1-19; cf. Hosea 11:1-12.
117. Cf. Exod. 32:7.
118. Cf. 12:9; 17:12; 20:49; 24:19.
119. Gen. 32:28.
120. Cf. 1 Kings 12:1-24.
121. There is a textual problem here. Most commentators hold that **'dwelling places'** is a corruption of 'turnings' or 'backslidings', the consonantal Hebrew behind these words being almost indistinguishable. Accordingly, Israel is to be saved from its sins (cf. 36:29). But this commentary stays with the Masoretic Text. See Block, *Ezekiel,* vol. 2, p.407, n.79 for details.
122. Cf. Lev. 26:3; Deut. 4:1,5,14,40; 5:1,31; 6:1-2,24-25; 7:11-12; 8:1; 11:1; 12:1; 27:1; 28:1,15; 30:10.
123. Cf. Gen. 28:13; 35:12; 48:21; 49:29-32.
124. Gen. 15:7-21; 2 Sam. 7:12-16.
125. Exod. 40:34-38.
126. To claim that, as Thomas says, chapter 37 is 'initially ... about the restoration of the exiles from Babylon' (*God Strengthens*, p.244), seems to me to miss the point. Ezekiel anticipates an ultimate regathering of Israel, after which there will be no further Diaspora.
127. Cf. John 14:20.
128. So Rom. 11:25-27.
129. See P. Naylor, *A Study Commentary on 1 Corinthians* (Darlington: Evangelical Press, 2004), p.460.
130. Dan. 7:8,20; 8:9-13; 11:36.
131. NKJV.
132. E.g. Lev. 26:14-39; Deut. 4:25-28; 28:15-68; 2 Chr. 36:21.
133. Cf. Isa. 46:1-7.
134. **'The mountains of Israel'**, 38:8; 39:2,4,17; **'the land of Israel'**, 38:18,19; Yahweh's own **'land'** (38:16).
135. This explains, for example, Matthew 5:5. In the future glory there will be one people who inherit one land.
136. For this reason I would not accept the view that, as Taylor suggests, 'chapters 38 and 39 are a separate composition, written in a different literary genre, which were added to 1 – 37 as a kind of postscript, and that 40 – 48 were a later appendix which built

on the concluding chapter of the original work, 1 – 37' (*Ezekiel,* p.242).
137. Klein, *Ezekiel: The Prophet and His Message,* pp.159-60. A Reubenite called Gog is mentioned in 1 Chronicles 5:4, but nothing more is known about him, and he was not the Gog mentioned here. Block observes that Gyges of Lydia is mentioned in six inscriptions of Ashurbanipal (668–631 BC), (*Ezekiel,* vol. 2, p.433). Herodotus notes that, having murdered his sovereign, he usurped the throne and reigned for thirty-eight years (*Book 1,* 8-15).
138. As is finely said by Cooke, *A Critical and Exegetical Commentary on ... Ezekiel,* p.406.
139. Cf. Rev. 20:8.
140. So Block, *Ezekiel,* vol. 2, p.434.
141. Cf. 27:13; 32:26; Gen. 10:2; 1 Chr. 1:5.
142. The notion that *Rôsh* (= Russia), Meshech (= Moscow) and Tubal (= Tobolsk) refer to Russia and two of her cities is dismissed here without discussion.
143. 2 Kings 19:28.
144. For **'Persia'**, cf. Dan. 10:1; Ezra 1:1-2; 6:14; 7:1; Esth. 1:3,19; 2 Chr. 36:20,22,23.
145. Cf. Gen. 10:2-3.
146. That is, if *'Rôsh'* means 'chief of'.
147. Cf. Lev. 26:5-6.
148. For the Hebrew behind **'villages'**, cf. 1 Sam. 6:18; Esth. 9:19; Zech. 2:4, and perhaps Judg. 5:7,11.
149. For **'Sheba'** and **'Dedan'**, cf. 25:13; 27:15,20,22-23. For **'Tarshish'**, cf. 27:12,25.
150 'Blitzkrieg' is a German Second-World-War term meaning 'lightning war': enemy forces sweep rapidly over their victim's terrain.
151. The pharaoh of the Exodus (Exod. 9:16; cf. Rom. 9:17), the Assyrians (Isa. 10:5-19), the Babylonians (Hab. 1:5-11), and even those who put Jesus to death (1 Cor. 2:8), were also instituted by God to act as his agents. But, like Gog, they were solely responsible for their evil deeds.
152. Cf. Isa. 25:5,10; 26:21; Jer. 30:23-24; Joel 3:9-17; Hag. 2:6.
153. So Block, *Ezekiel,* vol. 2, p.456.
154. Cf. S. of S. 2:14.
155. Exod. 19:16-19; cf. Heb. 12:26.
156. Cf. Judg. 7:22; 2 Chr. 20:23.
157. Cf. Josh. 10:11-13.
158. Gen. 19:24.
159. *Shishétikah.* Block states that the verb is 'inexplicable' (*Ezekiel,* vol. 2, p.460, n.2). Keil and Delitzsch suggest that it is related to an Ethiopian word meaning 'to proceed' or 'climb' (*Ezekiel,* p.171). The Septuagint gives 'lead you on'.

160. Cf. 26:15,18; 27:3,6-7,15,35.
161. Cf. Jer. 17:27; 21:14; 43:12; 49:27; 50:32.
162. 1 Kings 20:23.
163. Cf. Ps. 46:8-9; Isa. 2:4; 9:4-5; Micah 4:3.
164. Isa. 9:5; cf. Ps. 46:9.
165. Cf. Judg. 5:30; 8:24-26; 2 Kings 7:16; Isa. 9:3.
166. Cf. Num. 19:1-22; Deut. 21:22-23.
167. So Block, *Ezekiel,* vol. 2, p.469.
168. The Hebrew behind **'block off'** occurs in Deut. 25:4, with reference to muzzling an ox, and in Ps. 39:1, concerning muzzling the mouth.
169. Cf. Ps. 79:1.
170. Block argues, on the basis of 5:7 and 7:12-14, that the city named **'Multitude'** is Jerusalem (*Ezekiel,* vol. 2, p.472). But if the 'sea' (39:11) to the east of which the burial valley is situated is the Dead Sea, this cannot be the case. Further, would it be appropriate for the enemy dead to be interred in the environs of the holy city? Finally, taking into account that chapters 34 – 39 never mention Jerusalem, is 39:16 to be reckoned as the sole exception?
171. Cf. Isa. 34:5-7; Zeph. 1:7.
172. Cf. 'You shall eat neither fat nor blood' (Lev. 3:17).
173. Cf. the execution of justice in 18:8, and Exod. 12:12.
174. Cf. Rev. 20:8-10.
175. Block, *Ezekiel,* vol. 2, p.482.
176. Cf. Deut. 31:18.
177. Cf. 16:53; 29:14; Job 42:10; Ps. 14:7; 85:1; 126:1; Amos 9:14.
178. **'Sanctify myself'** translates the *Niph'al niqdashti*, this conjugation being primarily reflexive of *Qal*.
179. The Hebrew connecting link *asher* sometimes means 'forasmuch' or 'since' (cf. Gen. 30:18; 31:49). See Brown, Driver and Briggs, *A Hebrew Lexicon,* p.83.
180. Cf. Isa. 32:15; 44:1-5; Joel 2:28; Zech. 12:10. For the Spirit considered as a fluid, cf. 1 Cor. 12:13.
181. In the New Testament, cf., for example, Acts 2:17,33; 2 Cor. 1:21-22; 5:5; Gal. 3:2; Eph. 1:13-14; 4:30; 1 Peter 1:2.
182. Cf. John 14:17.
183. 2 Cor. 4:6.
184. Gen. 15:1-21.
185. See Lev. 26:40-45; Deut. 30:1-10.
186. John 6:37-40.
187. John 10:16.
188. Eph. 2:12; 3:3-6.
189. Ps. 122:6-7.
190. Matt. 15:26-27; Mark 7:27-28.
191. Luke 2:25,38.

13. The thirteenth series of prophecies (40:1 – 48:35)
1. Ellison, *Ezekiel: The Man and His Message,* p.142.
2. So Taylor, *Ezekiel,* p.253.
3. With the exception of 40:5,14,42; 41:3,8,22; 43:13-14, heights are never mentioned.
4. Block, *Ezekiel,* vol. 2, p.505.
5. Not all would agree with this approach. But nowhere does the New Testament employ chapters 40 – 48 in expounding our Lord as the Head of his church. Should not the silence be allowed to speak for itself?
6. Gal. 4:3,9; cf. Col. 2:8,20. It is important to note that Paul contemplates Moses' law as 'weak and beggarly' (i.e. leading its adherents to spiritual destitution) *only* if it is misinterpreted as an instrument for self-justification. It was, of course, never designed for this.
7. Although chapters 40 – 48 are in a relative sense loosely eschatological, does this compel us to comprehend them as pointing to a this-worldly scene? 'Post-eschatological' might be a more useful term.

Whereas in the Old Testament 'for ever' does indicate permanency, as with the institution of the Passover (Exod. 12:14,17), why cannot 43:7,9 lead us forward to an enduring state *following* the eschatological event?
8. Cf. Heb. 10:18.
9. 1 Cor. 11:26.
10. See Dan. 9:27; Matt. 27:51; Mark 15:38; Luke 23:45; Heb. 10:20.
11. Luke 2:25,38. Cf. Joseph of Arimathea (Luke 23:51).
12. Rev. 5:5-6.
13. Block notes that there is an analogy between chapters 40 – 48 and the departure from Egypt (*Ezekiel,* vol. 2, pp.498-9).
14. 1 Cor. 15:44.
15. Matt. 25:10.
16. Exod. 25 – 40; cf. Heb. 8:5.
17. Cf. Heb. 8:5.
18. 2 Kings 16:10-16.
19. 2 Chr. 36:21-23; Ezra 1:1-4; Jer. 25:12; 29:10.
20. Matt. 27:53.
21. Cf. 17:22-23; Isa. 2:2; Micah 4:1.
22. Dan. 9:16,20; cf. Ps. 2:6; 24:3; 68:15; Isa. 2:2; Micah 4:1.
23. Cf. chapter 1, where in his 'visions of God' Ezekiel beholds the components of the throne of Yahweh as resemblances.
24. Cf. Ps. 122:1-2. The Qumran Temple Scroll, dated to the second century BC, designates Jerusalem as 'the city of the sanctuary where I [Yahweh] cause my name to abide' (from G. Vermes, *The Dead Sea Scrolls in English,* p.143).
25. Cf. the measuring line of Zech. 2:1.

26. The Siloam inscription tells that Hezekiah's tunnel was 1,200 cubits in length, which implies that the length of one cubit was about 44·6 centimetres (or 17½ inches). If this figure is accepted as that of Ezekiel's normal cubit, and if one handbreadth (say, 11 centimetres, or a little over 4 inches) is added, the length of the measuring reed of 40:5 would have been 3·34 metres (or just under 11 feet). Herodotus, *Book 1*, 178, reveals that there was a difference of 'three fingers' between the 'royal cubit' and the 'common cubit'. Cf. also 2 Chr. 3:3. Measurements did vary.
27. Cf. 1 Kings 14:28; 2 Chr. 12:11. It has often been noted that Ezekiel's gate is similar to Solomon's city-gate at Megiddo, with three recesses on each side of the entrance (so Taylor, *Ezekiel*, p.255). 'The prophet was familiar with architectural convention' (Block, *Ezekiel*, vol. 2, p.519).
28. So Gardiner, *Ezekiel*, p.318.
29. But only half the height of the porch of Solomon's temple (2 Chr. 3:4).
30. I am indebted to Gardiner, *Ezekiel*, p.319.
31. Cf. 1 Kings 6:4.
32. Block translates the underlying Hebrew as 'niches' instead of **'windows'** (*Ezekiel*, vol. 2, p.522). If so, they might have been employed as storage spaces. However, without windows to let in light, a building nearly 30 metres (or over 90 feet) long would have been inappropriately gloomy.
33. Cf. 1 Kings 6:29-36.
34. Cf.1 Chr. 9:26; Neh. 10:37-39; Jer. 35:4; 36:10.
35. Or perhaps some were situated on the west side. We are not told.
36. Block would place eight along each of the north, south and east outer walls, and six on the west side (*Ezekiel*, vol. 2, p.525). He may be right.
37. One is reluctant to follow some commentators, who suggest that verse 30 is a dittograph of verse 29. But, as it stands, it is unintelligible unless one revocalizes it. So Gardiner, *Ezekiel*, p.320.
38. For **'rinse'**, cf. 2 Chr. 4:6; Isa. 4:4; Jer. 51:34.
39. Lev. 1:11; 6:25; 7:2.
40. Lev. 1:4. Cf. Lev. 3:2,8,13; 4:4,15,24,29,33; 8:14,18,22; Num. 8:12.
41. Lev. 16:21-22. J. D. Currid comments concerning Leviticus 1:4 that resting a hand on the animal's head 'merely symbolizes acknowledgement of one's sins, and the act is one of identification with the animal. This appears to be the proper interpretation of the passage' (*Leviticus*, p.31).
42. Heb. 10:18.
43. See Exod. 29:18; Lev. 12:8; 6:5; Num. 5:8.
44. The total of eight tables assumes that 40:41 adds the 2 + 2 and 2 + 2 mentioned respectively in 40:39-40. But Block, whose

interpretation commands respect, is uncertain (*Ezekiel,* vol. 2, p.533).
45. See 2 Chr. 5:12.
46. So Block, *Ezekiel,* vol. 2, p.536. Cf. 1 Chr. 6:31-48; 9:1-44 (particularly verse 33); Ezra 2:70; Neh. 7:73.
47. So Block, *Ezekiel,* vol. 2, p.538.
48. 1 Kings 1:7-8,39,45; 2:26-27; cf. 1 Kings 4:2.
49. Cf. 1 Kings 6:3; 2 Chr. 3:4.
50. Keil and Delitzsch, *Ezekiel,* p.223. Not a few modern commentators resort to the Greek Bible for help.
51. With reluctance, I have adopted the Septuagint's twelve in favour of the Masoretic Text's eleven because twelve fits exactly with an east-west length of 100 cubits for the porch, nave and holy of holies combined. Further, the Hebrew orthography behind **'twelve'** is almost the same as that for 'eleven'.
52. 1 Kings 7:15-22.
53. The Greek Old Testament states that there were ten steps.
54. E.g. 1 Kings 21:1; 2 Kings 20:18; Isa. 39:7.
55. Cf. Heb. 8:5.
56. 1 Kings 6:2,16-17.
57. In Moses' original tabernacle, the length of the holy place was twenty cubits, the width ten cubits. The holy of holies was ten cubits square (Exod. 26:15-27).
58. Lev. 16:17.
59. 1 Kings 6:20.
60. Cf. Gen. 2:21-22; 1 Kings 6:5.
61. 1 Kings 6:5-10.
62. This assumes that the **'rooms'** (*l'shakôt*), 41:10, were the side rooms (*tz'laôt*).
63. Cf. 1 Kings 6:29-30.
64. Cf. Mal. 1:7,12.
65. The altar of incense in Moses' tabernacle was 1 x 1 x 2 cubits (Exod. 30:1-3); the measurements of that in Solomon's temple are not given (1 Kings 6:22; 7:48).
66. Cf. Heb. 9:3-4.
67. 1 Kings 6:31,34.
68. See also 1 Kings 7:6.
69. 1 Kings 6:19-35.
70. So Gardiner, *Ezekiel,* p.326.
71. With acknowledgements to Cooper, *Ezekiel,* p.369.
72. Gardiner, *Ezekiel,* p.327. The Septuagint gives 100 cubits.
73. With acknowledgements to Block, *Ezekiel,* vol. 2, p.564.
74. **'Wall'** translates *gadér*, a protective wall or screen; cf. 13:5; 22:30; Num. 22:24.
75. So Gardiner, *Ezekiel,* p.328.
76. Cf. Lev. 6:16,26; 7:6.
77. Apparently, Exod. 28:43; Lev. 6:10-11; 16:23.

78. Here, as Block observes (*Ezekiel*, vol. 2, p.568, n.160), the Masoretic Text's 'five cubits of reeds' should read **'five hundred reeds'**. The Masoretic Text retains an error of metathesis between the Hebrew for 'cubit' and 'hundred'.
79. Cf. 1 Peter 1:11.
80. Exod. 40:34-35; 1 Kings 8:10-11; 2 Chr. 5:13-14; 7:1-3.
81. Cf. Deut. 33:2; Isa. 60:1-3; Hab. 3:3-4.
82. 1:4-28; 3:23; 8:4; 9:3; 10:1,15,22.
83. Cf. 32:18; Gen. 49:7; Isa. 6:10; Jer. 1:10.
84. So Block, *Ezekiel*, vol. 2, p.580.
85. Cf. 1 Chr. 28:2; Ps. 99:5; 132:7; Isa. 60:13; 66:1; Lam. 2:1.
86. 2 Kings 21:4-7; 23:7.
87. Cf. Zech. 2:2; Rev. 11:1.
88. Cf. Matt. 5:8.
89. But in general I have followed Block's exposition (*Ezekiel*, vol. 2, pp.598-604). K. W. Carley (*The Book of the Prophet Ezekiel*, The Cambridge Bible Commentary Series, Cambridge: CUP, 1974, p.288) provides an excellent three-dimensional sketch of the altar which reflects closely my own submission.
90. See Brown, Driver and Briggs, *A Hebrew Lexicon*, p.300, for examples.
91. For **'base'**, cf. 16:24,31,39, where *gab* denotes a raised platform.
92. Cf. Isa. 29:1-2.
93. Horovitz, ed., *An Introduction to the Language of Scripture*, p.25. Cf. 2 Sam. 23:20.
94. Cf. Exod. 29:12; Lev. 4:7; 1 Kings 1:50-53; Ps. 118:27.
95. Exod. 27:1; 2 Chr. 4:1. The Jewish author Josephus, who was alive at the time, relates that in Herod's temple the altar was fifty cubits square and fifteen cubits high, with horns at the corners and approached from the south (*Wars of the Jews*, 5.5.6).
96. Cf. Gen. 22:8; Heb. 9:22.
97. Cf. Heb. 8:5; 9:24.
98. Cf. Lev. 8:14-15; Ps. 51:9 (Hebrew text).
99. *The New Oxford Dictionary of English*, ed. J. Pearsall (New York: OUP, 2001), p.203.
100. Cf. Exod. 29:10,15,19.
101. Lev. 4:11-12,20-21; cf. Lev. 8:17; 9:11; 16:27; Heb.13:11.
102. Lev. 4:22-23.
103. Cf. Exod. 28:41; 29:9;33; Lev. 8:33; 16:32; 21:10; 1 Chr. 29:5; 2 Chr. 29:31.
104. A. M. Stibbs, *The Meaning of the Word 'Blood' in Scripture* (London: The Tyndale Press, reprint of second edition, 1958), pp.10,14.
105. Cf. Rom. 5:9.
106. Gen. 31:54; Exod. 18:12.

107. Cf. 1 Kings 11:7-8; 2 Kings 16:2; 21:4; 2 Chr. 24:18; 28:23; 33:1-9; cf. 2 Chr. 36:14.
108. With acknowledgements to Block, *Ezekiel,* vol. 2, p.620.
109. So Taylor, *Ezekiel,* p.270.
110. Cf. 2:4-8; 3:9,26-27; 17:12; 24:3.
111. Cf. Gen. 17:12 and Exod. 12:43 for a similar expression. The implication in 44:7 is that aliens who preferred to reject the stated terms of covenant admission had nevertheless been admitted to worship by an erring covenant people. Consider Lev. 26:41 and Jer. 9:25.
112. Lev. 17:10,12; Num. 15:14,26,29; cf. 1 Kings 8:41-43.
113. Cf. Lev. 3:11; 21:6.
114. Cf. Num. 18:1-7.
115. E.g. John 4:21; Acts 11:18; 15:1-29; Gal. 5:2; Eph. 2:13-22.
116. See Gen. 29:34; 34:25-30; 49:5; Exod. 32:26-29; Num. 3 – 4; 18:7,21-23; 35:1-8; Deut. 10:8-9; 1 Chr. 23:27-32; 2 Chr. 11:13.
117. Cf. 2 Chr. 11:13.
118. Cf. Num. 18:7.
119. See Lev. 1:5,11; 3:2,8,13; 4:14-15,24,29,33; 17:3-5; cf. Ezek. 40:38-39.
120. Cf. Deut. 10:8.
121. Cf. 16:53-54,60-63; 20:43; 36:31-32; 39:25-26; 43:10-11. Those who are forgiven and restored do not gloat.
122. Cf. Exod. 28:39-43. Ezekiel 40:3 employs the same Hebrew word for **'linen'** with regard to the flax line held by Ezekiel's guide.
123. Cf. Lev. 6:10; 16:4.
124. Cf. Exod. 29:37; 30:29; Lev. 6:11.
125. For a different view, see Block, *Ezekiel,* vol. 2, p.641.
126. See Lev. 10:6; 21:5-6.
127. For the deadening effect of wine, cf. Gen. 9:21; 2 Sam. 11:13; Prov. 20:1; 23:29-35; Hosea 4:11.
128. Lev. 21:7,14.
129. Contrast Jeroboam's practice, 1 Kings 12:31.
130. Cf. Deut. 24:1-4; Matt. 5:31-32.
131. Deut. 33:10; cf. Deut. 17:8-13; 19:17; 21:5.
132. 1 Sam. 8:5-6,20; cf. 2 Sam. 14:4; 15:2-4.
133. Cf. Gen. 2:17; Rom. 6:23.
134. As remarked by Block, *Ezekiel,* vol. 2, p.538.
135. Exod. 23:19; 34:26; Lev. 2:3; 6:25-26,29; 7:6-7; 27:21; Num. 15:19-21; 18:8-16,18-20; Deut. 10:9; 18:1-5.
136. Cf. Exod. 22:31; Deut. 14:21.
137. Lev. 16.
138. Cf. Matt. 5:13-14.
139. Luke 7:14-15; cf. Matt. 9:25 and parallels.
140. Luke 6:38.
141. Cf. Luke 11:13.
142. Cf. Exod. 25:2; 30:15; Lev. 7:14; Num. 15:19.

143. Cf. Num. 33:54; 34:13; 36:2-3.
144. Thus Gardiner, *Ezekiel,* p.335. But most modern commentators assume that the measure is the cubit. Remarkably, to my mind, Block (*Ezekiel,* vol. 2, p.652) does not even discuss the matter.
145. See the comments on 40:5.
146. Modern commentators, such as Wright, *The Message of Ezekiel,* and Thomas, *God Strengthens,* tend not to discuss the issue, assuming that the cubit is the unit of linear measurement.
147. Some commentators read 25,000 x 20,000, as in the Septuagint. Admittedly, this would simplify an explanation of the present verse. But, yet again, this commentary stays with the Masoretic Text.
148. Josh. 21:19.
149. Num. 35:1-8.
150. This suggestion accords with the Septuagint. The Masoretic Text translates as something like '... for a holding, twenty apartments', which seems to make little sense. The suggested emendation supposes that, prior to the text being preserved in square Hebrew, a *kaph* replaced a slightly similar *beth* in the last word, changing from 'apartments' to **'to live [in]'**.
151. Deut. 17:14-17; 1 Sam. 8:14; 22:7; 1 Kings 21:1-16. Cf. Isa. 5:8; Jer. 22:13-19.
152. 1 Sam. 8:11-18.
153. 1 Kings 21.
154. Cf. Lev. 19:35-36; Deut. 25:13-16; Hosea 12:7; Amos 8:5-6; Micah 6:10-11; Prov. 11:1; 16:11; 20:10.
155. D. J. Wiseman, 'Weights and Measures', *The New Bible Dictionary,* pp.1319-20.
156. Cf. Exod. 30:13; Lev. 27:25; Num. 3:47.
157. According to Block (*Ezekiel,* vol. 2, p.657, n.48), this is because weights in the Old Testament tend to be multiples of fifty (cf. Gen. 23:15; Exod. 30:24; Num. 31:52).
158. For the ***'maneh'***, cf. Ezra 2:69; Neh. 7:71-72.
159. Cf. 1 Kings 4:22; 5:11; 2 Chr. 2:10; 27:5. The appositional **'the bath, the oil'**, though supported by the Septuagint, is confessedly difficult and is deleted by many commentators.
160. Cf. Gen. 13:10, with reference to the Jordan valley.
161. For drink offerings, cf. Num. 15:5.
162. Cf. Gal. 3:28.
163. Lev. 23:15-21; Num. 28:26-31; Deut. 16:9-12.
164. The first day of the seventh month, Lev. 23:24-25; Num. 29:1-6.
165. Lev. 16:1-34.
166. Lev. 4:2-35; 16:14-15; 23:26-32; Num. 15:22-29; 28:11-15.
167. Block argues that the ritual described here is not an annual event, but a one-time inaugural procedure, analogous to the

decontamination of the altar described in 43:18-27 (*Ezekiel,* vol. 2, pp.662-4). Yet the once-for-all consecration of Moses' altar led to annual sacrifices. So, perhaps, here.

168. See Exod. 12:3.

169. 2 Kings 23:21-23; 2 Chr. 30:1-27; 35:1-19.

170. Passover sacrifices: Exod. 12:1-28; Lev. 23:4-8; Num. 28:16-25; Deut. 16:1-2.

171. Exod. 12:13-14.

172. Num. 29:12-38.

173. So Block, *Ezekiel,* vol. 2, p.671.

174. Cf. 45:22; Lev. 4:27.

175. For new-moon feasts, see 1 Sam. 20:5,18,24; 2 Kings 4:23; 1 Chr. 23:31; 2 Chr. 2:4; 8:13; 31:3, Ezra 3:5. Cf. Isa. 1:13-14; Hosea 2:11; Amos 8:5.

176. Lev. 23:4-44; Deut. 16:16.

177. Lev. 27:16-24; 25:10-13; cf. Jer. 34:8-17.

178. Jer. 31:31.

179. Cf. our Lord's statement that in performing their duties on the Sabbath, the priests 'profaned' the Fourth Commandment, yet remained 'innocent' (Matt. 12:5), 'profaned' being an exceedingly strong word. That command does not appear as an eternally (or universally) valid moral requirement.

180. Cf. 1 Cor. 14:33.

181. As suggested by the parallel in Rev. 22:1, which tells of water proceeding from 'the throne of God and of the Lamb'.

182. See 1 Sam. 10:1; 2 Kings 9:1,3.

183. Cf. Joel 3:18 and Zech. 14:8 for the metaphor. Ezekiel elaborates but does not innovate.

184. Cf. Rev. 22:2.

185. For **'region'**, or 'circle', cf. Josh. 22:10-11.

186. For 'Salt Sea', cf. Gen. 14:3; Num. 34:3,12; Deut. 3:17; Josh. 3:16; 12:3; 15:2,5; 18:19; 2 Sam. 8:13; 2 Kings 14:7; 1 Chr. 18:12; 2 Chr. 25:11; Ps. 60, introductory heading.

187. For **'Arabah'**, cf. Deut. 1:1; 3:17; 4:49.

188. Block (*Ezekiel,* vol. 2, p.695) gives a tentative identification with the Moabite Eglath-shelishiyah (Isa. 15:5; Jer. 48:34).

189. Taylor, *Ezekiel,* p.280. Also, Block, *Ezekiel,* vol. 2, p.695.

190. The Hebrew *g'bûl*, usually translated as 'border', can mean 'territory'; see Brown, Driver and Briggs, *A Hebrew Lexicon,* p.148.

191. Cf. Gen. 48:5,22; Josh. 17:14,17.

192. Gen. 13:14-17; 15:17-21; 17:8; 22:17; 28:13-14; cf. Ezek. 20:28.

193. Num. 33:54; 34:13.

194. Josh. 3.

195. 1 Kings 8:65; 1 Chr. 13:5; 2 Chr. 7:8; 2 Kings 14:25.

196. Block's map (*Ezekiel,* vol. 2, p.711) places Damascus and Gilead within the restored land of Israel. Yet does the Hebrew text of 47:18 actually indicate this?
197. Num. 20:1-14; 34:4.
198. Lev. 19:33-34.
199. Lev. 25:47-55.
200. Ruth 1:16-17.
201. Num. 32:1-42; Josh. 14:3.
202. Judg. 18:27-30; Josh. 19:24-31; 19:32-39; 17:7-13; 16:5-10; 13:15-23; 15:1-63.
203. Gen. 49:10.
204. Gen. 44:20.
205. It is to be stressed that 48:8 points only to the 25,000 x 10,000 reed strip allocated to the priests, and in which the central sanctuary would be placed, and not to the complete square of 25,000 reeds a side, embracing also the Levites' portion and then the possession of the city. The order of presentation is determined throughout by spiritual significance.
206. See 40:46; 43:19; 44:15.
207. Lev. 25:32-34.
208. Cf. Num. 35:2-5.
209. Josh. 18:11-28; 19:1-9; 19:17-23; 19:10-16; Num. 32:1-42; Josh. 14:3.
210. Cf. the new, heavenly Jerusalem, as outlined by Rev. 21:12-13,16-17.
211. But contrast Rev. 21:12.
212. Heb. 7:2; Ps. 46:4; 48:2; Isa. 60:14.
213. Titus 2:13.
214. Matt. 15:26-27; Mark 7:27-28.

Appendix A: The reed or the cubit?
1. Eichrodt, for example, assumes without discussion that the unit of measurement is the cubit (*Ezekiel,* p. 548). So also W. Zimmerli, *Ezechiel* (Neukirchen-Vluyn: Neukirchener Verlag, 1969, 2 vols), vol. 2, p.1066.
2. Holy Bible: English Standard Version (London: HarperCollins Publishers, 2002).
3. The identification of the linear unit as either the cubit or the reed also arises with respect to chapters 45 and 48.
4. New American Standard Bible (Nashville: Thomas Nelson, 1977).
5. Taylor, *Ezekiel,* pp.263-4.
6. Cf. John 2:20.
7. To accept that the temple is situated within a square of 500 cubits implies much too little space for the temple.
8. As do many commentators.
9. English Standard Version, pp.886, 889.

Appendix B: Ezekiel's city

1. 2 Sam. 24:18-25; 1 Chr. 21:28-30; 2 Chr. 3:1.
2. Acts 8:27.
3. Rev. 21:2,22.
4. One Greek *stadion* was about 184·9 metres, or 202 yards, and one reed was about 3·34 metres, or just under 11 feet. Each side of Ezekiel's square city was 5,000 reeds (including the open areas).

Appendix 'C': Romans 11:25-26

1. As well as Rev. 21 – 22. But these chapters have already been referred to in the body of the present commentary.
2. W. Hendriksen, *Romans* (Edinburgh: The Banner of Truth Trust, 1980), pp.377-84, states the case clearly.
3. J. Murray, *The Epistle to the Romans* (Grand Rapids: Eerdmans, 1987 [reprint of the 1968 one-volume edition]), part 2, p.84.
4. Thus 1 Cor. 2:7; 4:1; 15:51; Eph. 6:19. With acknowledgements to C. Hodge, *Commentary on the Epistle to the Romans* (Grand Rapids: Eerdmans, 1977 [reprint of the 1886 revised edition]), p.372.
5. So F. F. Bruce, *The Epistle to the Romans* (London: The Tyndale New Testament Commentaries, 1967 [reprint of the first edition, 1963]), p.222, *pace* Hendriksen, *Romans,* p.379. Cf. Acts 20:11; 27:17,44; 28:14; Rom. 5:12; Rev. 9:17.
6. Hendriksen, *Romans,* p.370.
7. Murray, *Romans,* pp.95-6.
8. Bruce, *Romans,* p.221.
9. Keil and Delitzsch, *Deuteronomy,* p.452.
10. Matt. 24:14; Mark 13:10; cf. Matt. 28:19.
11. 2 Thess. 2:3-10.
12. B. Vawter and L. J. Hoppe, *A New Heart: A Commentary on the Book of Ezekiel* (Grand Rapids: Eerdmans; Edinburgh: Handsel Press, 1991), pp.212-13.
13. J. Orton, *Memoirs of the Life, Character and Writings of the late Reverend Philip Doddridge, D.D. of Northampton* (London: J. Buckland, 1766), p.20.